ROSTER

of

REVOLUTIONARY SOLDIERS

in

GEORGIA
Volume I

Compiled
by
MRS. HOWARD H. McCALL
State Regent, Ga. D. A. R., 1916–1918
Vice-President General from Ga. N. S. D. A. R., 1922–1925

Published
by the
GEORGIA SOCIETY
DAUGHTERS OF THE AMERICAN REVOLUTION

MRS. THOMAS COKE MELL
State Regent, 1940–1942

CLEARFIELD

Originally Published
Atlanta, 1941

Reprinted
Genealogical Publishing Co., Inc.
Baltimore, Maryland
1968

Reprinted for
Clearfield Company, Inc. by
Genealogical Publishing Co., Inc.
Baltimore, Maryland
1996, 2004

Library of Congress Catalogue Card Number 68-9361
International Standard Book Number: 0-8063-0219-4

Made in the United States of America

"To be a Georgian, is not simply a piece of luck, but a priceless privilege, to be paid for in loyalty, and with love, and with life itself if the occasion demands. May the love of all thy children—O Georgia—encompass thee and may God make them worthy to be called Georgians."

GOLDEN JUBILEE PROJECT
1940

of the

GEORGIA SOCIETY
DAUGHTERS OF THE AMERICAN REVOLUTION

MRS. THOMAS COKE MELL (JOSEPHINE DAVIS)
State Regent (1940-42)

COMPILER'S PREFACE

The year 1940 will be written in the annals of the National Society, Daughters of the American Revolution as the *"Golden Jubilee Year."*

The Georgia Society presents as its Golden Jubilee Project, the publication of this Volume *"Roster of Revolutionary Soldiers in Georgia."*

The material for this volume was compiled, edited, and presented as a loving gift to the Georgia Society, D. A. R., by MRS. HOWARD H. McCALL (Ettie Tidwell), State Regent of Georgia D. A. R., 1916–1918, and Vice-President General from Georgia of the National Society, D. A. R., 1922–1925.

The work of compiling this material has been a labor of love by one who is proud to claim Georgia as the state of her nativity, and who has striven in this way to preserve some of the history of many *Revolutionary Soldiers*, participants in the struggle for our Independence, and who lie buried in Georgia.

The book is written as a dependable and authoritative reference book for libraries and patriotic organizations.

The records assembled have been compiled of *Revolutionary Soldiers* whose records of service to their Country in the War of the Revolution (1775–1783) should be easily available to all interested in genealogical research.

Care has been taken in compiling these records: from pension papers, family Bible and tombstone records, grants of land, lottery lists, wills, estates, and official records of military service. It is not a complete list, and some mistakes will occur. But all data has been verified and may be used for application papers in the National Society, Daughters of the American Revolution.

REVOLUTIONARY SOLDIERS

The graves of the following REVOLUTIONARY SOLDIERS in Georgia have been located by the Georgia Society, Daughters of the American Revolution. (Also included are the names of the Revolutionary Soldiers buried in Warren County, Georgia, whose names appear on tablet.) See Page 9.

Name	County
CHARLES ABERCROMBIE	Hancock
JAMES ACHESON	Warren
JAMES ADAMS	Elbert
THOMAS ADAMS	Elbert
SAMUEL ALEXANDER	Warren
HUGH ALEXANDER	Jefferson
WILLIAM ALEXANDER	Elbert
ELISHA ALLEN	Warren
JAMES ALLEN	Jefferson
WILLIAM ALLEN (age 112 years)	Lumpkin
LIEUT. COL. WILLIAM ALSTON	Elbert
JAMES AMOS	Hancock
LIEUT. COL. NICHOLAS ANCIAUX	Screven
KENNETH ANDERSON	White
WILLIAM ANDERSON	Baldwin
DAVID ANDREWS	Henry
JOHN ANDREWS	Oglethorpe
WILLIAM ANDREWS	Oglethorpe
HENRY ANGLIN	Jackson
THOMAS ANSLEY	Warren
JEAN PIERRE ARNAUD	Chatham
JOHN ARNETT	Screven
JOHN ARNOLD	Baldwin
WILLIAM ASH	Franklin
ICA ATKINS	Dodge
JOHN AUSTIN	Walton
SAMUEL J. AXON	Liberty
WILLIAM BABB	Baldwin
JOHN BACHOLTS	Glynn
CHARLES BAKER	Bartow
BEAL BAKER	Hall
JOHN D. BAGWELL	Gwinnett
JOHN BALL	Warren
ABNER BANKSTON	Butts
JOHN BARNETT	Oconee
ROBERT BARNETT	Wilkinson
ROBERT BARRETT	Irwin
JAMES BARROW	Warren
REUBEN BARROW	Warren
SAMUEL BARROW	Jones
THOMAS BARROW	Jackson
GEORGE BASSETT	Richmond
CORNELIUS BATCHELDER	Wilkinson
JESSE BATTLE	Hancock
WM. SUMNER BATTLE	Hancock
JAMES BAXTER	Baldwin
JOHN BAXTER	Murray
JAMES BEASLEY	Warren
THADDEUS BEALL	Warren

Name	County
WILLIAM BEAVERS	Coweta
LABAN BECKHAM	Pike
SAMUEL BECKHAM	Baldwin
PHILIP H. BEDFORD	Washington
EDWARD BEESON	Baldwin
FRANCIS BELL	Hall
JACOB BELLEW	Habersham
RICHARD BENNETT	(near Jesup, Ga.)
JOHN BERRIEN	Chatham
JOHN BERRY	(Ebenezer Cemetery)
WILLIAM BIRD	Warren
JAMES BISHOP	Warren
EDWARD BLACKSHEAR	Laurens
WM. BLACKWELL	Franklin
HENRY BONNER	Warren
ISAAC BORING	Jackson
LITTLEBERRY BOSTICK	Jefferson
NATHAN BOSTICK	Jefferson
FRANCIS BOYKIN	Baldwin
SAMUEL BOYKIN	Baldwin
BENJAMIN BRACK	Burke
JOHN BRACK	Burke
THOMAS BRADFORD	Irwin
JAMES BRADY	Warren
AMOS BRANTLEY	Hancock
JACOB BRASELTON, SR.	Jackson
JOSEPH BREED	Warren
STEPHEN BROCK	Burke
JOHN HANNA BROOKS	Jones
JOAB BROOKS	Warren
ANDREW BROWN	Elbert
BENJAMIN BROWN	Fayette
BENJAMIN BROWN	Elbert
JOHN BROWN	Pike
JOHN BROWN	Warren
JOHN R. BROWN	Camden
NATHAN BROWNSON	Jefferson
GEORGE BUCHANAN	Sumpter
JOHN BULL	Baldwin
HAWKINS BULLOCK	Clarke
WILLIAM BURFORD	Butts
JACOB BURKHALTER	Warren
JOSHUA BURKHALTER	Warren
MICHAEL BURKHALTER	Warren
PRESCOTT BUSH	Stewart
PATRICK BUTLER	Elbert
ZACHARIAH BUTLER	Elbert
JAMES BUTTS	Hancock
JOHN CALDER	McIntosh

Name	County
Peter Callaway	Laurens
James Cameron	(near West Point)
Samuel Camp	Hancock
William Candler	(near Augusta, Ga.)
James Cantey	Baldwin
Thomas P. Carnes	Baldwin
Patrick Carr	Jefferson
Thomas Carr	McDuffie
Wm. Carraway	Upson
Adam Carson	Jones
William Carson	Wilcox
Alexander Carswell	Burke
John Carswell	Burke
David Carter	Hart
James Carter	Baldwin
Thomas A. Carter	Elbert
Wm. Cheek	Bartow
Tully Choice	Hancock
Turner Christian	Elbert
Richard Christmas	Elbert
Christopher Clark	Elbert
John Clark	Florida
William Clark	Hall
Elijah Clarke	Lincoln
Larkin Clarke	Elbert
David Clay	Wilkinson
Jacob Cleveland	Elbert
Ezekiel Cloud	Henry
Daniel Clower	Gwinnett
John Coffee	Telfair
John Coleman	Burke
Jonathan Coleman	Burke
John Colley	Lincoln
Vines Collier	Oglethorpe
William Cone	Screven
Wilson Conner	Screven
Joshua Cook	Washington
John Cooper	Madison
Richard Cooper	Screven
Samuel Cooper	Muscogee
Thomas Cooper	Jasper
George Cowan	Jefferson
Cary Cox	Putnam
John Craps	Terrell
Peter Crow	Bartow
Angel Cunningham	Jackson
James Cunningham	Elbert
John Daniel	Elbert
Thomas Daniel	Washington
William Daniel	Washington
Cyrus Dart	Glynn
John Davidson	Jasper
Joseph Davidson	Wilkinson
George Dawson	Greene
Stephen Day	Columbia
Raymond Demere	St. Simons Is.

Name	County
James De Launay	Baldwin
John Dickinson	Coweta
Michael Dixon	Hancock
David Dickson	Clayton
Jesse Dismukes	Baldwin
James Dooly	Lincoln
Thomas Dooly	Lincoln
Andrew Du Bourg	Baldwin
Wilson Drew	Emanuel
Jacob Durden	Emanuel
Daniel Deupree	Oglethorpe
Nathaniel Durkee	Hart
James Duncan	Baldwin
John Duncan	Elbert
Elisha Dyar	Hart
Peter Early	Clarke
David Edenfield	Emanuel
William Edwards	Bartow
David Elder	Oconee
Joshua Elder	Oconee
Samuel Elbert	Chatham
Levin Ellis	Hancock
James Espy	Clarke
Hartwell Ezzell	Jasper
Peter Fair	Baldwin
Daniel Fane	DeKalb
Wm. Faris	Walker
Thomas Farrar	Franklin
William Fears	Jasper
William Few	Jefferson
Benjamin Fitzpatrick	Morgan
Lewis Flemister	Wilkes
William Fletcher	Telfair
Jonas Fouche	Greene
George Franklin	Washington
Wm. Franklin	Irwin
Colquitt Freeman	Madison
George Freeman	Wilkes
Holman Freeman	Wilkes
John Freeman	Wilkes
James Freeman	Richmond
Richard Fretwell	Newton
William Gainer	Washington
John Gamble	Jefferson
Lewis Gardner	Randolph
Jacob Garrard	Greene
Matthew Gaston	Butts
John Gator	Troup
Allen Gay	Coweta
John Gibson	Fulton
Young Gill	Hancock
James Gilmore	Washington
Wm. Giradeau	Liberty
William Glover	Hart

Name	County
SHADRACK GOODWIN	Harris
THOMAS GORDON	Gwinnett
NATHANIEL GREENE	Chatham
THOMAS GREEN	Lamar
DAVIS GRESHAM	Greene
ARCHIBALD GRESHAM	Greene
AARON GRIER	Taliaferro
CHARLES GRIFFIN	Clinch
JAMES GRIFFIN	Irwin
PETER GROOVER	Forsyth
MOSES GUEST	Franklin
JACOB GUNN	Baldwin
JAMES GUNN	Jefferson
RICHARD GUNN	Taliaferro
JOHN HABERSHAM	Chatham
JOSEPH HABERSHAM	Chatham
SIMON HADLEY	Thomas
WILLIAM HALEY	Elbert
LYMAN HALL	Richmond
JOHN HAMES	Murray
(now Marietta, Ga.)	
JAMES HAMILTON	Columbia
STEWART HAMILTON	Montgomery
ABNER HAMMOND	Baldwin
HENRY HAND	Sumpter
HENRY HARDIN	Walton
WILLIAM HARDWICK	Washington
WILLIAM HARPER	Hancock
JACOB HARRELL	Decatur
ABSOLEM HARRIS	Hancock
BENJAMIN HARRIS	Baldwin
JOHN THOMPSON HARRIS	Walton
MILES HARRIS	Hancock
SAMUEL HARRIS	Hancock
JOHN HART	Baldwin
DANIEL HARTLEY	Crawford
CHARLES HARVIE	Gordon
MICHAEL HARVIE	Baldwin
ZEPHANIAH HARVEY	Jasper
JOHN HATCHER	Wilkinson
BENJAMIN HAWKINS	"Old Agency"
BENJAMIN HAYGOOD	Monroe
MOSES HAYNES	Hart
GEORGE HAYNIE	Barrow
JOHN HAYS	DeKalb
JOHN HEARD	Greene
GOV. STEPHEN HEARD	Elbert
THOMAS HEARD	Greene
ELISHA HEARN	Putnam
ROBERT HENDRY	Liberty
JOSEPH HERNDON	Walton
EPHRIAM HERRINGTON	Emanuel
JACOB HIGGENBOTHAM	Elbert
SAMUEL HIGGENBOTHAM	Elbert
RICHARD B. HOOPER	Banks
JAMES HORTON	Jasper

Name	County
PROSSER HORTON	Jackson
VALENTINE HORSLEY	Upson
JOHN HOWARD	Baldwin
ISAAC HOWELL	Fulton
ISHAM HUCKABY	Coweta
DAVID HUDSON	Elbert
HOPE HULL	Clark
THOMAS HUMPHRIES	Baldwin
JAMES HUNT	Elbert
MOSES HUNT	Elbert
WILLIAM HUNT	(near Davisboro, Ga.
THOMAS HUMPHRIES	Baldwin
DANIEL INMAN	Burke
JOSHUA INMAN	Burke
ALEXANDER IRWIN	Burke
GOV. JARED IRWIN	Burke
JOHN LAWSON IRWIN	Burke
EPHRIAM IVEY	Baldwin
CHARLES JACKSON	Cumberland Island
DRURY JACKSON	Baldwin
EDWARD JACKSON	Walker
JOHN JAMES	Cobb
SERGEANT JASPER	Chatham
JOHN JENKINS	Lamar
LEVI JESTER	Butts
JOSEPH JETER	Hancock
WILLIAM JESTER	Butts
WM. JOHNSON	Oglethorpe
EZELL JOHNSTON	Jasper
JOHN JOHNSTON	Jasper
LITTLETON JOHNSTON	Jasper
ABRAHAM JONES	Burke
DANIEL JONES	DeKalb
JAMES JONES	Screven
JOHN JONES	Burke
SEABORN JONES	Burke
WILLIAM JONES	Columbia
WILLIAM JONES	Jasper
JOHN JORDAN	Washington
HENRY JOYCE	Toombs
DEMSEY JUSTICE	Baldwin
JOHN KENDRICK	Pike
WM. BIBB KEY	Elbert
HENRY KING	Taliaferro
JOHN KING	Jackson
RICHARD KING	Taliaferro
PETER KOLB	Meriwether
WILLIAM LANCASTER	Pulaski
ABRAHAM S. LANE	Screven
AUSTIN LANE	Screven
LEWIS LANIER	Screven
ALEXANDER LATTA	Monroe
JOHN LAWRENCE	Putnam

Name	County
Hugh Lawson	Jefferson
John Lawson	Burke
Roger Lawson	Jefferson
William Lee	Jackson
James Lester	Baldwin
John Lewis	Bartow
John Lindsey	Wilkes
James Little	Franklin
Wm. Little	Baldwin
Abraham Liveley	Burke
Matthew Liveley	Burke
Evans Long	(near Columbus, Ga.)
Amos Love	Laurens
Col. David Love	Greene
James Luckie	Oglethorpe
Jeremiah Lumsden	Jasper
Mayhen Lyle	Jackson
Wm. Lyon	Jefferson

"Light Horse" Harry Lee was buried at Cumberland Island; re-interred in Va.

Name	County
Charles McCall	Bulloch
Thomas McCall	Laurens
Thomas McCall	Bulloch
Thomas H. McCall (McCaule)	Chatham
William McCall	Screven
Hugh McCauley	DeKalb
Joseph McClendon	Coweta
William McGehee	Baldwin
William McIntosh	St. Simons Island
Samuel McClendon	Henry
Angus McCurry	Hart
John McElhammon	Jackson
John McGough	Greene
Charles McKimsey	Jackson
John McMullen	Hart
Neil McNeil	Terrell
James McPhail	Liberty

Name	County
Samuel Mackey	Franklin
John L. Marsh	Macon
Abraham Marshall	Columbia
John Marshall	Columbia
Daniel Marshall	Columbia
Joseph Marshall	Columbia
Levi Marshall	Columbia
Zacheus Marshall	Columbia
Beverly Martin	Elbert
Isaac Mathews	Jackson
James Mathews	Upson
William Mathews	Jackson
Nathan Mattox	Elbert
Obediah Mavis	Baldwin
John Maxwell	Fulton
Thomas Maxwell	Elbert
George Menifee	Talbot
Jacob Mercer	Jasper

Name	County
James Meriwether	Jefferson
Thomas Meriwether	Jasper
Jonathan Miller	Baldwin
John H. Milner	Pike
Henry Mitchell	Hancock
Thomas Mitchell	Henry
William Mitchell	Wilkinson
Claxton Mize	Banks
David Montgomery	Jackson
James Montgomery	Jackson
Francis Moreland	Jasper
Robert Moreland	Jasper
Clement Moore	Butts
James Moore	Taliaferro
William Moran	Baldwin
Obediah Morris	Butts
William Morris	Newton
William Morris	DeKalb
Oliver Morton	Jones
Samuel Moseley	Stephens
Miles Murphree	Burke
John Murphree	Burke
Edmund Murphy	Richmond
Nicholas Murphy	Richmond
John Myrick	Baldwin

Name	County
Basil O'Neal	Columbia
John Neely	Coweta
John Nelson	Lincoln
Thomas Nelson	Pike
John Newton	Oglethorpe
Moses Newton	Washington
John Nicholson	Union
Sanders Nobles	Clinch
William Norris	Newton
John Nunn	Wilkinson
James Nunnelee	Elbert
John Nunnally	Oconee

Name	County
Archibald Odom	Pulaski
William Ogletree	Monroe
Dionysius Oliver	Elbert
James Brush Oliver	Richmond
Daniel Orr	Spalding

Name	County
Richard Parham	Baldwin
James Park	Greene
Ezekiel Evans Parke	Greene
Daniel Parker	Upson
Henry Parks, Sr.	Franklin
Wm. Pate	Turner
John Patterson	Jefferson
Robert Patterson	Baldwin
Wm. Patterson	Baldwin
John Peel	Jefferson
Seth Peirce	Jefferson
William Penn	Jasper

Name	County
WILLIAM PENTECOST	Jackson
WILLIAM PETERS	Lowndes
JOHN PHINAZEE	Harris
FERDINAND PHINIZY	Oglethorpe
JAMES PITTMAN	Madison
ROBERT POLLARD	Columbia
THOMAS POLLARD	Columbia
HENRY POOL	Glascock
OLIVER PORTER	Newton
OTEY PROSSER	Baldwin
ANTOINE POULLAINE	Wilkes
JOHN POWELL	Jefferson
JOSIAH POWELL	Jefferson
ROBERT PULLEN	Newton
REUBEN RANSOME	Clarke
JOHN RAWLINS	Murray
ANDERSON REDDING	Monroe
JACOB REDWINE	Coweta
SAMUEL REID	Putnam
RICHARD RESPESS	Upson
AMOS RICHARDSON	Hart
JAMES RILEY	Elbert
MATTHEW RHODES	Habersham
REUBEN ROBERTS	Jones
JOHN ROBINSON	Hancock
RANDALL ROBINSON	Coweta
JOSEPH ROE	Burke
HARDMAN ROOKS	Washington
SHADRACK ROWE	Harris
JOHN ROWELL	Haralson
JOHN RUCKER	Elbert
WILLIAM RUCKER	Elbert
JOHN RUSHIN	Macon
JOHN RUTHERFORD	Baldwin
WILLIAM RYALS	Telfair
PHILIP RYAN	Clarke
MOSES SANDERS	Clarke
DANIEL SCHEE	Washington
JAMES SCOTT	Screven
JOHN EPPES SCOTT	Hancock
JAMES SCREVEN	Liberty
JOSEPH SESSIONS	Washington
JOHN SHACKELFORD	Hancock
JOHN SHIELDS	McDuffie
JOHN SHINE	Laurens
WM. STUDLEY SHIRLEY	Jones
HENRY SIMMONS	Camden
JOHN SIMMONS	Hancock
THOMAS SIMMONS	Jones
ABRAM SIMONS	Wilkes
ARCHIBALD SIMPSON	Wilkes
EDWARD SINGLETON	Lumpkin
JOHN SITTON	White
HENRY SLAPPEY	Jasper
SAMUEL SLAUGHTER	Baldwin

Name	County
DAVID SMITH	Barrow
HARDY SMITH	Laurens
ISAAC SMITH	Monroe
JAMES SMITH	Wilkinson
ROBERT SMITH, SR.	Butts
WILLIAM SMITH	Coweta
WM. (HELL NATION) SMITH	Coweta
GEORGE SNELLINGS	Elbert
LAZARUS SOLOMON	Wilkinson
RICHARD SPEAKS	Butts
JOHN SPEARMAN	Jasper
REV. JOHN SPRINGER	Wilkes
ROBERT STAFFORD	Glynn
GEORGE STAPLETON	Jefferson
BENTON STARK	Jackson
JOHN STEENSON	White
ALEXANDER STEPHENS	Taliaferro
DANIEL STEWART	"Midway"
WILLIAM STEWART	Schley
JOHN STONEYCIPHER	Stephens
CHARLES STRONG	Clarke
JOHN STRONG	Clarke
JOHN STROUD	Walton
PETER STROZIER	Wilkes
JOHN STUART	Washington
JAMES STUART	Washington
JOSEPH SUMNER	Emanuel
JOHN SUTTON	White
MATTHEW TALBOT	Washington
JOHN TALIAFERRO	Wilkinson
JOSIAH TATTNALL	Chatham
CLARK TAYLOR	Oglethorpe
FRANCIS TENNILLE	Washington
RICHMOND TERRELL	Newton
ANDREW THOMAS	Washington
JAMES THOMAS	Baldwin
WM. THOMAS	Banks
Aaron Tomlinson	Jefferson
Sherrod Thompson	Jackson
Dozier Thornton	Elbert
David Thurmond	Madison
John Thurmond	Coweta
Henry H.Tompkins	Oglethorpe
Andrew Torrance	Baldwin
PURNAL TRUITT	Wilkes
RICHARD TURNER	Chatham
ZADOC TURNER	Hancock
JESSE VAUGHAN	Wilkinson
JAMES WADSWORTH	Jones
DAVID WALKER	Putnam
ELISHA WALKER	Johnson
GEORGE WALKER, II	Bleckley
GEORGE WALKER, III	Bleckley
JAMES WALKER	Upson

Name	County
JOHN WALKER	Wilkes
WILLIAM WALKER	Jefferson
SANDERS WALKER	Oglethorpe
GEORGE WALTON	Richmond
FRANCIS WARD	Putnam
EDWARD WARE	Madison
JAMES WARE, SR.	Madison
ELI WARREN	Laurens
JEREMIAH WARREN	Hancock
JEREMIAH WARREN	Baldwin
JESSE WARREN	Hancock
JOSIAH WARREN	Laurens
JOHN WATSON	Baldwin
BENJAMIN WEAVER	Greene
CLAIBORNE WEBB	Jackson
JOHN WECHEL	Hall
SAMUEL WHATELEY	Greene
DANIEL WHATLEY	Greene
JAMES WHEELER	Jackson
HUDSON WHITAKER	Baldwin
EDWARD WHITE	Chatham
JOHN WHITE	Bartow
JOHN MARTIN WHITE	Hart
THOMAS WHITE	Columbia
FADDY WHITTINGTON	Spalding
JOHN WILLIAMS	Camden
JOHN WILLIAMS	Butts
THOMAS WILLIAMS	Stewart
JOHN WILLIAMSON, SR.	Butts
MICAJAH WILLIAMSON	Wilkes
JOHN WILSON	Effingham
JOHN WILSON	Greene
REUBEN WINDHAM	Taylor
HENRY WINTERWHEEDLE	Wilkinson
WILLIAM WISE	Bullock
JAMES WOOD	Heard
SOLOMON WOOD	Jefferson
WILLIAM WOOD	Coweta
AMBROSE WRIGHT	Chatham
SAMUEL WRIGHT	Glynn
WILLIAM WRIGHT	Henry
LEWIS YANCEY	Jasper
SOLOMON YOUMANS	Tattnall
JAMES YOUNGBLOOD	Baldwin

NOTE: Col. William Clark and his wife, Ruth Goodwin, were re-interred in cemetery at Gainesville, Ga. The graves of four REAL DAUGHTERS marked were MRS. ANN MARIA REDDING (1825-1910) and MRS. LUCY ANN GIBSON (1829-1905), both daus. of WILLIAM ANDERSON, of Va. and Ga., REV. SOL., and MARY (POOL) NEWSOM and SARAH POOL, Glascock Co. (both daus. of HENRY POOL of Ga.) These two daus. unveiled the marker placed over the grave of their father, HENRY POOL, REV. SOL. (1766-1808) on May 7, 1933.

NOTE: The Ga. Society D. A. R. marked the grave of ISAAC BOGAN at Union, S. C., together with the S. C. D. A. R. Also marked graves of JACOB GREEN, Gadsden, Ala., and JOHN LANDIS, Augusta Co., Va.

NOTE: Records of names of REV. SOL. in this list will be found in the Annual Proceedings of the Ga. Society D. A. R.

GOLDEN JUBILEE PROJECT—1890–1940

The Ga. Society, D. A. R., MRS. THOMAS COKE MELL, State Regent. MARKER erected by Burkhalter Chapter, D. A. R., Warrenton, Ga., June 14, 1940, MRS J. A. BRAY, Regent.

The inscription is as follows: "To the REVOLUTIONARY SOLDIERS found, to date, buried in Warren Co., Ga., who fought in the War for American Independence, 1776–1783."

JAMES ACHESON	JOAB BROOKS	GEORGE COOPER
SAMUEL ALEXANDER	JOHN BROWN	JAMES COOPER
ELISHA ALLEN	JACOB BURKHALTER	DANIEL CULPEPPER
THOMAS ANSLEY	MICHAEL BURKHALTER	WILLIAM CULPEPPER
JOHN BAKER	HENRY BURNLEY	CARY CURRIE
HENRY BARKSDALE	ISRAEL BURNLEY	JACOB DARDEN
JOHN BARKSDALE	THOMAS BUSH	STEPHEN DARDEN
JAMES BARROW	SAMUEL CAMP	DAVID DAVIS
REUBEN BARROW	JOHN CARSON	NATHAN DAVIS
THADEUS BEALL	JAMES CARTER	JAMES DOZIER
JAMES BEASLEY	ELPHINSTON CARY	JAMES DRAPER
COL. WILLIAM BIRD	WILLIAM CASON	JEREMIAH DUCKWORTH
JAMES BISHOP	JACOB CASTLEBERRY	SHADRACH FLEWELLEN
CAPT. HENRY BONNER	JOHN CHAPMAN	GIBSON FLOURNOY
JAMES BRADY	ISAAC COOK	NATHAN FOWLER
JOSEPH BREED	HEZEKIAH COOKSEY	WILLIAM FRANKLIN

PRYOR GARDNER
CHURCHILL GIBSON
PETER GOODWIN
JAMES GRAY
AARON GRIER
NICHOLAS HARBUCK
THOMAS HARDIN
HENRY HARP
ZACHERIAH HARRELL
ABRAHAM HEATH
JOSHUA HILL
RICHARD HILL
THOMAS HILL
CAPT. WILLIAM HILL
AMBROSE HOLLIDAY
JACOB HORNE
MATHEW HUBERT
EPHRIAM IVY
PEEPLES IVY
JOHN J. JACKSON
ARTHUR JENKINS
ROBERT JENKINS
WILLIAM JOHNSON
ABRAHAM JOHNSTON
JOHN KELLY
WILLIAM KENDALL
THOMAS W. KENT
ARCHIBALD LACY
BLAKE LASSETER
RICHARD LEE
JOHN LINN
DAVID LOCKETT
JONATHAN LOCKETT
SOLOMON LOCKETT
THOMAS LOCKETT, SR.
WILLIAM LOWE
LIEUT. WILLIAM LUCAS
JOHN McCORMICK

DRURY McCULLERS
REUBEN McGEE
JOHN McLAUGHLIN
JOSEPH McMATH
JOHN MAYES
JAMES MAYS
LIEUT.-COL. CHARLES MEDLOCK
MARTIN MIMMS
ABNER MITCHELL
SAMUEL MOON
MORDECAI MOORE
WILLIAM MORRISON
EDWARD MURPHY
JOHN MYRICK, SR.
JAMES NAPIER
CAPT. DAVID NEAL
SAMUEL NEAL
THOMAS NEAL
CAPT. THOMAS NEAL
BENJAMIN NEWSOME
SOLOMON NEWSOME
WILLIAM NICHOLS
JAMES NORRIS
BENJAMIN OLIVER
ROBERT PALMER
JOHN PARISH
JAMES PARKER
WILLIAM PARKER
JOSEPH PEAVY, SR.
PETER PERKINS
HENRY PERSONS
JOSIAH PERSONS
TURNER PERSONS
WILLIAM PILCHER
HENRY POOL
PHILIP POOL
JESSE RICKETSON

ELISHA ROBERTS
JAMES ROGERS
REUBEN ROGERS
JAMES ROQUEMORE
WILLIAM ROSE
SAMUEL RUTHERFORD
JOHN SALLIS
ABRAM SANDERS
JONAS SHIVERS
WILLIAM SHURLEY, SR.
SETH SLOCOMB
JOHN C. SMITH
NATHANIEL SMITH
THOMAS SMITH
JOSHUA STANFORD
ALEXANDER STEPHENS
WILLIAM STROTHER
CHARLES STURDIVANT
THOMAS TERRY
ALEXANDER THOMPSON
MOSES THOMPSON
JOHN TORRANCE
WILLIAM TRAVIS
JOHN TRENT
EZEMIA VERDON
GEORGE WAGGONER
JAMES WAGGONER
BENJAMIN WHEELER
WILLIAM WHITE
RICHARD WIGGINS
WILLIAM WILDER
DAVID WILSON
JOHN WILSON
NATHANIEL WOOTEN
JOHN WYNNE
ROBERT WYNNE
JAMES YOUNG

PARISHES OF GEORGIA 1775

The Colony of Georgia was divided into Parishes. *Christ Church* Parish, including Savannah; *St. Mathews* Parish, including Abercorn and Ebenezer; *St. George's* Parish, including Halifax; *St. Paul's* Parish, including Augusta; *St. Philips* Parish, including Great Ogeechee; *St. John's* Parish, including Midway and Sunbury; *St. Andrews* Parish, including Darien; *St. James* Parish, including Frederica. Public worship was ordered to be held in all Parishes. (One of the First Laws.)

When the Colonies found that there was no prospect of a settlement of the dispute between them and England, each of them, following the example of Massachusetts, appointed by action of the Provincial Congress, a committee to resist every attempt at executing the acts of Parliament. In some cases that Committee was called the "Committee of Safety," in others, as in Georgia, the "Council of Safety." Massachusetts set the example in Feb., 1775; Georgia followed suit June, 1775.

Before this, even as early as January, St. John's Parish, dissenting from the action of the Provincial Congress of Georgia in the delay to positively acquiesce in the proceedings of the other Provinces in regard to the authority of Continental Congress, appointed a committee to attend the meeting of the General Committee in Charleston, S. C., and present the side of St. John's Parish in the questions involved.

The dissatisfaction resulting from such delay, culminated in the determination of St. John's Parish to send delegates to the Continental Congress before the rest of the Province did so and on Mar. 21, 1775, DR. LYMAN HALL, afterwards one of the three Signers of the Declaration of Independence, from Georgia, was appointed a delegate to the Continental Congress from the Parish of St. John. This was the direct cause of the change of the name of the Parish to *Liberty Co.*, the first county in the Colony of Georgia. In 1777, the name of *Wilkes Co.* was given to the "Ceded Lands" of upper Georgia.

Georgia, at the outbreak of the Revolution, was a Province of divided households, for while the younger members of the family were ardent Whigs, the older ones, as a rule, were stout Loyalists, whose devotion to the Crown stood the supreme test. It required some courage on both sides to maintain a firm position; nowhere was this more noticeable than in Savannah, where the older members of many of the most prominent families were loyal to the Crown, and where the "Liberty Boys of Georgia" had as their leader ARCHIBALD BULLOCK, *President of the First Provincial Congress of Georgia.*

CEDED LANDS OF GEORGIA

In the year 1774, Governor Wright opened a Land Court in Georgia, where the Broad river joins the Savannah. A stockade fort was built for protection against the Indians, and here was sold the lands, ceded by the Creek and Cherokee Indians. On June 11, 1774, he issued a proclamation stating that the lands would be surveyed and parcelled out in tracts of 100 to 1,000 acres. To the head of each family was to be sold 100 acres, for each child 50 acres and 50 acres for the wife.

The "Ceded Lands" (now Wilkes Co.) was almost an unbroken wilderness. Men of energy and enterprise made clearings and built the first homes in upper Georgia. This region is rich in historic memories.

At the point where the Broad river flows into the Savannah, there were three towns bearing the imposing names of *Petersburg, Lisbon,* and *Vienna.* These towns constituted a great trading center, where goods could be brought by pole boats from Augusta and carried by wagons to upper Georgia.

The first settlements in the "Ceded Lands" were at *Dartmouth* (later the name was changed to Petersburg) located at the confluence of the Broad and Savannah rivers, and at *Lisbon,* located on the south side of the Broad river and east side of the Savannah. Across the Savannah river in South Carolina was the town of *Vienna.* At the present time Lisbon, in Lincoln Co., has only one store; of Petersburg, in Elbert Co., and Vienna, in South Carolina, not a vestige remains. Petersburg was the third largest town in Georgia, second in size only to Savannah and Augusta and having more than 50 stores and two newspapers.

Many of the men who settled in the "Ceded Lands" were REVOLUTIONARY SOLDIERS and many received their military training under GENERAL ELIJAH CLARKE, who served as Colonel at the Battle of Kettle Creek, Feb. 14, 1779.

Near Coody Creek (now Elbert Co.) stood the home of NANCY HART, the wife of BENJAMIN HART, *Rev. Sol.*, perhaps the most noted woman that the Southern Colonies produced during the Revolutionary War. It was in her home that she performed her celebrated feat of capturing single-handed a whole squad of British Soldiers and holding them at bay until her little daughter "Sukey" could summon her father and other patriots from the hiding places in the swamps. "A brave intrepid soul was she and a dear lover of Liberty."

From these "Ceded Lands" (Wilkes Co.) there moved out into the valleys of Georgia, Alabama, and Mississippi small armies of early settlers, the descendants of those early pioneers who settled there before and soon after the Rev. War. Wilkes Co. has been divided into Crawford, Taliaferro, Hart, Warren, Greene, Hancock, and other counties.

In 1792 there were 82,000 people in Georgia and 36,000 lived in Wilkes County.

NOTE: When the Land Court was opened 1773 at the point where the Broad river joins the Savannah river, a stockade fort was built and was called *Fort James,* with a garrison of 50 rangers, with barracks and officers' quarters. Each corner of the Fort had two-story houses with swivel guns placed and openings for small arms.

NOTE: The impelling motive which caused the families to emigrate from Va. to N. C. was that they could sell their lands in the more developed communities in Va. and buy advantageously in the newer settlements in N. C. Then in 1782 Ga. gave bounty grants of land, 287½ acres (and more to officers) to *Rev. Sols.* to induce them to settle in Ga.

REVOLUTIONARY SOLDIERS IN GEORGIA

JAMES BULLOCH OF GEORGIA

JAMES BULLOCH[1], b. Scotland 1701, came to S. C. 1729; d. Savannah, Ga., 1780. He wa: J. P., Colleton District, S. C., 1735–1737. Received a Royal Grant of land in Ga. 1765. Was : Member of the Patriotic Provincial Congress of 1775 for the Sea Island District of Ga. and receive permission to raise a company of *Continental Soldiers.* Mar. (1) JEAN STOBO (dau. of Archibal Stobo, from Scotland to S. C., 1700, and his wife, Elizabeth Park); mar. (2) Mrs. Ann Ferguson widow; mar. (3) Mrs. Ann (Cuthbert) Graham, widow; mar. (4) Mary Jones (dau. of Hon. Nobl Jones and Miss Wimberly). Among the children by (1) wife Jean Stobo were:

1. ARCHIBALD BULLOCH, mar. Mary De Veaux.
2. Jean Bulloch, mar. Josiah Perry.
3. Christina Bulloch, mar. Hon. Henry Yonge.

ARCHIBALD BULLOCH[2], b. Charleston, S. C., 1731; d. Ga. Feb., 1777. Buried in the Colonial Cemetery, Savannah, Ga. Was *President of the first Provincial Congress* assembled in Tondee's Tavern, Savannah, Ga., 1775. *Delegate to Continental Congress* 1775-1776. He was the leader of the party who burned every house on Tybee Island to prevent its use by the British Seamen from the Men-of-War anchored in the Roads, and first read the Declaration of Independence to the Townspeople of Savannah. Was the *President of the new Republic of Ga.* 1776-1777. Was *Commander-in-Chief of the Army in Ga.* and headed the famous "Liberty Boys" of Ga. Mar. Oct. 9, 1764, at "Argyll," Ga., MARY (called Polly) DE VEAUX (1748-1818), (dau. of COL. JAMES DE VEAUX, *Rev. Sol.* of Ga. in command of 1st Ga. Regiment of Militia, 1775, and his wife, Ann Fairchild).
Children:

1. JAMES, mar. Anne Irvine.
2. Archibald Stobo, mar. 1793 Sarah Glen.
3. Jane, mar. J. Benjamin Maxwell (son of Wm. Maxwell).
4. William Bellinger, mar. (1) 1798 Harriet De Veaux (dau. of Jacob De Veaux and his wife, Elizabeth Barnwell); mar. (2) Mary Young (dau. of Benjamin Young and his wife, Martha Allston).

In front of Tondee's Tavern, Savannah, Ga., June 5, 1775, was erected the famous *Liberty Pole*, which became the rallying center of Savannah; and from the porch ARCHIBALD BULLOCH, then *President of the Council of Safety*, read the Declaration of Independence to the assembled populace, after which 13 guns were fired from the old Battery on Bay street.

PETER TONDEE, owner of this famous Tavern, was a loyal *Patriot.* During the latter part of Feb., 1777, the President of Georgia d. and BUTTON GWINNETT was elected *President and Commander-in-Chief.*

JAMES BULLOCH[3], (son of Archibald Bulloch[2]), b. Ga. 1765; d. Savannah, Ga., Feb. 9, 1806. Was a *Rev. Sol.* of Ga. and Capt. of Va. Garrison troops 1778-1780 under Col. George Mister. Hon. member Ga. State Society of the Order of the Cincinnati. Mar. April 13, 1786, ANNE IRVINE (dau. of Dr. John Irvine and his wife, Ann Elizabeth Baillie).
Children:

1. John Irvine, mar. Charlotte Glenn.
2. JAMES STEPHENS, mar. (1) Esther Amarinthia Elliott; (2) Martha (Stewart) Elliott.
3. Jane, mar. 1808 in Liberty Co., Ga., John Dunwoody (1786-1856) (son of JAMES DUNWOODY, b. Chester Co., Penn., 1741; d. Liberty Co., Ga., 1807, *Rev. Sol.*, and his wife, Esther Dean Splatt).

JAMES STEPHENS BULLOCH[4], b. in Ga.; d. suddenly in the "Old Presbyterian Church," Roswell, Ga. Mar. (1) Dec. 31, 1817, Esther Amarinthia Elliott, b. 1797 (dau. of John Elliott and his (1) wife, Esther Dunwoody). He mar. (2) Martha (Stewart) Elliott, widow of the above John Elliott, as (2) wife, and dau. of GEN. DANIEL STEWART, *Rev. Sol.* of Ga. and his wife, Susanna Oswald.
Child by (1) wife:
    James D.
Children by (2) wife:
1. Charles Irvine, d. y.

2. (Lieut.) Irvine Stephens, mar. Ella Sears.
3. MARTHA (see later)—
4. Anna, mar. James K. Gracie.

MARTHA BULLOCH[5] (sometimes called Mitty), b. Hartford, Conn., July 8, 1834; d. Feb. 12, 1884. Mar. at Roswell, Ga., Dec. 22, 1853, THEODORE ROOSEVELT, b. New York City 1831, d. 1878. They lived in New York City. (The old *Bulloch* mansion is still standing (1940) in Roswell, Ga.)

Children:
1. THEODORE ROOSEVELT, Lieut.-Col. of the "Rough Riders" during the Spanish American War: *President* of the *United States of America.* Mar. (1) Alice H. Lee; (2) Edith Kermit Carow.
2. ELLIOTT ROOSEVELT, mar. Anna R. Hall.   Issue, ANN ELEANOR, Elliott, Gracie. (Their daughter, ANN ELEANOR ROOSEVELT, mar., 1905, her cousin, FRANKLIN DELANO ROOSEVELT, b. in Hyde Park, N. Y., Jan. 30, 1882.   Now (1940) *President of the United States of America.*
3. ANNA ROOSEVELT, mar. Commodore W. S. Cowles.
4. CORINNE ROOSEVELT, mar. Douglas Robinson, Jr.

In a beautiful spot in the heart of Liberty Co., Ga., the Congress of the United States reared a *Memorial* to the joint memory of GEN. JAMES SCREVEN and GEN. DANIEL STEWART, *Rev. Sols.* of Ga. (Gen. Daniel Stewart was the great grand-father of President Theodore Roosevelt and the g- g- grand-father of Eleanor (Roosevelt) Roosevelt, the wife of the President of the United States, FRANKLIN DELANO ROOSEVELT.)

GEN. JAMES SCREVEN was wounded and later d. Nov. 28, 1778, at the home of John Elliot, Sr., whither he had been taken after being wounded.

This Monument stands in the Old Midway Cemetery, next to the Old Midway Church, at the edge of the old Stage road from Savannah to Darien.   Upon the altars erected in this historic church were kindled the fires of Georgia's resistance to the dominion of England, and as a rebuke for her primacy in the cause of country, this Church and Parish sustained the full measure of royal vengeance. At Sunbury near this place was fought one of the most stubbornly contested engagements of the Revolution.

The old Church stands now (1940) like a sentinel in its isolated grandeur, at the intersection of two Colonial roads with a prospect down an avenue of ancient oaks, beneath which the Red Coats marched more than one hundred and fifty years ago, and under which the heavy tramp of the Union army in the War Between the States awoke the echoes of the quiet woods many years later.   The most historic highway in Georgia.

The present Church was built in 1792 upon the ruins of the edifice burned by the British.

The people of Midway, known as the Dorchester settlement but called Midway by reason of its equal distance from two of the principal rivers, came originally from Dorchester, S. C., to which point they had emigrated from Dorchester, Mass.

ARCHIBALD BULLOCH, NOBLE WIMBERLY JONES, JOHN HOUSTON, and GEORGE WALTON were the "Famous Quartette of Liberty" in Georgia.

EVAN DAVIS OF GEORGIA

EVAN DAVIS, b. Wales, emigrated from Wales to America (Philadelphia, Penn.), and then settled in Va., but came later to the new lands in Ga., and settled near Savannah. He resided there until the close of the Rev. War, in which he took an active part, serving in the Ga. Cavalry, under Count Pulaski. (A monument was erected in Savannah, in honor of Count Casimir Pulaski, and the Pulaski Chapter, D. A. R., Griffin, Ga., bears the name of this Polish nobleman.) Evan Davis mar. in S. C. Mary (Emory) Williams. Their son, SAMUEL DAVIS, b. Ga., was a *Rev. Sol.* of Ga. He commanded a company of irregular troops of horse in the Rev. War. He mar. Jane Cook in Ga, and they were the parents of JEFFERSON DAVIS (10th child), b. in Christian (now Todd) Co., Ky., June 3, 1808; d. in Miss., Dec. 6, 1889. He graduated at West Point and as Lieut. U. S. Army, mar. (1) Sarah Knox Taylor (dau. of Gen. Zachary Taylor, U. S. A.), mar. (2) Feb. 26, 1845, Varina Howell. This grandson of EVAN DAVIS, *Rev. Sol.* of Ga., and son of SAMUEL DAVIS, *Rev. Sol.* of Ga., became the most illustrious citizen of Miss. and the South, filling many positions of trust and was the *President* and official head of the *Confederate States of America* (1861-1865).

ELIJAH CLARKE OF GEORGIA

GENERAL ELIJAH CLARKE, b. Edgecomb Co., N. C., 1736; d. Ga., Dec. 15, 1799. Mar. in N. C. 1760, HANNAH ARRINGTON (1737-1827). He moved with his family to the "Ceded Lands" of Ga. 1774 (Wilkes Co., now). Both are buried at the home plantation (in now Lincoln Co., Ga.) "Woburn." (Their graves were marked by the D. A. R.). Three Ga. Chapters D. A. R. bear the names of Gen. Elijah Clarke, his wife, Hannah Clarke, and their son, Gov. John Clarke.

ELIJAH CLARKE was a *Rev. Sol.* of Ga. and the story of his life and bravery is told in detail in every history of Ga. He was the Col. at the Battle of Kettle Creek, and it has been said that this battle made possible Cornwallis' defeat. Was at the Siege of Augusta and King's Mt. Served as Captain of Rangers, Colonel and then Brigadier-General. His wife was one of the *Revolutionary heroines* of Ga. Her home was burned by the Tories while her husband was in the field and she, too, was at the Siege of Augusta.

Children of Elijah and Hannah (Arrington) Clarke:

1. JOHN CLARKE, b. N. C., 1776; d. Fla., Oct. 15, 1832. Mar. Nancy Williamson, (dau. of COL. MICAJAH WILLIAMSON, *Rev. Sol.* of Ga.), 2 children, 1 son and dau., mar. Col. John Campbell. JOHN CLARKE served as a *Rev. Sol.* under his father, distinguished himself at the Battle of Jack's Creek, became Major General in the *War of 1812*, was placed in charge of all forces destined for the protection of the Seacoast and Southern boundaries of the State. Elected *Governor of Ga.*, 1819, re-elected 1821. In 1827 he removed to Fla., where he died.

2. GIBSON CLARKE (1772-1820), mar. Susanna Clark. Moved to Miss.

3. ELIJAH CLARKE, JR., mar. Margaret Long.

4. NANCY CLARKE, mar. JESSE THOMPSON, b. Amelia Co., Va., 1754. Moved to Ga. with his brother, Robert Thompson and sister, Elinor (mar. Samuel Watkins). They settled in Wilkes Co. He served as *Rev. Sol.*, Ga. Line under Gen. Clarke. Received bounty land for his services. D. 1819.

5. ELIZABETH CLARKE, mar. BENAJAH SMITH, a *Rev. Sol.* of Ga. Served under Gen. Clarke.

6. POLLY CLARKE, mar. (1) COL. CHARLES WILLIAMSON (son of Col. Micajah Williamson), a *Rev. Sol.* of Ga. She mar. (2) William J. Hobby, b. Conn., came to Augusta, Ga., 1789.

7. FRANCES CLARKE, b. 1781, mar. EDWIN MOUNGER, a *Rev. Sol.* of Ga.

8. SUSAN CLARKE, d. y.

NOTE: Will of Charles Williamson, to wife, Polly, and son, Charles. . . . ."To son Charles, my bounty land as a late State Troop Officer," . . . ."money due me as a militia officer on the frontier of this State." Signed July 31, 1799. Probated Feb. 27, 1800. Wilkes Co. Records.

REVOLUTIONARY SOLDIERS

BUTTON GWINNETT, baptized Gloucester Co., England, April 10, 1735. Mar. Ann Bourne in England, April 19, 1757. Came to America 1765, his wife joined him in 1767 in Savannah, Ga. He bought St. Catherine's Island on the Ga. coast (formerly owned by MARY MUSGROVE). The "Olde House" was his plantation home. Feb. 2, 1771, he was elected a delegate from Ga. to the Continental Congress. Was elected Mar. 5, 1777 *President and Commander-in-Chief of the Continental Army* at the death of President Archibald Bulloch. He was one of the three Signers from Ga. of the Declaration of Independence. Was fatally wounded in a duel with Gen. Lachlan McIntosh and d. Savannah, Ga., May 19, 1777. His wife d. 1780.

Three children, all b. in England:

1. Amelia, b. 1758.

2. Ann, b. 1759.

3. Elizabeth, b. 1762, mar. Peter Belin of S. C.

(Ref. "Button Gwinnett," by Charles Francis Jenkins.)

ABRAHAM BALDWIN, b. Guilford, Conn., Nov. 6, 1754. D. Washington, D. C., Mar. 4, 1807, while serving in Congress as a Senator from Ga. He served as *Chaplain* in the Continental Army from Conn. Moved to Savannah, Ga., 1784, sent to Continental Congress, 1785. A member of the Congress, 1787, at the convention which framed the *Constitution of the U. S.*

(See life of Abraham Baldwin, by Dr. Harry C. White, Prof. of Chemistry at the University of Ga. 1870-1927.)

GEORGE WALTON, one of the three Signers of the *Declaration of Independence of Georgia.* B. Va. 1740; came to Savannah, Ga., and d. at his home in Augusta, Ga., "Meadow Garden," Feb. 12, 1804. Mar. 1779 Dorothy Camber of Chatham Co., Ga. Their son, GEORGE WALTON, was the first *Secretary of State of the Territory of Florida.* Dorothy (Camber) Walton d. Pensacola, Fla. Sept. 12, 1832. GEORGE WALTON, SR., purchased a country seat (in now Augusta, Ga.), 1791, which he called "Meadow Garden," where he spent the last 14 years of his life. He lies buried under the Monument erected to "the Signers," GEORGE WALTON, LYMAN HALL, and BUTTON GWINNETT in Augusta, Ga. *"Meadow Garden"* was purchased by the National Society, Daughters of the American Revolution, for memorial purposes. It is a patriotic museum for relics of the Revolutionary period. (The Augusta Chapter D. A. R. of Ga. are in charge of the home.) *Secretary First Provincial Congress, Governor of Georgia,* 1779, 1789-1790. Col. of Militia. Was captured at Savannah by British soldiers.

JOHN HOUSTON, b. Parish of St. George, Ga. Aug. 31, 1744; d. White Bluff, near Savannah, Ga., July 20, 1796. Member *Continental Congress.* Signed the famous "Card" which called the Ga. Patriots together at Tondee's Tavern. A leading *Patriot* and forwarded supplies to the closed port of Boston, Mass. Was elected *Governor of Georgia* 1778, and again in 1784.

SAMUEL ELBERT, b. Prince William Parish, Va., 1740; d. Great Ogeechee, Ga. Moved to Savannah, Ga.; made Captain of Grenadiers 1774; member Council of Safety 1775; was Lieut. Colonel 1776; Commandant of a Brigade at the Battle of Brier Creek, Ga. Was appointed Major-General of the Ga. Militia. Was *Governor of Georgia* 1785. He d. Nov. 1, 1788. Was member of the *First Provincial Congress,* July 4, 1775 (Grave marked). Mar. Nov. 29, 1769 Elizabeth Rae.

Children known:
1. Kitty, mar. 1791 Capt. John Burke.
2. Betsey, mar. 1798 Dr. M. Burke.
3. Celia Rae, mar. Allen Gay.
(Other Children.)

JAMES JACKSON, b. Devonshire England, Sept. 21, 1757; d. Washington, D. C., Mar. 16, 1806, while serving in Congress as *Senator from Ga.* Served from Savannah, Ga. as a *Rev. Sol.,* as Lieut. Captain, Brigade Major, and Colonel Legionary Corps, Ga. State Line. Escaped from the British at the capture of Savannah, Ga.; was at the Battle of Cowpens; later served with Gen. Washington. Member *Provincial Congress of Ga.* Elected *Governor* 1788 (but declined). Served as *Governor* 1786, (1798-1801). Mar. 1785 Mary Charlotte Young (dau. of Wm. Young (1743-1776) and his wife, Sophia Chappelle.) Had issue.

The story of the past played by Gen. James Jackson in the exposure of the Yazoo fraud can be found in all Histories of Ga. Buried Congressional Cemetery, Washington, D. C.

JARED IRWIN, b. N. C. 1750; d. Union Hill, Washington Co., Ga. Mar. 1, 1818. Entered the Continental Army as Captain, promoted to Colonel, then General. Was twice elected *Governor of Georgia.* As Governor, he signed the rescinding of the Yazoo act Feb. 13, 1796. Mar. his cousin, Isabella Erwin.

Had issue:
1. John, a *Soldier of 1812.*
2. Thomas.
3. Jane.
4. Elizabeth, mar. Simeon Whitaker.

With his three brothers, JOHN LAWSON, ALEXANDER, and WILLIAM, all of whom were *Rev. Sols.,* he built a fort near Union Hill, his home, to protect this section of Ga. from the Indians, called Fort Irwin. The first monument ever erected by the State of Ga. was erected to the memory of Gov. Jared Irwin at Sandersville, Ga.

NOTE: In Monterey Square, Savannah, Ga. a monument was erected to COUNT PULASKI, the Heroic Pole, who fell mortally wounded fighting for American Liberty at the Siege of Savannah, Oct. 9, 1779.

DAVID EMANUEL, b. Penn., 1742; d. Burke Co., Ga., 1808. Served in the Ga. Line under Brig.-Gen. John Twiggs of Ga. Was captured but escaped from the Tories. He was *Governor of Georgia* 1801. Mar. ANN LEWIS.

Children:
1. Rebecca, mar. Jacob Walker.
2. Ruth.
3. Martha.
4. Asenath, mar. Francis Wells.
5. Ann, mar. as (2) wife, James Welch.
6. Mary, mar. Thomas Blount.

JOHN ADAM TREUTLEN, b. Berchtesgaden, Austria 1726; killed in S. C. 1782 by the Tories. Buried near Metts Cross Roads, S. C. and grave was marked by the D. A. R. Chapter, St. Matthew, S. C. He came from Holland to America in 1735. Was at Frederica, St. Simons Island, later Vernonsburg near Savannah, Ga. He was a *Rev. Sol.*; member of the *First Provincial Congress of Ga.* (1775) and was elected as *First Governor of Georgia* under the Constitution of 1776 on May 8, 1777. Mar. (1) 1755 Margaretta DuPuis of Purysburg, S. C. (across the Savannah river from Ebenezer, Ga.). She d. 1777. Mar. (2) Mrs. Ann Unselt (widow of David Unselt).

Children by (1) wife:
1. Christiana.
2. Jonathan.
3. Dorothea.
4. Elizabeth, b. April 8, 1760, mar. WILLIAM KENNEDY, b. Aug. 12, 1757. *Rev. Sol.* (son of Hugh Kennedy).
5. Mary, mar. (1) Edward Dudley; (2) John G. Morel.
6. Hannah.
7. Christian Streit, mar. Mary.
8. John Adam, Jr., b. Aug 29, 1770, mar. (1793) Ann Margaret Miller (dau. of JOHN MILLER, *Rev. Sol.* of S. C. under COL. WM. THOMPSON.)
9. DuPuis.

JOSIAH TATTNALL (son of Josiah Tattnall, the Loyalist), b. at Bonaventure, near Savannah, Ga. 1762; d. Nassau, New Providence, Bahama Island, June 6, 1830. His remains were removed to the family burial ground at Bonaventure (now Chatham Co.), Ga. His father, during the Rev. War, removed with his family to the Bahama Island. But despite his father's care, JOSIAH TATTNALL escaped from home and in 1782 joined the Colonial troops under Gen. Anthony Wayne in Ga. in 1801 he was elected *Governor of Georgia*. He was *U. S. Senator* from Ga. (His son, Commodore Josiah Tattnall, Jr., served the United States with distinction upon the high seas.)

EDWARD TELFAIR, b. Scotland 1735, came to Va. 1758, then N. C. and later, 1758, settled in Savannah, Ga. Was a "Son of Liberty;" member Ga. Assembly 1776; member *Continental Congress*, and on July 24, 1778 signed the ratification of the Articles of Confederation. Was elected *Governor of Georgia.* 1787-1789, and as Governor (1791-1793) entertained GEORGE WASHINGTON, *President of the United States*, on his memorable visit to Ga. in 1791; d. Savannah, Ga., Sept. 17, 1807. Mar. Sarah (dau. of WILLIAM GIBBONS, *Rev. Patriot* of Ga.). Their sons were:

1. Edward.
2. Thomas, mar. Margaret Long (dau. Col. Nicholas Long).
3. Josiah G.
4. Alexander.
Daughters:
5. Mary.
6. Sarah.
7. Margaret.

OLIVER BOWEN, b. Rhode Island 1741, came to Savannah, Ga.; d. Augusta, Ga., July 11, 1800. Member of Council of Safety; Captain of Ga. Continental troops; *Commodore of the Navy,* placed in command of the first vessel, "The Dauntless," commissioned during the Rev. His vessel, officered by Commodore Bowen and Major Joseph Habersham, made the first capture of the

Rev. War, a British Schooner, a part of whose cargo was 14,000 pounds of gun-powder. He mar. Mar. 21, 1798 (widow) Ann Dorsey, of Liberty Co., Ga. He also served as captain of 2nd Co., Ga. Batt.

NOTE: On the evening of May 11, 1775, soon after the news of the Battle of Lexington, six adventurers broke into the powder magazine in Savannah, Ga., and took possession of the stores of ammunition. Some of the captured booty was for the use of Ga. troops, some sent to S. C., and some to Boston, and was used at the Battle of Bunker Hill. The beardless Captain of the band was JOSEPH HABERSHAM; the others were Noble W. Jones, Edward Telfair, Joseph Clay, William Gibbons, and John Milledge.

LYMAN HALL, b. Wallingford, Conn., April 24, 1724. Came to Dorchester, S. C., and later to Ga. with the famous Puritan Colony, which formed the Midway settlement in the Parish of St. John. Was sent from this Parish as a delegate to the Continental Congress in Philadelphia. Signer of The Declaration of Independence on behalf of Ga. with George Walton and Button Gwinnett. His property at Sunbury, Liberty Co., was confiscated by the British Government. Returned South in 1782, settled at Savannah, Ga. Was called (1782) to the office of *Governor of Georgia*. Mar. Mary Osburn. D. at his plantation home, "Shell Bluff," Burke Co., Ga., Oct. 19, 1790. Buried at the same place. His remains were re-interred 1848 and placed under the monument at Augusta' Ga., erected to the three Signers for Ga. of the Declaration of Independence.

GEORGE HANDLEY, was *Governor of Georgia* 1788. B. England Feb. 9, 1752; d. Roe's Hall, Ga., Sept 17, 1793. Came to the Colonies (Savannah, Ga.), 1775. As a *Rev. Sol.* was captured at Augusta and sent to Charleston, S. C. as a prisoner. In 1776 was Captain in Continental Army, then Lieut. Col. Moved to Glynn Co., Ga., and was appointed collector of the port by President George Washington. Charter member of the Order of the Cincinnati. Mar. SARAH HOWE (a niece of Major General Samuel Elbert). They had one son:

George Thomas Handley.

JOHN WEREAT, *Governor of Georgia* 1779, b. 1730. Member *First Provincial Congress* of Ga. and *Speaker of the Congress* 1776. When Savannah fell into the hands of the British, the legislature dispersed without appointing a Governor for the succeeding year. As President of the Executive Council, he served as Governor. D. Bryan Co., 1798.

WILLIAM EWEN, *Governor of Georgia* 1775, b. England 1720. Chairman 1775 of Council of Safety. Active in support of the Patriots.

STEPHEN HEARD, *Governor of Georgia* 1781, b. Ireland. Settled in Va., moved to Ga. 1773. Settled in the "Ceded Lands," on Broad river. Served in the Rev. Feb. 18, 1781, was elected *President of the Council*. Served as *Governor de Facto* until Governor Brownson was elected Aug. 16, 1781.

NATHAN BROWNSON, *Governor of Georgia* and *Congressman*, graduated from Yale, 1761. Came to Liberty Co., Ga., and was the *First Physician* to practice south of the Ogeechee river before the Rev. He was surgeon in a Ga. Brigade; member *Provincial Congress* 1775; of *Continental Congress* 1776–1778; member of the legislature 1784. D. Liberty Co., Ga. Nov. 6, 1796.

RICHARD HAWLEY, *Governor of Georgia* 1780, b. near Savannah, Ga., 1740. Represented Liberty Co. in State Assembly. Represented Ga. in *Continental Congress*. During his executive term of office, Ga. was overrun by the British. He d. Savannah, Ga., 1784.

JOHN MARTIN, *Governor of Georgia* (1782–1783). Appointed Naval Officer at the Port of Sunbury, by Governor Wright in 1761. A *Patriot*; member *Provincial Congress* 1775; Lieut.-Colonel of Continental Army 1781. As Governor of Georgia 1782, his administration saw the British evacuate Savannah, July 11, 1782. Appointed a commissioner to make treaty with the Cherokee Indians 1783, and the same year was elected Treasurer of State.

GEORGE MATHEWS, *Governor or Georgia* 1787, re-elected Governor in 1794–95. B. Augusta Co., Va., 1739. Made Colonel 1775 and fought under Washington at Brandywine and Germantown. Served as Colonel under Gen. Greene, located in Oglethorpe Co., 1785. D. Augusta, Ga., Aug. 30, 1812, age 73 years. Buried St. Paul's Churchyard, Augusta, Ga.

JOHN MILLEDGE, *Governor of Georgia* (1803-1806), b. Savannah, Ga., 1757. Active in the cause of "Liberty;" was one of the party that rifled the crown's powder magazine, and captured Governor Wright in his own house; participated in the futile assaults upon Savannah and Augusta;

elected to *Continental Congress;* was the FIRST who originated the idea of a State University, and gave 700 acres of land to the University; d. Feb. 9, 1818; buried Summerville Cemetery, Augusta, Ga.

JOHN CLARKE (son of Col. Elijah Clarke, *Rev. Sol.*), *Governor of Georgia* (1819-1823), b. N. C., 1766. At the age of 16 was appointed Lieutenant of a Co., then Captain of the Continental Militia. Under command of his father, he fought at the Siege of Augusta and the Battle of Jack's Creek. Major-General in War of 1812. Elected *Governor* in 1819 and 1821. Moved to Florida 1827, where he died Oct. 15, 1832.

MATTHEW TALBOT, *Governor of Georgia* (1819), b. Bedford Co., Va., 1756. Settled in Wilkes Co., Ga., 1785. Member of convention which framed the Constitution of Ga. President of the Senate. By the death of GOVERNOR WILLIAM RABUN (son of MATTHEW RABUN, *Rev. Sol.*), he became *Governor*, acting until the election of Governor John Clarke. D. in Wilkes Co. Ga., Sept. 17, 1827.

GOVERNORS OF GEORGIA WHO WERE REVOLUTIONARY SOLDIERS

WILLIAM EWEN, Chairman of "Council of Safety," 1775; ARCHIBALD BULLOCH, served as commander-in-chief and *President of Georgia* under the Provisional Assembly, up to the meeting of the first regular State Convention, Feb. 7, 1777, and was thus the first *Republican President of Georgia;* Governor 1776-7; BUTTON GWINNETT, 1777; JOHN ADAM TREUTLEN, 1777; JOHN HOUSTON, 1778-1784; JOHN WEREAT, 1779; RICHARD HAWLEY, 1780; STEPHEN HEARD, 1780; NATHAN BROWNSON, 1781; JOHN MARTIN, 1782-3; LYMAN HALL, 1783; SAMUEL ELBERT, 1785; GEORGE MATHEWS, 1787-1794-5; GEORGE HANDLEY, 1788; GEORGE WALTON, 1789-1790; JARED IRWIN, 1796; EDWARD TELFAIR, 1789-1791-93; JAMES JACKSON, 1786; DAVID EMANUEL, 1801; JOSIAH TATTNALL, 1802; JOHN MILLEDGE, 1803-1806; MATTHEW TALBOT, 1819; JOHN CLARKE, 1819-1821.

REVOLUTIONARY SOLDIERS

PART I.

Many years have rolled away since the stirring scenes of the Revolution were acted but the brilliant events of that period will live on the pages of history.

The names of those *Revolutionary Soldiers* who espoused the popular cause and threw the whole weight of their power and influence on the side of Liberty, are on the Nation's Roll of Honor.

While the Revolutionary Army of Georgia was small compared to many other Colonies, it was our State, Georgia, which offered land in quantity as an inducement to *Revolutionary Soldiers* of all the States to settle in Georgia.

Truly we can say these *Revolutionary Soldiers* from Georgia and the other Colonies helped to secure for us our glorious heritage.

CHARLES ABERCROMBIE (son of Robert Abercrombie, *Rev. Sol.* of N. C., b. Scotland, 1715), b. N. C., Mar. 4, 1742; d. Hancock Co., Ga. 1819. Served as Capt. 1778; Major 1780 N. C. Line; received bounty land in Ga. for his services. Mar. Edwina Booth (dau. of JOHN BOOTH, private N. C. Line. Capt. Raiford's Co., Col. Armstrong's Troop. B. N. C., d. Hancock Co., Ga. 1804.)

Children:

1. John, mar. Elizabeth Martin, widow.
2. Abner.
3. Leonard, mar. Sallie Comer.
4. Edmund (1773-1829), mar. Mary Pollard (1778-1810).
5. Anderson, *Sol. War of 1812*, mar. Sidney Grimes.
6. James, mar. Parthenia Ann (Brown) Ross.
7. Charles, mar. Elizabeth (Grimes) Martin.
8. Jane, mar. BOLLING HALL, *Rev. Sol.*, b. Va., 1767, d. Ala. 1836 (son of HUGH HALL, *Rev. Sol.* of Va. and his wife Mary Dixon.)
9. Nancy, mar. Mr. Barnes.
10. Sarah, mar. Thomas Baines.

ROBERT ABERCROMBIE (son Robert Abercrombie, *Rev. Sol.* of N. C.), b. Orange Co., N. C.; d. Hancock Co., Ga. Served as Major Col. John Butler's Reg. N. C. troops. Mar. Mary —.

JOHN ADAIR (son of JOSEPH ADAIR, *Rev. Sol.* of S. C. and his wife, Sarah Dillard, and grandson of JOSEPH ADAIR, *Rev. Sol.* of S. C. and his (1) wife Sarah Laferty), b. Duncan's Creek, S. C., 1753; d. Morgan Co., Ga. 1812. Entered service 1779; captured near Charlotte, N.C.; in prison Camden, S. C. Mar. Jane Jones. She mar. (2) Green Jackson; she d. 1852.

Children:

1. Joseph Alexander, mar. 1811 Elizabeth McCord.
2. John Fisher (1785-1856), mar. (1) Tylitha Brantley; (2) Mary Radcliff Slaven (dau. of Norcut Slaven and his wife, Ann Holliday, of Wilkes Co., Ga.)
3. Hiram, *Sol. of 1812.* Lived Upson Co., Ga.
4. Jones, mar. (1) Miss Woods, (2) Polly Ann Shields.
5. Elizabeth, mar. Miles Garrett, of Ala.
6. William, mar. — Lived Morgan Co., Ga.
7. Mary, mar. John Apperson, of Ala.
8. Farmar.
9. Susan.
10. Sarah, d. y.
11. James, mar. Sarah Dean.

Letter from Gen. Smallwood to Lord Cornwallis, Commander of the British forces, Southern Dept. Oct. 24, 1780. (Extract)

"Sir: . . . . . the prisoners taken in the neighborhood of Charlotte, N. C., viz: JOHN ADAIR; RICHARD THOMAS; WILLIAM RANKIN; ANDREW BAXTER; JOHN MCKAY; WILLIAM WILEY; WILLIAM WALLACE; and ALEXANDER BROWN, I understand are very desirous of obtaining an exchange. Perhaps your Lordship would have no objection to admit of a partial exchange of those persons for a like number now in our possession, whose situations or circumstances may not be altogether dissimilar. If this proposition should meet with your approbation, you will be so obliging as to signify it, that the exchange may take place." The exchange was made.

The Henry Laurens Chapter D. A. R. of Laurens, S. C. and the Musgrove Mill Chapter, D.A.R. of Clinton, S. C. placed a tablet in the Duncan Creek Presbyterian Church, Laurens Co., S. C. (This Old Church founded by the Scotch Irish, is a veritable mother of Presbyterianism in S. C.) The tablet placed in honor of and bears the names of 16 *Rev. Sols.*, viz:

1. Joseph Adair, Sr.
2. Joseph Adair, Jr.
3. Thomas Logan.
4. Robert Long.
5. Leonard Beasley.
6. John Copeland.
7. George Young.
8. Joseph Ramage.
9. Thomas McCrary.
10. Thomas Holland.
11. Robert Hanna.
12. John Craig.
13. J. Bell.
14. James Craig.
15. James Adair, Sr.
16. William Underwood.

Many of these men came to Georgia.

JAMES ADAMS (son of James and Cecily (Ford) Adams), b. Albemarle Co., Va., Oct. 18, 1753; d. Elbert Co., Ga., 1835. Served as Minute man and Orderly Sergeant Va. troops. Enlisted Fluvanna Co., Va., 1777 under Capt. Roger Thompson and Col. Charles Lewis; received pension; also land 1827 Cherokee Lottery. Mar. in Va. JANE CUNNINGHAM. Moved to Elbert Co., Ga., 1796.

Children:
1. William, mar. (1) Katherine Mansfield; (2) Sarah Head.
2. Samuel, mar. Martha Ann Thornton.
3. Ann Thompson, mar. HIRAM GAINES, *Rev. Sol.* of Ga.
4. Jane, mar. Isham Teasley.
5. Elizabeth, mar. IVY SEALS, *Rev. Sol.* of Ga.
6. John C., mar. Ann Dickerson.

JAMES ADAMS, b. S. C., d. Hancock Co., Ga. Served under Gen. Sumpter in S. C. Mar. Mary —.
Children:
1. Robert, mar. 1815 Frances Hudson (dau. of IRBY HUDSON, *Rev. Sol.*)
2. David.
3. Jonathan.
4. William.
5. James.
6. Rebecca, mar. — Hill.
7. Polly.
8. Nancy.
9. Jean.

DAVID ALDERMAN, b. N. J. 1749 (son of Daniel Alderman and his wife, Abigail Harris, of N. J. and Duplin Co., N. C.); d. Bulloch Co., Ga., 1831. Was a *Rev. Sol.* of N. C. Moved to Ga. 1815. Mar. 1773 JEMINA HALL (1753-1815), b. and d. at Duplin Co., N. C.)
Children:
1. Daniel, b. 1773, mar. (1) Ann Newton; (2) Mary Wilson; (3) Mary Williams; (4) Mary P. Wilson.
2. Ann (called Nancy) Nov. 11, 1775, mar. John Carlton.
3. Thomas, Aug. 7, 1777, mar. Susan Newton.
4. Mary, Aug. 29, 1779, mar. Timothy Murphy.
5. Elizabeth, April 20, 1781, mar. — Newton.
6. Phoebe, April 11, 1783, mar. John Matthis.
7. Lucertia, Mar. 19, 1785, mar. Joshua Herring.
8. Rachel, Jan. 12, 1787, mar. — Sloan.
9. Samuel, Mar. 13, 1789, mar. Sarah Chestnut.
10. Rebecca, Feb. 25, 1793, mar. Elisha Alderman (Daniel).
11. Susanna, Mar. 14, 1795, mar. William Bland.

12. William, Jan. 12, 1798, mar. Sarah Edmondson.

13. Timothy, Feb. 19, 1801, mar. Sarah Williams.

14. James, Feb. 19, 1801, mar. Anna Holloway.

Note: DANIEL ALDERMAN (brother of DAVID ALDERMAN) was a *Rev. Sol.* of N. C.; mar. Sarah Newton. He was b. 1745; d. in N. C., 1821. Children: Jemina, 1773; David, 1775; Rachel, 1779; Sarah, 1782; Isaac, 1784; Mary, 1786; Elisha, 1788; Elizabeth, 1791. Many of their descendants came to Ga.

JOHN ALDERMAN (brother of DANIEL and DAVID ALDERMAN), was also a *Rev. Sol.* of N. C. mar. Mary Cashwell.

Note: REV. JAMES ALLEN, who is buried in Columbus, Ga. (Grave located by Ala. D.A.R) when only a lad, took up arms in Va. Continental Line as a *Rev. Sol.* in defense of his country. He afterwards moved to Wilkes Co., Ga.

DR. ADAM ALEXANDER, b. Inverness, Scotland, Mar. 13, 1738; came to America and settled at Sunbury, Ga., 1776; served as surgeon in the Continental Army, Ga. troops; mar. (2) Louisa F. Schmidt (1775–1846).

Children:

1. Adam Leopold, b. Jan. 29, 1803, mar. Sarah Hillhouse Gilbert (dau. of FELIX GILBERT, *Rev. Sol.*, and his wife, Miss Hillhouse, and grand dau. of David and Sarah (Porter) Hillhouse, of Conn. and Ga.).

2. Louisa, b. 1807, mar. Major Anthony Porter.

SAMUEL ALEXANDER, b. N. C., 1757; d. Warren Co., Ga., 1817. In Col. Elijah Clarke's Reg. of Rifle Corps. Received 287½ acres of land for his services as a *Rev. Sol.* in Franklin Co., Ga. Mar. Olivia Wooten (or Norton), b. 1759.

Children:

1. Asa, mar. Fathia Wooten, of Greene Co., Ga.

2. Mary, mar. James Simmons, b. 1774.

3. Asenith, mar. Dr. Willis Roberts.

From *House Journal* of Ga. 1796:

"CAPT. SAMUEL ALEXANDER prays compensation for balance due him while serving as Capt. in Col. Elijah Clarke's Reg. Rifle Corps, raised to aid Gen. Wayne in 1782. Capt. Alexander satisfied claims for GEORGE BARNHARD; LEWELLYN INLOW; and WILLIAM CLINTON, privates in his Co. The Governor of Ga. was authorized to draw warrant out of taxes of 1794, for sum due him." Feb. 13, 1796.

WILLIAM ALEXANDER, b. Va.; d. Elbert Co., Ga., 1806. Received bounty land in Wilkes Co., Ga., 1784, for his services as a *Rev. Sol.* in Continental Army of Va. and Ga. Also drew land as a *Rev. Sol.* in Elbert Co., 1806. Mar. (1) (name unknown); (2) Nancy —.

Children:

1. Peter, mar. Nancy Shackelford (dau. of HENRY SHACKELFORD, *Rev. Sol.*).

2. James.

3. John.

4. George.

5. Elijah.

6. Ezza, mar. (as (1) wife) Standley Jones; mar (2) Frances Rucker (dau. of WILLIAM RUCKER, a *Rev. Sol.*).

7. Milly, mar. Willis Rucker.

8. Dau., mar. William Page.

9. Frances, mar. 1810 Bardin Rucker.

10. Dau., mar. Reuben Cleveland.

DREWRY ALLEN, b. Orange Co., N. C., Dec. 1, 1749; d. Pike Co., Ga., Jan. 20, 1826. Served as *Rev. Sol.*, N. C. troops. Mar. in Greene Co., Ga., Elizabeth Yarbrough (1753–1823).

Children:

1. Josiah, mar. Elizabeth Browning.

2. Clement, mar. Mary McKissick.

3. Stokes, mar. Susan Jane Fouche.

4. Nancy, mar. (1) — West; Feb. 4, 1817, mar. (2) James Ravens; mar. (3) John Yarborough.
5. Martha (1782–1853), mar. (as (2) wife) William Pyron.
6. Young David, mar. Jane Moore.

ROBERT ALLEN, b. N. C.; d. Ga. Received a grant of land for his services as a *Rev. Sol.* of N. C. Mar. (1) near Hepzibah, Ga., Elizabeth Anderson (dau. of Elisha Anderson and his (1) wife, Miss Brack); mar. (2) —; their dau., Hattie, mar. Henry Washburne, of Savannah, Ga.
Children:
1. Martha, mar. Judge William Rhodes.
2. Jane, mar. Edmund Palmer.
3. Elizabeth, mar. (as (1) wife) Alexander Murphy.
4. Rosa, mar. Benjamin Wooding.
5. Polly Crawford.
6. Sarah.
7. Jackson.
8. Emily.
9. Robert A., mar. (1) Priscilla Wood; (2) Caroline Walker, widow.
10. Elisha A., mar. Jeanette Evans (dau. of Daniel Evans).

BENJAMIN ALLISON, b. Montgomery Co., Md., 1760; d. Habersham Co., Ga., April, 1844. Mar. Md., 1786, CASSANDRA —. Moved to N. C., then to Ga. in 1824. His name is on the list of persons who have taken the Oath of Allegiance and Affirmation of Fidelity and Support to the State of Md. (Rev. Record), May, 1778.
Children:
1. Benjamin, Jr.
2. William, mar. Miss Padgett (their dau., Susan Clark, mar. Reaves Westmoreland).
3. Elizabeth.
4. Hamilton (or Hampton), mar. Margaret —.
5. Thomas, Mar. Clarisey.
6. Dau., mar. William Buchanan.
7. Dau., mar. William Hix.
8. Dau., mar. James Chambers.
9. Dau., mar. John C. Allen.

HENRY ALLISON, of Greene Co., Ga., and wife, MARTHA, of Richmond Co., Ga., Oct. 10, 1787, sold to Anderson Crawford, of Richmond Co., Ga., 460 a. on the Oconee river, Washington Co., on lands reserved by an act of the Assembly of the State, Feb. 12, 1784 for the payment of bounties and gratuities to the officers and soldiers of the Continental Establishments and the above mentioned tract of 460 a. of land being a gratuity ordered by the General Assembly of Ga. to HENRY ALLISON, formerly a Lieutenant in the Continental Troops, land in Greene Co. (formerly Washington Co.), Ga., granted April, 1784, by his Honor, Governor Mathews.

JAMES ALSTON, b. Chowan Co., N. C., about 1746; d. Elbert Co., Ga., 1815. He was an officer in N. C. Regiment. Mar. Orange Co., N. C., 1774, Grizell (Gilly) Yancey, b. N. C., 1752, d. Monroe Co., Ga., 1845.
Children:
1. Nathaniel (1775–1852), mar. Mary Grey Jeffrys.
2. Charity, mar. James Banks.
3. Sarah, mar. Joseph Groves.
4. Martha, d. unmarried.
5. John, mar. (1) Charity Tate; (2) Miss McGinty.
6. Hannah, mar. James Jones Banks (son of Ralph and Rachel (Jones) Banks).
7. Elizabeth, mar. John O. Glover.

LIEUT. COL. WILLIAM ALSTON, b. N. C., Dec. 25, 1736; d. Elbert Co., Ga., 1810. Member *N. C. Provincial Congress* 1775; of the Constitutional Convention, Halifax Co., N. C., 1776. Lieut.-Col. in 1776, 3d. Regiment N. C. troops under Gen. Jethro Summer. Mar. his cousin, Charity Alston. She d. 1823.

Children:
1. James, mar. Catherine Hamilton (dau. of MAJOR ANDREW HAMILTON, *Rev. Sol.* of Va., and his wife, Jane McGara).
2. William H., mar. Elizabeth Rucker.
3. Philip Rucker, mar. Miss Woolfolk.
4. Solomon.
5. George.
6. Mary, mar. Capt. James Clark.
7. Elizabeth, mar. — Thompson.
8. Christine.
9. Ann, mar. — Tait.
10. Sarah, mar. Thomas Chambers.

WILLIAM ANDERSON, b. Va., Jan. 8, 1763; d. Baldwin Co., Ga., May 6, 1844. Enlisted Wilkes Co., Ga., under Capt. Burwell, Col. Elijah Clarke's Ga. Line. At Siege of Augusta. Enlisted later at Wrightsboro, Ga., as a Volunteer Rifleman, stationed at Philip's Fort, Wilkes Co., Ga. Pension; widow's file No. 6855. Mar. (1) Wilkes Co., Ga., Sarah Finch (dau. of CHARLES FINCH, *Rev. Sol.*, d. Franklin Co., Ga., 1795, and his wife, Joyce); (2) Baldwin Co., Ga., Mar. 5, 1806, Mary Hunnicutt, d. 1844. She drew a pension, as widow of *Rev. Sol.* 1844. They had 15 children, 13 living in 1844, and mentioned in pension.
1. Louisa.
2. Sarah.
3. Allen G.
4. Thomas B.
5. Lazarus G.
6. Henry F.
7. David M.
8. Gilbert M.
9. Mary Ann.
10. Martha S., mar. George W. Rowell.
11. ANN MARIAH, b. May 19, 1825, mar. 1857 Thomas Parham Redding. She was a *Real Daughter* of the *National Society, Daughters of the American Revolution.*
12. LUCY ANN, b. 1829, mar. T. Marion Gibson. She was a *Real Daughter* of the *National Society, Daughters of the American Revolution.*
13. George Washington.

CHRISTOPHER ANTHONY, b. Va., 1744; d. while on a visit to Cincinnati, O., 1815. Served as a *Rev. Sol.* in Va. and drew land for his services in Wilkes Co., Ga. Mar. (1) JUDITH MOORMAN; mar. (2) MARY JORDAN, of Nansemond Co., Va. (dau. of Samuel and Mary (Bates) Jordan).

Children by (1) wife:
1. Mary, mar. David Terrell.
2. Joseph, mar. Rhoda Moorman.
3. Charles, mar. Elizabeth Harris.
4. Elizabeth, mar. William Ballard.

Children by (2) wife:
1. Christopher, mar. Annie H. Couch.
2. Samuel, mar. Mary Irwin.
3. Hannah, mar. (1) — Johnson; (2) John Davis.
4. Sarah, mar. Henry Davis.
5. Jordan.
6. Penelope.
7. Charlotte, mar. Eph Morgan.
8. Rachel, mar. Lot Pugh.

JOSEPH ANTHONY, b. Va., Mar. 28, 1750; d. Wilkes Co., Ga., 1810. He served as a *Rev. Sol.* of Va. and drew bounty land for his services in Wilkes Co., Ga. Mar. (1) Rhoda —. He mar. (2)

Ann Elizabeth Clark (called Betty), dau. of MICAJAH CLARK, *Rev. Sol.* of Va., and his wife Judith Adams.

Children by (1) wife:
1. Sanuel P.
2. Thomas C.
3. Charles.
4. Judith.

Children by (2) wife:
1. Mary, mar. Armistead Ellis Stokes.
2. Mark.
3. Ansel M. (1778–1868), mar. (1) 1806, Sarah Menzies of N. C.; (2) 1836, Catherine Blakely, of Wilkes Co.
4. Joseph.
5. Micajah.
6. Ann, mar. — Early.

JAMES ANTHONY, b. Bedford Co., Va., 1747; d. Wilkes Co., Ga., 1827. Served in Capt. Stubblefield's Co., Col. Parker's 5th Va. Reg., Mar. Ann (Nancy) Tate.

JOHN ANDREW, b. Midway, Ga., 1758; d. Clarke Co., Ga., Mar. 10, 1830. Served as private under Gen. Samuel Elbert Ga. Troops; Ensign under Gen. Wade Hampton. Mar. (1) in S. C., Feb. 10, 1779, ANN LAMBRIGHT. He mar. (2) at Colonels Island, Ga., Sept. 20, 1785, MARY BUER ANDREWS. He mar. (3) in Elbert Co., Ga., Dec. 11, 1791, Mary Overton Cosby.

One dau. by (1) wife:
1. Ann, mar. Abram J. Roberts. She was b. Jan. 20, 1780.

Children by (2) wife:
1. Mary Buer, b. 1786, mar. 1807, Samuel Le Seuer.
2. Matilda Hull, b. 1792, mar. 1809, Geo. C. Spencer.

Children by (3) wife:
1. James Osgood, b. Wilkes Co., May 3, 1794; mar. May 1, 1816, Ann Amelia McFarland, of Charleston, S. C. He was Bishop of Methodist Episcopal Church, South.
2. Charles Godfrey (1795–1796).
3. Lucy Garland, b. 1799, mar. (1) 1830, John Wright; (2) 1844, William R. Henry.
4. Betsey Sidnor, b. 1800.
5. Scynthia Fletcher (1802–1803).
6. Carolina Wesley, b. 1804.
7. Patsey Evelina, b. 1806.
8. Judy Harvey (1809–1833).
9. Hardy H. (1811–1854).
10. William Harvie.

JOHN ANDREW, after the Rev. War, was the first itinerant Methodist preacher in Ga., who was a native Georgian. He was the son of James Andrew, a member of the Puritan Dorchester settlement in Ga. This was the only congregation of Puritans, south of New England. They removed in a body from Mass. to S. C., then to Ga., and formed the famous "Midway Church" in St. John's Parish (now Liberty Co.). John Andrew, left an orphan when young, was brought up at the home of Pastor Osgood, in charge of the Midway Congregation.

NOTE: GARNETT ANDREWS, b. June 11, 1764; d. Oglethorpe Co., Ga., Oct. 5, 1807, mar. Jane (called Ginny) Woodson on Jan. 1, 1787, b. Mar. 26, 1767. Children: 1. William, b. 1787; 2. Susanna, b. 1789; 3. Betsey W., b. 1790; 4. Thomas, b. 1800; 5. Wyatt, b. Feb. 6, 1794, d. 1831, mar. 1816 Johanna Smith (dau. of Anthony Garnett Smith and his wife, Polly Allen); 6. Jacob Woodson; 7. Thomas Garnett, b. 1802; 8. Nancy; 9. Ave Pollard, b. 1807.

JOHN ANDREWS, b. Va., May 4, 1762, d. Oglethorpe Co., Ga., May 2, 1816. *Rev. Sol.* of Va. Mar. in Va. Mar. 17, 1789, NANCY GOODE. She d. after 1816. He was at Yorktown at surrender of Cornwallis; came to Ga.; received bounty grant of land for his services; settled in Oglethorpe Co.

Children:
1. Marcus, mar. Ann Connell.

2. Frances Garnett, mar. James Daniel.
3. John Garnett, mar. Mary Ann Polhill.
4. Garnett, mar. Annulet Ball.
5. Sarah Martha, mar. Dr. Isaac Bowen.
6. Elizabeth, d. y. (1800-1804).
7. Elizabeth, b. 1805, mar. Dr. Willis Green.
8. Emily, mar. Richard Jones.
9. James A.
10. Daniel Marshall, mar. Martha A. Wylie.

WILLIAM ANDREWS (son of Dr. Mark Andrews, *Rev. Sol.* of Va., and his wife, Avis Garnett), b. Va., 1758; d. Oglethorpe Co., Ga., May 3, 1821.   Allowed pension for his services as Sergeant in Capt. Mayo Carrington's Co. Va. troops.   Wounded at the Battle of Brandywine 1777. Mar. Mary Gaines.

Children:
1. William, b. 1796, d. 1875, mar. Elizabeth Smith (dau. of LARKIN SMITH, b. Va., 1760, d. Oglethorpe Co., Ga., 1834, *Rev. Sol.* of Va., and his wife, Avey Bradley).
2. Elizabeth G.
3. Ave.
4. Nancy.

THOMAS ANSLEY, b. 1737; d. Warren Co., Ga. 1809. Served as private Ga. troops. Received bounty land for his services. Mar. 1760 Rebecca Harrison, widow, d. 1804.

Children:
1. Thomas, Jr. (1767-1837), mar. Henrietta Ragland.
2. Abel, mar. Lydia Morris.
3. Samuel, mar. 1809 Mary Tillman.
4. Miller.
5. William.
6. James.
7. Joseph.
8. Rebecca, mar. —Duckworth.
9. Nancy.
(One step-son of Thomas Ansley, viz: Benjamin Harrison.)

JOHN APPLING, JR., b. Va.; d. Richmond Co., Ga. private Ga. troops, and granted land for his services. Member Constitutional Convention from Richmond Co. Mar. Rebecca Carter (dau. of LANGDON CARTER, *Rev. Sol.* of Va.).

Son: Col. Daniel Appling, A *Sol. of 1812.*

JOHN APPLING, SR., was a *Rev. Sol.* of Va. Mar. Martha —. After his death, Martha Appling moved with her children to Richmond (now Columbia) Co., Ga. and was given two tracts of land as the widow of a *Rev. Sol.* in 1785. Made will Aug. 17, 1788.

Their children were:
1. JOHN, JR.
2. Daniel.
3. William.
4. Elizabeth, mar. Joshua Wynne, of Richmond Co., Ga., *Rev. Sol.*
5. Lucy.
6. Patty.

JEAN PIERRE ARNAUD, b. Marseilles, France, 1751, came to America and settled in Md. D. Savannah, Ga., 1833. Served as private in Capt. Williamson Co. Md. Line. Later served as privateer, was captured and confined on the "Jersey" prison ship. Mar. ELIZABETH LELAND (1760-1853). Their dau.:
Elizabeth Cecil Virginia (1801-1839) mar. 1820, John James Penfield Boisfeuillet (1703-1864).

JAMES F. ARNOLD, b. Halifax Co., Va., 1754; d. Monroe Co., Ga., 1825. Served as Major N. C. Line. Mar. 1770 Bethany Bailey (1758-1850).

Children:
1. Elijah B., mar. Susan Ware.
2. Jesse.
3. Malina.
4. James.
5. Fielding.
6. Augustus.

JAMES ARNOLD, b. Augusta Co., Va., 1760; d. Wilkinson Co., Ga., 1823. Served as Corporal under Capt. John Gillison, Col. Stephens and Col. Russell, 6th and 10th Va. Regiment. Mar. ELIZA-BETH STROUD (dau. of JOHN STROUD (1745-1813) who served as private under Capt. Meriwether, 1st Va. Reg.) and his wife, Mary Margaret Dozier (1750-1812) (dau. of WILLIAM DOZIER, *Rev. Sol.* of Va. and his wife Elizabeth—).

WILLIAM ASHE, b. Penn.; d. Burke Co., Ga., 1831. Served in the Snow campaign in 1777 under Capt. Bratton, Col. Neal and Col. Lacey. Mar. 1783 Jane Fleming; d. 1854. She received a pension as his widow 1834 for his services.
Children:
1. John, mar. Miss Newton, moved to Ala.
2. Alexander (1785-1848), mar. 1824 Elizabeth McCracken (dau. of WILLIAM McCRACKEN who served with N. C. troops, and received bounty grant of land for his services 1784 in Franklin Co., Ga., and his wife Elizabeth McCord.)
3. James.
4. Dobey.
5. William, Jr., mar. Cynthia Turk.
6. Robert Rutherford.
7. Mary Hunter.
8. Janet.
9. Elizabeth.
10. Elijah.
11. Isabella.
12. Rachel.

ICA ATKINS (son of ICA ATKINS, *Rev. Sol.* of Cumberland Co., N. C. Private N. C. Line, and his wife, Nancy Hutchins), b. Mar. 7, 1763; d. Dodge Co., Ga., 1832. Mar. Mary Gordon. (His grave as a *Rev. Sol.* was marked).
Children:
1. Elizabeth.
2. Ann (1795-1885), mar. (1) William Martinleer; (2) John Miers; (3) Wm. Colbert.
3. Sarah.
4. Littleberry.
5. Ica.
6. Janet.
7. Mary.
8 Lillie.
9. Grace.
10. Richard Gordon.

NATHAN ATKINSON, b. S. C.; d. Greene Co., Ga. Served with S. C. troops and received bounty land for his services in Ga. Mar. Betsey Whitehead. Moved to Greene Co., Ga.
Children:
1. Betsey.
2. Patience.
3. Rhoda.
4. Thomas.
5. Jane.
6. Lazarus, b. 1791, d. Ala. Mar. July 13, 1813, Mary Ellen Lane (dau. WILLIAM D. LANE), *Rev. Sol.* Served with Ga. troops. D. Putnam Co., Ga., before 1785. Grant made to William Lane's

heirs (dec.) Feb. 15, 1785 on Certificate of service in 3d Ga. Continental Batt., NATHANIEL PIERCE, Lieut. and Adj.

THOMAS ATKINSON (son of Henry and Ann Atkinson, Quakers), b. Craven Co., N. C., Sept. 18, 1741; d. Ga. after 1815. Mar. (1) 1765, in N. C., RUTH CRUZE (dau. of John and Ann Cruze). She d. N. C., Jan. 17, 1779. He mar. (2) Sept. 5, 1781 RUTH HARVEY, of N. C.

He was a *Rev. Sol.* of N. C. Certificate of Payment on record, Hillsboro District, N. C. Moved to Ga. 1784.

Children by (1) wife:
1. JOHN, b. Nov. 25, 1766, mar. Mary Woody.
2. Thomas, b. Aug. 30, 1769.
3. Mary, b. April 5, 1771.
4. Ann, b. Feb .28, 1773.
5. Robert, b. Feb. 17, 1775.

Children by (2) wife:
6. William, b. July 18, 1782.
7. Elizabeth, b. Sept. 29, 1784.
8. Henry, b. Feb. 11, 1786; d. 1800.
9. Martha, b. June 10, 1787.
10. Rachel, b. Oct. 12, 1788.
11. Isaac, b. 1790; d. 1799.
12. Ruth, b. May 25, 1791.
13. Edith, b. June 29, 1795.
14. Nathan, b. 1795; d. 1800.
15. David, b. Aug. 21, 1797.

JOHN AVERY, b. (now Columbia) Co., Ga.; d. Columbia Co., Ga., 1847. (Had two brothers, Archer and Isaac Avery). Served in Ga. troops; wounded at Battle of Brier Creek, Ga.; was given grant of land for his services. Mar. MARY LOGGETT.

Children:
1. John.
2. Martha, mar. —Wellborn.
3. Elizabeth, mar. —Smith.
4. Miller.
5. Herbert.
6. Archer.
7. Asa, mar. Sarah Jones.

WILLIAM AYCOCK, b. Va.; d. Elbert Co., Ga., 1805. Served with Georgia troops. Received grant of land in Franklin Co., Ga., for his services. Mar. Patty Easter (dau. of James and Sarah Easter, of Elbert Co., Ga., *Rev. Sol.*)

Children:
1. James.
2. Richard.
3. Milton.
4. Juda.
5. Tabitha.
6. Terrell.

DANIEL AYERS, b. 1763; d. Ga., 1827. Drew land in Ga. for his services as a *Rev. Sol.* Mar. RHODA HOLTON.

Children:
1. Joseph.
2. Obediah.
3. Mary.
4. Priscilla.
5. John.
6. Rhoda.

JOHN BACHLOTT, b. St. Milo, France, 1760; d. Camden Co., Ga., June 6,1833. Came with LA FAYETTE to America. Was at the Battle of Yorktown. Drew land in Camden Co., Ga., for his services. Mar. 1785 MARY CONRAD in Va. Came to S. C. then to Amelia Island, Fla., 1799. Settled at St. Mary's, Ga., 1800. Their son:

JOSEPH BACHLOTT, b. Va., 1792; d. St. Mary's, Ga., 1822. Mar. Mary Frances Rudolph, b. 1805 (dau. of THOMAS RUDOLPH, b. 1760, buried St. Mary's, Ga. A *Rev. Sol.*; and his wife Elizabeth, who as his widow drew a pension for his services.) (The grave of John Bachlott has been marked by the D. A. R.)

THOMAS BACON, b. S. C., 1743. Came to Ga. 1755; d. Liberty Co., Ga., Jan. 26, 1812. Served as 3d. Lieut. under COL. JOHN BACON 1776; 1st Lieut. Liberty Co. Riflemen. Received bounty land for his services 1784. Mar. (1) CATHERINE WINN, June 7, 1770, at Midway Church. She d. Jan 4, 1778. Mar. (2) SARAH BAKER June 1, 1778; (3) MARTHA WHEELER 1779 in Carolina.
Children by (1) wife:
1. John.
2. Thomas, mar. (1) Elizabeth Sumner; (2) Sarah Holcombe.
3. William.
Child by (2) wife:
Sarah.
Children by (3) wife:
1. Catherine.
2. Joseph.
3. Henry.
4. Eliza Winn.

JOHN BACON, b. S. C., 1739; d. Ga., 1786. He served as Capt. Co. of Riflemen Liberty Co., Ga., 1777. Member Provincial Congress from St. John's Parish, Ga., 1775. Mar. (1) ANN ANDREW, Feb. 17, 1761; (2) Sarah Bacon, April 12, 1778; (3) ELIZABETH MORE, in Carolina, 1779. She mar. (2) William Kirkland.

GEORGE BAGBY, b. Va., 1751; d. Jackson Co., Ga., 1807. Drew bounty land in Ga. for his services as *Rev. Sol.* Mar. MARIANA—(or Miriam).
Children:
1. Ann.
2. John.
3. Joseph.
4. Flumes.
5. Abner.
6. Dicey.
7. Sally.
8. Rachel.
9. Henry.
10. William.
11. George. W.
12. Betty.
13. Jeffries.

BEAL BAKER, b. Baltimore, Md., 1756; d. Ga., 1842. Served as a *Rev. Sol.* of Md. Mar. 1782 SARAH BROWN, b. Burke Co., N. C., 1759; d. Ga., 1850. They moved to Hall Co., Ga.
Children:
1. John, b. Oct. 15, 1784, mar. Amelia Brawner.
2. Polly, mar. Isaiah Pritchet.
3. James, mar. Mary Sewell.
4. Joshua (1792–1842), mar. 1814 Mary (called Polly) Parks (1797–1876), dau. of HENRY PARKS, b. Albemarle Co., Va., 1758; d. Ga., 1825, and his wife, Martha Justice. He was a *Rev. Sol.* and drew bounty land for his services in Franklin Co., Ga.

COL. JOHN BAKER, b. Dorchester, Mass., 1722 (son of Benjamin Baker, of Dorchester, Mass., who came to Midway (Liberty Co.), 1752); d. Liberty Co., Ga., June 3, 1792. He was appointed member of the committee which met in Savannah, Ga., July, 1774, to discuss the British Port Bill. Appointed Colonel and served in Continental Army. Member Provincial Congress of Ga. Mar. (1) ELIZABETH FILBIN; (2) MARY (JONES) LAPIN (widow of CAPTAIN MATHIAS LAPIN, *Rev. Sol.* of Ga. Line, who lived at Sunbury, Ga.).

Daughter by (1) wife:

MARY ANN BAKER, mar. John J. Maxwell (son of CAPT. MAXWELL, *Rev. Sol.* of Ga.).

Daughters by (2) wife:

1. SARAH BAKER, mar. (in Liberty Co., Ga.) MICHAEL RUDOLPH, b. Elkton Co., Md.; d. at sea. Served as *Rev. Sol.* Captain 1781 of Ga. Dragoons under Col. Henry Lee, Ga. Line. Their dau., Amelia Rebecca Rudolph (1788–1814), mar. John Francis William Courvoisier, Jr. (son of JOHN FRANCIS WILLIAM COURVOISIER, b. Switzerland, 1750; d. Savannah, Ga., 1811. A *Rev. Patriot*, a Signer of the Resolutions presented by the City of Savannah about the condition of the Colonies in 1775. He mar. 1778 Mary Fox (1762-1816). Mary Fox Courvoisier (dau. of John Francis William Courvoisier, Jr.), was b. 1810; d. 1850. Mar. Robert Lundy (or Lunday) (1798-1860) (son of THEOPHILUS LUNDAY, b. Va.; d. Ga. Served as 2nd Lieut. Volunteer Co. of St. George's Parish, Ga. Received grant of land for his services in Effingham Co., Ga. He mar. 1790 Frances McLinn).

2. MATILDA AMANDA BAKER (dau. of John Baker), mar. Thomas Huston Harden (son of WILLIAM HARDEN, *Rev. Sol.* of S. C.).

AUGUSTUS BALDWIN (cousin of ABRAHAM BALDWIN OF GA.), b. Goshen, Conn., Aug. 27, 1764; d. Savannah, Ga., May 23, 1808. Served as Chaplain Rev. War. Mar. REBECCA COOKE, widow, 1799. She d. Augusta, Ga., May 25, 1828.

Children:

1. Louise, mar. Dr. Alexander Cunningham.
2. Augustus Collins, mar. Mary E. Allen.
3. William Henry.

DAVID BALDWIN, SR., b. 1725; d. Richmond Co., Ga., 1783. Will dated Aug. 24, 1782. Came to Ga. 1767. He was at second siege of Augusta, Ga., and served as Captain Ga. troops. *Rev. Sol.* Mar. 1745 SARAH OWEN (dau. of EPHRIAM OWEN and wife, Sarah —).

Children:

1. WILLIAM, b. May 22, 1746; d. Ga., 1819. Was a *Rev. Sol.* of Ga. Mar. Elizabeth Kimbrough (dau. of JOHN KIMBROUGH, *Rev. Sol.* of Ga.).
2. DAVID, served as *Rev. Sol.* in Capt. Baldwin's Co.; d. 1782.
3. Owen, mar. — Wiley.
4. Ephriam.
5. Sarah, mar. — Parks.

DAVID BALDWIN, SR., and his sons, DAVID BALDWIN, JR., and WILLIAM BALDWIN, each received 287½ acres of land, as bounty land for their services as *Rev. Sols.* in Washington Co., Ga.

WILLIAM BALDWIN, b. N. C., May 22, 1746; d. Columbia Co., Ga., 1819. Was a *Rev. Sol.* Sergeant of Minute Men. Received bounty land for his services in Ga. (son of CAPT. DAVID BALDWIN, *Rev. Sol.*). He was also a *Sol. of War of 1812.* Mar. Elizabeth Kimbrough, b. Wilkes Co., Ga.; d. Ala. (dau. of JOHN KIMBROUGH, *Rev. Sol.* of Ga.).

Children:

1. James (1780–1847), mar. Elizabeth White.
2. David, b. 1783, mar. Elizabeth Ousley.
3. William, b. 1786, mar. Celia Fitzpatrick.
4. John, b. 1790.
5. Sarah, b. Feb. 27, 1793, mar. Joseph Fitzpatrick.
6. Polly, b. Dec. 2, 1795, mar. — Hutchinson.
7. Jesse, b. Mar. 19, 1798, mar. Caleb Willingham.

LAURENCE BANKSTON, b. Va., 1748; d. Wilkes Co., Ga., 1844. Served in Continental Army with Va., N. C. and Ga. troops. Received grant of land in Wilkes Co., Ga., for his services. Mar. NANCY HENDERSON, b. Va., 1758; d. Wilkes Co., Ga., Sept. 26, 1849 (dau. of JOSEPH HENDERSON, *Rev. Sol.* of N. C., d. Wilkes Co., Ga., 1809, and his wife, Isabella Delphia Lea).
Children:

1. Isabella Lea (1784–1874), mar. 1800 Isaiah Tucker Irvine (1783-1855), son of CHRISTO-PHER IRVINE, *Rev. Sol* of Va. and g-son of WILLIAM IRVINE, *Rev. Sol.* of Va.).
2. Priscilla, mar. William Matthews.
3. Elizabeth, mar. Samuel G. Mozley.
4. Martha, mar. Caleb Sappington.
5. Delphia, mar. Jacob Shorter.
6. Esther, mar. Isaac Whitaker.
7. Hiram, mar. Susanna —.

MAJOR JOHN BARNARD (son of Col. John Barnard of the BRITISH ARMY, who came to Savannah, Ga., about 1743 in command of a Regiment called the "Rangers," held commission until his death, and his wife, Jane Bradley); b. Wilmington Island, Ga., Nov. 12, 1750; d. Ga., 1825. Member Provincial Congress 1775. Assisted in raising the "Liberty Pole" in Savannah. Commanded a Co. which attacked the crew of a British frigate, which had landed on Wilmington Island. Was taken prisoner, exchanged, and served until the end of the War. Mar. LUCY TURNER (dau. of Lewis and Jesten Turner, of Savannah, Ga.).
Children:

1. Timothy, b. 1775, mar. Amelia Guerard.
2. Lucy Wilmington, mar. (1) Henry Charles Jones; (2) Charles O. Screven.
3. Mary E.
4. John W.
5. James, mar. Catherine Guerard.
6. Henrietta, mar. Stephen Williams.
7. Georgia A., mar. Murdock Chisolm.

ABRAHAM BARNETT, b. Orange Co., N. C., 1751; d. Greene Co., Ga., 1792. Served in Capt. WM. JOHNSTON'S CO., 11th Va. Reg. and N. C. troops. Received bounty grant of land for his services. Mar. Mecklenburg Co., N. C., MARY BROOMFIELD (1757-1818).
Children:

1. William, moved to Miss.
2. Martha, b. 1798; d. Henry Co., Ga., 1851; mar. Dr. John S. Fall (as (2) wife).
3. Mary, mar. — King.
4. Margaret (called Peggy).
5. Ann, mar. — Dale.
6. Jane, mar. (1) — Elliot; (2) — Broomfield.
7. Elizabeth, mar. — Hart.

JOEL BARNETT, b. Amherst Co., Va., 1762. Moved to Ga.; d. on a visit to Miss. (Son of Nathaniel Barnett, *Rev. Sol.* of Va. and Ga.) Served as private Ga. Line; received bounty grant of land for his services in Washington Co., Ga. Mar. (1) Elizabeth Crawford; (2) Mildred Meriwether.
Child by (1) wife:
Joel, Jr.

Children by (2) wife:
1. Susan, mar. (1) John Gresham; (2) John Gilmer.
2. Charles (1800–1890), mar. Eliza Williamson Gresham.
3. Frank, mar. Eliza Goolsby.
4. Emily, mar. (1) Craven Totten; (2) — Stewart.
5. Ann, mar. — Burke.
6. Rebecca, mar. Michael Johnson.
7. Nathaniel.
8. Dau., mar. — Crawford.

JOHN BARNETT (son of Nathan Barnett, *Rev. Sol.* of Va., and his wife, Lucy Webb), b. Va., June 7, 1762; d. Clark Co., Ga., Mar. 1814. Served as private Ga. troops under Gen. Elijah Clarke and in S. C. troops under Gen. Francis Marion. Received bounty grant of land. Mar. July 13, 1783, Columbia Co., Ga., CAROLINE FLEMING TINDALL (1762-1842), dau. of WILLIAM TINDALL, a *Rev. Sol.* of Ga., and his wife, Betsey Ann Booker.

Children:

1. Nathan Bird (1784–1810), mar. Sarah Lumsden.
2. William Booker, mar. Miss Blakeley. Moved to Ky.
3. Lucy Greene (1790), mar. Elijah Brown (1781–1854), 10 children.
4. John F. (1793), mar. Nancy Briscoe. Moved to Miss., then Texas.
5. Mary Booker (1795), mar. 1815 William Griffin, of Henry Co., Ga.
6. Sarah Caroline, mar. John Griffin (bro. of William) (their son, Gen. Thomas Griffin, who mar. Sarah Colbert).

NATHANIEL BARNETT, b. Amherst Co., Va., 1727; d. Wilkes Co., Ga., 1824. Served as private Ga. troops. Was a prisoner of the British, confined at Augusta, Ga., when the Tories drove the Whigs into upper Ga. Mar. 1748 Susanna Crawford, b. 1728, d. before 1824.

Children:

1. Nelson, d. 1803.
2. David.
3. WILLIAM, mar. (1) Mary Meriwether; (2) Sally (Wyatt) Bibb. A *Rev. Sol.*
4. JOEL, mar. (1) Elizabeth Crawford; (2) Mildred Meriwether. A *Rev. Sol.*
5. Ann, mar. Joel Crawford.
6. Elizabeth, mar. —Spears.
7. Peter.

NATHAN BARNETT, b. New Kent Co., Va., 1729; d. Greene Co., Ga., 1805. Served as *Rev. Sol.* from Ga. in the Battle of Kettle Creek, Feb. 14, 1799, under Gen. Elijah Clarke. Was given land for his services. Mar. 1757, in Va., LUCY WEBB, b. 1731. Came to Ga. 1768, settled on Little Kioka Creek, St. Paul's Parish.

Children:

1. NATHAN BARNETT, Jr., b. 1758. *Rev. Sol.*
2. MIAL BARNETT, b. Va., 1760; living Greene Co., Ga., 1814. *Rev. Sol.* Mar. Polly —.
3. JOHN BARNETT, *Rev. Sol.*
4. CLAIBORNE BARNETT, *Rev. Sol.* Land Greene Co., Ga. Living 1806 Logan Co., Ky.
5. Leonard Barnett, living 1828 Greene Co., Ga.

SION BARNETT, *Rev. Sol.*, was present at Battles of Stono and Cowpens; published the first proclamation connected with the Mecklenburg Declaration. D. Jasper Co., Ga., 1854, age 82.

WILLIAM BARNETT, b. N. C., 1747; d. Wilkes Co., Ga., 1834. Commanded a troop of horsemen of Mecklenburg Co., N. C.; later served in S. C. under Gen. Sumpter. Received bounty land for his services, Wilkes Co., Ga. (He was son of JOHN BARNETT, b. Ireland, 1717; d. N. C., 1804, *Rev. Sol.* of N. C., and his wife, Ann Spratt (b. 1718, d. 1801). Mar. 1772 Jean Jack (1750-1811), (dau. of PATRICK JACK, *Rev. Patriot*, and his wife, Lillis McAdough (Adoo), of N. C.)

Children:

1. Samuel, mar. (1) —; (2) Elizabeth (Worsham) Welles, widow of Thomas Welles.
2. John, mar. Mary Jack.
3. William, mar. Nancy (or Mary) Ray.
4. Lilly.
5. Patrick, mar. Nancy Beall.

WILLIAM BARNETT, b. Ulster Province, Ireland, 1715; d. N. C., 1778. *Rev. Sol.* of N. C. Mar. 1749 MARY SPRATT (dau. of Thomas Spratt, of N. C.).

Children:

1. WILLIAM, *Rev. Sol.*
2. John.
3. Thomas, Caswell Co., N. C.
4. Abraham.

WILLIAM BARNETT (son of Nathaniel Barnett and Susanna Crawford), b. Amherst Co., Va. Lived in Ga. D. Ala., 1830. Served in Va. troops. Was given bounty land in Columbia Co., Ga., for his services. Mar. (1) MARY MERIWETHER (dau. of FRANCIS MERIWETHER, *Rev. Sol.* of Va., and his wife, Martha Jameson), b. 1766; d. 1805; Mar. (2) SALLY (WYATT) BIBB, widow of William Bibb (no issue).

Children by (1) wife:

1. Thomas Meriwether, mar. Margaret Micou.
2. Martha, mar. Francis M. Gilmer.
3. Mary, b. 1797, mar. David Taliaferro (brother of CAPT. BENJAMIN TALIAFERRO, *Rev. Sol.*).
4. Nathaniel (1793), mar. 1814 Polly Hudson (dau. of DAVID HUDSON, a *Rev. Sol.*, placed on pension roll 1833 from Elbert Co., Ga., for service in Major Andrew Pickens S. C. Regiment, and his wife, Mary Cobb Booker).
5. Lucy, mar. George Mathews.
6. Frances, mar. Isaac Ross.
7. Elizabeth, mar. William Mathews.
8. Peter, mar. Miss Saffold.

WILLIAM BARNETT, b. Va.; d. Greene Co., Ga. Served with Va. troops; received bounty land in Ga. for his services. Mar. MARY HEWEY.

One son:

JOHN BARNETT, b. Greene Co., Ga., 1784. Mar. Elizabeth Butrill (dau. of WILLIAM BUTRILL or BUTTRILL, *Rev. Sol.* of Va. and Ga., and his wife, Martha). They moved to Heard Co., Ga., 1827.

SAMUEL BARRON, b. Ga., Mar. 16, 1768; d. Washington (now Jones) Co., Ga., 1826. Served as a private, N. C. Regiment; received bounty grant of land in Washington Co., Ga., for his services. Mar. JOANNA BRASWELL.

Children:

1. Rebecca.
2. Nancy.
3. Sally.
4. Willis.
5. Jonathan.
6. Wiley.
7. Greene.
8. Abner.
9. Benjamin, mar. Sarah Barron.
10. William.
11. Thomas.
12. James.

WILLIAM BARRON, SR., b. Ireland, about 1740; mar. there 1760 PRUDENCE DAVIS. She d. 1815. They removed with their family to America and settled 1766 in Warren Co., Ga. He served as Captain in Rev. War and was wounded at the Siege of Augusta, Ga. He fell into the hands of the Tories and they lured the Indians to behead him. The Tories put his head, as a trophy of war, on a pole, placed erect in the center of Augusta, where it remained three weeks, until the Whigs regained control of the town and took it down.

Children:

1. John, b. Ireland, about 1763.
2. WILLIAM BARRON, JR., b. Ga., 1767; mar. Martha Farr. A *Rev. Sol.* of Ga.
3. SAMUEL BARRON, *Rev. Sol.* of Ga. Mar. Joanna Braswell.
4. (Mary) Elizabeth, mar. Jacob Garrard.

SAMUEL BARRON (brother of William, Sr.), mar. Ann —. A *Rev. Sol.* of Ga.

JOHN BARRON (brother of William, Sr., was a captain at the Siege of Augusta, and was wounded and captured by the British.

JAMES BARROW, b. Edgecomb Co., N. C., Jan. 31, 1757; d. Warren Co., Ga., Jan. 20, 1828. Served as private, N. C. Line, under Col. Jethro Summer. Served at Valley Forge, Brandywine, Savannah, and Charleston. Received bounty grant of land on Bark Camp Creek, Burke Co., Ga., 1784. Mar. (1) 1785 ANNE; (2) 1802 NANCY HARDWICK; (3) 1814 PATIENCE CRENSHAW, b. May 15, 1779; d. 1817 (dau. of Jesse Crenshaw and his wife, Precious Cain). Two children by (3) wife:

1. David Crenshaw, b. July 26, 1815; d. 1879. Mar. 1838 Sarah Eliza Pope. DAVID CRENSHAW BARROW, JR. (1852-1929), was Chancellor of the State University, Athens, Ga.; the only living man for whom a Co. in the State of Ga. was named—Barrow Co., 1915.

2. Precious Patience, mar. Wm. McKinley.

REDDICK BASS, d. Ga., 1828. Received bounty grant of land in Warren Co., Ga., for his services. Mar. OBEDIENCE —.

Children:
1. Buckner.
2. Elizabeth, mar. McTyre.
3. Nancy.
4. Larkin.
5. Perkins.

JESSE BATTLE, b. Hertford Co., N. C., July 8, 1738; d. Hancock Co., Ga., Aug. 25, 1805. A *Patriot*; furnished supplies for the American troops. Came to Ga. 1787. Mar. 1756 SUSANNA FAUCETTE (or Forsett), b. France, 1738; d. Hancock Co., Ga., May 8, 1819.

Children:
1. John.
2. Benjamin, mar. Christian Wyatt.
3. WILLIAM SUMNER, mar. Sarah Whitehead. *Rev. Sol.*
4. Priscilla.
5. Bathsheba.
6. Lewis.
7. Jesse.
8. Susan Faucette, mar. (1) John Ragan; (2) — Fairchild.
9. Mary (1774-1842), mar. 1793 WILLIAM RABUN, *Governor of Georgia*, 1819 (son of MATTHEW RABUN, *Rev. Sol.*).
10. Lazarus, mar. (1) Miss Cook; (2) Margaret (Porter) Fannins.
11. Isaac, mar. Martha (Patsey) Rabun.
12. Reuben Taylor (1784–1805), mar. Bethia Alexander.

WILLIAM SUMNER BATTLE, b. Nansemonde Co., Va., Oct. 26, 1761; d. Taliaferro Co., Ga., 1828. Came to Greene (now Hancock) Co., Ga., and served with Ga. troops. Received grant of land for his services. Mar. Edgecombe Co., N. C., SARAH WHITEHEAD, b. N. C., Mar. 9, 1766 (dau. Lazarus Whitehead).

Children:
1. Elizabeth (1784–1803).
2. Joseph John (1786–1858), mar. Rhoda Henrietta Whitehead.
3. Jesse Brown, mar. Martha Battle Rabun.
4. Sarah Whitehead, d. Texas, 1811. Mar. Christopher Anthony Carter.
5. John William, mar. (1) Elizabeth Atkinson; (2) Miss Asbury; (3) Sidney Lane Tuggle.
6. Mary Hale, mar. Herman Mercer.
7. Serena A. Hagan, mar. William Stroud.
8. Lazarus Whitehead, mar. Nancy Chevers.
9. Susan Faucetta, mar. Col. William Henry Long.
10. Selina C., mar. (1) Albert G. Bunkley; (2) Richard Felton.
11. Bennett W., d. y.
12. Betsey, d. y.

ANDREW BAXTER, JR. (son of ANDREW BAXTER (1725–1781), *Rev. Sol.* of S. C., Lieut. and Major, killed by the Tories, and his wife, Frances), b. S. C., Dec. 21, 1750; d. Wilkes Co. (now Greene), Ga., 1816. Served in Continental Army. Received bounty grant of land in Ga.

for his service.   Mar. 1784, ELIZABETH HARRIS (1764-1844), (dau. of CHARLES HARRIS, b. Mecklinburg Co., N. C., 1740; d. Greene Co., 1791. A *Rev. Sol.*   Received bounty land in Ga. for his service.   Mar.Elizabeth (Thompson) Baker).

Children:

 1. Thomas W. (1781-1844), mar. Mary Wiley (1798-1869), dau. of Moses Wiley and his wife, Ann Jack, dau. of JOHN JACK, *Rev. Sol.*, and his wife, Ann Barnett.

 2. Eli H., mar. Julia Richardson.

 3. Andrew.

 4. John.

 5. Cynthia.

 6. Eliza T.

 7. James.

 8. Richard.

 9. Mary, mar. Wm. Green Springer (son of John Springer, *Rev. Sol.*).

THADDEUS BEALL, b. Frederick Co., Md., 1745; d. Warren Co., Ga., 1815.   Private in Capt. Edward Burgess' Co.; 1st Lieut., Capt., Major on Gen. Resin Beall's Staff.   Flying Camp, Md. troops.   Mar. 1767 AMELIA JANE BEALL.

Children:

 1. Frederick, mar. Martha Beall.

 2. Jeremiah, mar. Elizabeth Catten.

 3. Josiah. mar. Miss Colton.

 4. Thaddeus, Jr.

 5. Samuel.

 6. Elias, mar. Mary Neal.

 7. Walton, mar. William Reese.

 8. Amelia, mar. William Dent.

 9. Anna, mar. Thomas Dent.

 10. Major.

SAMUEL BECKHAM (son of Simon and Susan Beckham), b. Nov. 24, 1760; d. near Milledgeville, Ga., Nov. 2, 1825.   His record as a *Rev. Sol.* found on his tombstone erected by the State of Ga. (grave marked by D. A. R.) Mar. Feb. 18, 1790 ELIZABETH HOUGHTON (1769-1805), (dau. of Joshua and Nancy Houghton).

Children:

 1. Nancy, mar. — Mitchell.

 2. Mary B.

 3. Elizabeth H.

 4. Erasmus G.

 5. Susan, mar. — Burch.

 6. Albert G.

FRANCIS BELL, b. Lynchburg, Va., 1750; d. Jackson Co., Ga., 1838.   Served in N. C. troops, in the Battle of Guilford C. H.   Mar. 1770 ESTHER MONTGOMERY (1754-1834).

Children: (known).

 1. Sarah, mar. Curtiss Greene.

 2. Mary, mar. John Bell.

 3. Joseph Scott, mar. Rachel Phinizy.

JAMES BELL, b. N. C., Oct. 4, 1747; d. Elbert Co., Ga., Oct. 23, 1809.   Mar. 1776 OLIVE MOSELEY, b. N. C. Jan. 1, 1760; d. Elbert Co., Ga., Oct. 22, 1822.   Served in N. C. Continental Line.   Moved to Ga. 1788.   He also served as J. P., Elbert Co., 1792.   (Record for Society Daus. of the War of 1812.)

Children:

 1. Joseph, mar. Mary —.

 2. James (1789-1848), mar. Susan Key (dau. of WILLIAM BIBB KEY, *Rev. Sol.*, b. Va., 1759; d. Ga., 1836, and his wife, Mourning Clark).

 3. William, mar. Elizabeth Thornton.

4. Thomas, mar. Polly (Hubbard) Dye.
5. David, mar. Elizabeth Snellings.
6. Polly.
7. Elizabeth, mar. William Moore.
8. Nancy.
9. Polly, mar. —Moore.
10. Martha, mar. Harmon Lovingood.

JOSEPH BELL, b. N. C.; d. Elbert Co., Ga., 1818. Served in N. C. Line. Received bounty grant of land for his services in Elbert (formerly Wilkes Co.), Ga., 1784. In 1825 his widow drew land in Land Lottery as widow *Rev. Sol.* Mar. in N. C. Elizabeth Moseley, b. N. C., 1765.
Children:
1. Anna, mar. 1807 Tapley Bullard (son of THOMAS BULLARD, *Rev. Sol.* of Ga., and his wife, Ann).
2. Thomas.
3. Mary.
4. Joseph, Jr.
5. Rebecca, mar. John Gunter.
6. Eleanor, mar. William W. Downer.
7. Elizabeth, mar. Burrell Dye.
8. Milly L., mar. Peter B. Butler.

SAMUEL BELLAH, b. Rowan Co., N. C., 1752; d. Morgan Co., Ga., 1833. Served as private, N. C. Line. Mar. in N. C. July 18, 1776, Jane Morgan.
Children:
1. James.
2. Robert.
3. Tempee.
4. Rachel.
5. Morgan, mar. Elvey Price.
6. Peggy.
7. Walter.
8. Steele.

NATHAN BENTON, b. Orange Co., N. C., 1764; d. Columbia Co., Ga., 1826. Served as private, N. C. Line, 10th Reg. Mar. 1796 Susanna Crawford (1776–1804).
Children:
1. Nelson Moore, mar. (1) Lucy Jones; (2) Martha Ann Wooding.
2. Parmelia Frances, mar. James Luckie.
3. Thomas H.
4. George Constantine.
5. Eugenius.

JOHN BERRY, b. 1762; d. Effingham Co., Ga., 1817. Served as private from Effingham Co., Ga. Line. Mar. Mary Reisser.
Children:
1. John.
2. Bananza.
3. Obediah.
4. Naomi.
5. Salome, mar. 1811 Emanuel Rahn (son of JONATHAN RAHN, *Rev. Sol.* of Effingham Co., Ga.)

MAJOR GEN. JOHN BERRIEN, b. near Princeton, N. J., 1759; d. Savannah, Ga., 1815. Came to Ga. 1775. Served as private, Lieut., Captain, Major 1782. Served at Valley Forge and Monmouth. Was Brigadier Gen., Northern Army, *Sol. of 1812.* Mar. (1) Margaret McPherson (1763–1785), (dau. of JOHN McPHERSON, *Rev. Sol.*, an officer in the Provincial Navy); (2) WILLIHAMENIA SARAH ELIZA MOORE.
One son by (1) wife:
John McPherson Berrien, b. Rockhill, N. J., 1781; d. Ga., 1856. Mar. (1) Eliza Richardson

Anciaux, d. 1828 (dau. of MAJOR NICHOLAS ANCIAUX, *Rev. Sol.*, who came to America with La Fayette and was under Command of COUNT DUPONTE; was at the surrender of Cornwallis at Yorktown. Lived and d. in Ga.); (2) 1833 Eliza G. Hunter.

Children by (2) wife (WILLIHAMENIA S. E. MOORE):
1. Richard.
2. Thomas.
3. Sarah.
4. Eliza.
5. Weems.
6. Ruth Lowndes, mar. Dr. James Whitehead.
7. Julia, mar. John Whitehead.

PAUL BEVILLE, b. Va., 1755; d. Ga., 1836. Served as private, Ga. Line. Received bounty land for his services. Mar. 1780 Sarah Scruggs (dau. of RICHARD SCRUGGS, *Rev. Sol.* of Ga.). Children:
1. Paul, Jr. (1788–1819), mar. 1810 Mary Pearce (1793–1816) (dau. of STEPHEN PEARCE, *Rev. Sol.* of Screven Co., Ga., and wife, Mary Mills).
2. James, mar. Delia Dell (dau. of PHILIP DELL, *Rev. Sol.* of Ga.).
3. Frances, mar. J. Garnett.

ROBERT BEVILLE, b. Henrico Co., Va., 1752; d. Screven Co., Ga., 1838. Served as private, Ga. Line. Received bounty of land in Ga. for his services. Mar. SARAH WILLIAMS HUDSON. Children:
1. Robert.
2. Granville (1785–1850), mar. Sarah Ann Bonnell (1800–1854), (grand-dau. of ANTHONY BONNELL, *Rev. Sol.*; served as Lieut., Ga. Line, and wife, Mary; d. Screven Co., Ga., 1805.)
3. Claiborne (1781–1852), mar. 1802 Susannah Daly (1784–1844), (dau. of BENJAMIN DALY (D'Oilly), *Rev. Sol.* of Ga., and his wife, Susanna Garnett).

WILLIAM BIBB, b. Hanover Co., Va., 1735; d. Wilkes (now Elbert Co.), Ga., 1796. Served in the Va. Continental Army. Member Va. Convention 1774. Com. of Safety of Va. 1775. Mar. (1) in Va. MRS. BOOKER (nee Clark); (2) SALLIE WYATT, b. Charlotte Co., Va., 1750, d. Autauga Co., Ala., 1826. (She mar. (2) William Barnett.)

Children by (1) wife:
1. Elizabeth, mar. (1) Capt. John Scott; (2) — Clarke.
2. Lucy.
3. Hannah, mar. (1) Peyton Wyatt; (2) Major John Tull.
4. Sallie Booker, mar. (1) Marable Walker; (2) Archelaus Jarrett.

Children by (2) wife (Sallie Wyatt):
1. William Wyatt, mar. Mary Freeman (dau. of HOLMAN FREEMAN, *Rev. Sol.* of Ga.). (He was appointed first *Governor of the Territory of Alabama*, then elected first *Governor of the State of Alabama.*)
2. Thomas, mar. Parmelia W. Thompson. He was also *Governor of Alabama.*
3. Peyton, mar. Martha Cobb.
4. John Dandridge, mar. Mary Xenia Oliver.
5. Joseph Wyatt, mar. (1) Louise DuBose; (2) Martha Dancy.
6. Benajah Smith, mar. Sophia Lucy Ann Gilmer.
7. Delia, mar. Alex Pope.
8. Martha, mar. Fleming Freeman (son of HOLMAN FREEMAN, *Rev. Sol.* of Ga.).
9. Lucy.

JOHN BILLUPS, b. Va., 1758; d. Oglethorpe Co., Ga., 1814. Served as Lieut. Gloucester Co., Va. Reg., Continental Line. Mar. 1798 Susanna Carleton (1761–1817). Child:
Thomas Carleton Billups (1804–1860), mar. 1823 Sarah Moore.

WILLIAM BIRD, b. Penn.; d. Warren Co., Ga., 1813. Served 1775 in Col. William Thompson's Batt. of Riflemen, the first troops south of New England to join Gen. Washington's troops at

Cambridge. Came to Warren Co., Ga., 1794. Mar. (1) Miss Wood of Penn.; (2) Catherine Dalton, of Va.

Children:
1. William.
2. Wilson.
3. John.
4. Fitzgerald.
5. Ariana.
6. Eliza, mar. 1808 James Lesley.
7. Emily, mar. as (3) wife Rev. Robert M. Cunningham.
8. Caroline, mar. Benjamin Cudsworth Yancey.
9. Louisa, mar. Capt. Robert Cunningham, a *Sol. of 1812*, and their dau., ANN PAMELA CUNNINGHAM, was founder and first Regent of the Mount Vernon Ladies Memorial Association.
10. Catherine.

WILLIAM BIVINS, b. April 2, 1748, buried in Bivins Estate, Wilkinson Co., Ga., Dec. 11, 1828. Mar. POLLY NELSON HALL, b. Sept. 17, 1770, d. Nov. 28, 1838; buried Marion Co., Ga. (8 miles from Buena Vista, Ga.) He was a *Rev. Sol.*

Son:
Martin Luther, b. July 18, (1816-1878). Mar. Winifred Powell (1818-1841) (dau. of William Powell, Jr. (1778-1852)), and mar. 1802 his wife, Nancy Edwards (1780-1857).

DAVID BLACKSHEAR, b. Jones Co., N. C., 1764; d. Laurens Co., Ga., 1837. Served as private N. C. Militia at the Battle of Moore's Creek, 1776. Moved to Ga. 1790, and was a Ga. *Sol. of the War of 1812*. Buried at Blackshear family burying ground, "Springfield," Laurens Co., Ga. Mar. Frances Hamilton. (Grave marked by D. A. R.)

Children:
1. James H., mar. Caroline L. Floyd (dau. of Col. John Floyd, a *Sol. of War of 1812*, and g-dau. of CHARLES FLOYD, *Rev. Sol.* of Va. and Ga.).
2. Mary.
3. William T.
4. Edward Jefferson.
5. Ann Elizabeth.
6. Eliza Ann.
7. David, Jr.
8. Everard.
9. Joseph.
10. Floyd.
11. Elijah.
12. John Duke.
(Other Children).

PHILIP BLASENGAME, b. S. C.; d. Greene Co., Ga., 1825. Served as a *Rev. Sol.* Mar. Frances —. Left in his will to his son, James, two draws of land received for his services as *Rev. Sol.* Other children mentioned in will were:
2. Benjamin.
3. Polly, mar. Absolom Awtrey.
4. Nancy, mar. —Awtrey.
5. Elizabeth, mar. — Bradshaw.

MILLER BLEDSOE, b. Va., 1761; d. Oglethorpe Co., Ga., 1841. Enlisted Henry Co., Va., at 15 years of age, under Capt. Ambrose Dudley, 2nd Va. Regiment. He was severely wounded at the capture of "The Hook." Was at Battle of Camden. In charge of Co. ordered to Henry Co., Va., and was at the surrender of Yorktown. Granted land 100 acres in Ky. as private, Va. Line. Mar. Jean Bowling.

Mentions children in will:
1. Polly, mar. — Swanson.
2. Sidney, mar. — Derby.

    3. Jane (1791–1861), mar. William Landrum.
    4. Unie, mar. Whitfield Landrum.
    5. Nancy, mar. Lemuel Edwards.
    6. Betsey, mar. — Elder.
    7. Moses.
    8. Peachy.
    9. Miller, Jr.

THOMAS BLOODWORTH, b. Wilmington Dist., N. C., 1755.; d. Morgan Co., Ga., 1836. Appointed Major Continental Army, N. C. Member N. C. Assembly 1781. Mar. 1802, FRANCIS PROCTOR (sometimes called Tamsie) (1774-1868).
Children:
    1. Hiram.
    2. Solomon (1806–1890), mar. (1) Lucy Thornton.
    2. David Madison.
    4. Thomas S. Morgan, mar. Caroline Maxey.
    5. Fanny, mar. — Brand.
    6. Lymise Proctor, mar. (1) James McNab; (2) Joe Hale.
    7. Mary Ann, mar. — Yarborough.
    8. Simeon Peter, mar. Elizabeth Crawford.

SAMUEL BLOODWORTH (brother of Thomas), drew land as a *Rev. Sol.* in Washington Co., Ga.

ANTHONY BONNELL, b. about 1752; d. Screven Co., Ga., 1805. Served as Lieut., Ga. Line. Mar. Mary —.
Children:
    1. William, b. 1774; d. 1830; mar. 1795 Rebecca Magee. Children: a. William, b. Mary Cassandra, c. Mary Ann, d. Sarah Ann (1800-1854), mar. as (2) wife Granville Beville (1785-1850), e. Jane, mar. Benjamin Lane.
    2. Daniel.
    3. Elizabeth.

NOTE: EDMUND BOTSFORD, b. Woburn, Bedfordshire, England, 1755. Arrived Charleston, S. C. 1766. Came to Ga. At this time, June 1771, there was only one ordained Baptist minister in Ga., viz: DANIEL MARSHALL, *Rev. Sol.* But in 1771, he preached his first sermon in Ga. and was ordained in Charleston, S. C., Mar. 14, 1773. He lived in Burke Co., Ga., but travelled over Ga. He served as Chaplain in the American Army, in S. C., N. C. and Va. Mar. 1773 SUSANNA NUN at Augusta, Ga. She was born in Ireland. He d. Georgetown, S. C. Dec. 25, 1819.

CHESLEY BOSTICK, b. Va.; d. Richmond Co., Ga., 1801. Served as Capt. 1st Ga. Reg. Jan., 1776. Was taken prisoner at Savannah, Ga. Living in Augusta, Ga., 1786. Mar. Jane Gervais.
Children:
    1. John, mar. Betsey Bostic.
    2. Chesley, Jr., mar. (1) Susanna Cobb; (2) Ann Matilda Hargrove.
    3. Elizabeth, mar. as (1) wife, Thomas P. Carnes.
    4. Sarah Maria, mar. —Shellman.
    5. Mary Ann, mar. — Thompson.
    6. Henrietta, mar. John Guyton.

LITTLEBERRY BOSTICK, SR., b. Goochland Co., Va., July 10, 1751; d. Ga., Sept 10, 1823. Served as private in Col. James McNeill's Ga. Regiment. Received bounty land grant for his services. (His father, John Bostick, and his 2 brothers, Nathan and Chesley, Jr., were all *Rev. Sols.*) Mar. July 27, 1773 (1) Rebeckah Beal (1752-1791); (2) Nov. 6, 1792 Mary Birdsong (1773-1820).
Children by (1) wife:
    1. Littleberry, Jr., mar. 1812 (1) Margaret Rudd Hancock; (2) 1820 Mary Ann Martha Walker.
    2. Jacob, mar. Rebeckah Beal.
    3. Betsey, mar. John Bostick (son of Chesley).
    4. Jeremiah.
    5. Nathaniel, mar. Sarah J. B. Brown.

Children by (2) wife:
1. Mary, mar. Jesse Roberson.
2. Susanna Addison, mar (1) Nicholas Connelly; (2) Marcus Flournoy.
3. Matilda Golden, mar. (1) Jacob Beal; (2) Don Frederick Bostick.
4. Caroline Verlinda, mar. — Todd.

NATHANIEL BOSTICK (called Nathan), b. Va., Jan. 26, 1746; d. Jefferson Co., Ga., Feb. 14, 1818. Served as private in Co. under COL. JAMES McNEILL, Ga. Regiment. Mar. 1769 Martha Gwinn, b. 1750.
Children:
1. Elizabeth (1770–1835), mar. 1798 WILLIAM WALKER, a *Rev. Sol.*, b. Va., 1762; d. Jefferson Co., Ga., 1818. He served as private in Col. John Twiggs Ga. Reg.
2. Hillery, b. 1771; mar. Elizabeth Jarvis.
3. John, b. 1773, d. 1839; mar. (1) Elizabeth Hayless; (2) Elviza Beal.
4. Nathan, Jr.; mar. Catherine Connoly.
5. Holmes G.
6. Mary Ann; mar. William Hayles.

ISAAC BORING (son of Joseph and Susanna Boring. She mar. as (2) wife, John Browning), b. N. C., Mar. 8, 1762. Served as private N. C. Caswell Co. troops. Given land for his services. D. Wilkes (now Jackson) Co., Ga., 1836. Mar. 1780 Phoebe Browning (dau. of JOHN BROWNING, *Rev. Sol.* of N. C.), d. Jackson Co., Ga., 1851.
Children:
1. David.
2. John.
3. Elizabeth, b. 1784; mar. Wm. Lyle.
4. Susannah.
5. Sarah (or Senah), b. 1789; mar. James Wafer.
6. Robert.
7. Rebecca.
8. Isaac, Jr.
9. Phoebe.

MATTHEW BOLTON, b. Va., about 1760; d. Columbia Co., Ga., 1824. Served in the Va. Line. His widow drew land in Warren Co., Ga., in 1827 for his services. Mar. Mar. 26, 1788, MARY CHAPMAN.
Children:
1. Martha, mar. James Mappin.
2. Mary, mar. Willis Roberts.
3. Robert, mar. Lydia —.
4. Thomas, mar. Martha Shipson.
5. Samuel, mar. Jane Phelps.
6. Elizabeth, mar. (1) H. T. Wade; (2) Joseph Elliott.
7. Nancy P., mar. Robert Markes.
8. John T.
9. Millie (1812–1813).
10. Elishap.

JOHN BOSTON, b. N. C., 1737; d. Effingham Co., Ga., May 8, 1810. He served as Major in Onslow Co., N. C., troops. Mar. REBECCA RANDAL (1740–1790).
Their son, James Boston (only child living to maturity), b. N. C., 1767; d. Effingham Co., Ga., 1837. A *Soldier of the War of 1812.* Mar. 1794 (1) ELIZABETH DELL BRIGGS; (2) 1814 SARAH KETTLES, widow; 11 children by (1) wife; 2 children by (2) wife.

BIUS (or Bias) BOYKIN, d. Ga., 1812. Served in N. C. Line and received bounty grant of land for his services. Mar. Sarah Peeples, b. Va., d. Ga., after 1812.

Children:
1. Thomas (1785–1829), a *Soldier of the War of 1812*, mar. Elizabeth Fennell (dau. of NICH-OLAS FENNELL, a *Rev. Sol.* of N. C., and his wife, Margaret Robinson). He received bounty grant of land in Ga.
2. John.
3. Solomon.
4. Nancy.
5. Jeany.

BURWELL BOYKIN, b. Va., 1752; d. S. C., 1817. Mar. (1) Elizabeth Whitaker; (2) Mary Whitaker. He had 17 children. (Bro. of Major Francis Boykin.)

MAJOR FRANCIS BOYKIN, b. S. C., 1745; d. Baldwin Co., Ga., 1821. Served as Major in the "Mounted Rangers" of S. C. (Grave marked by D. A. R.). Mar. CATHERINE WHITAKER.
Children:
1. Samuel (1786–1848), mar. (1) Sarah Maxwell, one son; (2) Narcissa Cooper, 9 children.
2. James, mar. (1) Miss Owens; (2) Miss Rutherford.
3. Elizabeth, mar. William Rutherford.
4. William.
5. Mary.

In 1785 MAJOR FRANCIS BOYKIN; CAPT. JAMES CANTEY, of Camden, S. C., and ENSIGN HUDSON WHITAKER, of N. C., all *Rev. Sols.*, came to Baldwin Co., Ga. CAPT. SAMUEL BOYKIN and CAPT. BURWELL BOYKIN, brothers of Major Boykin, remained in S. C.

JOHN BRADLEY, b. St. George's Parish, Ga., 1755; d. Oglethorpe Co., Ga., 1837. In 1780 he served as Captain of a Galley from St. George's Parish. Mar. MARY NOIL (or Neil).
Two children (known):
1. John A., mar. Martha Jameson Meriwether.
2. Mary Ardis, mar. 1820, Isham Weaver.

WILLIAM SCOTT BRANCH, b. Chesterfield Co., Va., 1760; d. Clarke Co., Ga., 1838. Served in the Va. Line. Drew land in the 1827 Ga. Lottery for his services as a *Rev. Sol.* Mar. DICEY JANE CALICUTT.
Children:
1. John, mar. Sarah Broughton.
2. James, mar. Leah —.
3. Arnistead, mar. Julia —.
7. Marcellus, mar. Malcolm Dawson.
5. Sarah, mar. William Walker.
6. Emily, mar. Malcolm O'Neill.
7. Judith and others.

JACOB BRASELTON, of N. C., b. Wales, June 27, 1749; d. Jackson Co., Ga., 1825. Served in Va., N. C., and Ga. Continental troops. Granted bounty land in Ga., 1790. Mar. 1772, HAN-NAH GREEN, b. April 8, 1757.
Children:
1. John (1774–1850), mar. Elizabeth Brown.
2. Elizabeth, 1775.
3. Henry, 1777.
4. William, 1779.
5. Hannah, 1781.
6. Mary (or Mart), 1783.
7. Jacob, Jr., 1785.
8. Green, 1786.
9. Reuben, 1788.
10. David, 1790.
11. Job, 1792, mar. Sallie Dowdy.
12. Rebecca, 1795.
13. Amos, 1797.
14. Sarah, 1799.

JACOB BRASWELL, b. Edgecombe Co., N. C., Mar. 7, 1763; d. Ga., July 25, 1839   Served with N. C. troops. Mar. July 9, 1789, NANCY COTTON, b. Dec. 1772.
Children:
1. Elizabeth.
2. Micajah, d. y.
3. Jacob, Jr.
4. Priscilla Macon.
5. Sallie.
6. Willie.
7. Peggy.
8. Tempsey.
9. Alexander Cotton.
10. Maria.
11. Micajah, b. 1811.
12. Rodia.

ALLEN BROOKS, JOAB BROOKS, JOHN H. BROOKS, JAMES BROOKS and MICAJAH BROOKS, five brothers, all *Rev. Sols.*, were b. near Fayetteville, N. C. (sons of John Brooks of Va., who moved to N. C. 1736); they moved to Ga. and all received land grants in Ga. for their services in Rev. War.

One brother ISAAC BROOKS, *Rev. Sol.* remained in N. C. (Grave of MICAJAH BROOKS, *Rev. Sol.*, marked by Ga. D. A. R. in Polk Co., five miles west of Rockmart, Ga.)

JOHN H. BROOKS, b. N. C.; d. Jones Co., Ga., 1811. (Grave marked by D. A. R.) Mar. Jane Terrell of N. C.
Children:
1. Philip H., *Sol. of the War of 1812.*
2. Charles E., *Sol. of the War of 1812.*
3. Samuel, *Sol. of the War of 1812.*
4. William T., *Sol. of the War of 1812.*
5. John, mar. 1816 Alice Waldrop, of Jones Co., Ga.
6. Isham.
7. Sarah, mar. Richard C. Shirley.

WILLIAM BROOKS, b. Va.; d. Greene Co., Ga. 1819. Mar. in Va., Mary— (called Polly). Was a *Rev. Sol.* of Va. Line. Moved to Oglethorpe Co., Ga. Received grant of land.
Three sons (known):
1. Thomas.
2. Wilson.
3. Robert.
Their son, WILSON BROOKS, b. Va. 1767.; d. Oglethorpe Co., Ga. Nov., 1846. Mar. in Ga. 1795 Mary Glover (dau. of EDMUND GLOVER, *Rev. Sol.* of Va., d. Oglethorpe Co., Ga.), *Sol. of the War of 1812.*
Their children:
1. Richard P.
2. O. P.
3. Elizabeth, mar. —Smith.
4. Edward G.
5. W. R.
6. Wilson Walter, mar. Katherine L. C. Yancey
7. Lucy R., mar. —Boggs.
8. Thomas P., mar. Mary L. Amis.
9. Mariah H., mar. —Zuber.
10. Martha, mar. —Zuber.
11. Sarah B., mar. —Stewart.
12. Mahala, mar. —Collier.
13. Mary, mar. —Collier.
(Names mentioned in will made Aug. 13, 1846; probated Nov. 9, 1846, Oglethorpe Co., Ga.)

JONATHAN BRYAN, b. S. C., 1708.; d. at "Brampton," near Savannah, Ga., 1788. Member Provincial Congress and Committee of Safety, Ga.; together with his son JAMES BRYAN *Rev. Sol.*, he was captured by the British 1779, and was a prisoner in New York two years. Mar Oct. 13, 1737, MARY WILLIAMSON (1722-1781).

Children:

1. HUGH, a *Rev. Sol.*
2. Jonathan, d. y.
3. Joseph.
4. WILLIAM, *Rev. Sol.*
5. JAMES, *Rev. Sol.*, mar. Elizabeth Langley.
6. Mary, mar. JOHN MOREL (1733-1776), *Rev. Sol.*
7. Josiah (1746-1774), mar. 1770 Elizabeth Pendarvis (after his death his widow mar. (2) LIEUT. JOHN SCREVEN, *Rev. Sol.* and they had 13 children.)
8. John.
9. Elizabeth.
10. Hannah, mar. JOHN HOUSTON, a *Rev. Sol.* and *Governor of Georgia* (son of Sir Patrick Houston, of Ga.)
11. Ann.
12. Sarah Janet.

BENJAMIN BRYANT, b. N. C. 1760; d. Jackson Co., Ga., 1796. Served as private Ga. troops. Mar. 1782 SARAH WHITFIELD.

Children:

1. William Lane, mar. Eliza H. Trout.
2. Hugh.
3. John, mar. Elizabeth Crockett.
4. Martha, mar. John Keith.

SHERWOOD BUGG, b. New Kent Co., Va., 1720; d Augusta, Ga., 1782. Commanded a Co. in Col. James Jackson's Ga. Regiment; was captured and confined in prison ship. His home at Beech Island, S. C., was raided by the British and Tories. Mar. ELIZABETH HOPSON, a *Revolutionary Patriot*, d. 1799.

Children:

1. Obedience (1753-1841), mar. 1790 William Newsome (1750-1851).
2. Sherwood, Jr., mar. Sarah Ann Jones.
3. Mary Elizabeth, mar. John Lamar.

THOMAS BULLARD, of Va. and Ga., b. Va.; d. Elbert Co., Ga. 1823. Drew land for his services in Wilkes Co., Ga. In 1825 his widow drew land as widow of *Rev. Sol.* Mar. Ann—, she d. 1827.

Children (mentioned in will):

1. Elizabeth, mar. Aug. 22, 1811 William Dye.
2. Temperance, mar. John Woodly.
3. Thomas P., mar. Eliz P. Gunter.
4. Sarah, mar.—Murphy.
5. Delilah, mar.—Cooks.
6. Tapley, mar. Ann Bell.
7. Nancy, mar.—Butler.
8. Allen.

HAWKINS BULLOCK, b. N. C.; d. Oglethorpe (Wilkes) Co., Ga. Nov. 1, 1833. Served under Capt. Twitty, Gen. Nathaniel Greene. Received bounty land in Wilkes Co., Ga. for his services. Mar. Mar. 12, 1789 Frances Roy Gordon (dau. CAPT. ALEXANDER GORDON, who received bounty land in Wilkes Co., Ga. for his services as a *Rev. Sol.*). (His sister, Susanna Bullock, mar. George Gordon.)

Children:

1. John Gordon (1790-1835).
2. Mary Wyatt (1791), mar. Richard A. Sims.
3. Alexander Gordon (1797), mar. Milly Sorrells.

4. Nathaniel H. (1798), mar. Setty Colbert.
5. William Gordon (1802), mar. Elenor Sorrells.
6. Richard Henley (1810), mar. (1) Mary H. R. Griffeth (2) Malinda Thompson.
7. Frances Roy (1806), mar. Hiram Hampton.
8. Hawkins Sherman (1812).
9. Louise Nance.

HAWKINS BULLOCK (was son of Nathaniel Bullock and his wife, Mary Hawkins.) They moved to Ga. during the Rev. War. He served as a *Rev. Sol.* in Ga. where he d. Wilkes Co.)

DANIEL BULLOCK, b. S. C. Oct. 25, 1762; d. Columbia Co., Ga., June 1834. Enlisted Edgefield Dist. S. C.; served as private 1779 in Capt. Tutt's and Capt. Maxwell's Companies, under Col. Hammond. Served under Gen. Pickens and Gen. Greene. Received Pension File W 8403. Mar. Columbia Co., Ga. JANE FINGUEFIELD. Nov. 12, 1789.

Children (known):
1. Zacheriah, b. 1790, mar. Dec. 7, 1812 Frances Edrington, b. 1795.
2. John.
3. Daniel, Jr.
4. Lucy L., b. 1804.
5. David, b. Aug. 25, 1796.

MICHAEL BURKHALTER, b. Germany, 1725; d. Warren Co., Ga., 1784. Served as private under Col. Elijah Clarke at Battle of Kettle Creek and at Siege of Augusta. Was living in Wilkes (now Warren), Co. Ga. (Inventory of Estate Oct. 8, 1784. (Grave marked). Mar. MARTHA NEWSOME, a *Rev. Patriot* who nursed the wounded soldiers, b. 1724, d. 1790.

Children:
1. John BURKHALTER, b. S. C. 1760; mar. 1798 Sarah (Hardin) Loyless. He was a *Rev. Sol.* at 13 years of age. (Grave marked at Buena Vista, Ga.)
2. Michael, Jr.
3. JOSHUA, *Rev. Sol.* (Grave marked.)
4. Jacob.
5. Jeremiah.
6. Isaac.
7. Mary.
8. Barbara.

HENRY BURNLEY, b. Bedford Co., Va., 1756; d. Columbia Co., Ga., Jan. 1835. He enlisted 1776 Bedford Co., Va. Served two years under Capt. Henry Terrell, Capt. William Jones, Col. Daniel Morgan. Then Ensign of Volunteers Oct. 28, 1782. Commissioned Lieut. in Militia Campbell Co., Va. Was at the Battles of Guilford C. H., Chestnut Hill, and others. Mar. (1) 1782 in Va., Lucy (Barksdale) Davenport (widow of JOHN DAVENPORT of Va., *Rev. Sol.* killed at Battle of Guilford C. H.), mar. (2) Widow Todd.

Children by (1) wife:
1. Richmond (1789), mar. Sally Veazey.
2. Sarah, mar. Hiram Hubert.
3. Lucy Barksdale (1799-1864), mar. J. Turner Dickson (1790-1864).
4. Elizabeth, mar. Spencer Seals.
5. Ann, mar. Archibald Seals, and others.

ISRAEL BURNLEY, b. Va. 1725; d. Wilkes Co., Ga., 1792. (Will recorded Mar. 15, 1793.) Mar. in Va. Ann (Hannah) Overton (1827- after 1793). He was a *Revolutionary Patriot.* Furnished supplies to the Continental Army in Campbell Co., Va. Was granted bounty lands in Ga. for his services.

Children:
1. Susan, mar. John Barksdale (came to Ga. 1789).
2. Dau. mar. John Colbert.
3. Dau. mar. George Smith.
4. HENRY (1756-1835), mar. Lucy (Barksdale) Davenport. He served as a *Rev. Sol.* of Va. Received bounty land in Ga.
5. Stephen G., mar. 1810 Warrenton, Ga., Partheny Garrett.

JOHN BURCH, b. Va. 1750; d. Hancock Co., Ga. 1818. Served in Henry Co., Va., on muster roll of Capt Jones Tarrant's Co. and Col. Abraham Penn's Regiment. Mar. in Va. SARAH PHILLIPS (1753-1840).

Children:

1. Gerard, b. Va. 1782; mar. (1) Susan Simms (dau. of ROBERT SIMMS, a *Rev. Sol.* and his wife, SARAH DICKINSON, a *Rev. Patriot* for whom the Sarah Dickinson Chapter D. A. R. of Newnan, Ga. was named.) He mar. (2) Elizabeth Beckham.

2. John, mar. (1) Miss Sampson; (2) Obedience Dutiful (Bugg) Cobb.

3. William P.

4. Richard C., mar. 1822 Martha Matilda Jernigan.

5. Jane, mar. Richard L. Watson.

6. Elizabeth, mar. Arthur Fort.

7. Saleta, mar. Needham Jernigan.

8. Morton Newman, mar. Mary (Ballard) Figg.

FORD BUTLER, b. S. C.; d. Wilkinson Co., Ga. 1817. Mar. Martha (called Patsey). A *Rev. Sol.* and received bounty land in Ga. for his services, 287½ acres in Franklin Co., Ga. Heirs in will Wilkinson Co., Ga., besides wife, were:

1. Malachi (Mallekia).

2. Sally.

3. Joel, mar. (1) —Culpepper; (2) Belinda Ashley.

(Perhaps other children.)

PATRICK BUTLER, b. Hanover Co., Va. Mar. 1, 1760; d. Elbert Co., Ga. 1838. Enlisted from Mecklenburg Co., Va. Served as private under Capt. James Anderson, Col. Nelson's Va. Reg. Received pension for services in 1833. Mar. REBECCA—.

Children:

1. John (1780-1830), mar. 1806 Elizabeth Hubbard.

(Other children not known.)

WILLIAM BUTTRILL, b. Va. 1763; d. Butts Co., Ga., 1858. Served under GEN. NATHANIEL GREENE in Ga. Mar. MARY WILLIAMS of Va. Lived in Jasper Co., Ga.

Children:

1. Thomas, mar. Luranie Bonner.

2. William, mar. Mary Fold.

3. Elizabeth, mar. —Barnett.

4. Nancy, mar. Dr. Jesse George.

5. Mary, mar. —Ford.

6. Burwell, mar. Marion Elizabeth Moseley.

7. Asa, mar. Lucile Manley.

8. Brittain, mar. (1) Louise Hudson; (2) Emmaline McCord.

9. John, mar. Anne Allston.

10. Jesse.

SAMUEL BUXTON, b. Va.; d. Ga. On muster roll of militia belonging to the upper counties of Ga.; served under Gen. Wayne at Ebenezer 1782. Mar. NANCY PLUMMER.

Their son:

William Buxton, b. Burke Co., Ga., 1791, mar. Rebecca Heath (dau. of JORDAN HEATH, b. in S. C.; d. Burke Co., Ga., a *Rev. Sol.*, wounded at the Siege of Charleston, and his wife, Christian Wimberly).

GEORGE CABANISS, b. Va.; d. Baldwin Co., Ga., 1815 (son of NATHAN CABANISS, *Rev. Sol.* of Va.) Served as a *Rev. Sol.* Mar. PALATIA HARRISON (dau. of Henry Harrison, of Berkeley Co., Va.)

Children:

1. Henry.

2. Elijah.

3. H. B.

4. Mathew.

5. George.
6. Eldridge Guerry.
7. Mary.
8. Sandall.
9. Rebecca.
10. Palatia.
11. Dau., mar. Elisha Greer.

JOHN CALLAWAY, b. Bedford Co., Va., 1750; d. Wilkes Co., Ga., 1821. Served as Major, Bedford Co. Va., Militia. Received bounty land for his services in Ga. Mar. 1770 BETHANY ARNOLD (1752-1840). (His brothers, JACOB, JOSEPH, and ISAAC CALLAWAY were also *Rev. Sols.*)
Children (from will):
1. John, Jr.
2. Lydia, mar. — Thrash.
3. Betsey, mar. — Jarrell.
4. Dau., mar. — Whittaker.
5. Pheribee, mar. REUBEN STROZIER, *Rev. Sol.*
6. Mary, mar. —Thrash.
7. Nancy, mar. Daniel Carrington.
8. Addah, mar. — Milner.
9. Bethany, mar. Joseph Talbot.
10. Enoch (1792-1859), mar. 1811 Martha Reeves.
11. Job (1780-1819), mar. Tabitha Lawrence.
(Other children.)

JOHN CALDER (CAULDER) (son of Alexander Calder of S. C.), b. S. C. 1762; d. McIntosh Co., Ga., Jan. 24, 1845. Received pension for his services as a *Rev. Sol.* 1832. Served as private Ga. Militia, commanded by Gen. Elijah Clarke; was at the Siege of Augusta. Served as a Soldier in S. C. (Light Horse) under Capt. Harvie, Col. Samuel Hammond. Was wounded at Battle of Eutaw Springs. Joined Col. Hammond's Reg. at Saluda. Marched in Indian Expedition at Battle of Little Terrapin under Gen. Pickens. Served under Captains Jesse and William Thompson and was discharged at Perkins Mill, S. C. (Record certified to by Allen B. Powell, of McIntosh Co., Ga., Nov. 21, 1833, President of Ga. Senate and *Sol. in War of 1812*). Mar. Dec. 24, 1787 (1) PHOEBE HAUGHTON (or Horton) in Liberty Co., Ga. She d. McIntosh Co., Ga., May 17, 1803. He mar. (2) Mar. 15, 1804 WINWOOD F. RICHEY, d. Feb. 10, 1854. He was also a *Sol. of War of 1812.* (The grave of JOHN CALDER, *Rev. Sol.*, at "Contentment," the Calder Plantation, McIntosh Co., Ga. has been marked.)
Children by (1) wife, Phoebe Haughton.
1. Sarah, b. Oct. 4, 1788, mar. William Houghton (Horton) Hazzard.
2. Mary, b. Nov. 9, 1790, mar. Allen Beverly Powell. (*Sol. of War of 1812*).
3. Ann, b. Mar. 8, 1792.
4. Esther, b. Mar. 1, 1794.
5. Henrietta, b. Feb. 3, 1796.
6. Maria, b. July 1, 1798.
7. Alexander H., b. July 6, 1801.
8. John, b. 1803.
Children by (2) wife, Winwood F. Richey.
1. John Morrison, b. Mar. 28, 1807; d. 1834.
2. James Richey, b. Oct. 22, 1808; d. 1837.
3. Catherine A., b. Oct. 21, 1810.
4. Robert Patrick, b. Nov. 23, 1813; d. 1818.
5. William McKay, b. Jan. 10, 1816; d. 1839.
6. Margery, b. Mar. 6, 1818.
7. Hugh P., b. April 20, 1820; d. 1822.
8. Allen Powell, b. June 25, 1822; d. 1824.
9. A. Seraphina, b. Dec. 8, 1824; d. 1824.
10. George W., b. May 27, 1827.
11. Eugene M., b. Sept. 9, 1830.

JAMES CAMERON, b. 1761; d. Ga. 1840. Served as *Rev. Sol.* Received land in Cherokee Land Lottery 1827 for his services while living in Jasper Co. Mar. SARAH BROWN.
Children:
1. David (1796-1849), mar. Mary Lyle.
2. Thomas, mar. Nancy Stephens.
3. James Hawthorne (1800-1850), mar. Emma Castleberry.
4. Flora, mar. —Lorrance.
5. Benjamin H., mar. Mrs. Eliza Gilmer.
6. Janie, mar. James Lloyd.
7. Susie, mar. Benjamin Wilson.
8. William.
9. Sarah, mar. James Wilson.

BENJAMIN CAMP, b. Va. 1757; d. Jackson Co., Ga., 1832. Served as private in Capt. Nathaniel's Welch's Co., Col. Wm. Brent, 2nd Va. Reg.; also N. C. Reg. Mar. 1776 ELIZABETH DYKES.
Their son:
Joseph Camp (1779-1854), mar. 1799 ELIZABETH CAMP (dau. of THOMAS CAMP, JR., b. Va.; d. S. C. Private 2nd Va. Reg. and his wife, Susan Wagner; and g-dau. of THOMAS CAMP, SR., b. Va. 1717; d. N. C. 1798; a *Rev. Sol.* and *Patriot* and his wife, Winifred Starling. They had 5 SONS who fought at the Battle of King's Mt. One son, JOHN CAMP, son of Thomas Camp, Sr., b. Brunswick Co., Va.; d. Jackson Co., Ga., 1818. Served as private Va. Troops. Mar. Mary Tarpley).

SAMUEL CAMP (son of ICHABOD CAMP, b. Milford, Conn., 1726; d. Ill., 1786; a *Rev. Sol.* of Conn., and his wife, Content Ward, b. Durham, Conn., May 14, 1752), d. Warren Co., Ga., Aug. 18, 1827. Quartermaster in Col. Gabriel Penn's Va. Reg., Albemarle Barracks, 1779. Also served Quartermaster Va. troops. Mar. 1776 Amherst Co., Va., MARY BANKS (1753-1799).
Children:
1. Madden.
2. Cecilius.
3. Chander, mar. Mary Harwell.
4. Sarah, mar. James Ledbetter.
5. Nancy, mar. —Williams.
6. Elizabeth, mar. John Smith, of Warren Co., Ga.
7. Mary, mar. Sims Kelly. Moved to Ala.
8. Telemachus, d. Evansville, Ill.
9. Hyppupile (called Lucy), mar. —Johnson.
10. Gerard, mar. Martha Lacey.
11. Claudely, mar. 1806 Ann Harry.

DAVID CAMPBELL, b. Augusta Co., Va., 1750.; d. Washington, Tenn. Served in Va. under GEN. NATHANIEL GREENE of R. I. and Ga. Mar. 1780 ELIZABETH OUTLAW (dau. of ALEXANDER OUTLAW, b. N. C., 1738; d. Ala., 1826. Served as private N. C. Reg. under Col. William Campbell at King's Mt., and his wife, Penelope Smith).
Children:
1. Alexander.
2. Penelope.
3. Polly.
4. Betsey.
5. Mary.
6. Thomas J., mar. 1817 Sarah Bearden.
7. Victor.
8. Moreen.
9. Caroline.
10. Letitia.
11. Margaret.
12. Harriet.

WILLIAM CANDLER, b. Ireland, 1735; d. Richmond (now McDuffie), Co., Ga. 1787. Served as Colonel of a Regiment known as the "Regiment of Refugees of Richmond Co., Ga." Served at Siege of Augusta, Kings Mt., and Siege of Savannah. Mar. ELIZABETH ANTHONY (dau. of JOSEPH ANTHONY, *Rev. Sol.* of Va. and Ga., and his wife, Elizabeth Clark). She mar. (2) Cornelius Dysart.

Children:

1. Mary, mar. MAJOR IGNATIUS FEW, b. Md., 1748 (a brother of WILLIAM and BENJAMIN FEW, all three *Rev. Sols.* of Ga.).
2. HENRY, *Rev. Sol.*, mar. Miss Oliver.
3. JOSEPH, a *Rev. Sol.*
4. WILLIAM, a *Rev. Sol.*, mar. Miss Guthrie.
5. JOHN, a *Rev. Sol.*
6. Charles, d. y.
7. Amelia.
8. Falby.
9. Elizabeth, mar. John A. Devereux.
10. Mark Anthony, mar. (1) —; (2) Lucy White.
11. DANIEL, b. Columbia Co., Ga., 1779; d. there 1816. Mar. 1779, Sarah Slaughter (dau. of SAMUEL SLAUGHTER, of Va. and Ga., a *Rev. Sol.* A brother, REUBEN SLAUGHTER, also a *Rev. Sol.*, of Baldwin Co., Ga.).

Field Officers of the "Regiment of Refugees," Richmond Co., Ga., at the organization 1780: COL. WILLIAM CANDLER; LIEUT. COL. DAVID ROBESON; MAJOR JOHN SHIELDS (killed in battle); ADJ. JOHN McCARTHY; and REV. LOVELESS SAVAGE, Chaplain. Some of the Line Officers were: CAPT. ROBERT SPURLOCK; CAPT. EZEKIEL OFFUT; CAPT. ABRAHAM AYERS; CAPT. JOHN SHACKELFORD; FREDERICK STALLINGS; CAPT. JAMES STALLINGS; LIEUT. EDMUND MARTIN; LIEUT. JAMES MARTIN. This was the *only* Ga. Regiment distinguished as "Refugees." So called because the families of all the men were in refugeeship in less dangerous parts of the country.

JAMES CANTEY, b. Camden Dist., S. C., 1755; d. near Milledgeville, Ga., Oct. 9, 1817. Served as Lieut. and Captain under Col. William Thompson's S. C. Rangers. Mar. in S. C., MARTHA WHITAKER (1765–1806).

Children:

1. John (1786), mar. Emma Susanna Richardson.
2. Zacheriah.
3. Mary, mar. William Whitaker (son of HUDSON WHITAKER, *Rev. Sol.*).
4. Sarah, mar. Henry Crowell, moved to Columbus, Ga.
5. James, mar. Camilla F. Richardson—a *Sol. of 1812.*

THOMAS PETERS CARNES, b. Prince Co., Md. 1762; will made Athens, Ga., Aug. 2, 1816, probated May 5, 1822. Served in the Maryland Line and was given bounty land for his services in Franklin Co., Ga. D. Milledgeville, Ga. Mar. (1) ELIZABETH BOSTWICK, dau. of CHESLEY BOSTWICK (Bostic), *Rev. Sol.* of Ga.; (2) SUSAN (KING) SCREWS, of Milledgeville.

Children by (1) wife:

1. Robert Watkins.
2. William W.
3. Ann Low.
4. Julia, mar. Augustin N. Clayton, of Athens, Ga.

Children by (2) wife:

1. Thomas P., Jr.
2. Peter Johnson.
3. Nancy Clarke.
4. Richard S.
5. Susan King.

WILLIAM CARRAWAY, b. N. C., 1754; d. Thomaston, Ga., Feb. 1, 1834. Enlisted at Cambridge, S. C., served as Sergeant. Discharged June 11, 1780. Served under Captains John Moore

and Smith, Col. Hayes. Enlisted while a resident of Cumberland Co., N. C. Moved to Lincoln Co., Ga. Allowed pension while a resident of Upson Co., Ga. Mar. 1784, Elizabeth —. (Grave marked.
Children:

1. John (called Jobe), 1787–1869, mar. Elizabeth McCorcle.
2. Charity, 1789, mar. Benjamin Bethel.
3. Robert, mar. — McCorcle.
4. Mildred, mar. — McCorcle.
5. James.
6. Charles.

NOTE: MRS. ELIZA (MAJORS) CARLTON, *Real Daughter N. S. D. A. R.* of Senoia, Ga., member Joseph Habersham Chapter Atlanta, Ga., b. Dec. 25, 1806; d. Oct. 10, 1906 (dau. of SAMUEL D. MAJORS and wife, Elizabeth Greene, who served as private, age 16, in the Halifax Co. Va., troops; also served in *War of 1812*.) She was mar. to Thomas W. Carlton, of Va. They removed to Oglethorpe Co., 1826, then to Coweta Co., Ga., 1845. They had 14 children. Their first son, Ethelbert Carlton.

THOMAS CARR, b. Spottsylvania Co., Va., 1758; d. Columbia Co., Ga., 1820. Served under Gen. Marion, was twice wounded. Was Col. of Militia. Mar. (1) —; (2) FRANCES BACON (1771–1812).
Children:

1. Alexander Walter, b. 1787.
2. Susanna Brooks (1789–1870), mar. Nickolas Ware.
3. Thomas Dabney, mar. Annie Belle Watkins.
4. Selina Agnes, mar. Rev. Ignatius Few. (He was the first President of Emory College, Oxford and Atlanta, Ga.)
5. William Anthony, mar. (1) Cynthia Walker; (2) Jane Aikens.

JOHN CARSON, b. Neury, Ireland; d. Crawford Co., Ga. Served as a minute man under Col. Elijah Clarke. Received bounty land for his services. Mar. ISABELLA M. GOUGH.
Their son:
Joseph Jefferson (1802-1875), mar. Martha Raines.
(Other children are not known.)

ALEXANDER CARSWELL, b. Ireland, 1727; d. Burke Co., Ga. (formerly St. George's Parish), 1803. Served as private from Ga. under Gen. Twiggs. Received bounty grant of land in Burke Co., Ga., for his services. Mar. LADY ISABELLA BROWN.
Children:

1. Edward (1755), mar. Jane Trimble.
2. Agnes (1757), mar. Andrew Templeton.
3. JOHN, b. 1760; d. Burke Co., Ga., 1817. Served as *Rev. Sol.* with his father in Ga. Line under GEN. TWIGGS, 4th Ga. Reg. Mar. Sarah Wright. Two of their children were: A. Alexander (1789-1848), mar. 1813 Mary Palmer (dau. of GEORGE PALMER (1753-1821), Burke Co., Ga., *Rev. Sol.*, who obtained bounty grant of land for his services, and his wife, Mary Cureton); B. Mathew (1795-1844), mar. Adelaide M. Williams.
4. Alexander, Jr. (1762), mar. Elizabeth Stiles.
5. James.
6. Matthew, mar. Sarah Martin.

CHARLES CARTER, b. Goochland Co., Va., April 19, 1752; d. Oglethorpe Co., Ga. *Rev. Sol.* Served 1778 in Capt. Taylors Co., Col. Moore and Col. Yancey's N. C. Regiment. Enlisted 1780 as private in Capt. Gillam's Co., Col. Joseph Taylor's N. C. Regiment. Received pension while a resident of Oglethorpe Co., Ga. (Had 3 brothers: John, Thomas, and Robert Carter.)

DAVID CARTER, b. New Jersey, Feb. 20, 1752; d. Ga., Dec. 16, 1849. Enlisted as private, 1775, under Col. Morgan. Private, Pickens District, S. C. Captured and confined on prison ship "Concord," 1781. Received pension for services. Buried Mt. Zion Methodist Church Yard, Elbert (now Hart) Co., Ga. Mar. MEHITABLE COBB.
Children (known):

1. Micajah, mar. (1) Nancy (Goolsby) Garrett.
2. Mehitable.
3. David, Jr.

THOMAS CARTER, b. Edgecomb District, S. C., 1750; d. Franklin Co., Ga., 1810. Was a *Rev. Sol.* of Ga. and received bounty grant of land for his services upon certificate of Col. Elijah Clarke, April 12, 1784, in Franklin Co., Ga. Mar. 1771, Mary —, (1753-1792).

Children (known):
1. John.
2. Thomas, mar. 1795 Sarah —. He was b. S. C., 1772; d. Hall (formerly Franklin) Co., Ga., July, 1857. Private in Capt. Tooke's Co. 1814. (Record for Society Daughters of the War of 1812.) 6 children.

THOMAS A. CARTER, b. Va., 1750; d. Elbert Co., Ga., 1807. He served as private, Va. Continental Line. Received bounty land for his services in Ga. Mar. (1) 1774, Lucy Farris (1755–1795); (2) Elizabeth Stubbs, widow, of Wilkes Co., Ga.

Children by (1) wife:
1. James, mar. Lucy Martin.
2. Thomas S., mar. (1) Mary Smith; (2) Matilda Harman.
3. Nancy M., mar. Richardson Hunt.
4. Frances.
5. George.

Child by (2) wife:
Thomas P., mar. Lucy Hudson.

JOSIAH CARTER, b. England, 1735; d. Putnam Co., Ga., 1827. Served as private, Ga. Line, under Col. Elijah Clarke. Mar. MARY ANTHONY.

Children:
1. Josiah, Jr.
2. Anthony.
3. James.
4. John.
5. Loula.
6. Wellen.
7. Nancy.
8. Christopher, mar. Sarah Whitehead Battle.

JOHN CHAPMAN, b. S. C., 1746; came to Richmond Co., Ga. Enlisted in the Ga. troops, was Sergeant of Minute Men. Received grant of land in Wilkes Co., Ga., 1784 for his services. He mar. 1768, MARY THOMPSON, b. 1749; d. before 1819. He d. Warren Co., Ga., 1818.

Children (known):
1. Nathan, b. S. C., Feb. 11, 1777; mar. Elizabeth Hart, b. Jan. 30, 1780 (dau. of SAMUEL HART, *Rev. Sol.* of Ga., and his wife, Susanna Boring).
2. Benjamin, mar. Susanna Hart.
3. Thomas, mar. Sarah Hart.
4. John.
5. William.

WILLIAM CHAPMAN, private in Capt. Uriah Goodwyn's Co., 3rd S. C. Regiment. Received 287½ acres of bounty land for his services, in Franklin Co., Ga. He served under Col. William Thompson. On pay-rolls Mar. 1, 1779 to Nov., 1779., to 1780. At Siege of Charleston, S. C.

BENJAMIN CATCHINGS, b. Va., Oct. 31, 1748; d. Wilkes Co., Ga., 1798. Served with Ga. troops; promoted to Major on the Battlefield of Kettle Creek. Received bounty lands for his services. Mar. 1769, MILDRED CRIDDLE CARLETON, b. 1749. D. 1840.

Children were:
1. Joseph (1782-1852), mar. 1801, Mary Holliday (dau. of THOMAS HOLLIDAY, b. Va., 1750; d. Wilkes Co., Ga., 1798. Served as private, Ga. troops, and his wife, Martha Dickerson).
2. Philip, mar. Jincey Barnes.
3. Seymore.
4. Silas.
5. Jonathan.
6. Benjamin.
7. Ann.

TULLY CHOICE, b. Va., June 17, 1753; d. Hancock Co., Ga., Dec. 19, 1837. Enlisted 1776 in Capt. Thomas Dillard's Co., Col. Charles Lewis' Va. Regiment, 2nd Lieut. 1775; in Col. Mason's Va. Regiment, 1779; and Capt. Henry Co , Va. Militia, 1780. Mar. Aug. 15, 1791, in Laurens Co., S. C., REBECCA SIMS, of S. C. They moved to Hancock Co., Ga., 1792.
Children:
   1. John.
   2. Fenton.
   3. Ann, mar. John Graybill.
   4. William, mar. — Fretwell.
   5. Tully, Jr.
   6. Ruth.
   7. Jesse, mar. Elizabeth Bass.
   8. Catherine, mar. James Bass.
   9. Martha, mar. Ingram Bass.
   10. Rebecca, mar. Benjamin Sanford.

ROBERT CHRISTIE, b. Scotland, 1750; d. Savannah, Ga., 1801. Served as Lieut. in CAPT. ZACHRAY SMITH BROOKS' Co., S. C. Cavalry. Mar. ANN MARSHALL (1755-1817).

Their son, ROBERT, JR. (1787-1822), mar. 1814, Hannah Rahn (dau. of JONATHAN RAHN, *Rev. Sol.* (1762-1840), Effingham Co., Ga., who served as corporal 2nd Co., Regiment of Ga., and his wife, CHRISTIANA BUNTZ (1763-1824)).

Other *Rev. Sols.* connected with this family are JAMES McCALL, S. C.; FRANCIS McCALL, N. C; THOMAS McCALL, S. C., and JACOB CASPAR WALDHAUER, of Ga.

CHRISTOPHER CLARK, b. Va., April 20, 1737; d. Elbert Co., Ga., 1803. Served with Va. troops; received bounty land for services. Mar. MILDRED TERRELL, b. June 7, 1741; d. 1800.
Children:
   1. MICAJAH, b. 1758, mar. Penelope Gatewood. *Rev. Sol.*
   2. CHRISTOPHER (1760-1819), mar. Rebecca Davis. *Rev. Sol.*
   3. DAVID (1762-1846), mar. Mary —. *Rev. Sol.*
   4. Mourning (1764-1840), mar. 1783, WILLIAM BIBB KEY, a *Rev. Sol.*; 15 children.
   5. Judith (1766-1812), mar. PETER WYCHE, *Rev. Sol.*
   6. Rachel (1768), mar. (1) JOHN BOWEN, *Rev. Sol.* of Va. (1758-1790); she mar. (2) John Daley.
   7. Agatha, mar. George Wyche.
   8. Mary, mar. Thomas W. Oliver.
   9. Samuel.
   10. Joshua.
   11. Millie, mar. Shelton White.
   12. Terrell, b. Va., 1781.
   13. Susan, b. Ga., 1783, mar. F. McCarty Oliver.
   14. Lucy, mar. as (2) wife, James Oliver.

CHRISTOPHER CLARK (son of Christopher Clark and his wife, Mildred Terrell), b. Va., Jan. 6, 1760; d. Elbert Co., Ga., Sept. 21, 1819. Served in Va. Line and received bounty grant of land in Ga. for his service. Mar. Oct. 17, 1799, REBECCA DAVIS (dau. of William Davis, *Rev. Sol.* of Va., and his wife, Mary Chisolm), b. 1780; d. 1857.
Children:
   1. Samuel (1800-1862), d. Ala.
   2. Margaret Ann, b. 1803; d. Texas, 1866; mar. 1821, James Opher Clark, her cousin (son of Micajah Clark, Jr.).
   3. William Davis (1805-1882), mar. 1830, Elizabeth Jane Hearn (dau. of Thomas Hearn).
   4. Christopher Hill (1807-1848).
   5. Thomas Jefferson.
   6. George Washington.
   7. Mary (1812-1848), mar. Thomas B. Burge.

DAVID CLARK, b. Va., April 8, 1762; d. Elbert Co., Ga., Sept. 10, 1846. Served as private, Ga. Militia. Received bounty grant of land for service. Mar. Dec. 10, 1794, MARY COBB (1775–1840).

Children:
1. Elizabeth, mar. Philip Matthews.
2. Mary, mar. Thomas Edwards.
3. Eliza, mar. Madison Hudson.
4. Lucinda, mar. Henry Cosby.
5. Christopher.
6. John T.
7. Mildred, mar. Thomas F. Willis.

JUDITH (ADAMS) CLARK, a *Patriot* (dau. of Robert and Mary (Lewis) Adams, of Va., and widow of MICAJAH CLARK, *Rev. Sol.* of Va.), b. Va.; d. Ga. After the death of her husband, the widow Clark moved to Ga. with her children; received land. Five sons were *Rev. Sols.*

Children of Micajah Clark and Judith (Adams) Clark were:
1. CHRISTOPHER (1737–1803), mar. Millicent (sometimes spelled Mildred) Terrell. A *Rev. Sol.*
2. ROBERT (1738), mar. Susanna Henderson. *Rev. Sol.*
3. WILLIAM, mar. Judith Cheadle. *Rev. Sol.*
4. Judith, mar. 1770 ANDREW MOORMAN, *Rev. Sol.*
5. MICAJAH, JR., mar. Mildred Martin. *Rev. Sol.*
6. JOHN (1743–1819), mar. Mary Moore. *Rev. Sol.*
7. Penelope, mar. (1) Reuben Rowland; (2) Jonathan Sanders.
8. Bolling, mar. Elizabeth Cheadle.
9. James C., mar. Lucy Cheadle.
10. Elizabeth, mar. JOSEPH ANTHONY, a *Rev. Sol.*

WILLIAM CLARK (son of JOHN CLARK, b. Va., 1728; d. S. C., 1794, and wife, Judith), b. Putnam Co., Ga., 1831. Served as private, Ga. Line, and received bounty for his service in Washington Co., Ga. Mar. 1792 MARY HARVEY (1776–1830), (dau. of Evan and Mary Harvey. EVAN HARVEY, b. 1753; d. Putnam Co., Ga., 1814. Served in S. C. and Ga. Line and received bounty grant of land in Wilkes Co., Ga.; for his service in Ga. Line under Col. Clarke.)

NOTE: Connected with the WM. CLARK line are ARTHUR FORT, *Rev. Sol.*; THOMAS WELLBORN, *Rev. Sol.*; EVAN HARVEY, *Rev. Sol.*; and EVANS LONG, *Rev. Sol.* (all of Ga.).

JOSEPH DAVID CLARK, b. Va., April 12, 1752; d. Orange Co., Va., Feb. 5, 1839. After Rev. War, moved to Elbert Co., Ga., where he remained until shortly before his death. Enlisted Culpeper Co., Va.; served as matross in Capt. William Murray's Co., in Capt. Eddin's Co., 1st Va. Artillery Regiment, Col. Charles Harrison. His children obtained pension Feb. 20, 1851. Mar. (1) Ann Haynes, b. 1758, 11 children; (2) 1812, Catherine (no issue).

Children by (1) wife:
1. Larkin, lived Morgan Co., Ga.
2. JAMES, b. Orange Co., Va., 1779, came to Elbert Co., Ga., where he d. 1826. *Sol. of 1812*; drew land in Lottery of 1806; Lieut. of Militia 1809; Capt. 1812. Mar. April 8, 1812, Mary Alston (1783–1871), (dau. of LIEUT.-COL. WILLIAM ALSTON, *Rev. Sol.*, and his wife, Charity Alston).
3. Mary, mar. Col. Barnard Heard, Wilkes Co., Ga.
4. Ann P., mar. Adj. Gen. John C. Easter.
5. Elizabeth, mar. Col. Thomas White, Jones Co., Ga.
6. Sallie T., mar. Lewis Shirles, of Va.
7. Tabitha, mar. Cuthbert Reese, of Jones Co., Ga.
8. Eunice H., mar. Solomon H. McIntyre, of Va.
9. William David, of Orange Co., Va., mar. Jane Mary Eliason.
10. Bethsheba.

JOSEPH CLAY (son of Ralph Clay and Elizabeth Habersham, of England), b. Beverly, England, 1741; d. Savannah, Ga., 1805. Member Provincial Congress, Ga., 1777, and of Council of Safety. Served as Paymaster of the Southern Division Continental Army. Mar. Ann Legardiere (1745–1821).

Children:

1. Joseph, mar. Mary Ann Savage.
2. Ann, mar. Thomas Cummings.
3. Elizabeth, mar. Thomas Young.
4. Betsey, mar. Dr. James Box Young.
5. Sarah, mar. William Wallace.
6. Kitty, mar. 1793, Joseph Stiles.

BENJAMIN CLEVELAND, b. Prince Wm. Co., Va., April 26, 1738; d. 1806. Served as Ensign, N. C. troops, Howe's Reg. Mar. MARY GRAVES. Several children.
One dau.:
JEMIMA CLEVELAND, mar. James Wiley, and their son, James Rutherford Wiley, of Ga., mar. Sarah Hawkins Clark, dau. of William Clark and his wife, Elizabeth Sevier, dau. of Gen. John Sevier, *Rev. Sol.*, of Tenn.
One son:
JOHN CLEVELAND, *Rev. Sol.*, mar. Catherine Montgomery Sloan.

LARKIN CLEVELAND, brother of Benjamin Cleveland, b. Va., 1748; d. Ga., 1814; mar. Frances —. He served as Lieut. under his brother as Colonel.

EZEKIEL CLOUD, b. Wilkes Co., N. C., 1762; d. Henry Co., Ga., 1850. Served as private, Ga. Line. Received pension for his service 1831. Mar. ELIZABETH HARMON.
Children (known):

1. Nancy (Ann), mar. Col. William Hardin (son of Valentine and Margaret (Castleberry) Hardin); a *Sol. of the War of 1812.* They lived at New Echota (house built for the Moravian Missionaries). 7 children.
2. Levi, mar. Elizabeth Brown.
3. Mary Elizabeth, mar. Jacob Hale Stokes.

JEREMIAH CLOUD, of Wilkes Co., Ga., (wife Sarah), drew 287½ acres of land on Rocky Creek, Washington Co., for his service as a *Rev. Sol.*

DANIEL CLOWER (son of Michael Clower and his wife, Catherine Morgan, sister of Gen. Daniel Morgan, *Rev. Sol.* of Va.), b. Penn., July 18, 1762; d. Gwinnett Co., Ga., Sept. 30, 1842. (Grave marked by D. A. R.) Enlisted Orange Co., N. C., and drew pension 1835 for his service, while residing in Gwinnett Co. He was a Methodist preacher.
Children:

1. Sarah, b. 1787; mar. John Moorman Venable, of Jackson Co., Ga. 10 children.
2. Elizabeth, d. y.
3. Jonathan, d. y.
4. John (1794), mar. 1816, Nancy Winn. 10 children.
5. Nancy (1799), mar. 1824, John W. Stell.
6. Jane (1802), mar. George Witherspoon.
7. Daniel, Jr. (1805), mar. Parthenia Carter Brandon.
8. Mary (1807), mar. John Brown.
9. Searcy, d. y.

GEORGE CLOWER (bro. of Daniel Clower) moved from Penn. to Jasper Co., Ga., then to Wilkerson Co., Ga. He was a *Rev. Sol.* (Also his brother, JONATHAN CLOWER, enlisted as a *Rev. Sol.*, Orange Co., N. C.) Moved to Jasper Co., Ga.; d. Bibb Co., Ala. Mar. Berks Co., Penn., MARY SULAR.

ZEBULON COCKE, b. N. C., 1734; d. Burke Co., Ga. Served in N. C. and Ga. Line. Mar. (2) SARAH (PERRY) FIELD and moved to Burke Co., Ga., 1764.
Children:

1. CALEB, a *Rev. Sol.*
2. Isaac Perry, mar. Almeda Griffin (dau. of WILLIAM GRIFFIN, *Rev. Sol.*, and his wife, Mary Booker Barnett, of Henry Co., Ga.).
3. John, b. 1784. *Sol. of War of 1812.* Mar. Lydia Davis, b. Burke Co., Ga., 1791 (dau. of BENJAMIN DAVIS, *Rev. Sol.* of Ga., and his wife, Elizabeth Daniell). Their son, Benjamin E., mar.

1841 Margaret Cameron (dau. of ALEXANDER CAMERON, *Rev. Sol.* of N. C., and his wife, Nancy McCarty; they moved 1828 from Cumberland Co., N. C., to Early Co., Ga., where they died.) (Perhaps other children).

GEORGE COCKBURN, b. 1746; d. Franklin Co., Ga., 1834. Served in Rev. troops in Col. John A. Patrick's Regiment, under Major Shackelford, and drew land as a *Rev. Sol.* in 1827 Cherokee Land Lottery. Mar. ELIZABETH —

Children (not in order of birth):
   1. Archibald.
   2. George.
   3. John.
   4. Josiah.
   5. Russell.
   6. Jeremiah, mar. Joanna Henson.
   7. Clark.
   8. Jerusha, mar. — Blackwell.
   9. Rachel.
   10. Malissa.
   11. Sarah.

JONATHAN COLEMAN (son of THOMAS COLEMAN, *Rev. Sol.* of Va., and his wife, Mildred Richards), b. Va., came to St. George's Parish (now Burke Co.), Ga. Served as Sol., Ga. Line, under Gen. Wayne. Buried at old Bark Camp Church, near Midville, Ga. Mar. MILDRED (Milly) PITTMAN. (His grave marked).

Children (known):
   1. Charles, mar. Amelia Garner.
   2. Lindsey, lived Jefferson Co., Ga.
   3. Elisha, mar. (1) Miss Whitfield; (2) Mary L. Scott (dau. Brig. Gen. John Scott; g-dau. of CAPT. JAMES SCOTT, *Rev. Sol.*, and his wife, Frances Collier).

VINES COLLIER, b. Brunswick Co., Va., 17—; d. Oglethorpe Co., Ga., Sept. 1795. Served as private, Va Line Received bounty grant of land in Ga. for his services as a *Rev. Sol.* Mar. 1760 ELIZABETH WILLIAMSON (dau. of Benjamin Williamson, of Va.).

Children:
   1. Molly, b. 1760; mar. John H. Owens.
   2. Elizabeth, mar. Rev. Thomas Dunn.
   3. Sarah, mar. Harrison King Smith.
   4. Isaac.
   5. Ann, mar. (1) John Hardman; (2) Geo. Menefee.
   6. Thomas.
   7. John, mar. Patsey Gresham.
   8. William, mar. Sally Powell.
   9. Vines, Jr., b. 1777, mar. Dorothy Rafferty.
   10. Benjamin, mar. Ann Howard.
   11. Williamson, mar. Jemena Powell.
   12. Robert, mar. Martha Booker.
   13. Cuthbert, mar. Nancy Dickey.

PETER COFFEE, b. Ireland 1750, landed in America from Ireland; d. Hancock Co., Ga., 1820. Served in the Va. Continental Army, private, Capt. Benjamin Casey's 12th Va. Regiment; also Capt. Michael Bower's Co., Col. James Wood's Regiment. Drew pension for his service. Mar. SARAH SMITH, of Prince Edward Co., Va.

Children:
   1. Elizabeth, b. 1775, mar. (1) Charles Daniels; (2) —.
   2. Susanna, mar. T. Randall.
   3. Nancy, mar. (1) Abram Heard; (2) —.
   4. JOHN, mar. Ann Penelope Bryan (dau. of JOHN HILL BRYAN, *Rev. Sol.*). He was *Gen. in the War of 1812.*
   5. Sarah, mar. William Harris.

    6. Joshua.
    7. Mary, mar. Henry Gibson.
    8. Cynthia, mar. Thomas Stocks.
    9. Martha, mar. George Heard.
    10. Joshua.

JOSHUA COFFEE, brother of Peter Coffee, came with him to America. Was a *Rev. Sol.* Both Peter and Joshua Coffee had each a son, John Coffee, both of whom were *Generals in the War of 1812.*

JOSEPH COLLINS, b. 1755; d. Twiggs Co., Ga., 1839 (at the home of his daughter). Had grant of land, 287½ acres, in Washington Co., Ga., certified by Col. Elijah Clarke for his service as a *Rev. Sol.* He lived in Washington, Wilkes, and Macon Counties, Ga. Mar. NANCY CONNER. Children:
    1. Ruth, mar. — Norris.
    2. Martha, mar. —Cunningham.
    3. Mary, mar. W. H. Owens.
    4. Sarah, mar. Alexander Nelson.
    5. Wilson, mar. Martha Cunningham.

WILLIAM CONE, b. N. C., 1745; d. Bulloch Co., Ga., 1815. Served as private, McLean's Regiment, Ga. Troops. Mar. 1765, KEZIAH BARBER. They had 3 sons and 9 daughters.
    1. Aaron (1766–1830), mar. Susanna Marlow. 12 children.
    2. Joseph, removed to Thomas Co., Ga.
    3. William, Jr. (1777–1857), mar. Sarah Haddock, moved to Camden Co., Ga.
    4. Sarah, mar. Wm. A. Knight.
    5. Nancy, mar. Edwin Morris.
    (Names of other children not known.)
    (Wm. Cone descended from Daniel Cone of Haddam, Conn.)

THOMAS CONNALLY, b. Va., 1718; d. at the age of 82 (in 1800) in Gwinnett Co., Ga. (Buried in the Strickland grave yard near Sewanee, Ga.) He mar. POLLY PRICE (dau. of John E. and Elizabeth (Lindsey) Price), b. Va.; d. Madison Co., Ga. He served as a recruiting officer in Va. during Rev. War.
Children:
    1. John, mar. Biddy King.
    2. Thomas, mar. (1) Temperance Porter; (2) Susan Bagley.
    3. Charles, mar. Nancy Stokes.
    4. George.
    5. David, mar. in Va., Elizabeth Christian, b. Orange Co., N. C., Oct. 31, 1776; d. Fulton Co., Ga., 1848.
    6. Abner, mar. Lucy Bagley.
    7. Nathaniel, mar. Eliz Nailer.
    8. Price, mar. Sally Corker.
    9. William, mar. Cenas Christian.
    10. Christopher, mar. Elizabeth McIntyre.
    11. Samuel, mar. Pyrene Christian.
    12. Elizabeth, mar. Thomas Gaddis.
    13. Margaret, mar. Thomas Jones.
    14. Sallie, mar. Abner Barnes.
    15. Mary, mar. Wilson Strickland.

BENJAMIN COOK, of Monroe Co., Ala., applied for pension Sept. 15, 1828, on account of his Rev. Service. Served as private under CAPT. WILLIAM McINTOSH and MAJOR JOHN HABERSHAM, of Ga., from Aug. 19, 1782, until Dec. 10, 1783. Discharged at Savannah, Ga. He was also engaged in recapturing three vessels which had been taken by the enemy in the harbor of Savannah. He enlisted from BULLOCH CO., GA. He was b. 1760; d. Union Co., Ark., Feb. 27, 1846, where he resided with his children. Grave marked by the Pine Bluff Chapter, D. A. R., of Ark. Buried in the cemetery at the old Shady Grove Church, 8 miles east of El Dorado.

RICHARD COOPER, b. Duplin Co., N. C., 1758; d. Screven Co., Ga. Served as private under Capt. Wm. Kenson, Col. Charles Ward, N. C. Regiment. Mar. in S. C., LUCRETIA HOWARD.

Children (known):
1. David.
2. William.
3. Jane, mar. James Middleton.
4. Rachel, mar. Rev. Richard Parker.
5. George (1783–1862), mar. Mary Conner (dau. of REV. WILSON CONNER, of Ga., *Rev. Sol.*, and his wife, Mary Cook).

THOMAS COOPER, b. Frederick Co., Va., 1733, d. Greene Co., Ga., 1799. Served as Capt., Va. troops; also gave civil service; was *Sol. of War of 1812*; mar. 1762 Sarah Anthony, b. 1742 (dau. of JOSEPH ANTHONY, *Rev. Sol.* of Va., and his wife, Elizabeth Clark).

Children:
1. Penelope, mar James Nisbet.
2. Elizabeth, mar. Thomas Stovall.
3. Joseph.
4. Agnes.
5. Thomas.
6. Polly.
7. John.
8. Sarah.
9. Micajah.

JOHN COX, b. Jan 6, 1737; d. Ga., Oct. 1, 1793. Received grant of land for his service as a *Rev. Sol.* Mar. Francinia —, b. July 25, 1737, d. Dec. 2, 1811.

Children:
1. Thomas (1759–1817).
2. Mary.
3. Nancy Clark (1763), mar. REUBEN RANSOME, a *Rev. Sol.* (His grave in Clarke Co., Ga., marked by the D. A. R.)
4. Letitia, mar. — Mattox.
5. John.
6. Francinia (1769–1801), mar. THOMAS GREER (1760–1843), a *Rev. Sol.* 10 children.
7. Elizabeth, mar. — Turner.
8. Richard (1776–1837), mar. Eliza Massey Mead.
9. Martha, mar. — Colleran. Moved to La.
10. Bolling, d. Ala., 1842.

JOHN CRAPS (CRAPPS), b. Lexington Co., S. C., 1768; d. Randolph (now Terrell) Co., Ga., 1853. Served as private, 4th S. C. Artillery Regiment. Mar. Catherine Lowman, b. S. C., 1770; d. Ga., 1850.

Children:
1. George (1799), mar. Harriet Rogers.
2. Elizabeth, mar. Martin Stampes.
3. John Jacob.
4. Anna Barbara (1796), mar. Major David Kaigler. (Grave marked by D. A. R.)

Connected with the CRAPS family are ANDREW KAIGLER, *Rev. Sol.*, d. in Tenn.; JACOB SAYLOR, *Rev. Sol.*, d. S. C.; and Jack Dennard, d. at Jeffersonville, Ga.

JOHN CRATON (OR CRATIN), b. Md.; d. Wilkes Co., Ga., 1826. Buried near Petersburg, Ga. Served as *Rev. Sol.*, Lieut. 2nd Md. Regiment. Drew bounty land in Ga. Mar. 1780, Mary Ann Lanham, d. 1835.

Children:
1. Sylvester D.
2. Dau., mar. Richard H. Stokes.
3. Susanna, mar. (1) Raphael Wheeler; (2) Lewis R. Beaman.

4. Elizabeth Matilda, mar. — Wilkinson.
5. Eliza Sophia, mar. — Walton.
6. Dau., mar. — Bray.

Will made Feb. 3, 1826, pro. Jan. 1, 1827. G-children mentioned in will: Bennett, Jefferson, Washington, and John S. Wheeler; Julian Bray; John Walton; and Richard and John C. Stokes.

JOEL CRAWFORD, b. Hanover Co., Va., 1736; moved to Amherst Co., Va., 1750. Moved to Edgefield District, S. C., 1779; d. Wilkes Co., Ga., 1788. Enlisted Amherst Co., Va.; was in Chester District, S. C., 1780. Soon after this he was captured by the British, placed in Camden prison, released several months later. Removed, 1783, to Kioke Creek, Columbia Co., Ga. Mar. in Va., 1760, Fannie Harris (dau. of BENJAMIN HARRIS, *Rev. Sol.*, of Rockfish Valley, Va.).
Children:

1. Ann, mar. Joel Barnett (her cousin).
2. Robert, mar. Elizabeth Maxwell.
3. Joel, Jr., mar. Ann Barnett (his cousin). He was *Sol. of War of 1812.*
4. David, mar. Mary Lee Wood.
5. Lucy, mar. James Tinsley.
6. William Harris, mar. Susanna Girardin (Gerdine).
7. Elizabeth, mar. (1) William Glenn; (2) William Rhymes.
8. Charles, d. unmarried.
9. Fanny, mar. David Crawford.
10. Nathan, d. unmarried.
11. Bennett, mar. (1) Nancy Crawford; (2) Martha Crawford (dau. of Thomas Crawford).

DAVID CULBERTSON (son of JOSEPH CULBERTSON, *Rev. Sol.* of Va., and his wife, Agnes), b. Va., 1762; d. Greene Co., Ga., 1796. Served in N. C. troops; received bounty lands in Franklin Co., Ga., for his service. Pension granted to his widow for his service in 1830. Mar. Caswell Co., N. C., 1782 CLARA BROWNING (dau. of JOHN BROWNING, *Rev. Sol.* of N. C., who died in Ga.). She mar. (2) Jonathan Haralson.
Children by (1) husband:

1. Isaac, mar. Mary Houston.
2. Jeremiah.
3. John.
4. James, mar. (1) Sarah M. Wilkerson; (2) Libby Ashford, widow.
5. David, mar. Lucy Wilkerson.
Children by (2) husband:
1. Jonathan.
2. Kinchen.
3. Hugh. A.

(Allied with this family are ROBERT MORROW, *Rev. Sol.* of Md.; THOMAS EWING, *Rev. Sol.* of Md.; JOHN WILKERSON (OR WILKINSON), *Rev. Sol.* of Ga.)

JAMES CULBERTSON, b. 1764; d. 1823 (son of JOSEPH CULBERTSON, *Rev. Sol.* of Va., and his wife, Agnes). Served with N. C. troops. Received pension. Mar. MARY KILGORE. (Brother of DAVID CULBERTSON.)

JOHN CUNNINGHAM was a resident of Abbeville District, S. C., where he enlisted in the Continental Army, 1776. Served as Captain, Major, and Colonel of Ga. Militia. Served 2nd Ga. Batt. Received pension for his service. D. Elbert Co., Ga., Mar. 12, 1829. Mar. Aug 10, 1781, at Clark's Fort, Ga., ANN DAVIS.
(Four of the brothers of Ann Davis were *Rev. Sols.*) She was allowed a pension as the widow of a *Rev. Sol.* Sept. 18, 1838. She d. 1845, Elbert Co., Ga.
Children:

1. Elizabeth, b. 1783.
2. Franklin, b. 1784, lived in Elbert Co.
3. Johnson (1786–1809).
4. Joseph, b. 1788.
5. James S.
6. John A., b. 1799.

BENJAMIN DALEY (D'OILEY), b. S. C., 1750; d. Ga. Served in Ga. Militia. Received bounty grant of land in Effingham Co. for his service. Mar. in Effingham Co., Ga., Jan. 6, 1774, Susanna Garnett (sister of THOMAS GARNETT, *Rev. Sol.*, Lieut. of Ga. troops), and both served under CAPT. ABRAHAM RAVOT, of Ga.

Children (known):
1. Elizabeth, b. Effingham Co., Ga., Dec. 22, 1774.
2. Susanna, mar. Clayborne Beville (son of ROBERT BEVILLE, *Rev. Sol.* of Ga.).

ALLEN DANIEL, b. Va., 1738; d. Madison Co., Ga., 1814. Served as Captain 8th Va. Regiment. (Was J. P. Elbert Co. Representative from Elbert Co., Ga. *War of 1812 Record*). Mar. MARY ALLEN.

Children:
1. Elizabeth, mar. Aaron Johnson.
2. ALLEN, JR., b. Va., 1772; d. Ga., 1836. Brig.-Gen. in *War of 1812*. Representative 1821; mar. Mary Jones. (dau. of Russell Jones).
3. James, mar. (1) Elizabeth Jones (dau. of James and Elizabeth Jones); (2) Delilah Eurenice Wilson.
4. Charity, mar. Elisha Johnson.

JOHN DANIEL (DANIELL), b. Wake Co., N. C., May 23, 1760; d. Elbert Co., Ga., 1841 Enlisted Wake Co., N. C.; Captain in Col. Malmadge's N. C. Regiment. Served under Col. Farmer, 1780; was granted pension. Mar. MARGUERITE MEANS.

Children:
1. James J.
2. David.
3. John.
4. Allen.
5. Nancy, mar. — Cunningham.
6. Mary, mar. — Craft.
7. Sarah, mar. — Cunningham.
8. Lucinda, mar. — Prewitt (Pruitt).

JOHN DANIEL, b. Marlboro District, S. C., 1760; d. Dodge Co., Ga., 1830. Served as private in Capt. Moses Pearson's Co., Col. Marion's S. C. Regiment. Mar. 1799 REBECCA STEPHENS. (Grave marked by the D. A. R.)

Children:
1. Jack, mar. Eliza Mitchell.
2. Moses, mar. Lucinda Evans.
3. Matthew.
4. James, mar. Elizabeth Wilcox.
5. Nancy, mar. 1827 Simeon Bishop (b. N. Y., 1799; d. Ga., 1836).
6. Sallie, mar. George Wilcox.
7. Mary, mar. John Wilcox.
8. Sophronia, mar. Norman McDuffie.

BENJAMIN DANIEL, b. N. C., 1740; d. Laurens Co., Ga., 1818. Served in Ga. Line; certified to by Gen. John Twiggs. Mar. LUCRETIA BERGAMONT, d. 1830.

Children:
1. William.
2. James.
3. John, mar. Elizabeth Hudson.
4. Mary.
5. Elizabeth, mar. Benjamin Brantley.

WILLIAM DANIEL, b. N. C., 1747; d. Laurens Co., Ga., 1807. Served as private, S. C. Line, under Gen. Sumpter. Mar. LUCRETIA BELL.

Children (from will):
1. John.
2. Elizabeth, mar. Philip Raiford.

3. Martha, mar. — Marsh.
4. Jesse.
5. James.
6. Mary, mar. — Hatcher.
7. Catherine, mar. (1) Lewellyn Threwitz; (2) — Griffin; (3) — Ball.

WILLIAM DANIELL, b. N. C., Nov. 25, 1743; d. Clarke Co., Ga., Sept. 5, 1840. Mar. (1) Rachel —; (2) June 11, 1787 Mary Melton, b. Mar. 11, 1770; d. Oct. 3, 1843 (dau. of Moses and Nancy (Keen) Melton). Served as private, N. C. troops. Certified to by Col. Elijah Clarke, Feb. 2, 1784, that "WILLIAM DANIELL was a Refugee Sol. of N. C. and entitled to draw a bounty grant." He received 287½ acres of land in Franklin Co., Ga. (Grave marked by the D. A. R.) He had 26 children—12 by first marriage, 14 by second marriage.
By (1) wife:
1. William, Jr., b. Sept. 22, 1767, mar. Elizabeth Davis.
2. Elizabeth.
3. Mary.
4. Rebecca.
5. Nathaniel, mar. — Brantley.
6. Isaac, b. 1781, mar. Polly Johnson.
7. George, mar. Ellen Barber.
(Five other children, names not known).
By (2) wife:
1. Rachel, mar. William Barber.
2. Josiah (1792–1845), mar. (1) Sarah Ann (Owen) Burrough; (2) Elizabeth Jeffries.
3. Susannah, mar. Treman Fuller.
4. Jeremiah Melton, mar. (1) Nancy Burnett; (2) Sarah Wise.
5. Eleanor, mar. — Brandey.
6. Beadon, mar. Patsey Hodges.
7. Masters, d. at Sea.
8. Clarissa, mar. John Hodges.
9. Alfred, mar. (1) Mary Hodges; (2) Mary Dinard.
10. Stephen, mar. (1) Elizabeth Melton; (2) Louise Hodges.
11. Moses (1811–1892), mar. Eliza Hamby.
12. Robert, mar. (1) Naomi Burnett; (2) Margaret Fleming.
13. Olive, mar. David Hamby.
14. Cary, mar. — Hodges.
(See DANIELL Family in "McCall-Tidwell and Allied Families" Book published by the author, Mrs. Howard H. McCall).

STEPHEN BEADON DANIELL, b. N. C., 1745; d. Ga. Served as Ensign, 1776; was transferred Aug., 1777, from N. C. to S. C. Regiment. Member Com. of Safety, Brunswick, Co., N. C. (Home on Little River, N. C., burned by the British.) Mar. 1769, REBECCA HOWE (dau. of GEN. ROBERT HOWE, *Rev. Sol.* of N. C., and his wife, Sarah Grange), d. Ga. about 1820. Six children (3 known):
1. GEORGE W., b. N. C., 1782, d. Laurens Co., Ga., 1845; mar. (1) Lucrety Smith; (2) Mary Gonto; (3) Sarah Garnett, widow. 12 children by (2) wife; 1 by (3) wife. He was a *Sol. of 1812.*
2. Amos.
3. Robert Howe.

WILLIAM DANIELL (DANIEL), b. Ireland, 1745; d. Washington Co., Ga., 1836. Served as private, Ga. Line. Mar. 1772, Elizabeth Skinner, d. 1837.
Children:
1. William, mar. Temperance Ellis.
2. Elizabeth, mar. — McDonald.
3. Thomas M. (twin).
4. Theophilus (twin).
5. Frances, mar. Delano Renfroe.
6. Young.

7. Thomas.
8. Kenoth.
9. Abel (1794–1885), mar. 1825, Penelope (Jones) Sullivan (dau. of THOMAS JONES, b. England, 1755, d. Ga., 1809, *Rev. Sol.*, and (2) wife, Elizabeth Boyd).

THOMAS DARRACOURT (name spelled Darricott; Derrecot), b. Va.; d. Wilkes Co., Ga. (Made will Sept. 4, 1792, pro. Dec. 19, 1793.) He was a *Rev. Sol.* Mar. Elizabeth —.
Children:
1. Cecelia, mar. Richmond Terrell.
2. JOHN, *Rev. Sol.* Certificate of Col. Leonard Marbury for Quartermaster-Sergeant.
3. Mary, mar. John Wingfield.
4. Margaret (called Peggy), mar. — Borum.
5. William.
6. Elizabeth.
7. Francis.
8. James.

CYRUS DART, b. Haddon, Conn., June 11, 1764; was drowned near St. Simons Island, Ga., 1817. (He was the son of JOSEPH DART, a *Rev. Sol.* of Conn., and his wife, Abigail Brainerd.) Enlisted as private in Capt. Stillwell's Co., 1st Conn. Regiment, April 1, 1782. Came to Glynn Co., Ga., 1792, and lived in the "old town of Frederica." Mar. May 7, 1796, ANN HARRIS; they lived at "Coleraine." (Dead town of Ga.)
Children:
1. Erastus.
2. Horace.
3. Urbanus, b. 1800, d. Brunswick, Ga., 1883; mar. 1836, Eliza Moore. 8 children.
4. Alfred.
5. Theodore.
6. Ann Marie, mar. Dr. Du Pree.
7. Eliza Ann, mar. (1) Cyrus Paine; (2) Schupert Burns.
8. Edgar C. P., mar. Ellen Moore.

"Coleraine" was an Indian town (now a dead town of Ga.) on the North side of St. Mary's river, where the Treaty of peace and frienship was made June 29, 1796, between the President of the United States and the Kings, the Chiefs, and Warriors of the Creek nation of Indians, ratified Mar. 18, 1797. The Commissioners on the part of the United States were BENJAMIN HAWKINS; George Glymer; and ANDREW PICKENS. (The Lyman Hall Chapter, D. A. R. of Waycross, Ga., marked the site of Coleraine).

JOHN MARTIN DASHER, b. N. C., 1738; d. Effingham Co., Ga., 1802. Served as private under Capt. Kubler in St. Mathew's Parish, Ga. Mar. Susanna Shaffer (dau. of BELTHAZAR SCHAFFER (SHAFFER), *Rev. Sol.* of Ga.).
Children:
1. John.
2. Solomon (1791–1854), mar. Maria Wylly (dau. of THOMAS WYLLY, b. West Indies, 1762; d. Effingham Co., Ga., 1846. *Rev. Sol.* Asst. Quartermaster under his uncle, RICHARD WYLLY, *Rev. Sol.* of Ga.).
3. Naomi, mar. 1802, William C. Wylly.
4. Susanna, mar. — Franklin.
5. Martin, mar. Lydia Wiltman.
6. Christopher, mar. Ann Bird.
7. Joshua, mar. Dolly Moore.

REV. JONATHAN DAVIS, b. England about 1730; d. Wilkes Co , Ga., Mar., 1818. Mar. 1756, Lucy Gibbs, b. Va., 1738; d. Wilkes Co., Ga., about 1818. *Rev. Sol.* Served in Va. Line.
Children:
1. James.
2. Mary, mar. in Va., David Phillips; came to Wilkes Co., Ga.
3. John, b. 1759, mar. Mary Easton.
4. WILLIAM, mar. Nancy Easton. *Rev. Sol.*

5. Lucy, mar. (1) — Richardson; (2) — Goodall.
6. Mildred, mar. Thomas Phillips.
7. Susannah, b. Oct., 1769; mar. Benjamin Goss.
8. Elizabeth, mar. James Hitchcock.

WILLIAM DAVIS, b. Va., 1748; d. Wilkes Co., Ga., May 14, 1818. Served as Lieut, Col. in 5th Va. Regiment. Moved to Wilkes Co., Ga., 1795. Mar. Brunswick Co., Va., Aug. 28, 1769, AGNES LANIER, d. Feb. 21, 1813 (dau. of Sampson Lanier of Va., and his wife, Elizabeth Chamberlain).
They had 11 children.
One child (known):
Lewis Lanier Davis (1792-1832), mar. 1818 in Wilkes Co., Louise Tucker Irvine (dau. of Isaiah Tucker Irvine and his wife, Isabella Lea Bankston).

WILLIAM DAVIS, b. 1748; d. Ga., 1801. Served in S. C. Regiment. Received bounty grant of land for his service. Mar. in S. C., ANNE McLEOD.
Children:
1. John.
2. Charles.
3. Rebecca.
4. Ulysses.
5. Jane.
6. Martha.
7. Elizabeth.
8. Maria.

REV. WILLIAM DAVIS, b. Va., Jan. 7, 1765; d. Oct. 31, 1831; mar. in Va., Nancy Easton, b. Philadelphia, Pa.; d. 1841. Moved to Wilkes Co., Ga., 1793. Rev. Sol. of Va. Served under Gen. De La Fayette and was at the surrender of Cornwallis.
Children:
1. Reuben E., b. Oct. 8, 1790; d. age 21.
2. Lucy, d. y.
3. Elizabeth, b. Feb. 16, 1793; mar. — Orr.
4. Lucy Gibbs, b. May 7, 1795; mar. Rev. Wm. Henderson.
5. William, b. Dec. 8, 1796; mar. Joice Johnson.
6. Jonathan, b. Nov. 17, 1798; mar. (1) Mary Elizabeth Johnson; (2) — Mary Bledsoe.
7. Nancy E., b. June 10, 1800.
8. Jeptha Vining, b. Dec. 10, 1801; mar. (1) —; (2) —.
9. Isaac Newton, b. June 1, 1803; mar. — Meddis.
10. James, b. Jan. 22, 1805; mar. Louisa Hudson.
11. Jesse Mercer, b. Jan. 25, 1807; mar. (1) Sophie Burton; (2) Mrs. Elizabeth Gilbert; (3) widow McGouldrick.
12. Tabitha, b. June 10, 1809.

STEPHEN DAY, b. Penn., 1742; d. Columbia Co., Ga., 1825. Received bounty land in Ga. for his service, upon certificate of Col. James McNeil. Mar. Margaret Jones, b. 1744 (dau. of JAMES JONES, Rev. Sol. of Ga., and his wife, Mary —).
Children:
1. John, mar. Feribee Bulloch.
2. Stephen, Jr.
3. Jonathan.
4. Joseph.
5. Dau., mar. Thomas Kendrick.
6. REBECCA, mar. JOHN KENDRICK, Rev. Sol., b. Frederick Co., Md., 1759; d. Pike Co., Ga., 1843. Served as Lieut.; received bounty land in Ga. for his service. Granted pension. They had 7 children: a. Sylvanus K., mar. Elizabeth Park; b. John, mar. Nancy Locklin; c. William A. mar. Mary McLean; d. Adeline Eliza, mar. William Freeman; e. Sarah Rebecca, mar. Jonas Shivers; f. Theodate, mar. Daniel Carroll; g. Cornelia.

WILLIAM DENMARK, b. N. C.; d. Ga, age 102 years. Served as *Rev. Sol.* Settled in Screven Co., Ga., 1770. Mar. (1) Miss Moye; (2) Emma Moye.

Children:
1. REDDEN, b. Screven Co., Ga., 1770, d. Ga., 1813; mar. Lavinia Wise (dau. of William Wise, *Rev. Sol.* of Va., who settled in Screven Co., Ga.). She mar. (2) Mr. McNeely.
Children of Redden Denmark: a. Elizabeth, mar. James Groover; b. Clarissa; c. Sarah, mar. William Lastinger; d. John, d. Perry, Fla., 1844; e. Thomas Irving, b. 1809, mar. Amanda Groover (dau. of Charles Groover).

JACK (JOHN) DENNARD, b. S. C., 1750, d. Ga., 1810.   Enlisted in S. C. 6th Regiment, 1776. Served as Lieut. in Capt. McBee's Co.; also Capt. Mapp's Co., Col. Roebuck's S. C. Regiment. Mar. Harriet —.

Children (known):
1. Shadrack.
2. Isaac, mar. Mary Harris. A *Sol. of 1812.*
3. William.
4. Thomas.
5. John.
6. Bird, b. 1780, mar. Rhoda Marshall. A *Sol. of 1812.*

PETER DE VEAUX, b. Ga., 1752; d. Ga., 1826; mar. Martha Box. He was a member of the *Provincial Congress.* (From certificate of John Armstrong, Adj. General of the Southern Department at Philadelphia, Penn.: "14th May, 1780 that Peter DeVeaux was appointed an aide de camp to Major Gen. Gates.") Aug. 2, 1780, he was at Masks' Ferry on the Peedee river, S. C., and continued to serve in that capacity during the time Gen. Gates commanded the Southern Department.

One child, dau.:
Eliza Sarah De Veaux, b. 1798, mar. 1816, John Morel.

DAVID DICKSON, b. Pendleton District, S. C., 1750; d. Clayton Co., Ga., May 23, 1830. Served at Snow Camps, Speedy river, 1775. Commanded a Volunteer Co. under Gen. Williamson, 1776, in the Cherokee Nation against the Indians and Tories. Commanded a Co. of Minute Men on the Frontier. Received bounty grant of land in Ga. for his service. Mar. (1) Sarah — (1750-1785); (2) Martha Cureton (1764-1796); (3) Anne Allen (1772-1840). (Grave marked by the Ga. D. A. R.)

Children (mentioned in will):
1. William H.
2. Michael.
3. David.
4. John Orr, mar. Mary Glass.
5. Nancy Campbell, mar. — Smith.
6. Martha Easley, mar. — McConnell.
7. Thornton Smith.
8. Robert David.
Step-son, Chandler Aubrey.

JOHN DOOLY, b. N. C.; came from S. C. to the Ceded Lands of Ga. (now Wilkes Co.), with a wife, 3 sons, and 3 orphan nephews in 1762. Served as Captain of the 2nd Continental Ga. Brigade, later Colonel. Was killed by the Tories, 1780. Several of these Tories crossed the Savannah river and were later captured by the "War Heroine of Ga., NANCY HART."

Others were also captured and hanged at TORY POND in Wilkes Co.

(Dooly Co., Ga., was named for Col. Dooly and formed in 1821). His brother, THOMAS DOOLY, *Rev. Sol.*, was killed July 22, 1776, in a skirmish with the Indians, while returning to Ga. with a band of recruits for the Ga. Continental Army. Another brother, GEORGE DOOLY, served under Capt. Hart.

JAMES S. DOZIER, b. Lunenburg Co., Va., 1739, d. Warren Co., Ga., 1808. Served as Sergeant, Va. Militia, and in Artillery. Mar. MARY DUNWOODY (OR DINWOODY), b. 1740.

Their son:
Leonard Wesley Dozier, b. Va.; d. Warren Co., Ga.; mar. Nancy Staples.

WILLIAM DRANE. *Rev. Sol.*, b. Va.; d. Ga.   Mar. Cassandra Magruder.
Children (only two known):
  1. Eleanor, b. Columbia Co., Ga.; d. Coweta Co.; Mar. Anselm B. Leigh, a *Sol. of 1812*.
  2. William, Jr., b. Columbia Co., Ga., 1800. Mar. Martha H. Winfrey (dau. of JESSE WIN-
FREY, *Rev. Sol.*, Capt. in Ga. Line).

JAMES DUNWOODY (son of John Dunwoody of Chester Co., Penn., and his wife, Susanna
Cresswell, dau. of William Cresswell, of Fogg's Manor, Penn.), b. Chester Co., Penn., 1741; d. Liberty
Co., Ga., 1807. Came to Ga. 1770. Member Ex. Council of Ga. Mar. 1774, Esther (Dean) Splatt
(dau. of Abraham Dean and his wife, Ann Du Pont).
Children:
  1. James, Jr., mar. Elizabeth West Smith.
  2. John, mar. Jane Bullock.
  3. Esther, mar. Hon. John Elliott as (2) wife.

Note: WILLIAM DUFFEL, DANIEL SHINE, and CHARLES RALEY, all *Rev. Sols.* of
Ga., went to Milledgeville, Ga., 1825, to see Marquis de La Fayette when on his visit to America.

ELISHA DYAR (OR DYER), b. Va., 1763, near the Potomac river; d. Franklin Co., Ga., Sept.
4, 1839. Enlisted Granville Co., N. C., 1778, under Gen. Abram Potter and Col. Farrow. Was at
the Battle of Briar Creek. Enlisted, 1780, under Capt. Peter Burnett, Col. Ambrose Dudley. Came
to Ga., 1800; received land in Cherokee Land Lottery, 1827, as a *Rev. Sol.* Mar. MALVINA
WHEELER in 1790 (1760–1820).
Children:
  1. Martin.
  2. John.
  3. Joel H., mar. Rachel Sanders.
  4. Rebecca, mar. 1820, William S. P. Crawford.
  5. William.
  6. Polly, mar. William Smith.
  7. Elizabeth, mar. Jeremiah Wells.
  8. Melvina, mar. George Hornbuckle.

JOHN EADY, SR., b. Ireland, settled on Black Creek, Wilkinson Co., Ga. He was a *Rev.
Sol.*, and his service was certified to by Col. Elijah Clarke; mar. —.
Children:
  1. Margaret, mar. John William Gay (son of ALLEN GAY, *Rev. Sol.* of Ga., and his (1) wife,
Celia Elbert).
  2. John, Jr.
  3. Henry (1786–1847), mar. 1807, Elizabeth Gay (dau. of ALLEN GAY, *Rev. Sol.*, and his
(2) wife Abigail Castleberry).
  (Perhaps other children).

JACOB EARLY (son of JEREMIAH EARLY, *Rev. Sol.* of Va.), d. Ga., 1794. Served as
Capt. Va. Line; received bounty grant of land for his service in Wilkes Co., Ga. Mar. 1767, ELIZA-
BETH ROBERTSON. His will was probated Clarke Co., Ga.
Children:
  1. Ann (called Nancy), b. 1769, mar. BUCKNER HARRIS, a *Rev. Sol.* (son of WALTON
HARRIS, *Rev. Sol.*, and his wife, Rebecca Lanier).
  2. Mary.
  3. Elizabeth.
  4. Alicey.
  5. Sally.

JOHN EARLY (son of JEREMIAH EARLY, *Rev. Sol.* of Va.), b. Va.; d. at his home "Early's
Manor," Greene (formerly Wilkes) Co., Ga., 1807. Served in Va. Line, Lieut. stationed 1781 at
Travis Point; delegate to Va. Convention from Culpeper Co. Moved to Ga., 1791; mar. 1772, LUCY
SMITH.
Children:
  1. PETER, b. 1773, elected *Governor of Georgia*, 1813; mar. Ann Adams Smith. She mar. (2)
Rev. Adiel Sherwood.

2. Elizur, mar. Miss Patterson.

3. Mary (called Polly), mar. Major George Watkins.

4. Clement, mar. Sarah Terrell.

5. Joel, Jr., mar. Miss Singleton.

6. Jeremiah, mar. (1) Jane Sturgis; (2) Ann Billups. She mar. (2) John Cunningham.

7. Lucy, mar. Col. Charles Lewis Mathews (youngest son of *Governor* GEORGE MATHEWS, of Ga.).

JAMES EASTER, b. Va.; d. Elbert Co., Ga. (will made May 19, 1791, pro. Feb. 11, 1792). Served in Va. Line. Received 287½ acres of bounty land in Franklin Co., Ga., 1784. Mar. SARAH —. She mar. (2) 1792, EDMUND BREWER; (3) ROBERT MOORE.

Children of James and Sarah Easter (mentioned in will, not in order of birth):

Daus:

1. Mary Ann.

2. Elizabeth.

3. Dolly.

4. Lotty.

5. Sophia, mar. Joseph Howard.

6. Teary, mar. Jasper Smith of Bedford Co., Tenn.

7. Patty, mar. William Aycock.

8. Tabitha (called Tabby), mar. Thomas Napier.

9. Marjery.

Sons:

10. William Thompson.

11. Booker Burton, mar. Catherine Youmans.

12. Lewis.

13. Champion.

ELI EAVENSON, b. Chester Co., Penn., Jan. 12, 1760; d. Elbert Co., Ga., July 29, 1829. Mar. 1781, RACHEL SEAL, b. April 25, 1760; d. after 1829. He was a *Rev. Sol.* and drew two lots in Lottery of 1806; one, 1825, for Rev. service in Elbert Co. Was also a *Sol. of 1812.* Came to Ga. 1791.

Children:

1. George, b. Nov. 7, 1782, mar. Polly Hilly.

2. Susanna, b. Jan. 4, 1784, mar. John Higgenbotham.

3. Hannah, b. Nov. 2, 1786, mar. Matthew Pulliam.

4. Elizabeth, mar. Beverly Teasley.

5. Polly, b. 1791.

NEHEMIAH EDGE, b. Md., 1754; d. Ga., 1806. *Rev. Sol.;* served in N. C. troops. Received land in Wilkes Co., Ga. Mar. ELIZABETH DOSTER.

Children:

1. John, b. 1784; d. Cave Spring, Ga., 1844; mar. Sarah Miller (1780–1840).

2. James.

3. Reason, mar. (1) —; (2) Susan J. Deloney (1816).

ISAAC EDMONDSON, b. England, 1760; came to America. *Rev. Sol.;* served in S. C. Line. Moved to Bulloch Co., Ga.; d. Savannah, Ga., 1811. Mar. 1785, NANCY COX (1765–1842); moved to Brooks Co., Ga.

Children:

1. Susanna, mar. John Mathis.

2. Elizabeth, mar. William Holoway.

3. James.

4. John b. 1806, mar. Martha Strickland (dau. of Archibald Strickland, of Tattnall and Brooks Cos., Ga., formerly of N. C.).

5. David, mar. Tabitha Tillman.

6. Sally, mar. William Alderman.

FRANCIS EDMUNDS, made his will in Wilkes Co., Ga., Feb. 16, 1795; pro. July 9, 1799. He was a *Rev. Sol.* Received bounty grant of land for his service. Mar. RACHEL —.
Children:
1. William.
2. Richard.
3. John.
4. Catherine.
5. Mary.
6. Dolly.
7. Eloi.
8. Ann, mar. — Dixon.
9. Sally, mar. — McClendon.
10. Elizabeth, mar. — Bailey.

JOHN EDWARDS, b. England, 1759; d. Meriwether Co., Ga., 1833. Served as private, Ga. troops, Capt. Eldredge's Co., Col. Elliott's Regiment. Mar. 1786, ELIZABETH RAINEY.
Children:
1. Sterling (1788–1853), mar. 1816, Susan Hicks.
2. Patsey.
3. Paulina, mar. John Rainey.
4. Mary, mar. George Crinder.

WILLIAM EDWARDS, b. about 1741; lived in N. C.; died Effingham, Ga., 1833. Served in Capt. Elliott's Co., Col. Charles Pinckney's S. C. Regiment; enlisted 1775. Served also in Col. William Caldwell's S. C. Regiment. Drew land as a *Rev. Sol.* Cherokee Lottery, 1827. Mar. 1761, Chloe Stokes (1744–1803).
Children:
1. William (1770–1833), mar. Elizabeth Beall.
2. Obediah, mar. 1799, Tabitha Pitts (dau. of JOHN PITTS, *Rev. Sol.* of N. C., and his wife, Frances Griffin).
3. Henry.
4. Chloe.
5. Beall.
(Other children).

SOLOMON EDWARDS, b. Va., 1756; d. Clarke Co., Ga., 1844. Served as private, Va. Line; received bounty land in Ga. for his service. Mar. SARAH MATTHEWS.
Children:
1. William, mar. Kate Coleman.
2. Sarah Matthews, mar. Wylie Jones. She mar. (2) Mr. Dennis. 10 children.
3. Richard, mar. (1) Polly Harper; (2) Amanda Cunningham.

JOHN EPPINGER, b. Wermender, Wurtenburg, May 8, 1730; went to London 1749; came to America, 1749. Settled in N. C.; came to Savannah, Ga., Oct. 15, 1759. He was a *Rev. Patriot* and *Sol.* Many patriotic meetings were held in his home, "The Eppinger Tavern," Savannah, Ga. He d. 1776. Mar. BARBARA MAYERS (dau. of Jacob Mayers (or Majes)), b. in Wurtenburg, Germany, July 10, 1732; d. Savannah, Ga., Jan. 5, 1812.
Children:
1. Margaret, b. Wilmington, N. C., Jan. 1, 1755; d. 1793. Mar. BALTHAZER SCHAEFFER on May 30, 1772. He was a *Rev. Sol.*
2. Anna Magdaline, d. y.
3. Wenafoother (or Winifred), b. Savannah, Ga., July 1, 1763; mar. Joseph Roberts.
4. John, b. July 21, 1769, d. July 23, 1823; mar. Hannah Elizabeth Cline. He was United States Dist. Marshal 1808–1812. (*1812 Record*).
5. Sarah, mar. (1) John Miller; (2) John Jones.
6. James, mar. Elizabeth Shandley.
7. Matthew.
8. George.

WILLIAM EVANS, b. Va., Dec. 26, 1746; d. Wilkes Co., Ga., 1806. Served as private, Va. Line; received bounty grant of land, 1784, in Washington Co., Ga., for his service. Susanna Clement (dau. of Benjamin Clement, of Pittsylvania Co., Va.).
Children:
1. John (1772–1825), mar. Bessie Morton.
2. Stephen, mar. (1) Elizabeth Bennett; (2) — Jackson.
3. James, mar. Sallie Bennett.
4. Arden, mar. Elizabeth —.
5. William (1776–1822), mar. Elizabeth C. Hammock.
6. Sallie, mar. (1) Samuel Slaton; (2) William Combs.
7. Susan, mar. Kellis Slaton.
8. Annie, mar. Jonas Starke.
Widow Susanna (Clement) Evans, mar. (2) Daniel Slaton.

HARTWELL EZZELL (EZELL), b. S. C., 1764; d. Jasper Co., Ga., 1836. Served as private, Ga. Troops. Received bounty grant of land for his service. Mar. 1793, Sealy Lowry (1767–1814).
His son:
Braxton Rogers Ezzell (1798-1888), mar. Elizabeth Jackson (1804-1889).

EBENEZER FAIN, b. Chester Co., Penn., 1762; d. Habersham Co., Ga., 1842. Served as private with Penn.. S. C., and Ga. troops, under Capt. James Montgomery, Capt. William Trimble, and Col. Elijah Clarke. Mar. 1781 in Tenn., MARY BLACK; she d. Gilmer Co., Ga., 1846.
Children:
1. David, b. Gilmer Co., Ga., 1782.
2. Margaret.
3. Mercer, moved to Texas.
4. Elizabeth, b. 1791, mar. John Trammell, of Habersham Co., Ga. (son of WILLIAM TRAMMELL, Rev. Sol. of Ga.).
5. Mary Ann.
6. Sallie.
7. John.
8. Rebecca Ann.
9. Polly.

THOMAS FAIN (son of WILLIAM FAIN, Rev. Sol. of Ga. and Tenn., and his wife, Miss Knox.; grave marked by Tenn. Society D. A. R.); b. N. C., 1760; d. Decatur Co., Ga., 1832. Place of residence during Rev., Orange Co., N. C.; served as private, N. C. Line. Mar. 1781, MARY PARRAMORE (1762–1832). Lived in Decatur Co., Ga.
Children:
1. Matthew, b. Aug. 11, 1782.
2. Betty, b. Feb. 17, 1785.
3. Lavinia, b. 1787, mar. William McMullen.
4. Nancy, b. 1789.
5. Mary, b. 1791, mar. — Martin.
6. Rebecca, b. 1793, mar. James McMullen.
7. Clara, b. 1795, mar. — Strickland.
8. Ann, b. 1798, mar. — Whiddon.
9. Luvenicia, b. 1801, mar. 1817, George Robert Francis McCall (son of WM. McCALL, Rev. Sol., and (2) wife, Mary Pearce, of Screven Co., Ga.); both buried old Columbia Primitive Baptist Church.
10. Thomas, Jr., b. 1802, mar. —.
11. William, b. 1807.
12. Levice, b. 1810, mar. — Marshall.
13. L., b. Jan. 15, 1817.

JOHN FAIR, b. 1760; d. Ga., 1850. Served as a Rev. Sol. Received grant of land. Mar. Polly Waldener.
Children:
1. Sally.

  2. Nancy.
  3. William.
  4. Alexander.
  5. Elizabeth.
  6. Rhoda.
  7. Rebecca.
  8. Polly.
  9. Susan.
  10. Effie.

PETER FAIR, b. France, came to America and served under La Fayette. Mar. Susanna Bone, of Charlestor, S. C. On his tombstone in Milledgeville, Ga., 1824: "A Frenchman who came to S. C., later to Ga. *Rev. Sol.*"

ANDERSON FAMBROUGH, d. Clarke Co., Ga., Nov., 1815. Served as *Rev. Sol.*; drew Lottery land in Ga. Mar. Elizabeth —.
Children:
  1. Gabriel.
  2. John Anderson.
  3. Joshua.
  4. Jesse.
  5. Jane.
  6. Lucy.
  7. Polly, mar. — Thompson.
  8. Nancy, mar. — Thompson.
  9. Susanna, mar. — Ward.
  10. Elizabeth, mar. — Cole.

JAMES FANNIN, b. Nov. 28, 1739; d. Ga., Nov. 4, 1803. Served in *Rev. War* and received Lottery land in Ga. for his service. Mar. ELIZABETH SAFFOLD (1748–1814).
Children:
  1. Ann, mar. Littleton Mapp.
  2. Sarah, mar. James Allison.
  3. William, mar. C. Martin.
  4. Joseph Decker (1776–1817), mar. Betsey Lowe.
  5. John H., mar. Mary Wright.
  6. James W., mar. Ann P. Fletcher.
  7. Japtha, mar. Katie Porter.
  8. Eliza, mar. Setphen Bishop.
  9. Isham (1778–1819), mar. Patsey Porter.
  10. Abram, mar. Jane Williamson.

ROBERT FARQUHAS, b. Scotland, 1743; d. Charleston, S. C., 1784; was a *Rev. Patriot;* loaned money to the State of Ga. during Rev. War to help "carry on."

WILLIAM FARRIS, lived in Rabun Co., Ga., prior to 1834; d. 1835. Buried near town among the pines, but was removed to La Fayette Cemetery. The old stone marker bears this inscription: "WILLIAM FARRIS, died 1835 in the 85th year of his age. A Soldier of the Revolutionary War." Grave marked by D. A. R.

WILLIAM FEARS, b. Va., Feb. 16, 1766; d. Jasper Co., Ga., May 13, 1820. He served in the Va. Line and, in the Cherokee Lottery, 1827, in Ga., drew two lots of land for his service as a *Rev. Sol.* and for being wounded in the service. Mar. 1771 in Va., Ann Bulger, b. Va., Feb. 13, 1752.
Children:
  1. James, b. April 28, 1772, mar. Mary Anthony Porter.
  2. William, b. Jan. 31, 1774, mar. (1) Mary (Polly) Griffin; (2) Joicy T. Bowdre.
  3. Mary, b. Nov. 20, 1775, mar. (1) — Crenshaw; (2) Henry Fulke, of Va.
  4. Elizabeth, b. Dec. 18, 1777, mar. — Petty.
  5. Rebecca, b. May 20, 1779, mar. Bartholemew Roberts.
  6. Ezekiel, b. Sept. 30, 1781, mar. Alice Stringfellow.

7. Thomas, b. Oct. 30, 1783, mar. 1833 (no issue).
8. Frances, b. Nov. 5, 1786, mar. — Parks.
9. Zacheriah, b. July 3, 1789, mar. Elizabeth Mathews.
10. Samuel, b. Oct. 13, 1791, mar. Mary Ballard.
11. Robert, b. Aug. 21, 1793, mar. — Smith.
12. Sarah, b. 1796, mar. — Chaplaine. Moved to Tenn.
13. Nancy. b. Oct. 30, 1799, mar. William Roberts.

ISAAC FELL, came to America, d. Ga. Was serving in a Company, stationed at the Springfield Redoubt, when Savannah, Ga., was besieged by the British; he lost an arm in the conflict, was captured, placed aboard a ship, and conveyed to England. He was also a *Sol. of the War of 1812.* Mar. Mar. 10, 1774, in Savannah, Ga., ELIZABETH SUSANNAH SHICK (dau. of JOHN SHICK, a *Rev. Sol.* of Ga., and his wife, Margaret Ritter). He was the son of William and Isabella (Lambert) Fell.

JOHN FIELDER, b. Goochland Co., Va., 1752; d. Walton Co., Ga. Enlisted as sergeant, 1775, in Capt. John Clark's Co., Col. John H. Meade's Regiment, Va. troops. Mar. 1778, Nancy Hawkins.

WILLIAM FEW, SR., b. Kennett, Penn., 1714; came to Ga. from N. C.; d. near Wrightsboro, Ga. Mar. 1743, MARY WHEELER. Received bounty land (for his service in N. C. Line) in Washington Co., Ga.
Children:
1. BENJAMIN FEW, b. Md., 1744; came to Ga.; d. on a visit to Ala., 1805. Mar. in N. C., RACHEL WILEY. Served as Col. in Richmond Co., Ga. Militia.
2. WILLIAM FEW, JR., b. Md., June 8, 1748; d. at Fishkill on the Hudson, N. Y., July 16, 1828. Mar. Catherine Nicholson (dau. of COMMODORE JAMES NICHOLSON, N. Y., a *Rev. Sol.*). Served as Lieut. Col., Richmond Co., Ga., Militia; member of Executive Council 1777–1778, and of *Continental Congress* 1780–1782. Moved to N. Y. One of the first Trustees of the University of Ga.
3. JAMES FEW, b. 1746, was murdered by the Tories during the Regulator movement. Mar. SARAH WOOD.
4. IGNATIUS FEW, b. Md., 1750; d. Columbia Co., Ga., 1810. Served as 1st Lieut., Capt. and Major, Ga. Troops. Mar. (1) MARY CANDLER; (2) Lavinia —.
5. HANNAH FEW, mar. RHESA HOWARD, *Rev. Sol.* of Ga.
6. Elizabeth Few, mar. COL. GREENBERRY LEE, *Rev. Sol.*
Note: Rev. Ignatius Alphonso Few, b. Columbia Co., Ga., 1789; d. 1845; was the first President of Emory College, Oxford, Ga. (now Emory University, Atlanta, Ga.).

BENJAMIN FITZPATRICK, b. Va., 1745; d. Buckhead, Morgan Co., Ga., 1821. Served as private, Va. Line; received bounty grant of land in Ga. for his service. Mar. (1) MARY PERKINS; in 1784, (2) SARAH JONES. His grave marked by D. A. R.
Children by (1) wife:
1. Nancy, mar. John High.
2. Constantine (1771–1845), mar. Mary Perkins (1778–1856); 5 children.
3. Frances, mar. — Stewart.
Children by (2) wife:
1. Elizabeth, mar. Samuel Clay.
2. William, b. 1786, mar. Nancy Green.
3. Joseph, mar. Nancy Hunter.
4. Alexander, mar. Nancy Hill.
5. Susan, mar. (1) Charles Matthews; (2) John Emerson.
6. Bennett, mar. Eliza Shackelford.
7. Mary, mar. Thomas Brown.
8. James, mar. Sarah Harris.
9. Jesse, mar. (1) Nancy McGowan; (2) Mrs. Phillips.

RENE FITZPATRICK, b. S. C.; d. Ga., 1839. Served as private, Ga. Line; received bounty grant of land in Ga. for his service. Mar. 1797, MOLLIE HARDWICK (dau. of WILLIAM HARDWICK, *Rev. Sol.*, and his wife, Cynthia Parker).

LEWIS FLEMISTER, b. Essex Co., Va., 1746; d. Wilkes Co., Ga., 1807. Enlisted 1775, Chesterfield C. H., Va.; served as private, 7th Va. Regiment, Capt. William Moseley; transferred to Morristown, N. J., Capt. Caleb Gibbs' Co. Sergeant 1783, discharged Newburg, N. Y., 1783. (Grave marked by D. A. R., 1930.) Mar. Feb. 27, 1790, ELLENDER CHISM (dau. of James and Barbara Chism), b. Halifax Co., N. C., 1773; d. near Monticello, Ga. 1855.

Children:

1. William L., mar. Micha Wilson.
2. James, mar. Ailsa Wilson.
3. Lewis Fielding, mar. Lucy Wilson.
4. John, mar. Huldah Woodruff.
5. Catherine, mar. John Lindsay.
6. Euramie Elizabeth, mar. Isaac Parker.

JOHN FLERL (OR FLOERL), b. Salzburg, Germany; d. Ga., 1776. Came to America, settled at Ebenezer, Ga. (Salzburger Colony). Member First Provincial Congress of Ga., 1775. Capt. Ga. troops 1776 under Gen. Samuel Elbert. Mar. (1) Jan. 15, 1765, HARRIET ELIZABETH BRAND-NER (1743-1773); (2) 1774, DOROTHY KIEFFER.

Children:

1. Judith, d. y.
2. Margaret or Mary (1767), mar. J. C. WALDHAUER, a Rev. Sol.
3. John, d. y.
4. Israel (1771-1813), mar. Sarah Salome Waldhauer. She mar. (2) Lewis Weitman.

WILLIAM FLETCHER, b. Accomac Co., Va., 1729; d. Telfair Co., Ga., after 1837. He is buried in Telfair Co. Place of residence during the Rev. was Marion District, S. C., 50 miles above Georgetown. He served as a Rev. Sol. and is recorded in the pension claim (granted) his son, JOHN FLETCHER, in 1832. He was given land in the Cherokee Land Lottery in Ga., 1827, as a Rev. Sol. of Telfair Co. He mar. (1) in Va. (name unknown); (2) Elizabeth McIntosh, in Georgetown, S. C., at St. Philips Parish Church; (3) Louisa Hendricks.

Children by (2) wife:

1. GEORGE, b. S. C., Dec. 28, 1752; Rev. Sol. Moved to Effingham Co., Ga.
2. JOSEPH, mar. Elizabeth Lanier; Rev. Sol. Lived in Bulloch Co., Ga.
3. JOHN, b. S. C., 1765; mar. Susan Mizell. Rev. Sol. Moved to Ga., then Fla.
4. ANN (called Nancy), mar. WILLIAM McCALL, Rev. Sol. of S. C.; moved to Ga. (Effingham and Screven Cos.).
5. Elizabeth, mar. (1) — Barton; (2) JOSEPH MORRISON, of S. C., Rev. Sol.
6. Rebecca, mar. JOSHUA HODGES, Rev. Sol. They lived in Screven and Bulloch Cos.

Children by (3) wife:

1. Sarah.
2. Thomas.
3. Wiley.

JOHN FLETCHER, b. S. C., Jan. 14, 1765; d. Gadsden, Fla., May 30, 1860. Rev. Sol., served 1780 under Capt. James Gregg, Lieut. Col. Thomas Davis, Col. Hugh Giles, Gen. Francis Marion. After Gates' defeat he was under Major David Thornley, Col. Baxter and others. Served as private to 1782. Lived in Marion Dist., 50 miles above Georgetown; moved to Ga., 1784, to Gadsden, Fla., 1825. (Applied for pension Nov. 9, 1832). Was living as a minor with his father during Rev. His father, WILLIAM FLETCHER, and three brothers were Rev. Sols. He was Capt., Bulloch Co., Ga. Militia, 1796. (Sol. 1812 record). He was H. R. Telfair Co., Ga., 1816-17. Mar. (Telfair, formerly Bulloch, Co.), SUSAN MIZELL.

Children (known):

1. Zecheriah.
2. John, moved to Opelika, Ala.
3. Nancy, mar. Leonidas Lott.
4. Sarah.
5. Zabud.
6. Ziba, mar. Blanche Reese.

CHARLES FLOYD, b. Northampton Co., Va., Mar. 4, 1747; came to Charleston, S. C.; d. "Bellevue," Camden Co., Ga., Sept. 9, 1820. In Charleston, S. C., raised a Co. of guards; served with the "Liberty Boys" of Ga.; was captured by the British, carried to Savannah, then Charleston, and remained a prisoner until the end of the War. Mar. 1768, MARY FENDIN, of Greene's Island, S. C., b. April 15, 1747; d. McIntosh Co., Ga., Sept. 18, 1804.

Their only child:

MAJOR GEN. JOHN FLOYD, of the *War of 1812*, of Ga., b. 1769; d. 1839; mar. 1793, Isabella Maria Hazzard (dau. of Richard Hazzard, of S. C., and his (1) wife, Phoebe Loftain, of Fla.). They had 12 children.

ROBERT FORSYTH (buried in St. Paul's Churchyard, Augusta, Ga.). From tombstone record: "Sacred to the memory of ROBERT FORSYTH, Federal Marshal of Ga., who in the discharge of the duties of his office fell a victim to his respect for the laws of his Country and his resolution in support of them on the 11th of January 1794, in the 40th Year of his Age.

His virtues as an Officer of rank and unusual Confidence in the War which gave Independence to the U. S. and in all the tender and endearing relations of social life, have left impressions on his Country and his Friends, more durably engraved than this monument."

His wife, FANNY FORSYTH, d. Louisville, Ga., Sept, 1805, age 46. Buried in Summerville Cemetery, Augusta, Ga.

Their son:

JOHN FORSYTH, was *Governor of Georgia*. Mar. Clara Meigs.

NOTE: The act granting the Charter to Franklin College (now the State University at Athens, Ga., Clarke Co.), was passed Jan. 27, 1785. (The first of American State Universities. Ref. "Abraham Baldwin," by Prof. Harry C. White, Prof. of Chemistry, University of Ga.)

ABRAHAM BALDWIN, the first President, called in 1800 to be Professor of Mathematics at Franklin College; JOSIAH MEIGS of Conn. was later President of the College; b. Middleton, Conn., Aug. 21, 1757 (son of RETURN MEIGS, *Rev. Sol.* of Conn., and Elizabeth Hamlin); d. 1822. He mar. Clara Benjamin, b. Stratford, Conn., May 5, 1762 (dau. of JOHN BENJAMIN (1730–1796), *Rev. Sol.* of Conn., and his wife, Lucretia Backus). Their dau., Clara Meigs, mar. JOHN FORSYTH, *Governor of Ga.* (son of Robert Forsyth, of Va. and Augusta, Ga.).

NOTE: ALONZO CHURCH (1793–1862), President of University of Ga. (1830–1860) (then Franklin College), Athens, Ga. (was the grand-son of TIMOTHY CHURCH, b. South Hadley, Mass., 1736; d. Brattleboro, Vt., 1823, *Rev. Sol.* of Vt., and his wife, Abigail); mar. SARAH TRIPPE (1800–1861), of Putnam Co., Ga.

ARTHUR FORT, b. —, Jan. 15, 1750; d. Twiggs Co., Ga., June 15, 1833. Served Ga. troops, living in Burke Co., Ga., 1775. Mar. SUSANNA (TOMLINSON) WHITEHEAD (1755–1820) (widow of Richard Whitehead. They had one son, Richard Whitehead, Jr., b. 1776).

Children:

1. Sarah, b. 1779, mar. Appleton Rossiter (son of TIMOTHY ROSSITER, a *Rev. Sol.*, b. 1752; d. Hancock Co., Ga., 1848, and his wife, Mary Dinsmore).

2. Moses, mar. Eudlocia Walton Moore.

3. Arthur, mar. Mary Newson (or Munson).

4. Tomlinson (*Sol. of 1812*), mar. Martha Fannin. They had 13 children.

5. Susanna, mar. (1) Robert Jamison; (2) Samuel B. Hunter.

6. Elizabeth, mar. Lovett B. Smith.

7. Zachariah C., mar. Amanda Beckham.

8. Owen Charlton, b. 1798; d. 1829.

THOMAS FORSTON, b. Orange Co., Va., May 1, 1742; d. Wilkes (now Elbert) Co., Ga., Feb. 15, 1824; received bounty land in Wilkes Co. for his service, Va. troops. Mar. (1) in Va., RACHAEL WYNN.

Children:

1. Benjamin, mar. Elizabeth —.

2. William, mar. Eliza Lane.

3. Jesse (1783–1827), mar. Mary B. White.

4. Richard (1778–1836), mar. (1) Lucy Arnold.

5. Elizabeth , mar. William Gibbs.

6. Milly, mar. JOHN WILLIS, d. 1822, a *Rev. Sol.*; she drew land as widow of *Rev. Sol.*, in Elbert Co., Ga., 1827; (also drew land for her orphan children: Banjamin, Elizabeth C., Louisa Willis).

7. John (1794), mar. (2) Elizabeth Gaines.

8. Thomas, mar. Mary —. She mar. (2) Samuel Kerlin.

REV. GEORGE FRANKLIN (son of Rev. William and Sarah (Boone) Franklin, who moved from Va. to Curituck Co., N. C., 1780), b. Va., 1744; d. Jan. 1816. He was a *Rev. Sol.* Mar. Vashti Mercer (a half-sister of Rev. Silas Mercer of Ga.). (His grave was marked by the D. A. R.)
Children:

1. Vashti, mar. (1) — Boyd; (2) Daniel Harris as (2) wife.

2. Owen, mar. Eliza Floyd.

3. George.

GEORGE FREEMAN (son of Holman Freeman, Sr.), b. Va., 1758. Mar. in Va. FRANCES (called Fanny) TAYLOR. Moved to Wilkes Co., Ga. (then the "Ceded Lands") in 1772. Served under Gen. Elijah Clarke in Ga. Militia and was at the Siege of Augusta. He d. Wilkes Co., Ga., May 12, 1796. She d. 1820.
Children:

1. Wesley.

2. Allen.

3. HENRY, moved to Fayette and Coweta Cos. Mar. 3 times: (1) Elizabeth Hinton; (2) Lucinda Weatherly; (3) Nancy Moody.

4. Elizabeth.

5. Alicy.

6. George, Jr.

7. Joseph.

HOLMAN FREEMAN, JR. (son of Holman Freeman, Sr.), b. Va.; came with his parents to the "Ceded Lands," now Wilkes Co., Ga., 1772. He served during the Rev. under Gen. Elijah Clarke; was at the Siege of Augusta and served throughout the War. He also was a *Sol. of the War of 1812*, as Col. of Batt. He mar. about 1783, PENINAH WALTON (sister of Josiah Walton, of the Broad river Settlement). She was b. Va.; d. Ala., where she removed after her husband's death in Wilkes Co., 1817.
Children:

1. Fleming, mar. Sally Bibb; moved to Ala.

2. John, mar. Miss Callaway; moved to Ala.

3. Mary, mar. Dr. William Bibb, the *Territorial Governor of Ala.*, 1816.

JAMES FREEMAN (son of Holman Freeman, Sr.), mar. Rhoda —. Was a *Rev. Sol.* of Ga.

JOHN FREEMAN (son of Holman Freeman, Sr.), b Va., 1756; d "Poplar Grove," Wilkes Co., Ga., Jan. 7, 1807. Served under Gen. Elijah Clarke; was at the Siege of Augusta and Charleston, S. C.; fought under Pickens, Sumpter, and Morgan in S. C. Was with Count D'Estaing at Savannah, Ga. After Savannah was siezed by the British, the FREEMAN BROTHERS joined the Va. Army; he was made Captain; later joined Gen. Greene and was at Battle of '96. He mar. 1785, CATHERINE CARLTON (dau. of ROBERT CARLTON, a *Rev. Sol.* of Va., d. Wilkes Co., Ga., and his wife, Rebecca).
Their only child:

REBECCA FREEMAN (1786-1843), mar. Oct. 6, 1803, Shaler Hillyer (son of ASA HILLYER, *Rev. Sol.* of Conn., and his wife, Rhoda Smith). He was b. Conn., Aug. 2, 1775; d. Wilkes Co., Ga., Mar. 22, 1820.

WILLIAM FREEMAN (son of Holman Freeman, Sr.), mar. Sally. —. Lived in Augusta, Ga. Was a *Rev. Sol.* of Ga.

NOTE: The five sons of Holman Freeman, Sr., were *Rev. Sols.* of Ga., viz: HOLMAN, JR. WILLIAM, GEORGE, JAMES, and JOHN FREEMAN.

ELIJAH FREENY, b. Sussex Co., Del.; d. Baldwin Co., Ga., Oct. 1798. Mar. Elizabeth —, b. Del., d. Baldwin Co., Ga., 1808. He was a *Rev. Sol.* of Del. Received land in Ga.
Children:
1. Elizabeth, mar. (1) Tilghman Buckner, d. 1810; (2) Enoch Underwood, July 23, 1815.
2. Nancy, mar. Mar. 20, 1814, Baldwin Co., Ga., Amos Fox Byington, a *Sol. of the War of 1812*.
3. Clement.
4. Charlotte.
5. William.
6. Elijah, Jr.
7. Eliza.
8. Robert.

RICHARD FRETWELL, b. Va., 1752; d. Ga., 1843. Enlisted 1776, Cumberland Co., Va.; received, in Newton Co., Ga., pension for service as private, 4th Va. Regiment, under Capt. Holcomb, Col. Robert Lawson. Moved to Hancock Co., Ga., 1784. Mar. FRANCES —. His will mentions grand-sons, Richard, Leonard, William A., and Philip Z. Fretwell; grand-daus., Patsey Brown, and Frances Kennon, wife of M. L. Kennon; Nancy and Elizabeth Fretwell; son, Leonard, and wife, Polly; daus., Lucy, mar. — Clifton; Nancy, mar. — Burge; and Patsey, mar. Jackson Harwell.

WILLIAM FURLOW, b. Ireland; d. Greene Co., Ga.; came to Md., then S. C. Served with Col. Elijah Clarke at the Siege of Augusta. Mar. MARGARET (OR ELIZABETH) NIDY.
Children:
1. James.
2. John.
3. William.
4. David.
5. Charles.
6. Sallie, mar. — Neal.
Two other daus. (names unknown).

WILLIAM GAINER, b. Petersburg, Va., 1758; moved to Ga. and settled on Augusta Road near Davisboro; d. Washington Co., Ga.; buried near Sandersville, Ga. Served as private, 12th Va. Regiment, under Capt. Benjamin Speller; Col. Smith and William Brent's Regiment. Received land grants in Washington Co., Ga. Mar. 1778, Martha Williams, b. 1762.
Children:
1. Mary (1779–1846), mar. Jordan Smith.
2. Rebecca (1794), mar. Jesse Wall.
3. Penelope, mar. Jason Bryan.
4. James (1783–1869), mar. Mrs. Priscilla Brantley.
5. Nancy, mar. Zadoc Salter.
6. Miriam, mar. Bythal Hynes.
7. Dau., mar. Allen Fort.
8. Elizabeth, mar. —Britt.
9. Sallie, mar. Solomon Brown.
10. Tempe, mar. — Smith.

DANIEL GAINES, b. Va., 1745; moved to Wilkes Co., Ga., 1785; d. Wilkes Co., Ga., 1803. He was a *Rev. Sol.* of Va., Major of Batt. of Minute Men from the Cos. of Albemarle, Amherst, and Buckingham, Va.; served under Col. Charles Lewis and Gen. La Fayette in Yorktown and Va. Mar. (1) Mary Hudson (dau. of John and Anne (Jones) Hudson, of Va.); (2) Mary Gilbert (dau. of Henry Gilbert, of Amherst Co., Va.).
Children:
1. Gustavus.
2. Hippocrates.
3. Zenophen.
4. Daniel.
5. Archimedes.
6. Henry Gilber.
7. Bernard, the eldest (1767–1839), mar. 1812, Sarah Force Cook.

THOMAS GARNETT (GARNET) (son of ANTHONY GARNETT and wife, of Va., a *Rev* *Sol.* of Va., Continental Line, d. Columbia Co., Ga., 1794), b. Essex Co., Va., 1750; d. Chatham Co., Ga., 1793. At a meeting of the Ga. Council of Safety, June 25, 1776, commissions were issued to "ABRAHAM RAVOTT, Captain; THOMAS GARNETT, First Lieut.; DANIEL HOWELL, 2nd Lieut.; JAMES DELL, 3rd Lieut., of a Co. of Militia, Second Batt., First Regiment, Upper District of St. Mathews Parish, Ga." Mar. at the Ebenezer Jerusalem Church, Effingham Co., Ga., Jan. 8, 1772, RACHEL WILLSON. (She mar. (2) WILLIAM G. PORTER, a *Rev. Sol.* of Effingham Co., Ga.)

One child:

JOHN GARNETT (1776), mar. 1794, Mary Bostwick (dau. of Samuel Bostwick and his wife, Ann Mary Maner). He was a *Sol. of War of 1812.*

JACOB GARRARD, b. Sept. 4, 1763; d. Putnam (Baldwin) Co., Ga., 1819. Served as private, Ga. troops; was at Battle of Cowpens; received bounty grant of land in Ga. for his service. Mar. June 22, 1786, MARY ELIZABETH BARRON, b. 1765; d. Baldwin Co., Ga., 1827 (dau. of WILLIAM BARRON, *Rev. Sol.*, and his wife, Prudence Davis).

Children:

1. Nancy, b. 1787, mar. (1) Thomas Roquemore, (2) Samuel Johnson; (3) Green Simmons.
2. William, b. 1791, mar. (1) Delilah Clements; (2) Mary Ann (Roquemore) Allen.
3. John, b. 1790.
4. Jacob, b. 1794.
5. Mary Rebecca.
6. Hiram.
7. Zillah Ann, b. 1802; d. Texas; mar. Rev. James Roquemore, (who (2) mar. Martha Goss).
8. Eliza Maria.
9. Anna Lucinda.

JOHN GARRARD, b. 1730; d. Jones Co., Ga., 1807. Served as private; received 287½ acres of land for his service in Wilkes Co., Ga. Mar. (1) 1758 in S. C., MARY BOLT; (2) ELIZABETH —.

Children by (1) wife:

1. Robert.
2. Frances, mar. John Barron.
3. Nancy.
4. JACOB, *Rev. Sol.*, mar. Mary Elizabeth Barron.

ALLEN GAY (son of JOHN THOMAS GAY, *Rev. Sol.* of N. C.), b. Northampton Co., N. C., 1765; d. Coweta Co., Ga., June 18, 1847. Buried at Macedonia Baptist Churchyard. (Grave marked by D. A. R.) Served as private in Capt. Robert Raiford's Co., Col. Dickerson N. C. Regiment. Mar. (1) Sept. 5, 1787, CELIA RAE ELBERT, of Savannah, Ga. (dau. of MAJOR GEN. SAMUEL ELBERT, *Rev. Sol.* and his wife, Elizabeth Rae), d. 1793; (2) in Ga., ABIGAIL CASTLEBERRY; (3) 1824, widow ANNIE BENTON, of Coweta Co., Ga.

Children by (1) wife:

1. John William, mar. Margaret Cady.

Children by (2) wife:

1. Elizabeth, b. 1790, mar. Henry Eady.
2. Gilbert, b. 1811, mar. Sarah Stamps.
(Perhaps other children.)

HEROD GIBBES, b. Va.; d. Morgan Co., Ga. Served seven years in Va. Continental Army; removed to Pickens, S. C., then to Morgan Co., Ga. Mar. in Va., LUCY ANDERSON.

Son:

Thomas A., b. S. C., 1786; mar. Martha Maddox, of Greene Co., Ga.; d. Walton Co., Ga.

JOHN GIBSON (son of Gideon Gibson), b. S. C., 1759; d. Fulton Co., Ga., 1832. Served as private, S. C. Regiment, under Col. Charles Pickney. Mar. 1779, (1) FANNIE FLEWELLYN, d. 1807 (dau. of ABNER FLEWELLYN, *Rev. Sol.*); (2) 1809, ELIZABETH DOZIER; (3) CLARA BUTTS (widow of Wm. Butts). She d. 1842.

Children:

1. John.

2. Churchill.
3. Nancy, b. 1796, mar. John Gorman. Moved to Gwinnett Co., Ga.
4. Wylie Jones (1801–1868), mar. Sarah Ann Bennett.
5. Sarah, mar. Isaiah Tucker, b. Amherst Co., Va., 1761; came to Warren Co., Ga., 1794.
6. Ann, b. 1810; d. 1863; mar. Horatio Whitfield.
7. Henry.

JOHN GIBSON, b. 1750; moved to Cheraw District, S. C., then to Warren Co., Ga., 1784.
Served in S. C. Line. Mar. (1) 1777, ANN CRAWFORD; (2) WIDOW FULLER.
Children by (1) wife:
1. Thomas, b. 1786, mar. Martha Neal.
2. John, b. 1778.
3. Susan G., b. 1780.
4. William, b. 1783.
Children by (2) wife:
1. Mary Anne.
2. Ferriby.
3. Lucy.
4. Elizabeth.
5. David Neal.

FELIX GILBERT, b. Scotland; came to Va.; d. Wilkes Co., Ga., 1801. Served as a private.
Va. troops. Mar. MISS GRANT (dau. of Peter Grant, of the Broad river Settlement, Ga.).
Children:
1. Dau., mar. Henry Gibson.
2. Ann, mar. John Taylor.
3. Elizabeth, mar. Dr. Gilbert Hay.
4. Maria, mar. (1) — Christmas; (2) Andrew Shepherd.
5. William.
6. Felix, b. Rockingham Co., Va.; mar. Miss Hillhouse.

WILLIAM GILBERT, b. Va., 1758; d. Gwinnett Co., Ga., 1830. Served in Va. and Ga.
Troops; received bounty grant of land in Ga. for his service. Mar. 1785, TAMAR STRICKLAND,
b. 1768.
Children:
1. Isaac (1790–1863), mar. 1813, Elizabeth Allbright; 9 children.
2. Jacob.
3. Nancy.
4. John.
5. William.
6. Oliver.

PETER GILLIAM, b. Va., 1737; d. Wilkes (now Elbert) Co., Ga., 1809. Served as a Rev.
Sol. from Pittsylvania Co., Va., under Gen. Daniel Morgan; received grant of land in Wilkes Co.,
Ga., for his service. Mar. 1758, ANN HEARD (dau. of Stephen Heard and Mary Falkner), b.
Va., 1744; d. Greene Co., Ga., 1821.
Children:
1. Charles.
2. Sarah, mar. Ewing Morrow (son of ROBERT MORROW, b. Ireland, 1742; d. Md., 1782;
a Rev. Sol., Ensign in 2nd Md. Batt. Flying Camp, and his wife, Margaret Ewing (1751-1803),
dau. of COL. THOMAS EWING (1730–1790), Rev. Sol., Col. 3rd Batt. Flying Camp, Md., and his
wife, Margaret).
3. Mary, mar. — Reeves, of Va.
4. Patsey, mar. — Williams, of Greene Co., Ga.
5. Elizabeth.
6. Ann, mar. Joseph Morrow (brother of Ewing Morrow).

JOHN BLAIR GILMER (son of GEORGE GILMER and his (3) wife, Harrison Blair, Rev.
Patriot of Va.), b. Williamsburg, Va., 1748; d. Broad river settlement, Ga., 1793. Served under

Marquis de La Fayette. Was at the Siege of Yorktown; received bounty grant of land, Wilkes Co., for his service. Mar. 1770, MILDRED THORNTON MERIWETHER, d. 1826.
Children:
  1. John Thornton (1774–1831), mar. 1803, Martha Gaines Harvie. Moved to Ky., then to Ill.
  2. Nicholas, b. 1776, mar. Amelia Clarke.
  3. Francis Meriwether (1785–1864), mar. 1808, Martha Barnett (1790–1855) (dau. of WILLIAM BARNETT, Rev. Sol., and his wife, Mary Meriwether); 5 children.
  4. George Oglethorpe, mar. Martha Johnson (dau. of Nicholas Johnson).
  5. David H., mar. Virginia Clark.
  6. Harrison Blair, mar. 1808, Gabriel Christian.
  7. Betsey, mar. Thomas McGehee.
  8. Sally, mar. Burton Taliaferro.
  9. Jane, mar. (1) Thomas Johnson; (2) Abner McGehee of Ala.

THOMAS MERIWETHER GILMER (son of Peachy Ridgeway Gilmer and his wife, Mary Meriwether of Va.), b. Va., 1760; d. Broad river settlement, Ga., 1817. Served under Marquis de La Fayette and also had active service in Ga.; received grant of land for his service. Mar. 1783, ELIZABETH LEWIS (1765–1855), dau. of THOMAS LEWIS (1718–1790), Rev. Sol. of Va., and his wife, Jane Strother.
Children:
  1. Peachy, mar. (1) Mary Boutwell Harvie; (2) Caroline Thomas, widow. Moved to Ala.
  2. Mary, mar. (1) Warren Taliaferro (son of ZECHERIAH TALIAFERRO, b. Va., 1730, d. S. C., 1811, a Rev. Sol., and his wife, Mary Boutwell). She mar. (2) Nicholas Powers.
  3. Thomas Lewis, mar. (1) Nancy Harvie; (2) Ann Harper.
  4. GEORGE ROCKINGHAM, b. 1790, mar. Eliza Frances Grattan (dau. of ROBERT GRATTAN, Rev. Sol. of Va., and his wife, Elizabeth Gilmer). He was a Sol. of 1812, and also Governor of Georgia.
  5. John (1792–1860), mar. (1) Lucy Johnson; (2) Susan (Barnett) Gresham.
  6. William Benjamin Strother, mar. Elizabeth Marks. Moved to Ala.
  7. Charles L., mar. (1) Nancy Marks; (2) Matilda Kyle, widow.
  8. Lucy Ann Sophia, mar. Senator B. S. Bibb, of Ala.
  9. James Jackson, mar. Elizabeth Jordan.

HENRY GINDRAT, b. Purysburg, S. C., 1740; d. Effingham, Co., Ga., 1801. Served as an officer under Gen. Nathaniel Greene and was wounded at Eutaw Springs; received bounty land in Ga. for his service in S. C. and Ga. Mar. (1) MARY MAY (dau. of John May and his wife, Mary (Stafford) Patterson, dau. of COL. WILLIAM STAFFORD, Rev. Sol. of S. C.; she mar. (3) James Mullet and d. 1820, age 106 years); (2) DORCAS (WILLIAMS) STAFFORD (widow of COL. SAMUEL STAFFORD, Rev. Sol. of S. C.).
Children by (1) wife:
  1. Abraham, mar. Barbara Clark, widow of William Clark.
  2. John.
  3. Mary, mar. Dr. Benjamin St. Mark.
  4. Rhoda, mar. William Gilleland.
Children by (2) wife:
  1. Dorcas, mar. — Washburn.
  2. Henrietta, mar. 1823, JOSIAH CLARK, a Rev. Sol.; served as officer under Gen. Nathaniel Greene; lived at Beech Island, S. C., and Effingham Co., Ga.
  3. Henry, Jr.

THOMAS GORDON, b. Spottsylvania, Co., Va., Dec. 12, 1758; d. Gwinnett Co., Ga., 1826, Served as private, S. C. Regiment; received bounty grant of land in Ga. for his service. Mar. 1777. Mary Buffington, b. Chester Co., Penn., 1760; d. Ga., 1837 (dau of JOSEPH BUFFINGTON, b. Penn., 1737; d. Penn.; mar. Mary Few (1741–1807), a Rev. Sol. of Chester Co., Penn.).
Children (known):
  1. John Few.
  2. Joseph Roy.
  3. Charles.

4. Samuel.
5. Alexander.
6. George Aston.
7. FEW (1797-1857), mar. Clarissa Hardin (dau. of HENRY HARDIN, a *Rev. Sol.*, b. N. C., 1761; d. Monroe Co., Ga., 1843).
8. Buffington.
9. Caroline Matilda.
10. Mary.
11. William.
12. James (1801-1863), mar. Sarah Laird (1804-1868).

PHOEBE BUFFINGTON (dau. of Joseph and Mary Buffington), b. Chester Co., Penn., 1764; mar. 1785 in Spartanburg, S. C., John White, b. Va., Aug. 8, 1765 (son of Henry and Frances White).

DANIEL GRANT, b. Va., 1724; d. Wilkes Co., Ga. 1793 (will dated July 4, 1793). Removed to N. C. 1765. Served with N. C. troops; received bounty grant of land in Ga. for his service. Mar. 1750, ELIZABETH TAIT.
Children:
1. Amelia, mar. Lieut. John Owen.
2. Fannie, mar. — Gafford.
3. THOMAS, mar. Frances Owen.
4. Isabella, mar. — Davis.
5. Anna, mar. — Wilkins.

THOMAS GRANT, b. Hanover Co., Va., 1757; d. Jasper Co., Ga., Nov. 27, 1827. Served as Lieut. in N. C. troops with his father, DANIEL GRANT, *Rev. Sol.*; they received land in Ga. and moved there with their families. Mar. FRANCES OWEN (dau. of John and Mildred (Grant) Owen).
Children:
1. Daniel, mar. Lucy Crutchfield.
2. Mildred, mar. J. Billingsley.
3. Thomas, Jr., mar. Mary Baird.
4. William, mar. Ritura Mills.
5. Elizabeth, mar. William Love.

DR. ROBERT GRANT, b. Scotland July 15, 1762; came to S. C. Served as Surgeon on Gen. Marion's Staff, S. C.; d. St. Simon's Island, Ga., 1843. Mar. April 5, 1799, SARAH FOXWORTH, b. S. C., 1778; d. N. Y., 1859.
Children:
1. Robert.
2. Elizabeth Helen, mar. Dr. Robert Hogan.
3. Amelia.
4. Harry.
5. Charles, mar. Cornelia Bond.
6. Hugh F., mar. Mary Elizabeth Fraser.
7. Harry Allen, mar. (1) Louisa Bloodgood; (2) Laura Thompson.
8. Sarah Ann.
9. James Couper.

JAMES GRAVES, b. Culpeper Co., Va., 1730; d. Lincoln Co., Ga., 1796. Mar. 1750, MARY COPELAND, b. Va., about 1732; d. Lincoln Co., Ga., 1801. He served as a *Rev. Sol.* of Ga., private, under Gen. Elijah Clarke, at the Battle of Kettle Creek. Certificate of Gen. Clarke, April 9, 1784; received 287½ acres of land in Franklin Co., Ga., bounded N. W. by land given by Ga. to COUNT DE ESTAING, *Rev. Sol.* from *France.*
Children:
1. Richard, mar. Mary —.
2. John.
3. Robert.
4. Thomas.
5. Mary, mar. SAMUEL WHITTAKER, *Rev. Sol.*

6. Sally, mar. — Ried.
7. Susannah.
8. Francis, mar. Rebecca —.
9. William, mar. Nancy —.

JOHN GRAVES, b. Culpeper Co., Va., 1748; d. Wilkes Co., Ga., 1824. A *Rev. Sol.* Was at Brandywine, Germantown, and Monmouth. When Gen. Greene crossed the Yadkin river in 1780, Col. Graves was ordered to protect the Troops from Cornwallis; received bounty grant of land in Ga. Settled near Graves Mt. (named for him); moved to a place named French Mills, in Wilkes (now Lincoln) Co., Ga., where he d.; buried in family graveyard at the home of his son. Mar. Catherine West. Had issue.

WILLIAM GRAVES, b. 1746; d. Ala., 1802.; received land in Ga. for his service; moved later to Ala. Mar. SARAH SMITH.
Their dau.:
Dorothy Graves, mar. as (1) wife, Bird Fitzpatrick (son of WILLIAM FITZPATRICK (1746-1809), who received bounty grant of land in Ga. for his service); lived in Savannah, Ga., and his wife, Anne Philips (dau. of JOSEPH PHILIPS, *Rev. Sol.* of Ga., who served under Col. Elijah Clarke (1734-1800) in Ga., and his wife, Sarah Lyndes (Lindes)).

HENRY GRAYBILL, b. Lancaster Co., Penn., 1734; d. Washington Co., Ga., 1816. Served as private, Ga. Line, under Gen. Elijah Clarke; received bounty land in Ga. for his service. Mar. MARY RUTHERFORD.

JOHN GREEN, his claims as a *Rev. Sol.* paid to him Jan. 27, 1784, then Sheriff of Effingham Co. Mar. MARTHA REBECCA —. He d. Effingham Co., Ga., 1819, age 55 years. Served as Capt., 6th Co. Batt., Continental Army of Ga.

McKEEN GREEN, JR. (son of McKEEN GREEN, SR., *Rev. Sol.* of Ga.), d. Tattnall Co., Ga. On certificate of Col. Caleb Powell, he received bounty grant of land on the Altamaha river, Washington Co., Ga., for his service as a *Rev. Sol.*, June 9, 1784. Mar. at Ogeechee, Ga., July 3, 1786, Elinor McCall (dau. of CHARLES McCALL, *Rev. Sol.* of S. C. and Ga., and grand-dau. of FRANCIS McCALL, *Rev. Sol.* of N. C.).
Children:
1. Harris.
2. Selete, mar. Daniel Sauls, April 24, 1811.
3. Ann.
4. William.
5. Jane, mar. CAPT. MICHAEL HENDERSON, *Rev. Sol.*
6. Sarah Hull, mar. BASIL O'NEAL, *Rev. Sol.*
7. James.
McKeen Green and John Green were appointed Members of the Ex. Council of Ga., Jan. 5, 1786. McKEEN GREEN, JR., JOHN GREEN, and BENJAMIN GREEN, all *Rev. Sols.* of Ga., were brothers.

PETER GREENE, JR., b. R. I., 1725; d. Hancock Co., Ga., Oct. 20, 1807. Lived in Brunswick Co., Va. during the Rev. and served as a *Rev. Sol.* of Va. as private. Mar. 1750, Judith Love (dau. of Allen Love). She was b. Oct. 1727; d. Hancock Co., Ga.
Children:
1. JAMES, b. 1751; d. Jan. 5, 1806; mar. April 25, 1781, Elizabeth Bass. A *Rev. Sol.*
2. Sarah Ann. b. April 27, 1753.
3. Nathaniel, moved to N. C.
4. Frederick.
5. Elizabeth, b. May 24, 1758.
6. Peter, b. 1760 (twin).
7. Judah, b. 1760 (twin).
8. Alexander, b. Sept. 1, 1764.
9. Myles (Miles), b. June 26, 1767, Va., d. Monroe Co., Ga., 1853; mar. (1) Oct. 15, 1789, Elizabeth Hunt (dau. of CAPT. JUDKINS HUNT, *Rev. Sol.* of Va.), b. 1769, d. 1809; (2) Nancy Bass; (3) Widow McGhee.

MAJOR GEN. NATHANIEL GREENE, b. Warwick, R. I., May 27, 1741; d. at his plantation home, "Mulberry Grove," in Ga., June 9, 1786. (Plantation presented to him for his Rev. service, by the State of Ga.; formerly the confiscated estate of Lieut. Gov. of Ga., John Graham, 14 miles from Savannah, Ga.) He served as Col., was made Major Gen. by act of Legislature and in 1783 was voted a resolution of thanks for his service by the Congress of the United States. Monument erected to his memory, Savannah, Ga. Inscribed on monument: "Major Gen. Nathaniel Greene. Soldier, patriot, and friend of GEN. GEORGE WASHINGTON, *Rev. Sol.* and later *President of the United States.*" Mar. July 20, 1774, CATHERINE LITTLEFIELD. She mar. (2) at Philadelphia, Penn., 1796, Phineas Miller.

Children:
1. George Washington, d. unmar.
2. Martha Washington, mar. (1) 1795, John Nightengale, of Warwick, R. I., 3 children; (2) Henry Turner, 4 children.
3. Cornelia Lott, mar. (1) Peyton Skipwith; (2) Edward Littlefield.
4. Nathaniel R., mar. Ann Maria Clark.
5. Louisa Catherine.

CHARLES JACKSON, *Rev. Sol.* of Mass., b. Newton, Mass., 1767; d. at the home of Phineas Miller, Cumberland Island, Ga., 1801.

WILLIAM GREENE, SR., b. Va., 1734; removed to Warren Co., N. C. Mar. there, SARAH ANN ALSTON. Served in 1st N. C. Regiment as Captain; was granted 500 acres bounty land as an officer for service in Washington Co., Ga., Jan. 24, 1784.

WILLIAM GREENE, JR., b. N. C., 1764; d. Greene Co., Ga., Dec. 13, 1819. Will on record, made Dec. 8, 1819. Served as private in N. C. and Ga. Militia; of the First Batt. Richmond Co., Ga., Militia; received 287½ acres of bounty land for his service in Greene Co., upon certificate of Gen. Elijah Clarke, 1785. He was also a *Sol. of the War of 1812* from Greene Co., Ga. Mar. June 17, 1784, RUTH HUNTER, b. Warren Co., N. C., Sept. 24, 1764; d. Greene Co., Ga., May 15, 1826 (dau. of JESSE HUNTER, *Rev. Sol.* of N. C., and his wife, Ann Alston, dau. of SOLOMON ALSTON, *Rev. Sol.* of N. C., and his wife, Nancy Hinton).

Children:
1. Lemuel, b. Mar. 29, 1785, mar. (1) Ann Merritt; (2) Eliza Coleman.
2. Sarah, b. June 12, 1786, mar. (1) Douglass Watson; (2) Drury Towns; (3) John Mercier.
3. ALSTON HUNTER, b. Mar. 31, 1788 (*Sol. of War of 1812*), mar. Cynthia (Clay) Barrett (dau. of James and Margaret (Muse) Clay).
4. Nancy, b. 1790, mar. Wm. Fitzpatrick.
5. Nathaniel, d. y.
6. William (1795–1818).
7. Augustine, mar. (1) Phoebe Burke; (2) Mrs. Baldwin; (3) Miss Fisher (or Fish).
8. Elizabeth, mar. — Sledge.
9. Philip, d. La Grange, Ga., Dec. 2, 1871. Mar. Mildred Washington Sanford.
10. Ruth Hunter, b. Feb. 26, 1804.

JOHN GRESHAM, b. Va., 1759; d. Oglethorpe Co., Ga., 1818; received bounty land for his service, 3 years Va. Line; in Ga. service, 3 years. Mar. 1784, dau. of JOHN SCOTT, (*Rev. Sol.*, and his wife, Elizabeth Upshaw, and grand-dau. of THOMAS SCOTT, *Rev. Sol.* of Va. (1730-1801), and his wife, Elizabeth Wingfield).

Children (known):
1. Eliza Williamson (1801–1876), mar. 1824, Charles Barnett.
2. John, Jr. (1799–1827), mar. in Miss., Susan Crawford Barnett (1798–1874) (dau. of JOEL BARNETT (1762–1851), *Rev. Sol.* of Ga., and his wife, Mildred Meriwether).

JAMES GRIFFIN, b. Edgecomb Co., N. C., 1753; moved to Irwin Co., Ga., 1815; d. Irwin Co., Ga., Dec. 1836. Enlisted in Continental Army at Edgecomb Co., N. C., 1777, and as Corporal served in companies under Captains Blount and Euglas, Colonels Buncombe and Harney's N. C. Regiment. He was in the Battles of Brandywine, Monmouth, Guilford C. H., and was with GEN. GEORGE WASHINGTON at Valley Forge; discharged 1783. Mar. April 1, 1780, Sarah Ledge

of N. C. They moved to Irwin Co., Ga., 1815, from N. C. His wife d. near Hahira, Ga., after 183₆
Both are buried 8 miles from Ocilla, Ga., in Irwin Co.
They had 9 children (7 known):
1. Noah.
2. Joshua.
3. Thomas.
4. Rhoda.
5. Shadrack, mar. Jan. 27, 1814, NANCY BRADFORD, b. N. C., 1792. (dau. of THOMAS
BRADFORD, *Rev. Sol.*, b. Edgecomb Co., N. C.; buried by the side of James Griffin. He served a
Lieut. in N. C. Regiment with Corporal James Griffin. (Their graves were marked by the D. A. R.
6. Solomon.
7. Elizabeth.

JOHN GRIFFIN, b. Powhatan Co., Va., Sept. 3, 1740; d. Oglethorpe Co., Ga., Feb. 1819
Served as Sergeant in Capt. William Earle's 1st N. C. Regiment, then as Lieut. and Capt. From
N. C. he moved to Wilkes Co., Ga., where he received bounty land for his service. Mar. Powhatan Co., Va., Nov. 19, 1772, MARY ANN ANDREWS, b. 1754; d. before 1816. (His will is on
file at Lexington, Ga.)
Children:
1. Sarah, b. Sept. 1, 1773.
2. Ann Garnett, b. June 20, 1776, mar. — Barnett.
3. David, b. 1778 (twin).
4. Jesse Andrews, b. 1778 (twin).
5. Mary, b. Sept 11, 1781, mar. as (1) wife, WILLIAM FEARS (son of WILLIAM FEARS
Rev. Sol.; d. Jasper Co., Ga., and his wife, Ann Bulher).
6. William, b. Jan. 21, 1790, mar. Mary Booker Barnett.
7. Thomas, b. Sept. 24, 1787.
8. John, b. Jan. 21, 1790, mar. Sarah Caroline Barnett.
9. Wyatt Andrews.
10. George W., b. 1796.
11. Susanna, mar. — Hubbard.

JOHN GRIMES, b. Va.; d. Wilkes Co., Ga. Came to Ga. from Va.; received bounty land
for his service as a *Rev. Sol.* Mar. Elizabeth Wingfield (dau. of THOMAS WINGFIELD, *Rev.
Sol.*, and his wife, Elizabeth Terrell).
Children:
1. Thomas Winfield.
2. John, mar. 1792, Sarah Wharry.
3. STERLING, b. 1782; d. 1826; mar. 1810, MARIA MERVIN FONTAINE (1790–1822),
(dau. of AARON FONTAINE, *Rev. Sol.* of Va. and Ky.)
4. Lucy (mentioned in deed of gift, 1789).
The orphans of John Grimes drew land in Ga. 1803 Lottery.

JOHN GROOVER (spelled Gruber), b. Ga., 1738; a *Rev. Sol.* and was killed by the Tories
at his home on Cowpens Branch, Effingham Co., Ga., in 1780. The State at this time was overrun by the British. He mar. at Ebenezer, Jerusalem Church, June 4, 1765, MARY MAGDALEN
KALCHER, (dau. of RUPERT KALCHER, of Ebenezer, Ga., from London, Eng.)
Children (all baptized at Jerusalem Church):
1. John, b. 1766; d. Brooks Co., Ga.; mar. Hannah Lastinger.
2. Joshua, b. 1772.
3. Solomon, b. 1769, mar. Nov. 11, 1798, Elizabeth Wise.
4. William, b. 1780.

MOSES GUEST, b. Fauquier Co., Va., 1750; d. Franklin Co., Ga., 1837. Enlisted in Wilkes
Co., N. C.; removed to Pendleton, S. C.; served as Capt; received pension for his service as a *Rev.
Sol.* while a resident of Franklin Co., Ga. Mar. MARY BLAIR. Widow allowed pension.
Children:
1. Sanford.
2. Susanna.

3. Morgan.
4. William.
5. Moses, Jr.
6. John.
7. Hall.
8. Nathaniel.
9. Cobb.
10. Burton.
11. Giles.
12. Elizabeth.
13. Mary.
14. Celia, mar. Archibald Cogburn.
15. Cynthia.
16. Susan.
17. Annie.

RICHARD GUNN, SR., b. Brunswick Co., Va., June 6, 1761; d. Taliaferro Co., Ga., June 30, 1840. Served in the Va. Continental Line; received bounty land in Ga. for his service,in Oglethorpe Co. Mar. in Va. about 1784, ELIZABETH RADFORD, b. Va., May 16, 1761; d. Taliaferro Co., 1847.
Children:
1. Jane (called Jincy), b. July 31, 1785, mar. 1805, Jeremiah Holden.
2. Nelson (1787), mar. Jane Reynolds.
3. William (1789), mar. Pleasance Stephens.
4. John, d. y.
5. Richard, Jr. (1795); moved to Ala.
6. Radford, b. Va., 1797, mar. (1) Peggy Rhodes, of Oglethorpe Co.; (2) Ann J. S. Beck, of Warren Co.
7. Elizabeth, b. Ga., 1799, mar. Mr. Rhodes.
8. Larkin R. b. 1802, mar. Cynthia Darden; moved to Ala.
9. Jonathan b. 1809, mar. 1830, Elizabeth D. Wynne.

WILLIAM GUNN, b. Va.; d. Wilkes Co., Ga., after 1814. Served in the Augusta Co., Va. Militia; received bounty grant of land for his service in Wilkes Co., Ga. Mar. in Va. —.
Children:
1. Elizabeth, mar. 1807, Harrison Mallory.
2. John, mar. 1810, Catherine Hammack.
(Perhaps other children).

JAMES HABERSHAM, b. Ga., 1744; d. Savannah, Ga. Served as Lieut. Ga. Batt. under his brother, JOSEPH HABERSHAM. Made Major, served throughout the war. Was known as the "rebel financier." Mar. Sept. 20, 1769, ESTHER WYLLY.
Children:
1. Richard Wylly, mar. 1808, Sarah Elliott.
2. John, mar. 1812, ANN MIDDLETON BARNWELL (dau. of CAPT. JOHN BARNWELL, Rev. Sol. of S. C.).
3. Alexander.
4. Mary, mar. Benjamin Maxwell.
5. Esther, mar. Hon. Stephen Elliott.
6. Joseph Clay, mar. Ann W. Adams.

JOHN HABERSHAM, b. Ga., Dec. 23, 1754; d. Chatham Co., Ga., Nov. 19, 1799. Served as 1st Lieut., Ga. Batt., 1776 Brigade. Major under Gen. Lachlan McIntosh and Col. Samuel Elbert. Member Continental Congress. Mar. 1782, SARAH ANN CAMBER, of Bryan Co., Ga.
Children:
1. Ann, d. y.
2. James Camber, d. y.
3. Joseph Clay, mar. Ann Wylly Adams (1795).

4. John Harris, d. y.
5. John Bolton, d. y.
6. Mary Butler, mar. her cousin, Joseph Habersham.
7. Susan Dorothy.

JOSEPH HABERSHAM, b. Savannah, Ga., 1751; d. same place Nov., 1815. Served as Major, Lieut.-Col. of 1st Ga. Regiment, Ga. Line Continental troops throughout the War. *Member Provincial Congress.* Charter member Order of the Cincinnati. Mar. May 19, 1776, at "Brampton," ISABELLA RAE (sister of Elizabeth Rae who married GEN. SAMUEL ELBERT, *Rev. Sol.*).
Children:
1. James.
2. John.
3. Mary.
4. Isabella.
5. Joseph.
6. Robert, mar. (1) Mary O'Brien; (2) Elizabeth Neyle.
7. William, mar. Mary Elliott.
8. Eliza A.
9. Susan Ann.
NOTE: JAMES, JOHN, and JOSEPH HABERSHAM were sons of JAMES HABERSHAM, *Royalist* of Ga.

WILLIAM HALEY (OR HAILEY), b. Va., 1748; d. 1830; living on Cody's Creek, Elbert Co., Ga., 1792; drew land in Wilkes Co., Ga., for his service in Continental Army; also drew land 1806 and 1825 Lottery as a *Rev. Sol.* A *Sol. of the War of 1812.* Mar. 1771, MARY TURMAN (dau. of Martin and Ann Turman (or Tureman)).
Children mentioned in will made Oct. 2, 1830:
1. John, mar. Polly Underwood.
2. Thomas.
3. James.
4. William.
5. Reuben, mar. Sally Wood.
6. Mary, mar. Jesse Cash.
7. Ritta (or Polly), mar. James B. Adams.
8. Tabby (Tabitha), mar. Easton Forston.
9. Lucy, mar. Benajah Teasley (son of Isham Teasley).
10. Sally, mar. Henry Mann.
11. Betsey, mar. John A. Teasley.
He also mentions in will the children of THOMAS LANE, dec. 1829, a *Rev. Sol.* who drew land in Ga., 1784, as a *Refugee Sol.*, viz: JOHN FORSTON; ELIZA (LANE) FORSTON, wife of William Forston (son of THOMAS FORSTON).

LEWIS HALL, b. N. C., 1746; d. Ga., 1822. Served as Lieut. in Ga. and N. C. troops. Captured by British, wounded in prison, Charleston, S. C. Released and served again till close of War. Mar. (1) —; (2) 1790, NANCY COLLEY (1767–1858).
Children:
1. Instance, 1797.
2. James, of Montgomery Co., Ga.
3. Seaborn, of Tattnall Co., Ga., b. 1808; mar. (1) Ann Gannay; (2) Chrissie Quinn.
4. W. L.
5. Flora, mar. James Kemp.
6. Piety (or Polly), mar. 1822, Henry Cook.
7. Priscilla, mar. Benj. H. Smith.
8. Rebecca, mar. D. D. David.
9. Elpheus.
10. Mary. mar. George Wilcox.
11. John.

GEORGE HAMILTON, b. Md., 1722; d. Ga., 1798. Served as Captain Md. Militia; received bounty grant of land for his service in Washington Co., Ga. Mar. ELIZABETH SCHUYLER.

Their son:
GEORGE HAMILTON, JR., b. Md., 1754; d. Wilkes Co., Ga., 1826. Served as private in his father's Co.; received land for his service in Wilkes Co., Ga. Mar. AGNES COOPER (dau. of THOMAS COOPER, *Rev. Sol.*, served in Va. Militia, and wife, Sarah Anthony; they removed to Ga. 1794; he d. Greene Co., Ga., 1797).

Their dau.:
Sarah, mar. James Render.
(Martha Wellborn Render (1811–1877), mar. Joseph Anthony (1805–1875)).

JAMES HAMILTON, b. Ireland; d. Ga., July 31, 1817. Served as Ensign, 1777; Lieut., 1778, 6th Va. Regiment; prisoner at Charleston, S. C. Mar. ANN FOX NAPIER; d. 1807 (dau. of THOMAS NAPIER, *Rev. Sol.*, b. 1740; d. Ga., 1802).

Children (known):
1. Thomas Napier, mar. Sarah Sherwood Bugg (dau. of Sherwood Bugg, Jr., and wife, Sarah Ann Jones; g.-dau. of SHERWOOD BUGG, *Rev. Sol.* of Ga. and S. C., and his wife, ELIZABETH HOPSON, a *Patriot*).
2. Ann Elizabeth, mar. Samuel Goode.
3. James Fox, mar. (1) Frances Harris; (2) Emily Bowden.
4. Patsey, mar. — Porter.
5. Dorothea, mar. Richard Randolph.

JOHN HAMILTON, b. Amelia Co., Va., 1747; d. Hancock Co., Ga., 1829. Served in Va. troops. Mar. Tabitha Thweatt, b. Va., 1747; d. Ga., 1805 (dau. of James Thweatt and wife, Sarah Studevant, of Va.).

Children:
1. Marmaduke (1770–1832), mar. Elizabeth Scott.
2. James Thweatt.
3. John.
4. Thomas P., mar. Elizabeth Freeman.
5. George, mar. Elvira Eavens.
6. Sarah Thweatt (1775–1850), mar. ROBERT RAINES, a *Rev. Sol.*, Ga. troops, of Hancock Co., Ga.; d. 1816.
7. Frances (1781–1827), mar. Brig.-Gen. David Blackshear, Laurens Co., Ga.
8. Martha.
9. Mary, b. Hancock Co., Ga., 1778; d. Thomas Co., Ga. Mar. George White Hayes.
10. William, mar. (1) Mary —; (2) Elizabeth Bryan.
11. Everard. *Sol. of 1812.* Mar. Mary H. Floyd (dau. of Gen. John Floyd, *Sol. of 1812*).

STEWART HAMILTON, b. N. C.; d. Montgomery (now Telfair Co.), Ga., 1831. Served as private, Capt. Bailey's 10th N. C. Regiment. Mar. CLARISSA STRINGER, d. 1840.

Children:
1. Benjamin.
2. Solomon.
3. Rebecca, mar. — Stoney.
4. Strother.
5. Joshiah.
6. William, mar. Elizabeth Brown.
7. Sarah, mar. Benj. Burch.
8. Rosannah, mar. — Gillis.

JOHN HAMMOCK. b. Va., 1758; d. Lincoln Co., Ga., 1831. Served as private, Va. troops; received bounty land for his service, 1784, Washington Co., Ga. Mar. (1) 1778, PHOEBE PASCHALL, b. 1760; d. about 1808; (2) SARAH THORNTON, widow. Lived in Wilkes (now Lincoln), Co., Ga.

Children by (1) wife:
1. Samuel, mar. Elizabeth —.

2. Paschall, mar. (1) Zilpha Green; (2) Miss Hughes.
3. William.
4. John, mar. Ann —.
5. Elijah, mar. Polly Chapman.
6. Charles.
7. Thomas.
8. Feraby, mar. — Mumford.
9. Margaret, mar. — Green.
10. Elizabeth, mar. — Roling.
11. Reliance.
12. David.

ROBERT HAMMOCK, b. Va.; d. Wilkes Co., Ga., July 1779. (Will made July 9, 1779). Was a *Rev. Sol.* and a *Patriot*; wife, MILLENOR —.
Children:
1. Lewis.
2. Robert.
3. McFarlane.
4. John.
5. Joshua.
6. William.
7. Edward.
8. Anna, mar. — Ray.
9. Betsey, mar. — Moncreif.
10. Lucy.
11. Polly.
12. Lurina.
13. Katie.
14. Millie, mar. — Bentley.

ABNER HAMMOND, b. 1762; d. Milledgeville, Ga., 1829 (son of CHARLES HAMMOND, *Rev. Sol.* of S. C., and his wife, ELIZABETH STEELE; they had four sons who were *Rev. Sols.*, viz: ABNER, CHARLES, killed as *Rev. Sol.*, LEROY, SAMUEL, and one dau., Elizabeth). AB-NER HAMMOND raised a Volunteer Co., joined his brother, Samuel, at the Siege of Augusta, Ga. Was Lieut., S. C. troops, later Capt. Mar. (1) ANN JONES; (2) 1803, SARAH DUDLEY.
Children by (2) wife:
1. John, mar. (1) —; (2) Caroline Fort.
2. Anne, mar. Peter Stubbs.
3. Eliza, mar. Baradell Palmer Stubbs.

LE ROY HAMMOND, b. Va.; d. Beech Island, S. C. Lived at Augusta, Ga. Served under Gen. Andrew Williamson; appointed 1778. Mar. Miss Tyler.
One son:
LEROY HAMMOND, JR., a *Rev. Sol.* at the age of 16 years.

SAMUEL HAMMOND, b. Richmond Co., Va., Sept. 21, 1757; d. at his home on Horse Shoe Creek, Beech Island, S. C., Sept. 11, 1842. Monument erected to his memory in Augusta, Ga. He served as aide to Gen. Hand; fought at King's Mt. and Siege of Augusta. Was *Military Governor of Mo.*, 1805, later *Governor of Mo.* Mar. (1) REBECCA, widow of John Rae, d. 1788; (2) May 5, 1802, ELIZA AMELIA O'KEEFE. 8 children.
One dau.:
Mary Ann, mar. James R. Washington. She was charter member N. S. D. A. R. of Mary Hammond Washington Chapter D. A. R., Macon, Ga., which bears her name.

HENRY HAND, b. Va., 1753; d. Talbot Co., Ga., 1835; received bounty land in Ga. for his service as private. Mar. ELIZABETH HARRISON.
Children (known):
1. William.
2. John.

3. Henry Harrison.
4. James.
5. Rev. Thomas.
6. Joel.
7. Rev. Joseph.

JOHN HARVIE, b. Scotland, 1706; came to Va., 1730; d. Va., 1767. Mar. MARTHA GAINES, b. Va., 1719; d. Oglethorpe Co., Ga., 1801. In 1780, during the Rev., MARTHA HARVIE, widow, a *Patriot* during the Rev. War, moved with most of her children to Ga. and settled on the Broad river, Wilkes Co. (JOHN HARVIE, *Rev. Sol.*, remained in Va., mar. Margaret Jones).

Other children were (all came to Ga.):

1. Richard.
2. Daniel, mar. Sally Taliaferro (sister of COL. BENJAMIN TALIAFERRO, *Rev. Sol.*).
3. Richard.
4. WILLIAM, *Rev. Sol.* of Va., mar. Judith Cosby.
5. Martha, mar. John Moore.
6. Mary, mar. DAVID MERIWETHER, *Rev. Sol.*
7. Martha, mar. John Davenport.
8. Genette, mar. Reuben Jordan
9. Elizabeth, mar. James Marks

JAMES HANES (HAINES), (son of David and Elizabeth (Callaway) Hanes, of Del.), b. New Castle Co., Del., Oct. 12, 1762; d. (now Clayton Co.), Ga., 1862. Served as private. Enlisted May 18, 1781, as *Rev. Sol.* under recruiting officer Thomas Keane in New Castle Co. for the Del. Regiment as per Muster Roll in Dept. of Public Archives Del. Mar. 1790 New Castle Co., Del., JEMINA CALLAWAY.

Children:

1. Ephriam, b. Sept. 13, 1791, killed at Savannah, Ga. *Sol. of War of 1812.*
2. Joshua, b. Aug. 1796, mar. Miss Allen. 11 children.
3. Elijah, b. Aug. 1798, mar. Celia Rountree.
4. James, b. Jan. 5, 1808, mar. Malinda Lasseter.
5. David, b. Aug. 18, 1803; d. Oct. 10, 1866, Mar. (1) 11-11-1823, Elizabeth Lasseter; (2) Martha Barnes. He had 8 children.

WILLIAM HARDWICK, b. S. C., June 6, 1727; d. Greene Co., Ga., Feb. 24, 1803. Buried near Davisboro, Ga. Served as private 3rd S. C. troops, and Sergeant 6th S. C. troops. Mar. Cynthia Parker, April 22,—.

Children (not in order of birth):

1. Martha, mar. —Jones.
2. Nonaly, mar. —Dawkins.
3. Nancy, mar. —Daniell.
4. Molly, b. 1763, mar. Renée Fitzpatrick.
5. WILLIAM, b. 1760, mar. Nancy Shipp, *Rev. Sol.*
6. Garland, b. May 22, 1768.
7. James, b. Dec. 16, 1750.
8. George, b. 1766.
9. Peggy, b. June 7, 1773.

WILLIAM HARDWICK, JR., b. 1760; d. Ga., Mar. 1, 1826. Received bounty land in Ga. for his service as *Rev. Sol.* Mar. April 22, 1780, Nancy Shipp.

Children:

1. Betsey, mar. 1808 Allen Roberts.
2. William.
3. Franky.
4. Richard.
5. Eliza, mar. —Hart.
6. Nancy, mar. James Darrow.
7. Jefferson.

8. Patsey, mar. 1809 David Lewis.
9. Sophie Garland, mar. Stephen Jones.
10. Polly, mar. Adam Jones.

HENRY HARDIN, b. Johnston Co., N. C., May 8, 1750; d. Walton Co., Ga., 1843. Served in the N. C. Continental Line under Capt. Smith, Col. Brevard, and Col. Hunter. Mar. (1) Sarah Cook; (2) Matilda Jones.

Children:
1. Effie, mar. Richard Fletcher.
2. Judith, mar. Thomas Stephens.
3. Elizabeth, mar. (1) — Eads; (2) — Taylor.
4. Mark, mar. Mary Hadley.
5. Benjamin Cook.
6. Edward J., mar. Jane Louise Barrett.
7. Clarissa Warren, mar. Few Gordon.
8. Harriet Hargrove, mar. Wiley Thornton.

JOHN HARDY, b. Tyron Co., N. C., 1756; d. Warren Co., Ga., 1818. Member of a Company of *Patriot Troops* under Col. Elijah Clarke; received bounty land in Ga. for his service. Mar. 1778, Sarah Sutton (1758-1812).

Children (known):
1. John, Jr.
2. Jesse.
3. Penelope.
4. Sutton.

SAMUEL HARRIS, b. Va., —; d. Greene Co., Ga., 1789. Served as a *Rev. Patriot.* Mar MARTHA —.

Children:
1. Robert.
2. James.
3. Thomas.
4. Samuel, Jr.
5. John.
6. William.
7. Laird.
8. Mathew.
9. Dau., mar. Samuel Ross.
10. Jane, mar. THOMAS McCAULE (McCALL), *Rev. Sol.*
11. Dau., mar. William Wylie.

WALTON HARRIS, b. Va., 1739; d. Greene Co., Ga., 1809. Served as private, Ga. Line, under Gen. Elijah Clarke at the Battle of Kettle Creek. Was made prisoner at Augusta, Ga. Mar. REBECCA LANIER (dau. of Sampson Lanier, of Va.).

Children:
1. BUCKNER HARRIS, b. Va., 1761; d. Ga., 1821. *Rev. Sol.*; served as private under Gen. Elijah Clarke, Ga. Line. Lived in Wilkes Co., Ga. Mar. Nancy Matilda Early.
2. SAMPSON HARRIS, b. 1763. Served as a *Rev. Sol.* Mar. Susan Terrell Willis.
3. Joel.
4. Edwin.
5. Nathan.
6. Simeon.
7. Augustine (1767-1836), mar. Ann Byne.
8. Walton, mar. Virginia Beverly Billups. 11 children.
9. Elizabeth.
10. Littleton.
11. Jeptha V. (1778-1856), mar. Sarah Hunt.

BENJAMIN HART (son of Thomas Hart and his wife, Susanna Rice), b. Hanover Co., Va., 1730; d. Brunswick, Glynn Co., Ga., 1802. He moved with his parents to Orange Co., N. C.; then to Edgefield Co., S. C., and in 1771 moved with his family to the "Ceded Lands" of Ga., formerly Wilkes Co., now Elbert Co., Ga. He is buried in the old cemetery, Wright's Square, Glynn Co. He served as Lieut., Ga. Militia, 1777 to Nov. 9, 1782; was also a musician (cornet) and served as regimental quartermaster of the 3rd Continental Dragoons, July 26, 1778. Mar. ANN (called Nancy) MORGAN (dau. of Thomas and Rebecca (Alexander) Morgan, of Bucks Co., Penn.). She d. Henderson Co., Ky., 1840. (Her grave has been marked by the Samuel Hopkins Chapter, D. A. R. of Henderson, Ky.; grave in Hart Cemetery, 12 miles from Henderson).

NANCY HART moved to Kentucky after her husband's death and lies buried in the Blue Grass State. Among the heroines of the Rev., an exalted place must be assigned to NANCY HART, of Ga. The story of her bold capture of a band of Tories single-handed, electrified the whole theatre of War, during the troublous times of Toryisms in upper Ga. In the dangerous, infested districts in Ga., in the darkest hour of the struggle for Independence, she not only outwitted and out-braved the whole band of Tories, but added another name to the heroic Roster of the Rev.

On another occasion she built a raft of logs, and crossed to the Carolina side of the Savannah river to obtain information for the Ga. troops. While in the fort with other women and children, while the men were away in the field, she ably defended it many times from the Tories and Indians who attacked it. Georgia is very proud of her "Nancy Hart" and her name is commemorated in the State; she is known as the "Heroine of the Battle of Kettle Creek." Hart Co., the only Co. in Ga. named for a woman, is named for her; also the "Nancy Hart Highway" and the "Nancy Hart Chapter," D. A. R., of Milledgeville, Ga., bears her name. A splendid picture of "Nancy Hart Capturing the Tories" hangs on the wall of the Genealogical room at the State Department of Archives, Atlanta, Ga., and a memorial built by the Federal Government at Hartwell, Ga., was unveiled and dedicated by a descendant of the heroine.

Children of Benjamin and Nancy (Morgan) Hart:

1. THOMAS MORGAN (called Morgan), name appears on list of Georgians who fought at the Battle of Kettle Creek, at War Hill, Wilkes Co. (adjoins Elbert), together with the names of BENJAMIN HART, and NANCY HART.

2. JOHN, b. 1762; d. Henderson Co., Ky., 1821. He was a *Rev. Sol.* of Ga., and also a *Sol. of 1812.* Lived in Oglethorpe Co., Ga., 1788, Sparks Fort, near Athens, Ga., 1791. Mar. 1787, Patience Lane (dau. of JESSE LANE, *Rev. Sol.* of Ga., and his wife, Winifred Aycock).

3. Sally, mar. — Thompson.

4. Keziah.

5. Benjamin, Jr., mar. Mary —.

6. Mark.

7. Lemuel.

8. SUKEY (Susanna). The "Sukey Hart Chapter," C. A. R., of Milledgeville, Ga., bears her name.

JOHN HART, b. S. C.; d. Ga. Served as an officer in the 2nd S. C. Regiment. Was taken prisoner at Charleston, May 12, 1780. Mar. MARY SCREVEN (dau. of GEN. JAMES SCREVEN, *Rev. Sol.* of Ga.; killed at the engagement at Midway Church, Nov. 24, 1778).

Their dau.:

Elizabeth Hart, mar. CAPT. JOSEPH JONES, of Liberty Co., Ga. (son of MAJOR JOHN JONES, a *Rev. Sol.*, who served on the staff of GEN. McINTOSH and was killed at the Siege of Savannah, Ga.).

SAMUEL HART, b. Caswell Co., N. C., 1755; d. Hancock Co., Ga., 1808. Served as a *Rev. Sol.* of 10th N. C. Regiment. Private 10th N. C. Regiment, Capt. Carter; Lieut. 9th N. C. Regiment, 1776; received bounty grant of land in Ga. for his service. Inventory of his estate in Hancock Co., Ga., made July 8, 1808. Mar. Susannah Boring (dau. of Joseph and Susannah Boring, of Caswell Co., N. C. Mrs. Susannah Boring, mar. (2) John Browning, *Rev. Sol.* of N. C. and Ga.). She d. Taliaferro Co., Ga., 1837.

Children:

1. William, mar. Nancy Bell.

2. Samuel, Jr., mar. Martha Veazey.

3. Eli.

4. James, mar. Mary Bell; moved to Ill.

5. Elizabeth, mar. Nathan Chapman.
6. Sarah, mar. Thomas Chapman.
7. Susannah, mar. Benjamin Chapman.
8. Martha, mar. James Veazey.
9. Mary.
10. John.

WILLIAM HARTSFIELD, b. 1748; d. Oglethorpe Co., Ga., 1830. Served as private, N. C. Line; received bounty land in Ga. for this service. Mar. 1771, Anna —.
Children:
1. Henry.
2. Mary.
3. John.
4. Becky.
5. Jacob.
6. Tempe.
7. Sally.
8. Betsey.
9. James.
10. Haskey.
11. Andrew.
12. William, Jr.

JOHN HATCHER, b. Henrico Parish, Va., 1750; mar. in Va., about 1772, Mary Brady, of Va. They came to Ga. He served as a *Rev. Sol.* in Col. William Candler's Regiment; received bounty land, 287½ acres, in Washington Co., Ga., 1785. Lived in Columbia Co., Ga., then Warren Co., Ga. Served as Major in Ga. Militia, 1800. (This is *1812 War Record*). Moved to Wilkinson Co., Ga., 1810, where he d. and is buried in old family cemetery on plantation in Passmore District, near Oconee river.
Children:
1. Jane Elizabeth, mar. — Thorpe.
2. Willie E., mar. — Mitchell.
3. Susan.
4. John.
5. Robert.
6. William Green, mar. Elizabeth Webb.
(Perhaps other children).

NOTE: During the years following the *Rev. War.*, the Indian troubles, together with their British sympathizers, which were drenching the Oconee Frontier of Ga. in blood, made it necessary for every able-bodied man to arm and equip himself and be ready to perform military service.

BENJAMIN HAWKINS (son of Col. Philemon and Delia Hawkins), b. Butte (now Warren)' Co., N. C., 1754; d. at his home, "Creek Agency," on the Flint river, Crawford Co., Ga., June 8, 1816. His four brothers, JOHN, PHILEMON, BENJAMIN and JOSEPH HAWKINS, were also *Rev. Sols.* BENJAMIN HAWKINS was a member of the Senior Class at Princeton when selected by Gen. George Washington as French interpreter on his official staff; was at the Battle of Monmouth, afterwards a *Sol. of 1812.* Member *Continental Congress,* 1782. He was buried on a bluff overlooking Flint river, in Crawford Co., and his grave was marked by the Ga. D. A. R. Fort Hawkins, on the Ocmulgee river, Macon Ga., named in his honor, and the Benjamin Hawkins Chapter, D. A. R., Cuthbert, Ga., bears his name.

MOSES HAYNES, b. Va.; d. Wilkes (now Hart) Co., Ga., 1829. Served in Va. Continental Line; received bounty land in Wilkes Co., Ga., for his service. Mar. SARAH —.
Children:
1. Stephen.
2. William.
3. Moses, Jr.
4. Thomas.
5. Nancy.

6. Elizabeth.
7. Polly.
8. Sarah.
9. Jane.

PARMENAS HAYNES (son of Henry Haynes (1701-1782) and wife, Mary; *Rev. Sol.* of Va.), b. Bedford Co., Va., July 1, 1742; d. Oglethorpe Co., Ga., Mar. 1, 1813. Served as Captain, Va. Continental Line. Mar. (1) Dec. 15, 1767, ELIZABETH BABER; (2) Dec. 2, 1781, DELIA GREER (dau. of AQUILLA GREER, b. Surry Co., Va., 1710, a *Patriot* who signed the Oath of Allegiance in Henry Co., Va., 1777, and with his wife, Elizabeth, moved to Greene Co., Ga., where he d.).

Children by (1) wife:
   1. Nancy, b. Dec. 10, 1768, mar. (1) James Shackelford; (2) Jesse Eley.
   2. Robert, b. 1770, mar. 1794, Lucy Phelps.
   3. Richard, b. 1773, mar. 1800, Abi Ragan (dau. of JONATHAN RAGAN, *Rev. Sol.* of Ga., and wife, Ann).

Children by (2) wife:
   1. Parmenas, Jr. (1783-1849), mar. 1807, Jane Phelps.
   2. Sally, b. 1785, mar. Woody Jackson.
   3. Delia, b. 1788, mar. 1808, William Greer, of Greene Co., Ga.
   4. Polly, mar. John Thorington, of Oglethorpe Co., Ga.
   5. Jasper, mar. Lucy Slaton.
   6. Henry.

JAMES HEAD, b. Orange Co., Va.; d. Elbert Co., Ga. (Will made Oct. 23, 1795, pro. Jan. 7, 1796.) Lived on Kettle Creek, Wilkes Co. Served as *Rev. Sol.* of Va.; received bounty land in Ga., 1793. Mar. ELIZABETH JANET POWELL (dau. of SIMON POWELL, *Rev. Sol.*, Sergeant in Co. of Rangers under Capt. Hogg., Orange Co., Va.).

Children:
   1. Lucy, mar. James Allen (son of DAVID ALLEN, b. Va., 1755; d. Morgan Co., Ga., after 1827, and his wife, Eliza Caroline —. He was a *Rev. Sol.*; drew land in Cherokee Land Lottery, Ga., 1827).
   2. Elizabeth, mar. Reuben White.
   3. Martha, mar. John Lewis.
   4. James, mar. Elizabeth Seals.
   5. Sarah, mar. Benjamin Forston.
   6. Benjamin.
   7. Simon.

BARNARD HEARD, b. 1739; d. Wilkes Co., Ga., 1798. Served as Major, Ga. troops; made prisoner by the British, escaped, and was at the Siege of Augusta.

JESSE HEARD, b. Augusta Co., Va., 1749; d. Wilkes Co., Ga., 1803. Served as private, Ga. troops, under Gen. Elijah Clarke; received bounty grant of land for his service in 1784. Mar. (1) JUDITH WILKINSON; (2) ELIZABETH —.

Children by (1) wife:
   1. Stephen.
   2. Lucy Wilkinson (1779-1843), mar. 1806, Wm. Weare Harman.
   3. Sarah, mar. Stephen Martin. Moved to Mo.
   4. Judith, mar. her first cousin, William Smith. Moved to S. C.
   5. Mary, mar. — Grier. Moved to Ala.
   6. Jesse Falkner (1785), mar. Caroline Wilkinson (dau. of BENJAMIN WILKINSON, of Wilkes Co., Ga., *Rev. Sol.* who fought at Battle of Kettle Creek).
   7. Elizabeth, mar. John Stanton. Moved to Mo.
   8. Susan, mar. (1) Thomas Beatty; (2) — Robbins.

THOMAS HEARD, b. Va., 1742; d. Greene Co., Ga., 1808. Served as Capt., Va. State troops. Mar. in Va., Aug. 2, 1767, Elizabeth Fitzpatrick (1750-1790) (dau. of JOSEPH FITZPATRICK,

Rev. Sol. of Va., b. Va., 1720; d. Greene Co., Ga., and his wife, Martha Napier, d. age 106 years); mar., (2) Mary Veazy (dau. of JAMES VEAZY, *Rev. Sol.*).
Children by (1) wife:
   1. Catherine, mar. (1) Isaac Stokes; (2) Pressly Watts.
   2. Abram (1769-1822), mar. Nancy Coffee.
   3. Joseph, mar. (1) — Stuart; (2) — Clark; (3) Mary Allen.
   4. Mary, mar. John Cook.
   5. Thomas, mar. Polly Whatley.
   6. Elizabeth, mar. (1) — Peeples; (2) Michael Whatley.
   7. Sally, mar. Wilson Whatley.
   8. Woodson, mar. Mary Peeples.
   9. George, mar. Martha Coffee.
   10. Falkner, mar. Mary Robinson (dau. of RANDALL ROBINSON, *Rev. Sol.*, and his (1) wife, Lydia Walker).

STEPHEN HEARD (son of JOHN HEARD, *Rev. Sol.*, and his wife, Bridget Bouton, of Va. and Ga.), b. Va., 1740; d. Elbert Co., Ga., Nov. 13, 1815. Commanded a Co., member of Ex. Council and also President. Was *Governor of Georgia* and for a time the seat of the Government of Ga. was at his home, "Heard's Fort," Wilkes Co., while Savannah was in the hands of the British. He was also taken prisoner by the British. Mar. (1) Jane Garmany. She was driven from her home by the Tories and d. from exposure; (2) Aug. 25, 1785, Elizabeth Darden (called Betsey) (1766-1848).
Children:
   1. Barnard, b. 1787, mar. Mary Hutson.
   2. Martha Burch, b. 1788, mar. Bartlett Tucker.
   3. George Washington, b. 1791.
   4. John Adams, b. 1793; d. Mar. 17, 1829.
   5. Bridget Carroll, b. 1795, mar. (1) Simeon Henderson; moved to Miss.; (2) — Thompson.
   6. Jane Lanier, b. 1797, mar. Singleton W. Allen.
   7. Pamela Darden (1799-1816).
   8. Thomas J. (1801-1876), mar. Nancy Middleton.
   9. Sarah Hammond, b. 1804, mar. Dr. Jarrett.

NOTE: For Heard, Fitzpatrick, and Evans families, see *"Southern Lineages,"* by Adelaide Evans Wynn, of Atlanta, Ga.

ELISHA HEARN, b. Somerset Co., Md., 1754; d. Putnam Co., Ga., 1812. Served as a private and a sailor in Va.; in 1831 widow received bounty land for his service in Va. Mar. FEREBY JOHNSON.
Children:
   1. Elisha, Jr.
   2. Francis, mar. Elizabeth White.
   3. Joshua.
   4. Huldah.
   5. Polly.
   6. Benjamin.
   7. Thomas.

JONATHAN HEARN (son of Samuel and Elizabeth Hearn), b. April 11, 1760; d. Putnam Co., Ga. Mar. 1783, Rhoda Parker (dau. of Jacob and Mary Parker), b. Dec. 17, 1763; d. —. They lived in Sussex Co., Del., and he served from this Co. as a *Rev. Sol.* Came to Hancock Co., Ga., Mar., 1792.
Children:
   1. Asa, b. Dec. 17, 1783.
   2. Zabed, b. Nov. 22, 1785.
   3. Seth, b. Jan. 2, 1788.
   4. LOT, b. Sussex Co., Del., Mar. 18, 1790. Came with his parents to Hancock Co., Ga.; moved to Jackson Co., 1800; to Putnam Co., 1809. Mar. Frances McClendon, Jan. 13, 1813. *Sol. of 1812.*
   5. Polly, b. April 20, 1792.

6. Samuel, b. June 31, 1795.
7. Jacob, b. July 29, 1797.
8. Elizabeth, b. Jan. 29, 1799.
9. Judith, b. July 2, 1801.
10. William, b. Dec. 17, 1803; d. 1873; mar. 1821, Anna Pennington.
(Perhaps other children).

WILLIAM HENDLEY, b. Scotland, came to Va. Served in the Va. Continental Line. Settled in Bulloch Co., Ga., then Telfair Co. Mar, MILLIE ANN HORTON.
Children:
1. William, mar. — Harrell.
2. Sophia, mar. W. L. Harrell.
3. Nancy, mar. — Roundtree.
4. Jeanet, mar. Daniel McCranie (son of JOHN H. McCRANIE, *Rev. Sol.*, and his wife, Katherine Lashley).
5. Horton, mar. Polly Ann Daniel.
6. Dau., mar. — Fletcher.
7. Dau., mar. — Posey.
8. Dau., mar. — Jarnigan.

JAMES HEUSTON, *Rev. Sol.* Buried 6 miles from Madison, Morgan Co., Ga. His wife, MARY —, buried there also. She d. Oct. 11, 1828, age 66 years. They were living in Greene Co., Ga., 1806. Drew land in 1825 Lottery of Ga., as a *Rev. Sol.* in Morgan Co., Ga. Had 2 draws as *Rev. Sol.*, in 1806 Ga. Lottery.
Children:
1. Nancy, mar. — Hargrove.
2. Polly, mar. 1807, Isaac Culberson (son of DAVID CULBERSON, *Rev. Sol.* of Caswell Co., N. C., and Greene Co., Ga.).
3. Peggy, mar. — Avery.
4. Prudence, mar. — Johnson.
5. Young.
6. James Ross.
7. John.

JOHN HEUSTON (HUSTON), bro. of JAMES HEUSTON, was a *Rev. Sol.* of Ga.

ABRAHAM HILL, b. Chowan Co., N. C., 1732; d. Wilkes Co., Ga., Feb. 4, 1792. Served as private, under Lieut. John Cropper, in Va. troops. Moved from Wake Co., N. C., 1785, to Wilkes (now Oglethorpe) Co., Ga. Mar. Christian Walton (dau. of THOMAS WALTON, member N. C. House of Assembly).
Children:
1. John —.
2. ABRAHAM, JR. (1759-1818), mar. Elizabeth McGehee. *Rev. Sol.*
3. Judith, mar. Josiah Jordan.
4. Clara (1763-1798), mar. Henry Augustus Pope.
5. Sarah (1765-1816), mar. Benjamin Blake.
6. Henry (1767-1829), mar. Betty Andrew (dau. of BENJAMIN ANDREW, a *Rev. Patriot* and Member of Council of Safety, Ga.).
7. Theophilus (1769-1829), mar. Polly Jordan.
8. Noah (1771-1805), mar. Ann Pope (1780-1805) (dau. of BURWELL POPE, a *Rev. Sol.*, b. Va., 1752; d. Wilkes Co., Ga., and his wife, Priscilla Wooten).
9. Miles (1774-1844), mar. Tabitha Pope (dau. of BURWELL and PRISCILLA (WOOTEN) POPE).
10. Wylie Pope (1775-1844), mar. Martha Pope (dau. of BURWELL and PRISCILLA (WOOTEN) POPE).
11. Mary (1777-1849).
12. Thomas, mar. Sally McGehee. She mar. (2) Dyonosius Oliver.

ABRAHAM HILL, JR. (1759-1818) (son of ABRAHAM HILL and Christian Walton), was murdered by the Tories in Oglethorpe Co., Ga. He was a *Rev. Sol.*; served as private in Capt. John

Reid's Troops of Light Dragoons, Lieut.-Col. Wade Hampton's N. C. Regiment. Mar. May 5, 1791, Elizabeth McGehee (1773-1816) (dau. of MICAJAH McGEHEE, Rev. Sol. (1745-1816), and his wife, Ann Baytop Scott (1753-1876)).

Children:
1. Abram Scott (1807-1866), mar. Susan F. Halsey.
2. Elizabeth (1810-1844), mar. Blanton Meade Hill.
(Perhaps other children).

HENRY HILL, b. N. C., 1730; d. Wilkes Co., 1804. Served as Rev. Sol. Mar. SARAH COTTEN, d. 1814.

Children:
1. John.
2. Abram (1778-1852), mar. in Wilkes Co., Ga., 1806, Clarissa Callaway (1790-1855) (dau. of Joseph Callaway, g.-dau. of JOB CALLAWAY and JONATHAN RAGAN, both Rev. Sols.).
3. Theophilus.
4. Henry, Jr.
5. Nancy (1770-1839), mar. COL. WILLIAM JOHNSON (1755-1821), Wilkes Co., Ga. (a Rev. Sol. who was granted bounty land for his service in Washington Co., Ga.). They had 10 children: 1. Elizabeth, mar. Drury Cunningham; 2. Mary, mar. Henry Spratlin; 3. Susan, mar. Judge James Dabney Willis; 4. John Pope, mar. Prudence Irvine; 5. Nancy, mar. her cousin, Col. Lodwick M. Hill (as 1st wife); 6. William; 7. Stephen; 8. Martha Pope, mar., as (2) wife, Burwell Pope Hill; 9. Catherine; 10. Sarah.

(See "The Hills of Wilkes Co., Ga.," by Lodowick J. Hill).

ISAAC HILL, b. 1748; d. Clarke Co., Ga. (will made Nov. 9, 1829; pro. Oct. 7, 1833). Served as Rev. Sol. Mar. NANCY CRAIN (a Patriot and wounded in War).

Children:
1. Middleton.
2. Isaac, Jr.
3. Elender, mar. — Hopkins.
4. Charlotte, mar. — Burney.
5. Olivia, mar. — Harvey.
6. Elizabeth, mar. Joseph Lane, Jr.
7. Sally, mar. John Love.
8. Catherine, as (2) wife, mar. John Love.
9. Nancy, mar. — Seavers.
10. Eudocia, mar. — Anderson.
11. Roderick.

WILLIAM HILL (1760-1850), served as private, Ga. Line. Mar. 1782, PHOEBE FLOURNOY (1764-1819).

Children:
1. John.
2. Robert.
3. Frances, mar. John Ashurst.
4. Phoebe, mar. Frederick Crow.
5. Winifred, mar. Eli Lester.
6. Virginia, mar. Harmon Hubert.
7. William, Jr.

CHRISTOPHER HILLARY, b. 1735; d. St. Simons, Ga., Feb. 18, 1796. Served in Ga. Line under Gen. Elijah Clarke. Captured by the British 1781, exchanged 1782; received bounty land in Glynn Co., Ga., 1787. Mar. Mar. 20, 1787, Agnes Hightower. She mar. (2), as (2) wife, COL. JOHN McINTOSH, Rev. Sol. of Ga.

One dau.:
Marie Hillary, b. Ga., 1788, mar. Major William Jackson McIntosh (son of Col. John McIntosh, and his (1) wife, Sarah Swinton).

JAMES HIGHSMITH, b. —; d. Elbert Co., Ga., Mar. 10, 1824. He was a *Rev. Sol.* Mar. Milly —. She drew land as widow of *Rev. Sol.* in 1827 Land Lottery of Ga.

Children:
1. Susanna, mar. Benjamin Bobo.
2. Lucretia, mar. —Skelton.
3. John.
4. Sarah, mar. —Bobo.
5. Winney, mar. —Griffin.
6. Nancy, mar. 1823, Daniel M. Johnston.
7. Thomas, mar. Elizabeth Parks.

DAVID HILLHOUSE, b. Conn. —; d. Wilkes Co., Ga. Moved before 1787 from New Haven, Conn. to Washington, Wilkes Co., Ga. He owned and edited the "Monitor," of Washington, Ga. (This was the first town in the United States to be named in honor of President George Washington and the "Monitor" was the first newspaper to be published in Ga.) He mar. SARAH PORTER (dau. of ELISHA PORTER, b. Hartford, Conn. (or Hadley, Mass.), 1742; d. Springfield, Mass., 1796. He was a *Rev. Sol.*; commanded a Regiment at the Lexington alarm; was at the Battle of Saratoga, and also escorted Gen. Burgoyne to Boston. He mar. Sarah Jewett).

Children (2 known):
1. Dau., mar. Felix Gilbert, of Wilkes.
2. Mary Hillhouse, mar. Andrew Shepherd as (2) wife.

JOSHUA HODGES, SR., b. N. C., Oct. 13, 1736; d. Bulloch Co., Ga., Mar. 13, 1809. Served in the Militia from Martin Co., N. C. under Capt. Kenneth McKenzie on a tour of duty, 1780; received land grant in Burke Co., Ga., for his service. Mar. in N. C., ANN RAIFORD. All of their children lived and d. in Bulloch Co., Ga., except dau., Alcy, who mar. and removed to Lowndes Co., Ga.

Children:
1. Joseph, mar. Celeanor, Denmark. 9 children.
2. Catherine, b. 1762, mar. Jarvis Jackson.
3. Benjamin, mar. Dorothy Carr.
4. Joshua, Jr., b. 1766, mar. Rebecca Fletcher (dau. of WILLIAM FLETCHER, *Rev. Sol.* and his (2) wife, Elizabeth McIntosh).
5. Essenurer (called Alcy), mar. 1801, John Dampier.
6. Rhoda, mar. Lemuel S. Lanier.

HENRY HOLCOMBE, b. Prince Edward Co., Va., Sept. 23, 1762. Removed with parents to S. C. Served as an officer in S. C. Line. Mar. 1786, FRANCES TANNER. Was called to the First Baptist Church, Savannah, Ga., 1799, then to Philadelphia, Jan. 1, 1812; d. Philadelphia, Penn., May 22, 1821.

WILLIAM HOLLIDAY, SR., b. Ireland, 1723; d. Wilkes Co., Ga., 1786. Will made July 7, 1786. Served as private in Ga. Line; received bounty grant of land for his service, in Wilkes Co., Ga. Mar. ANN—.

Children:
1. WILLIAM, JR., mar. Jane Cooper.
2. Thomas, mar. Rebecca Ragan.
3. Robert.
4. Abraham.
5. Ayers.
6. John.
7. Jane.
8. Mary.
9. Ann.
10. Elizabeth.
11. Margery.

WILLIAM HOLLIDAY, JR., b. Ireland, 1750, came to America before the Rev. and settled in Laurens Co., S. C. Moved to St. Paul's Parish, Richmond Co., Ga.; d. Laurens Co., S. C. (on

visit) Nov., 1826. Served as private Ga. troops under Gen. Elijah Clarke; fought at the Battle of Kettle Creek; received bounty land for his service, Wilkes Co., Ga. Mar. JANE COOPER.
Children:
1. William, b. S. C., moved to Miss.
2. Robert Alexander, b. S. C., 1787, moved to Ga., where he d. Nov. 1862. Mar. Rebecca Burroughs. 12 children.
3. Mathew, mar. Miss Dean, moved to Cass Co., Ga, then to Miss.
4. Martha Ann (called Nancy), mar. John Russell—, moved to Cass Co., Ga.
5. Margaret.

WILLIAM HOLLOWAY, SR., lived in Swains District, Thomas (now Brooks Co.) Co., Ga. Was a *Rev. Sol.* Mar. ELIZABETH EDMUNDSON (dau. of ISAAC EDMUNDSON (OR EDMONDSON), *Rev. Sol.* and his wife, Nancy. They lived in Bulloch Co., Ga.; d. in Brooks Co., Ga.)
Children (mentioned in will of William Holloway, made May 4, 1839, pro. Jan. 18, 1859).
1. William, Jr.
2. James.
3. Griffin.
4. Nancy, mar. Ansel Parish.
5. Roxy Ann, mar. James Alderman
6. Harriet, mar. —Yates.
7. Lavinia, mar. Canneth Yates.
8. Katherine, mar. J. I. Albritton.
9. Susanna, mar. William Smith.
10. Orphelia, mar. Lasa Adams.

DAVID HOLLIMAN (OR HOLLAMOND), b. 1757, came from N. C. to Wilkes Co., Ga. Will made Oct. 30, 1779, pro. July 1, 1783. Served in N. C. Line; received grant of land, Wilkes Co., Ga. for his service.
Will mentions:
Sons:
1. David, Jr.
2. Mark.
3. Samuel.
Dau.:
Aley (or Alcy).
Wife not named. (Absolem and Charity Holliman, Exs.)

JOHN HOLMES, b. Caroline Co., Va., 1747. Came to the Carolinas, then Ga.; d. Wilkes Co., Ga., 1803 (will pro. Mar. 8, 1803). Served in Ga. Militia as chaplain; received grant of land in St. Andrew's Parish, Ga., and was licensed to teach English and Latin at Savannah, Ga. Rector of Burke Co., Ga., Church 1776 and on Feb. 16, 1776 was appointed Chaplain of 1st Ga. Regiment. Mar. 1767 CHLOE BENTLEY (1747-1813), (dau. of WILLIAM BENTLEY, b. Fairfax, Va.; d. DeKalb Co., Ga., 1802; served as Lieut. and then Captain; received land grant for service. Mar. Mary Elliott).
Children:
1. Apsylla (1770-1815), mar. 1789, PITT MILNER (son of JOHN MILNER, a *Rev. Sol.* and his wife, Elizabeth Godwin.)
2. Penelope, mar. Benjamin Milner.
3. Mary, mar. (1) —Parks; (2) Elisha Kendall.
4. Elizabeth.
5. Josiah.
6. John, Jr.
7. James.
8. Moses.

JOHN HOOD, b. Amelia Co., Va.; d. Wilkes Co., Ga. Served in the Va. Continental Line, discharged at Augusta, Ga.; received bounty land, Wilkes Co., Ga. Mar. REBECCA REEVES, of Wilkes Co.
One of their children:
Joel Hood, b. Wilkes Co., Ga., 1789; d. Meriwether Co., Ga., 1861. Mar. Martha Dowdy (dau. of MARTIN DOWDY, *Rev. Sol.* of Va., who d. Oglethorpe Co., Ga., and his wife, Mary Temple).

JOHN HOWARD, b. S. C., Oct. 4, 1761; d. Baldwin Co., Ga., April 18, 1822. Served as a private in Capt. Putnam's Co. under Brig. Gen. Sumpter's S. C. troops; rose to the rank of Major. (Grave marked by D. A. R.) Mar. JANE VIVIAN (1770-1837).
Children:
1. Mary, mar. Seaborn Jones.
2. Elizabeth, mar. (1) Robt. Rutherford; (2) Edward Cary.
3. John Harrison, mar. Caroline Bostick.
4. Thacker, mar. Elizabeth Thweatt.
5. Homer, mar. Eleanor Sewell.
6. Augustus, mar. (1) Miss Wimberly; (2) Ann Lindsay.
7. Ann.
8. Melton.
9. Sarah.

NEHEMIAH HOWARD, living in Edgefield District, S. C., was a *Rev. Patriot.* Mar. EDITH SMITH, b. 1733. Moved to Elbert Co., Ga., where he d. 1798.
Children:
1. Nehemiah, Jr.
2. Mark.
3. Benjamin.
4. James.
5. Joseph.
6. JOHN, mar. Jane Vivian.
7. Isiah, mar. —Pittman.
8. Hester, mar. —Torrance.
9. Nancy, mar. Elisha Owens.
10. Mary, mar. (1)—Woodward; (2) John Barrett.
    NOTE: Mary Ann Howard[4] (John[3], John[2], Nehemiah[1]) of Columbus, Ga., mar. Charles H. Williams and originated "Memorial Day for the Confederate Soldiers."

JOSEPH HOWELL, JR. (son of Joseph and Margaret Howell), b. N. C., 1733; removed to Cabarrus Co., N. C.; d. DeKalb Co., Ga., 1835, age 102 years. Member N. C. Assembly. Served in the Mecklinburg Co., N. C. Militia. Fought at Guilford C. H. and King's Mt. Mar. in Anson Co., N. C., 1768, MARGARET ELEANOR GARMON, who d. after 1795.
Children:
1. John, mar. Essena Osbourne.
2. Joseph, mar. 1789, Sylva Robinson (1773-1853).
3. Elizabeth, mar. (1) Eli Green; (2) Jacob Smith; d. Ala.
4. Eli, mar. 1801, Nancy Love, d. Ala.
5. Margaret, mar. Edmund Smith, d. Ala.
6. William, mar. Elizabeth Sides.
7. Isaac, mar. 1805, Margaret Tucker, d. Ga.
8. Evan, b. Cabarrus Co., N. C., 1781; d. Gwinnett Co., Ga , 1868; mar. (1) Martha Love; (2) Mary Elliott; (3) Harriet Himes (Owens); (4) Jane Brooks; (5) Teziah Brombelow.
9. Michael, mar. Mary Freeman, d. Ark.
10. Eleanor, mar. John Kiser, d. Ga.
11. Henry, b. 1775, mar. Mary Miller.

JOSEPH HUBBARD, b. Va., 1760; d. Ga., 1830. Mar. 1778, Cynthia Bennett, (1763-1835). Served as *Rev. Sol.* and also in *War of 1812.*
Children:
1. Elizabeth (1778-1840), mar. Jacob Wise, of Butts Co., Ga.
2. Susan.
3. William.
4. Susannah.
5. Bennett.
6. John.
7. Mildred.

JOHN HUBBARD, lived in Petersburg, (Elbert Co.) Ga. where he d. Feb. 15, 1800; received 287½ acres bounty land on certificate of Gen. Elijah Clarke for his service. Mar. SALLY—.
(Children mentioned in will):
1. Mary, mar. —Puryear.
2. Joseph.
3. Rhoda, mar. —Burton.
4. Benjamin.
5. Susanna.
6. John, mar. (1) Betsey Cook; (2) Ann Nunnellee.
7. Richard, mar. Patsey Jones.

MATTHEW HUBERT, b. Va., 1757; d. Warren Co., Ga., 1812. Served as private under Captains Edmunds and Gregory in Va. Lived Caswell Co., N. C.; moved to Wilkes Co., Ga. Mar. 1775, MARTHA WALLACE (1753-1835), dau. of Robert Wallace.
Children:
1. Nancy, b. N. C., 1776, mar. William Flournoy, of Putnam Co., Ga.
2. Hiram, mar. Sarah Burnley.
3. Mary, mar. John Vining. Moved to Ala., then to Texas.
4. Benjamin (1782-1812).
5. Archibald.
6. Elizabeth.
7. William, b. Ga., 1784, mar. Rebecca Hawkins, of Putnam Co., Ga. Moved to Texas.
8. John, mar. Sally Wright.
9. Harman, mar. Virginia Hill.

CUTHBERT (called Cutbird) HUDSON, b. Va.; d. Elbert Co., Ga., 1801. Served as *Rev. Sol.*; received bounty grant of land on Eastanollee Creek, Franklin Co., Ga., 1785. His widow received land as widow of *Rev. Sol.*, 1827, Cherokee Lottery. Mar. ELIZABETH —.
(Children mentioned in will, not in order of birth):
1. Christopher.
2. Joacim.
3. Joshua, mar. Elizabeth —, 1799. Lived Franklin Co., Ga. 9 children: a. Mary; b. Nancy; c. Bathsheba; d. Betsy; e. Lotty; f. Maria; g. Milton Pierce; h. Martha Waver; i. Sally Melissa.
4. Gilliom.
5. Thomas.
6. Amphelady, mar. John Westbrook.
7. Elizabeth, mar. —Northington.
8. Mary, mar. Richard Burton.
9. Bathsheba, mar. Abraham Burton, Jr.
10. Susanna.

DAVID HUDSON, b. Prince Edward Co., Va., 1762; d. Elbert Co., Ga., 1831. Placed on Pension roll for service as private in Capt. Moore's Co., Major Picken's S. C. Regiment. Mar. MARY COBB BOOKER (1765-1830).
Children (known):
1. Charles.
2. William.

IRBY HUDSON, SR., b. 1750; d. Hancock Co., Ga., 1806. Mar. Dec. 4, 1778, Orange Co., Va., Phoebe Featherstone, b. 1754; d. Dec. 16, 1821. Served in Capt. Robert Bolling's Co., Dinwiddie Co., Va., under Col. Parker, Gen. Mecklenburg's Brigade.
Children:
1. Elizabeth, b. 1779; d. Jan. 5, 1834, mar. Thomas Little.
2. William, mar. Aug. 23, 1806, Frances Long.
3. Sarah, mar. July 17, 1806, Woodlief Scott.
4. Thomas, mar. Jan. 20, 1809, Sophie Thurmond.
5. Irby, Jr., mar. Dec. 22, 1812 (1) Jane Frances Flournoy; (2) Martha (Flournoy) Marshall.
6. Charles, mar. Elizabeth Reese.
7. Mary, mar. Oct., 1808, Frederick Scott.

8. John, b. Jan. 4, 1794; d. June 5, 1859, mar. (1) June 8, 1820, Nancy Gaither; (2) Elizabeth D. Jarrett.

9. Lewellyn (1795-1836), mar. 1821, Evelina Alexander.

10. Frances, mar. Robert Adams.

JAMES HUNT, JR., b. Va., June 6, 1762; d. Elbert Co., Ga., Mar. 23, 1832. Served as a *Rev. Sol.* Va. Continental Line. Mar. Va., JEMINA CARTER, b. 1772; d. Hart Co., Ga., Jan. 7, 1869.

Children:

1. Elizabeth, b. 1791, mar. Jesse M. Redwine.

2. Henry.

3. William, b. 1795.

4. Sion, mar. Priscilla Thornton.

5. James (1800-1838).

6. Moses, b. 1802.

7. Drucilla, mar. Nicholas M. Adams.

8. Willis, b. 1808, mar. Priscilla Teasley.

9. Hullium, mar. Harriet C. Ward.

10. Richard Carter, b. Elbert Co., Ga., 1813; d. Ark., mar. (1) Mary Harris.

11. Mary, mar. 1826, Wm. (Buck) Page.

CAPTAIN JUDKINS HUNT, b. 1747; d. Hancock Co., Ga., 1817. Will pro. Hancock Co., Ga., Jan. 5, 1818. Mar. Martha Batte at Brunswick Co., Va. (1749-1809). A *Rev. Sol.*

Children:

1. Nancy Porter (1784-1828), mar. ALLEN J. GREEN, Captain Va. troops, Sussex Co., Va., *Rev. Sol.*

2. Elizabeth, mar. Myles Green.

3. Sally, mar. —Rives.

4. William.

5. Judkins, Jr.

MOSES HUNT, b. June 8, 1760; d. Elbert Co., Ga. Served in Major Dobbs Battalion; received bounty land for his service in Ga. Militia. Mar. MARY TAMAR TYNER (1760-1840). (She was captured as a girl and held in captivity several years by the Indians.) Will made June 6, 1839, pro. Mar. 12, 1842. A *Rev. Sol.*

Children:

1. Mary (1779-1863), mar. James Adams.

2. James.

3. John S., mar. 1825, Mary Gaines.

4. Nancy, mar. Lawrence M. Adams.

5. Joel.

6. Henry.

7. Joshua.

8. Richard.

9. George.

DANIEL INMAN, b. N. C., 1751; d. Burke Co., Ga., 1837. Served in Burke Co., Ga. troops. Mar. (1) AVA ALLEN; (2) —. A *Rev. Sol.*

Children:

1. Alfred.

2. Rachel, mar. (1) Levi Spain; (2) Francis Jones.

3. Elizabeth.

4. Allen.

5. Sophie.

6. Mary.

7. Jeremiah.

8. Daniel, Jr.

SHADRACK INMAN, b. 1750; killed at the Battle of Musgrove's Mill. Entered service as Lieut. Ga. Line; his widow, Elizabeth —, was granted land in Ga. as the widow of a *Rev. Sol.*

JOHN GODHILP ISRAEL SMITH, b. 1755; d. Ga., June 4, 1820. Served as *Rev. Sol.*; received bounty land for his service. Mar. CHRISTINIA (KIEFFER) MINGLEDORF (1755-1851). (See page 157.)

Children:

1. Christinia, mar. Charles Ryall.
2. Hannah Elizabeth, mar. Matthew Carter.
3. Sarah, mar. James Bird, of Bryan Co.
4. David.
5. Solomon.
6. Joshua.
7. Salome.

CHRISTOPHER IRVINE, b. Ireland, 1725; d. Wilkes Co., Ga., 1815. Served as Captain of Co. 5th Ga. Regiment 1776; received bounty land for his service in Wilkes Co., Ga. Mar. 1779 (1) LOUISA TUCKER, of Amherst Co., Va. (dau. of Mathew Tucker, of Va.), d. 1795; (2) 1797, PRUDENCE ECHOLS, of Wilkes Co., Ga., d. 1821.

Children by (1) wife:

1. Isaiah Tucker, b. Va., 1783; d. Ga., 1855. (*Sol. of 1812.*) mar. 1801, Isabella Lea Bankston (dau. of LAWRENCE BANKSTON, *Rev. Sol.* of Va. and Ga., and his wife, Nancy Henderson.) 10 children.
2. Charles Mallory.

Children by (2) wife:

1. John.
2. William.
3. David (1808-1865), mar. Sarah Baldwin Royston, of Greene Co., Ga.
4. Christopher, Jr.
5. Smith, killed by Indians.

JOHN LAWSON IRWIN (son of HUGH IRWIN, b. Ireland, 1725; d. 1805; granted bounty land for his service in Ga. Line, and his wife, Martha Alexander), b. Mecklenburg Co., N. C., 1755; d. Washington Co., Ga., 1822. Served as private, Ga. Line, under his brother, COL. JARED IRWIN. *Rev. Sol.* of Ga. Mar. 1790, REBECCA SESSIONS (1773-1839).

Their son:

Alexander Irwin (1792-1843), mar. 1824, Margaret Moore Lawson (1798-1853), (dau. of ANDREW THOMPSON LAWSON, b. Ga., 1760; d. Augusta, Ga., 1822., *Rev. Sol.* of Ga., and his wife, Mary Moore Barry, dau. of ANDREW BARRY, b. Penn., 1746; d. S. C., 1811. He was a *Rev. Sol.*, commanded a Co. of S. C. Rangers. Mar. MARGARET MOORE, a *Patriot* of the Revolution).

JAMES JACK (son of PATRICK JACK, Lieut. 3rd Lancaster Co., Penn. Battalion and member of N. C. Council of Safety. *Rev. Sol.* of Penn. and N. C., and his wife, Lillis McAdoo), b. Penn., 1731; d. Wilkes (now Elbert) Co., Ga., 1826. Served in N. C. Line. Carried the *Mecklenburg Declaration of Independence* to Philadelphia for the Congress; received bounty land for his service in Wilkes Co., Ga., 1784. Mar. MARGARET HOUSTON.

Children:

1. William, mar. Miss Cummings.
2. Patrick (1769-1820), *Sol. of 1812*. Mar. Harriet Spencer. 8 children.
3. Catherine, mar. Sidnor Cosby.
4. Archibald.
5. James.

JOHN JACK (son of Patrick Jack), b. N. C.; d. Wilkes Co., Ga. Served in N. C. Line; received bounty land for his service in Wilkes Co., Ga. Mar. MARY BARNETT (dau. of JOHN BARNETT, *Rev. Sol.* of N. C., and his wife, Ann Spratt, b. 1725, the first white child born in N. C. between the Yadkin and Catawba rivers).

EDWARD JACKSON, b. Craven Co., S. C., Feb. 14, 1755. Enlisted Chesterfield Dist., S. C., private in Capt. Griffeth's and Capt. Lloyd's Co., Col. Benton's S. C. Regiment; allowed a pension while a resident of Gwinnett Co., Ga., 1832; d. Walker Co., Ga., Feb. 22, 1845; buried Poe's Cemetery, Trion, Ga. (Grave marked). He mar. (2) Mary Hall, Jackson Co., Ga., June 1803; she received pension for his service 1853; d., age 84 years, Gwinnett Co., Ga., 1854.

Child by (1) wife:
    William, b. 1790.

DANIEL JACKSON, b. S. C., 1735; d. Wilkes Co., Ga., 1794. Served as private under Col. John Brandon in S. C. Mar. 1770 NANCY HIGH.

Children (known):
    1. Samuel (1786-1830), mar. 1807, Orrie Cox.
    2. Elizabeth (1792-1872), mar. Jack Wilburn (son of THOMAS WILBURN, b. N. C.; d. Greene Co., Ga., and Martha Wilburn (or Wellborn); Rev. Sol. of Ga.; served as private Ga. troops).

DRURY JACKSON, b. England; d. Wilkes Co., Ga., 1794. Served as private, S. C. troops; received bounty land in Ga. for his service. Mar. 1768, NANCY MAYFIELD (1749-1837).

Children:
    1. Nancy.
    2. Greene.
    3. Edward.
    4. Hartwell (1777-1859), mar. (1) 1801, Elizabeth Bostic (Bostwick); (2) Margaret Bradford.
    5. Wynche (1780-1854), mar. (1) Polly Dyer; (2) —.

WILLIAM JENNINGS, b. Nottoway Co., Va., 1726; d. Wilkes Co., Ga.. 1793. Mar. Agnes Dickerson. He was a Rev. Sol.

Children:
    1. Dickerson.
    2. John.
    3. Moody.
    4. James.
    5. Robert.
    6. Thomas.
    7. Henry.
    8. Elizabeth, mar. — Anders.
    9. Sarah, mar. — Robertson.
    10. Mary, mar. OLIVER JETER, Rev. Sol.
    11. Nancy, mar. — Hix.

OLIVER JETER (son of Thomas and Winneford Jeter), b. Caroline Co., Va., about 1742. Mar. Mary Jennings (dau. of WILLIAMS JENNINGS and his wife, Agnes Dickerson, of Amelia Co., Va., and Wilkes Co., Ga.). They lived in Amelia Co., Va., until after 1790; moved to Edgefield Co., S. C.; d. Lincoln Co., Ga. (will recorded there). He served as a Rev. Sol. of Va.

Children:
    1. Samuel.
    2. Thomas.
    3. William, mar. Mary Lamar.
    4. James.
    5. Virginia, mar. — Harding.

JOHN JOHNSON, b. Va.; d. Elbert Co., Ga., 1802; received bounty grant of land in Ga. for his service, certified to by Col. Elijah Clarke, Feb. 2, 1784. Mar. CATHERINE JOHNSON (sister of two Rev. Sols., ANGUS JOHNSON and ARCHIBALD JOHNSON, who drew land in Ga. for their service, Monroe Co. (Lottery)).

Children:
    1. Mary.
    2. Elizabeth.
    3. Angus.
    4. Nancy.
    5. Alexander.
    6. Peter.
    7. Donald.

8. John, Jr.
9. Malcom.
10. Neil.

JOHN JOHNSON, b. Va., d. Ga., 1792. Served in Ga. Line; received land for his service on Shoals Creek, Franklin Co., Ga. Mar. SARAH —; she d. after 1792.
Children:
1. Walter.
2. Joseph.
3. Isaiah.
4. Darcus.
5. Upton.
6. Elizabeth.
7. Precious, mar. — Cash.
8. Sarah.

NATHAN JOHNSON, b. Ireland, 1720; d. Oglethorpe Co., Ga., 1805. Served as private, Ga. Line; received bounty grant of land for his service. Mar. ELIZABETH HUTCHINS. A *Rev. Sol.*
Children:
1. Aaron, b. 1762, mar. Elizabeth Daniel (dau. of ALLEN DANIEL and wife, Mary Allen, a *Rev. Sol.* of Va. and Madison Co., Ga.).
2. Thomas, mar. Mary Susan Griffeth (dau. of JOHN GRIFFETH, a *Rev. Sol.*, and his wife, Ann McCraft).
3. Nathan, Jr., mar. Rebecca Elliott.
4. Elisha, mar. Charity Daniel (dau. of ALLEN DANIEL, *Rev. Sol.*).
5. Luke, mar. Elizabeth Ellsbury.
6. Mary.

NICHOLAS JOHNSON, b. Va.; d. Ala. Lived on the Broad river, Wilkes Co., Ga. Served in Ga. Line; received bounty grant of land for his service. (He was son of THOMAS JOHNSON (1735–1803), *Rev. Sol.* of Va., and his wife, Elizabeth Ann Meriwether, of Va.) Mar. MARY MARKS, of the Broad river Settlement, Ga. (dau. of JAMES MARKS, *Rev. Sol.* of Va., b. Amherst Co., Va., 1745; d. Ga. 1816, and his wife, Elizabeth Harvie).
Children:
1. Nancy, mar. Reuben Jordan.
2. Betsey, mar. Louis Bourbon Taliaferro.
3. Martha, mar. George Oglethorpe Gilmer.
4. Lucy, mar. George Gilmer.
5. Barbara, mar. — Fraser.
6. Rebecca, mar. Charles Jordan.
7. Sarah, mar. Morgan Smith.
8. Frank.
9. James.
10. Edward.

THOMAS JOHNSON, b. S. C., Mar. 10, 1742. Moved to Greene Co., Ga., where he d. Mar. 5, 1816. Served as Lieut., Ga. troops, *Rev. War.* Mar. Agnes Grier, b. Penn.; removed with parents to S. C.; d. Dallas Co., Ala., Sept. 5, 1820.
One child (known):
Bernard (1782–1843), mar. (1) Sarah Ann Taylor; (2) Sarah Craig; (3) Martha (Norwood) Hines.

WILLIAM JOHNSON, b. Scotland, 1734; d. Hancock Co., Ga., 1806. Served as private; received bounty grant of land for his service. Mar. MARGARET SCOTT, 1757.
Children:
1. William.
2. Samuel.
3. Laban Scott.
4. Margaret.
5. Green (1797–1852), mar. 1827, Martha W. Adams, d. 1881.

WILLIAM JOHNSON, b. 1755; d. Wilkes Co., Ga., 1821. Will pro. Sept. 1821; was granted land for his service as a *Rev. Sol.* in Washington Co., Ga., 1785. Was also a *Sol. of 1812.* Mar. in Wilkes Co., Ga., Nancy Hill, b. 1770; d. Meriwether Co., Ga., 1839.
Children:

1. Elizabeth, mar. Drury Cunningham.
2. Mary, mar. Henry Spratlin.
3. Susan, mar. Judge James Dabney Willis.
4. William, Jr., d. unmar.
5. John Pope, mar. Prudence Irvine.
6. Nancy (1808–1846), mar. 1824, Col. Lodowick Meriwether Hill. He mar. (2) Martha Strother Wellborn.
7. Martha Pope (1814–1893), mar. (1) 1829, Burwell Pope Hill as (2) wife; (2) Rev. Wm. D. Martin.
8. Catherine, mar. George W. Chatfield.
9. Stephen, d. unmar.
10. Sarah, d. unmar.

ABRAHAM JONES, b. Va., about 1749; lived in Halifax Co., N. C., then Florida and, 1773, moved with his widowed mother to St. George's Parish, Ga. (He was the son of ABRAHAM and MARTHA (JONES) JONES, of Prince George Co., Va., who had SEVEN sons (all *Rev. Sols.*) viz: JOHN, ABRAHAM, JAMES, BATTE, SEABORN, WILLIAM, THOMAS).

He served as Lieut., 2nd Ga. Regiment. At the fall of Charleston, S. C., 1780, he was taken prisoner by the British; d. Montgomery Co., Ga., 1811. Mar. (1) SARAH BUGG, of Beach Island, S. C.; (2) the widow of Zephaniah Beale.
Children by (1) wife:

1. Martha Bugg, b. 1785, mar. Dr. Thomas Moore, of Md., and Augusta, Ga.
2. Seaborn, d. Columbus, Ga., 1874. Mar. in Milledgeville, Ga., Mary Howard.
3. John A. (1790–1880), mar. Martha Jenkins.
4. Eliza Agnes.
5. Elizabeth.
6. Sarah Keziah Paris, mar. Dr. Charles Williamson.

ADAM JONES, b. Va., was a *Rev. Sol.* Settled near Long Creek at Meeting House (as he was a preacher) on the Ogeechee river in 1785; d. Oct. 1, 1830, Ga.

BATTE JONES, b. Edgecombe Co., N. C., Mar. 4, 1754; d. Burke Co., Ga., 1821. Served as 1st Lieut., 6th Co. Ga. Militia, under Col. John Thomas; granted bounty land for his service. Mar. his first cousin, MARY JONES (dau. of HENRY JONES, *Rev. Sol.* of Ga.).
Children:

1. Harriet Eliza (1791–1863), mar. 1822, as (2) wife, Rev. James Hall T. Fitzpatrick.
2. Henry Seaborn (1793–1838), mar. Margaret Torrence.
3. Mary Thomas, mar. (1) James E. Hines; (2) Everet Sapp.
4. Sarah M.
5. James Burwell.
6. Jane Margaret.

BRIDGER JONES (name sometimes written "Bridgeon"), b. N. C., Aug. 11, 1753. Will made Jan. 1, 1815, Pro. Nov. 12, 1819, Bulloch Co., Ga. Mar. Rachel Barry, b. 1762; d. 1816. Lived in Bulloch Co., Ga. *Rev. Sol.*; served in Continental Line; received bounty grant of land for his service. 12 children.
Children:

1. Barry, mar. Rebecca Wise.
2. Polly, d. y.
3. Bridger, Jr.
4. John F.
5. Josiah.
6. Bazel (or Basil).
7. Buckner.
8. Nancy, mar. — Jones.
9. Payne.
10. Lincy.
11. Polly (Mary), mar. Joshua Everett.
12. Rachel (1791–1871), mar. John Wise.

GEORGE JONES (son of Hugh and Elizabeth Jones), b. 1743; d. Ga.   Served as a private, Ga. Line.   Mar. 1769, Phoebe Foster, b. 1749.

Children:

1. Delphia Garnett (1770–1857), mar. 1808, Andrew Bryan.   8 children.
2. Edmund.
3. George.
4. Larkin.
5. Catlett.
6. John.
7. Ann F.
8. Phoebe.
9. Hugh.
10. Elizabeth.
11. Lucy.
12. Thomas.
13. Matilda.

HENRY JONES (son of Henry and Winny (Elder) Jones), b. near Petersburg, Va., 1762; d. while on a visit to Ala., 1818.   Removed after the War to Guilford C. H., N. C., then to Hancock Co., Ga.   Served three enlistments under Capt. B. Jones in Va., and was at the Battle of Camden, S. C.   Mar. (1) SARAH LIGHTFOOT; (2) MARY HOGAN; (3) NELLIE PAYNE.

Child by (1) wife:

Henry L.

Children by (2) wife:

1. William.
2. Thomas.
3. Cannon.
4. Seaborn.
5. John.
6. Reuben.
7. Allen, mar. Mary Jane Moody; moved to Wis.
8. Nancy.
9. Sarah.
10. Mary.

Children by (3) wife:

1. Joseph.
2. Minnie.
3. Benjamin.

HENRY JONES, b. Va., 1727; moved to Ga., 1770; d. Burke Co., Ga., 1803.   One of the two representatives from St. George's Parish to the Provincial Congress, meeting in Savannah, Ga., 1774–1775.   Appointed Magistrate by the Council of Safety; on July 6, 1780, his name appears as the "Rebel Colonel."   Mar. Keziah Jones.

Children:

1. Sarah, b. Amelia Co., Va., 1761, mar. her first cousin, James Jones.
2. Mary, b. 1764, mar. her first cousin, Batte Jones.
3. Henry, b. 1766, mar. Fannie (Miller) Jones (the widow of his uncle, Robert Jones).
4. Thomas.
5. Daniel.
6. Margaret, b. 1772, mar. (1) Capt. John Evans, of Ga.; (2) Dr. Job S. Barney, of Philadelphia, Pa.

JAMES JONES (son of Abraham Jones), b. Edgecomb Co., N. C., about 1752; d. near Waynesboro, Ga., 1810.   Enlisted from St. George's Parish, Ga.; captured at the fall of Charleston, S. C., and confined as a prisoner at Augusta, Ga., until that place was captured by the Americans.   Mar. his first cousin, SARAH JONES.

Children:

1. Mary, mar. Alexander W. Allen.

2. Jane Ann, mar. Thomas Cooper Butler, of N. Y.; they moved to Ohio.
3. Seaborn, mar. Margaret A. Jones.
4. James W., mar. Elizabeth H. Blount.

JAMES JONES, b. Va., April 28, 1764; d. Elbert Co., Ga., 1807. Served in the Va. Continental Line; received bounty grant of land in Ga. for his service. Mar. —.

Children:
1. James, Jr.
2. John.
3. Stanby.
4. George.
5. Thomas.
6. William.
7. Nancy.
8. Polly, mar. Gillam Hudson.
9. Dau., mar. Richard Hubbard.
10. Dau., mar. Shadrick Floyd.

JAMES JONES (son of Francis Jones), b. S. C., April 28, 1764; d. Screven Co., Ga., 1828. Served as private, Ga. Line; received bounty grant of land for his service. Mar. 1791, ELIZABETH MILLS, b. June 1774; d. 1836.

Children:
1. Francis, b. Jan. 27, 1792, mar. Rachel Spain.
2. Matthew, b. Oct. 11, 1795, mar. Elizabeth Inman.
3. Benjamin (Benny), b. Sept. 10, 1797.
4. Thomas, b. May 14, 1802, mar. Lavinia Young.
5. Brady Michael, b. Sept. 27, 1805.
6. Lavinia, b. July 9, 1795, mar. James Young.
7. Harriet, b. Mar. 21, 1817, mar. James B. Blackshear.
8. Elizabeth, b. April 20, 1813, mar. Joseph S. Neely.

JOHN JONES, b. Penn., 1720; d. Wrightsboro Township, Ga., 1782. Served in S. C.; received bounty land for his service in Ga., upon certificate of Col. Lee. Mar. MARY —.

Children:
1. Richard.
2. Ann, mar. — Brown.
3. Phillipine, mar. — Stanfield.
4. Margaret, mar. STEPHEN DAY, a *Rev. Sol.*
5. Mary, mar. — Anglin.
6. James.
7. Jonathan.
8. Nathan.

JOHN JONES, b. N. C., 1745; d. Ga., 1817. Served in Ga. Line under Gen. Clarke; received a bounty grant of land for his service. Mar. Susanna Strobhar.

One Child:
Obedience Jones (1764–1832), mar. JESSE OFFUTT, b. Ga., 1760; d. Richmond Co., Ga., 1830. He served as a private in Ga. Militia, under Col. Few.
Their dau., Frances Offutt (1787–1833), mar. John Goldwire (1779–1830), (the son of JAMES GOLDWIRE, b. Augusta, Ga., 1747; d. Mt. Pleasant, Ga., 1810; commanded a Co. of Militia, 1777, from St. Mathews Parish (now Effingham Co.), Ga., and his wife, Sarah King; mar. 1763. She was b. 1749; d. 1810).

JOHN JONES, b. Charleston, S. C., 1749, lived at Sunbury, Liberty Co., Ga. Served as Major, Ga. Line, Continental Troops, and killed at the assault on Spring Hill Redoubt, near Savannah, Ga., Oct. 9, 1778. Mar. MARY SHARPE (dau. of James and Mary (Newton) Sharpe).
Their son, JOSEPH JONES, *Rev. Sol.*, commanded the Liberty Co. Independent Troops in the War of 1812. Mar. Elizabeth Hart (dau. of JOHN HART, a *Rev. Sol.* of S. C., and his wife, Mary Esther Screven, dau. of BRIGADIER GEN. JAMES SCREVEN, *Rev. Sol.* of Ga., who was killed at Midway Church, Ga.).

MOSES JONES, b. Va., 1765; d. Ga., 1830. Served as private, Ga. Militia; received grant of land in Wilkes Co., Ga., for his service. Mar. Mary Florance, d. 1826.
Children:
1. Solomon.
2. Mason.
3. Anderson.
4. Moses, Jr., d. Harris Co., Ga., 1864.
5. Sarah, mar. John Mays (son of WILLIAM MAYS, *Rev. Sol.*, granted land in Ga., and his wife, Mary Wadkins).
6. Genevieve.
7. Armand.
8. Lucinda.
9. Toliver, mar. Hannah Gideon (dau. of FRANCIS GIDEON, *Rev. Sol.*, and his wife, Elizabeth Hopkins, of Wilkes Co., Ga. He served as Capt., Ga. Line).

NATHAN JONES (son of John and Mary Jones, Quakers from N. J., to Cane Creek M. M., N. C.), b. N. C. Came with parents to Wrightsborough, Ga. He served as a *Rev. Sol.* of Ga.; received bounty land for his service, upon certificate of Col. Greenberry Lee, Feb. 23, 1784. (Dismissed from Quaker M. M.) Mar. CARTNA — (Land deeds). He d. Elbert Co., Ga., 1807.
Children:
1. Allen, mar. Amelia —.
2. Dau., mar. John Hatchcock.
3. Polly, mar. Oct. 26, 1806, Debton Hatchcock.
4. Dau., mar. James Childers.
5. Arthur.
6. Thomas.
7. John.
8. Dau., mar. Darvin Harris.
9. Jesse.
10. Davis, mar. Dec. 31, 1820, Rhody Jones.

JONATHAN JONES and JOHN JONES, brothers of Nathan Jones, were also *Rev. Sols.* of Ga. (settled with their parents in Wrightsborough Settlement of Quakers, Ga., 1773).

NOBLE WIMBERLY JONES, b. England, 1725; d. Ga., 1805. Signed the call for the earliest meeting of the *Patriots of Ga.*, held in Savannah. Member House of Assembly; Speaker of Provincial Congress, 1775; member Ga. Council of Safety, 1776; member Continental Congress, 1775, and again in 1781-82. Mar. SARAH DAVID.
Children:
1. John.
2. Edward.
3. Sarah.
4. Catherine.
5. George.

RUSSELL JONES, d. Franklin Co., Ga., Feb., 1828; received his discharge as a *Rev. Sol.* from Lieut.-Col. Marbury, as a Continental Sol. of Dragoons; received bounty land in Ga., April 23, 1785. Mar. SARAH —.
Children (not in order of birth):
1. Polly, mar. Allen Daniel, Jr., Gen. of Militia in War of 1812.
2. Dudley.
3. Lewis.
4. Arglin, mar. Benjamin Cleveland.
5. Dau., mar. Charles Sorrells.
6. Amelia, mar. — Allen.
7. Thomas.
8. William.
9. James.
10. Russell, Jr.

SEABORN JONES (son of Abraham and Martha (Jones) Jones), b. Halifax Co., N. C., June 15, 1759; d. Augusta, Ga., July 24, 1815. Served in the Va. Continental Line; was taken prisoner at Charleston, S. C; discharged and fought as a Refugee Sol., 1781. Mar. (1) Wilkes Co., Ga., SARAH HARWOOD WILKERSON, d. Nov. 1806; (2) 1807, ELIZABETH HARRIS, widow. Lived at Augusta and Screven Co., Ga.

Children (who reached maturity), by (1) wife:
1. Augustus Seaborn, mar. Emily Robert of S. C.
2. Martha Melvina Milledge, mar. Rev. Woderwell.
3. Sarah Seaborn Rebecca Weed, mar. Governor Charles J. Jenkins, of Ga.

Child by (2) wife:
Elizabeth, b. 1816, mar. Dr. John Valentine Freeman Walker.
Sarah Ann Jones (sister of Seaborn Jones), b. N. C., 1763; mar. 1788, SHERWOOD BUGG, JR., a Rev. Sol. of Augusta, Ga., and Beach Island, S. C. She was a Patriot.

SOLOMON JONES, b. Va., 1760, lived in Liberty Co., Ga. Applied for a pension as a Rev. Sol. and musician. "That he enlisted in the Rev. War in Va. in Continental service, 1776. Andrew Getle, recruiting Sergeant, brought from there to Savannah, Ga.; served under Capt. Andrew Getle, Col. Stark, commander of Regiment 3 years; discharged at Charleston, S. C., by Gen. McIntosh; returned to Va.; re-enlisted in N. C. in Co. of Militia and came to Charleston on 9 months' tour. Re-enlisted with COL. WILLIAM WASHINGTON; served as trumpet major in Col. Washington's Dragoons. Discharged at end of Rev. War at High Hills of Santee. Was in Battles of Eutaw Springs and Cowpens; horse shot from under him in the first and wounded in second. Wife (living 1826, b. 1772.) One dau., now in S. C.; one son in Miss." (On file in records of Bryan Co., Ga., May 25, 1826).

WILLIAM JONES, b. King and Queen Co., Va., 1762; d. Columbia Co., Ga., 1834. Served in the Va. Continental Line in Va. and Ga.; received bounty grant of land in Ga. for his service. He mar. 4 times and had 21 children. Mar. (4) 1826, Elcie V. (Tankersly) Pace (dau. of JAMES TANKERSLY, Rev. Sol. of Va., and his wife, Susan Brooks).

Children (known):
1. Edwin Thomas (1831-1867), mar. Martha Dillon Wright.
2. MARY S., b. Columbia Co., Ga., Dec. 18, 1828; d. Dec. 6, 1899. Was a REAL DAUGHTER, National Society D. A. R. She mar. 1846, John M. Cutliff (1823-1907), (son of John Cutliff and Lucinda Ragan, and grand-son of ABRAM CUTLIFF, JONATHAN RAGAN, and JOHN RAY, all Rev. Sols. of Ga.).

WILLIAM JONES, b. Va., 1759; d. Jasper Co., Ga., Feb. 1841. Enlisted Va., Sept. 1, 1776, as a private and Sergeant in Capt. Joseph Parnell's Co. Served in Col. Samuel Elbert's Regiment, later in Col. Meriwether's Va. Regiment. Applied for pension April 21, 1829, age 70 years; pension granted. His widow was allowed pension as a widow of a Rev. Sol. Mar. in Va., MARY —; mar. (2) EMILIA PATTERSON.

Children by (1) wife (known):
1. William, Jr., b. S. C.; moved to Ga.
2. Mary Amelia, b. S. C., 1786; mar. Putnam Co., Ga., William Tidwell (son of WILLIAM TIDWELL, d. S. C., and his wife, Mary De Graffenreid. A Rev. Sol. of S. C.).

Children by (2) wife:
1. Jane; 2. Lucy; 3. Nancy; 4. Milly; 5. Joseph.

WILLIAM JONES, b. Amherst Co., Va.; d. Ga., Feb. 12, 1809. Served as private, S. C. Troops, under Gen. Nathaniel Greene. Served in Va. and S. C. throughout the war. Mar. 1781, ANN FREEMAN (dau. of James and Ann Freeman). She mar. (2) JOHN PARKER. He d. 1831; she d. June 3, 1847.

His daughter, Elizabeth Jones, made application for service of WILLIAM JONES while a resident of Sumpter District, S. C., Feb. 2, 1854. Granted.

Children of William and Ann Freeman Jones:
1. James.
2. Elisabeth, b. Dec. 5, 1784.
3. Mary.
4. Peggy.

    5. Nancy.
    6. Eli.
    7. William, Jr.
    8. Leonard.
    9. Wylie.
    10. Betsey Ann.
    11. Sarah.
    NOTE: Rev. Dabney P. Jones, preacher and first Ga. Temperance Lecturer, of Coweta Co., Ga. (1791–1866), mar. Mary Penn (1798–1858), dau. of Wilson Penn, and his wife, Frances Taliaferro (dau. of ZECHERIAH TALIAFERRO, *Rev. Sol.*, and his wife, Mary Boutwell).

    JOHN JORDAN, b. Va., 1756; d. Washington Co., Ga., Aug. 20, 1828. Mar. N. C., 1786, WINIFRED JORDAN, his cousin. Served in N. C. Troops, joined Gen. Samuel Elbert's Regiment in Ga.; was taken prisoner and exchanged; was at the surrender at Yorktown; received grant of land for his service, Washington Co., Ga. Pension granted to his daughter, Mary (Jordan) Newton of Athens, Ga. Buried near Sandersville, Ga.
Children:
    1. Britton (1787-1806), mar. 1814, Peggy (Margaret) Bell. 7 children.
    2. Green, mar. Elizabeth Sanford.
    3. Burwell, mar. Lavinia Holland.
    4. John (1800-1852), mar. Eliza Smith.
    5. Patience, mar. Isom Saffold.
    6. Persilla, mar. William Tennille (son of LIEUT. COL. FRANCIS TENNILLE, *Rev. Sol.*, and wife, Elizabeth Dixon).
    7. Mary, mar. John H. Newton.

    REUBEN JORDAN, b. Va., 1754; d. Broad River Settlement, Wilkes Co., Ga., 1816. Mar. Genette Harvie. (This record is only information for Genealogical Research).
Children:
    1. Martha, mar. Dr. Bradley.
    2. Reuben, Jr., mar. (1) Nancy Johnson (dau. COL. NICHOLAS JOHNSON, *Rev. Sol.* of Ga.); (2) the dau.of COL. CHARLES WILLIAMSON, *Rev. Sol.* of Ga., and his wife, Nancy Clarke, dau. of GEN. ELIJAH CLARKE, *Rev. Sol.* of Ga.)
    3. Fleming, mar. Anna Meriwether (dau. of THOMAS MERIWETHER, *Rev. Sol.* of Ga.) They moved to Jasper Co., Ga.
    4. Margaret, mar.—.
    5. Betsey, mar. Dr. George Meriwether.
    6. Mortimer, mar. dau. of Hezekiah Gray.
    7. Charles, mar. (1) Rebecca Johnson (dau. of COL. NICHOLAS JOHNSON, *Rev. Sol.*); (2) Elizabeth Yancey Reid.

    MICHAEL JOHNSTON KENAN, b. N. C., 1746; d. Hancock Co., Ga., 1817. Served in N. C. Troops and was a member of the N. C. Convention 1777. Took Oath of Allegiance, 1775 in N. C. Mar. Ann Holmes of N. C. Had two brothers, JAMES KENAN, who rose to rank of General in N. C. and OWEN KENAN, N. C., killed by the Tories.
Child:
    Thomas Holmes Kenan, mar. Amelia (Gray) Powell.

    JOHN WALTER KEY, b. Va., May 11, 1751; d. Franklin Co., Ga., 1828. Served as private Va. Line; received grant of land for his services in Franklin Co., Ga. Mar. VIRGINIA (called Jenny) WADE.
Children:
    1. Lucinda, mar. —Steel.
    2. Agnes, mar. Bradley Harrison.
    3. Elizabeth, mar. —Embry.
    4. Patty (Martha), mar. Beasley Thomas.
    5. Peirce (Price), mar. Sarah Hix.
    6. Winney, mar. Boley Embry.

7. Tolbert (or Talbird), mar. (1) 1816, Elizabeth Embry; (2) Effie Burgess; (3) 1850, Mary Wooten.

8. Sarah, mar. —Bailey.

9. George W., mar. Delilah Embry.

WILLIAM BIBB KEY, b. Albemarle Co., Va., Oct. 2, 1759; d. Elbert Co., Ga., Dec. 7, 1836. Served as *Rev. Sol.*; received bounty grant of land for his service Mar. Mourning Clark, b. Aug. 12, 1764 (dau. of CHRISTOPHER CLARK, *Rev. Sol.* of Ga., and his wife, Millicent Terrell).

Children:

1. Charles Terrell, b. 1784, mar. Mary Ann Clark.
2. Martha, mar. Nicholas Good.
3. James, b. 1788, mar. Rebecca Grizzle.
4. Milly, b. 1790, mar. Humphrey Posey.
5. Nancy, mar. Simeon Glenn.
6. Elizabeth, mar. Thomas Bell.
7. Margaret, mar. Thomas Good.
8. Keturah, mar. James Hamm.
9. Mary (Polly), mar. Joseph Bell.
10. Henry, d. y.
11. Thomas, d. y.
12. Susan, b. 1799, mar. James Bell, Jr.
13. Jane, b. 1801, mar. John Grizzle.
14. Sarah, b. 1803, mar. Thomas C. Elliott.
15. Lucy, b. 1809, mar. Nathan Mattox.

WILLIAM KIDD, b. Mecklenburg Co., Va., Dec. 16, 1763; d. Oglethorpe Co., Ga.; moved to Ga. 1799. Served as a *Rev. Sol.* of Va.; was allowed a pension in Ga. Mar. Oct. 6, 1781, Judy Carter.

Children:

1. Carter.
2. William.
3. Lucy, mar. Johnson Wright.
4. Elizabeth, mar. Dean Tucker.
5. Webb, mar. Malinda —.
6. Mary.
(Perhaps other children).

ROSWELL KING, b. Sharon, Conn., May 3, 1765. Served as private, 1782. Moved to Darien, Ga., McIntosh Co. Mar. CATHERINE BARRINGTON (dau. of Josiah Barrington, a kinsman OF JAMES EDWARD OGLETHORPE, the Founder (1733) of the Province of Georgia. (Fort Barrington, on the Altamaha river, in Ga., an outpost built long before the Revolution for defense against the Spaniards, was named for him). Their son, Barrington King, b. 1798, moved to Roswell, Ga. (named for his father). Mar. Catherine Nephew (dau. of JAMES NEPHEW, *Rev. Sol.* of Ga., Lieut. in Col. John Baker's Regiment of Liberty Co., Ga. Militia).

SAMUEL KNOX, b. Rowan Co., N. C., 1747; d. Jackson Co., Ga., 1835. Mar. 1774, Mary Luckey, b. 1758. Received a pension for service as private, N. C. Troops, under Col. Davie and Col. Locke.

PETER KOLB, b. Craven Co., S. C., 1762; d. Meriwether Co., Ga., Dec. 8, 1835. Served with S. C. Troops under Capt. Abel Kolb and Gen. Francis Marion. Mar. THERESY GALES.

Children:

1. Martin.
2. Elizabeth.
3. Nancy.
4. Mary.
5. Wilds.
6. Valentine.
7. William.
8. Linnie.
9. Hariot.

ARCHIBALD LACY, b. Va. 1758; d. Warren Co., Ga., 1822. Received pay, 1783 as a Va. Sol. for service in Va. Continental Line. His widow, living Newton Co., Ga., drew land in 1827 Lottery in Ga. as a widow *Rev. Sol.* He mar. in Va., 1787, SARAH MARTIN. Came to Wilkes (now Warren) Co., Ga.

Children:
1. Polly, b. Va., 1788, mar. as (2) wife, Fisher Gaskin.
2. Betsey, b. Wilkes Co., Ga., 1791, mar. Wm. Smith.
3. John Butler, d. Thomas Co., Ga., 1878.
4. Martha, b. Warren Co., 1796, mar. Gerard Camp.
5. Nancy, b. 1799, mar. 1814, William Candler.
6. Pleasant Martin, mar. Nancy Reynold.
7. Sally, mar. John K. Johnson; moved to Miss.
8. Randolph Grief (1807-1825).

CAPT. JOHN LAMAR, b. 1740, killed near his home in Hancock Co., Ga., 1799. Served in Ga. Militia; received bounty grant for his service as a *Rev. Sol.* Mar. (1) Elizabeth Bugg (dau. of SHER-WOOD BUGG, *Rev. Sol.* of S. C. and Ga., and his wife, Elizabeth Hopson, a *Patriot.*); (2) PRIS-CILLA BUGG (dau. of SHERWOOD BUGG, JR., and his wife, Obedience Jones, a *Rev. Sol.* of Ga.); (3) LUCY APPLING.

BASIL LAMAR (son of John Lamar and Priscilla Bugg), b. 1764; d. Ga., May 5, 1827. Served in Ga. Militia; received grant of land for his service. Mar. 1794, Rebecca Kelly (1762-1829).

Children:
1. Priscilla, b. 1795.
2. John Thomas, b. 1797.
3. Gazaway Bugg, b. 1798.
4. James Jackson, b. 1800.
5. George Washington (1801-1892), mar. 1841, Sarah Walker Harlow (dau. of Dr. Southwell Harlow, of Plymouth, Mass.)
6. Oswald.
7. Zecheriah.
8. Rebecca J., mar. Hugh McLeod.
9. Thomas Jefferson.

THOMAS LANDRUM, b. Orange Co., Va., Oct. 6, 1759; d. near Lexington, Oglethorpe Co., Ga., 1833. Enlisted Feb. 23, 1778, private in Va. Co. under Capts. Burnley —, Lipscomb, Cols. Heath, Parker and Morgan; while a resident of Oglethorpe Co., Ga., 1832 he was allowed a pension for his service. (He served as Col. Ga. Troops, *War of 1812*). Mar. 1784 NANCY BELL, of Orange Co., Va.

Children:
1. Elizabeth, b. 1785, mar. Bledsoe Brockman.
2. John, b. 1787.
3. James B., b. 1789.
4. William H. (1793-1867), mar. 1820, Jane Bledsoe.
5. Mary, b. 1791, mar. —Norton.
6. Joseph, b. 1795.
7. Hay T., b. 1799.
8. Whitfield, b. 1797, mar. Eunice Bledsoe.
9. Nancy, b. 1801, mar. — Jennings.
10. Sarah B., b. 1803, mar. — Wray.

ABRAHAM SHEPHERD LANE (son of Christian Lane), b. Raleigh, N. C., 1759; d. Eman-uel Co., Ga., 1849. Served as private Ga. Troops; received bounty grant of land in Ga. for his serv-ice; was also a Sol. of the *War of 1812*, from Bulloch Co., Ga. Grave marked by D. A. R. Mar. 1782, N. C. Betsey Mills.

Children (known):
1. Benjamin Lane (1797-1860), mar. Jane Bonnell (1804-1861) (g-dau. of ANTHONY BON-NELL, *Rev. Sol.*, and his wife, Mary, of Ga.)
2. Edward Wood (1788-1851), mar. Susanna Lanier.

JESSE LANE, b. Halifax Co., N. C., July 3, 1733; d. on a visit to his children in Ky., Oct. 18, 1804. He served as an officer in 3d N. C. Regiment; was given bounty grant of land in Ga. for his service. Mar. Halifax Co., N. C., 1755, WINIFRED AYCOCK (dau. of William Aycock of N. C., and Wilkes Co., Ga. (*Rev. Sol.*), and his wife, Rebecca (Pace) Bradford.) She was b. April 11, 1741, and d. Dec. 16, 1794 of pleurisy, caused from exposure of being driven from home by the Indians. He moved with his family, 1784, to Wilkes (now Elbert) Co., Ga., then to Sparks Fort (now Clarke Co.), Ga.

Children:
1. CHARLES, b. Oct. 2, 1756, mar. Elizabeth Mallory. A *Rev. Sol.*
2. Richard, b. 1759, mar. Mary Flint.
3. Henry, d. y.
4. Caroline, b. May 26, 1761, mar. (1) DAVID LOWRY, a *Rev. Sol.*; (2) George Swain.
5. Rhoda, b. May 1, 1763, mar. John Rakestraw.
6. Patience, b. May 8, 1765, mar. John Hart (son of BENJAMIN HART, *Rev. Sol.* of Ga. and his wife, NANCY MORGAN, known in history as the heroine, "NANCY HART").
7. Jonathan, b. April 3, 1767, mar. (1) Patience Rogers; (2) Mary Colley.
8. Jane, b. Dec. 25, 1769, mar. Elizabeth Street (the parents of GOV. JOSEPH LANE of Oregon).
9. Simeon, b. 1771, mar. Judith Humphries.
10. Rebecca, b. Mar. 5, 1773, mar. JAMES LUCKIE, a *Rev. Sol.*
11. Joseph, b. Mar. 28, 1775, mar. Elizabeth Hill.
12. Mary, b. June 18, 1777, mar. Thomas Kirkpatrick. Moved to Ill.
13. Sarah, b. June 18, 1777, mar. John Kirkpatrick. Moved to Ill.
14. WINIFRED, b. Oct. 11, 1780, mar. JAMES PELEG ROGERS.
15. Jesse, Jr., b. June 12, 1782, mar. Rhoda Jolly.
16. Elizabeth, b. Sept. 6, 1786, mar. William Montgomery. Moved to Miss.

THOMAS LANE, b. Va., 1764; d. Elbert Co., Ga., Nov. 2, 1829 (will pro.). He was a *Rev. Sol.*; received 1784, bounty land of 287½ acres for his service. Mar. in Ga. 1800, NANCY HALEY (dau. of WILLIAM HALEY, and his wife, Mary Turman; *Rev. Sol.* of Wilkes (then Elbert Co.) Co., Ga.)

Children:
1. ELIZA, b. 1802, Mar. (1) Aug. 10, 1820, Elbert Co., William Forston; (2) Nathaniel Dortch. Moved to Miss. 5 children.
2. John Allen, b. Elbert Co., Sept. 13, 1806. Mar. Nancy P. Mayfield; was living 1831 in Ala.; in 1838 in Miss. and d. in Chicot Co., Ark., Aug. 15, 1883. 8 children.

WILLIAM LANE, b. Fairfax Co., Va.; d. Elbert Co., Ga. Mar. Nancy Allen. They moved to Wilkes Co. 1784, then to Elbert Co., Ga. 1791. His wife d. about 1804. He was a *Rev. Sol.* of Va.

Ten children (4 names unknown):
1. THOMAS, b. Va., 1764; came to Ga. Mar. 1800, Nancy Haley. He was a *Rev. Sol.*
2. Sampson, a Methodist Preacher; mar. —, and had 10 children.
3. William, mar. Miss Bailey. 3 children.
4. Allen.
5. Henry.
6. (Rev.) John, b. April 8, 1789, mar. Sarah Vick, of Vicksburg, Miss. 3 children.

BENJAMIN LANIER (son of Byrd Thomas Lanier and wife, Mary), b. N. C., Dec. 14, 1740; d. Screven Co., Ga., 1817. Served in Ga. Line from Effingham Co.; appointed in 1778 to purchase supplies for American Army. Was a member of the Ga. Assembly. Mar. (1) SUSANNA ANN JONES (1744-1805).

Children:
1. John Lewis, b. 1774, mar. HANNAH MILLS (dau. of THOMAS MILLS, *Rev. Sol.* of Ga., and his wife, Lucy).
2. CLEMENT, a *Rev. Sol.* of Ga.
3. Mary, b. Dec. 25, 1759.
4. Berryman, b. 1776.
5. Bird.

    6. Betsey.
    7. Hannah, mar. Robert Dickson.
    8. Lucy, mar. Philip Newton.
    9. Nancy, mar. Thomas Mills.

    LEWIS LANIER, b. Va., 1756; d. Screven Co., Ga., 1839. Enlisted Essex Co., Va. as a private was promoted to Captain. Was taken prisoner and held for nine months on a British vessel. (His son Thomas B. Lanier, applied for pension of Lewis Lanier, 1846. BENJAMIN TAYLOR of Screven Co., Ga., in the application stated that he knew him and had served with him as a *Rev. Sol.* of Va.) He mar. (1) Sept. 21, 1788, ANN BUTLER (dau. of THOMAS BUTLER, *Rev. Sol.* of Va.); (2) Ga., 1803, Esther (called Hester) Thorn (1775-1855). Will of Lewis Lanier recorded Screven Co.
Children by (1) wife:
    1. James.
    2. Thomas Butler.
    3. Mary (called Polly), mar. Robert McCall (son of CHARLES McCALL, *Rev. Sol.* of S. C. and Ga., and g-son of FRANCIS McCALL, *Rev. Sol.* of N. C.)
    4. Elizabeth, mar. Charles McCall (brother of Robert McCall).
Children by (2) wife:
    1. Noel (1811-1890), mar. 1839, Sarah Tullis.
    2. Isaac (1806-1885), mar. Sarah Hurst.
    3. Sarah, mar. Henry Strickland.
    4. Amy, mar. (1) James Johnson; (2) — Kelly.
    5. Clarissa, mar. William S. Jackson.

    TOBIAS LASSITER, b. Nash Co., N. C.; d. Greene Co., Ga., 1801. *Rev. Sol.* of N. C.; received bounty grant of 287½ acres in Ga. for his service. Mar. SARAH —. Moved to Greene Co., Ga. after 1782. Made will there, July 18, 1801 (pro. 1801).
Children (perhaps others):
    1. Benjamin.
    2. Joseph Jesse, b. N. C., Dec. 6, 1781; d. Fayette Co., Ga., Sept. 21, 1848. Mar. Henry Co., Ga., Feb. 6, 1806, Sophie McClendon. 11 children.
    3. John.
    4. Hardy, b. 1780, mar. Elizabeth Kieth.
    5. Christiana.
    6. Rebecca.

    JOHN LASTINGER, b. Germany about 1740, came to America, landed at Charleston, S. C., then settled at Ebenezer, Ga. Served as private Ga. Troops; received bounty land. Mar. 1765, ANNA BARBARA —. (She came over on the same ship with him).
Children:
    1. Hannah, b. Aug. 25, 1768, mar. JOHN GROOVER (or Gruber), *Rev. Sol.* of Ga.
    2. John George, b. Nov. 24, 1776.
    3. Barbara, mar. James English. 9 children.
    4. Abner, mar. Ann Beasley.
    5. Andrew, b. Feb. 12, 1778, mar. Mary Parker.
    6. Elizabeth, b. Feb. 12, 1778, mar. — Millen.
    7. Mary, b. May 22, 1780.
    8. David, mar. Sarah —. Lived Bulloch Co., Ga.
    9. Tabitha.
    10. Sarah.

    ROGER LAWSON, b. Va., 1715; d. (now Jefferson Co.), Ga., Aug. 6, 1803. Lived in Rowan Co., N. C. Served with Ga. Troops; received bounty grant of land in Ga. for his service (Washington Co.). Mar. (1) 1752, HANNAH THOMPSON (dau. of Rev. John Thompson, of Penn. and N. C.); (2) Margaret McGill.
Children by (1) wife:
    1. HUGH LAWSON, b. 1755; d. Ga., 1802. Served at Capt. Ga. Militia; wounded at Augusta, Ga. Mar. (1) Ann —; (2) Sarah Whitaker.

2. JOHN THOMPSON LAWSON, b. Brunswick Co., Va., 1757; d. Twiggs Co., Ga., 1816. Served as Capt., then Colonel Ga. Militia; was given bounty grant of land in Liberty Co., Ga. Mar. Columbia Co., S. C., Sept. 1, 1778, ALICE MOORE, b. 1760, d. 1798. She was a *Rev. Patriot*; deeds recorded in S. C. History.

Their children were: 1. Roger, b. 1799, mar. Lucy Smith; 2. Charles Moore; 3. Andrew; 4. Hannah, b. 1785, mar. 1804, Archibald McIntyre, b. N. C., 1776; d. Thomas Co., Ga., 1830.

3. ROGER LAWSON, JR., *Rev. Sol.*, d. 1801.

4. WILLIAM LAWSON, killed as a *Rev. Sol.* of Ga.

5. ANDREW THOMPSON LAWSON, b. Ga., 1760; d. at Augusta, Ga., 1822. Served in Ga. Militia. Was a refugee after the fall of Charleston, S. C.; received bounty land in Ga. for his service. Mar. (1) 1792, Mary Moore Barry (dau. of ANDREW BARRY, *Rev. Sol.*, b. Penn., 1746; d. Spartanburg, S. C., 1811, and his wife, MARGARET CATHERINE MOORE, a *Rev. Patriot*); (2) Elizabeth Eakin.

6. ANDREW BARRY LAWSON, mar. Jane Patterson, lived in Jefferson Co., Ga.

7. MARY LAWSON, mar. Michael Burke.

8. HANNAH THOMPSON LAWSON, mar. Moses Speer.

Child of Roger Lawson and (2) wife, Margaret McGill.

Margaret McGill Lawson, mar. JOHN GAMBLE of Jefferson Co., Ga. He was a *Rev. Sol.*

Children of ANDREW THOMPSON LAWSON and his wife, Mary Moore Barry (1779-1802): 1. Margaret, mar. Alexander Nevin; 2. Mary Barry (1802-1869), mar. Benjamin Sessions; 3. Elizabeth Hannah; 4. Andrew Barry, b. 1794.

HENRY LEE (Light Horse Harry Lee), Col. of Cavalry in Rev. War, b. Va., 1756; d. Dungeness, Cumberland Island, Ga., Mar. 25, 1818. He was buried in chapel of Washington and Lee University, Va. after removal from Dungeness, Cumberland Island, Ga. He mar. (1) His cousin, Matilda Lee (dau. of Philip Ludwell Lee); (2) Ann Hill Carter.

Child by (2) wife:

ROBERT EDWARD LEE, b. Jan. 19, 1807; d. Oct. 12, 1880, mar. Mary Ann Randolph Custis (GEN. ROBERT EDWARD LEE of the Confederate States Army) (1861-1865).

On the Stone at the Grave of Henry Lee, at Dungeness, Cumberland Island, Ga. was the following inscription: "Sacred to the Memory of General Henry Lee, of Virginia. Obiit 25, March, 1818; aet 63.

ROBERT LEVERETT, d. Lincoln Co., Ga., 1806; received grant of land for his service as a *Rev. Sol.* Mar. Patsey Hammock.

Children:

1. Nancy.
2. Jordan.
3. Patsey.
4. Betsey.
5. Absolem.
6. Sallie.
7. Robert.
8. Hardy.
9. Polly.
10. Gricy.
11. Peggy.

JOHN LEWIS, b. Chowan Co., N. C., 1733; d. Burke Co., Ga., Jan. 3, 1818. Mar. 1768, Nancy Lavinia Ward, b. N. C., 1744; d. Ga., 1784. Served as private N. C. Line.

Children (known):

1. Jesse.
2. Mary.
3. James.
4. Matthew.

JOHN LEWIS (son of John Lewis and his wife, Sarah Taliaferro of Va), b. Albemarle Co., Va., 1757; d (now Cass Co.), Ga., Nov. 4, 1840. Served in the Va. Army at Brandywine, Monmouth and

Yorktown, under Marquis de La Fayette. Mar. 1786, Ann Berry Earle, b. 1763; d. (Cass Co.), Ga. 1845 (dau. of JOHN EARLE, b. in Va., 1737, a *Rev. Sol.* of S. C. Rangers and his wife, Thomasine Berry) (Grave of John Lewis marked by Ga. D. A. R. Inscription on tomb: *A Soldier of the Revolution*). Buried at Baptist Church Cemetery, near Adairsville, Ga. They removed to Ga. 1836. They reared 7 children.

JOHN LINDSEY, b. Halifax Co., Va., 1750; d. Wilkes Co., Ga., 1808. Served as Major and Colonel; wounded and known as "Old Silver Fist." Placed on Invalid Pension Roll for his service in S. C. and Ga. Mar. Clarissa (Bullock) Sims (dau. of NATHANIEL and MARY BULLOCK, a *Rev. Sol*; Wilkes Co., Ga.)

Children:

1. Clarissa Harlow Bullock Lindsey.
2. Numesis Creswell Christmas Lindsey, mar. 1807, John Gordon.
3. Matilda Marbury Somervill Lindsey (1789-1826), mar. Andrew Baskins Stevens.
4. Sallie Collier Billingsea Lindsey.
5. Jackson Clark Watkins Lindsey.
6. Jennie M. Lindsey, of St. Mary's, Ga.
7. Benjamin Fero Hamilton Lindsey.

He had brother, Benjamin Lindsey (name spelled Lindsay).

JAMES LITTLE, b. Va., 1737; d. Franklin Co., Ga., 1807. Served as Capt., Ga. Militia; for a time in charge of a block-house at Cherokee Ford, on Savannah river. Fought in 22 battles; received bounty grant of land in Franklin Co., Ga., for his service, June 6, 1784. Mar. 1765, ISABELLA HAMILTON (1741-1821).

Children:

1. James H. (1769-1856), mar. Annie Young.
2. John.
3. Ellen.
4. William.

(Perhaps other children).

MICAJAH LITTLE, b. Martin Co., N. C.; d. Wilkes Co., Ga., 1809. Served as Lieut. in Capt. William Brinkley's Co., 3rd N. C. Regiment; received bounty land in Ga. for his service. Mar. 1781, MARY BRACKENBERRY.

Children:

1. Cherry, mar. 1801, John Bethune.
2. Littleberry.
3. John E.
4. William.

NOTE: Found in the Department of Archives, Atlanta, Ga. (1935), claims for *Revolutionary Services* of JOHN LEFTWICK and JOHN LYNCH, Nov. 7, 1814, in the office of Ordinary, Putnam Co., Ga.; also in same office the claims of ABRAHAM CUTLIFF and WILLIAM J. STEPHENS, Sept. 20, 1823, *Rev. Sols.* of Putnam Co., Ga.

EVANS LONG, b. Culpeper Co., Va.; d. Twiggs Co., Ga., 1819. (He was the youngest of five brothers who all served as *Rev. Sols.*, viz: GABRIEL LONG, ANDERSON LONG, NICHOLAS LONG, NIMROD LONG and EVANS LONG).

He served as private, Capt. Long's Co., Col. Morgan's 11th Va. Regiment. Mar. LUCY APPERSON.

Children:

1. Mary (1783-1872), mar. William Crocker (1777-1835).
2. Margaret, mar. Elijah Clarke, Jr. (son of GEN ELIJAH CLARKE, of Ga.).
3. Frances, mar. William Hudson.
4. Lunceford, mar. Nancy Jackson.
5. Lucinda, mar. John Owens.
6. Sarah Ann, mar. Tuttle Moreland.
7. Nimrod Washington, mar. Catherine Davis.

NICHOLAS LONG, d. Wilkes Co., Ga., 1819. Served in N. C. Line; received bounty land in Ga. for his service as a *Rev. Sol.* He also served as Colonel of the 43d Regiment in the *War of 1812.* Member *Provincial Congress.* Mar. (1) —; (2) MARY McKINNEY.

Children:

1. Margaret, mar. Thomas Telfair (son of Gov. Edward Telfair, of Ga., a *Rev. Sol.*). Lived at Savannah, Ga.
2. Sarah Rebecca, mar. James Rembert.
3. Eliza, mar. — DuBose.
4. Eugenia, mar. Lock Weems.
5. Richard H., mar. Nancy Hay.
6. John, lived in Washington Co., Ga.

REUBEN LONG, b. Va.; d. 1792. Served as a *Patriot* of Va. Mar. MARY —. They were the parents of GABRIEL, EVANS, ANDERSON, NICHOLAS, and NIMROD LONG. They also had 3 daughters:

1. Fannie, mar. Daniel Richardson.
2. Peggy, mar. Robert Kay.
3. Polly, mar. John Nash.

SAMUEL LONG, b. Ireland, 1753; d. Paoli, Madison Co., Ga., July 7, 1822; came to Penn., 1762. Served in the Penn. Army, and served also as Capt. under Marquis de La Fayette, and was at the surrender of Cornwallis at Yorktown. Served Cumberland Co., Penn., Militia, 2nd Batt., 1781. Mar. ANN WILLIAMSON, b. Ireland, 1757; d. 1829. They moved to Madison Co., Ga., 1792.

Children:

1. JAMES, b. Penn., 1781, mar. in Ga., Elizabeth Ware. Their son, CRAWFORD W. LONG (1815-1876), mar. 1842, Mary Caroline Swain (dau. of George Swain). A statue of DR. CRAWFORD W. LONG has been placed, by Ga., in "Statuary Hall of Fame," National Capitol, Washington, D. C., as the *"Discoverer of Anesthesia."*
2. Thomas, mar. Isabella McCurdy.
3. Ann.
4. Mary.
5. Joseph.
6. Samuel, Jr.

CHARLES LOWRY (son of CHARLES LOWRY, *Rev. Sol.* of Va.), b. Va.; d. Cass Co., Ga., 1847. Served in the Va. Continental Army and moved to Franklin Co., Ga., 1812. Mar. in Va., Miss Reese.

Children:

1. David.
2. James.
3. Solomon.
4. John.
5. Samuel.
6. Elizabeth.
7. Mary.
8. Martha.
9. Sarah.
10. Thomas.
(5 other children d. y.)
David, James, Solomon and John were all *Sols. of the War of 1812.*

DAVID LOVE, b. Anson Co., N. C., 1740; d. Greene Co., Ga., Nov. 30, 1798. Served as Lieut. Col., N. C. Troops. Member Provincial Congress. Mar. Oct. 22, 1772, JEAN (JANE) BLEWETT (1756-1817). Grave marked.

Children:

1. d. y.
2. Robertus.
3. Acksah, mar. Thomas Sparks.

4. Vertus Mary.
5. Beloved.
6. Chaste Easter, mar. Abner Turner. (Had 15 children).
7. Allelujah, mar. 1812, Henry Rogers.
8. Ovid Blewett.
9. Josephine.
10. Friend Ovid.

JAMES LUCKIE, b. Va., 1761; d. Oglethorpe Co., Ga., April 6, 1822. He served as a *Rev. Sol.*; drew land in Ga. for his service. Mar. Rebecca Lane, b. 1773 (dau. of JESSE LANE, *Rev. Sol.*, and his wife, Winifred Aycock). They are both buried in cemetery at Cherokee Corner Church, Oglethorpe Co., Ga.

Children:
1. David, mar. Margaret Buyers (Byers).
2. Lorena, mar. Gen. Williamson.
3. Alexander.
4. William Dickinson (1800–1870), mar. Eliza Buckner.
5. Mary, mar. Columbus D. Pace.

GEORGE LUMPKIN, b. King and Queen Co., Va., 1723; d. Wilkes Co., Ga., 1799. Served as Capt. in *Rev. Army* in Va. Removed to Ga., 1784. Mar. (1) 1748, in Va., Mary Cody (1728–1799); (2) 1780, Lucy Hopson (1764–1820), dau. of HENRY HOPSON, *Rev. Sol.* of Va., and his wife, Martha Nevil (Neville).

Child by (1) wife:
JOHN LUMPKIN, b. Va., 1763; d. Ga., 1834.

Children by (2) wife:
1. William.
2. Wilson.
3. Jack.
4. George.
5. Henry Hopson.
6. Samuel.
7. Robert.
8. Martha.
9. Joseph Henry (1799–1867), mar. Callender Grieve.
10. Thomas Jefferson.
11. James Nevil.

JEREMIAH LUMSDEN, b. Va., 1753; d. Ga., Jan. 18, 1837. Served as a private, Va. Troops; received bounty grant of land for his service. Mar. ELIZABETH BELCHER (1757–1830).

Children:
1. Wilmoth (1779).
2. Lucy (1780).
3. Elizabeth.
4. Sally.
5. Amy.
6. Polly.
7. Susanna.
8. Phoebe.
9. John, mar. Susanna Jones.
10. Nelly P.
11. Jeremiah, Jr.
12. Charles W.
13. Jesse M.

CHARLES McCALL (son of FRANCIS McCALL, a *Rev. Sol.* of N. C.), b. Penn. (on Va. Line), 1732; d. Bulloch Co., Ga., 1816. He was a *Patriot* who rendered material aid during the

Rev. War, and also served in S. C. Troops at the "Battle of McCall's Field," his home place in S. C., on Lynch's Creek.

Five of his sons were *Rev. Sols.* of S. C., viz:

1. JOHN.
2. DAVID.
3. GEORGE.
4. HENRY.
5. WILLIAM.

All but John removed to Ga. with their father.

CHARLES McCALL received bounty land in Effingham Co., Ga., for his service. Also served as H. R. and in civil offices in Ga. (Record for Society of War of 1812.) Mar. (1) in S. C., 1755, CELETE ANN (called Nancy) WILLIAMS (dau. of REV. ROBERT WILLIAMS, First Pastor Welch Neck Baptist Church, Society Hill, S. C., and his wife, Ann Boykin); (2) Bulloch Co., Ga. Hannah Everett.

Children by (1) wife:

1. JOHN, remained in S. C. A *Rev. Sol.*
2. DAVID, mar. Frances —. Moved to Ga. A *Rev. Sol.*
3. GEORGE, mar. (1) Elizabeth Burnett; (2) Elizabeth Sanders. Removed to Ga., then to S. C., where he d. A *Rev. Sol.* of S. C.
4. WILLIAM, mar. (1) Ann (called Nancy) Fletcher (dau. of WILLIAM FLETCHER, *Rev. Sol.* of Ga., and his wife, Elizabeth McIntosh); (2) Mary Pearce (dau. of JOSHUA PEARCE, JR., *Rev. Sol.* of Ga.).
5. HENRY, private, S. C. Troops, from Cheraw District. Returned to S. C. *Rev. Sol.*
6. Eleanor, mar. Ogeechee, Ga., 1786, McKEEN GREEN, JR., a *Rev. Sol.* of Ga. (son of McKEEN GREEN, SR., *Rev. Sol.* of Ga.).
7. Nancy, mar. STEPHEN McCOY, a *Rev. Sol.*
8. Robert, mar. Bulloch Co., Ga., Mary (called Polly) Lanier (dau. of LEWIS LANIER, *Rev. Sol.* of Ga.).
9. Francis, mar. (1) Sarah Pearce (dau. of JOSHUA PEARCE, JR., *Rev. Sol.*); (2) Sarah Mattox, widow, of Tattnall Co., Ga.
10. Charles, Jr., mar. Betsey B. (Lanier) Stith (dau. of LEWIS LANIER, *Rev. Sol.*).
11. Nathaniel, mar. 1807, Mary Johnson.
12. Mary, mar. William Wright.

Children by (2) wife, Hannah Everett:

1. Sarah.
2. John.

Grave of CHARLES McCALL, *Rev. Sol.* located in the Everett family burying ground in Screven Co., Ga.

DAVID McCALL (son of CHARLES McCALL, *Rev. Sol.* of S. C. and Ga.), b. S. C.; d. Ga. Served as private, 1782, in Capt. Giles' Co., Col. William Hill's S. C. Regiment; received land, 1786, in Effingham (now Bulloch) Co., Ga., for his service. Mar. Frances (called Fanny) —.

Children:

1. Selaway, moved to Irwin Co., Ga.
2. John, moved to Irwin Co., Ga.
3. David, Jr., mar. Ellender Johnson. Lived in Lowndes Co., Ga. 8 children.
4. James, mar. Rebecca McMullan, moved to Lowndes Co., Ga.

(Perhaps other children).

HUGH McCALL (son of JAMES McCALL, *Rev. Sol.* of N. C., and his wife, Janet Harris, and brother of CAPT. JAMES McCALL, *Rev. Sol.* of S. C.), was a *Rev. Sol.* of N. C.; received bounty grant of land in Wilkes Co., Ga., for his service. (He was an uncle of HUGH McCALL (son of Col. James McCall), who was a *Sol. of 1812*, and the State Historian of Ga., and who d. in Savannah, Ga., unmar.).

GEORGE McCALL (son of CHARLES McCALL, *Rev. Sol.*), b. Lynch's Creek, S. C., Pedee District, Mar. 10, 1760; came to Effingham Co., Ga., 1786; returned to S. C., where he d. at Society Hill, Jan. 9, 1837. He served under Capt. James Gregg, Major Thornby. Later, together with his three brothers, JOHN, HENRY, and WILLIAM McCALL, joined the command under Gen. Francis Marion. Mar. (1) Elizabeth Burnett; (2) Elizabeth Sanders (dau. of NATHANIEL SANDERS, *Rev. Sol.* of S. C.).

Children by (1) wife, Elizabeth Burnett:
1. Nathaniel, mar. Sabrina B. Long.
2. Elhannon.
3. David.
4. Harriet.
5. Robert.
6. Francis.
7. William.

Children by (2) wife, Elizabeth Sanders:
1. James Sanders, mar. Elizabeth Ellen Lucretia Muldrow.
2. Moses Sanders, mar. Elizabeth Gregg.
3. George Jay Washington (1801–1871), mar. (1) Harriet Harlee; (2) Louisa Caroline Huggins.

JOHN McCALL (son of THOMAS McCALL, *Rev. Sol.*, and his wife, Rachel McCall), b. S. C.; d. Ga. Served as private in Capt. Giles' Co., Col. William Hill's S. C. Regiment. State Troops. Served 10 months in Sumpter's Brigade. Mar. Sarah —.

Children:
1. James.
2. Elizabeth, mar. Rev. Mann Dutton, of Gloucester Co., Va. Their dau., Henrietta Dutton, mar. Robert Raines Terrell.
3. Henrietta.
4. George E.
5. Thomas.
6. John, Jr.
7. William.
8. Hannah.
(Will on file, Effingham Co., Ga.)

SHERROD McCALL (son of THOMAS McCALL, *Rev. Sol.*, and his wife, Rachel McCall), b. S. C., 1766; d. Gadsden Co., Fla. Moved to Ga.; received a grant of land in Effingham Co., Ga., for his service as a *Rev. Sol.* of S. C., Dec., 1784. Was a member of Ga. State Legislature, 1808–1813. (Record for papers for War of 1812.) Mar. Margaret —, of Bulloch Co., Ga.

Children:
1. Elizabeth, mar. Eli Kennedy of Bulloch Co., Ga. (son of FRANCIS KENNEDY, *Rev. Sol.* of S. C. and Ga., and his wife, Sarah McGee), b. S. C., 1785.
2. William.
3. Sarah.
4. Jesse.
5. Thomas.
6. Allen.
7. Seaborn.
8. John.
9. Margaret.
10. Sherrod, Jr.
11. George.

(REV.) THOMAS McCALL (changed his name to McCaule while at College, son of JAMES McCALL and Janet Harris), b. Penn.; d. Savannah, Ga., Sept. 13, 1796. Served as Chaplain in S. C. Regiment. "He fanned while preaching the flames of patriotism in his Church and cherished the spirit of Independence." (From funeral notice.) Mar. (1) Jane Harris; (2) Mar. 8, 1796, Eliza H. Montfort (widow of Robert Montfort of Savannah, Ga.).

THOMAS McCALL (son of CAPT. JAMES McCALL, *Rev. Sol.*, b. Penn., 1741; d. S. C., April 16, 1781, and his wife, Elizabeth McCall), b. Mecklenburg Co., N. C., Mar. 19, 1764; d. Laurens Co., Ga., 1839. He served as private, S. C. Troops; received bounty grant of land in Ga. for his service. Was appointed Surveyor General of Ga., and also served as a *Sol. of the War of 1812.*

Mar. (1) April 1, 1787, Henrietta Fall (1767–1797); (2) July, 1798, Elizabeth Mary Ann Smith (1775–1831). Buried in old cemetery, Dublin, Ga., by the side of his (2) wife, Elizabeth Mary Ann McCall. (Grave marked).

Children by (1) wife:

1. Eliza Henrietta (1788–1795).
2. Selina Mary Ann, mar. Virgil H. Vivien.
3. Louisa Freeman, mar. George Gaines.
4. Thomas William.
5. James, d. y.

Children by (2) wife:

1. Sarah Georgiana, mar. Col. Eli W. B. Spivey.
2. Elizabeth Smith, mar. as (3) wife, Dr. Thomas Moore.
3. Margaret, d. y.
4. Harriet Moore, mar. Major Luke Mizell.
5. Janet Harris, mar. Ira Stanley.
6. Margaret Sanders, mar. Jeremiah H. Yopp.

NOTE: Elizabeth McCall (wife of JAMES McCALL) was the dau. of THOMAS McCALL, *Rev. Sol.* of N. C., and his wife, Margaret Greenfield (dau. of Samuel Greenfield, of Md. His dau., Elizabeth Greenfield, mar. James Barr., *Rev. Sol.* of S. C.).

THOMAS McCALL (son of FRANCIS McCALL, *Rev. Sol.* of Mecklenburg Co., N. C.), mar· his cousin, RACHEL McCALL (dau. of JAMES McCALL, *Rev. Sol.* of Mecklenburg Co., N. C.)· He was b. Va., near Penn. line, 1740; moved with his parents to N. C. Served in the S. C. Militia; received, in 1784, bounty grant of land in Effingham Co., Ga., for his service; d. Bulloch Co., Ga., 1818. His wife d. at same place, 1821.

Children:

1. ALEXANDER, *Rev. Sol.* of S. C.; received bounty grant of land in Wilkes Co., Ga.
2. JOHN, *Rev. Sol.*, mar. Sarah —.
3. SHERROD, *Rev. Sol.*, mar. Margaret —.
4. George.
5. Francis, mar. Miss Rawls.
6. Thomas, Jr., mar. Sarah —.
7. Jesse, mar. Mary —.
8. Marcia, mar. JOHN MOORE, *Rev. Sol.* of S. C. and Ga.; private in Capt. Giles' Co., Col. Wm. Hill's Regiment. Moved to Ga.
9. Ann, mar. — Musgrove.
10. Sarah, mar. Henry Williams.
11. William.
12. Abraham.
13. Eliza.

WILLIAM McCALL (son of CHARLES McCALL, *Rev. Sol.* of S. C. and Ga., and his wife, Celete Ann Williams), b. Lynche's Creek, near Society Hill, S. C., 1766; d. Screven Co., Ga., Jan. 12, 1830. Served as private in S. C., under Gen. Francis Marion. Was at Snow Island. Moved with his family to Effingham (now Screven) Co., Ga.; received land grant for his service; also was *Sol. of 1812.* Mar. (1) in S. C., 1789, Ann (called Nancy) Fletcher (dau. of WILLIAM FLETCHER, *Rev. Sol.* of S. C. and Ga., and his (2) wife, Elizabeth McIntosh); (2) 1800, Mary Pearce (dau. of JOSHAU PEARCE, JR., *Rev. Sol.* of Effingham Co., Ga., d. in Miss.).

Children by (1) wife:

1. Selete (Celete).
2. William, d. y.
3. George Robert Francis, mar. Luvincia Fain (dau. of THOMAS FAIN, *Rev. Sol.* of Ga.).
4. MOSES NATHANIEL (1792–1885), mar. (1) 1820, Caroline Griner (dau. of PHILIP GRINER, *Rev. Sol.* of Ga.). He was a *Sol. of the War of 1812*; mar. (2) April 1836, Catherine (Porter) Dopson (widow of William Dopson). He had 14 children.

Children by (2) wife:

1. Joshua William Pearce (1801–1864), mar. Mary Trowell.

2. Mary.
3. William.
4. Charles H., mar. (1) Miss Boynton; (2) Lucinda (Tharpe) Lowe.
5. Francis Stephen, mar. Ann Dopson.
6. John G., mar. Jane Dopson.
7. Sarah, mar. James Griner.
He was also a Baptist Minister. His grave, as a *Rev. Sol.*, has been marked by the Briar Creek Chapter, Ga. D. A. R., Sylvania Ga.

NOTE: For McCall history, see *McCall-Tidwell and Allied Families*, by Ettie Tidwell McCall.

STEPHEN McCOY, b. S C.; d. Ga. Mar. Jan. 27, 1792, Nancy McCall (dau. of CHARLES McCALL, *Rev. Sol.* of S. C. and Ga.). He was a *Rev. Sol.* of S. C. in 1782.
Children (known):
1. Robert.
2. Mary (called Polly), b. 1798, mar. (1) — Ellerbe; (2) Jan. 16, 1820, Reuben H. Jones. 9 children.

THOMAS McCLENDON, b. Edinburg, Scotland, 1734; d. Henry Co., Ga., 1798. Place of residence during the War was Montgomery Co., N. C. Served in N. C. Militia; received grant of land in Ga. for his service. Mar. Sarah Cooper, d. Ala.
Children (known):
1. Jacob.
2. Jeptha.
3. Wylie.
4. Cynthia.
5. Lydia.
6. JOSEPH, b. June 1751; d. Ga., 1837. Served as *Rev. Sol.* in Ga. Militia; received grant of land in Ga. for his service. Mar. OLIVE BLAKE.
7. THOMAS, JR., b. 1758; d. Ga. Served in Ga. Line. Mar. ELIZABETH —. Their dau., Sophia, mar. Joseph Jesse Lasseter (son of TOBIAS LASSETER, *Rev. Sol.* of Ga.).

ISAAC McCLENDON, b. Scotland, 1754; d. Wilkes Co., Ga., 1819. Lived in N. C.; moved to Wilkes Co., Ga., 1775. Mar. in N. C., 1775, MARY FINCHER. Was a *Rev. Sol.*; received bounty grant of land in Wilkes Co., Ga., for his service.
Children:
1. William.
2. Simpson.
3 Penelope, mar. Burwell Aycock.
4. Clarissa, mar. Zimri Tait.
5. Lewis.
6. Dorothy, mar. James Walker.
7. Francis.

JACOB McCLENDON, SR., b. 1725; came to Ga., Oct. 10, 1774; d. Wilkes Co., Ga., 1791. Served as *Rev. Sol.* of Ga. under Gen. Clarke; received bounty grant of land for his service. Mar. Martha —, d. 1827.
Children:
1. Isaac.
2. Samuel.
3. TRAVIS, a *Rev. Sol.* of Ga.
4. Dennis.
5. Amos.
6. Jemina.
7. Laney.
8. Penelope.
9. NANCY, b. about 1758, mar. WILLIAM HEARD, *Rev. Sol.* of Va.
10. Betheny.
11. Francis.
12. Jacob.

JOSEPH McCLENDON (son of THOMAS McCLENDON, SR., *Rev. Sol.* of N. C. and Ga.), b. June, 1751; d. Coweta Co., Ga., 1837. Served as private, Ga. Militia, under General Elijah Clarke. Mar. Olive Blake (dau. of WILLIAM BLAKE, *Rev. Sol.*, and his wife, Lucy (Allen) Mobley of Elbert Co., Ga.). He was also a *Sol. of the War of 1812.*

THOMAS McCLENDON, JR. (son of THOMAS McCLENDON, SR., *Rev. Sol.* of N. C. and Ga.), b. 1758; d. Ga. Served as private, Ga. Militia, under Gen. Elijah Clarke; received bounty grant of land in Ga. for his service. Mar. ELIZABETH —. Their dau., Sophie McClendon, mar. Henry Co., Ga., Joseph Jesse Lasseter.

JOHN H. McCRANIE came from Scotland to N. C. Settled Montgomery Co., Ga., then Telfair Co., Ga. Mar. Katherine Lashley. He was a *Rev. Sol.* of N. C.

Children:
  1. Daniel, mar. Jeanette Hendley.
  2. Neal.
  3. John.
  4. Malcom.
  5. Roderick.
  6. Katherine, mar. John Watson.

ALEXANDER McDONALD, b. 1750; d. McIntosh Co., 1844. Served as Sergeant, 2nd S. C. Regiment, under Lieut. Col. Francis Marion. Enlisted Nov. 4, 1775; on pay rolls to Nov. 1, 1779. Mar. 1771, CHRISTINE McLEOD. They lived and d. in McIntosh Co., Ga.

Children (known):
  1. William, b. 1772; d. McIntosh Co., 1845; mar. (1) Feriby Farrar; (2) Zilpha Farrar. *Sol. of the War of 1812.* Enlisted at Darien, Ga.
  2. Daniel, mar. Margaret Buchan. They d. in Thomas Co., Ga. *Sol. of the War of 1812.* Enlisted at Darien, Ga.
  3. Alexander.

DAVID McCURDY, b. County Antrim, Ireland, 1709; came to America and located in Penn. Was a *Patriot* and *Rev. Sol.* of Penn. Mar. SUSAN MADDEN. In 1787 he moved with his son John's family to Ga., where he d. 1833, at the age of 124 years.

Children:
  1. JOHN, *Rev. Sol.* of Penn., b. Westmoreland Co., Penn., moved to Madison Co., Ga., 1787. Served as private, Penn. Militia. Mar. Elizabeth Groves.
      Children: 1. Stephen; 2. John S., b. 1790, mar. (1) Rebecca Woods; (2) Mary Kelly; 3. William; 4. James; 5. Alexander; 6. Samuel; 7. Robert.
  2. DAVID, *Rev. Sol.* of Penn.
  3. ROBERT, *Rev. Sol.* of Penn.
  4. SAMUEL, *Rev. Sol.* of Penn.
  5. DANIEL, *Rev. Sol.* of Penn.

ANGUS McCURRY, SR., b. Scotland, about 1755; settled N. C. 1774. Served as private, N. C. Militia; received bounty land in Elbert (now Hart) Co., Ga., for his service. (Grave marked.) Buried Mt. Zion Methodist Churchyard; d. after 1839. Mar. Catherine —.

Children:
  1. Margaret, mar. John McDonald.
  2. Sarah, mar. John Gordon.
  3. John, mar. his cousin, Sarah McCurry.
  4. Daniel L.
  5. Angus, Jr., mar. Elizabeth Davis (dau. of JOHN DAVIS, *Rev. Sol.* of Va., and his wife, NANCY WOMACK. Children of John Davis were: 1. John; 2. Elizabeth; 3. Julia; 4. Lucy; 5. Sally; 6. Lucretia; 7. Nancy; 8. Polly; 9. Frances; 10. James; 11. Richard Davis.

MICAJAH McGEHEE, b. Augusta Co., Va., 1735; d. Broad river Settlement, Wilkes Co., Ga., July 31, 1811. Served with Va. Troops; received bounty land in Wilkes Co., Ga., for his service. Mar. 1769, ANN BAYTOP SCOTT (dau. of CAPT. JAMES SCOTT, *Rev. Sol.* of Va., and later of S. C., and his wife, Frances Collier).

Children:

1. Thomas, mar. Betsey Gilmer. Moved to Ala.
2. James.
3. Frank.
4. Abner, b. Prince Edward Co., Va., 1779; d. Ala., 1855; mar. (1) Charlotte Spencer; (2) Jane (Gilmer) Johnson (dau. of John Gilmer and his wife, Mildred Meriwether, and widow of Thomas Johnson); (3) Mary Russell Graves.
5. William, mar. (1) Miss Taliaferro; (2) Miss Watkins. Moved to Miss.
6. Edmund, mar. Miss Cosby. Moved to La.
7. Jack, mar. Melinda Hill (dau. of Miles Hill). Settled in Wilkes Co., Ga., then Miss.
8. Abram.
9. Hugh, mar. Miss White.
10. Betsey, mar. Abram Hill.
11. Sally, mar. (1) Thomas Hill; (2), as (2) wife, Dyonosius Oliver.
12. Lucinda, mar. Dyonosius Oliver.

MICAJAH McGEHEE was the first of the settlers of Wilkes Co., Ga., to plant a peach orchard on the waters of Broad river, and first to turn the fruit into brandy; it was said, too, that he built the first comfortable house on Broad river.

JOHN McGOUGH, b. Ireland, 1761; d. White Plains, Greene Co., Ga., 1847. Served in the S. C. Militia, from Abbeville District; received bounty land in Ga. Mar. MARGARET E. MILL. One son:

Robert, b. S. C., Mar. 28, 1786; d. Ga. *Sol. of War of 1812.* Mar. 1810, Sanda Cabaniss. 10 children.

JOHN McLAUGHLIN, b. Ireland, Jan. 1756; came to N. C.; d. Warren Co., Ga., 1836. Enlisted 1776, served under Capt. Robert Smith, Col. Polk, 4th N. C. Regiment. In Battles of Sullivan's Island; Brandywine; Germantown. Sergeant under Gen. Davidson and Gen. Rutherford. On Pension Roll, Warren Co., Ga., 1832. Mar. Oct. 1825, ELEANOR WILLIAMS, widow. She mar. (3) John Matthews. She drew pension as widow of a *Rev. Sol.* in Ga.

MAJOR GEN. LACHLAN McINTOSH, b. Scotland Mar. 17, 1725; d. Savannah, Ga., Feb. 20, 1806; came to Ga. 1735. (In Jan. 1775, a District Congress was held in St. Andrew's Parish, Ga., endorsing the "Resolutions of the Great American Congress," and LACHLAN, WILLIAM, and GEORGE McINTOSH, brothers, signed this endorsement.) He served as Colonel of the 1st Batt. of Troops appointed from Ga. by the Continental Congress, Jan. 6, 1776. Member of the Council of Safety. Transferred (after his duel with Button Gwinnett at Savannah, Ga.) 1779 for his service in Va. under Gen. Washington's immediate command. His son, CAPT. LACHLAN McINTOSH, JR., and JOHN BERRIEN were with him, serving as Staff officers. Served with Troops in Western Va. and Penn. Was returned to Ga. as second in command under Gen. Lincoln at the Siege of Savannah. When Charleston, S. C., was surrendered to Gen. Clinton, he was taken prisoner and later exchanged for Gen. O'Hara. Delegate to Continental Congress, 1784. Mar. SARAH THREADCRAFT (left no descendants in male line).

Daus.:

1. Catherine McCauley, mar. Charles Harris.
2. Hetty, mar. 1793, John Peter Warde.

Sons:

1. Lachlan, Jr., d. at Camden Co., Ga., Feb. 15, 1783.
2. Hamden, mar. Catherine C. Nephew.

COL. WILLIAM McINTOSH, b. Scotland; d. McIntosh Co., Ga. Served as Capt., later Col. of Ga. Continental Troops. Member Provincial Congress 1775. Mar. MARY MACKEY. Two of their children were:

1. Margery (1754–1818), mar. James Spalding. They lived at St. Simons Island, Ga.
2. John, a *Rev. Sol.* and a Maj.-Gen. in the *War of 1812*, mar. (1) Agnes Hightower Stevens; (2) Mrs. C. Hillary; (3) Sarah Swinton.

LIEUT. CHRISTOPHER HILLARY, a *Rev. Sol.*, had dau., Maria, who mar. Major William J. McIntosh (son of COL. JOHN McINTOSH, *Rev. Sol.*).

JAMES McMULLEN, SR., b. Scotland, 1758; came to Halifax, N. S., then to Mass. Served with Mass. Troops as drummer boy, at Lexington, Mass. Moved to S. C. and served with S. C. Troops; received bounty grant of land. Moved to Bulloch Co., Ga. Mar. SARAH MINTON of S. C., b. 1765. D. Bulloch Co., Ga.

Two sons:
1. William, b. S. C., 1782; d. 1847; mar. 1803, Lavinia Fain.
2. James, b. Ga., Mar. 6, 1788, mar. 1811, Rebecca Fain.
   Both brothers moved, 1846, to Lowndes (now Thomas) Co., Ga.

JOHN McMULLEN (OR McMULLAN, McMULLIN), b. Dublin, Ireland, 1740; came to Orange Co., Va.; d. Elbert (now Hart) Co., Ga., Dec. 1817. Served in Col. William Johnson's 11th Va. Regiment; was granted land for his service on Swift Run, Orange Co., Va., by the commonwealth of Va. Mar. (1) 1759, THEODOSIA ELIZABETH BEASLEY; (2) Elizabeth Stowers (1763–1848), Ga. (dau. of MARK STOWERS, *Rev. Sol.*).

Children by (1) wife:
1. James.
2. Mary, mar. Lewis Powell.
3. PATRICK, *Rev. Sol.*, b. Va., 1761; d. Ga.; mar. (1) —; (2) — Dobbs; received bounty land in Ga. One son, Sinclair, mar. Elizabeth Ballenger.
4. Catherine.
5. John.

Children by (2) wife:
1. Neal, mar. Polly Thornton.
2. Jeremiah, mar. Sarah Harper.
3. Lewis, mar. Francis Stowers.
4. Thomas, mar. Sally Gaines.
5. Fielding, mar. Polly Dollar.
6. Nancy.
7. Sinclair, mar. Clarissa Richardson (dau. of AMOS RICHARDSON, *Rev. Sol.* of Va. and Ga., and his wife, Susan Smith).
8. Daniel, mar. Sallie Wilson.
9. Elizabeth.
10. Lavinia (1806–1896), mar. Archibald Smith.
    (Last four children born in Elbert Co., Ga.)
    (Perhaps other children).

DANIEL McMURPHY, b. Ireland, 1735; d. Augusta, Ga., Oct. 27, 1817. From inscription in City (now Magnolia) Cemetery, Augusta, Ga. "Capt. Daniel McMurphy, d. Oct. 27, 1817, aged 82 years. Born in Antrim, Ireland. Came to Ga. 1756." In 1780 was a member of the Council when it was decided to evacuate Augusta; removed to Va. with his family, then returned South with Gen. Nathaniel Greene's Army, a Capt.; received public thanks for his care of the wounded at Cowpens, Eutaw Springs, and Guilford C. H. Mar. 1778, SUSANNA CROSSLEY (dau. of William and Martha Crossley, and sister of Henry and Mary Crossley).

Children:
1. George G. A. Y., mar. Kezia Martin.
2. Ann, mar. Henry Ware.
3. Jane, mar. William A. Cobb.
4. Daniel, mar. Mary Lamb.
5. Barbara, mar. David Reid.

DAVID McNAIR, b. Scotland, 1748; d. Richmond Co., Ga., 1811. (Buried near the old Martin McNair house, near Blythe, Ga.) First settled in Va., then N. C., then Ga. He served in the Ga. Militia, and Jan. 1, 1784 received 287½ acres bounty land for his service in Washington Co., Ga. Mar. (1) Catherine —; (2) ELEANOR MARTIN.

Children by (1) wife:
1. Samuel, mar. Anna McNair.
2. John (twin), mar. Mary Lucky.

    3. Daniel (twin).

Children by (2) wife:
    1. Anna, mar. Andrew McDonald.
    2. Martin, mar. Mary Donnelly.
    3. Robert, mar. Mary —.
    4. Harriet, mar. John Patterson.
    5. James S., mar. Martha Fudge.

NEIL McNEIL, b. Roberson Co., N. C., 1766; d. Randolph (now Terrell) Co., Ga., 1845. Served as Corporal in CAPT. JOHN JOHNSTON'S Co., Maj. John Collier's N. C. Regiment. (Grave marked).

BENJAMIN MADDOX, b. Va., July 4, 1760; d. Atlanta, Ga., 1864. Served as private, Va. Regiment. Settled in Elbert Co., Ga., 1804. Mar. ELIZABETH WALDROOP.
Children:
    1. Fielding.
    2. Sarah, mar. John Bush.
    3. Themie, mar. — Prior.
    4. Stansfield.
    5. Posey.
    6. James A., mar. Martha Tate.
    7. Walter.
    8. John.
    9. Henley.

SAMUEL MAGRUDER, b. Prince George Co., Md., 1708; d. Columbia Co., Ga., 1786. Served as Capt., Md. Militia. Member of Observation for Frederick Co., Md. Took *Patriots'* Oath. Mar. MARGARET JACKSON (1712-1806).
Children:
    1. NINIAN BEALL, a *Rev. Sol.*
    2. Ann.
    3. Ruth.
    4. Margaret.
    5. Sarah.
    6. Elizabeth.
    7. Samuel B.

NINIAN BEALL MAGRUDER (son of Samuel), b. Md., Nov. 22, 1736; d. Columbia Co., Ga., 1809. Took *Patriotic* Oath, Montgomery Co., Md., 1778. Appointed Sergeant, Md. Regiment, 1780. Mar. REBECCA YOUNG (1739-1811).
Children:
    1. Samuel, mar. Martha Ellis.
    2. William.
    3. Eleanor.
    4. Alitha, mar. — Drane.
    5. Sassandra, mar. — Drane.
    6. Margaret, mar. — Sims.
    7. Elizabeth, mar. Basil Magruder.
    8. Susanna, mar. — Silvers.
    9. Rebecca, mar. — Robertson.

BASIL MAGRUDER, b. Md.; d. Columbia Co., Ga., 1801. Mar. Elizabeth Magruder (dau. of NINIAN BEALL MAGRUDER and Rebecca Young). Private, 1778, 3rd Co. Middle Batt., Montgomery Co., Md.

NINIAN OFFUTT MAGRUDER (McGRUDER), b. Md., 1744; d. Richmond (now Columbia) Co., Ga., 1800. Enlisted Montgomery Co., Md., Sergeant 2nd Co., Md. Troops. Mar. 1765, Mary Harris (1748-1820) (dau. of Thomas and Sarah (Offutt) Harris).
Children:
    1. ZADOC, b. Montgomery Co., Md., 1766; d. Columbia Co., Ga., 1820. Served as private, Md. Troops, as a *Rev. Sol.* He mar. (1) Miss Talbott; (2) Tracey Rearden.

Children by (1) wife: 1. Ninan; 2. Sophronia; 3. Selina.
2. George (1772–1836), mar. (1) Elinor Shaw; (2) 1805, Susanna Williams.
3. Archibald.
4. John, mar. Sarah Prior.
5. Eleanor, mar. Williamson Wynne.
6. Sarah, mar. John Oliver.
7. Basil, mar. Elizabeth Magruder (dau. of Ninian Beall Magruder).

GIDEON MALLETTE, b. Purysburg, S. C., June 14, 1759; d. Effingham Co., Ga., Sept. 3, 1822. Served under Gen. Francis Marion, S. C. Troops. Mar. 1783, HANNA ELIZABETH A. De ROCHE (1767–1848).

Children:
1. Gideon, Jr.
2. Mary Ann.
3. Abraham (1790–1867), mar. Catherine Kennedy.
4. Daniel, mar. Susanna Zeigler.
5. Lewis.
6. John Henry.
7. Margaret.
8. Jeremiah (1802–1865), mar. (1) Emma Metzger; (2) Mary Porter (dau. of William G. Porter).
9. Eliza M , mar. John William Exley.

WILLIAM MANLEY, b. Cecil Co., Md., Nov. 24, 1761; d. Oconee Co., Ga., 1824. Served as private in Capt. Price's Co., Md. Line. Mar. in Dinwiddie Co., Va., 1785, LUCY FREEMAN (1767–1830).

Children:
1. William, mar. Mary Robinson Brown.
2. Joseph Parson (1789–1872), mar. 1814, Elizabeth Calhoun Bailey (1800–1876).
3. John.
4. Greene.
5. Infant.
6. Nancy, mar. — Morton.
7. Lourraine, mar. — Gresham.
8. Mary, mar. — Gill.
9. Elizabeth, mar. — Jackson.
10. Puss, mar. — Atkins.

JAMES MANN, b. —; d. Elbert Co., Ga., 1816. Served as *Rev. Sol.* Mar. JUDITH —. She drew in 1825 Ga. Lottery, as wife of *Rev. Sol.*

Children (mentioned in will; not in order of birth):
1. John, mar. 1816, Polly Harper.
2. Joel.
3. Jeremiah.
4. Asa, mar. Betsey White.
5. James, Jr., mar. Esther Lewis.
6. Henry, mar. Sarah Haley.
7. Martha, mar. HENRY SHACKLEFORD, of Elbert Co., Ga. (b. Orange Co., Va. *Rev. Sol.*).
8. Elizabeth, mar. (1) George Roebucks; (2) Johnston Maley.
9. Jesse.

JOHN MANN, b. 170–; d. Liberty Co., Ga., 1789. Member Provincial Congress 1775. Mar. 1732, Anne Vincent, d. 1775.

Children:
1. LUKE.
2. Mary Sophy.

LUKE MANN, b. Ireland, 1736; d. Great Ogeechee, Ga., April 7, 1802. Member Provincial Congress from Parish of St. Philips (now Bryan Co.), Ga. Served as Capt. in Gen. Greene's Army. Mar. 1756, ANNE BUTLER, d. Great Ogeechee, Ga., 1788.

Children:

1. Mary, mar. Samuel Sleigh.
2. Sarah, mar. (1) Josiah Stewart; (2) George Foster; (3) — Grover.
3. Martha, mar. William A. Dunham, of McIntosh Co.
4. Jane, mar. 1803, James P. Heath. Living Baltimore 1808.
5. Thomas, b. 1780, mar. (1) —; (2) Harriet.
6. Susan, mar. 1805, Samuel Lewis, of Liberty Co.
7. Frances, mar. Arthur M. Charlton, of Wilkes Co. (son of THOMAS CHARLTON, *Rev. Sol.*, and wife, Lucy Kenan).
8. Rebecca, mar. Thomas Day.
9. Harriet, mar. Samuel Dewse, of Liberty Co.
10. Ann, mar. John Pray, of Bryan Co.
11. Luke, Jr., mar. (1) Margaret —; (2) Eliza —.

JAMES MARKS, b. England, 1745; came to Albemarle Co., Va.; d. Wilkes Co., Ga., 1816. Signed Oath of Allegiance, Albemarle Co., Va. Served with Va. Army; was given grant of land in Ga. for his service. Mar. 1771, Elizabeth Harvie (1754–1793).

Children:

1. John, b. 1773, mar. Susan M. Tompkins.
2. Meriwether, mar. Ann Mathews. Moved to Ala.
3. Martha, mar. James Watkins.

ELIJAH MARTIN, b. Va., 1751; d. Jones Co., Ga., 1819. Served in Penn. Troops. Mar. in Penn., 1774, Mary Van Der Burg (1753–1833).

Children:

1. Elya.
2. Shadrack.
3. Israel, mar. Grace Martin.
4. Levi, mar. Jemina Harris.
5. Nancy, mar. — Coulter.
6. Rachel, mar. — Witt.
7. Elizabeth, mar. — Chapman.
8. Martha, mar. — Lambert.
9. Dau., mar. Robert Henderson.

Two other daughters.

Note: HENRY MITCHELL, President of the Senate of Ga., d. May 7, 1837, age 75 years. Lived in Warren Co., Ga.; d. Hancock Co., Ga. Served as Ensign, at 18 years of age, in Va. Was wounded and captured at Hanging Rock, N. C.

JAMES MARTIN, b. Va., 1749; d. Ga., 1785. Served as Col., Va. Army. Mar. Obedience Bugg (dau. of SHERWOOD BUGG, SR., *Rev. Sol.* of S. C. and Ga.).

Children:

1. Prudence.
2. Keziah.
3. Elizabeth.
4. Letitia.
5. Mary.
6. James, Jr.

REV. DANIEL MARSHALL, b. Windsor, Conn., 1706; d. Columbia Co., Ga., Nov. 2, 1784. He was the famous Pastor of the *first* Baptist Church in Ga., the Kiokee Church, on Kiokee Creek. He moved through Conn., to Penn., Va., and the Carolinas, to Ga. He was an ardent *Patriot*, imprisoned several times by the British. Served as Chaplain. Mar. (1) Hannah Drake; (2) in 1747, MARTHA STEARNS.

Child by (1) wife:

DANIEL, *Rev. Sol.*

Children by (2) wife:

1. ABRAHAM, b. Windsor, Conn., 1748; d. Ga., 1819. Served as Chaplain in Col. Stewart's Regiment of Minute Men from Augusta, Ga. Mar. 1792, ANN WALLER, d. Aug. 15, 1815.

2. LEVI, b. Winchester, Va., 1754; d. Columbia Co., Ga., 1809. Served as private, Ga. Troops; received bounty grant of land for his service. Mar. Sarah Wynne.

3. Mary, mar. ELIAS WELLBORN, *Rev. Sol.* Their son, James M. (1809–1879), mar. Louisa Cody (dau. of Michael Cody and Rebecca Rogers, dau. of REUBEN ROGERS, *Rev. Sol.* of Ga.).

4. Eunice, mar. JOHN PITTMAN, *Rev. Sol.* of Ga.

5. JOHN, *Rev. Sol.*

6. JOSEPH, *Rev. Sol.*

7. ZACHERIAH, *Rev. Sol.*

(The graves of the five sons, JOHN, ABRAHAM, LEVI, JOSEPH, and ZACHERIAH, all *Rev. Sols.* of Ga., have been marked by the Ga. D. A. R.)

The grave of DANIEL MARSHALL, who organized the Kiokee Baptist Church in 1772, near the town of Appling, the county seat of Columbia Co., is a little south of the Appling Court House, on the side of the road to Augusta, Ga.

GEORGE MATHEWS (OR MATTHEWS), b. Amherst Co., Va., 1739; d. Augusta, Ga., Aug. 30, 1812. Buried in old St. Paul's Churchyard. Served as Lieut. Col., 1775, 9th Regiment, Va. Troops, stationed at Chesapeake Bay under Gen. Andrew Lewis; was at Brandywine and Germantown; was taken prisoner, sent to British prison in N. Y., exchanged and placed in command of 3d. Va. Regiment. Removed to Goose Pond Tract, Wilkes Co., Ga. Elected *Governor of the State of Ga.*, 1786; Representative from Ga. to the First Continental Congress; again elected *Governor of Ga.*, 1794–95. Removed to Florida, then returned to Ga. Mar. (1) ANN (called Polly) PAUL (dau. of John Paul and half-sister of COL. JOHN STUART, *Rev. Sol.* of Va.); (2) MRS. REED, of Va.; (3) MRS. FLOWERS, of Miss.

Children by (1) wife:

1. John, mar. his cousin, Elizabeth Mathews (dau. of Archer Mathews). 5 children.

2. William, mar. Elizabeth (Meriwether) Thornton (dau. of Frank Meriwether, of Wilkes Co.).

3. George, mar. his step-sister, Miss Flowers, moved to Miss.

4. Charles Lewis, mar. Lucy Early (sister of Gov. Peter Early, of Ga.). Moved to Ala.

5. Ann, mar. Samuel Blackburn. Moved to Va.

6. Rebecca (1770–1825), mar. THOMAS MERIWETHER (1750–1831), a *Rev. Sol.* Lived in Jasper Co., Ga.

7. Jane, mar. Mr. Telfair.

From tomb-stone: "In memory of Gen. George Matthews, Aug. 30, 1812, age 73."

JAMES MATTHEWS, b. Va., Oct. 15, 1755; d. Wilkes Co., Ga., 1828. Enlisted, 1775, in 2nd S. C. Regiment under Col. William Thompsons and Gen. Francis Marion. Mar. (1) widow Jenkins; (2) 1786, Rebecca Carleton (1762–1840) (dau. of ROBERT CARLETON and his wife, Miss Wafford. He was a *Rev. Sol.* of Va., who moved to Ga. 1785).

Child by (1) wife:

One son. He moved to Ga. 1782.

Children by (2) wife:

1. Abraham (1786–1850), mar. (1) Polly Easton; (2) Elizabeth Burroughs.

2. James, mar. Keturah Pope. She mar. (2) Henry Long.

3. Philip, mar. (1) Elizabeth Clark (dau. of DAVID CLARK, *Rev. Sol.*); (2) Widow Wilkes.

4. Isaac Newton, mar. Catherine Ruddell.

5. Jacob Gibson, mar. Winny Jordan.

6. Mary.

7. Martha.

8. Rebecca.

MOSES MATTHEWS, b. Halifax Co., Va., 1725; d. Wilkes Co., Ga., 1806. Was a *Rev. Sol.*; served as a gunsmith in Gen. Sumpter's S. C. Regiment; received grant of land in Ga. for his service. Mar. in Va., Sarah Findley.

Children:

1. JAMES, mar. (1) Widow Jenkins; (2) Rebecca Carleton.

2. Moses, Jr.
3. Philip, mar. —.
4. Jesse, mar. Sarah Spinks.
5. William, mar. —.
6. Sally, mar. Henry Smith.
7. Mary (Polly), mar. Nicholas Ware.

PHILIP ¡MATHEWS, Rev. Sol., was b. 1752; d. Crawford Co., Ga., 1857. Mar. Priscilla —, d. Aug 4, 1875. Both are buried in the Old Providence Church Cemetery, near Roberta, Ga. He was allowed a pension for his service, 1840. Age 88 years.
One child:
Dr. Alfred Clark Mathews (son of Rev. Philip Mathews), was the grandfather of Corra May White, who married Rev. Lundy Harris. She was the well known Southern author and writer of Georgia—"CORRA HARRIS," of Rydal, Ga.

JOHN MATTOX, b. Colleton District, S. C., about 1765; d. Tattnall Co., Ga., 1826. He was a Rev. Sol. of Ga.; received bounty land in Washington Co., Ga., for his service as a Minute Man of Ga., while a resident of S. C. Mar. S. C., Sarah —. They removed to Tattnall Co., 1803. He also served as a Sol. in the War of 1812. (From deeds in Co.)
Children:
1. Elijah, mar. Lavinia Johnson (dau. of William Johnson, of Tattnall Co., Ga.)
2. Michael.
3. Joseph Allen.
4. John.
(Perhaps other children).

MICHAEL McKENZIE MATTOX (brother of JOHN MATTOX), b. Colleton District, S. C. Served in S. C. Militia as a Rev. Sol.; received discharge and payment for 104 days in S. C. Militia. Mar. Elizabeth Hartridge. They removed to Tattnall Co., Ga.
Children (from will):
1. Aaron.
2. John.
3. Elijah, mar. Candace Tippins (dau. of PHILIP TIPPINS, Rev. Sol.).
4. Elizabeth, mar. — Addison.
5. Dau., mar. William Eason.

AUDLEY MAXWELL, d. Ga. Served as Col. of Ga. Troops; member of First General Assembly of Ga. Mar. MARY STEVENS (dau. of John and Mary Stevens).
One child:
JAMES MAXWELL, a col. in Ga. Regiment; member Provincial Congress, which met at Savannah, Ga., 1775; Secretary of State 1778. Mar. Ann Way.
In 1756 JOHN STEVENS deeded to Audley Maxwell and others, 2½ acres of land on which the "Old Midway" Church was built.

WILLIAM MAXWELL (son of James Maxwell and his wife, Mary Simons, of S. C., who came to Ga., 1752, and settled on Midway river (now Bryan Co.), Ga.), b. Amelia Township, S. C., 1739; d. Bryan Co., Ga., 1807. He served as Capt. and as privateersman, commanding his own armed vessel, 1779; was captured, kept under parole by the British, until after the evacuation of Savannah, Ga., July 11, 1782. Mar. 1763, CONSTANTIA BUTLER, of Great Ogeechee, Ga.
Children:
1. Elizabeth.
2. John Jackson (1784–1855), mar. MARY ANNE BAKER (dau. of COL. JOHN BAKER, Rev. Sol. of Ga.).

WILLIAM MAY, b. Essex Co., Va., May 3, 1764; d. Mar. 4, 1844. Served as a Rev. Sol. (1779–1780) in Capt. John Dillard's Va. Co.; he then entered for 3 months, served under Lieut. Laurence and Robert Bolt; served in 1780 under Capt. Hamby. Ect. Applied for pension as a Rev. Sol., Aug. 2, 1833, while a resident of Murray Co., Ga.; pension allowed 1834 as a private. Place of residence during Rev. War. was Henry Co., Va. Mar. RHODA —, July 1783. She was b. Feb.

3, 1765; received pension as widow of *Rev. Sol.*, May 6, 1844, while residing in Polk Co., Tenn. (See pensions).

Children:
1. Arpah, b. May 6, 1784.
2. John, b. Jan. 3, 1786.
3. Daniel, b. April 16, 1788.
4. William, b. Jan. 11, 1790.
5. Ruth, b. Oct. 8, 1792.
6. Mary Ann, b. Feb. 8, 1795.
7. James, b. April 29, 1800.

DAVID MERIWETHER, b. Albemarle Co., Va., 1755; d. Clarke Co., Ga., Nov. 16, 1822. Served as Lieut., Va. Troops; was at the Siege of Savannah, Ga.; was taken prisoner at Charleston, S. C., released and served until the end of War; received bounty grant of land, Wilkes Co., Ga., for his service. Mar. 1782, FRANCES WINGFIELD, of Wilkes Co., Ga.

Children:
1. John, moved to Ala.
2. James, moved to Tenn.
3. William, mar. Sarah Mallory.
4. Francis.
5. George, mar. Martha Williams.
6. David (1800), mar. (1) Henrietta Collier; (2) Eliza Dabney.
7. Judith, mar. Rev. Hemming.

JAMES MERIWETHER, b. Va., 1755; d. Louisville, Ga., 1817. He served in the "Silk Stocking" Co. of Richmond, Va. Continental Troops; received bounty grant of land in Ga. for his service. Mar. SUSAN HATCHER.

Children:
1. James, Jr.
2. Alexander.
3. Dau., mar. Thomas M. Berrien.
4. Dau., mar. Eleazur Early (brother of Gov. Peter Early).
5. Dau., mar. Daniel Sturgiss.

FRANCIS MERIWETHER (son of THOMAS MERIWETHER and his wife, Elizabeth Thornton), b. Va., Oct. 3, 1737; d. Ga., Jan. 1803. Served with the Va. Troops; received bounty grant of land for his service in Ga. Mar. in 1765, MARTHA JAMESON (dau. of James and Mary (Gaines) Jameson). They moved to Wilkes Co., Ga., 1784.

Children:
1. THOMAS, *Rev. Sol.*, mar. Rebecca Mathews.
2. Valentine, b. 1768, mar. Barbara Cosby.
3. Nicholas, mar. Mary D'Yempest.
4. Mary, mar. William Barnett.
5. Mildred, mar. Joel Barnett.
6. Elizabeth, mar. William Mathews.
7. Margaret, mar. Dr. John A. Bradley.
8. Nancy, mar. William Glenn.
9. Sarah, mar. James Olive.
10. Lucy, mar. Grover Howard.

THOMAS MERIWETHER, b. Va., 1714; d. Va., 1756. Mar. Elizabeth Thornton.

Children:
1. NICHOLAS, *Rev. Sol.*, mar. Margaret Douglas.
2. FRANCIS, *Rev. Sol.*, mar. Martha Jameson.
3. DAVID, *Rev. Sol.*, mar. Mary Harvie.
4. Mildred, mar. JOHN GILMER, *Rev. Sol.*
5. Elizabeth, mar. THOMAS JOHNSON, *Rev. Sol.*
6. Sally, mar. Michael Anderson.
7. Mary, mar. PEACHY R. GILMER, *Rev. Sol.*

8. Nancy, mar. Richard Anderson.
9. LUCY, mar. (1) WILLIAM LEWIS, *Rev. Sol.*; (2) JOHN MARKS, *Rev. Sol.*
Children by (1) husband: 1. Meriwether, *Governor of Mo.*; 2. Reuben, mar. Mildred Dabney;
3. Jane, mar. Edmund Anderson. Children by (2) husband: 1. John; 2. Mary.
10. Jane, mar. Samuel Dabney. 11 children.

THOMAS MERIWETHER (son of FRANCIS MERIWETHER and his wife, Martha Jameson), b. Va., 1766; d. Jasper Co., Ga., 1831. Served as a private under Gen. La Fayette; received bounty land for his service in Wilkes Co., Ga. Mar. REBECCA MATHEWS (dau. of Gov. George Mathews).
Children:
   1. Frank, mar. Miss Butler.
   2. George, mar. (1) Miss Jordan; (2) Miss Watkins.
   3. Ann, mar. Fleming Jordan, of Jasper Co., Ga.
   4. Mary, mar. Dr. David Reese.
   5. David, mar. (4 times).

NOTE: WILLIAM MERIWETHER, b. Va., 1730; d. 1790.
Children:
   1. Elizabeth, mar. Nicholas Meriwether.
   2. DAVID WOOD, mar. Mary Lewis. A *Rev. Sol.*
   3. William, Jr., Mar. Sarah Oldham.
   4. Mildred, mar. Thomas Mitchell.
   5. Sarah, mar. Gen. D. L. James.
   6. Valentine, mar. Priscilla Pollard.
   7. Ann, mar. Major John W. Hughes.

ISAAC MIDDLEBROOKS, b. Md., 1753; d. Morgan Co., Ga., 1823. Served as private, Ga. Troops. Mar. 1780, Elizabeth Perkins (dau of ARCHIBALD PERKINS, b. N. C., 1746; d. Greene Co., Ga., 1840. Private, N. C. and Va. Troops, and his wife, Elizabeth Gibbs).
Children:
   1. Isaac, Jr., mar. Elizabeth Thompson.
   2. James, mar. Miss Hays.
   3. Bethenia, mar. Jesse Wade (son of PEYTON WADE, *Rev. Sol.*).
   4. Fannie, mar. — Thompson.
   5. Elizabeth, mar. — Chaney.
   6. Lea, mar. — Chaney.
   7. Polly, mar. Jeremiah Boggess.

ISAAC MIDDLEBROOKS was at the Battle of Savannah, Ga., and assisted in carrying the body of Count Casimir Pulaski from the field where he was killed, at the Siege of Savannah.

JOHN MIDDLEBROOKS, b. Caswell Co., N. C., 1755; d. Newton Co., Ga., 1830. Private, Capt. Root's Co., Col. Lytle's Caswell Co., N. C. Troops. Mar. (1) MARY WARE; (2) MILLY SUTTON.
One child by (2) wife: (Perhaps others).

ELIZABETH (1790-1865), mar. Aquilla Cheney, Jr. (1790-1867) (son of AQUILLA CHENEY, a *Rev. Sol.* of Mass., and his wife, Julia Benson, and grandson of LEVI CHENEY, a *Rev. Sol.* of Mass., and his wife, Mehitable Morse).

ELISHA MILLER, b. N. C., 1715; d. Ga., 1800. Served as private, Ga. Line. Mar. 1736, MARTHA COLSON (1720-1790). A *Rev. Sol.*
One child: (perhaps others).

Sarah (1737-1835), mar. 1755, JOHN CONYERS, b. Ga., 1725; d. Screven Co., Ga, 1814. Served as Capt. under COL. JOHN THOMAS, in Ga. Militia; *Rev. Sol.*
Their dau., Lucy Conyers (d. 1822), mar. 1790, ROBERT WILLIAMSON, d. Screven Co., Ga., 1810; he received a grant of land in Ga. for his service as a *Rev. Sol.*, Ga. Line, as Col.
Their son, Benjamin Williamson (1792-1881), mar. 1821, Elizabeth Roberts (1790-1829) (the dau. of JAMES ROBERTS (1744-1814), Screven Co., Ga.; served as Lieut., Ga. Militia, and his wife, Emily Williamson).

JESSE MILLER, b. York Co., S. C., 1750; came to Ga.; returned to S. C., where he d., Pendleton District, S. C., 1819. Served under Col. Greenberry Lee and received bounty grant of land in Washington Co., Ga., for his service. Mar. about 1780, Martha (called Patsey) Rose (dau. of WILLIAM ROSE, *Rev. Sol.* of S. C. and Ga., and his wife, Amy Langston).

Children (mentioned in will):
1. Amy.
2. Susan.
3. Empson, mar. Elizabeth —.
4. Archibald.
5. William.
6. Rebecca.
7. Mary.
8. Margaret, mar. Michael Burtz (son of MICHAEL BURTZ, *Rev. Sol.*).
9. George.
10. James.
11. Howell.
12. Sarah, mar. — Bruce.

JACOB MILLER, b. England, 1752; d. Columbia Co., Ga., about 1820. Settled with his parents in Fredericksburg, Va., from there to N. C. and S. C. Served as a private in Capt. George Liddell's S. C. Militia; received land in Camden District, S. C., for his service. Later removed to Columbia, S. C. Mar. in S. C., CATHERINE MALOY.

Children:
1. Francis, b. S. C., 1773.
2. John.
3. Elizabeth, mar. James Bradley.
4. Flora, mar. Harry Skinner.
5. William, mar. Phyllis Ellis.
6. Jacob, Jr., mar. Martha Newsom.
7. Mary, mar. Samuel McNair.
8. Catherine, mar. Hugh Smith.
9. Nancy, mar. William Newsome.
10. Francis II, mar. Hannah Mercer.
11. John II, mar. Mary Dayon.
12. Margaret.

WILLIAM MILLER, b. N. C., April 8, 1759; d. Ware Co., Ga., Nov. 27, 1837. Served as private, N. C. Line, and in Ga. Militia. Mar. 1785, AMEY BARKER, d. Oct. 23, 1831; buried Kettle Creek Churchyard, Ware Co., Ga.; received pension at Jackson Co., Ga.

Children (known):
1. Mary Ann, b. S. C., 1790. Mar., as (1) wife, Daniel Blackburn.
2. Barbara, b. Bulloch Co., Ga. Mar., as (1) wife, Gen. Thomas Hillard, b. Appling Co., Ga., 1805.
3. Elsie, b. 1785, mar. Benjamin Fordham.

THOMAS MILLS, b. Rowan Co., N. C., 1740; d. Screven Co., Ga. Served as 2nd Lieut. 1st. Regiment, 2nd Batt., Ga. Militia, 1776. Mar. 1760, LUCY —.

Children:
1. Hannah, mar. 1792, John Lewis Lanier (1762–1812).
(Other children not known).

JOHN MILNER, b. England, May 16, 1746; d. Wilkes Co., Ga., 1812. Served under Gen. Pickens and Gen. Sumpter in S. C. A captain; received bounty grant of land for his service, in Wilkes Co., Ga. Mar. 1765, ELIZABETH GODWIN, of Va., d. 1812.

Children:
1. Willis (1768–1790), mar. Sarah Ballard.
2. Pitt, mar. Apsyllah Holmes.
3. Simeon.
4. Benjamin.

 5. John (1775–1841), mar. Eunice Callaway. 12 children.
 6. Jonathan.
 7. Lucy.
 8. Nancy.
(Two other daus., names not known).

JOHN HAMILTON MILNER, b. Va., 1769; was a *Rev. Sol.* of Va. at the age of 14 years, and was present at the Battle of Yorktown. Mar. Miss Fairfax, of Va. Moved to Pike Co., Ga., and d. at Cleola, Harris Co., Ga.

JOHN MILTON, b. Halifax Co., N. C., 1740; d. Jefferson Co., Ga., 1803. He moved early to Ga., and was *Secretary of State*, 1777, and in charge of the great Seal of Ga. After the red-coats over-ran Ga., he secured the State Official Records, removed first to Charleston, then New Bern, N. C., then to Md., where they remained until after the War. Obtained in N. C. a commission of Lieut., later Lieut.-Col., in Continental Army, from Continental Congress. Was taken prisoner at the surrender of Fort Howe and was in prison at St. Augustine, Fla. Was *Secretary of State* again in 1781–3–9. Mar. Hannah E. Spencer. He was charter member of the Cincinnati Society.
Children:
 1. Homer Virgil, *Sol. of 1812*, mar. Elizabeth Robinson.
 2. Anna Maria, b. Ga., 1781. Mar. Benjamin F. Harris, of Ga.

PHILIP MINIS, b. Savannah, Ga., July 11, 1734 (the FIRST male white child b. in Ga.); d. there Mar. 6, 1789. Gave active support to the Colonists, and named in the *Royal Disqualifying Act of 1780.* Mar. JUDITH POLLOCK, of R. I. They had 5 children.
One child:
 ISAAC MINIS, b. Charleston, S. C. (after the British captured Savannah); d. Philadelphia, Penn., 1856. Mar. Dinah Cohen, of Georgetown, S. C., b. 1787; d. Savannah, Ga., 1874. He was a *Sol. of the War of 1812.*

 Note: The parents of Philip Minis were ABRAHAM and ABIGAIL MINIS, who, with their daus., Esther and Leah, arrived in Savannah, Ga., July 11, 1733. The history of their organization in London, England, for the journey, their trials and tribulations, as well as their successes, until they landed on Ga. soil in 1733, forms one of the interesting romances of the colonization of the new world.
 JUDITH POLLOCK was a member of one of the first Jewish families that settled in R. I. It is an interesting fact that R. I. and Ga. were the only Colonies where Jews were not prohibited from settling.

WILLIAM MITCHELL, came to America from Ireland at the age of 17 years; landed in Delaware Bay, and settled in Penn., July 3, 1770; he was granted 200 acres as a settler in Wrightsborough, St. Paul's Parish, Ga., a Quaker Settlement. He served as a *Rev. Sol.* of Ga. and was disowned by the Quakers. In 1784 was given a bounty grant of 287½ acres of land for his service in Washington (later Hancock) Co., Ga. In 1805 he removed to Wilkinson Co., Ga., where he d. He mar. Ruth Jackson (dau. of BENJAMIN JACKSON, a *Rev. Sol.*, who d. in Hancock Co., Ga., 1798). Had issue.

WILLIAM MITCHELL, b. Va., April 1, 1761; d. Franklin Co., Ga., 1840. Entered service as *Rev. Sol.* while a resident of Union District, S. C., July 1780, under Capt. Duff and Capt. Samuel Atterson; served as a Volunteer Horseman under Capt. George Avary, June 1781; received pension while a resident of Franklin Co., Ga. Mar. ELEANDER —.
Children:
 1. William.
 2. Eleander.
 3. Dau., mar. Thomas Whitlow.
 4. Dau., mar. David Barton.
 5. Dau., mar. John Savage.

WILLIAM MITCHELL, b. Va., 1748; d. Carnesville, Ga., 1819. Mar. 1770, Harriet Randolph, of Va. (1752–1824). *Rev. Sol.* and *Sol. of War of 1812.* Served as private, Ga. Line.
Children:
 1. Robert, b. 1771.
 2. James.

3. William, b. 1772, mar. Catherine Moulder.
4. John, b. 1774.
5. Joseph, b. 1776.
6. Martha, b. 1779.

THOMAS MITCHELL, b. England, 1755; d. Henry Co., Ga., 1840. Served as Lieut. in Col. Elijah Clarke's Regiment. Mar. MARY BARNETT. A *Rev. Sol.*

One child: (Others not known).

William Mitchell (1777-1859), mar. Eleanor Thomason (1780-1860) (dau. of JOHN THOMASON, *Rev. Sol.* who served as Corporal of Artillery, N. C. Troops, d. 1831 in Ala., and his wife, Eleanor Diamond).

THOMAS GOODWIN MITCHELL, b. Va., 1756; d. Thomas Co., Ga., 1826. Served in the 11th Va. Regiment under Col. Daniel Morgan; received bounty grant of land for his service in Montgomery Co., Ga. Mar. 1779, Anna Raines (1762-1832) (dau. of NATHANIEL RAINES, *Rev. Sol.* who served in Va. Troops, d. Va., 1789, and his wife, Susanna Parham).

Children:

1. Susanna (1785-1850), mar. Littleton Wyche.
2. Amy Goodwin (1782), mar. Gen. Edward Blackshear.
3. Hartwell, mar. Martha Jordan.
4. Nathaniel Raines, mar. Temperance Jordan.
5. Richard (moved from Va. to Old Hartford, Pulaski Co., Ga.); mar. Sophronia Dickey.
6. Thomas Goodwin, Jr. (1793-1862), mar. 1818, Elizabeth Alston (1796-1880) (dau. of JAMES ALSTON (1761-1825), *Rev. Sol.*, and his wife, Jane Wilcox, and g-dau. of PHILIP ALSTON, Col. in Rev. Army of N. C.).
7. Tabitha, d. y.
8. John, d. y.
9. Robert, d. y.
10. Nancy, mar. (1) Thomas Gatlin; (2) — Stone; (3) E. Alexander.

JOHN MOORE, b. 1763; d. Screven Co., Ga., 1848. Served as a *Rev. Sol.*, private in Capt. Giles' Co., Col. Hill's Regiment of S. C. State Troops, 1782. Moved to Screven Co., Ga. Mar. Jan. 16, 1792, MARCIA McCALL (dau. of THOMAS McCALL, *Rev. Sol.*, and his wife, Rachel McCall).

Children:

1. Sarah, mar. Hezekiah Evans(son of RUEL EVANS, *Rev. Sol.* of S. C., and his wife, Sarah Slater).
2. Thomas.
3. Elizabeth.
4. John.
5. James.
6. William.

DR. GEORGE MOSSE, b. England, 1741; d. Beaufort District, near Black Swamp, S. C., 1807. He settled at St. Helena's Island, S. C. Served in S. C. Was taken prisoner but escaped from the prison ship at Charleston, S. C., and returned to his duties as Surgeon in the Continental Army. Mar. (1) MISS MARTIN; (2) DOROTHY PHOEBE NORTON (dau. of Jonathan Norton and his wife, Mary Ann Chaplin).

Children:

1. Esther, b. 1772, mar. PAT McKENZIE, who served as a *Rev. Sol.* in the Md. Line.
2. Elizabeth, mar. James Stoney.
3. Phoebe, mar. Joseph J. Lawton.
4. Jane, mar. Benjamin Themistocles Dion Lawton.
5. Mary, mar. Adam Fowler Brisbane.
6. Martha, mar. Alexander J. Lawton.
7. Sarah, mar. Robert G. Norton.

NOTE: Closely connected with the Mosse family is the Lawton family of S. C.   ROBERT LAWTON, b. S. C., 1753; d. S. C., 1819; a *Rev. Sol.* of S. C.   Mar. Mar. 18, 1773, Sarah Robert (1755–1839).

Children:

1. Wm. Henry, mar. Catherine Maner (dau. of WM. MANER, *Rev. Sol.* of S. C.).
2. Joseph J., mar. Phoebe Mosse.
3. Rev. Winborn Asa, mar. (1) Mary (Cater) Rhodes; (2) Mrs. Perry; (3) Lucinda Landrum.
4. Thirza, mar. as (1) wife, Thomas Polhill.   He mar. (2) Matilda Rebecca Jaudon.
5. Benjamin Themistocles Dion, mar. Jane Mosse.
6. Charlotte Ann, mar. her first cousin, James Jehu Robert.
7. Alexander James, mar. Martha Mosse.

OLIVER H. MORTON, b. Boston, Mass., Sept. 6, 1763; d. Jones Co., Ga., Jan. 19, 1848. Served on board the Brigantine "Independence," commanded by Col. Simeon Samson, 1776–77. Later he joined the Militia at Plymouth, Mass., under Capt. Partridge.   Mar. SARAH EVERETTE, of Ashe Co., N. C., b. June 10, 1777; d. July 31, 1828.

Children:

1. Silas, mar. (1) Miss Hunter; (2) Selina Archer.
2. Daniel E., mar. Salome Hearst.
3. Mary, mar. Anthony Everett.
4. Ann Elizabeth, mar. Thomas Sharpe.
5. Martha.
6. Sarah.
7. Jesse.
8. Oliver H., Jr. (1803–1890), mar. Catherine Harris, b. S. C., 1808; d. Ga., 1871.
9. Lemuel B. (b. Samuel), mar. Sarah Feagin.
10. Jane, mar. Edward Chapman.
11. Thomas, mar. Martha Cole.

HENRY MOUNGER, b. Prince William Co., Va.; d. Wilkes Co., Ga., 1795.   Served under Gen. Elijah Clarke; received bounty land, 575 acres in Washington Co., Ga., for his service.   Mar. Mary —.

Children:

1. Thomas, mar. Lucy Grimes (dau. of JOHN GRIMES, *Rev. Sol.*, and his wife, Elizabeth Wingfield, of Wilkes Co., Ga.).
2. Edwin, b. 1781; (*Treasurer of the State of Ga.*); mar. Frances Clarke, b. 1787 (dau. of COL. ELIJAH CLARKE, *Rev. Sol.* of Ga.).
3. Henry, moved to Ala.
4. Sidney, mar. Dr. Thomas Wingfield.
5. Mary Ann, mar. Gen. David Terrell.
6. Lucy, mar. Mr. Woodruff.
7. Julia, mar. Mr. Bozeman.
8. Elizabeth, mar. Matthew Talbot, June 18, 1812.
9. James.

HENRY MOUNGER was also J. P. of Wilkes Co., and in Militia, 1790.   (Record for Society of 1812).

SAMUEL MORDECAI, b. S. C.; d. Savannah, Ga., 1820.   Served with the S. C. Troops, as a grenadier.   Mar. Miss Andrews.

One child (known):

Rachel Mordecai, mar. Isaac Harby (son of Solomon Harby and his wife, Rebecca Moses, dau. of MEYER MOSES, b. England, 1735; d. Charleston, S. C., 1800; rendered material aid to the Rev. Army and to the cause of the Colonies, and his (2) wife, Rachel Andrews).

THOMAS MORGAN (son of James Morgan, of Penn.), b. Buck's Co., Penn.; moved to Orange Co., N. C., then to Ga.; d. Savannah, Ga., 1778.   Mar. in Md., REBECCA ALEXANDER (dau. of Martin and Susanna Alexander, of Md.)   He served as a *Rev. Sol.*; received a bounty grant of land for his service.   His wife d. before 1778.   (Will on file, Savannah, Ga., mentions the following children):

1. John.
2. Thomas.

3. Luke.

4. Lemuel.

5. Sarah, mar. John Blair.

6. Ann (called Nancy), mar. BENJAMIN HART, *Rev. Sol.*, whose name appears on monument erected on the Kettle Creek Battleground by the U. S. Government for the men who fought at Kettle Creek.

NOTE: (The D. A. R. accept the statement that Thomas, James, and Sarah were children of James Morgan.) SARAH MORGAN mar. Squire Boone and they were the parents of DANIEL BOONE, of Ky., b. Bucks Co., Penn., Feb. 11, 1734 or 1735. The family settled on the Yadkin river, Orange Co., N. C., 1750. JAMES MORGAN d. 1782, mar. Eleanora —. They were the parents of GENERAL DANIEL MORGAN, *Rev. Sol.*, b. 1736. He mar. Abigail Bailey. THOMAS MORGAN was the father of Georgia's war heroine, NANCY HART.

EDMUND MURPHY (son of Nicholas Murphy, who settled in Augusta, Ga., 1736), b. Augusta, Ga., 1745; d. Ga., Dec. 10, 1821. Enlisted, Ga. Troops; was captured by the British, imprisoned at Fort Grierson (afterwards at Fort Augusta), and was only released when Fort Augusta was captured and its garrison surrendered to Gens. Pickens and Lee in 1782. Mar. (1) BETSEY ANN —; (2) Feb. 10, 1785, NANCY RHODES (sister of Aaron Rhodes, who mar. Nancy Murphy).

Children by (1) wife:

1. James.

2. Nancy, mar. Aaron Rhodes.

Children by (2) wife:

1. Nicholas, mar. (1) Nancy Collins, d. Mar. 20, 1819; (2) 1820, Nancy Carswell (dau. of JOHN CARSWELL, *Rev. Sol.*, and g-dau. of ALEXANDER CARSWELL, *Rev. Sol.*).

2. Alexander, mar. (1) Elizabeth Kinlow; (2) Elizabeth Allen; (3) Margaret Jones (widow of Henry Seaborn Jones).

3. Leroy, mar. Lucinda Brown.

4. John.

5. Edward.

6. Elizabeth Ann, mar. Robert Evans.

7. Levicy, mar. — Hull.

8. Mary, mar. Charles Rheny.

9. Maria, mar. — Brown.

10. Harriet.

JOHN MYRICK, b. York Co., Va., 1751; d. Baldwin Co., Ga., 1835. Served as private, Ga. Line; received bounty grant of land for his service. Mar. 1778, AMY GOODWIN (1755–1786).

Children (known):

1. Goodwin (1779–1831), mar. 1809, Martha Parham.

2. John.

3. Polly, mar. — Jones.

4. Martha, mar. — Horton.

5. Elizabeth, mar. — Green.

6. Lucy, mar. Drury Jackson (1767–1823).

7. Amy, mar. Thomas Stith Parham.

THOMAS NAPIER, b. Va., 1758; d. Bibb. Co., Ga., Sept. 30, 1838. Mar. (1) in Va., 1790, Tabitha Easter (dau. of JAMES EASTER, *Rev. Sol.*), b. Goochland Co., Va., 1771; d. 1800; (2) Nancy Moultrie. He was a *Rev. Sol.* of Va.; received bounty grant of land in Ga. for his service. Was also a *Sol. of 1812.* He is buried in Cherry St. Cemetery, Macon, Ga.

Children by (1) wife:

1. Leroy S., mar. 1825, Matilda Louise Moultrie (1808-1892).

2. Thomas.

3. Martha.

4. TABITHA, mar. Nathan C. Munroe.

5. Freeman.

6. Skelton, mar. 1820, Jane Gage (1804-1890).

One child by (2) wife:

William.

RENÉ NAPIER, b. Goochland Co., Va., 1734; d. Elbert Co., Ga., 1807. Mar. 1755, REBECCA HURT WARD; received bounty grant ot land in Washington Co., Ga., for his service as a *Rev. Sol.* of Va., and for service in Ga. under Col. Elijah Clarke.

Children:

1. Thomas, b. Nov. 1, 1758; d. Bibb Co., Ga., 1838. Mar. (1) Tabitha Easter (1771-1800) (dau. of JAMES EASTER, *Rev. Sol.*); (2) Nancy Moultrie. He was a *Rev. Sol.*, private under Gen Clarke, of Ga.
2. Skelton, d. unmar.
3. Sarah Garland, mar. Matthew Duncan.
4. Walker, mar. Miss Minter.
5. Chloe, mar. — Kelsey.
6. Dollie, mar. — Shorter.
7. Lucy.

BASIL O'NEAL, b. Md., 1758; moved to Va., 1775; came to Ga., 1780; d. Columbia Co., Ga., Oct. 14, 1849. Served as private, Va. Militia, Henry Co., Va., Sept. 20, 1777; served under Capt. Daniel Chadwell, 1778, Major John Graves; served two terms in Va. and one in Ga. (Grave marked by Ga. D. A. R.) Mar. (1) ELLEN BRISCOE (dau. of Dr. Briscoe and Ann Stuart, of Va.); (2) 1825, SARAH HULL GREENE (1798-1875) (dau. of McKEEN GREENE, JR., *Rev. Sol.* of Ga. and his wife, Eleanor McCall, dau. of CHARLES McCALL, *Rev. Sol.* of S. C. and Ga.).

Children by (2) wife:

1. Sarah Jane, mar. Lycurgus Rees.
2. Amanda, mar. Simpson Booker.
3. Fannie, mar. Jeremiah Jones.
4. Basil Lewellyn, d. 1927, mar. Martha Palmer.
5. Augustus A., mar. Scott Fortson.

THOMAS NEAL, b. N. C.; d. Warren Co., Ga., 1807. Served as *Rev. Sol.* Mar. SARAH —.

Children:

1. Polly Gardner.
2. Diana.
3. Esther.
4. Betsey.
5. Sally.
6. Rebecca.
7. Patsey.
8. Drucilla.
9. Elisha.

(CAPT. DAVID NEAL, CAPT. THOMAS NEAL, THOMAS NEAL, and SAMUEL NEAL, all *Rev. Sols.*, buried in Warren Co., Ga.)

JAMES NESSMITH (NESMITH, NESMITH) (son of James Nesmith and Miss Young, *Loyalists*, who came to Ga., 1760), b. St. George's Parish (now Screven Co.), Ga., 1765. Was a *Rev. Sol.*; served in S. C. after the fall of Savannah, Ga.; also *Sol. of the War of 1812*; Capt. of 38th District (Screven Co); d. Screven Co., Ga., Feb. 14, 1845. Mar. Elizabeth —. She d. before 1845.

Children (known):

1. Frances, mar. — Williams.
2. James.
3. John, mar. Elender —.
4. Elander, moved 1833 to Thomas Co., Ga.
5. CHARLES H., b. Screven Co., Ga., 1794; d. Thomas Co., Ga. Mar. in Screven Co., Patience Roberts (dau. of Thomas Roberts, a *Sol. of 1812*, and his wife, Mary Ponder, and g-dau. of ELIAS ROBERTS, *Rev. Sol.*, and JAMES PONDER, *Rev. Sol.*, both of Screven Co., Ga.).

WILLIAM NEVER, b. 1758; d. while on a visit to Ala., 1852. Served as a private in Va. Troops seven years. Also *Sol. of the War of 1812*. Came to Ga., 1787, and settled in Putnam Co. Mar. in Va., Miss Ballard (1768-1850).

Children:

1. William.

2. Elizabeth, mar. Capt. Jones.
3. John, mar. (1) Garnett Smith; (2) Julia Smith (dau. of David Smith, of Va. and Jones Co., Ga.)
4. Alsy.
5. Mary, mar. William Hardin.
6. Charlotte.
7. Daniel.

JOHN NEVILLE, JR., b. Va., 1750; d. Bulloch Co., Ga., July 30, 1804. Was a *Rev. Sol.*, private; place of residence during the Rev. War, Va. and S. C. Mar. about 1768, FRANCES ANN NIXON (1752–1815).
Children mentioned in Will made April 12, 1803:
   Jacob, b. 1769; d. Statesboro, Ga., 1873 (age 104 years). Mar. in Bulloch Co., Nov. 11, 1798, Nicey Henderson (1780–1889), age 109 years.
   Four daus.

REV. JOHN NEWTON, b. Aug. 7, 1732; d. Nov. 20, 1790. Served as a *Rev. Sol.* Mar. 1753, Keziah Dorsett.
Children:
   1. JOHN, JR., b. July 5, 1755; d. as a *Rev. Sol.* in a British prison. A monument was erected to his memory by the City of Savannah, Ga.
   2. Jemina, b. 1757.
   3. Philip Dorsett, b. 1760.
   4. James.
   5. MOSES, b. Aug. 14, 1766; d. 1826. Served as *Rev. Sol.* under his father, REV. JOHN NEWTON. Was at Savannah, Ga., and was taken prisoner at Charleston, S. C. Mar. 1793, Elizabeth Hudspeth.
   Children of MOSES NEWTON and Elizabeth Hudspeth: 1. Mary Early, mar. James Marcellus Johns; 2. John Hamlin, mar. Mary Jordan; 3. Isaac; 4. Nancy; 5. Elizabeth, mar. Andrew Howard; 6. Grace, mar. George Baskerville Lucas; 7. Sarah Baker.
   (The grave of MOSES NEWTON was marked by D. A. R.)

JOHN NEWTON, b. Penn., Feb. 20, 1759; d. Lexington, Oglethorpe Co., Ga., 1798; buried under the pulpit of the Presbyterian Church at Lexington. Served as private and Chaplain, N. C. Troops. Mar. in N. C., 1783, CATHERINE LOWRANCE, b. East Jersey, 1756; d. Athens, Ga., Oct. 12, 1846. They had 3 sons and 3 daus. Among these:
   1. Fidelia, b. Ga., 1786.
   2. Josiah.
   3. Betsey (Elizabeth).
   4. Elizur Lowrance (1796), mar. Eliza T. Collier.

JULIUS NICHOLS, b. Granville Co., N. C., 1759; d. Franklin Co., Ga., 1838. Entered service Wake Co., N. C., Volunteer in Militia, 1776, under Capt. James Jones' Light Horse Co.; entered Militia at Salisbury, N. C., under Capt. John Lopp and Col. Purvard; received pension for his service. Mar. SARAH —.
Children:
   1. Agnes, mar. — Anderson.
   2. Sarah.
   3. Jane.
   4. Candace Sabella.

JOHN NICHOLSON, b. Scotland; d. Oglethorpe Co., Ga., 1818; moved to Mecklinburg Co., N. C. Served as private, N. C. Troops. Mar. (1) in N. C., 1770, PENELOPE MANN, of Edgecomb Co., N. C.; they moved to Oglethorpe Co., Ga.; she d. before 1802.; (2) SUSAN BROWN.
Children by (1) wife:
   1. John.
   2. George.
   3. Joseph.

4. Jennie (or Jane), mar. David McLaughlin.
5. Peggy.
6. Sally.
7. Mary.
8. Ann.

One child by (2) wife:
Sarah, b. 1803, mar. John Erwin.

WILLIAM NORRIS, b. Harford, Md., Dec. 1760; d. Newton Co., Ga., 1852 or 1853; buried in family cemetery near Covington, Ga. Signed Oath of Allegiance; was in Capt. Francis Martin's Co., Md. Troops; received bounty land in Ga. 1827. (Grave marked). Mar. in Abbeville Dist., S. C., Nancy Cornelius, b. Va., 1771; d. Ga., about 1850.
Children:
1. Nancy, b. S. C., 1792.
2. Breward, mar. Vashti Cowley.
3. Willis Cornelius, mar. (1) Rebecca Mann; (2) Eliza Ruhlman.
4. William Pendleton, mar. Narcissus Respess.
5. Nancy, mar. Jackson Kilgore.

THOMAS NORTON, b. N. C.; d. Oglethorpe Co., Ga., 1801. (Will made June 18, 1801, on file Lexington, Ga.) Served as private in N. C. Line under Capt. Carr; drew land for his service in Griffin's District, DeKalb Co., Ga., in Cherokee Lottery. Mar. MARY —, about 1760.
Children (mentioned in will):
1. John.
2. James.
3. William (1765–1843), mar. Mary Landrum.

WILLIAM NORTON, b. S. C., 1744; d. Savannah, Ga., 1800. Served with S. C. Troops. Mar. in S. C., MARY GODFREY.
Children:
1. Alexander.
2. ROBERT GODFREY, b. Bluffton, Beaufort District, S. C., mar. his cousin, Sarah Mosse (dau. of GEORGE MOSSE, Rev. Sol., and his wife, Dorothy Phoebe Norton). He served as private, S. C. Troops. Their son, Alexander Robert Norton, b. S. C., 1812; d. 1869. Mar. Julia Elizabeth Green (dau. of DR. JOHN GREEN, of Screven Co., Ga. He and his wife are buried in Burke Churchyard on Briar Creek, Screven Co., Ga. Rev. Sol.).

WILLIAM NORTHERN, b. Va.; came to Edgecombe Co., N. C. Served with N. C. Troops. Mar. MARGARET DICKEN, of N. C.; they moved to Powellton, Ga., 1800.
Their son, PETER, b. N. C., 1794; d. Ga., 1863. Was Sol. of War of 1812. Mar. 1817, Maria Davis. Their son, WILLIAM JONATHAN, was Governor of Ga.

JOHN NUNNALLY, b. Va., Feb. 12, 1758; d. Clarke Co., Ga., June 10, 1825. Served in the 1st and 11th Va. Regiments. Mar. SUSAN VIRGINIA BURTON (called Sukey), b. Oct. 25, 1766; d. Mar. 14, 1849. (Both buried in Old Cemetery near Bishop, Oconee, Co., Ga.) His widow received a pension for his service as a Rev. Sol. They had children.

WILLIAM NUNNELEE (name also spelled NUNNALLY), b. Chesterfield Co., Va.; d. Elbert Co., Ga., 1804. Served as a Rev. Sol. of Va. Mar. in Va., SUSANNA HUBBARD (dau. of Thomas Hubbard).
Children:
1. JAMES FRANKLIN, b. Va., Jan. 3, 1760; d. Elbert Co., Ga., Feb. 12, 1838. Served as a Rev. Sol. Mar. (1) KEZIAH —; (2) Oct. 28, 1810, JANE NASH.
Children by (1) wife: 1. Willis; 2. Howell; 3. Osamin; 4. Simeon; 5. Charlotte, mar. — Bentley; 6. Sarah, mar. — Bolton.
Children by (2) wife: 1. Elizabeth (1812–1888), mar. 1825, Nicholas Burton; 2. Nancy (1813–1880), mar. 1830, Abraham Burton; 3. Martha, mar. 1830, Bud Wall; 4. Sophia, mar. 1833, Henry P. Mattox; 5. James Franklin, Jr., mar. 1836, Rachel McKinley; 6. Jane, mar. James Nelms; 7. Frances Elizabeth, mar. Richard Ware Snellings.
2. Elizabeth, mar. Col. Robert Middleton.

3. Nancy, mar. THOMAS BURTON, *Rev. Sol.*, b. Va.; d. Petersburg, Ga., 1828. He served as private, Ga. Troops, under Col. Elijah Clarke.

Children: 1. Leroy; 2. Nicholas; 3. Malinda, mar. John Childers; 4. Sophia. 4. Priscilla, mar. William Hatcher. 5. Walter.

THOMAS OGLESBY, b. Va., 1750; d. Elbert Co., Ga., 1832. Served as private, Ga. Troops; drew bounty land. Mar. 1776, MISS PARTEIS, d. 1825.

Children:

1. William (1777–1852), mar. (1) Mary Christian; (2) Paulina Wiley.
2. Leroy.
3. Garrett, mar. Ruth Bradley.
4. Drury.
5. Thomas, Jr.
6. Lindsay.
7. George.
8. Robert.
9. James.
10. Mary Lucinda, mar. William E. Morgan.

Note: Found on a tomb-stone of a *Rev. Sol.* in the "Old Sapp" grave-yard on lower river road to Eastman, Ga., about 4 miles from Hawkinsville, Ga.: "Sacred to the Memory of ARCHIBALD ODOM, a Minister of the Gospel, a Gentleman, and a REVOLUTIONARY SOLDIER."

WILLIAM OGLETREE (OR OGLITREE), b. Scotland Jan. 18, 1765; d. Wilkes Co., Ga., 1837. Mar. Mary Bird, b. Mar. 18, 1769; d. 1830. He was a *Rev. Sol.*, served as private, Va. Line. (Grave marked by D. A. R.)

Children:

1. Frances, b. Aug. 8, 1789.
2. Philemon, b. 1791, mar. (1) — Harper; (2) — Harper.
3. Elizabeth Crawford, mar. Glynn Tigner.
4. Nancy, b. 1793.
5. William, b. 1795.
6. John B., b. 1798.
7. James, b. 1800.
8. Elizabeth Bird, b. 1803, mar. Hiram Phinazee.
9. Buford B., b. 1806.
10. David, b. 1809, mar. Frances Fletcher.
11. Absolem, b. 1811, mar. Matilda Stewart (dau. of Thomas and Nancy (Russell) Stewart, of Oglethorpe Co., Ga.).
12. Mary B., b. 1814, mar. Harris Phinazee.

Note: MAJOR JAMES BUSH OLIVER, of London, England, who assembled and equipped his own Co. of *Rev. Sols.*, buried in old St. Paul's Churchyard, Augusta, Ga.

DYONISIUS OLIVER (son of Thomas Oliver and wife, Mary McCarty), b. Va., 1735; d. Wilkes Co., Ga., 1808. (He lived from 1793 on Wahatchie Creek, near Stencombs Meeting House, where he d. and was buried). Served as Captain of a privateer of Ga.; was with Gen. Lincoln at Kettle Creek, was captured and imprisoned by the British. Mar. (1) in Va., 1758, Mary Ann Winfrey (dau. of Valentine Winfrey, of Chesterfield Co., Va.). They moved before 1779 through S. C. to Wilkes (now Elbert) Co., Ga. She was b. Va., 1740; d. Elbert Co., Ga., 1802; (2) Jane Jackson, of S. C.

Children by (1) wife:

1. Peter, b. 1763, mar. his cousin, Betty Oliver (dau. of Francis Oliver, of Va.). (His only son, Dyonisius, moved to Miss.)
2. John (1765-1816), mar. his cousin, Frances Thompson (dau. of William and Mary (Wells) Thompson).
3. James, b. 1767, mar. (1) Mary Thompson (dau. of William and Mary (Wells) Thompson); (2) Lucy Clark (dau. of Christopher Clark).
4. Dyonisius, Jr., b. 1768, mar. his cousin, Frances Oliver (dau. of Francis Oliver, of Va.). They lived Edgefield District, S. C.

5. Thomas Winfrey, mar. Mary Clark (dau. of Christopher Clark); both are buried in the yard of the "Old Tavern," Elberton, Ga.

6. William, mar. (1) Barbara Tait; (2) Frances Ragland.

7. Eleanor, mar. John Goss, of Ga.

8. Martha, b. 1773, mar. her cousin, Thomas Hancock, of S. C.

9. Florence McCarty, a Methodist minister, b. Va., 1775; mar. 1796, Elbert Co., Ga., Susanna Clark (dau. of Christopher Clark); moved to Ala.

10. Frances, mar. William T. Cook, of Va.

Child by (2) wife:

Jackson, mar. Polly Maxwell.

EPHRIAM OWENS, b. N. C.; d. Ga. Mar. Sarah —. Lived Richmond Co., Ga. Was a *Rev. Sol.*; received bounty land, upon certificate of Col. Greenberry Lee, in Ga., 1784.

Children:

1. John, b. 1790.
2. Benjamin, b. 1792.
3. Mary, d. y.
4. Ephriam, b. 1797.
5. Elizabeth, b. 1799.
6. Sarah, b. 1801.
7. Ruth, b. 1803.

NATHANIEL PACE, b. July 16, 1743; d. Ga., Oct. 1, 1798. Came to Washington Co., Ga., with his wife, Amelia (Mildred) Boykin (sister of MAJOR FRANCIS BOYKIN. *Rev. Sol.* of S. C.).

Their dau., Frances (called Nancy) Pace, mar. Richard Whitaker (son of HUDSON WHITAKER, *Rev. Sol.* of S. C., who d. in Ga.).

THOMAS PACE, b. N. C., 1745; lived in N. C. until 1768, when he moved to Ga.; was granted land in St. Paul's Parish. He served as an officer in Ga. Troops and was on the British Black list in Ga. as a *Revel Officer*; was granted land in Washington Co., Ga. He moved back to N. C., and d. there, 1795. Mar. CEBELLE MATHEWS. She mar. (2) Benjamin Carr, and moved back to Ga.; settled in Newton Co. with her 8 children by (1) husband.

Children:

1. William.
2. Nannie.
3. John.
4. Mary.
5. Martha.
6. James.
7. Elizabeth.
8. Hardy Pace (1784–1836), mar. (1) Susan Turner; (2) Fannie Hopkins.

MAJOR WILLIAM PAGE, of St. Simon's Island, Ga., a *Rev. Sol.* of S. C., had an only child, ANNA MATILDA, who mar. 1824, Thomas Butler King, b. Mass., 1797; d. Waresboro, Ga., 1864 (son of CAPT. DANIEL KING, b. Mass., 1749; d. Mass., 1815, *Rev. Sol.* at the Alarm at Lexington, and his wife, Hannah Lord, of New London, Conn.).

DANIEL PARKER, b. Albemarle Co., Va., 1756; d. Ga., Aug. 11, 1844. Entered service at Chatham Co., N. C., Sept. 15, 1780, under Capt. Mark Patterson; also served under Capt. William Griffin; received pension for his service, 1832. (Grave marked.) Mar. MARY LUCY WHITE, b. Va., 1766; d. Upson Co., Ga., Nov. 14, 1845. Mentions his wife, Lucy, and the following children in his will, made Dec. 15, 1840, pro. Sept. 6, 1844.

Children:

1. Mary, mar. — Hudson.
2. Nancy, mar. — Meadows.
3. Faythia, mar. — Dark.
4. Stephen.
5. Daniel, Jr.
6. Philemon.

7. Sherwood.
8. Lucy.
9. Thomas.
10. Susanna, mar. — Meadows.

EZEKIEL EVANS PARKE, b. Va., 1757; d. Greensboro, Ga., 1826. Served under Gen. Nathaniel Greene; wounded at the Battle of Guilford C. H. Mar. SUSAN SMYTHE.
Children:
1. James, mar. Frances Wingfield.
2. Griffen, mar. Louise Starke.
3. Richard, mar. Frances Redd.
4. Joseph.
5. Thomas Payton, mar. Caroline Russell.
6. Katherine, mar. Eugene Van Valkinburg.
7. Lucinda, mar. Peter Jones Williams.

JACOB PARKER (son of George and Sarah Parker, of Md.),b. Somerset Co., Md., 1724; d. Greene Co., Ga., 1791. Served in 2nd Md. Regiment. Moved to Hancock Co., Ga., on Rocky Creek, 1790. Mar. 1748, MARY SMITH (dau. of George and Judith (Turner) Smith, of Md.).
Children:
1. Elisha, remained in Md.
2. George, mar. 1780, Rhoda Evans, of Md.
3. Jacob, Jr., mar. Widow Spurlock, of Ga.
4. Nancy, mar. Wm. Beauchamp, of Md. They came to Ga.
5. Rhoda.
6. Polly, mar. in Ga., 1793, Chris Simmonds.
7. Judith, mar. in Md., 1786, PHILIP TURNER, *Rev. Sol.* They came to Ga. He was the youngest son of ZADOC TURNER, SR., *Rev. Sol.* of Md., who d. at the home of his son in Hancock Co., Ga., 1819, and his wife, Sarah Hicks.

JOHN PARKER, b. Sussex Co., Del., Sept. 25, 1740; d. Ga., Mar. 3, 1825. Mar. in 1760, Sarah Gordy. She was b. 1743; d. 1793. Served as *Rev. Sol.* under Capt. Charles Pope, Capt. Joseph Vaughn, Col. John Haslet and others, of Del.
Children:
1. Hannah, b. Apr. 21, 1761.
2. Jacob, b. Aug. 2, 1764.
3. Priscilla, b. Apr. 12, 1767.
4. John, Jr., b. June 22, 1769.
5. Elizabeth, b. Apr. 28, 1772.
6. Mary (Polly), b. Aug. 20, 1774.
7. WILLIAM, b. Aug. 27, 1778; d. 1857. Mar. 1800. Kitty Matthews (1780–1845).
8. Peter, b. Oct. 20, 1780.
9. Elisha, b. Dec. 5, 1782.
10. Nancy, b. Aug. 4, 1787.

MOSES PARKER, b. Mass., 1725; came to Chowan Co., N. C., about 1750, then to Cheraw District, S. C., 1760. Served as private, S. C. Militia, and also furnished forage and provisions to the Militia. Mar. SUSANNA —. Moved to Greene Co., Ga., where he d. Dec. 1798.

Their son, MOSES, JR., b. Mass., 1748; d. Greene Co., Ga., 1799. Served as private, S. C. Militia. Mar. (1) Miss Breedlove; (2) Ann Parker.

Children by (2) wife: 1. John; 2. Daniel; 3. Priscilla Ann (1796–1880).

HENRY PARKS, b. Albemarle Co., Va., May 31, 1758; d. Franklin Co., Ga., May 18, 1845. Served with the Continental Army in Va.; received land grant in Ga. for his service. Mar. (1) 1782, Martha Justice (1753–1818); (2) Emma Crutchfield; (3) Sarah Pullian.
Children by (1) wife:
1. John, b. 1784, mar. Betty Meadows.
2. Henry, Jr., mar. Mary Ann Dorsey.
3. Mary (Polly), b. 1797, mar. 1814, Joshua Baker (1794–1834).

4. Elizabeth, mar. James Hargroves.
5. Charles, d. y.
6. William Justice, mar. (1) Naomi Pickett; (2) Dolly Varden, widow; (3) Mrs. Burgess.
Children by (2) wife:
1. Frank A.
2. Sallie, mar. Levi Shankle.
3. Matt Henderson.

SAMUEL PARSONS, b. Va., 1762; d. Fayette Co., Ga., 1832. Served as private, Va. Line; was at the Battle of Guilford C. H., and was at the surrender at Yorktown. Mar. ANN —.

Their dau., CATHERINE (1784-1855), mar. Pernal Patrick (son of JOHN PATRICK, b. Ireland, 1751, a Rev. Sol. of S. C.), b. Md., 1776; d. Ga., 1856.

WILLIAM PASCHALL (PASKAL, PASCHEL), b. Apr. 15, 1753; d. Wilkes Co., Ga., Mar. 1807; received bounty land in Ga. for his service as a Rev. Sol. Mar. Mary —, b. June 13, 1753; d. Jan 11, 1837.
Children:
1. William, b. 1776.
2. Thomas, b. 1778.
3. Susanna, b. 1782, mar. 1799, John Gresham.
4. Margaret.
5. Samuel, b. 1788.
6. Polly.
7. Isaiah (twin), b. July 14, 1793.
8. Jeremiah (twin), b. July 14, 1793.
9. Dennis, b. 1796, mar. 1820, Dicy Gresham, b. 1802; d. 1868.

WILLIAM PATMAN, b. Henrico Co., Va., 1760; d. Lexington, Ga., 1821. Served as Sergeant of Artillery 3 years, Va. Line; obtained grant of land in Ga. for his service. Mar. SUSANNA BIGGER in Prince Edward Co., Va. A Rev. Sol.
Children:
1. Mary.
2. John.
3. Elizabeth.
4. Watson.
5. James.
6. Nancy.
7. Susannah.

JOHN PEACE, b. on voyage to America from Eng.; mar. Elizabeth Wade, b. Wales. Served in the Rev. Army in Va.; Came to N. C., then to Ga. Received bounty land in Hancock Co., Ga., where he d.
Children:
1. Major, b. N. C., 1790; d. 1854; mar. (1) Biddy Gilleland; (2) Sarah Vincent.
2. John.
3. Daniel.
4. Elizabeth, mar. — Johnson.
5. Nancy, mar. Lemuel Lovett.
6. Jane, mar. Peter Bray.
7. Martha, mar. Robert McCook.
8. Temperance, mar. Wm. Brewster.

WILLIAM PEARMAN, b. Va., 1760; d. Ga., after 1802. Served as Sergt., Capt. Ree's Co.; also under Capt. John Peyton's Va. Troops. Mar. Miss Weakley. A Rev. Soldier.
Children:
1. Elizabeth, mar. W. S. Douglas.
2. Robert, mar. Elizabeth Worthington (?).
3. Mary, mar. A. M. Duke.
4. Sarah, mar. Henry Duke.

5. Susan, mar. Thomas Douglas.
6. William.
7. Samuel.
8. Weakley.

HENRY PECK, b. Va., Dec. 25, 1764; d. Ga., 1855. Mar. Taliaferro Co., Ga., 1798, Polly Lockett. Enlisted Jan. 7, 1781 in Capt. John Peck's Co., Col. Elijah Clarke's Regiment, Ga. Troops; was at the Siege of Augusta.

Children:

1. William Winfrey, mar. Elizabeth Reed.
2. James, mar. Polly Swain.
3. Thomas, mar. Miss Jarrold.
4. Elizabeth.
5. Sarah, mar. Adam Hunter.
6. Mary, mar. — Trippe.

JONES PERSONS, b. Bute Co., N. C., 1760; d. Upson Co., Ga., 1850. Served as private, from Bute Co., N. C. Line; received bounty land in Ga. for his service. Mar. 1790, Diana Neal.

Children:

1. Thomas, mar. Nancy Freeman.
2. Pinckney, mar. Sarah Ann Williams.
3. Benjamin.
4. Lovett, mar. Malinda Lyons.
5. Jones, Jr., mar. Miss Neal.
6. Martha, mar. Stanley Purefoy.
7. Mary, mar. — Allison.
8. Sarah, mar. — Smith.

JOSHUA PEARCE, JR. (son of Joshua and Hannah Pearce, name sometimes spelled Pierce), b. St. Mathews Parish (now Screven Co.), Ga.; d., 1822, while on a visit to his brother, WILLIAM PEARCE, Rev. Sol. of Ga., who moved first to Miss., with his wife, Sarah Bray, and family. They moved later to La. His brother, STEPHEN PEARCE, was also a Rev. Sol. of Ga.; all lived in Effingham (later Screven) Co., Ga. JOSHUA PEARCE, JR. was a Rev. Sol. of Ga. and S. C.; received a grant of land in Effingham Co. for his service. Mar. (1) Mary —; (2) in La., 1821, Ann B. Bray.

Two of the daus. of Joshua Pearce, Jr., and his (1) wife, Mary —:

1. MARY PEARCE, mar., as (2) wife, WILLIAM McCALL, Rev. Sol. of Ga.
2. SARAH PEARCE, mar. Francis McCall, brother of WILLIAM McCALL, as (1) wife.

ISHAM PHILIPS, b. 1741; d. Henry Co., Ga., Dec. 14, 1837. Served as a private under Col. Greenberry Lee and in Md. Troops. Mar. Mary Dawson.

Their dau., Mary Phillips, mar., as (1) wife, John Dorsey.

JOHN PHINAZEE, b. Ireland, 1760; d. Harris Co., Ga., 1837. Served as private, S. C. Line; received bounty grant of land in Ga. for his service. Mar. 1788, SARAH HARRIS (1765–1856).

Children:

1. William, mar. Jane Potts.
2. James, mar. Polly Baldwin.
3. Harris, mar. Mary Ogletree.
4. Jonathan, moved to Cal.
5. Hiram (1802–1883), mar. Elizabeth Bird Ogletree (1803–1884). 9 children.
6. Rachel, mar. Joseph Bell.
7. Margaret, mar. George Bell.
8. Sallie, mar. Nathan Bramblett.
9. Polly, mar. Griffin Read.
10. Elizabeth, mar. Benjamin Read.
11. Mahala, mar. (1) Arthur Herring; (2) — Watts.

WILLIAM PIERCE (OR PEARCE), b. Ga., 1740; d. Savannah, Ga., Dec. 10, 1789; entered the Continental Army and became aide-de-camp to Gen. Nathaniel Greene. Member *Sons of*

Liberty, Savannah, Ga.; charter member *Society of the Cincinnati*. Mar. CHARLOTTE FEN-WICK (dau. of Edward Fenwick, of S. C.). After his death, she mar. (2) EBENEZER JACKSON, of Mass., *Rev. Sol.* (son of GEN. MICHAEL JACKSON, of Mass.). In 1781 Continental Congress presented a sword to MAJOR WM. PIERCE for his service.
One child:
  WILLIAM LEIGH PIERCE, of Savannah, Ga.
  (In 1791 GEN. GEORGE WASHINGTON, on his memorable visit to Ga., spent the night at the home of JOSHUA PEARCE (PIERCE), brother of MAJOR WILLIAM PIERCE, a *Rev. Sol.*, of Effingham Co., Ga. His homestead was built on the original grant of land given to him by George, III, of England. This home was made doubly historic, for in 1825 his son, STEPHEN PEARCE, entertained Marquis de La Fayette on his visit to the South, in 1825).

  JAMES PITTMAN, b. Amelia Co., Va., Mar. 4, 1756; d. Madison Co., Ga., 1850. Enlisted Columbia Co., Ga.; served under Capt. Germaine, Col. Marbury's S. C. Regiment, under Capt. Wm. Grier and under Col. Clarke on his expedition to Fla.; served in Va., 1781. Pensioned as private and Lieut., 1833, at Madison Co., Ga. Mar. July 5, 1781, Martha Taylor (dau. of JAMES TAYLOR, of Henry Co., Va., a *Rev. Sol.* of Va.; d. Tenn., and his wife, Nancy Owen), b. May 4, 1763; d. Va., 185-.
Children:
  1. John Green (1782–1873), mar. 1804, Polly Moore (dau. of JOHN MOORE, *Rev. Sol.*).
  2. Pleasant Owen, mar. Susanna Benton.
  3. Martin Hughes, mar. Nancy Smith.
  4. James, d. Miss., mar. Nancy Benton.
  5. Elizabeth Alice, d. Ala., mar. Samuel Barnett.
  6. Nancy, mar. Silas Smith.
  7. Lucinda, mar. Henry Harris.
  8. Timothy F., mar. Mary Ann Harris.
  9. Sarah Ann, mar. Sampson Lay.
  10. Martha Diana, mar. Abner Wells.
  11. Noah Washington, mar. (1) Lucinda Strickland; (2) Martha Smith.
  12. America Taylor (1805–1872), mar. Benjamin Woods.
  13. Teresa, mar. Wilson Strickland.

  JOHN PITTMAN, b. Va., 1723; settled in S. C., 1771; d. Richmond Co., Ga., April 19, 1785. Served in 4th Artillery, S. C. Regiment, under Capt. Harman Davis. Mar. in Va., 1747, MARY (called Polly) ROWE (OR BOW). She was a *Rev. Patriot* and was crippled by the Tories.
Children:
  1. BUCKNER, b. 1748; d. Adams Co., Mo., after 1805. A *Rev. Sol.* of Ga.
  2. Lucy (1750-1774).
  3. Sarah (1763-1771).
  4. JOHN, JR., b. 1752; a *Rev. Sol.*, mar. Eunice Marshall (dau. of REV. DANIEL MAR-SHALL, *Rev. Sol.* of Ga.).
  5. Mary, b. 1754, mar. PELEG ROGERS, a *Rev. Sol.* 10 children.
  6. JAMES (1756–1850); received pension as a *Rev. Sol.*; mar. Martha Taylor. 13 children.
  7. Patsey (1760), mar. David Langston, of S. C.
  8. Zilpha (1762), mar. Blanton Nobles.
  9. PHILIP, b. 1765; d. Decatur Co., Ga., 1849; a *Rev. Sol.* at 16 years of age. Mar. 1792, Epsie Jasper.
  10. Timothy, b. 1767; d. Ga., 1854.
  11. Grace, mar. Jamerson Andrews.

  JOHN PITTS, b. N. C., 1740; was murdered by the Tories in Effingham Co., Ga., 1787. Served as Capt., 1st Regiment, N. C. Militia, under Col. Samuel Jarvis. Mar. 1781, FRANCES GRIF-FIN. She mar. (2) — Marks.
Children:
  1. Tabitha (1782–1863), mar. 1799, Obediah Edwards (1777–1857) (son of WILLIAM ED-WARDS, a *Rev. Sol.*, and his wife, Chloe Stokes).
  2. Lorena.

3. Daniel, moved to Tenn.

4. Hardy Griffin (1787-1840), mar. (1) Widow Porter (she received part of Benjamin Porter's estate); (2) Elizabeth Scruggs (dau. of Gross Scruggs). Buried Colonial Cemetery, Savannah, Ga.

5. Elizabeth, mar. DANIEL DAMPIER (1757-1847), a *Rev. Sol.*

JAMES PONDER, b. S. C.; d. Screven Co., Ga., 1826., a *Rev. Sol.*; served as "Commissary and Wagon Master," S. C. Troops; received pay for Rev. service in S. C., June 10, 1785. Mar. in S. C., REBECCA ROBINS. They removed to Screven Co., Ga., where she d. 1828.

Their dau., MARY PONDER, mar. in Screven Co., Ga., Thomas Roberts, a *Sol. of the War of 1812* (son of ELIAS ROBERTS (ROBERT), *Rev. Sol.* of S. C., b. S. C.; d. Screven Co., Ga., and his wife, Mary Rue). MARY (PONDER) ROBERTS mar. (2) George Smith of Screven Co., Ga.

They had 4 children: 1. Elias, mar. Nancy Nevils; 2. Elizabeth, mar. Charles H. Johnson; 3. Patience, mar. Charles H. Nessmith (or Nesmith); 4. Polly Ann (possibly by (2) mar., to George Smith), mar. James Cone.

CHARLES POPE, b. Smyrna, Del.,1748-1784; d. Columbia Co., Ga., 1803. Served as Lieut. Col., Del. Regiment; was wounded 1776. Mar. (1) JANE STOKELEY (1752-1793); (2) 1799, SARAH SIMPSON (dau. of Thomas and Janet Simpson).

Children by (1) wife (only three known):

1. Benjamin Stokeley, mar. Eliza Wyatt.

2. Alexander (1777-1845), mar. Dorothy Bibb.

3. William, d. Petersburg, Ga., 1803.

OLIVER PORTER (son of John Porter, *Rev. Sol.* of Va., and Mary Anthony), b. Prince Edward Co., Va., 1763; d. Greene Co., Ga., 1838. Enlisted in the Regiment of his brother, WILLIAM PORTER, and was at the Siege of Yorktown; received land in Greene Co., Ga., for his service. Mar. Margaret Watson, b. 171- (dau. of DOUGLASS WATSON, b. Va., 1750; d. Wilkes Co., Ga., 1797; served in Va.; received bounty grant of land in Wilkes Co., Ga., for his service, and his wife, Margaret Parker. A *Rev. Sol.*)

Children known:

1. Ann (1793-1875), mar. 1815, Adam Goudylock Saffold (son of WILLIAM SAFFOLD, *Rev. Sol.*, who received land in Ga. for his service; he d. Ga.).

2. Douglass Watson, mar. Annabelle Burwell (dau. of JOHN BURWELL, *Rev. Sol.*, and his wife, Ann Powell).

3. James, b. Greene Co., Ga.; mar. Athline (or Abijah) Cox, b. Morgan Co., Ga. (dau. of John Cox, and his wife, Elizabeth Hyde) (dau. of JAMES HYDE, *Rev. Sol.*, who d. from effects of wounds received in service).

WILLIAM PORTER, b. Va.; d. Effingham Co., Ga., May 1791. Served in Va. Line; received bounty grant of land as a Refugee Soldier in Effingham Co., Ga. Mar. ELINOR STEWART. (His estate was administered by his son, David Porter, and appraised by Christian Treutlen, Samuel Bostwick and John Boykin).

Children:

1. Susanna, mar. Wm. Cox, of Barnwell, S. C.

2. James, mar. Elizabeth —.

3. William, Jr., mar. (1) Miss Treutlen; (2) Rachel (Wilson) Garnett (widow of THOMAS GARNETT, *Rev. Sol.*, of Effingham Co., Ga.).

4. Benjamin, mar. Elizabeth —.

5. David, mar. 1797, Sally Bostwick (dau. of Samuel Bostwick, and his wife, Ann Mary Maner).

DR. ANTOINE POULLAINE, b. France; d. Washington, Wilkes Co., Ga., 1794. Sailed to America from Bordeaux, France; served as *Rev. Sol.*, *Surgeon*, and private physician to Marquis de La Fayette. Mar. at Hanover Co., Va., about 1787, SARAH GARLAND WINGFIELD.

One child:

Dr. Thomas Noel Poullaine (1792-1889), Greensboro, Ga., mar. 1814, Harriet Bryan Wray.

HENRY POOL, b. England, 1759; mar. (1) in England, Susan Ratchett; they came to America; (2) Mary Hutchinson; (3) Eleanor Hutchinson; had many children. He served as a *Rev. Sol.* and was present at the Battles of King's Mt., Cheraw, Cowpens, and others; he drew land as a *Rev. Sol.*, in Warren Co., Ga., and the Cherokee Land Lottery of 1827. His grave marked by the D. A. R.

Two of his children were MARY and SARAH; both became members of the National Society, Daughters of the American Rev. as "Real Daughters."
Mary mar. ARCH NEWSOM; d. 1937.
Sarah lived at Gibson, Ga.; d. 1939.
(HENRY POOL and PHILIP POOL, *Rev. Sols.*, buried in Warren Co., Ga.)

BURWELL POPE, b. N. C., 1751; d. Wilkes Co., Ga., Jan. 9, 1800. Served in N. C. Line; received bounty grant of land in Ga. for his service in Oglethorpe (formerly Wilkes) Co. Mar. in N. C., 1772, PRISCILLA WOOTEN (1756-1806).
Children:
1. Robert (1775-1831).
2. Tabitha Christian (1778-1852), mar. 1795, Miles Hill.
3. Ann (1780-1805), mar. 1796, Noah Hill.
4. Martha (called Patsey) (1782-1853), mar. Wylie Hill.
5. Wylie, mar. Sallie Davis; removed to Ala.
6. Sarah, mar. Robert Holmes.
7. Burwell, Jr., 1790 (*Brig.-Gen., War of 1812*), mar. 1815, Sallie Key Strong.

JOHN POPE, b. Halifax Co., N. C., 1755; d. Wilkes Co., Ga., 1819. Served as Capt., Ga. Troops; received bounty grant of land in Ga. for his service. Mar. ELIZABETH SMITH, d. 1829.
Children:
1. Huldah, mar. Henry Jossey, Jr.
2. Keturah, mar. James Mathews, Jr.
3. Mary L., mar. — Henderson.
4. Wylie.
5. Rowena.
6. Louisa.
7. Martha, mar. Rev. William Callaway.
8. Augustine Burwell.

JAMES POWELL—Certificate that he was a prisoner and subsequently a *Refugee Sol.*, John Baker, Col., Aug. 19, 1784. Prays for bounty land.

LEWIS POWELL, b. Bladen Co., N. C., 1750; d. Dooly Co., Ga.; pension for service under Col. Thomas Robeson, N. C. Continental Line. Mar. 1777, Martha Thompson, b. Va.
One son:
Thompson Powell (1771-1844), mar. Charlotte H. Bridgers; moved to Macon, Ga.
(Perhaps other children).

MOSES POWELL, b. S. C., about 1755; d. Jasper Co., 1821. Served as private under Gen. Elijah Clarke of Ga.; received bounty land, 287½ acres, in Washington Co., Ga., for his service. Mar. 1777, Sarah —.
Children (not in order of birth):
1. George.
2. William.
3. Evan.
4. Benjamin.
5. Nancy, mar. — Respess.
6. Charity, mar. — McMichael.
7. Sarah, mar. — Goolsby.
8. Civility, mar. — Marks.
9. Catherine, mar. — Maddox.
10. Martha, mar. — Marchman.
(From will).

MOSES POWELL, b. 1760; d. Ga., 1834; a *Rev. Sol.*; mar. Nancy Pope (dau. of Wiley Pope).
Children:
1. Moses.
2. Alcamy.
3. Asa.

4. Chapman.
5. Bennett.
6. Silvey.
7. Pleasant.
8. Burchey.
9. Nancy.
10. Emily.
11. Francis.
12. Wiley Pope.
(From will).

WILLIAM POWELL, b. N. C., 1759; d. Ga., 1792. A *Rev. Sol.*; served as private in Col. Abraham Shepard's N. C. Regiment. Mar. Mariam Lamb.

Their dau., Mariam, mar. Jonathan Cloud.

GEORGE PURVIS, b. England, settled in Del.; came to Glynn Co., Ga., 1789, where he d. 18—. Enlisted in Del. Regiment, 1775; Second Lieut. in Capt. Patten's Co., Col. Hall's Regiment, April 1777. First Lieut. Oct. 1777. Was in Battles of Monmouth, Germantown, and Brandewine; was captured at Camden, S. C., and exchanged. Made Capt. 1782. Member of the Cincinnati. Mar. ELIZA —.

Children:
1. Polly, mar. Benjamin Franklin.
2. Sarah A., mar. 1821, John Flinn.
3. Martha Eliza, mar. James Hatcher.
4. William G., mar. Martha Goodwin Bills (dau. of Jonathan and Lucy Bills, who came to Glynn Co., Ga., from Middletown, Conn., 1819).

JOHN QUATERMAN, of Liberty Co., Ga., a *Rev. Sol.*, mar. Elizabeth —.

(Four of their sons, JOHN, JR., ROBERT, THOMAS and WILLIAM, were *Rev. Sols.*)

ROBERT QUATERMAN, b. 1744; d. Liberty Co., Ga., 1786. Served as private in Ga. Militia. Mar. (2) 1771, Elizabeth Baker, b. 1756.

Children:
1. Mary Ann, mar. 1797, Micajah Andrews (son of ISHAM ANDREWS, *Rev. Sol.*, Va. Troops, and his (1) wife, Rebecca Way).
2. Elizabeth (1776), mar. as (1) wife, Joseph Quaterman (her cousin).
3. Rebecca.
4. Joseph.
5. Sarah.
6. William.
7. Thomas.
8. John.
9. Susannah.

THOMAS QUATERMAN, b. S. C., Mar. 27, 1738; came with his parents to (now Liberty Co.), Ga., 1754; d. Medway, Ga., May 31, 1791. Served as private, Ga. Militia. Mar. (1) 1758, REBECCA BACON, d. 1775; (2) 1776, REBECCA SMALLWOOD; (3) Rebecca (Baker) Ball.

Children by (1) wife:
1. Rebecca, mar. 1775, John Norman.
2. JOSEPH (1764–1801), mar. his cousin, Elizabeth Quaterman. He served as private, Ga. militia. Their son, Joseph (1796–1863), mar. Harriet Stevens.
3. Thomas, Jr., mar. 1787, Renchie Norman.
4. William.
5. Sarah.

Child by (2) wife:
John.

Children by (3) wife:
1. Susanna.

2. Robert, mar. 4 times.
3. Thomas.

WILLIAM QUATERMAN, b. 1746; d. Ga., 1794. Served as *Rev. Sol.*, Ga. Line; received bounty land for his service. Mar. SARAH STEWART (1751–1832).

Children:
1. William, Jr.
2. Susanna.
3. John Stewart.
4. Cynthia B.
5. Sarah.
6. Richard.
7. Elizabeth.
8. Rebecca, mar. John Stacy.
9. Arlissa (a son).

NOTE: At the beginning of the Rev., the British occupation drove the inhabitants away from Medway and the famous Medway (Midway) Church.

MATTHEW RABUN, b. Halifax Dist., N. C., May 15, 1744; d. Hancock Co., Ga., May 14, 1819. Served with N. C. Troops. Commissioner of specific supplies and Assistant Quartermaster, General Commissioner for Halifax Co., N. C., 1781; mentioned as Staff Officer, N. C. records. Mar. in N. C., SARAH WARREN; came to Ga.

Children:
1. Jane (1766–1855), mar. 1790, JOHN VEAZEY (1760–1847), a *Rev. Sol.*
2. Elizabeth, d. y.
3. Sarah, mar. (1) — Moss; (2) Nathan Morris.
4. Martha, mar. Isaac Battle.
5. Mary, mar. (1) — Biggers; (2) — Brown; (3) Rev. Haygood; (4) John Bishop.
6. WILLIAM, b. 1771, mar. Nov. 21, 1793, Mary Battle. Was elected *Governor of Ga.*, in 1819.

JONATHAN RAGAN, b. Nottoway Co., Va., April 11, 1744; d. Washington Co., Ga. Will made in Wilkes (now Oglethorpe) Co., Ga., April 6, 1813; Pro. Mar. 1814. Served as private, Ga. Line, under Gen. Elijah Clarke; received bounty land for his service. Mar. ANN —, b. Va., 1745; d. Ga., before 1813.

Children (mentioned in will):
1. Nathaniel, b. 1762, mar. Elizabeth (Ray) Griffen.
2. Polly, mar. — Phillips.
3. John.
4. Nancy, mar. Joseph Callaway.
5. Rebecca, mar. — Callaway.
6. Winnie, mar. Isaac Callaway.
7. Abigail (Abi), mar. Richard Haynes.
8. Elizabeth, mar. William Lumpkin.
9. Asa.
10. Jonathan, Jr.
11. Jeremiah.
12. David, mar. (1) Elizabeth Simmons.
13. Jehu.
14. Marcus B.

JONATHAN RAHN, b. 1762; d. Effingham Co., Ga., 1840. Corporal, 2nd Ga. Batt. Mar. 1783, Christiana Buntz (1763–1824) (dau. of URBAN BUNTZ, *Rev. Sol.* of Ga.).

Children (2 known):
1. Emanuel, b. 1789, mar. 1811, Salome Berry (dau. of JOHN BERRY, b. 1762; d. Effingham Co., Ga., 1817; served as private, Effingham Co., Ga., Militia, and his wife, Mary Reisser).
2. Susannah (1798–1863), mar. 1820, John Wilson (son of JAMES WILSON (1745–1825) *Rev. Sol.* of N. C. and Effingham Co., Ga.).

REUBEN RANSOME, d. Clarke Co., Ga., 1833. (Will made Oct. 11, 1832, Pro. Mar. 4, 1833). He was a *Rev. Sol.*; drew land as a *Rev. Sol.* in 1827 Cherokee Land Lottery. (Grave marked by the D. A. R.) Mar. NANCY C. —.

Children:
1. Dudley.
2. Reuben, Jr.
3. Nancy, mar. — Perkins.
4. Polly.
5. Jane, mar. — Turner.
6. Joseph.
7. Elizabeth, mar. — Cook.
8. Richardson D.
9. William.
10. Dau. mar. Isaac Knowles.

ABRAHAM RAVOT, b. S. C.; d. Ga. (son of Gabriel Frances Ravot and his wife, Louise Catherine Malette). Served as Capt., Effingham Co., Ga., Militia. Mar. (1) —, d. July 16, 1795; (2) Mary Mikell, widow, d. 1811.

Children by (1) wife:
1. Abraham, Jr., b. 1773.
2. Henrietta, b. 1775, mar. 1795, John Porter.

Children by (2) wife:
1. Margaret Marie, mar. William King, Jr.
2. Mary.
3. Elizabeth, mar. John Palmer.
(Perhaps other children).

ANDERSON REDDING, b. Va., 1764; d. Monroe Co., Ga., 1845. Buried Salem Churchyard, near Bolingbroke, Ga. Served as private, Va. Line; was at the surrender at Yorktown. Mar. DELILAH PARHAM.

Children:
1. William Chambless, mar. Margaret Flewellyn (dau. of ABNER FLEWELLYN, *Rev. Sol.*).
2. Elizabeth, mar. John Green.
3. Rowland.
4. Thomas (1794–1877), mar. Maria Searcy.
5. Lourania.
6. Mary.
7. James M.

WILLIAM REDDING, b. Va., 1736; d. Ga., 1822. Served with Va. Troops; received bounty land in Ga. for his service; moved to Ga., 1785. Mar. PATTY PARHAM.

Children (known):
1. CHARLES, b. Va., 1756; d. Ga., 1815, a *Rev. Sol.*; mar. Edith —.
2. Arthur, mar. Frances Wynne.
3. ANDERSON, b. Va., 1764; d. Ga., 1845; a *Rev. Sol.*; mar. Delilah Parham.

JACOB REDWINE, b. Oct. 12, 1751; d. Coweta Co., Ga., 1840. Removed from Montgomery Co., N. C. Served as private in Capt. John Johnston's Co., Col. John Collier's Regiment of Militia. Moved to Ga., 1784. Mar. ROWENA RHINEHEART, b. 1755; d. Elbert Co., Ga., July 4, 1831.

Children:
1. Elizabeth, b. 1778, mar. John W. Carroll.
2. Mary, b. 1777, mar. William Ballinger.
3. Jemina, mar. — McGee.
4. Sally, mar. — Larramore.
5. Kate, mar. — Hearn.
6. Barbara, mar. Joseph Parker.
7. Nancy, mar. — Underwood.

8. Lewis, mar. Mary Merritt.
9. Jacob, mar. — Tuble.
10. Michael, mar. — Hart.
11. John, mar. — Crawford.

SAMUEL REID, b. Rowan Co., N. C., 1728; d. Putnam Co., Ga., 1810. Lived in Iredell Co., N. C.; a member of the Council of Safety; Capt. in Col. Alexander's Regiment, Gen. Rutherford's N. C. Brigade; received bounty land in Ga. for his services. Mar. 1753, AGNES KAY (OR McKAY) She d. 1806.
Children:
1. Samuel, Jr., b. 1758; d. Jasper Co., Ga., 1842; mar. Emily Elizabeth Hurt.
2. Alexander (1769–1810), mar. Elizabeth Brewer.
3. William.
4. James.
5. John.
6. Andrew.
7. Mary Hall.
8. Margaret.
9. Jean.
10. Agnes.
11. Sarah.

JOHN REMSHART, b. England; came to Ga. With Gen. James Edward Oglethorpe on his second voyage to Ga.; joined the Salzburger Colony at Ebenezer. Made will Aug. 15, 1782, Pro. Nov. 20, 1782, Effingham Co., Ga. Was a *Rev. Patriot.* Mar. Feb. 14, 1764, ANNA MARGARET MUELLER.
Children:
1. DANIEL, b. Oct. 26, 1765; mar. Elizabeth Waldhauer. A *Rev. Sol.*
2. Catherina.
3. Judith.
4. Asa.
5. Christine.
6. Christian.
7. Elizabeth.

JOSHUA RENDER, b. —; made will in Wilkes Co., Ga., April 1, 1817; Pro. Nov. 2, 1818. He was a *Rev. Sol.* Mar. Susan (or Susanna) —, d. Wilkes Co. Ga., 1820.
Children:
1. Christopher, mar. 1810, Elizabeth Wilkerson. He d. 1826.
2. James.
3. Susan, mar. Johnson Wellborn.
4. Joshua, Jr., d. 1824.
5. Martha, mar. Abner Wellborn.
6. Elizabeth, mar. 1820, Nathan Truitt.
7. Nancy, mar. Nicholas Wiley.
8. Dau., mar. Joshua Callaway and their dau. mar. Purnal Truitt.

AMOS RICHARDSON, b. —; d. Elbert (now Hart) Co., Ga. Served as private, Ga. Line. (Grave in Sardis Churchyard, Hart Co., marked by the D. A. R.) Mar. SUSAN SMITH.
Children:
1. Mahlon, mar. Sallie Self (dau. of Samuel E. Self).
2. Crissa, mar. 1824, Sinclair McMullen.
3. James V., mar. (1), 1830, Milly Bobo; (2) Elizabeth McMullen.
4. Willis, mar. Drucilla Gaines.
5. Annie, mar. John Farmer.

DANIEL RICHARDSON, b. England; came to America, settled in Culpeper Co., Va.; moved to S. C., then to Ga. D. Hancock Co., Ga., 1796. Enlisted in Capt. Levine's Co., 9th Va. Regiment., Col. George Mathews, as Lieut. Mar. FRANCES LONG, d. Ga., 1796 (dau. of REU-

BEN LONG, a *Rev. Sol.*, who had 7 sons as *Sols. in Rev. War.* She was g.-dau. of COL. BLOOM-FIELD LONG, *Rev. Sol.* of Va.).

Children:
1. Thomas.
2. Obediah, mar. Jane Bush.
3. Polly, mar. — Thomas.
4. Elizabeth, mar. — Harris.
5. Katie, mar. — Lamar.
6. Nancy, mar. Sam Dent.
7. Margaret, mar. — Williams.
8. Gabriel.
9. Sally.
10. Julia, mar. — Baxter.
11. Armistead, b. 1788; d. Putnam Co., Ga. *Sol. of 1812.* Mar. Elizabeth Griggs, Putnam Co., Ga.

JOEL RIVERS, b. Prince George Co., Va., April 6, 1761; d. Sparta, Hancock Co., Ga., 1829; received bounty land in Ga. as a *Rev. Sol.* Mar. before 1789, JEMINA BONNER, b. Mar. 11, 1761.

Children:
1. William, b. 1790.
2. Jane, b. 1792.
3. Jacobus.
4. Nancy.
5. Henry.
6. Robert.
7. Sarah Ann, b. 1808, mar. James Robert Lewis.
8. Bonner, b. 1810.
9. Lucy, b. 1813.
(Perhaps other children).

ELIAS ROBERTS (ROBERT), b. Santee District, S. C., 1745; d. Screven Co., Ga., after 1815. Served in the S. C. Militia. Mar. in S. C., MARY RUE, b. France; d. Yamacraw Bluff, Ga., 1815, "leaving 5 adult children." They were living in Savannah, Ga., 1789.

Children:
1. Mary.
2. Elias, Jr.
3. Thomas. (See later.)
(Two other children, names unknown).

THOMAS ROBERTS, b. S. C., 1787; d. Screven Co., Ga., 1816. Was a *Sol. of the War of 1812.* Mar. Mary Ponder (dau. of JAMES PONDER, *Rev. Sol.* of Ga.). She mar. (2) George Smith, of Screven Co., Ga.

Children:
1. Elias, mar. Nancy Nevils (dau. of JACOB NEVILS, *Rev. Sol.* of Ga.).
2. PATIENCE, mar. Charles H. Nessmith.
3. Elizabeth, mar. Charles H. Johnson.
4. Polly Ann, mar. James Cone. (Perhaps Polly Ann Smith by (2) marriage).

WILLIAM ROBERTSON, b. —; d. Franklin Co., Ga., 1803. *Rev. Sol.*; received bounty land in Ga., on certificate of John Twiggs, Mar. 23, 1784; also certificate of Col. Elijah Clarke, April 20, 1784. Mar. Majeen (Jane), d. 1830.

Children:
1. William.
2. Samuel.
3. Margaret.
4. Elizabeth, mar. — Brixy.
5. Sarah, mar. — Ragsdale.

6. Rebecca, mar. — Toney.
7. Rhoda, mar. — Williams.
(Perhaps other children).

JOHN ROBINSON (OR ROBERSON), b. May 6, 1756; d. Baldwin Co., Ga., Dec. 18, 1832. Applied for pension Nov. 1832. Served in Va. Enlisted after Battle of Trenton for 3 years with Wm. Porter, recruiting officer; served in Capt. William Taylor's 2nd Va. Regiment; taken prisoner at Charleston, but escaped. Mar. Mar. 27, 1788, JERIAH —, b. Columbia Co., Ga., Aug. 19, 1769. His wife applied for pension May 8, 1839, as the widow of a *Rev. Sol.*

Children:
1. Solomon, b. 1789.
2. John, b. 1792.
3. Sally, b. 1794.
4. Luke, b. 1797.
5. William, b. 1798.
6. Maria, b. 1801.

JERIAH ROBINSON, widow, was living in Baldwin Co., Ga., Dec. 6, 1843.

RANDAL ROBINSON, b. Granville Co., N. C., May 2, 1762; d. Newnan, Ga., Feb. 27, 1842. Served in N. C., Jan. 1, 1777 to Nov. 15, 1778; moved to Edgefield District, S. C., 1779, and served 189 days in Capt. Waters' S. C. Regiment. Mar. (1) 1789, LYDIA WALKER, d. 1790; (2) PHERIBY HILL (1767-1874).

Child by (1) wife:
Mary, mar. Falkner Heard.

Children by (2) wife:
1. Martha.
2. Elizabeth, mar. Peyton Prichard.
3. Samuel, d. y.
4. Alma, mar. Turner Persons.
5. Permilia, mar. Caleb Cook.
6. John Evans, mar. (1) 1829, Mary Wingfield; (2) 1835, Sarah Ramey.

REUBEN ROGERS, b. Northampton Co., N. C., Nov. 1, 1735; d. Warren Co., Ga., 1794. Served as private under Col. Elijah Clarke; captured by British and held as prisoner of war. Name appears on monument erected by the Government and D. A. R. at Kettle Creek; received bounty land for his service in Wilkes (now Warren) Co., Ga. Mar. Dec. 15, 1767, TEMPERANCE JAMES, b. Aug. 24, 1751.

Children:
1. John (1769), mar. 1802, Nancy Swain.
2. Faith (1771), mar. — Darden.
3. Mary.
4. Clary.
5. Nancy, mar. — Saxon.
6. Reuben, Jr., mar. Elizabeth Emerson. She mar. (2) Elias Wilson.
7. Phoebe, mar. Frederick Brown.
8. Temperance, mar., as (2) wife, Thomas Lockett.
9. Joseph (1784), mar. Frances Gardner. She mar. (2) — Stafford.
10. Rebecca (1786), mar. Michael Cody. Their dau., Louise Amanda Cody, mar. JAMES M. WELLBORN (son of ELIAS WELLBORN, *Rev. Sol.*).

WILLIAM ROSE, b. N. C., about 1725; d. Ga. Enlisted, 1776, in Capt. Nelson's Co., Col. Thomas Polk's N. C. Regiment of Militia. Mar. Amy Langston.

Children (from will; bro.-in-law, James Langston, Ex. of will):
1. JOHN, b. N. C., 1746; d. Ga., 1846. Served as private in Col. Thomas Polk's Regiment, N. C. Militia, and also with Ga. Troops under Col. Elijah Clarke. Mar. 1778, Mary Washington.
2. Frederick.
3. William.
4. Howell.

5. Martha (called Patsey), mar. JESSE MILLER, *Rev. Sol.* of S. C., who received land grant in Ga. for his service.

6. Sarah.

7. Elizabeth.

8. Winifred.

JOHN RUSHIN (RUSHING), b. Cheraw, S. C., 1764; d. Ga., on Flint River, 1843; buried Montezuma, Ga. Served as Lieut. in Col. Benton's S. C. Regiment; was also a *Sol. in War of 1812.* Mar. 1780, Rachel Renfro (1765–1833).

Children:

1. Joel, b. 1785.

2. John, b. 1791.

3. William, b. 1794; d. 1843, mar. Mary (Polly) Cox.

4. Mary, b. 1801.

5. James, b. 1787.

6. Elizabeth, b. Wilkes Co., Ga., 1792; d. Brooks Co., Ga., 1875. Mar. (1) 1810, Elisha Gardner; (2) John French.

7. Matilda, b. 1797.

8. Caroline, b. 1807.

9. Evelyn, b. 1805.

(Grave marked by Ga. D. A. R.)

JOHN RUTHERFORD, b. S. C., 1760; d. Baldwin Co., Ga., 1833. Served under Gen. Nathaniel Greene; received bounty grant of land in Wilkes Co., Ga., for his service. Mar. (1) Mary (Polly) Hubert (dau. of BENJAMIN HUBERT, *Rev. Sol.* of Warren Co., Ga.); (2) Sally Gordon, widow. On his tombstone, 3 miles from Sandersville, Ga., on Milledgeville Rd., is the following inscription: "To the memory of JOHN RUTHERFORD, a Soldier of the Revolution who lived long to share the honors of his countrymen. Died Oct. 31, 1833. Buried at his request by the side of his first wife, Polly Hubert." He was the son of ROBERT RUTHERFORD, of N. C., *Rev. Sol.* (His brother, THOMAS, mar. Nancy Harvey).

Children by (1) wife:

1. William, mar. Eliza Boykin (1806–1837) (dau. of MAJOR FRANCIS BOYKIN, *Rev. Sol.*, who moved from S. C. to Milledgeville, Ga. Grave marked by the Ga. D. A. R.).

2. Dorothy, mar. (1) Samuel Wiggins; (2) Joshua Bigham.

3. Francis Jeter.

Children (mentioned in will of John Rutherford, Baldwin Co., Ga., present wife, SALLY GORDON widow):

1. John G.

2. Nathaniel.

3. Robert's (dec.) heirs.

4. Benjamin.

5. William.

6. Dorothy, and the children by her first husband, Samuel Wiggins.
   John W. Gordon, son of Sally Gordon by previous marriage.

SAMUEL RUTHERFORD, *Rev. Sol.*, buried in Warren Co., Ga.

BALTHAZER SCHAEFFER, b. Seckback, Frankfort on the Main, Germany, April 1, 1742; came to Savannah, Ga., 1770; mar. there (1) May 30, 1772, Margaret Eppinger, b. Wilmington, N. C., Jan. 14, 1755; d. Savannah, Ga., Oct. 1793; (2) Widow Unselt. He d. Savannah, Ga., May 1, 1811. Served as a *Rev. Sol.*, private, Ga. Troops, under Gen. Lachlan McIntosh.

Children:

1. John W., b. 1773, mar. Mary Lawrence.

2. George, b. 1775, mar. Mary Morgan of N. Y.

3. James, b. 1777, mar. Susan Dasher.

4. Ferderick, b. 1779, mar. Mary Cole.

5. Margaret, b. 1781, mar. Mr. Gugle.

6. Jacob, b. —, mar. the widow of his brother, John W.

7. Sarah, b. 1787.

8. Hannah Eppinger, b. 1789.
9. Elizabeth.
10. Simon Peter, b. 1792; d. N. Y., 1849.

WILLIAM SCOTT, b. Louise Parish, Va., 1754; d. Monroe Co., Ga., 1806. Served as Capt., Ga. Troops, under Gen. Elijah Clarke. Mar. 1784, JANE THOMAS (1763–1808).
Children:
1. Annie (1785–1850), mar. 1806, Charles H. Willingham.
2. Daniel (1787), mar. Jemina Walker.
3. Jane, mar. — Sanford.
4. Polly, mar. —Welch.
5. Darius.
6. James.
7. Isaac.
8. John.
9. Sarah.
10. Samuel.
11. Benjamin.

JEREMIAH SANFORD, b. Loudon Co., Va., Nov. 4, 1739; d. Greensboro, Ga., Aug. 11, 1825. On his tombstone the epitaph reads: "A Rev. Soldier, an honest man, a Friend of Gen. George Washington." Served as private, Ga. Militia. Mar. 1766, MARY MODESSETT (1746–1793).
Children:
1. Vincent, b. April 17, 1770, mar. Priscilla Palmer.
2. Benjamin, b. Nov. 26, 1771, mar. Jane Armour.
3. Jeremiah, Jr., b. Sept. 24, 1772, mar. 1798, Ada Palmer (1776–1864).
4. Daniel, b. Jan. 28, 1778, mar. Elizabeth Totley.
5. Mildren Washington, b. July 12, 1781, mar. Israel Palmer.
6. Thomas, b. 1783; d. y.

RICHARD SASNETT, JR. (son of RICHARD SASNETT, of France, S. C., and N. C., *Rev. Sol.* of N. C., and his wife, Henrietta), b. Edgecomb Co., N. C., 1758; mar. (1) —; (2) 1786, REBECCA BORDEN (dau. of Joseph Borden, of N. J. and N. C.). Served as private in Capt. Joseph Borden's Co. of Mounted Riflemen, under Gen. Morgan; was in Battles of King's Mt., Cowpens, and Guilford C. H. Moved with his family, 1800, to Hancock Co., Ga., and settled on Buffalo Creek. Here they both d. and are buried on the old Arnold Plantation, Hancock Co., Ga.
Children:
1. Mary Elizabeth, b. 1787, mar. Henry Harris.
2. Sarah Jane, b. 1789, mar. William Hall.
3. Joseph Richard, b. Feb. 12, 1793, mar. June 16, 1812, Rhoda Henderson Turner (dau. of Philip and Juda (Parker) Turner). He d. Hancock Co., Ga., 1849. 4 children.

BRIGADIER-GENERAL JAMES SCREVEN, b. James Island, S. C., 1744; d. Nov. 24, 1778, from a wound received in a skirmish with British Soldiers near Midway Church, Ga. (In 1915 U. S. Congress erected a monument jointly to the memory of GEN. SCREVEN and GEN. DANIEL STEWART, and this monument marks the spot where Gen. Screven was buried in old Midway Churchyard near Darien, Ga.). He mar. 1764, MARY ESTHER ODINGSELL (dau. of Charles Odingsell), d. Jan. 6, 1779.
Children:
1. ESTHER (1765–1801), mar. Thomas Smith.
2. MARY ESTHER (1767–1845), mar. CAPT. JOHN HART (son of REV. OLIVER HART, a *Rev. Sol.*, and his wife, Sarah Breese), b. 1758; d. 1814. A *Rev. Sol.* of S. C., Lieut, 1777, 7th S. C. Regiment, then Capt.; captured at Siege of Savannah. In 1815, his widow moved to Liberty Co., Ga., where she d.; received pension as widow of *Rev. Sol.* Children: 1. Oliver James; 2. Esther Mary; 3. Martha Lee; 4. John S.; 5. Charles T.; 6. Henry William; 7. Elizabeth Screven Lee; 8. Odingsell W.; 9. Smith Screven.
3. Martha.
4. James.

5. CHARLES ODINGSELL, b. 1773; d. N. Y., 1830. Mar. (1) Lucy (Barnard) Jones; (2) Barbara Rankin Golphin. They lived at Sunbury, Ga.
6. Thomas.

REV. OLIVER HART, b. Warminster, Penn., July 5, 1723; d. Hopewell, N. J., Dec. 31, 1795. As a minister of the First Baptist Church, Charleston, S. C., he was appointed by the Council of Safety to reconcile the settlers on the frontier. He served as Chaplain in Continental Army. Mar. (1) Sarah Breese (1729-1772); (2) 1774, Ann Marie (Sealy) Grimball.

JOHN SCREVEN (bro. of Gen. James Screven), b. James Island, S. C., 1750; d. S. C., 1801. (Lived in Ga. and known as the Ga. Screvens.) Served as Lieut. of the St. John Rangers of Liberty Co., Ga. Mar. (1) 1772, PATIENCE HOLMES; (2) 1776, ELIZABETH (PENDARVIS) BRY-AN, widow of Josiah Bryan.
Children by (2) marriage:
1. John (1777-1830), mar. Hannah Proctor.
2. Richard Bedon, mar. (1) Alice Pendarvis.
3. Sarah (1780-1841), mar., as (2) wife, MAJ. WM. HAZZARD, of S. C. (1759-1821), who served as Aide to Gen. Anthony Wayne and was wounded at Siege of Savannah.
4. Martha, mar. James West, of S. C.
5. Elizabeth, mar. John Brooks Posey (son of GEN. POSEY, *Rev. Sol.* of Orange Co., Va.).
6. Mary Bedon, mar. Stephen Royer Proctor.
7. Thomas Edward, mar. Cornelia Ann McNich.

THOMAS SEMMES, b. Md., 1753; d. Wilkes Co., Ga., 1823. Served in Capt. Walter Hanson's Co., as Lieut., Md. Regiment. Mar. in Charles Co., Md., Feb. 1779, Mary Ann (Radcliff) Brawner.
Children:
1. Roger Semmes, b. Dec. 1779; d. 1804; mar. Jane Sanders.
2. Andrew G.
3. James R.
(Two bros. of Thomas Semmes were JOSEPH SEMMES, *Rev. Sol.* of Md., mar. Henrietta Thompson; and ANDREW SEMMES, killed at one of the Battles on Long Island).

SAMUEL SENTELL, b. 1759; d. Ga., 1844; received bounty grant of land in Ga. Mar. NANCY STEPHENS. A *Rev. Sol.*
Children:
1. William, b. 1783.
2. Nathan.
3. Elizabeth, mar. Larkin Cardin.
4. Samuel, Jr.
5. John.
6. Sarah, mar. Andrew Griffin.
7. Brittain.
8. Hetty Louise, mar. Rev. Edmund R. Reynolds.
9. Martin.
10. Nancy, mar. Ingram Love.

EDMUND SHACKELFORD, b. Va.; d. Elbert Co., Ga., 1821. Served in Va. Militia; his widow drew land as widow of *Rev. Sol.* in Cherokee Land Lottery, 1827, while a resident of Jackson Co., Ga. Mar. JUDITH —.
Children (mentioned in will):
1. Philip.
2. Edmund.
3. John, mar. Martha Mann.
4. Reuben.
5. Jefferson.
6. Nancy, mar. Drury Oglesby.
7. Elizabeth, mar. John Seal.
8. Judith, mar. Mordecai Alexander
9. Polly, mar. John Harris.

JOHN SHACKELFORD (son of Roger and Carey (Baker) Shackelford), b. Parish of Stratton Major (now King and Queen Co.), Va., 1750; d. Hancock Co., Ga., April 3, 1800. A *Rev. Sol.* of Va., served with the Va. Army in Ga.; received bounty land for his service in Ga. Mar. Hanover Co., Va., 1775, FRANCES WADE BUTLER (dau. of Edmund and Susanna Butler, of Va.), b. Va., 1755; d. Hancock Co., Ga., Sept. 23, 1811.

Children:

    1. Anna, b. April 2, 1776, unmar.

    2. Elizabeth (1781-1860), mar. GEN. EPPS BROWN, of Hancock Co., Ga. (1765-1827), a *Rev. Sol.* of Ga.

    3. Mary, mar. Charles Wingfield, of Wilkes Co., Ga.

    4. Nancy (1785-1858), mar. George Rives, of Hancock Co., Ga. (son of CAPT. GEORGE RIVES, *Rev. Sol.* of Va.).

    5. Susanna, d. 1815, mar. — Lawson.

    6. Frances Wade, mar. David Edward Butler.

    7. Edmund, mar. Miss Broadnax.

    8. John, d. unmar.

    9. James, mar. Martha Broadnax.

HENRY SHACKELFORD, b. Va. —; d. Elbert Co., Ga. Will made April 5, 1808, Pro. Jan. 5, 1819. Was a *Rev. Patriot.* Mar. —, wife d. before 1808.

Children (mentioned in will):

    1. Henry, Jr.

    2. Edmund, mar. Judith —.

    3. Nancy.

    4. Betsey.

    5. Jenny.

    6. Fanny.

    (G.-son, Edmund Alexander).

JOHN SHEFFIELD (SHUFFLE OR SHUFFIELD), father of West Sheffield, was a *Rev. Sol.* and received a bounty grant of land in Ga. for his service. He mar. ELIZABETH GRADDY. (widow of William Graddy, by whom she had one son, William Graddy, Jr.).

Children (not in order of birth):

    1. Ephriam.

    2. WILLIAM, a *Rev. Sol.*; received bounty grant in Ga. for his service.

    3. Wright.

    4. ISHAM, b. 1750; d. Duplin Co., N. C., 1784. Served as *Rev. Sol.*, private in Duplin Co., N. C. Militia. Mar. Barbara Boney (1753-1819) (dau. of WIMBECK BONEY, *Rev. Sol.* of N. C., and his wife, Catherine Mallard). Descendants came to Ga.

    5. Bryan.

    6. WEST, b. N. C., 1747; d. Wayne Co., Ga., 1830. (See West Sheffield, below).

    7. Arthur.

    8. Nancy, mar. — Screws.

    9. Levisa.

   10. Polly.

   11. Catherine.

   12. Tabitha.

WEST SHEFFIELD, son of John Sheffield (Shuffle or Shuffield), b. N. C., 1747; d. Wayne Co., Ga., 1830. Removed to Ga. before the *Rev. War.* and settled in St. George's Parish. (Wayne Co. is now a part of this Parish.) Served as a private in Ga. Troops; received a bounty grant of land in Ga. for his service. Mar. (1) 1774, Susanna Sherrard, b. 1752; d. 1802; (2) 1803, Elizabeth —, b. 1765.

Children by (1) wife:

    1. Sidnah, b. Nov. 11, 1775, mar. Job. Tison, b. 1770.

    2. Aaron.

    3. Sherrard, b. 1782.

    4. Bryant (1784-1855), mar. Elizabeth Ogden (1804-1887).

5. Pliny.
6. Flora.
7. Catherine.
8. Randall.
9. John (1804–1883), mar. 1825, Sarah Ann Cook (1806–1895).

JOHN SHICK, b. Germany, 1726; d. Savannah, Ga., 1797. Served as Lieut. in Continental Army of Ga.; was wounded and lost his right arm; was prisoner on British ship; received bounty grant for service. Mar. MARGARET RITTER.

Children:
1. Elizabeth Susanna, mar. ISAAC FELL, *Rev. Sol.*
2. Peter.

When the British took Savannah, one of their prisoners was ISAAC FELL, the fiance of ELIZABETH SUSANNA SHICK, and in her efforts to secure his freedom, the British officers offered her wine and insisted upon a toast. She gave the following toast impromptu. "Here's to those who were turned out and not to those who turned them out; I hope to see a turn about of those turned in who were turned out." She secured the release of her lover.

JOHN SHINE, b. Jones Co., N. C., May 13, 1759; d. Twiggs Co., Ga., Mar. 10, 1832. Served as private, 1780, N. C. Troops, under Col. Caswell. Mar. Clarissa Williams (dau. of James Williams of N. C.), d. Nov. 24, 1817.

Children (known):
1. Daniel W., b. 1786; *Sol. of 1812;* mar. (1) Mary Womble; (2) 1826, Nancy Glenn.
2. Cassandra (1788), mar. 1806, James Harrison.
3. Sarah Williams (1784), mar. James Miller.

JOHN SHINE was a guest in Milledgeville, Ga., when LaFayette visited there in 1825.

SAMUEL SHY (SHI), b. 1765; d. Jasper Co., Ga., Dec. 13, 1830. Buried about a mile from Pennington, Morgan Co., Ga. Served as a private; received land in Hancock Co., Ga., for his service. Mar. JANE —. She d. Sept. 12, 1843.

Children:
1. Sarah, mar. Thomas Tyler.
2. Nicey, mar. Thomas Aikens.
3. Eleanor, mar. Joseph Howard.
4. Polly, mar. James Aikens.
5. Eliza, mar. Samuel Pennington.
6. Mariah, mar. Ransom Harwell.
7. Seaborn.

JONAS SHIVERS, b. Va., 1749; d. Warren Co., Ga., Nov. 12, 1826. Will made Sept. 6, 1825, Pro. Dec. 1826. Mar. LILLIORY GODWIN; she d. Aug. 8, 1826. Served as private, Ga. Line; received grant of land in Ga. for his service.

Children:
1. Barnaby.
2. Willis.
3. William.
4. Thomas.
5. James.

WILLIAM STUBLEY SHIRLEY (son of Richard Shirley, who came with his brother, William, from Augusta Co., Va., and settled in Ga.), b. Washington Co., Ga., 1757; d. Ga. Oct. 10, 1833. Served as private, Ga. Troops. Mar. Washington Co., Ga., 1780, Elizabeth Maxwell.

Children:
1. Richard Charles, b. 1781, mar. (1) Sarah Brooks; (2) Nancy Porter.
2. James.
3. John.
4. Samuel.
5. Edward.
6. Mahaley Parker.

7. Mary.
8. William S., Jr.
9. Elizabeth.

James, John and Samuel were triplets, b. 1783. William S., Jr., and Elizabeth were twins.

ABRAHAM SIMONS, d. Wilkes Co., Ga., 1823. He was a Rev. Sol. and a Jew. Mentions in will: step-son, Owen Holliday; dau., Nancy, mar. William Grant of Washington, Ga., and their children: Nancy Richardson Grant; Augustin and Thomas Grant; Elizabeth, his dau., mar. Christopher Brooks; wife, NANCY. He lived six miles from Washington, Ga., the house still standing. According to his expressed desire, he was buried in an erect position, with his gun, by the side of the road. The widow, NANCY MILLS SIMONS, mar., 1827, Jesse Mercer (son of Silas Mercer, both noted Baptist Preachers of Ga.) and the fortune of her first husband, the Colonial Jew, helped to build Mercer (Baptist) University of Ga.

ADAM SIMMONS, b. Va.; d. Wilkes (Oglethorpe) Co., Ga., 1810. Mar. Rebecca —. He was a Rev. Sol.; received bounty grant of land in Ga. for his service as private Va. and Ga. Line.
Children:
1. Rebecca, mar. 1817, James Tucker.
2. Adam, Jr., mar. Elizabeth —. He d. Oglethorpe Co., Ga., 1819. (His mother, Rebecca Simmons was living with him.) 10 children.

JAMES SIMMONS, drew 287½ acres of bounty land in Washington Co., Ga., April 8, 1785.
HENRY SIMMONS, Rev. Sol., drew land Wilkes Co., 1788. Mar. Margaret —.

JOHN SIMMONS, JR., b. Va. (son of John Simmons and (1) wife); moved to Wilkes Co., Ga., where he d. Served as private Va. Continental Army. Mar. Ann Freeman (dau. of Holman Freeman, Sr., of Wilkes Co., Ga.) Eleven of his bros., all Rev. Sols. of Ga., Va. and N. C. came to Wilkes Co., Ga., viz: WILLIAM, SR.; JAMES; HENRY; STERNE, SR.; ADAM; RICHARD; ASA; JESSE; PHILIP; STEPHEN; THOMAS.
Children (mentioned in will):
1. Moses W.
2. John, Jr.
3. Holman F.
4. Susanna, mar. John L. Richardson, of Nacoochee, Ga.

JOHN SIMMONS, b. Scotland, 1712, came to America and settled in Va. Mar. (1) name unknown. He moved to Wilkes Co., Ga., 1773; (2) REBECCA —. He served as Rev. Sol. in Va. and in Ga.; served under Gen. Elijah Clarke at the Battle of Kettle Creek; received a grant of 287½ acres land for his service on Shoulderbone Creek, Washington Co., Ga. Sept 1, 1794 he willed "the 650 acres where I now reside (formerly Wilkes Co.) and the 287½ acres in Hancock Co., received for my service as a Rev. Sol." to his children by (2) wife. He d. 1797; his (2) wife d. before this, about. 1795.

Children by (1) wife:
1. William, Sr.
2. Thomas.
3. John, Jr.
4. Richard.
5. James.
6. Adam, Sr.
7. Asa.
8. Henry.
9. Jesse.
10. Sterne, Sr.
Others.

These sons were all Rev. Sols. of Ga., Va., and N. C. They moved with their families to Wilkes Co., Ga., where they received bounty land for their services.
Children by (2) wife:
1. Thomas, lived in Lincoln Co., Ga.
2. Rebecca, mar. Joseph Westmoreland.
3. Elizabeth, mar. Ishmael Davis.

4. KEZIAH, b. Wilkes Co., Ga., 1784; d. "Poplar Grove," DeKalb Co., Ga., Mar. 8, 1868. Mar. Feb. 14, 1805 in Miss. as (2) wife, Reuben Westmoreland (son of JOSEPH WESTMORELAND, *Rev. Sol.* of Va., and his wife, Martha Shores, of Va. and Ga.)

    5. Susannah.
    6. Ruth.
    7. David, moved to Miss.
    8. Elijah, moved to Miss.

(The grave of JOHN SIMMONS, *Rev. Sol.*, has been marked by the D. A. R. Grave located 8 miles from Sparta, Hancock Co., Ga.)

JOHN SIMMONS, b. Va., moved to N. C., then to Ga.; d. Talbot Co., Ga., 1837. Wounded at Battle of Cowpens; served in N. C. Militia. Mar. Miss Nutt in 1756.

Children (known):

    1. WILLIAM, b. N. C., 1758. Served in N. C. Militia as *Rev. Sol.*; obtained bounty land in Ga. for his service; obtained a pension and was living in Ga., 1832. He changed his name to Isaac for his uncle, ISAAC NUTT, a *Rev. Sol.* of N. C., killed at the Battle of Cowpens.
    2. Rhoda.
    3. Winnie.
    4. Sarah.
    5. John.

STERN SIMMONS, b. Va., came to the "Ceded Lands" of Ga. from S. C., and d. Wilkes (now Lincoln) Co., Ga., 1828; received a bounty grant of 287½ acres in Wilkes Co. for his service as a *Rev. Sol.* of Ga. Mar. Gracey —.

Children:

    1. John.
    2. Thomas.
    3. Sterne, Jr.

(Children of his son, John Simmons, were mentioned in will, viz: Sarah; John, Jr.; Sterne and Mary Ann Simmons).

WILLIAM SIMMONS, b. Va.; d. Wilkes (now Oglethorpe) Co., Ga., 1808. *Rev. Sol.*; warrant for 287½ acres bounty land, certificate of Col. Elijah Clarke in Franklin Co. Mar. (1) Mary —; (2) Patience —.

Children (mentioned in deed of gift), 1798. Not in order of birth:

    1. Willis.
    2. Solomon.
    3. John.
    4. Henry.
    5. Asa.
    6. Polly.
    7. Nancy.
    8. Rachel.
    9. Celinda.
    10. William, Jr.
    11. Samuel.
    12. Dau., mar. her cousin, Jesse Simmons.

HENRY SLAPPEY, b. S. C., 1758; d. Twiggs Co., Ga., 1820. Served in S. C. Light Dragoons under Capt. William Alexander; wounded at King's Mt. Mar. 1778, ANN RUTHERFORD (dau. of ROBERT RUTHERFORD, b. Va., 1734; d. S. C., 1814, *Rev. Sol.*, and wife, Dorothy Brooks, b. 1753; d. 1795).

Children (known):

    1. Dorothy, mar. Capt. Ezekiel Wimberly.
    2. John G., mar. Margaret Monroe.

EZEKIEL SLAUGHTER, b. Va., 1729; d. Greene Co., Ga., Aug. 20, 1792. Served as private in Col. Thweatt's Va. Regiment; received bounty grant of land for his service in Ga. Mar. SARAH

BUTLER (dau. of Samuel and Barsheba Butler, of Hanover Co., Va.) She was b. Oct. 1, 1727; d after 1792.

Children:
1. Mary, b. Oct. 15, 1748.; mar. — Worsham.
2. JOHN (1750-1805), mar. Mary Hendricks. He was a *Rev. Sol.* of Va.; d. Va.
3. Sallie, mar. Peter Robert.
4. James.
5. Betty, b. Jan. 11, 1753, mar. — Jones.
6. Juda, b. Oct. 17, 1754, mar. —Hill.
7. SAMUEL, mar. Fanny —.
8. Ann (or Nancy), b. July 5, 1760; mar. — Stillwell.
9. Patty, b. July 3, 1764, mar. John Gill.
10. Susanna, b. 1768, mar. SAMUEL HAWKINS, *Rev. Sol.* of Ga. (bro. of BENJAMIN HAWKINS, *Rev. Sol.*; Col. of Ga. Regiment and Indian Commissioner).
11. Lucy, b. April 30, 1769.
12. Ezekiel, b. April 30, 1756.
13. REUBEN, mar. (1) Ann; (2) Polly Lawson.

REUBEN SLAUGHTER, b. Va., Nov. 4, 1766; d. Greene Co., Ga. after 1792. Served as private Bedford Co. Militia; received grant of land in Ga. for his service. Mar. (1) Ann —; (2) 1789, Polly Lawson. Had 12 children by each marriage.

SAMUEL SLAUGHTER, b. Va.; d. Baldwin Co., Ga., 1821. Will made April 5, 1820; pro. July 4, 1821. Served in the Bedford Co., Va. Militia; received land grant in Ga. for his service (Grave marked by D. A. R.) Mar. Fanny —.

Children:
1. Daniel.
2. John.
3. Reuben.
4. Prudence A., mar. Isaiah Chapman.
5. Sally, mar. (1) 1799, Daniel Candler; (2) 1819, D. S. Chapman.

CHARLES SMITH, b. S. C., 1764; d. Cherokee Co., Ga., Jan. 28, 1843. Enlisted 1781; served two months as private in Cav. under Capt. Jacob Barnett, Col. Hampton's S. C. Regiment. He was living in Habersham Co., Ga., 1838; his widow was granted pension for his service, April 10, 1847. Mar. Elizabeth Gillespy, d. 1865.

Children (mentioned in pension):
1. Jemina, b. Dec. 11, 1785, mar. — Hyde.
2. James, b. 1788.
3. Anna, b. 1790, mar. — Conn.
4. Elizabeth, b. Mar. 21, 1793, mar. — Boling.
5. Edward G., b. 1798, mar. Elizabeth —.
6. Charles, Jr., b. 1800.
7. John, b. 1803.
8. Noah.

FRANCIS SMITH, b. Va., came to Ga.; d. on Fishing Creek, Wilkes Co., Ga., 1814; received grant of land in Ga. for his service as a *Rev. Sol.* Mar. LUCY WILKERSON.

Children:
1. John, mar. Miss Walker. Moved to Tenn., then to Mo.
2. Ebenezer, of Wilkes Co., mar. Frances Anderson.
3. William Wilkerson, mar. Judith Heard. Moved to Ala.
4. Thomas, mar. Cynthia White. Moved to Mo.
5. Francis, mar. Mrs. Toombs (formerly Miss Kelne). She mar. (3) Andrew White, of Tenn. (4) Gov. Blount, of Tenn. (She married 4 times before she was 21 years of age).
6. Reuben, mar. —. Moved to Mo.
7. Ann Adams, mar. *Governor* Peter Early, of Ga.; and had children: 1. Augustus; 2. Thomas; 3. Alexander; 4. Francis; 5. Peter; 6. Lucy; 7. Cynthia. She married (2) Rev. Adiel Sherwood.

HARDY SMITH, b. Johnson Co., N. C., 1757; d. Laurens Co., Ga., 1852. Served as private N. C. Troops under Col. Armstrong and Col. Johnson; received bounty land in Ga. on Oconee river and was also granted pension for his service. Mar. (1) —; (2) 1796, Rebecca Thompson, d. 1835.

Children (by (2) wife, known):
1. Hardy, Jr. (1801-1864), mar. (1) —; (2) 1836, Ann Anderson (dau. of Gaillard Anderson of N. C.)
2. Thompson.
3. Loftin.
Perhaps other children.

JOHN SMITH, b. N. C.; d. Wilkes Co., Ga., Jan. 1795. Mar. Sarah — in N. C. Came to Ga. from N. C. with wife and two children in 1773. He was a *Rev. Sol.* (called Capt. John Smith); received bounty grant of land in Ga. for his service.

1. Elizabeth.
2. MARTHA, b. Nov. 15, 1770, mar. JOHN WALKER, *Rev. Sol.*
3. John Taylor, mar. Margaret (called Peggy) —. Their children were: 1. Elizabeth; 2. Timothy; 3. Nicholas; 4. Francis; 5. Jean.
4. Nancy.
5. Franky (Frances), mar. Harris Coleman, *Rev. Sol.*, d. 1816.
6. Margaret, mar. John Pope, *Rev. Sol.*
7. Mary (Polly), mar. James Wooten, *Rev. Sol.* J. P. Wilkes Co., 1812.
8. Charles, mar. Nancy —.
9. Benjamin.
10. William.
11. Mildred (Milly), mar. Thomas Wooten, Jr.
12. Alexander.
13. David, mar. Elizabeth —.

JOHN GOTTLEIB ISRAEL SMITH, b. 1755; d. Bryan Co., Ga., 1820. Served as private Ga. Troops; in 1782 he petitioned Council of Safety for a discharge in order to help the suffering in Savannah after the evacuation by the British. Mar. at Ebenezer, Ga., Christiana Kieffer (1755-1841) (dau. of Emanual Kieffer of Savannah, Ga.). His will on record Bryan Co., Ga. He was a J. P., Bryan Co., 1804; Record for Society of War of 1812.

Children:
1. Christiana Smith, mar. Charles Ryals.
2. David, mar. Eliza —.
3. Sarah, mar. James Bird.
4. Salome.
5. Solomon.
6. Joshua.

ROBERT SMITH, b. Feb. 20, 1760; d. and was buried near Cork, Butts Co., Ga. He was a *Rev. Sol.* Mar. FERGUSON WILSON, b. Nov. 1767 on ship-board in passage from Ireland to America. She was named "Ferguson" after the name of the Capt. of Boat. (information supplied by Marjorie Thomas Schairer, descendant, Aug. 1938).

Children:
1. Hugh, b. Nov. 27, 1787.
2. Elizabeth, b. July 4, 1789.
3. Jane, b. May 19, 1792.
4. Robert Wilson, b. Mar. 10, 1794. *Sol. War of 1812.*
5. Ann Adair, b. Aug. 16, 1796.
6. Mary, b. Dec. 14, 1798.
7. David, b. Sept. 16, 1801.
8. Rosannah, b. May 4, 1804.
9. William, b. June 12, 1811.

ROBERT SMITH, b. Ireland; emigrated to Charleston, S. C. Was a *Rev. Sol.*; d. Campbell Co., Ga. Grave marked by D. A. R. of Ga.

GEORGE SNELLINGS, b. Va., came to Elbert Co., Ga., 1797, where he d. Oct. 1818.   Served in Va. Militia.   (Grave marked by D. A. R., Elberton, Ga.)   Mar. Rebecca Hudson, of Nottoway Co., Va.   She d. Elbert Co., Ga., Sept. 1826.
Children:
  1. John (1787–1856), mar. Nancy Butler.
  2. Hannah (1788–1839), mar. Peter Patrick Butler.
  3. Elizabeth, mar. Joseph Brawner.
  4. Samuel (1793–1876), mar. 1815, Elizabeth Neal Burton (dau. of Thomas and Rhoda (Hubbard) Burton).
  5. Rebecca, mar. John Taylor.
  6. Martha, mar. John Hudson.
  7. Mary, mar. (1) Richard Burton; (2) Richard D. Hudson.
  8. Richard Ward, mar. Elizabeth Nunnellee.

JOHN SPRINGER, b. Del. 1744; d. Washington, Ga., 1798.   He was a *Rev. Sol.*; received bounty land for his service in Ga.; his widow drew land in 1804, 1819 and 1832 Lotteries as the widow of a *Rev. Sol.*   He mar. ANN GREEN (dau. of WILLIAM GREEN (1739–1819), a *Rev. Sol.* of N. C., and his wife, Mary Christmas), d. 1836.
Children:
  1. William Green (1790–1840), mar. 1808, Mary Baxter (1794–1847) (dau. of ANDREW BAXTER, JR., *Rev. Sol.* of Ga., grand-dau. of ANDREW BAXTER, SR., *Rev. Sol.* of N. C.).
  2. Lucinda, mar. Robert M. Garvin.
  3. Katherine, mar. James Alexander.
  4. Sally.
  5. Elizabeth.
  6. Nancy.
  7. Susanna.
  8. Mary Ann.

REV. JOHN SPRINGER was the first Presbyterian Minister to be ordained south of the Savannah river.   He was ordained by the S. C. Presbytery at Washington, Ga., in 1790.

JOHN STACY, b. St. Mary's Co., Md., 1725; d. Ga., May. 12, 1781.   Was a member of the "Sons of Liberty"; of the Committee of Correspondence. Lived in the "Old Midway Colony," Liberty Co., Ga.   Mar. (2) SARAH (DUNHAM) WAY; d. June 15, 1782.
Children:
  1. JOHN, JR., b. Ga., Dec. 10, 1761; d. April 7, 1817.   Served as *Rev. Sol.* with Ga. Troops. Mar. (1) May 3, 1787, Margaret W. Quaterman; (2) Nov. 23, 1797, Sarah Quaterman
  2. James, b. 1763.
  3. Margaret, b. 1765.
  4. Mary, b. 1767.
  5. William, b. 1769.
  6. Jonathan, b. 1771.
  7. Elizabeth, b. 1773.
  8. Susanna, b. 1775.
  9. Thomas, b. 1776.
  10. Sarah, b. 1778.
  11. Robert, b. 1780.

ROBERT STAFFORD, b. S. C.; d. Wayne Co., Ga., Feb. 1829.   He mar. Jane Blair (dau. of WILLIAM BLAIR (name spelled Blayer), *Rev. Sol.*, and his wife, Sibbiah Earl).   Moved to Effingham Co., then Screven Co., Ga., from S. C., 1790.   He was J. P., Screven Co. (Record for Society, Daughters of 1812).   Moved to Wayne Co., Ga., in 1810.   (Grave marked).
Children:
  1. Martha (1797–1866), mar. Joseph Wiggins (1789–1855).
  2. Sibbiah, mar. Wayne Co., Ga., Capt. Thomas O'Neal, d. 1830.
  3. Jane Amanda, mar. 1821, John Hatcher.
  4. Mary (1804–1864), mar. 1827, Wayne Co., Ga., George W. McDonald, of McIntosh Co., Ga.   He was b. Dec. 30, 1802.

5. Robert (1808–1863), mar. (1) 1830, Martha Ann Ratcliffe (1812–1850) (dau. of James and Martha (May) Ratcliffe, of Glynn Co., Ga.); (2) Smithie Haile.

6. James (1812), mar. (1) 1833, Wayne Co., Martha (Mundie) Bryant; (2) 1845, Elizabeth Burney.

ALEXANDER STEVENS, b. England, 1726; d. Warren (now Taliaferro) Co., Ga., 1813. Served seven years as Capt. of Penn. Troops. Buried 2 miles from Crawfordville, Ga. Mar. in Penn., Catherine Baskins, d. Ga., 1794.

Children (not in order of birth):
1. Nehemiah, moved to Tenn.
2. James (1778), mar. 1800, Elizabeth Garrett.
3. Jane.
4. Mary.
5. Catherine.
6. Elizabeth.
7. ANDREW BASKINS (1782–1846), lived on Kettle Creek, Ga., mar. (1) Margaret Greer (dau. of AARON GRIER, Rev. Sol., who moved to Ga. from Penn., and sister of Robert Grier (of Grier's Almanac)); (2) 1814, Matilda M. Lindsey.
Children by (1) wife: 1. Mary; 2. Aaron; 3. ALEXANDER HAMILTON STEVENS, *Vice-President of the Confederate States of America,* and *Governor of Georgia* in 1882.
Children by (2) wife: 1. John; 2. Andrew B., Jr.; 3. Benjamin; 4. Linton; 5. Catherine, mar, 1833, Thomas Grier.

JOHN STEVENS, b. S. C., 1737; d. Liberty Co., Ga., 1777. Delegate to Provincial Congress, 1775. Mar. Margaret McCarty.

Children:
1. Elizabeth.
2. Mary.
3. Margaret.
4. John, Jr., mar. Araminthia Way.
5. Munroe.

DANIEL STEWART (son of JOHN STEWART, *Rev. Sol.,* and his (1) wife, Susanna Bacon) b. St. John's Parish (now Liberty Co.), Ga., Dec. 20, 1760; d. 1829 and is buried at The Cemetery of Midway Church. At 15 years of age, he enlisted and served under Col. Harden, Gen. Marion, and Gen. Sumpter, in S. C.; was taken prisoner but made his escape and served throughout the war. He was a *General* in the *War of 1812.* (The British Army laid waste St. John's Parish and burned the famous Midway Church of the Dorchester Settlers.) He mar. (1) at Dorchester, S. C., Feb. 20, 1783, Martha Pender, b. there Nov. 1763; (2) Jan. 1, 1786, Susanna Oswald, b. Nov. 2, 1770, at Newport, Liberty Co., Ga.; (3) Mar. 6, 1810, Sarah (Hines) Lewis, widow of Capt. Elijah Lewis.

Child by (1) wife:
John, b. 1784; d. y.

Children by (2) wife:
1. Mary, b. Feb. 12, 1788, mar. Major Josiah T. Wilson.
2. Daniel McLaughlin, b. Oct. 4, 1791, mar. 1824, Elizabeth Eichenberger, of Glynn Co., Ga.
3. Sophia, b. 1792.
4. Susanna, b. 1794.
5. Joseph Oswald, b. 1797.
6. MARTHA, bap. Aug. 15, 1799, mar. (1) Jan. 6, 1818, Hon. John Elliott; (2) 1832, Major James S. Bulloch.
7. John, mar. Hepworth Carter.
8. Sarah Caroline, d. y.
9. Georgia Druscilla, d. y.

(MARTHA (STEWART) (ELLIOTT) BULLOCH was the maternal grandmother of PRESIDENT THEODORE ROOSEVELT and a great grandmother of ELEANOR ROOSEVELT, the wife of FRANKLIN DELANO ROOSEVELT, the *President of the United States*).

HENRY STEWART (son of MATTHEW STEWART, b. Scotland, 1720; d. N. C., 1808 a *Rev. Sol.* of N. C., and his wife, ELIZABETH McCALL, of N. C.), b. Anson Co., N. C., 1759; d. Ga., 1861. Enlisted in N. C. Aug. 1776 under Capt. Charles Polk; transferred to Capt. Thomas Ray, and then served under his father, CAPT. MATTHEW STEWART. After the war, removed with his brother, James Stewart, also *Rev. Sol.*, to Wilkes Co., Ga.; received land in this Co. for his service. Removed to Greene (now Taliaferro) Co. Applied for and was granted a pension.

JAMES STEWART (sometimes spelled STUART), b. Dorchester Co., S. C., Aug. 3, 1732; d. 1784. Came to Liberty Co., Ga., 1752 (then St. John's Parish). Served in Ga. Militia from Liberty Co. Member of the House of Assembly and of Executive Council, 1783; bounty grant of land (250 acres) on certificate of Col. John Baker, Liberty Co., was receipted for by his son, James M. Stewart. He mar. (1) Susanna —; (2) 1782, Elizabeth Jackson. She mar. (2) Sept. 1785, as (2) wife, Thomas Stone and d. Dec. 1785.
Children:
1. William.
2. John, b. 1764, mar. 1798, Susanna Graves.
3. Josiah, b. 1771; d. 1805; mar. Sarah Mann.
4. James (1766–1805).
5. Charles, mar. Christian Graham.
6. Susanna, mar. William Thompson.

JOHN STEWART, b. S. C., 1740; d. Liberty Co., Ga., 1815. A member of "Legionary Corps" of Ga. Was at the Battle of Midway Church and also at the Siege of Savannah.

JOHN STEWART, came to Wilkes Co., Ga.; made will there June 26, 1829, Pro. Sept. 1, 1829; received grant of land for his service as a *Rev. Sol.* Mar. MARY —.
Children (mentioned in will):
1. Dogel (or Dugald).
2. James.
3. Charles.
4. Dau., mar. Wylie Pope.
5. Ann, mar. William Smith.

JOHN STEWART, b. S. C., Feb. 23, 1726; d. Liberty Co., Ga., Sept. 4, 1776. Served as Col. Artillery, Ga. Brigade. Mar. (1) Susanna —; she d. Oct. 21, 1766; (2) Aug. 7, 1769, Sarah Nichols.
Children by (1) wife:
1. Sarah, b. 1751, mar. William Quaterman.
2. Ann, d. y.
3. Susanna (1758), mar. Joseph Fox.
4. DANIEL, mar.(1) Martha Pender; (2) Susanna Oswald; (3) Sarah (Hines) Lewis. A *Rev. Sol.*
5. Mary, d. y.
6. John, d. y.
Child by (2) wife:
Elizabeth, b. 1774, mar. John Jones.

WILLIAM STEWART, b. Hanover Co., Va., 1762; d. Monroe Co., Ga., 1848. Served as private and Sergeant of Va. Militia; placed on Pension Roll for his service, 1834. Mar. Mary (called Molly) Penn(dau of Joseph Penn and wife, Mary Taylor, dau. of JOHN TAYLOR of Va. (1696–1780), a *Patriot*, and his wife, Catherine Pendleton), d. 1816.
Children:
1. John.
2. Thomas (1792–1871), mar. Nancy Jane Russell.
3. Charles.
4. James.
5. Blanton, mar. Regina Maria Dyson.
6. Richard (1808–1850), mar. Elizabeth Booty.
7. Nancy.
8. Frances, mar. — McCommon.
9. Polly.

THOMAS STONE, b. S. C., came to St. Philip's Parish (now Bryan Co.), Ga. Was a J. P., 1774–1778; was appointed on the commission for confiscated estates from Chatham Co., in 1782, to the House of the Assembly. Gave material aid and support to the cause of the Colonies. Mar. (1) May 3, 1759, Frances Guerin; (2) 1785, Elizabeth (Jackson) Stewart, widow of James Stewart, of Midway, Ga.; (3) May 19, 1799, in Glynn Co., Ga., Elizabeth Clubb, widow of Thomas Clubb, of St. Simons, Ga. They lived in Brunswick, Glynn Co., Ga., where he d.

Children by (1) wife:
1. Susanna.
2. Elizabeth Frances, mar. 1791, William Maxwell.
3. Henry Dassex, mar. (1) 1788, Susanna McClelland; (2) Ann (Maxwell) Oswald.

HENRY STONEHAM, b. Amherst Co., Va.; d. Jackson Co., Ga., Jan. 18, 1815. Served as private, Va. Troops, under Capt. Campbell; wounded at Guilford C. H. Mar. JANE DILLARD (1759 – after 1856). She was living 1856 in Grimes Co., Texas, when she was allowed 160 acres of bounty land as the widow of a *Rev. Sol.*

Children (known):
1. George, b. Va., 1786.
2. John D., b. 1795.

ANTHONY STOREY (son of GEORGE STOREY, *Rev. Sol.* of Penn. and S. C., and his wife, Nancy Cantor), b. 1746; d. Jackson Co., Ga., 1799. Served in Capt. Robert Farris' Co., Col. Brandon's S. C. Regiment. Mar. SARAH FARRIS (1748–1795).

Their son, Edward Storey (1772–1852), mar. Margaret Thompson (dau. of JOHN THOMPSON, *Rev. Sol.* of S. C., and his wife, Margaret Ann Wallace).

THOMAS STOVALL, b. Henry Co., Va.; d. Hancock Co., Ga., 1806. Served under Gen. Clark, Va. Line. Mar. (1) 1781, Elizabeth Cooper (1762–1843) (dau. of Capt. THOMAS COOPER, b. Va.; d. Greene Co., Ga.; served as Capt., Va. Line, and his wife, Sarah Anthony).

Children (born in Henry Co., Va.):
1. George, b. 1783, mar. Elizabeth Jeter.
2. Joseph, mar. Mary Pleasant Bonner.
3. Pleasant, mar. (1) Miss Lucas; (2) Miss Trippe; (3) Mrs. Hill.
4. Sallie, mar. Benjamin Simmons, of Sparta, Ga.
5. Ruth, mar. Mr. Hunt.
6. Polly.

WARREN STOW (OR STOE), b. Sheffield, Conn., 1755; moved to Wake Co., N. C.; d. Franklin Co., Ga., after 1823. Enlisted in the Sheffield, Conn., State Troops, under Capt. Noah Phelps; served under Capt. Remington in Conn., then later served in N. Y., then in S. C., where he was discharged from service; received pension for service. Mar. SALLY —.

Children:
1. Hudson.
2. Pressley.
3. William.
4. Martha.
5. Nancy, mar. James McCarty.

JACOB STRICKLAND, b. N. C., 1741; came to Ga., 1769, and settled, with his brothers, HENRY, ISAAC, and SOLOMON, all *Rev. Sols.* of N. C., on Rocky Comfort Creek (now Wilkes Co.), Ga.; d. Franklin Co., Ga., 1804. Served in N. C. Line; received bounty grant of land 1784 in Franklin Co., Ga., for his service. Mar. in Guilford, N. C., 1765, Priscilla Young (1747–1825).

Children:
1. Faith, b. Aug. 13, 1767, mar. — Myers. Moved to Miss.
2. TAMAR, b. Oct. 13, 1768, mar. WILLIAM GILBERT, *Rev. Sol.* They lived in Madison Co., Ga.
3. Isaac (1770–1857), mar. 1799, Mary Hargroves. Settled in Madison Co., Ga.
4. Jacob, b. May 6, 1772, mar. Clarissa Sanders, widow.
5. Mary, b. 1773, mar. (1) JOHN GILBERT, a *Rev. Sol.* Settled in Franklin Co., Ga.; (2) James Allen, of Habersham Co.

6. Hardy, b. 1775, mar. Susan Pyron, of Jackson Co., Ga. Settled in Madison Co.
7. Priscilla, mar. her cousin, Hardy Strickland. Settled in Jackson Co., Ga.
8. Selah (or Celia), mar. Robert Young, of Hall Co.
9. Henry, b. 1781, mar. Elizabeth Wilkins, of Franklin Co. Settled in Hall Co.
10. Wilson, mar. Polly Connally. Settled in Gwinnett Co.
11. Betsey, mar. — Eubanks. Moved to Tenn.
12. Nancy, mar. James Ryley, of Franklin Co.
13. Sarah, mar. Berry Vaughan.

SOLOMON STRICKLAND, b. N. C., 1735; d. Madison Co., Ga., 1818. Served in N. C. Line. Mar. Amy Pace, b. N. C., 1739; d. Ga., 1815.

Their dau., Eunice, mar. 1794, Alexander Thompson (1771–1845).

CHARLES STRONG, b. Hanover Co., Va., Jan. 18, 1764; d. Clarke Co., Ga., Oct. 16, 1848. Served as private, Va. Line; then Capt.; on Pension List of Ga., 1831, from Oglethorpe Co. Mar. Nov. 29, 1785, SARAH THOMPSON (sister of JOHN THOMPSON, *Rev. Sol.* of Ga.), b. July 25, 1764; d. May 27, 1849.

Children:
1. Elizabeth (1787–1807), mar. Obediah Echols.
2. William (1789–1795).
3. Elisha (1792–1879), mar. Ann Scott Hill (dau. of Thomas Hill).
4. Sarah Key (1795–1877), mar. Burwell Pope.
5. Ann T. (1797), mar. Ebenezer Newton (1789).
6. Susan (1799–1875), mar. Thomas W. Golding.
7. Charles (1801–1870).
8. Nancy, d. y.
9. Martha (1805–1877), mar. 1824, John D. Moss, Athens, Ga.

JOHN STROTHER, b. Va.; d. Hancock Co., Ga., 1796; received pay for service, N. C. Line, at Hillsborough District, Orange Co., N. C. Moved to Franklin Co., then to Hancock Co., Ga. Mar. Jane Fussell. (Will Pro. May 1830).

Children:
1. David.
2. Aaron.
3. John, mar. Hannah —.
4. James.
5. Richard.
6. Anna, mar. — Moody.
7. Elizabeth, mar. — King.
8. Martha, b. Va., 1765; d. Clarke Co., Ga.; mar. (1) Amos Thompson; (2) MARK STROUD a *Rev. Sol.*, d. Hancock Co., Ga.

JOHN STROUD, b. Amwell, N. J., 1732; d. Clarke Co., Ga. Buried Mars Hill Cemetery, Clarke Co., Ga. (Grave marked by Ga. D. A. R.) Joined the Colonial Army in Penn.; fought in the French and Indian Wars; served as *Rev. Sol.* in N. C. under Major John Ashe, 1st N. C. Regiment, 1777–1779. Moved to Burke Co., Ga., then to Hancock Co., Ga., then to Clarke Co., Ga. (Will made Jan. 21, 1805, Pro. Jan 6, 1806.) Mar. 1756, SARAH CONNALLY (CONNELLY).

Children:
1. Margaret (1757–1834), mar. STEPHEN CROW, b. N. C., 1750; d. Clarke Co., Ga., 1830, a *Rev. Sol.* of Ga.
2. William.
3. John.
4. Betty.
5. Hannah, mar. — Melson.
6. Mary, mar. William Haygood.
7. Sarah.
8. James.
9. MARK.

10. Tabitha (not in order of birth).
11. Isaac.
(Rachel Crow (Stephen), mar. Jeremiah Burnett).

MARK STROUD, b. Hillsborough District, N. C., Feb. 27, 1763; d. Hancock Co., Ga., while enroute to Clarke Co., July 2, 1798. Member N. C. State Reserves, and was at the Battle of Guilford C. H. Mar. 1784, Martha (Strother) Thompson.

Children:
1. William, mar. Serena A. Regan Battle.
2. Levi, mar. Fannie Haygood.
3. Eli.
4. Mary (twin), mar. William Haygood.
5. Sarah (twin), mar. James Haygood.
6. Albion.
7. Orion.
8. Tillitha.

GEORGE SWAIN, b. Mass., came to Wilkes Co., Ga., and was a J. P. there 1787; d. Oglethorpe Co., Ga., 1819; mar. Caroline (Lane) Lowry, widow of David Lowry (name spelled Lowrey), d. Wilkes Co., Ga., 1788, and dau. of JESSE LANE, *Rev. Sol.* of Ga. Children of DAVID LOWRY and Caroline Lane were: 1. Mary, mar. John Hanson, d. Wilkes Co., 1814. She d. 1820; 2. James; 3. Patience, mar. — Irwin.

Children:
1. Cynthia Coleman.
2. Caroline.
3. Matilda.
4. Althea.
5. Polly.
6. George, Jr.
7. James L.
8. DAVID LOWRY SWAIN, Gov. of N. C.
This family was not related to the SWAIN family of Tyrrell Co., N. C.

JOB SWAIN, b. Me., Feb. 20, 1747; d. Warren Co., Ga., Feb. 12, 1819. Mar. in Warren Co., Ga., 1786, Susan Smith, b. April 11, 1762; d. May 27, 1832; a *Rev. Sol.*

Children:
1. Nancy, mar. — Rogers.
2. Thomas, mar. Rebecca Prigden.
3. Jonah.
4. Margaret.
5. Richard.
6. James.
7. William.
8. John.

STEPHEN SWAIN, b. Chowan Co., N. C., about 1746; d. Montgomery (formerly Laurens) Co., Ga., 1796; a *Rev. Sol.* of N. C. as Ensign of 8th Co. Regiment Batt. of Foot in 1775; resigned Aug. 1777; received grant of land on the Oohoopee river, Ga., in 1790. Mar. in N. C., Ann Elizabeth —, of Tyrrell Co.

Children (known):
1. Stephen (served as a member of the Ga. Legislature, from Montgomery and Emanuel Cos., for 33 years).
2. Canneth, b. N. C., 1770, mar. Rebecca Johnson. They moved to Thomas Co., Ga., where he d. 1832. They had 10 children. She mar. (2) John Chason, of Decatur Co., Ga.
3. Sherrod, of Emanuel Co., Ga., mar. Mary Lane.

JOHN TALBOT, b. Va., July 15, 1735; d. Wilkes Co., Ga., Aug. 1798. One of the signers of the Declaration of Independence, at Williamsburg, Va., 1774; a *Rev. Sol.* of Va.; received bounty grant of land for his service in Ga. He settled in Wilkes Co., Ga., 1783; was buried in graveyard at Old Smyrna Church, Wilkes Co., Ga. In the will of his wife, Phoebe Talbot, is found this: "My body to be buried in the Meeting House lot, as near the grave of my dear deceased husband, JOHN TALBOT, as it can be placed." Mar. (1) Sarah Anthony (no issue); (2) Phoebe Mary Moseley (dau. of Col. William Moseley of Va.), b. Va.; d. Wilkes Co., Ga., July 1806.

Children by (2) wife:

1. Matthew, mar. Elizabeth Mounger (Munger).
2. John, Jr.
3. Phoebe, mar. DAVID CRESSWELL, *Rev. Sol.* (son of Rev. James Cresswell, of Va.); received bounty grant of land for his service in Ga.; d. Wilkes Co., Ga.
   Children: 1. Mary Garlington, mar. Freeman Walker; 2. John Talbot; 3. Phoebe; 4. Elizabeth; 5. Zulenia.
4. Elizabeth, mar. George Walker.
5. Thomas, mar. —.
6. Mary (Polly), mar. WILLIAM TRIPLETT, *Rev. Sol.*
7. Eliza Ann, mar. Nathaniel Cox.
8. Williston, mar. Hester Carper.

MATHEW TALBOT, b. Bedford Co., Va., 1729; d. Morgan Co., Ga., Oct. 12, 1812. Served in Bedford Co., Va., Militia. Mar. (1) Mary Williston; (2), June 1753, Mary (Haile) Day, widow of Thomas Day. As a *Patriot*, settled, 1778, on the Watauga river, Ga. Fort Wautauga was built on his place. He was at the retaking of Augusta, Ga., June 5, 1781, as a *Rev. Sol.*

Children:

1. Hale, b. 1754.
2. Mathew, b. 1756.
3. Thomas.
4. William, b. 1760, mar. Mary Bailey.
5. Edward.
6. Clayton.
7. Mary.

BENJAMIN TALIAFERRO (son of ZACHARIAH TALIAFERRO, *Rev. Sol.* of Va., and his wife, Mary Boutwell), b. Va., 1750; d. Wilkes Co., Ga., Sept. 3, 1821. Served as Col. under Gen. Lee and Gen. Lincoln in Southern Army; captured at Charleston, S. C. Mar. (1) MARTHA MERIWETHER, 10 children; (2) MISS COX.

Children by (1) wife:

1. Emily, mar. Isham Watkins.
2. Louis Bourbon, mar. Betsey Johnson.
3. Betsey.
4. Mary.
5. Benjamin, Jr., mar. Martha Watkins (dau. of James Watkins, Sr., of Elbert Co., Ga.).
6. Martha, mar. William McGehee.
7. David, mar. Mary Barnett.
8. Thornton, mar. (1) — Green; (2) Widow Lamar.
9. Margaret (1794-1836), mar. (1) John Brown; (2) Joseph Green.
10. Nicholas M. (1801-1871), mar. 1824, Ann Hill (1804-1868) (dau. of Miles Hill and Tabitha Pope; g.-dau. of ABRAHAM HILL, *Rev. Sol.* of N. C. and Ga., and Christian Walton; also g.-dau. of BURWELL POPE, *Rev. Sol.* of Va. and Ga., and Priscilla Wooten).

Child by (2) wife:
   Zacheriah.

JOHN TALIAFERRO, b. Caroline Co., Va., 1733; d. Ga., 1791. Served as Capt. of Minutemen of Va. Troops. Mar. Mary Hardin (dau. of HENRY HARDIN, *Rev. Sol.* of Va., and his wife, Judith Lynch).

Children:

1. RICHARD, b. Amherst Co., Va., 1759; d. N. C., 1781; a *Rev. Sol.* of Va. Mar. Dorcas Perkins.
2. Charles.
3. Benjamin.

4. Judith.
5. Rosa.
6. Elizabeth.
7. Anna.
8. Betheland.
9. Sally.
10. Lucy.

CALEB TALLEY, b. Hanover Co., Va.; d. Greene Co., Ga. Served as private, Va. Line. Mar. Elizabeth Stuart; moved to Lincoln Co., Ga., 1797.

Children:
1. Dau.
2. William.
3. Nicholas.
4. Alexander.
5. Caleb, Jr.
6. Elknah.
7. Nathan.
8. John Wesley, b. 1800; d. Texas, 1885; mar. Rosetta Ralston.
(Five of the sons of Caleb Talley were Methodist ministers).

JOHN TATE, b. Ireland 1758; came to America 1763 and settled with his parents in Shippensburg, Penn. Entered service as *Rev. Sol.* in Penn. Militia 1776; volunteer under Capt. Robert Culbertson at Shippensburg, Cumberland Co., Penn. Removed after war to Baltimore, Md., then to Burke Co., N. C., and 1796 removed to Franklin Co., Ga., where he received pension. D there. Mar. ANN (called Nancy) —.

Child:
William.

WILLIAM TAYLOR, JR. (son of William Taylor, *Rev. Sol.* of S. C., and his wife, Nancy Johnson), b. Edgefield Dist., S. C., 1765; d. Ga. Served as private and Serg. in Capt. Joseph Harley's Co., 3d Regiment, S. C. Troops. Mar. Molly Clarke (dau. of GEN. ELIJAH CLARKE, *Rev. Sol.* of Ga., and his wife, Hannah Arrington).

JOHN TEASLEY, b. Va., 1755; d. Ga. Served as private, Va. Troops, and in N. C. Lived in Washington Co., N. C. Moved to Wilkes Co., Ga., where he received bounty grant of land for his service. Mar. LUCY HUNT.

Children:
1. Isham, b. Wilkes Co., Ga.; d. Elbert Co., Ga., 1834. Mar. Jane (called Jency) Adams (dau. of JAMES ADAMS, a *Rev. Sol.*).
2. John.
3. James.
4. George.
5. Peter.
6. Aquilla.
7. Priscilla, mar. Lemuel Rucker.
8. Thomas.

WILLIAM TEASLEY, b. Va.; d. Ga., 1824. Served as private, Va. Line. Mar. SARAH —; she received land, 1825, as the widow of a *Rev. Sol.*, in Elbert Co., Ga.

Children (mentioned in his will):
1. Anna, mar. Wesley Christer.
2. Amelia, mar. William Lumsford.
3. Winny, mar. John Horton.
4. Elizabeth, mar. Thomas Horton.
5. Levi.
6. Thomas J.

FRANCIS TENNILLE, b. Prince William Co., Va., 1747; d. Ga., 1812. Enlisted in Washington Co., Ga., 2nd Batt. Served as Lieut., Capt., and Lieut. Col., Ga. Militia. Mar. Mary Elizabeth Bacon Dixon (dau. of ROBERT DIXON, a *Rev. Sol.*, and his wife, Ann Bacon, of Ga.).
Children:

1. Francis (1799–1877), mar. Miss Jordan.
2. William, mar. Priscilla Jordan.
3. Robert.
4. John.
5. Benjamin.
6. Algernon.
7. Sidney, mar. Louise Dunbar Roe.

SIMON TERRELL, b. Orange Co., N. C., Mar. 27, 1755; d. Franklin Co., Ga., 1836. Placed on Pension Roll of Franklin Co., Ga., 1836, for service as Dragoon, N. C. Militia. Mar. 1775, Sarah Thompson. (His twin bro., AARON TERRELL, *Rev. Sol.* of N. C., d. S. C., mar. Ann Thompson, sister of Sarah).
Children (known):

1. William, b. 1784; d. 1827, mar. 1818, Sarah Kendrick.
2. Thompson, mar. Miss Baker.
3. Hannah, mar. James Allen.
4. Timothy, b. 1777, mar. Mary (Polly) Davis.
5. Elizabeth, mar. — Martin.
6. Amelia, mar. Thomas Hollinsworth.

VINCENT A. THARP, b. Wales, 1760; came to Va., then to S. C.; d. Twiggs Co., Ga., 1825. Served as private in S. C. Troops under Gen. Francis Marion. Was a gun-smith by trade and was detailed to make guns for Continental Army. After the war, was a Baptist minister of Ga. Mar. (1) name unknown; (2) Sarah Persons.
Children (known):

1. Jeremiah Allen, a *Sol. of 1812*, mar. Jane Dunn.
2. William, mar. Martha Davis.
3. Chadwick, mar. Elizabeth —.
4. John, mar. Obedience Elizabeth Hatcher.

PHILIP THOMAS, b. Charles Co., Md., 1753; d. Franklin Co., Ga., 1821. Served as corporal in Capt. Yates' Co., Col. Josiah Hawkins' Charles Co., Md., Regiment. Mar. Elizabeth Covington Wailes.
Children:

1. John W.
2. Philip W.
3. Elizabeth.
4. Edward Lloud (1778-1850), mar. Mary Hogue.
5. James L., mar. Rebecca Avery.
6. Levin Wailes, mar. Thursa Farrar.

ALEXANDER THOMPSON, b. Penn.; d. Ga., 1808. Served as a *Rev. Sol.* of N. C., from Burke Co.; received grant of land for his service in Ga. Mar. 1760, ELIZABETH MARY HODGE.
Children (not in order of birth):

1. William, mar. Mary Tillman (dau. of William and Mary (Farrow) Tillman).
2. Alexander, Jr. (1771–1845), mar. Eunice Strickland (dau. of SOLOMON STRICKLAND, *Rev. Sol.*, b. 1735; d. Madison Co., Ga., 1818, and his wife, Amy Pace).
3. Ruth.
4. James.
5. Robert.
6. John.
7. Sarah.
8. Esther.

ANDREW THOMPSON, b. S. C., 1762; d. 1819. Served in the S. C. Militia, and was captured by the British. Mar. MARY McBRIDE.

Their dau., MARY McBRIDE, b. Union District, S. C., Nov. 30, 1807; d. Coweta Co., Ga., Oct. 2, 1902. She was a *Real Dau.* of the National Society, D. A. R.

BENJAMIN THOMPSON, b. Ireland; d. Hancock Co., Ga., 1796. Served as private, Ga. Line; received land grant for service as *Rev. Sol.* Mar. Ann —. She d. after 1802.

Children (known):
1. John.
2. William, moved to Miss.
3. Jesse.

DANIEL THOMPSON, b. Ireland, 1759; d. Moreland, Ga., 1841. Served in the Va. State Line 3 years; was given bounty grant of land in Ga., 1783, for his service. Mar. 1785, JANE BOYD, b. 1760.

One of their sons, James (1793-1847), mar. 1820, Elizabeth Carmichael (1804-1866), dau. of Arthur Carmichael and his wife, Frances Bell (dau. of JOHN BELL, *Rev. Sol.* of S. C., and his wife, Sophia Patrick).

JOHN THOMPSON, b. Va., 1762; d. Clarke Co., Ga., 1810. Served 2 years in Va. Continental Line. Mar. Sarah Strong (sister of CHARLES STRONG, *Rev. Sol.* of Ga.).

Children:
1. Richard.
2. Frances, mar. — Price.
3. Elizabeth, mar. — Middleton.
4. Polly.
5. Sarah.
6. Martin.
7. William.

JOSEPH THOMPSON, b. Spartanburg Dist., S. C., 1765; d. Ga., July 1, 1802. Served in S. C. Troops under Gen. Francis Marion; received bounty grant in Ga. for his service, upon certificate of Gen. John Twiggs, at New Savannah, 1785. Mar. JANE DILL, b. Penn., 1770; d. S. C., April 7, 1802.

Children:
1. Alexander (1791-1877), mar. (1) Betsey Alexander; (2) Elizabeth Pedon.
2. James, d. unmar.
3. John, d. unmar.
4. Joseph, b. S. C., Sept. 29, 1797; d. Atlanta, Ga., Aug. 21, 1885. Mar. (1) May 21, 1827, Mary Ann (Tomlinson) Young (dau. of George Tomlinson and his wife, Avaline Reynolds, of De Kalb Co., Ga.); 9 children; (2) 1851, Mrs. Reeder; (3) Mrs. Thomson.

DOZIER THORNTON (son of Mark and Susanna (Dozier) Thornton), b. Lunenburg Co., Va., April 14, 1755; d. Franklin Co., Ga., Sept., 1843. Enlisted from Surry Co., N. C., then Wilkes Co., N. C. Served in N. C.; pension granted to him for his service while a resident of Franklin Co., Ga. He was a Baptist preacher and a Missionary to the Cherokee Indians; received land grant, 1825 as a *Rev. Sol.*, recorded in Elbert Co., Ga. Mar. (1) in Lunenburg Co., Va., Feb. 6, 1779, Lucy Hill, b. Jan. 13, 1760; (2) Jane (Gilbert) Pulliam (dau. of Rev. Thomas Gilbert).

Children:
1. Jeremiah.
2. Reuben, mar. (1) Elizabeth Adams; (2) Katherine Richardson; (3) Elizabeth Waters.
3. Green.
4. Sanford.
5. Jonathan.
6. Dozier, Jr.
7. Evans.
8. Benjamin (1781-1854), mar. (1) Sarah Upshaw; (2) Rebecca Upshaw.
9. Percilla.
10. Martha Ann, mar. Samuel Adams (son of James and Jane (Cunningham) Adams).

SOLOMON THORNTON, b. Va., 1745; d. Savannah, Ga., 1809. Served as private, Ga. Line; received bounty grant of land, 1785, in Wilkes Co., Ga., for his service. Mar. Sarah —.
Children (mentioned in will):
1. William (1765-1825), mar. Mary Carter.
2. Martian.
3. Nancy.
4. Judy, ma.. Samuel Hunter.
5. John.
6. Joshua.
7. Polly.
8. Aggy.
9. Caty.
10. Samuel.

JOHN TILLMAN, b. Somerset Co., Md., 1751; d. Bulloch Co., Ga., 1830. Served in the 2nd Batt., N. C. Continental Line; received land for his service. Settled in Bulloch Co., Ga., 1810. Mar. SARAH EGGERTON (OR ERGARTON).
Children:
1. JAMES (1776-1855), mar. Martha Marlow.
2. John, b. 1777.
3. Mary, b. 1780, mar. 1800, Henry Simmons.
4. Elizabeth, mar. William Rushing.
5. Nancy, b. 1782, mar. 1811, Daniel Simmons.
6. HENRY (1790-1851), mar. Aleph Simmons.
7. JOSEPH ISAIAH, mar. (1) Catherine Chewing; (2) Cassandra C. Everett.

WILLIAM TILLMAN (son of George and Goudeth Tillman, of Va. and N. C.), b. Bristol Parish, Va., 1748; d. Burke Co., Ga., 1785. A Rev. Patriot of S. C., who gave material aid. Removed to Burke Co., Ga. Mar. in Va., 1768, Mary Farrow.
Children:
1. William (1770-1825), mar. Polly —.
2. James (1778-1837), mar. Nancy Vinson.
3. Sarah (1769-1837), mar. Nathaniel Trout.
4. Polly, mar. William Long.
5. Penelope, mar. James Carithers.
6. Nancy, mar. 1800, William Thompson, of Madison Co., Ga.

WILLIAM TINDALL, b. Va., 1717; d. Columbia Co., Ga., July 22, 1804. Served in the Va. Continental Army; received a bounty grant of land for his service in Franklin Co., Ga. Mar. about 1758, Betsey Ann Booker, d. Sept. 24, 1804, age 62 years.
Children:
1. John, b. 1759, mar. Mary —.
2. Caroline Fleming, b. 1762, mar. 1782, JOHN BARNETT, Rev. Sol. of Ga. (son of NATHAN BARNETT, Rev. Sol of Ga.).
3. William, b. 1764, mar. Elizabeth —.
4. Jonathan, b. 1766, mar. Betsey —.
5. Pleasant, mar. Polly Hobbs, of Richmond Co., Ga.
6. Sealy Ann, mar. (1) — Davis; (2) — James.
7. Elizabeth.
8. Bird Booker, mar. Nancy —.

JAMES TINSLEY, b. Richmond, Va., 1764; d. Columbia Co., Ga. Moved to S. C., near Charleston. Served as a private, Va. and S. C. Troops. Came to Ga. 1790. Mar. (1) ELIZABETH ZACHERY, of S. C.; 7 children; (2) Lucy Ann (Crawford) Richards (sister of Hon. William Harris Crawford); 3 children.

PHILLIP TIPPINS, b. N. C., 1754; d. Tatnall Co., Ga., 1826. Moved to S. C., 1777, then to Warren Co., Ga.; a Rev. Sol. of Ga. under Capt. Abner Hickman, Aug. 15, 1781; discharged in

Ga., Feb. 1782; received bounty land for his service.   Mar. (1) Mary Underwood; (2) Nancy Philips. Moved to Tattnall Co., Ga., 1802.

Children by (1) wife:
1. George Underwood, mar. Penny Durrence, d. in Fla.
2. Cynthia, mar. — Durrence.
3. James Augustus, mar. Eliza Edwards.
4. Cecelia.
5. Lemuel.
6. Candace, mar. Elijah Mattox (son of MICHAEL McKENZIE MATTOX, *Rev. Sol.* of Tattnall Co., Ga.).
7. William Wayne, mar. Mary Mason.
8. John, killed by the Indians in Fla.

Children by (2) wife:
1. Simeon.
2. Jeptha.
3. Phillip Henry.

GABRIEL TOOMBS, b. Va.; d. Wilkes Co., Ga.   A *Rev. Patriot*, too old fo r active service Moved to Ga., 1784. Mar. Ann —; she d. before 1807.

Children:
1. ROBERT.
2. Dawson Gabriel, mar. Mary —.
3. Mary, mar. Dr. Lewis Barrett.
4. Elizabeth.
5. Sallie D., mar. Robt. Dawson.
6. Ann D., mar. John Spearman.

ROBERT TOOMBS, b. Va.; d. Wilkes Co., Ga., 1815.   Served as Maj. commanding a Regiment of Va. Troops. Moved to Wilkes Co., Ga., 1783, where he received bounty grant of land for his service.   Mar. (1) MISS SANDERS, no issue; (2) SARAH CATLETT; (3) CATHERINE HULING (dau. of JAMES HULING, *Rev. Sol.* of Va. and Wilkes Co., Ga.).

Child by (2) wife:
Laurence Catlett, mar. in Wilkes Co., Ga., 1822, Harriet E. DuBose (dau. of EZEKIEL DU-BOSE, *Rev. Sol.* of Lincoln Co., Ga., and his wife, Mary Rembert).

Children by (3) wife:
1. Sarah Ann, mar. Henry J. Pope.
2. ROBERT A. (1810–1885), mar. 1830, Mary Julian DuBose. (This was the famous "BOB TOOMBS" of Ga. History and a *Confederate Sol.*)
3. Gabriel.
4. James H.
5. Augustus.

ANDREW NICHOLSON TORRANCE, b. Scotland, settled in Va., 1766.   Served as private, Va. Troops and as quarter-master. Moved to S. C., then to Baldwin Co., Ga., where he d. July, 1811.   Mar. 1789, Hester Howard.

Children:
1. William Howard, *Sol. of the War of 1812.*, mar. Miss Crawford. Both d. 1837.
2. Aurelins.
3. Mansfield.
4. Harriet.
5. Clara.
6. Maria.
7. Matilda.

JOHN TOWNS, b. Va., 1758, moved to Wilkes Co., Ga.; d. Morgan Co., Ga., 1825.   Served as Lieut. in Capt. John Cropper's Co., Col. Daniel Morgan's Va. Regiment. Mar. Margaret Hardwick, widow of JAMES HARDWICK, *Rev. Sol.*, killed in battle; received bounty land in Wilkes Co., Ga., for his service. They had seven children, four sons and three daus.

One son, GEORGE WASHINGTON BONAPART, b. Wilkes Co., Ga., 1801, moved to Greene Co., then to Morgan Co., where he d. Mar. (1) Miss Campbell; (2) Mary Jones. He was elected *Gov. of the State of Ga.*

FREDERICK TREUTLEN, b. Holland, came with his brother to America, settled at Frederica, St. Simons Island, Ga.; then moved to Savannah, Ga., in 1735. Made will Feb. 17, 1798, Pro. Nov. 15, 1798. Served with Ga. Troops. Mar. Margaret Schadd (dau. of COL. SOLOMON SCHADD, *Rev. Sol.* of Ga., who lived at Wilmington Island), b. Switzerland, 1728; d. St. Simons Island, Ga., 1807.

Children:

1. Catherine, mar. John Tebeau (son of JAMES TEBEAU, *Rev. Sol.* of Ga., who mar. Susan Henks; had 6 children, viz: 1. John; 2. Samuel; 3. Norris; 4. Charles; 5. Daniel; 6. Ann Mary).
2. Ann, mar. Peter Provost.
3. Elizabeth.
4. Frederick.
5. Charles.
6. Edmund.

PURNAL TRUITT, b. Del., Feb. 26, 1757; d. Wilkes Co., Ga., 1844. Served as private from Del. in Capt. John Patten's Co., Col. David Hall's Regiment, 1778. In 1779 transferred to Col. Charles Pope's Regiment; received pension for his service; moved to Wilkes Co., Ga. Mar. (1) POLLY GODFREY, b. Jan. 26, 1758; 7 children; (2) RACHEL RENDER, b. Wilkes Co., Ga., 1762.

Children by (1) wife:

1. Sarah, b. 1784, mar. — Montgomery.
2. Nancy, b. 1786, mar. — Collins.
3. Riley, mar. Bonetta Smith.
4. Thomas.
5. Nathan.
6. John.
7. Purnal, Jr., b. Dec. 24, 1795, mar. 1819, Nancy Callaway, b. 1796; 10 children.

ISAIAH TUCKER, b. Amherst Co., Va., about 1761; came to Warren Co., Ga.; d. Ga. Served in Va. Militia; was given grant of land for his service in Wilkes Co., Ga. Mar. Oct. 5, 1793, Sarah Gibson.

ZADOC TURNER, b. Worcester Co., Md., 1729; d. Hancock Co., Ga., 1820. Served as private, 2nd Regiment, Md. Militia. Came to Ga., 1793, and settled at Mt. Zion, Hancock Co., Ga. Mar. (1) Sabra Hicks; (2) Eliza.

Children:

1. Philip, mar. Judith Parker.
2. Henry.
3. Joshua.
4. Zadoc, Jr.
(Perhaps other children).

NOTE: ZADOC TURNER came with his family and household goods on a sailing vessel from Chesapeake Bay; after a stormy passage, the vessel was driven to the West Indian Islands, and finally landed at Savannah, Ga. One of the daus. d. at sea and is buried in the Colonial Cemetery at Savannah. From Savannah, the Turner family took boats on the Savannah river to Augusta, Ga., whence they crossed Ga. on horseback and in wagons and finally settled in Hancock Co., east of the Oconee river, just after the Indians had removed a little farther West. He was in the Battles of Brandywine, Trenton, and Valley Forge.

JOHN TWIGGS, MAJOR GENERAL of Ga. Troops, b. Md., June 5, 1750; d. Richmond Co., Ga., Mar. 29, 1816. Served with Ga. Troops, also as Capt., Col., and was made Brig. Gen. in 1781. Mar. Ruth Emanuel, b. 1744 (a sister of DAVID EMANUEL, a *Rev. Sol.* of Ga., and *Gov. of the State of Ga.*).

Children (mentioned in will; not in order of birth):

1 Abraham.
2. Levi.
3. Asa.
4. George, mar. Sarah Lowe.

5. David Emanuel, b. Richmond Co., Ga., 1790, *Sol. of the War of 1812*, and Brig. Gen. in the *War with Mexico*, mar. (1) Elizabeth Hunter; (2) Miss Hurt of New Orleans, La.
6. Asenath, mar. Frances Wells.
7. Ruth, mar. Henry Greenwood.
8. Sarah, mar., as (2) wife, Henry Greenwood.

JAMES VEAZEY, b. Md., Aug. 27, 1727; d. near Powelton, Ga., Oct. 1, 1789. A *Patriot* and private, Md. Line; served in Lee's Legion, Md. Troops, 1776, and private in Ga. Militia; mar. 1750, Elizabeth (Hollinsworth) Johnson (1727–1812).
Children:
   1. Zebulon (1751-1827), mar. Nancy Cain.
   2. Mary, mar. (1) Dr. Wilson; (2) John Tapperly; (3) Thomas Heard.
   3. William (1756–1806), mar. Ann Armistead.
   4. Ezekiel (1759–1837), mar. Elizabeth Veazey.
   5. Jesse (1762–1813), mar. Sarah Peek.
   6. Francinia, mar. William McClellan.
   7. JOHN (1760–1847), *Rev. Sol.*, mar. Jane Rabun; he served as private, Ga. Line; received bounty land in Ga. for his service. His wife was the dau. of MATHEW RABUN, *Rev. Sol.* of N. C., and his wife, Sarah Warren.

JOHN VEAZEY, b. Md., Mar. 29, 1760; d. Ga., Nov. 8, 1847. He was a *Rev. Sol.*; received bounty grant of land in Ga. for his service. Mar. Feb. 4, 1790, Jane Rabun (dau. of MATTHEW RABUN, a *Rev. Sol.* of N. C. and Ga., and his wife, Sarah Warren), b. Jan 1, 1766; d. Jan 10, 1855.
Children:
   1. Sallie (Sarah), mar. 1810, Richmond Burnley, b. 1789 (son of HENRY BURNLEY, *Rev. Sol.* and Grandson of ISRAEL BURNLEY, *Rev. Sol.* of Va. and Ga., and his wife, Ann Hannah Overton).
   2. William, d. y.
   3. Lovett, d. y.
   4. Elizabeth, b. Oct. 3, 1795, mar. her cousin, Henry McLellan.
   5. John, b. Dec. 8, 1797, mar. Elizabeth Gardner.
   6. Polly (Mary) (1800–1828), mar. 1822, Thomas Whaley.
   7. Eli (1801–1844).
   8. Lemuel (1804–1828).
   9. Nancy (twin), b. Sept. 16, 1806, mar. Thomas Neel (or Neal).
   10. Martha (twin), b. Sept. 16, 1806, mar. Samuel Hart.

JOHN VENABLE, b. Va., 1740; d. Jackson Co., Ga., 1811. Served with the rank of Capt. and was the assistant Commissioner of Provision Laws, Bedford Co., Va. Was at the Battle of Guilford C. H. Mar. in Va., 1780, Agnes Moorman (dau. of CHARLES MOORMAN, of Va.). They moved to Wilkes Co., Ga., where he received a bounty grant of land for his service in Va. as a *Rev. Sol.*
Children:
   1. Robert (*Sol. of War of 1812*), mar. Judith Jackson.
   2. Charles.
   3. Abram.
   4. William.
   5. John Moorman, mar. Sarah Clower.
   6. Nathaniel, mar. Sarah Montgomery.
   7. Mary, mar. Jacob Venable.

JOHN VERNER, JR. (son of JOHN VERNER, SR., *Rev. Sol.*, and his wife, Mary Pettigrew, 8 children: 1. David; 2. John, Jr.; 3. Samuel; 4. George; 5. Charles; 6. Dinah; 7. Nancy; 8. Jane), b. Granville Co., N. C., Mar. 5, 1763; d. Elbert Co., Ga., 1853. Was a *Rev. Sol.*; drew bounty land for his service. Mar. (1) 1785, JANE EDMUNDSON (1767–1792); (2) July 18, 1793, Rebecca Dickey (1774–1849).
Children by (1) wife:
   1. Mary P., b. 1786, mar. William Cockerman.
   2. William, mar. Elinor Hooper.
   3. James, b. 1790.

Children by (2) wife:

1. Nancy, d. y.
2. Jane, b. 1796, mar. Thomas Humphries.
3. John Augustus, b. 1799.
4. David O., b. 1799.
5. Charles, b. 1801, mar. Mary L. Davis.
6. Rebecca.
7. Lemuel H.
8. Samuel, b. 1808, mar. Malinda Crawford.
9. George W., b. 1810, mar. 1833, Harriet Harris.
10. Anna, mar. W. L. Stribling.
11. Ebenezer Pettigrew, mar. Emma Foster.

JACOB CASPAR WALDHAUER, b. Austria before 1734; d. Savannah, Ga., May 1804. Mar. Mary Virginia Flerl (dau. of Capt. JOHN FLERL, *Rev. Sol.*, and his wife, Dorothy Brandeis). He came to America with Gen. James Edward Oglethorpe; represented St. Mathew's Parish in the first Provincial Congress of Ga., assembled at Savannah, Ga., 1775. Served as Capt., Ga. Militia, 1776; member Council of Safety, 1776.

Children:

1. Salome, mar. Israel Floerl. (Flerl)
2. John C., mar. Margaret Floerl.
3. Israel.
4. Elizabeth, mar. Daniel Remshart (son of JOHN REMSHART, *Rev. Sol.*, and his wife, Anna Margaret Mueller), b. Oct. 2, 1765.
5. Hannah, mar. Lewis Weitman.
6. Margaret, mar. David Gugel.

EDWARD WADE, b. Va., —; d. Greene Co., Ga., 1790. Was a *Patriot*; took the Oath of Allegiance, Pittsylvania Co., Va., 1770; also was private in Va. Troops under Capt. William Witcher. Mar. 1746, Mary —.

Their son, PEYTON WADE, b. Halifax Co., Va., 1755; d. Morgan Co., Ga., 1831. Took Oath of Allegiance and also served under Capt. WILLIAM WITCHER, *Rev. Sol.* Mar. Martha Perkins.

Children:

1. Archibald.
2. Jesse.
3. Peyton L.
4. Edward.
5. Frances, mar. Henry Vidette.

ELISHA WALKER, b. Va., about 1761; d. Washington Co., Ga., 1802. Mar. 1787, ELIZABETH BOWERS, d. 1839; she drew land in Lottery as the widow of a *Rev. Sol.* He served as private, 1777, 1st Batt., Richmond Co., Ga. Militia, commanded by Col. James McNeill; drew bounty land for his service in Washington Co., Ga.

Children:

1. Noah, b. 1790, mar. Charlotte Calhoun.
2. Jeremiah, mar. Joanna —.
3. Henry, mar. Charity Fox.
4. Judy, mar. Johnson.
5. Perusila, mar. Arthur Rawls.
6. Annie, mar. — Parker.
7. Lott, mar. Mary (Polly) Walters.

JEREMIAH WALKER, b. N. C., 1747; d. Elbert Co., Ga., Oct. 1792. Mar. (1) —; mar. (2) MILLY COLSON, widow of Jacob Colson. He served as a *Rev. Sol.* of N. C. and a *Sol. of 1812* in Ga. (1st wife d. N. C., before 1780).

Children:

1. Polly, mar. John Coleman. Her 3 daus. were named Elizabeth, Narcissa, and Melanda.
2. Henry Graves.

3. Memorable.
4. James Sanders.
5. Elizabeth, mar. — Marshall.
6. John Williams.
7. Jeremiah.

Bro. SAUNDERS WALKER and wife, Sarah, of Wilkes Co., *Rev. Sol.*

JAMES WALKER, b. N. C., 1753; d. Upson Co., Ga., June 24, 1849. He commanded a Brigade at the Battle of Cowpens; received bounty land in Ga. for his service. Mar. CHARITY SMITH. They moved to Washington (now Putnam) Co., Ga., then to Upson Co., Ga.

Children:
1. Nathaniel F. (1783–1823), mar. Susan N. Palmer.
2. William W., mar. Mary Smith.
3. Benjamin, mar. Elizabeth Swinney.
4. Allen, mar. Elizabeth A. Owen.
5. Lucretia, mar. Martin Stamps.
6. Mary, mar. Elisha Perryman.
7. Sarah, mar. Daniel Grant.
8. Nancy Milledge, mar. Enoch Womble.
(Grave marked).

JOEL WALKER, b. Mar. 10, 1733; d. Jefferson Co., Ga., Jan. 19, 1796. Served as a *Rev. Sol.*; received bounty land in Ga. Mar. (1) Judith — (1733–1782); mar. (2) 1784, Barbara Beal.

Children by (1) wife:
1. Arthur, b. 1756.
2. Joel, Jr., b. 1758.
3. William (1762–1818), mar. 1798, Elizabeth Bostic.
4. David, b. 1765, mar. Elizabeth —.
5. Charles.
6. Elizabeth, b. 1760.
7. Betsey.
8. Sarah.
9. Mary, b. 1773.

Children by (2) wife:
1. Jeminah.
2. Peggy, b. 1787 (twin).
3. Patty, b. 1787 (twin).
4. Henry.
5. Nancy.
6. Sally, b. 1795 (twin).
7. Grace, b. 1795 (twin).

JOHN WALKER, b. Hampshire Co., Va., Dec. 7, 1765; d. Danburg, Wilkes Co., Ga., Oct. 10, 1826, a *Rev. Sol.*; served as private under Col. Elijah Clarke, 1780, having been transferred from Col. Baker's N. C. Regiment; was granted 287½ acres of land in Wilkes Co., Ga., for his service, 1784. (In 1790, he served for a short time in the U. S. Congress as *Senator*.) Mar. Feb. 11, 1790, MARTHA SMITH (dau. of John and Sarah Smith), b. Nov. 17, 1770; d. Danburg, Wilkes Co., Ga.

Children:
1. William (1791–1823).
2. John S., b. May 12, 1793; d. Mar. 1892.
3. Taylor (1795–1817).
4. James, b. Aug. 6, 1798; d. Ala., 1876; mar. Dolly McLendon.
5. Nancy, b. Feb. 24, 1801; d. West Point, Ga., 1876; mar. Joel Callaway.
6. George (1803–1824).
7. Richard, b. May 13, 1805; d. 1869.
8. Robert, b. Danburg, Wilkes Co., Ga., Oct. 10, 1807; d. Griffin, Ga., April 1882. Mar. 1827, Elizabeth West Cain, b. 1811; d. Aug. 6, 1868. Lived in Pike and Spalding Cos., Ga. They had 18 children.

9. Sophia, b. Aug. 13, 1810; d. Oct. 4, 1857; mar. Dr. William Quarles Anderson.

10. Martha, b. April 13, 1813; d. 1885; mar. Thomas Smith.

JAMES WALKER (bro. of John Walker), was a *Rev. Sol.*; served under Col. Clarke; mar. Dorothy McClendon (dau. of Isaac and Mary McClendon, of Wilkes Co., Ga.).

WILLIAM WALKER (son of JOEL WALKER, *Rev. Sol.*, and his wife, Judith —), b. Buckingham Co., Va., 1762; d. Jefferson Co., Ga., 1818. Private in Ga. Militia, under MAJOR GEN. JOHN TWIGGS. Served as scout. Mar., Jefferson Co., Ga., Elizabeth Bostic (1770–1835) (dau. of NATHAN BOSTIC (OR BOSTWICK), b. Suffolk Co., Va., 1746; d. Jefferson Co., Ga., 1818; received bounty grant of land for service as private in Ga. Militia. Mar. Martha Gwinn, b. 1750).

Children:

1. Charles Hillary, b. 1812, mar. Caroline E. Jones (dau. of William Hardwick and etencia (Abercrombie) Jones).

2. Arthur.

3. William H.

4. Anthony Winston.

5. Martha (or Mary) Ann, b. 1806, mar. Littleberry Bostic, Jr.

JOHN WALLER, SR., b. Md., Mar. 13, 1749; d. Hancock Co., Ga., 1808. Served as private, Md. Troops. Mar. Elizabeth Rhodes (Rodes).

Children:

1. HANDY, b. Md.; d. Putnam Co., Ga., 1845. Served as private, Md. Troops. Mar. 1792, MARTHA TEASLEY; received bounty land.

2. James, b. Dec. 15, 1768; d. Hancock Co., Ga., 1817; *Sol. of 1812.* Mar. Elizabeth Ellis (1772–1845) (dau. of LEVIN ELLIS, a *Rev. Sol.*, b. Va.; d. Hancock Co., Ga., and his wife, Isobel).

Children: 1. Mary Elizabeth; 2. Martha; 3. Ellis M.; 4. Elizabeth K.; 5. James B.; 6. Phyllis; 7. Ibby C.; 8. Irwin.

3. Daniel.

4. John.

5. William.

6. Charles R.

7. Elizabeth.

8. Nathaniel E.

GEORGE WALTON, b. Prince Edward Co., Va., 1724; d. Columbia Co., Ga., 1796. Served as 1st Lieut. in Col. McIntosh's Command, Ga. Line. Mar. (1) Martha Hughes (1734–1815); 13 children.

One dau., Nancy Hughes Walton (1760–1809), mar. 1776, THOMAS MOORE, *Rev. Sol.*, b. Prince Edward Co., Va., 1756; d. Columbia Co., Ga., 1806.

JOHN WALTON, b. Va., 1743; moved to Richmond Co., Ga. Member of Provincial Congress of Ga. Mar. Elizabeth Claiborne.

(JOHN, ROBERT and GEORGE WALTON (*the Signer*) were *Rev. Sols.* of Ga., and were the sons of Robert Walton and Sallie Hughes, of Va.).

WILLIAM WALTON, b. Va., d. Columbia Co., Ga. Served in Va. Continental Army; received grant of land for service. Moved to Ga., 1790. Mar. Sallie Grinage.

JESSE WARREN, b. Va. —; d. Hancock Co., Ga., 1827. (Will made Jan. 16, 1826; Pro. Feb. 12, 1827). Served as *Rev. Sol.* of Va.; drew land for his service, in Lottery of 1827. Mar. Elizabeth —.

Children:

1. Jeremiah.

2. William.

3. Robert.

4. Jesse, mar. Timley —.

5. Sally, mar. Lott Harton.

6. Mary.

7. Susannah.
8. Elizabeth, mar. — Smith.
(Grave marked).

JOSIAH WARREN, b. Va., 1759; moved to Onslow Co., N. C.; d. Burke (now Laurens) Co., Ga., 1804. Served as Capt. at the Coast of Ga. for its defense; received pay for his service in 1782, and 287½ acres of land in 1785. Mar. 1774, NANCY DOTY, b. N. J. Children:

1. Josiah, Jr., b. Onslow Co., N. C.
2. Richard, b. Onslow Co., N. C.
3. Benajah.
4. Hinchey.
5. Kittrell.
6. Silas.
7. Eli, a *Sol. of War of 1812*; Gen. in Ga. State Militia.
8. Rachel, mar. Charles Culpepper.
9. Sarah, mar. Ichabod Scarborough.
10. Mary.
11. Lott, b. 1797.

NOTE: JOSIAH WARREN was known as "the Lone Horseman" from Burke Co., Ga., who rode upon the excited scene before the State House in Louisville, Ga., at the very moment when the papers of the Yazoo Act were about to be burned and drawing from his pocket the sun-glass, suggested to his friend, James Jackson, of Ga., that the accursed document be consumed by fire drawn from Heaven.

WILLIAM ALEXANDER WARE, b. Amherst Co., Va.; came to Ga.; lived on Line Creek, Fayette Co., where he d. unmar.; *Rev. Sol.*, present at the surrender of Cornwallis at Yorktown.

EDWARD WARE, b. Amherst Co., Va., 1762; came to Ga.; d. Danielsville, Ga., Nov. 3, 1836; *Rev. Sol.*, present at the surrender of Cornwallis at Yorktown; pension granted him, 1836, for his service; enlisted Va., 1776, under Capt. James Higgenbothem, 1778 under Capt. Rucker, Col. Fontaine. In 1780 Serg. under Capt. Samuel Higgenbothem, Capt. Dillard, and Col. Lynch; Second Lieut. Came to Ga. about 1790, lived in Richmond (then Madison) Co., Ga. Mar. 1781, Sarah Thurmond (dau. of Philip Thurmond, of Va.), b. 1764; d. 1812.

Children (known):
1. Philip (1786–1853), mar. Mary (Polly) Strickland.
2. Henry (1788–1822), mar. Melinda Strickland.
3. Elizabeth, mar. James Long. (They were the parents of Dr. Crawford W. Long, of Ga., the famous *discoverer of "Anesthesia."*)
4. Letty, mar. her cousin, James Ware, Jr.

JAMES WARE, b. Amherst Co., Va.; d. Madison Co., Ga. Moved to Ga. about 1790. *Rev. Sol.*, present at the surrender of Cornwallis at Yorktown. Commissioned Second Lieut, 1775, in Va. Continental Line. Mar. Mary Veal.

Children (known):
1. Edward, mar. Sarah Daniel Penn.
2. James, Jr., mar. his cousin, Letty Ware. They had 14 children.

ROBERT WARE, *Rev. Sol.* of Va., moved to Ga.; had son, Nicholas Ware, b. Caroline Co., Va., 1769.

MOSES WAY, b. S. C., 1734; d. Liberty Co., Ga., 1786. Came to Ga., 1754; settled at Midway. Served as Lieut., then Capt., Ga. Militia. Mar. (1) 1756, LYDIA MITCHELL, d. 1765; mar. (2) 1766, ANN WINN.

Children by (1) wife:
1. Lydia, mar. (1) 1774, Peter Sallens; mar. (2) John Foster.
2. John, mar. 1790, Sarah Goulding.
3. William.

Children by (2) wife:
1. Mary, b. 1767, mar. Samuel Jones, Jr. (son of Samuel Jones and Rebecca Baker, dau. of William Baker and Sarah Osgood).

   2. Susanna, mar. — White.
   3. Patty.
   4. Moses, Jr., mar. Susanna Dowse, widow.
   5. Rebecca T., mar. — Shearer.

JAMES WATKINS, *Rev. Sol.*, b. Va., 1728; d. Wilkes Co., Ga., 1801; buried Petersburg, Ga., on the North side of the Broad river, just before the waters empty into the Savannah river. (Will made, Wilkes Co., Ga.; Pro. July 27, 1801.) Mar. Martha —; she d. Nov. 22, 1803, age 69 years. Children:
   1. Robert.
   2. Joseph.
   3. Isham.
   4. William.
   5. James.
   6. Samuel.
   7. Thompson.
   8. Sally, mar. Robert Thompson.

THOMAS WATKINS, JR. (son of THOMAS WATKINS, *Rev. Sol.* of Powhatan Co., Va.) b. Va.; a *Rev. Sol.*, killed by the Indian Allies of the British. Mar. 1763, Sallie Walton, of Richmond Co., Ga. (sister of GEORGE WALTON, *Signer of the Declaration of Independence* from Ga) She mar. (2) Joshua Morris of Ky. Children:
   1. Robert, mar. Elizabeth Walton (dau. of John Walton); lived in Richmond Co., Ga.
   2. Thomas, III, Lieut. in Indian Wars.
   3. Anderson, mar Catherine Eve.
   4. George, b. 1770, mar. Mary (called Polly) Early (dau. of Joel Early); lived in Wilkes Co., Ga.
   5. Claiborne, mar. Elizabeth Craig. (dau. of Capt. Robert Craig, *Rev. Sol.* of Va.). She mar. (2) Mr. Clapp.
   6. Isaac, mar. twice; settled in Ark.
   7. Polly, mar. William Nichols of Ky.

BENJAMIN WEAVER, b. Halifax Co., N. C., 1760; d. Greene Co., Ga., 1816. Served as private in Capt. Raiford's Co., N. C. Regiment. Mar. (1) MISS DREWRY; mar. (2) ELIZABETH DANIEL.
Children by (1) wife:
   One son and two daus.
Children by (2) wife:
   1. William Wylie, mar. Caroline Mounger.
   2. Travis A. D., mar. Caroline Cook.
   3. Henry, d. y.

CLAIBORNE WEBB, b. Albemarle Co., Va., 1760; d. Elbert Co., Ga., 1818. Name appears in list of *Rev. Sols.* of Va., who received pay for their service, 1784, and also received grant of land in Wilkes Co., Ga., 1785. Mar. Margaret —, b. Va., 1765; received land, 1827, as widow of *Rev. Sol.*, living in 1832. Children:
   1. Bridges, *Sol. of 1812.*
   2. Margaret, mar. Joseph Glenn.
   3. William.
   4. Claiborne, Jr.
   5. Milton Pope, mar. Alice Deadwyler.
   6. Abner, mar. Nancy Deadwyler.
   7. Evelina, mar. Mial Smith.
   8. Elijah, mar. Ann B. Deadwyler.
  10. Martha P., mar. 1825, Joseph Deadwyler.

FRANCIS WEBB, b. Essex Co., Va., 1759; d. Hancock Co., Ga., 1811. Served as Midshipman in Navy, under Com. Capt. Travis, on the ship "Dragon"; was wounded. Mar. 1786, FRANCES WALKER (1764–1809) (dau. of Freeman Walker and his wife, Frances Belfield). They moved to Ga. 1810, where he received land.

Children:
1. Bathurst, d. y.
2. Thomas.
3. James (1792–1853), mar. 1813, Rachel Elizabeth Lamar (dau. of Col. Thomas Lamar, of Hancock Co., Ga.).
4. John, b. 1794; d. Aug. 19, 1870; mar. Ann (Nancy) Thomason (dau. of John Connor Thomason and his wife, Narcissa Jane Lewis). He was a *Sol. of 1812*.
5. Frances Belfield, d. y.
6. Richard W., d. y.
7. Wm. Meriwether.
8. Frances W., d. y.

ELIAS WELLBORN, b. Randolph Co., N. C., 1759; d. Columbia Co., Ga., 1836. Placed on Pension Roll. Served as private, N. C. Militia; received land in 1827 Lottery. Mar. Mary Marshall (dau. of ABRAM MARSHALL, *Rev. Sol.* of Ga.). Received pension.

Children:
1. Ruby, mar. Dr. Davis.
2. Marshall H., mar. (1) Miss Hill; mar. (2) F. Hardaway.
3. Stephen.
4. Lucy, mar. (1) George Lewis; mar. (2) — Morrow.
5. James Madison, mar. Louise Amanda Cody.
6. Martha, mar. William Briscoe.
7. Selina H., mar. Theophilus Hill.
8. Mary, mar. — Fleming.
9. Abner W., mar. — Heard.
10. Nancy, mar. Nathaniel Bailey.

WILLIAM WELLBORN, b. N. C., 1733; d. Ga., 1792. Served as private, N. C. Militia; was at the surrender of Cornwallis at Yorktown. Mar. Hepzibah Stearns (dau. of Isaac Stearns and his wife, Rebecca Johnson, g.-dau. of Charles Stearns, of Mass., and his wife, Rebecca Gibson).

Children:
1. Abner, mar. Martha Render.
2. ELIAS, b. Randolph Co., N. C., 1759; d. Columbia Co., Ga., 1836; received pension as *Rev. Sol.* Mar. Mary Marshall. 10 children.
3. Johnson, mar. Sallie Render.
4. Clara, mar. — Dennis.
5. James.
6. William.
7. Chapley.
8. Samuel.
9. Isaac.
10. Mary.

NOTE: April 10, 1815, William Wellborn was appointed attorney for the following *Rev. Sols.* "to apply for whatever money was due them for their service in the 5th N. C. Militia stationed at Norfolk and under the command of Col. Richard Atkinson, viz: SAMUEL MILLICAN; NATHAN WOODRIDGE; THOMAS WHITE; THOMAS LAIN (or LANE); ISAAC COLTRANE; SETH DIXON.

JOSEPH WESTMORELAND, b. Dinwiddie Co., Va., 1740; d. Va., 1784. He served as private, Va. Continental Line; received bounty land in Ky. for his service. He enlisted from Mecklinburg Co., Va. Mar. 1764, Mecklenburg Co., Va., MARTHA SHORES; she was in the 1785 Census of Va., a widow with 8 children. Moved, after the Rev. War, to N. C., then to Baldwin (later Putnam) Co., Ga., and d. Fayette Co., Ga., 1834.

Children:
1. Joel, moved West.

2. Joseph, mar. (1) Rebecca Simmons (dau. of JOHN SIMMONS, *Rev. Sol.*); mar. (2) a Creek Indian princess and moved to Indian Territory.

3. REUBEN, b. Va., 1770; d. Coweta Co., Ga., Aug. 1845. *Sol. of the War of 1812.* (Pension granted to his widow.) He mar. (1) in N. C., Rebecca Jane Jackson; two sons, James and Mark Jackson; mar. (2) in Miss., Keziah Simmons (dau. of JOHN SIMMONS, a *Rev. Sol.*). 6 children.

One dau., Angelina, mar. William de Graffenreid Tidwell, a descendant of WILLIAM TID-WELL, *Rev. Sol.* of S. C., and TSCHARNER DE GRAFFENREID, *Rev. Sol.* of Va.

4. Robert, mar. Ann Foreman.

5. John, mar.; moved to Pike Co., Ga.

6. Sybilla, mar. Benjamin Moody.

7. Martha, mar. — Linch.

HUDSON WHITAKER, b. N. C., Oct. 23, 1757; d. Washington Co., Ga., July 5, 1817. Served as Ensign 7th Regiment N. C. Troops, 1776. Mar. SUSANNA THOMAS, who d. 1839. She mar. (2) Miles Young.

Children:

1. Jordan John, b. 1778.

2. Simon (1780-1849), mar. (1) Elizabeth Mary Irwin (dau. of GOV. JARED IRWIN, of Ga.); (2) Nancy Pierce.

3. Richard, b. 1782; *Sol. of War of 1812*; mar. Frances Pace (dau. of NATHANIEL PACE, *Rev. Sol.* of N. C. and Ga., and his wife, Amelia Mildred Boykin, sister of Maj. Francis Boykin).

4. Samuel, *Sol. War of 1812*; mar. Margaret Young; moved to Fla.

5. William, mar. Mary Cantey.

6. Willis, mar. Rebecca Britt.

7. Edwin, mar. (1) Theresa Goode; (2) Martha Cobb.

8. Nancy, mar. John Davis, of Baldwin Co., Ga.

9. Hannah, mar. Mr. Dee, of Washington Co., Ga.

SAMUEL WHITAKER (bro. of Ensign Hudson Whitaker), b. N. C. Came from Halifax Co. to Ga. where he d.; received bounty land in Ga. for his service in N. C. Line. Mar. Elizabeth Williams.

Children:

1. Winifred Mary, b. 1789.

2. Ooroondatus (1791-1842), mar. Martha Rivers Harris.

3. John.

4. Katherine Boykin, mar. Major John Broadnax.

5. Elizabeth Carr, mar. James Gray.

JOHN M. WHITE, b. Spottsylvania Co., Va., June 27, 1743; d. Elbert Co., Ga., Feb. 6, 1833. Served as Capt. Spottsylvania Co., Va. Troops; received land, 1827, as a *Rev. Sol.* in Cherokee land lottery. Mar. 1775, Mildred Thornton Ballenger (dau. of JOSEPH BALLENGER, *Rev. Patriot,* and his wife, Sarah H. Franklin of Amherst Co., Va.) She was b. Oct. 23, 1756; d. Elbert Co., Ga., Sept. 2, 1840.

Children (mentioned in will):

1. Milly, mar. John Morris.

2. Mary, mar. — Jones.

3. Nancy, mar. Asa Mann (son of JAMES MANN, SR., *Rev. Sol.* of S. C.)

4. Lucy K., mar. Thomas Thornton.

5. Frances (d. before 1832), mar. Robert Roebuck, Jr.

6. Eliza, mar. 1823, Richard Rice.

7. Patsey, mar. Martin White.

SAMUEL WHITTAKER, b. Chester Co., Penn., about 1753 (son of William Whittaker, b. England, 1721; d. Rowan Co., N. C. after 1778, and his wife, Elizabeth Carlton); d. Franklin Co., Ga., 1802. Mar. MARY GRAVES (dau. of JAMES GRAVES, *Rev. Sol.* of Ga., and his wife, Mary Copeland), b. Va.; d. Wilkinson Co., Miss. after 1809. He served as a *Rev. Sol.* of Ga.; received bounty land, 287½ acres, for his service as a *Rev. Sol.* in Ga. Certificate of Col. G. Lee.

Children:

1. Mark (1783-1852), mar. Feb. 8, 1808, Richmond Co., Ga., Mary Brooks.

2. Joshua, b. 1779.
3. William, b. 1781.
4. John.
5. Joel
6 Sarah.
7. Elizabeth.

FADDY WHITTINGTON, b. Johnson Co., N. C., Feb. 12, 1752; d. Pike Co., Ga., Oct., 1855. Served 6 weeks as a *Rev. Sol.* in Capt. Jonathan Smith's Co. N. C.; 3 months in Capt. John Whitley's Co. N. C.; received pension May 1, 1832; received bounty land in Polk Co., Ga., Mar. 3, 1855; pensioner of Pike Co., Ga.; drew land in lottery as a *Rev. Sol.*, living in Jasper Co., Ga., 1820. Buried in "Seagrave's Cemetery, 4 miles frim Griffin, Ga. Mar. Johnston Co., N. C., 1778, REBECCA ROPER (dau. of JAMES ROPER, a *Rev. Sol.* of N. C., and his wife, Alice), b. N. C., 1761; d. Johnston Co., N. C., 1803.

Children (known):
  1. Mary, b. and d. in N. C.
  2. Thaddeus (a doctor of Pike Co.), b. N. C. 1791; d. Pike Co., Ga., 1840. Mar. Dec. 2, 1825, Sarah Burt, b. Ala., 1809; d. S. Ga., 1845.

ELISHA WILKERSON, b. Sussex Co., Va., 1763; d. Franklin Co., Ga., 1837. Entered Militia at Sussex Co., Va., under command of Capt. Green Hill; Col. Joseph Jones; Gen. Lawson; received pension for his service in Franklin Co., Ga. Lived in Dinwiddie Co., Va. 1789, then Mecklinburg Co., Va. until 1807, when he removed to Franklin Co., Ga. Mar. LUCY ABERNATHY (dau. of Tignal Abernathy of Mecklinburg Co., Va., d. 1808).

Children (not in order of birth):
  1. Elisha.
  2. Tignal.
  3. Thomas.
  4. Polly, mar. Wright Bond.
  5. Patsey, mar. — Mitchell.
  6. Sophia, mar. Thomas G. Edwards.
  7. Fanny, mar. — Baldwin.
  8. Sally, mar. — Cawthorn.
  9. Silva, mar. — Baker.

BENJAMIN WILKINSON (WILKERSON), b. Va., Sept. 23, 1748; d. Wilkes Co., Ga., 1817. Mar. 1777, Ann —, b. Aug. 25, 1758; d. Wilkes Co., Ga., 1825. He was a *Rev. Sol.*
Children:
  1. Eliza, b. Dec. 29, 1782.
  2. Polly, b. July 28, 1784.
  3. Elizabeth (Betsey), b. June 21, 1786.
  4. Nancy, b. July 15, 1788.
  5. Jeannett, b. April 18, 1790.
  6. CAROLINE, b. Dec. 31, 1792, mar. JESSE F. HEARD, b. June 17, 1785. He was a *Sol. of War of 1812,* as Capt. 165th Co. of Militia, July 7, 1812. Mar. Mar. 5, 1809. 13 children.
  7. John, b. Jan. 21, 1796.

CHARLES WILLIAMS, b. S. C., 1740; d. Wilkes Co., Ga., 1782. Mar. S. C. 1765, Susanna —, b. 1746; d. 1815. Came to the ceded lands of Ga. 1773. Served as a *Rev. Sol.*, Lieut. in Minute Battalion of Ga.; his widow drew land as Widow of *Rev. Sol.* in Washington Co., Ga., 1784.

Children (known):
  1. Joshua, mar. Peggy Williams, both d. Jones Co., Ga.
  2. Charles, Jr.
  3. Susanna.

JAMES WILLIAMS, b. S. C.; d. Jones Co., Ga., July, 1819. *Rev. Sol.* of Ga. Mar. Sally —; she drew land in 1827 lottery as the Widow of *Rev. Sol.*
Children (known):
  1. Eliza D., mar. Thomas McDowell.

2. Martha, mar. — Moore.
3. Rebecca M., mar. — Bunkley.
4. Mary W.
5. J. Howell Flewellyn, mar. Lucy Slatter.
6. William.

JOHN B. WILLIAMS, b. Bertie Co., N. C , about 1730; came to Wilkes Co., Ga. (ceded lands) Moved to Crawford Co., Ga., 1823; d. there 1836. Served as a *Rev. Sol.* under Gen. Elijah Clarke in the 1st Battalion of Minute Men. Mar. Columbia Co., Ga., Susannah Mourning Smith (widow of Lieut. Thomas Smith). Grave marked.
Children:
1. James, mar. Jemina Wilson.
2. Tryphena, mar. (1) — House; (2) Wiley Witchard.
3. Rachel, mar. George Moore.
4. Louisa, mar. Nathan Respess.

JOSEPH WILLIAMS, b. N. C., 1760; d. Ga., 1850. Served Ensign and Lieut. Duplin Co., N. C. Militia March, 1779 to May, 1781. Mar. Duplin Co , N. C., MARY ERWIN. He d. Telfair Co., Ga. and is buried at "China Hill" plantation.
Children:
1. William H.
2. Daniel.
3. Joseph, Jr.
4. Mary.
5. Rebecca.
6. Phoebe.
7. Nancy.
8. Elizabeth.

WILLIAM WILLIAMS, b. N. C., 1751; moved to St. Mary's, Ga. Served as an officer and was killed in S. C. after the War, by Tory sympathizers, at a meeting held in 1799. Mar. Hannah Blewett.
Children:
1. Sarah, mar. — Thomas, of S. C.
2. William, Jr., b. St. Mary's, Ga., 1791; d. Bainbridge, Ga., 1860. Mar. (1) Keziah Ashley; mar. (2) Cassandra Sheppard; mar. (3) Mrs. Root of Mass; mar. (4) Mrs. Cook.
NOTE: From Dept. of Archives and History, Atlanta, Ga. "The original claims of WILLIAM WILLIAMS, *Rev. Sol.* 2-24-1823. and of FOUNTAIN JORDAN, 2-18-1822, *Rev. Sol.* found in the office of Clerk of Court, Wilkes Co., Ga.

WILLIAM WILLIAMS, b. Va., 1761; allowed pension, 1835, while a resident of Washington Co., Ga.; enlisted, 1777, served as private in Capt. Isaac Moore's Co., Col. Abraham Shepard, and Col. Thomas Clark's N. C. Regiment. Was in Battle of Monmouth; captured at Paramus, N. J. Released and captured again, May 12, 1780 at Charleston, S. C.

MICAJAH WILLIAMSON, b. Bedford Co., Va., 1735; d. Wilkes Co., Ga., 1795. Served as Lieut.-Col. and a General in Ga. Army; served with Gen. Elijah Clarke to protect the frontier of Ga. Mar. 1770, SALLY (SARAH) GILLIAM, b. Henrico Co., Va., 1745; d. Ga. They moved to (now) Wilkes Co., Ga., 1768. She was a *Rev. Patriot.* During his absence in the field, the Tories burned their home and hanged their 12 year old son.
Children:
1. CHARLES, mar. Nancy Clarke (dau. of GEN. ELIJAH CLARKE, of Ga.) He made his will Feb. 27, 1800. His widow mar. (2) William J. Hobby, of Conn., and Augusta, Ga.
2. Micajah, Jr.
3. Thomas Jefferson.
4. Peter.
5. William.
6. Sally, mar. (1) Judge John Griffin; mar. (2) Judge Chas. Tait.
7. Nancy, mar. GEN. JOHN CLARKE (son of Gen. ELIJAH CLARKE) a *Rev. Sol., War of 1812,* and *Governor of Georgia,* 1819 to 1823.
8. Susan, mar. Dr. Thompson Bird.

9. Martha, mar. Thomas Fitch, of New England.

10. Mary, mar. 1808, Duncan G. Campbell (son of Archibald Campbell, of Orange Co., N. C. and Wilkes Co., Ga.)

11. Elizabeth, mar. Peterson Thweatt. Their dau., Sarah (1805-1879), mar. Thacker Brock Howard (son of JOHN HOWARD, b. S. C., 1761; d. Baldwin Co., Ga., 1822; a *Rev. Sol.* and his wife, Jane Vivian).

ROBERT WILLIAMSON, b. 1760; d. Screven Co., Ga., 1810. Served with Ga. Troops; received grant of land in Ga. for his service. Mar. Lucy Conyers (dau. of JOHN CONYERS (1725-1814) in Ga., who served in the Ga. Line under Col. John Thomas, and his wife, Sarah Miller (1737-1834), dau. of ELISHA MILLER, b. N. C., 1715; d. Ga., 1800; served as Capt. of Ga. Militia, and his wife, Martha Colson (1720-1790).

One of their sons, Benjamin (*Sol. War of 1812*), b. Ga., 1792; d. Ga., 1881; mar. 1821, Elizabeth Roberts (1799-1879), dau. of JAMES ROBERTS (1744-1814) in Ga.; served Ga. Line and received bounty grant for his service, and his wife, Emily Williamson. (All lived in Screven Co., Ga.)

JOEL WILLIS, b. —; d. Jones Co., Ga., June 10, 1822. He served as a *Rev. Sol.* Mar. (1) Amy —; mar. (2) Sarah —. His (2) wife, Sarah — (listed in will) of Jones Co., Ga. Drew land in 1827 as widow of *Rev. Sol.*

Children:

1. Joel, Jr.

2. William, b. N. C., Nov. 5, 1782; d. Upson Co., Ga., Aug. 11, 1851. Mar. Mar. 18, 1812, Nancy Middlebrooks (1797-1866). He was son of (1) wife Amy —.

3. Hosea, d. 1858.

4. Anaam, b. 1798; d. Oct. 24, 1878, mar. Mary Ann P. Means, d. 1906.

5. Rhesa, mar. Robert Hartley.

6. Rebecca, mar. —Gammon.

7. Hannah, mar. Jacob Lamb.

8. Sarah, mar. — Cadinhead.

9. Thomas, mar. Delaney Lord.

10. Nahum.

JAMES WILSON, b. Ireland, 1745; d. Effingham Co., Ga., 1825. Served as Capt. 10th N. C. Regiment; also Capt. 4th S. C. Troops; was captured at Charleston, S. C., 1780; received bounty grant of land in Ga. for his service. Mar. (1) Sarah —; mar. (2) Ann (Gordon) (Woodward) Pace.

Children by (1) wife:

1. John, b. 1768, moved to Texas.

2. James, Jr., b. 1773; d. Ga., 1833; mar. 1794, Elizabeth Morgan.

3. Jesse, b. 1774, mar. Eliza Cook; moved to Ill.

Children by (2) wife:

1. Luke, mar. (1) Patience Crawford; mar. (2) Ann Catherine Griner.

2. Allen Fulford, mar. (1) Mary Hurst; mar. (2) Serena Hurst; mar. (3) Margaret Fulford.

3. Elihu, mar. (1) Catherine Tullis (their son, Stephen, mar. Tabitha Edwards). He mar. (2) Ann (Achord) Warren.

4. Gabriel, mar. Sarah Oglesby.

5. Jeremiah, mar. Elizabeth Lucas.

JOHN WILSON, b. England, 1735; was killed in Battle in N. C., 1779 by the British. Mar. 1766 (2) Martha McKemie (sometimes spelled McKemy or Makemie) (dau. of George McKemie, b. Ireland; d. N. C., and his wife, Margaret Hutchinson, whose sister, Elizabeth Hutchinson, mar. Andrew Jackson, Sr., the parents of ANDREW JACKSON, *President of the United States.* Another sister, Jane Hutchinson, mar. James Crawford), b. 1739; d. 1790.

Their son, John McKemie (1769-1839), mar. Mary (called Pretty Polly) Erwin (dau. of ALEXANDER ERWIN, *Rev. Sol.* of N. C., and his wife, SARAH ANN ROBINSON, a *Rev. Patriot* of N. C.) Their descendants came to Ga.

JOHN WILSON, b. Buckingham Co., Va., Feb. 12, 1755; d. Greene Co., Ga., July 24, 1834; mar. in Prince Edward Co., Va., Sept. 2, 1780, Elizabeth Moore; she was b. 1761; d. Jan. 1840. He served in Va. Continental Line; received bounty land in Ga. for his service.
Children:

1. Sally, b. Va., Nov. 25, 1782; d. July 2, 1863; mar. Thomas Glass (1769–1846).
2. John, b. Mar. 14, 1789, mar. Polly Anderson.
3. Jesse, b. Dec. 14, 1792.
4. Silas (1795–1818).
5. Polly (1803–1808).

JOHN WILSON, b. Dec. 31, 1756; d. Feb. 15, 1847. From tombstone in McDuffie Co., Ga., near Thomson, Ga.: "Sacred to the Memory of JOHN WILSON, who died Feb. 15, 1847, age 91 years, 1 mo. and 15 days, an OFFICER IN THE REVOLUTION." Served as Capt., Ga. Troops. Mar. Oct. 2, 1783, MARY ROBERTSON (1763–1826).
Children:

1. Jonathan, b. Sept. 4, 1784.
2. David, b. April 7, 1786.
3. Sarah, b. Sept. 8, 1788, mar. William Scott.
4. Elias, b. Nov. 18, 1790, mar. (1) Margaret Scott; mar. (2) Temperance Saxon (mother of all his children); mar. (3) Mary Bacon; mar. (4) Elizabeth Rogers, widow.
5. Rebecca, b. June 9, 1793.
6. Elizabeth, b. July 19, 1795.
7. Mark, b. Dec. 1, 1797.
8. John, b. May 14, 1800.
9. Joel, b. Sept. 13, 1802.
10. Daniel, b. May 13, 1805.

JOHN WIMBERLY (son of EZEKIEL WIMBERLY, Rev. Sol. of Va. and N. C., and his wife, Mary Davis), b. Va., 1755; moved to Bertie Co., N. C., then to Ga.; d. Jones Co., Ga., 1835. Served in N. C. Continental Troops and in Ga. Militia. Mar. 1779, Penelope Perry.
Children:

1. Chloe, mar. Elijah Watson, of Edgefield Co., S. C.
2. James, mar. (1) Elizabeth Bryan; mar. (2) Mrs. Cook; mar. (3) Mrs. Jamieson.
3. Abner, mar. Miss Childers.
4. Perry, mar. and moved to Miss.
5. Lewis, mar. Matilda Garrett.
6. William, mar. and moved to Miss.
7. Henry, mar. Miss Childers.
8. John (Jack), mar. Narcissa Garrett.
9. Ezekiel, mar. 1807, Dorothy Brooks Slappey.

JOHN WINGFIELD, b. Va., July 20, 1723; d. Wilkes Co., Ga., Feb. 3, 1793. Mar. in Hanover Co., Va., Frances Oliver Buck, b. May 5, 1725; d. Wilkes Co., Ga., Feb. 25, 1795. He was a Rev Patriot and Sol; received grants of land for service, 1784–1785.
Children:

1. Thomas, b. Sept. 17, 1745, mar. Elizabeth Nelson.
2. Mary, b. Oct. 15, 1747, mar. Peter Terrell.
3. Elizabeth, b. Aug. 30, 1752, mar. Edward Butler.
4. Sarah, b. Aug. 28, 1754, mar. Stephen Pettus.
5. Charles, b. Jan. 17, 1756.
6. Garland, b. Oct. 17, 1757, mar. Mrs. Sarah Poullain.
7. Ann, b. May 22, 1759, mar. Rev. Hope Hull.
8. John, III, b. July 31, 1761, mar. Mary Darracourt.
9. Frances, b. Feb. 20, 1763, mar. David Meriwether.
10. Rebecca, b. July 12, 1765, mar. John Darricourt.
11. Martha (Patsey), b. May 30, 1767, mar. John Hardin Foster.

JOHN WINGFIELD, b. New Kent Co., Va., 1690; d. Wilkes Co., Ga., 1785. He was a Rev. Patriot who furnished supplies for the Rev. Army in Va. Mar. in Va., Sarah Garland. They moved to Wilkes Co., Ga.

Their dau., Elizabeth (1725–1755), mar. as (1) wife, CHARLES COSBY (1726–1800). He served as private under Capts. Tebb. and Briscoe, Va. Troops; received bounty land in Ga.; came from Hanover Co., Va., to Wilkes Co., Ga., 1784. Had issue.

JOHN WINGFIELD, b. Va., July 31, 1761; d. Wilkes Co., Ga. He was a *Rev. Sol.* Mar. Mary Darracott (dau. of Thomas Darracott).

Children:
1. Patsey.
2. Garland.
3. John L.
4. Frances, mar. — Meriwether.
5. Sarah Garland.
6. Overton.
7. Ann O., mar. 1818, Lucius Q. C. D'Yampert.

THOMAS WINGFIELD, b. Va., 1745; d. Wilkes Co., Ga., July 24, 1797. Served as a *Rev. Sol.*; received bounty grant of land in Ga. for his service. Mar. 1768, Elizabeth Nelson, b. 1749; d. 1802.

Children:
1. Samuel, b. 1772.
2. Mary, b. 1774.
3. THOMAS, b. 1777. (See below).
4. John, b. 1780.
5. Elizabeth, b. 1782.
6. Charles, b. 1784.
7. Francis Nelson, b. 1787.

THOMAS WINGFIELD (son of Thomas Wingfield), b. 1777; d. Wilkes Co., Ga., 1820. Mar. Elizabeth —. Children: Charles Ann Catherine; Virginia N.; Sophia H., mar. 1825, William A. Terrill; Elizabeth; Mary S.; Patsey Wade.

THOMAS WINGFIELD, b. Va.; d. Wilkes Co., Ga., 1806. Served in the Va. Continental Line. Mar. 1764, Elizabeth Terrell. Signer of Hanover Petition, Va.

Children (mentioned in will):
1. John.
2. Sarah G., mar. — Powell.
3. Mary, mar. RICHARD WORSHAM, *Rev. Sol.*, b. Va., 1746; d. Wilkes Co., Ga., 1826; drew pension for his service as Lieut. in 10th Va. Regiment; their dau., Elizabeth (1791–1836), mar. 1822, as (2) wife, Samuel Barnett (1775–1843), (son of WILLIAM BARNETT, *Rev. Sol.*, and his wife Jean Jack.). She mar. (2) JOHN GRIMES, b. Va., 1758; d. Wilkes Co., Ga. Served as private, Ga. Troops
4. Mildred, mar. John Simms (or Sims).
5. Sarah G., mar. (1) Anthony Poullain; mar. (2) Garland Wingfield.
6. Nancy.
7. Thomas, Jr.
(G.-children mentioned were: Wm. Garland Grimes; Wm. G. Thomas; Lucy and John Griffin; Henry P. and Thomas Wingfield; and Benjamin D. Simms).

WILLIAM WISE, b. Va., 1755; d. Bulloch Co., Ga., May 13, 1816. Served as private, Ga. Line. Certificate signed by Gen. E. Clarke. Mar. Sarah Margaret —; she d. after 1816.

Children:
1. Elizabeth, mar. Nov. 29, 1798, Solomon Groover.
2. Lavinia, b. Ga., 1787; d. Brooks Co., Ga., 1857; mar. (1) Aug. 17, 1802, Redden Denmark, b. 1770; d. 1813; mar. (2) Wm. McNeely.
3. Preston, mar. (1) Margaret Lee; mar. 1808, (2) Amy Jones.
4. Zilpha, mar. Jan. 7, 1811, Jesse Goodman.
5. Henry, mar. 1802, Elizabeth Groover.
6. Susanna, mar. 1802, James Denmark.
7. Rebecca, mar. 1809, Derry Jones.

8. John (1790–1834), mar. 1816, Rachel Jones (1791–1871) (dau. of BRIDGER JONES, *Rev. Sol.*, and his wife, Rachel Barry). 9 children.

9. Jincey, mar. Mr. Denmark.

SOLOMON WOOD, b. Va., 1726; d. Jefferson Co., Ga., 1815. Moved to N. C., then to Ga. Served as Capt. in Ga. Line and was promoted to Gen. Built "Wood's Fort" at his own expense. Mar. (1) Lydia Valentine of Va.; mar. (2) Elizabeth (Eason) Morton (1751–1826).

Children by (1) wife:

1. William, b. 1745.
2. John
3. Mark.
4. Elizabeth
5. Solomon, Jr.
6. Willis.
7. Lydia.
8. Joshua.
9. Sally.

Children by (2) wife:

1. Elizabeth, b. 1788, mar. John Mitchell.
2. Eason.
3. Nancy, b. 1781, mar. (1) Henry Willis Braezal; mar. (2) Eason Allen.
4. Mary, mar. — Mitchell.
5. William.
6. Mark Red.
7. John White.
8. Green, b. 1792.

THOMAS WOOTEN, b. N. C., 1720; d. Wilkes Co., Ga., 1791. Served as Lieut. under Col. Holman Freeman, 7th Ga. Regiment; received bounty land in Wilkes Co., Ga., for his service. Mar. (1) 1754, Sarah Rabun; mar. (2) —.

Children:

1. THOMAS, a *Rev. Sol.*, mar. Millie Smith.
2. Lemuel, mar. Nancy Smith.
3. James, mar. Polly Smith.
4. RICHARD B., b. Ga., 1760; d. Wilkes Co., Ga., 1798; served as Lieut. in Capt. John Pope's Co., 7th Ga. Batt. Col. Holman Freeman. Mar. Lucretia Cade (dau. of DRURY CADE, b. Va., 1743; d. Ga., 1809, and his wife, Winfred, d. 1812. He was a *Rev. Sol.*; served as Capt. under Col. Dooly, Col. Elijah Clarke, and Gen. Andrew Pickens).
5. Mary, mar. James Cade.
6. John.
7. Daniel.
8. Robert.

NOTE: "Died Feb. 3, 1797 at Savannah, Ga. MRS. ELIZABETH WRIGHT, widow of the late Mr. William Wright, a charitable and benevolent lady, who during the Americal Revolution, assisted many of the officers and soldiers that were on board the prison ships in the Savannah river, and through whose means, many valuable citizens were restored to their families. *A Rev. Patriot.*"

RICHARD WYLLY, b. Coleraine, Ireland, 1744; d. Savannah, Ga., 1801. Member of the *Provincial Congress* and the *Committee of Safety*. Commanded a Ga. Brig. as Colonel. Mar. 1784, MARY ANN (BRYAN) MOREL.

One child:

Mary Ann Wylly, mar. Nathaniel Adams.

THOMAS WYLLY, b. West Indies, 1762; d. Effingham Co., Ga., 1846. Served as assistant quartermaster to his uncle, Col. RICHARD WYLLY, *Rev. Sol.*; received land for his service. Mar. (1) Susanna Dawson; mar. (2) Naomi Rosenburg; mar. (3) Sarah (King) Goldwire.

Child by (1) wife:

William C.

Children by (2) wife:

1. Elisha.

2. Naomi, mar. three times.
3. Thomas, Jr.
4. Leonidas.
5. Frederick.
6. Sarah Ann.
7. Eliza, mar. Richard Williams.
8. Maria, mar. 1813, Solomon Dasher.

JOSHUA WYNNE, b. Va.; d. Columbia Co., Ga., 1805. Served as Maj., Ga. Line; received bounty land for his service. Mar. Elizabeth Appling.

Their son, WILLIAMSON WYNNE, b. Pendleton District, S. C., 1760; d. Greene Co., Ga., 1828. Served as private, S. C. Line, and in Capt. Dixon's Co., 1st N. C. Regiment. Mar. Eleanor Magruder (dau. of NINIAN OFFUTT MAGRUDER, a *Rev. Sol.* of Md. and Ga., and his wife, Mary Harris).

ROBERT WYNNE (WINN), b. Va., 1746; d. Warren Co., Ga., 1811. Mar. in Va., Elizabeth —. He was a *Rev. Sol.*; drew land Feb. 23, 1784. Certificate of Col. Greenberry Lee, in Franklin Co., Ga. Made will April 23, 1811; Pro. Dec. 1811. (Name on marker, Warren Co., Ga., by D. A. R.) (His bro., JOSHUA WYNNE, of Richmond Co., Ga., was a *Rev. Sol.* of Ga.; mar. Elizabeth Appling).

Children:
1. Lucy, b. 1768, mar. — Mullins.
2. CLEMENT, *Sol. of 1812*, mar. Frances Dewberry (dau. of Irby Dewberry, of Franklin and Warren Cos., Ga.).
3. Elizabeth, mar. — Walker.
4. Peter, mar. Sarah Dewberry (dau. of Irby Dewberry, of Franklin and Warren Cos., Ga.).
5. Mary. mar. — Walker.
6. Robert.
7. Dudley.
8. Nancy.
9. Susanna, mar. — Edwards.
10. Lydia, mar. — Hunter.
11. Cynthia.
12. Frances, mar. — Culpepper.
13. Thomas.
14. William.

WILLIAM YATES (son of WILLIAM YATES, *Rev. Sol.* of N. C., and his wife, Mary —), b. Wake Co., N. C., 1762; d. Montgomery (formerly Laurens) Co., Ga., 1850. Mar. in N. C., MARY WIMBERLY, b. N. C., 1770; d. Ga., before 1850. He served as private, N. C. Militia; drew land in Laurens Co., Ga., Lottery of 1827 as a *Rev. Sol.* in Ga.

Children (known):
1. Eli, mar. 1815, Molly Bancon.
2. Joseph, b. N. C., 1795; d. Brooks Co., Ga., 1862; mar. Cynthia Swain.
3. WILLIAM, b. Montgomery Co., Ga., 1801; d. Brooks Co., Ga., 1874; mar. Emanuel Co., Ga., 1823, Elizabeth Swain (1807–1871) (dau. of Canneth Swain and his wife, Rebecca Johnson, of Emanuel and Thomas Cos., Ga.).

WILLIAM YOUNG, b. New York—; d. Screven Co., Ga. Was a member, 1775, of the *Council of Safety*, Savannah, Ga.; also member of the *First Provincial Congress*. Mar. MARY HENDER-SON (dau. of Michael Henderson and wife, Miss Remer, of N. Y.).

Children:
1. James, b. Screven Co., Ga., Sept. 25, 1784; d. Ga., 1859; lived in Bulloch Co., Ga. Mar. Lavinia Jones, b. 1795 (dau. of James Jones, b. April 24, 1764; d. Ga., 1822, and his wife, Elizabeth Mills, b. 1774). They had 10 children.
2. Michael, b. Screven Co., Ga., 1797; d. Thomas Co., Ga., 1856. Mar. Sarah Everett (dau. of Joshua Everett and his wife, Jane Carter, of Bulloch Co., Ga.). They had 9 children.
3. Willis, b. 1786, mar. Mary Everett, of Bulloch Co.
4. Remer, b. 1788, mar. Mary Donaldson, of Decatur Co., Ga.

5. Elizabeth, b. 1790, mar. James Blackburn, of Ga.
6. John, b. 1793, mar. Elizabeth Price, of Chattooga Co., Ga.
7. David, b. 1799, mar. Mary Ann Thompson, of Decatur Co., Ga.
8. Sarah, b. 1802, mar. James Price, of Chattooga Co., Ga.
9. Lavinia, b. 1808, mar. Thomas Jones, of Burke Co., Ga.

REVOLUTIONARY SOLDIERS

PART II

DAVID ADAMS, b. Waxhaw, S. C., Jan. 28, 1766; d. Zebulon, Ga., 1834. Served under Gen. Henderson in S. C.; was at the Battle of Eutaw Springs; received bounty lands in Washington Co., Ga. for his service. Mar. BETSEY BRADFIELD (1799-1833).

NATHANIEL ADAMS, b. 1747; d. Ga., Mar. 7, 1806. A *Rev. Sol.* Qualified as a member of the Board of Commissioners of White Bluff Road, Ga. Mar. ANNA BOLTON (1752-1818).

THOMAS ADAMS, b. Fluvanna Co., Va., 1758; d. Elbert Co., Ga., 1836. Received pension as Sergeant Va. Troops under Col. Francis Taylor. Mar. 1786, Sallie Ford. Their son, John Adams (1798—) mar. Feb. 27, 1823, Nancy Davis.

WILLIAM ADDINGTON, b. S. C., 1759; d. Union Co., Ga., 1845. Served as private and Lieut. in Col. Brandon's S. C. Regiment. His widow received pension for his service as *Rev. Sol.*, 1848. He mar. 1783, DELILAH DUNCAN, b. 1765.

CHARLES ADKINS made declaration in Ga., dated Aug. 30, 1832, and filed in Upson Co., Ga., when he was 72 years of age. Served in N. C; applied for pension.

WILLIAM ADKINS received land April 6, 1784, upon certificate of Col. Elijah Clarke "that he hath steadfastly done his duty and is entitled to bounty land as a *Rev. Sol.* of 250 acres in Ga."

JAMES AIKENS, b. Penn., 1762. Lived Mecklinburg, N. C. Enlisted 1778, N. C. Troops under Capt. Brownfield; granted a pension Sept. 5, 1832, while a resident of Coweta Co., Ga.; d. there April 12, 1843. Mar. Greene Co., Ga., Mar. 16, 1791, Frances —; she drew pension as Widow of *Rev. Sol.* in 1844.

JOHN ALBRITTON, b. Hanover Co., Va., Dec. 6, 1747. Private in Capt. George's Co., Col. Charles Scott's Va. Regiment; then S. C. Regiment. Taken prisoner at Siege of Augusta. D. Ga., 1833.

JOHN ALEXANDER, b. S. C.; d. Gwinnett Co., Ga., 1830. Served in S. C. Troops. Mar. MISS WILLIAMSON (dau. of WILLIAM WILLIAMSON, *Rev. Sol.* "who commanded the troops, 1776 that checked the invasion of the Tories and Cherokees.") He and his three brothers joined the "TIGER IRISH CO." under Gen. Francis Marion.

HUGH ALEXANDER, b. 1747, d. Ga., 1835. Served as Lieut. Ga. Troops. Was at the Siege of Savannah, Ga. Mar. 1769, MOLLY WOODS (1751-1837).

LODOWICK ALFORD, b. N. C., 1715; d. Ga., 1789. Served in the Gen. Assembly of N. C. from Wake Co. A *Patriot.* Mar. REBECCA FERRELL. Children: 1. Jacob; 2. James, mar. Lurania Boykin; 3. Lodwick, Jr., mar. Judith Jackson. (Perhaps others).

JAMES ALLEN, b. Belfast, Ireland, 1750; d. Burke Co., Ga., 1835. Private Ga. Militia; received land grant, Washington Co. Mar. 1784, FRANCES SIMMONS.

JOHN ALLEN, b. 1760; d. Ga., 1828. Served as private Ga. State Troops. Mar. 1777, ELIZABETH INMAN, b. 1762.

PHILIP ALLEN, drew bounty land for Rev. service in Va. while living in Clarke Co., Ga., 1835, age 76.

NICHOLAS ANCIAUX, who came to Ga., where he d.; first came to this country with the French army, under command of Capt. DuPonte. He held a Captain's commission signed by Louis XVI of France. B. at Frankfort-on-the-Main, Germany, son of Chevalier De Wilterino. Mar. Lydia —.

GEORGE ANDERSON, b. N. Y.; d. Savannah, Ga. Served as a *Rev. Sol.* from Ga. Mar., N. Y., Feb. 18, 1761, DEBORAH GRANT (1736-1812). Moved to Ga., 1763, Their son, George Anderson, Jr., b. Savannah, Ga., 1767; d. 1847. Mar. 1794, Elizabeth (Clifford) Wayne.

JAMES ANGLIN, *Rev. Sol.*, b. N. C.; d. Wilkes Co., Ga., 1777. Four sons: JOHN; DAVID; WILLIAM; and HENRY were all *Rev. Sols.* of Ga.

JAMES ARNOLD, b. Augusta Co., Va., 1760; d. Wilkinson Co., Ga., 1823. Served as private N. C. Troops; received bounty grant of land for his service in Ga., 1784. Mar., 1794, ELIZABETH STROUD (1770-1859), of Elizabeth, N. C. (dau. of JAMES STROUD, Rev. Sol. of Va.)

RICHARD ASBURY, b. Va., 1761; d. Taliaferro Co., Ga., 1845 (son of HENRY ASBURY, Rev. Sol. and Patriot of Va., and his (1) wife, Emily Reade). Served as 2nd Lieut. under Major Redmond, Va. Troops. Mar. (1) 1780, ELIZABETH THORNTON (called Betty).

JOSEPH AVANT, b. Paris, France, 1720; d. Washington, Ga., 1798. Enlisted in Col. George Mathew's Va. Regiment.; was at Germantown and Brandywine. Mar. MELINDA DAVIS.

DR. SAMUEL JACOB AXON, b. S. C., 1751; d. Liberty Co., Ga., 1827. Served as Surgeon 1st S. C. Regiment. Mar. (1) MARY ANN GIRADEAU at "Midway" Church; 3 daus. She d. 1799. Mar. (2) ANN (LAMBRIGHT) DICKS (DIX), 1806. Their dau., SACCHARISSA, mar. Moses Jones.

JOHN ATKINSON, b. Northampton Co., Va.; d. Camden Co., Ga., 1808. Private Capt. Bentley's Co., Col. Thomas Marshall, 3rd Va. Regiment, 1777. Mar. 1756, ELIZABETH GARDEN.

MOSES AYERS, b. Snowden, Wales, 1747; came to Va., then to N. C. Served at the Battle of King's Mt. and Yorktown. Lived in Franklin (now Hart) Co., Ga., where he d. Mar. many times. Last wife, ABIGAIL PAYNE.

WILLIAM ANDERSON, b. S. C., 1763; d. Walton Co., Ga., 1837; received pension, 1836 for his service as private Va. Troops. Mar. 1786, ELIZABETH LEWIS.

JOHN DANIEL BAGWELL, b. N. C.; d. Gwinnett Co., Ga.; buried seven miles from Lawrenceville, Ga., Primitive Baptist Church Cemetery. Served as Rev. Sol. of N. C.

WILLIAM BABB, b. N. C.; lived in Oglethorpe Co., Ga. Rev. Sol.; d. Baldwin Co., Ga. Mar. Henryetta (called Patsey) Yates (dau. of WILLIAM YATES, b. Va., 1727; d. Wake Co., N. C., 1808, and his wife, Mary — (1732-1812). William Yates served as private N. C. Militia as a Rev. Sol). In 1823, William Babb gave power of Attorney to his bro-in-law, Willis Yates, for share in estate of William Yates of Chatham and Wake Counties, N. C.

JOHN BALL, b. near Fredericksburg, Va., about 1740; moved to Camden Dist., S. C.; d. Warren Co., Ga., 1815. Served with Ga. Troops, as private in Col. John Stewart's Regiment; received bounty land, certified to by Col. Samuel Jackson. Mar. MISS ROBINSON.

Anson Ball, Senator from Wilkinson Co., Ga., mar. Phoebe Jenkins. (Descendants say he is buried in Warren Co., Ga.)

EDWARD BALL, b. S. C.; d. Ga., 1779; came to St. John's Parish, Ga., 1767. Member of Provincial Congress, 1775, from St. John's Parish. Lieut, in Capt. John Bacon's Co. of Riflemen, 1777. Mar. 1773, REBECCA BAKER.

EDWARD BARNARD, Lieut. 2nd Regiment, Augusta Division, Capt. Troop of Horse, Sept. 6, 1775.

ABNER BANKSTON, Rev. Sol. Grave marked by the D. A. R., in Ga., on Indian Springs Road to High Falls, Butts Co.

LIEUT. WILLIAM BALDWIN, b. Va., 1736; d. Savannah, Ga., 1796. Lieut., Va. Line; mar. Ebenezer —, b. 1758. Children: Charles; Robert; Samuel; Henry; William, Jr.; Elizabeth; John, mar. Martha Speight.

ROBERT BARNETT, b. Sumpter, S. C., 1754; d. Wilkinson Co., 1827; received land in Carroll Co., Ga., for his service. Mar. (1) 1778, SARAH LOVE (1755-1806).

Graves of ROBERT BARNETT, DAVID CLAY, and WILLIAM MITCHELL (Rev. Sol.) marked by the D. A. R.

JAMES BARR, b. Guilford Co., N. C., Feb. 7, 1762; served in Capt. Daniel Gillespie's Co. of Minute Men, in Col. John Paceley's N. C. Regiment; allowed pension claim, 1832, while a resident of Jackson Co., Ga. His father was living, 1781, Pittsylvania Co., Va.

MOSES BARROW, b. N. C., 1755; d. Ga., 1801. Served as private in Capt. Bacot's Co., 10th Regiment, N. C. Line. Mar. 1790, MILDRED POWELL (1770-1812).

JOHN HICKS BASS, b. Brunswick Co., Va., 1763; d. Putnam Co., Ga., 1850. Served as private, Va. Troops; received bounty land in Ga. Mar. (1) 1791, REBECCA PATTILLO (1774–1834). Dau., Martha, mar. Thomas G. Frazer (1805–1873).

WILLOUGHBY BARTON, b. Scotland, 1750; d. Wilkes Co., 1800. Received bounty land in Ga. for services as private under Gen. Clarke. Mar. Rebecca McCoy.

JOHN BECK, b. Albemarle Co., Va., 1756; d. Ruckersville, Ga., 1821. Served as Ensign, 9th Va. Regiment. Mar. 1784, SARAH WANSLEY (1766–1860), (dau. of JOHN WANSLEY, b. Louisa Co., Va., 1738; d. Ruckersville, Ga., 1842. Mar. 1762, Amelia Barber, b. Va., 1744. Served as private, Va. Line.; received a pension for his service).

ROBERT BELCHER, b. S. C., 1758; d. Twiggs Co., Ga., 1848. Enlisted in Capt. James Foster's S. C. Co., 1776; served in Battles of Brandywine and Monmouth; received pension for three years' service, Va. Line. Mar. NANCY HOPKINS.

JAMES BLAIR, b. Va., 1761; d. Habersham Co., Ga., 1839. Served as private under Col. McDowell at King's Mountain, N. C. Line. Mar. ELIZABETH POWELL.

HENRY BONNER, b. Va., 1724; d. Warren Co., Ga., 1822. Served as Capt., Va. Continental Army. Mar. Ann Cate. Children (known): Robert; Henry; Richard.

JOHN BOOTH, b. N. C.; d. Hancock Co., Ga., 1804. Served as private, N. C. Line.

PHILIP BOX, Major, 1st Regiment, Foot Militia, Savannah, Ga. Division, Mar. 20, 1775.

JOHN BRADDOCK, of McIntosh Co.; d. Darien, Ga., 1797. Commanded a Co. of Ga. Troops. Mar. LUCY ANN COOK.

SPENCER BRANHAM, b. Goochland Co., Va.; d. Wilkes Co., Ga., 1803. Served as private, Va. Line. Mar. 1785, ELIZABETH RICHARDSON.

CHARLES BRAWNER, Rev. Sol. of Ga.; received certificate from Lieut. Col. James Jackson, of Ga., July 30, 1784: "That he served in the Ga. State Legion Infantry from the reduction of Augusta to the evacuation of the State by the British," and received 287½ acres of land in Washington Co., Ga.

ADAM BRINSON, b. June 10, 1751; d. Ga., Nov. 23, 1825, Rev. Sol.

MATTHEW BRINSON, b. Sept. 16, 1763, Rev. Sol. of Ga., mar. Sarah —, b. Dec. 4, 1760. Children: Gathara, b. Sept. 3, 1785; Catherine, b. Feb. 12, 1787; Adam, b. Aug. 6, 1789; Thomas H., b. Jan. 9, 1792; Rebecca, b. Jan. 31, 1794; Saba, b. Jan. 30, 1796; Matthew, b. Mar. 27, 1798; Sarah, b. Sept. 16, 1800; Nancy, b. Aug. 21, 1803.

ADAM FOWLER BRISBANE, b. Charleston, S. C., 1754; d. Ga., 1799. Delegate to the First Provincial Congress, held in Savannah, Ga., 1775. Mar. 1775, (1) MARY CAMBER, d. 1820.

BENJAMIN BROWN, Rev. Sol., served with N. C. Regiment. Grave marked by D. A. R. He is buried in Brown's Cemetery, 11 miles from Fayetteville, Ga.

EZEKIEL BROWN, Rev. Sol., b. 1769; d. Harris Co., Ga., 1863. Mar. ELIZABETH MERRITT.

JOHN BROWN, b. Scotland, 1729; d. Burke Co., Ga., 1786. Served as private, Burke Co., Ga. Militia, under Col. Elijah Clarke. Mar. 1754, REBECCA YATES (1732–1795).

JOHN BROWN, b. Kingston, R. I., 1764; d. St. Mary's, Ga., 1826, Rev. Sol. He lies buried in the ancient Burial Ground of St. Mary's, Camden Co., Ga.

NATHAN BROWNSON, b. Woodbury, Conn., May 14, 1742; removed to St. John's Parish, 1764. Member Provincial Congress; delegate from Ga. to Continental Congress; Surgeon, Ga. Brigade, Continental Army. Elected Governor of Georgia, 1781. D. Liberty Co., Ga., Oct. 18, 1796. Mar. (1) Elizabeth —, d. 1775.

BLAKE BRYAN (son of WILLIAM BRYAN, Rev. Sol. of N. C.), b. Johnston Co., N. C.; d. Twiggs Co., Ga. Served as private in Capt. Bryan Whitfield's Co., N. C. Militia. Mar. ELIZABETH BLACKSHEAR, 1791. His dau., Elizabeth (Patsey) Bryan, mar. James Wimberly (son of JOHN WIMBERLY, Rev. Sol.)

GEORGE BUCHANAN, b. Sept. 9, 1759. Served as Corp. and Serg. in Capt. Henry Hampton's Co., 6th Regiment, in S. C., under Lieut. Col. William Henderson; enlisted 1777, in Col. John Buchanan's Regiment; served at Siege of Savannah; prisoner, 1789, on Sullivan Island; allowed pension, 1833, at Marion Co., Ga. Buried in family cemetery (now Schley Co., Ga.).

WILLIAM BUGG, *Rev. Sol.*, b. 1757; d. Jan. 29, 1804. Buried in the Bugg cemetery near Augusta, Ga.

WILLIAM BURGAMY, b. France, 1739; d. Ga., 1819. Served as private, Ga. Line. Mar. 1759, SUSAN HAWKINS.

CHARLES BURCH and EDWARD BURCH came to Ga. and settled on the waters of Big Spirit Creek. Their names appear on the pay-roll of the Burke Co., Ga., Rangers, commanded by COL. PATRICK CARR, of Jefferson Co., Ga., 1782. CHARLES BURCH left 4 sons: Charles, Jr.; Joseph E.; Blanton; Kilt, of Richmond Co., Ga.

THOMAS BURTON, b. Va.; d. Elbert Co., Ga., 1828. Served as private under Col. Elijah Clarke. Mar. NANCY NUNNELLEE.

HEZEKIAH BUSSEY and Amey, his wife, sold to JONATHAN RAGAN, *Rev. Sol.* of Wilkes Co., Ga., Jan. 30, 1788, 287½ acres of land granted to said Hezekiah Bussey for his service as a *Rev. Sol.* Land on Oconee River, Washington Co., Ga., 1785.

EDMUND BUTLER, b. 1755; d. Hancock Co., Ga., 1802. Private under Col. Elijah Clarke's Ga. Troops; received bounty land for his service. Mar. FANNY GARRETT.

ROGER CAMERON, b. Va.; d. Walton Co., Ga. Private 1st S. C. Regiment. Mar. 1795, Ann (Spaulding) McPherson (1767-1855).

JOHN CARGYLE, b. Va.; d. Greene Co., Ga. Served as private under Capt. Porterfield, Col. Daniel Morgan, Va. Continental Line. Mar. 1746, CATHERINE RENEAU (1726-1774).

JOHN CARTER, b. Va., Dec. 18, 1761; d. Aug. 1820. Buried City Cemetery, Augusta, Ga. Mar. ANNE WRAY.

HOWARD CASH, original settler, Habersham Co., 1818; came from Va. to Elbert Co., Ga. Grave marked and monument unveiled as a *Rev. Sol* May 29, 1939. Drew land in 1827 lottery.

WILLIAM CASON, b. S. C., April 17, 1749; d. Ga. Enlisted Fairfield Co., S. C; drew pension for service, 1833, while a resident of Warren Co., Ga. Drew land as *Rev. Sol.* Cherokee Lottery, 1838.

JOSEPH CATCHINGS, b. Md., 1762; d. Greene Co., Ga., 1805; received bounty grant of land Wilkes Co., Ga. for service as private. Mar. MARTHA TOWNSEND.

WILLIAM CARRAWAY, b. 1754; d. Upson Co., Ga., 1834. Applied for pension; entered service Camden District, S. C.; resident of Cumberland Co., N. C. Served under Capt. James Moore, 3rd Co.; was Orderly Ser. at Siege of Savannah, Ga. in Col. Hugers Brigade S. C, Serg. Mar. Elizabeth — (1764-1838). Dau., Charity (1785-1845), mar. Benjamin Bethel (1782-1815).

LARKIN CLARK, b. Orange Co., Va., 1760; d. Elbert Co., Ga., 1843. Served as private Major Allen's Ga. Troops. Mar. LUCY SIMPSON WELCH (1780-1852).

ROBERT CLARK, JR., b. Halifax Co., N. C., 1757; d. Elbert Co. Served as private Ga. Line; received bounty grant of land in Ga. for his service. Mar. Rebecca Sledge.

JOHN CHRISTIAN, b. Va.; d. Franklin Co., Ga., 1820. Served as private and Capt. in Col. Vance's Va. Troops. Mar. MARY —.

WILLIAM CHEEKE, b. Randolph Co., N. C., 1752; d. Franklin Co., Ga., 1845. Placed on pension roll, 1833, for service as private Va. Troops. Mar. (1) 1775, MARY VINES (called Polly) (1750-1818).

DAVID CLAY, b. Duplin Co., N. C., about 1756; d. Wilkinson Co., Ga., 1818. Served as private N. C. Troops under Capt. Hall and Capt. Komegay. Widow applied and received pension 1852. Mar. 1792, EVE HARDIN (1772-1855.)

JEREMIAH CLOUD, b. Va.; d. Wilkes Co., Ga., 1783. Served with Ga. Troops under Col. Elijah Clarke. Mar. (1) 1742, ANN BAILEY; (2) SARAH —.

BLANCHARD COLDING, b. S. C., 1756; d. Ga., 1816. Served as Sol. S. C. Line. Mar. ANN GIBBON, b. 1756; d. Screven Co., Ga., 1818. Their son, Thomas (1773-1847), mar. Ann Dell (dau. PHILIP DELL, *Rev. Sol.* of Ga.)

JAMES THOMAS COMER, b. Va., 1729; d. Jones Co., Ga., 1837. Served as private Ga. Line. Mar. 3 times.

JOHN COLLINS, b. Frederick Co., Md. Mar. Burke Co., Ga., Nov. 30, 1786, PHOEBE SAILORS; she received a pension as widow of a *Rev. Sol.*, Jan. 31, 1853, while a resident of Cobb Co., Ga.

NOTE: From Augusta Chronicle. "CAPT. THOMAS COBB, ago 110 years, a native of Buckingham Co., Va. Came to Ga. 1784. A REV. SOLDIER. His patriotism induced him to take part with his country for the Independence of these States and he was often associated in the Councils of the Chiefs in those startling times."

JONATHAN COLEMAN (son of Thomas Coleman and wife, Mildred Richards), b. about 1750. Moved from Williamsburg, Va., to Augusta, Ga. Served as *Rev. Sol.* in Burke Co., Ga., under Gen. Wayne. Mar. 1784, Milly Pittman. Had issue.

PIERRE CONSTANTINE, b. Toulouse, France, 1736; d. Savannah, Ga., 1811. Came from France with Count Rochembeau and served as a grenadier with him at Yorktown. Mar. MARIE LOUISE BIDOT.

JOHN COOPER, b. Ga., 1751; d. Ga., 1816. Raised the Company known as "The Liberty Independent Troop," and served as Lieut. and Captain. Mar. ELIZABETH GIGINILLAT.

JOHN COOK, b. Va. —; d. Hancock Co., Ga. Served as Capt. under Gen. William Washington throughout the War; was at the Battles of Eutaw Springs, Cowpens, Guilford C. H. and others. Mar. (2) MARTHA PEARSON; two of their children were: Philip b. S. C., 1775; d. Twiggs Co., Ga., 1841. Mar. Martha Wooten; Martha, mar. John Daniel.

WILLIAM CORAM, b. Va., 1756; d. Wilkes Co., Ga. Mar. Mar. 1783, ANN HODO (1755-1829) (dau. of PETER HODO, *Rev. Sol.* of Warren Co., Ga.) He was a *Rev. Sol.* and served as Serg.

JOHN COLQUITT, b. Va.; d. Oglethorpe Co., Ga., 1800. Served as private Va. Troops. Mar. ELIZABETH HENDRICKS. Their son: ROBERT COLQUITT, b. Va.; d. Oglethorpe Co., Ga. Served as private Va. Troops; drew land as a *Rev. Sol.*, 1827, lottery in Ga. Mar. SUSAN HUBBARD.

REUBEN COOK, b. Hanover Co., Va., 1740; d. Elbert Co., Ga., 1820. Served as private, Va. State Troops. Mar. MOLLY DANIEL, d. 1828.

JAMES COOK, *Rev. Sol.*, Elliott's Dist., Jefferson Co., Ga.

CARY COX, b. S. C., Oct. 1744; d. Putnam Co., Ga., Oct. 24, 1814. Served as private, S. C. Troops. Mar. 1762, MARY HORNE, d. 1823. Children: William G., mar. Catherine Roberts; Ichabod (1767-1869), *Sol. of 1812*, mar. Mary Rowan; Asa, mar. Maria Rountree; Cary, Jr., mar. Martha Rountree; James, mar. Elizabeth Martin; Clara, mar. — Southall.

HENRY COOPER, b. N. Y., 1759; d. Putnam Co., Ga., 1840. Served as private in Capt. Jonathan Lawrence's Co.; Col. Harper's Regiment of Levies, N. Y. Mar. FRANCES PERRY.

JOHN COOPER, b. Henry Co., Va., 1742; d. Wilkes Co., Ga., 1835. Served as private, Ga. Line; received bounty grant of land for service. Mar. 1778, ELIZABETH WILSON. Drew land in 1827 Lottery.

CHARLES CRAWFORD, b. Amherst Co., Va., 1738; d. Ga., 1813; Capt. Commanded a Co. under GEN. ROBERT HOWE, 2nd N. C. Regiment. Mar. 1763, JANE MAXWELL. She was b. 1743.

THOMAS CRAWFORD, b. Va., 1729; d. Ga., 1794; received bounty land in Ga. for service as private, Va. Line. Mar. Mary Smith.

ALEXANDER CUMMINS, b. Va.; d. Oglethorpe Co., Ga., 1811. Commanded a Co. under under Col. Thomas Meriwether, Bedford Co., Va., Militia. Mar. ELIZABETH —.

ANSEL CUNNINGHAM, b. Ireland 1763; d. Jackson Co., Ga., 1837; received pension 1832 as a private, Va. Troops, under Col. Tucker. Mar. (1) —; mar. (2) MARY —.

MICHAEL CUP (OR CUPP), b. N. C., 1740; d. Wilkes Co., Ga., 1821. Served in Ga. Troops under Col. Elijah Clarke. Came to Ga., 1773, to the Ceded Lands; given bounty land for service as *Rev. Sol.*, 1785. Mar. Barbara Layle. They had dau., Mary, mar. Lazarus Summerlin (son of Henry Summerlin, of Wilkes Co.).

RICHARD CURD, b. Va.; d. Henry Co., Ga., May 16, 1827. Served in Va. Troops. Was a Juror in the trial of Aaron Burr, at 65 years of age. (From records at Milledgeville, Ga.)

HENRY CUYLER, b. New York City, 1754; d. Savannah, Ga., 1781. Commissioned Capt. of Light Infantry, Rev. War, by Gov. John Houston. Mar. 1778, DOROTHY MARTIN, d. 1786.

JOHN DALLAS, served as private, Va. Inf.; b. Va., 1748; d. Wilkes Co., Ga., 1815. Mar. 1774, MARY WALKER.

FREDERICK DANIEL, b. Brunswick Co., Va., 1755. Enlisted Nash Co., N. C. Moved to Ga. 1795. Applied for pension.

JEPTHA DANIEL, b. Va. Certified to by Gen. John Twiggs. Mar. Nov. 12, 1808, SARAH ROWLAND.

THOMAS DAVENPORT, b. Charlotte Co., Va.; d. Ga., 1808. Served as private, Ga. Line; received bounty grant of land for his service in Ga.

JOHN DAVIS, b. N. C., 1759; d. Morgan Co., Ga., 1818. Private, N. C. Line. Mar. NANCY PATTERSON.

JOHN DAVIS, b. King William Co., Va., 1754; d. Elbert Co., Ga., 1843. Placed on Pension Roll, Elbert Co., 1833, for service as private, Va. Militia. Mar. SARAH —.

NOTE: JOHN DAVIS. From pension. *Rev. Sol.* of Va.; pension issued April 5, 1833, service private; applied Sept. 30, 1830, age 100 years, living then in Gwinnett Co., Ga. Served from Prince William Co., Va., 1777. 4 years, 4 months, under Capt. Andrew Leach, Lieut. Valentine Peyton, Col. Philip Lee's Brigade. Removed to Pendleton Dist., S. C., settled Gwinnett Co., Ga., 1824.

RICHARD DAVIS, b. N. C., 1751; d. Ga., 1817. Served 1777-8 as private, 1st N. C. Regiment, under Maj. John Baptiste Ashe. Mar. 1777, Isabella Grant.

JOHN DENMAN, an Englishman, who came to America about 1760, served as a *Rev. Sol.* and after the War, he removed to Franklin Co., Ga., where he d.

JACOB DENNARD, b. Edgefield Dist., S. C., 1750; d. Jeffersonville, Ga., 1810. Served as Lieut. under Capt. Mapp and Capt. McBee, Col. Robuck Regiment. Mar. 1772, Harriet —.

GEORGE DENT, b. Md., 1756; d. Ga., 1813. Served as Lieut., 1776, 3rd. Md. Flying Camp. Mar. before 1779, Anna Maria Freeman (1762-1822).

REUBEN De JARNETTE, b. Va.; d. Putnam Co., Ga., 1830. Served in the Va. Continental Line. Mar. MISS BIRD.

MICHAEL DICKSON, b. Lunenburg Co., Va., 1743 Will filed Sparta, Hancock Co., Ga., 1803. Served as Capt. in Ga. Militia. Mar. LUCY CRAWFORD ATWOOD.

JOHN DIXON, b. N. C., 1758; d. Ga., 1835. Served as private. 1st Batt. of N. C., under Capt. McRee and Col. Clark. Mar. 1796, ELIZABETH POYTHRESS (1771-1842).

ISAAC DuBOSE, b. S. C.; d. Columbia Co., Ga. Served in S. C. as Lieut., under Gen. Morgan and Gen. Sumpter. Mar. his cousin, SARAH DuBOSE.

JAMES De LAUNAY, buried in City Cemetery, Milledgeville, Ga. "A Rev. Soldier" on tombstone.

JOHN DOBY, b. Sussex Co., Va., 1755; d. Jasper Co., Ga., 1836. Served as private in Capt. Cade's Co., Col. Keenan's N. C. Regiment. Mar. 1784, Sarah White (1757-1815), dau. of WILLIAM WHITE, a *Rev. Sol.*, and his wife, Sarah Lucas.

JOHN DOLLAR, b. 1742; d. at his plantation home "Antrim" near Sunbury, Ga., Oct. 20, 1797. A *Rev. Sol.* Capt. of Continental Artillery in the American War. (From Ga. Gazette Funeral Notice).

AMBROSE DUDLEY, b. Spotsylvania Co., Va., 1750; d. Fayette Co., Ga., 1825. Commanded a Co. of Va. Troops. Mar. 1773, ANN PARKER.

ROBERT DUNWOODY, b. Chester Co., Penn., 1744; d. Screven Co., Ga., 1794. Served as private 1781, in Capt. Allen's Co., Chester Co., Penn. Militia. Mar. MARY CRESSWELL. Their dau., Mary Dunwoody (1793-1870), mar. Benjamin Archelus Saxon (1796-1855).

ANDREW DUKE, b. Cabarrus Co., N. C., 1730; d. Ga., 1798. Served as Lieut. N. C. Line. Mar. KEZIAH ANDERSON. They lived Hancock Co., Ga.

MAJOR NATHANIEL DURKEE, buried in "Old Redwine Cemetery," Franklin (now Hart) Co., Ga., 1823. Mar. MALINDA —. (Grave marked by the D. A. R.) He was a nephew and namesake of Gen. Nathaniel Greene, *Rev. Sol.*)

JESSE EMBREE, b. 1750; d. Oglethorpe Co., Ga., 1800. Served as private, Ga. Line. Mar. 1773, NANCY EMBRY (1755-1805).

JOHN EMBREE, b. Little Egg Harbor, N. J., 1721; d. Wrightsboro, Ga., June, 1826. Was a *Patriot*, 1775. Mar. 1752, ELIZABETH HARRISON, Columbia Co., Ga.

JAMES EPSY, b. Cumberland Co., Penn., Dec. 7, 1759; d. Athens, Ga., 1834. Served in Col. Charles McLain's N. C. Regiment as private from Tryon Co., N. C.; drew pension for his service in 1832. Mar. (1) SARAH BAKER, d. 1829.

WILLIAM R. EVANS, b. Va., 1751; d. Ga., 1827. Served as Lieut. in Col. John Grimes Co. of Foot 6th Va. Regiment; mar. 1776, Ellie Graves Cooper.

JOHN EVANS, b. Ga., 1765; d. Ga., 1821. Served as a private Ga. Line; received grant of land for his service. Mar. 1795, ELIZABETH MURRAY (d. 1845).

DANIEL EVANS, a *Rev. Sol.* of Burke Co., Ga., whose name appears on the "Roster of Capt. Patrick Carr's Co. of Burke Co. Rangers 1782"; mar. MARY JONES (dau. of William and Mary Jones); their dau., Martha Jones Evans, mar. Reuben Walker (son of THOMAS WALKER, *Rev. Sol.* of Ga.)

JOHN FAVER, of Va., d. Coweta Co., Ga. Served at the Battle of Kettle Creek; granted land for his service in 1784. (A monument has been erected at his grave by D. A. R., Newnan, Ga.). He mar. in Va., MARY BOLTON.

WILLIAM FITZPATRICK, b. Va., 1746; d. Ga., 1809; was a *Rev. Sol.*; received bounty grant of land for his service. Mar. Celia Ann Phillips (dau. of JOSEPH PHILLIPS, b. 1734; d. Morgan Co., Ga., 1800; a *Rev. Sol.*, who served in Ga. Troops under Gen. Elijah Clarke).

MATTHEW FINLEY, b. Ireland, 1758; d. Ga., 1818. Served as private under COL. ELIJAH CLARKE. Mar. JANE McCORD.

ABNER FLEWELLYN, b. Halifax Co., N. C., 1760; d. Bibb Co., Ga., 1815. Served as private and his tombstone gives record as a man and a *Rev. Sol.*, N. C. Troops. Mar. Ann Lane (1766-1846). 1 dau. (known), Betsey Lane, b. 1793; mar. 1809, Tarpley Holt. Other children.

JAMES FLOURNOY, b. Chesterfield Co., Va., 1763; d. Ga., 1858; received a pension for his service as private in Capt. Cheatham's Co., Col. Robert Good's Regiment. Va. Mar. (1) 1785 PEGGY CUNDIFF (1763-1824). Their dau., Lucinda, mar. Silas Taylor.

JOHN FLOURNOY, b. Chesterfield Co., Va.; d. Ga. Served as private Ga. Line. Mar. his cousin, MARY ASHURST. He was the son of SAMUEL FLOURNOY, *Rev. Sol.* of Va. and his wife, Elizabeth Harris.

ROBERT FLOURNOY, b. Prince Edward Co., Va., 1763; d. Lexington, Ga., 1825. Served at age of 17 years as a private in Ga. Militia. Mar., 1780, Mary Willis Cobb, d. 1830. Record on Tombstone, Sparta, Ga.

WILLIAM FOSTER, b. England; came to Md., then to S. C.; then to Ga. Mar. in Ga., Polly Powell. Enlisted, 1776, in Ga.; served in S. C. 5th Regiment. D. Butts Co., Ga., April 22, 1852, age 106 years. (Grave marked by the D. A. R.)

OWEN FLUKER (son of Thomas Fluker, of Mass., and his wife, Hannah Waldo, of Boston, Mass.), b. 1756; d. Wilkes Co., Ga., 1819; received bounty land in Wilkes Co., Ga. for his service. Mar. MARY ANN BALDWIN (called Nancy). Mentions in will: Sons, Isaac; John; dau., Betty; Daus: Lucy, mar. — Ashmore; Mary, mar. — Jackson; Susanna, mar. — Morgan.

JOHN FOSTER, b. Southampton Co., Va., 1761; d. Columbia Co., Ga., 1821. Served as Serg. in Capt. Augustin Tabb's Co., 2nd Va. Regiment under Cols. Gregory, Smith, and William Brent. Mar. 1785, ELIZABETH SAVAGE (OR SAVIDGE) (1769–1830).

THOMAS FARRAR, b. Farrar's Island, Va., 1726; d. at the home of his son, Abner, Franklin Co., Ga., 1810. Served as Col. S. C. Militia. Mar. ELIZA HOWARD; two of their children were: Abner, mar. Katie Malone; Absolom, mar. Phoebe Avary.

PRIOR GARDNER, b. 1755; d. Warren Co., Ga., 1808. Served in N. C. Troops (Riflemen), and was at the Battle of Guilford C. H.

ANTHONY GARNETT, b. Va.; d. Columbia Co., Ga., 1794. Mar. in Va., Elizabeth —; granted land in Ky. for his service, Va. Line. Moved to Ga. Three children known: Thomas, a *Rev. Sol.* of Ga.; Joseph; and Susannah.

ANTHONY GARRARD, b. Va., 1756; d. Wilkes Co., Ga., 1807. Served in N. C. Continental Army; was given a grant of land in Ga. for his service. Mar. Elizabeth —.

THOMAS GILBERT, b. Orange Co., Va., 1730; d. Ga., 1820, age 90 years. A *Rev. Sol.* and a Baptist preacher.

EZEKIEL GILLIAM, b. Va.; d. Oglethorpe Co., Ga. Served as private S. C. Troops. Mar. Sarah Clemens.

WILLIAM GLOVER, b. Prince George Co., Md., 1760; d. Ga. Enlisted Wilkes Co., N. C., 1778; private under Capt. Sheppard, and Col. Gordon; received a pension for his service. Grave in Elbert (now Hart) Co., Ga., marked by the U. S. Government.

WILLIAM GOBER, b. N. C., 1744; d. Newton Co., Ga., 1826. Private in N. C. and Ga. Militia. Mar. 1762, Lucy —.

THOMAS GLASCOCK (son of William Glascock, the *"Rebel Counsellor"*) of Ga., and his wife, Elizabeth, are both buried on the Glascock plantation near Augusta, Ga. He was Capt. in the famous Legion of Cavalry under Count Pulaski. He was made a Brig.-Gen. in Continental Army, and d., age 54, at his country home, "The Mill," near Augusta, Ga.

JAMES GOLDWIRE, b. Augusta, Ga., 1747; d. Mt. Pleasant, Ga. Commanded a Co. of Ga. Militia, 1776, from St. Matthew's Parish (now Effingham Co.), Ga. Mar. Sarah King, b. 1749. Their son, John Goldwire (1779–1830), mar. 1809, Frances Offutt (dau. of JESSE OFFUTT (1760–1830), a *Rev. Sol.*, b. 1764; d. Richmond Co., Ga., 1832; served as private, Ga. Troops, under Col. Few; received bounty grant of land for his service; and his wife, Obedience Jones, dau. of JOHN JONES and Susanna Strobhar).

COL. AMBROSE GORDON, b. N. J., June 28, 1751; d. Augusta, Ga., June 28, 1804. A *Rev. Sol.*; will probated in Chatham Co., Ga. Mar. ELIZABETH MEAD.

LEWIS GRAVES, b. Spotsylvania Co., Va., 1760; d. Newton Co., Ga., 1839. Served as private, S. C. Troops, under Capt. Griffeth, Col. Murphy. Mar. 1781, Ruth Graves. Applied for pension.

ISAAC GRAY, b. S. C., 1750; d. Franklin Co., Ga., 1831. Served in S. C. Troops under Capt. John A. Patrick, Chandler's Batt. Drew land as a *Rev. Sol.* in the Lottery of 1825.

JAMES GRAY, b. S. C., 1758; d. Ga., 1834. Served as private, Ga. Line; received bounty land in Ga. for his service. Mar. Mary — (1769–1836). Their dau., Susan Gray, mar. Robert Howe (1782–1858).

STEPHEN GROVES, b. England, 1740; d. Madison Co., Ga., 1839. Placed on Pension Roll of Madison Co. for service as private in Penn. Militia. Mar. Isabella Weakley.

DANIEL GUNN, b. N. C., 1757; d. Jones Co., Ga., 1825. Served as orderly and Serg. in Capt. Lawson's N. C. Co. Mar. 1786, SUSAN STREET. Had issue.

GEORGE GUNN, b. Va.; d. Wilkes Co., Ga., 1807. Served as private, Augusta Co., Va., Militia; received bounty grant of land for his service, Wilkes Co., Ga. Mar. ANNE (called Nancy) —. She d. 1819. Had several children.

JACOB GUNN, b. Va.; d. Ga. Served as Maj., 2nd Regiment, Augusta Co., Va., Militia. Buried near Milledgeville, Ga. Inscription on tombstone: "Major Jacob Gunn."

JAMES GUNN, b. Va., 1739; d. Louisville, Ga., July 30, 1801. Enlisted in Va. Continental Army, as Capt. of Dragoons. Served under Gen. Anthony Wayne at the Siege of Savannah, Ga., 1782. Was Col. and Gen., State Militia, after War. *Member Continental Congress*, 1787. *Senator U. S.*, 1795. Mar. Sarah —. Had children.

DANIEL GUNNELS (OR GUNNALS), b. N. C.; d. Wilkes Co., Ga., 1815. Served as private, Ga. Troops. Came to Ga., 1773, to Ceded Lands, with wife and 4 sons; received bounty land for his service. Mar. Miss Akins. One son, Nathan, mar. Nancy Hunt.

BENJAMIN HAMBRICK, 1839 pension; b. Prince Edward Co., Va., July 9, 1739. Lived Wilkes Co., N. C., then Wilkes Co., Ga., Jasper Co., and Upson Co., Ga. Entered service under Capt. John Cleveland, Co. of Light Horse, under Col. Benj. Cleveland, Col. Wm. Lenoir, and Gen. Rutherford, N. C. Line. Was at Battle of Kings Mt.

JAMES HALL, late of N. C. Regiment, Capt. John Richards' Co., appointed Francis Baldwin, Attorney, to ask and receive his pay as a *Rev. Sol.*, N. C. Line. Lived in Greene Co., Ga.

HUGH HALL, b. Ireland, d. Hancock Co., Ga. Served as private, N. C. Line. Mar. in Penn., MARY REID. Their son, Alexander, b. N. C.; d. Meriwether Co., Ga., 1828; mar. ELIZABETH BROWN (dau. of Reuben and Betsey (Long) Brown). Their dau., Nancy, mar as (2) wife, Philip Tigner, b. Va., 1760. He mar. (1) Nancy Forbish. Perhaps other children.

JOHN HAMES, b. 1735; d. 1852; buried Murray Co., Ga.; reinterred 1911 in National Federal Cemetery, Marietta, Ga. (By D. A. R.) Served as private, Capt. and Maj., Ga. Troops. Mar. Miss Jasper (sister of SERG. JASPER, killed in Battle; monument to his memory erected on Bull St., Savannah, Ga.).

JOHN HAMMOND, b. Richmond Co., Va., 1722; d. Jackson Co., Ga., 1781. Served as Capt. under Col. Le Roy Hammond and Gen. Andrew Williamson in Drayton's Campaign. Mar. ANN COLEMAN.

JOHN HARDEE, b. Pitt Co., N. C., 1747; d. Camden Co., Ga., 1809. Served as private and Capt. of Continental Galley on the Coast of Ga. for 3 years. Later Capt. Ga. Militia; given bounty grant of land, Camden Co., 1786. Mar. 1768, CAROLINE T. ALDRICH. JOHN HARDEE, JR., b. 1769, mar. Sarah Ellis (1774–1848).

MARK HARDIN, b. Fauquier Co., Va., 1750; d. Warren Co., Ga. Served as private, Va. Militia. Mar. (1) Mary Hester Hunter; mar. (2) 1797, MARTHA FRANCES NEWSOME.

WILLIAM HARDIN, b. S. C., 1741; d. Ga., 1810. Served as private, S. C. Militia, under Gen. Francis Marion. Mar. SARAH BLEDSOE.

GEORGE HARLAN, b. Chatham Co., S. C., 1756; d. Ga., 1813. Served as private in Capt Henry Key's Penn. Militia. Mar. ANN BREEDE.

WILLIAM HARPER, b. Va.; *Rev. Sol.*; buried in family cemetery, Hancock Co., Ga.; drew pension. Mar. MARY INGRAM.

JACOB HARRELL, b. N. C., 1763; d. Decatur Co., Ga., Feb. 1837. Served as a *Rev. Sol.*, N. C. Line. Mar. Polly Whiddon, b. N. C.; d. Decatur Co., Ga., 1838. Son, John, and other children.

ABSOLOM HARRIS (son of Benjamin Harris (1732–1812), *Rev. Sol.* of Va., and his wife, Mourning Glenn), b. Greenville Co., Va., 1750; d. Hancock Co., Ga., 1824. Enlisted 1778 as private, Va. Line. Lieut., Brunswick Co., Va. Militia. Mar. (1) ELIZABETH (LOWE) TARVER; mar. (2) SARAH CLARE JETER.

BENJAMIN HARRIS, b. Sampson Co., N. C., 1761; d. Walton Co., Ga., 1840. Served as private, N. C. Line; received bounty grant. On Pension Roll, 1832.

THOMAS HARRIS, b. Mecklenburg Co., N. C., 1740; d. Green Co., Ga., 1790. Served as Capt., 4th N. C. Regiment. Mar. —. Their dau., Elizabeth Harris, mar. ANDREW BAXTER, JR., *Rev. Sol.*, of N. C. (1750–1814), son of ANDREW BAXTER, SR., of N. C.

JAMES, WILLIAM, STEPHEN, and JOHN HAWTHORNE, Ga. Sols. of the Line. JOHN HAWTHORNE drew land as *Rev. Sol.* in 1820 in Twiggs Co. WILLIAM HAWTHORNE drew land as *Rev. Sol.*, Decatur Co., in Lottery of 1827. Mar. Bethany Odom (1770-1854) (sister of the three brothers, ELKANAH, HALATIA, and DELDATHA ODOM). A son, Henry H., mar. 1814, Lucinda Pittman.

NOTE: JOSHUA HAWTHORNE was father of Kedar Hawthorne, and grandfather of Dr. J. B. Hawthorne, pastor of First Baptist Church, Atlanta, Ga.

JOHN HARRIS, b. Va., 1738; d. Walton Co., Ga., 1810. Served as gunner in Col. Charles Harrison's Va. Regiment of Artillery. Mar. MARY WALKER.

EDWARD HARRISON, b. England; d. Hall Co., Ga. Served as private, Ga. Troops; received bounty land for his service. Mar. (3) SUSAN GIDEON.

BENJAMIN HAYGOOD, b. N. C., June 30, 1758; d. Ga., June 4, 1841. Served under Capt. George Herndon, Gen. Folsom's N. C. Brig. from Chatham Co., N. C. Mar. Dec. 25, 1777, MARY STEWART (dau. of JAMES STEWART and his wife, Elizabeth), b. Dec. 25, 1760; d. Sept. 20, 1854. Children: John, b. 1778; Nancy, mar. John Thompson; James, mar. Sarah Stroud; William, mar. Polly Stroud; Elizabeth, mar. — Findley; Frances, mar. Levi Stroud; Sarah, mar. — Trammell; Benjamin, b. 1799.

THOMAS HAYNES, b. Mecklenburg Co., N. C., 1748; d. Columbia Co., Ga., 1823. Member *Council of Safety*, Halifax Co., N. C. Mar. 1782, FRANCES STITH.

JOSIAH HATCHER, b. Va., 1761; d. Pike Co., Ga., 1847. Served as private, Ga. Line. Mar. LEVINIA CLAY.

JOHN HAYS, b. Nov. 2, 1751; d. June 2, 1839. His wife, Mary, b. Dec. 19, 1760; d. June 19, 1839. Tombstone marked, Decatur, Ga., "A Revolutionary Soldier."

WILLIAM HATCHER, b. Va., 1755; d. Wilkinson Co., Ga., 1833. Served as private; received bounty land for his service. Mar. 1782, PRISCILLA STOUT.

JOHN HEARN, b. Va., 1767; d. Putnam Co., Ga., after 1808. Served as a *Rev. Sol.* of Va., 1781-1782. Came to Hancock Co., Ga. Mar. NANCY LYNCH.

ROBERT HENDERSON, b. Augusta Co., Va., 1750; d. Jackson Co., Ga., 1839. Served in Augusta Co., Va., Militia, under Capt. William Robinson and Capt. Henry Watterson. Removed to Jackson Co., Ga., 1796; drew land as a *Rev. Sol.* 1838, in Ga. Mar. Mary Carroll.

JOHN HENDRICK, b. Lincoln Co., N. C., 1754; d. Monroe Co., Ga., 1820. Served as private, Capt. Robt. Porter's Co., Col. John White, Va. Regiment. Mar. 1793, LUCY HUNT (1760-1808).

WYATT HEWELL, b. Spottsylvania Co., Va., 1756; d. Ga., 1842; received pension 1832, for service as private and Sergt., Va. Troops. Mar. 1777, SARAH WORTHEY (WORTHY).

ROBERT HENDRY, b. Scotland, 1752; came to New Hanover Co., N. C.; d. Liberty Co., Ga., 1830. Served as private under Light Horse Harry Lee at Yorktown. Mar. 1778, ANNE LEE Son, William Hendry (1783-1840), mar. in Lowndes Co., Ga., 1807, Nancy McFail (1786-1840), dau. of JAMES McFAIL, *Rev. Sol.*, of Lowndes Co., Ga., and his wife, Judith —.

DAVID HICKS, b. Brunswick Co., Va., 1739; d. Elbert Co., Ga., 1812. Served as Sargt., Va. Inf. Mar. 1763, MARY JOHNSON, d. 1820.

NATHANIEL HICKS, of Ga., Courier on the staff of Gen. Nathaniel Greene, lived after the War on the Ohoope river (now in Emanuel Co., Ga.). Mar. —. One son, JAMES, b. Ga., 1799, mar. Mary Hightower (dau. of JOSHUA HIGHTOWER, of Laurens Co., Ga., a *Rev. Sol.*, b. Va.; d. Ga.).

ISAAC HILL, b. Charles Co., Md., 1748; d. Warren Co., Ga., 1827. Served as drummer, 3rd Md. Regiment. Mar. 1772, LUCY WALLACE (1746-1798).

MATHEW HOBSON was a *Rev. Patriot*, at whose house the Council of Safety of Ga. held their meeting in Augusta, Ga. It was his dau., AGNES, who swam the Savannah river at Augusta, to carry important information to the American forces.

JAMES HINES, b. 1760; d. Effingham Co., Ga., 1804. Served in N. C. Line from Pitt Co., N. C. Mar. DRUCILLA —. They had 10 children.

BENJAMIN HODNETT, b. Va., 1761; d. Jasper Co., Ga., 1820. Served as private Va. Troops.. Mar. (1) 1784, ELIZABETH WYATT COLLIER.

LEWIS HOGG, b. S C., 1750; d. Ga., 1820. Served as private S. C. Militia. Mar. 1777 CLARA SMITH (1747-1838).

JESSE HOLBROOK, b. Va., 1764; d. Elbert Co., Ga., 1844. Placed on Pension Roll for service in *Rev. War*, as private Va. Line. Resident of Elbert Co., Ga. Mar SUSANNA —.

NATHAN HOLBROOK, b. Burlingham, Mass., 1745; d. Savannah, Ga., 1819. Served as Lieut. and Capt. Mass. Troops. Mar. SUSANNA WADHAMS (1760-1839), dau. of JONATHAN WADHAMS, b. Wethersfield, Conn., b. 1730; d. Goshen, Conn., 1812. A *Rev. Sol.* of Conn.; volunteer from Goshen for relief at Danbury, Conn. He mar. 1754, Judith Howe (1730-1818). Their dau., Ann Holbrook (1786-1878), mar. 1806, REV. THOMAS GOULDING of Ga. (1786-1848).

WILLIAM HUDGINS, age 70 in 1832. Had wife and 13 children living Upson Co., Ga. Served as a *Sol.* in N. C. under Capt. Oldham, Col. Wm. Moore. (Pension).

THOMAS HOLLIDAY (HOLLODAY), b. Va., 1750; d. Wilkes Co., Ga., 1798. Served in Ga. Troops under Gen. Elijah Clarke; received bounty land for his service, Washington Co., Ga. Mar. ELIZABETH or MARTHA —. Children: Dickinson; John; Lucy; Allen; Polly; Thomas; Ivey.

WILLIAM HOLT, b. Louisa Co., Va., 1757; d. Elbert Co., Ga., 1826. Served as Surgeon in Va. Militia, with the rank of Capt. Mar. 1784, LUCY SANDERS (1765-1847).

WILLIAM HOOD, b. N. C., 1739; d. Washington Co., Ga., 1809. Enlisted, 1782, in Capt. Brevard 10th N. C. Regiment. Mar. CHRISTIANA HOOD (1746-1807).

JOHN HOUSTON, b. Ireland, 1760; d. Coweta Co., Ga., 1835. Served as private under Capt. Thomas Dugan and Col. John Purvis; he was allowed pension, 1832. Mar. 1788, MARY WILSON (1768-1849).

VALENTINE HORSLEY, b. 1758; d. Upson Co., Ga., Sept. 8, 1843. Lived in Va.; moved to Monroe Co., Ga.; drew land in 1827 Lottery as a *Rev. Sol.* Mar. Sarah Kendrick (1766-1836). Children: Joseph; Thomas; James (1794-1886), mar. Elizabeth Bullard; John; Green; Anna, b. 1792, mar. James Brandon; Elizabeth.

SOLOMON HOWARD, b. Bertie Co., N. C., 1758; d. Washington Ga., 1834. Record of service Bureau of Pensions, Washington, D. C. Mar. MOANING BARRON.

HENRY HUGHES, b. England; d. Burke Co., Ga., April 27, 1814. Served as Capt. Va. Line. Mar. Jane Cooper (dau. of Thomas Cooper), d. 1826.

JENNENS HULSEY, b. King's Mt., N. C., 1765; d. Henry Co., Ga., 1850. Served as private at the Battle of King's Mt. Mar. 1806, REBECCA PATE (1788-1827).

HOPE HULL, b. Somerset Co., Md., Mar. 13, 1763; d. Athens, Ga., 1818. Served as a *Rev. Sol.*, together with his two brothers, THOMAS HULL AND JOHN HULL. Moved to Salisbury Dist., N. C., 1785, then to Wilkes Co., Ga., 1788. Mar. in Va., ANN WINGFIELD, of Hanover Co., Va. He was a Methodist minister.

THOMAS HUMPHRIES—Name found in list of *Rev. Sol.*, Baldwin Co., C. H., Milledgeville, Ga. In old book labelled, "Watson's Battalion District." Registered by Robert Winn, Jr. Mar. 15, 1819.

TURNER HUNT, b. N. C., 1756; d. Monroe Co., Ga., 1847. Served as private N. C. Line. Mar. Mary —.

WILLIAM HURT, b. N. C.; d. Hancock Co., Ga., 1812. Served as private Ga. Line, where he was wounded; received bounty land in Ga. for his service. Mar. (1) Priscilla Yancey; mar. (2) 1794, POLLY (BASS) HUNNICUTT.

HUGH IRWIN, b. Ireland, 1727, emigrated to America, and settled in N. C.; moved to Ga., 1757; d. Burke Co., Ga., 1805. Mar. — and had 4 sons and 1 dau: JARED; JOHN LAWSON; ALEXANDER; WILLIAM; Margaret. Was a *Patriot* during the Rev. and was given a grant of land in Ga. for his service, Aug. 20, 1781.

EDWARD JACKSON, b. S. C.; d. Walker Co., Ga., 1845. Name appears in *Rev. War*. Claims; on Pension Roll 1830, living in Gwinnett Co., Ga.

ROBERT JARRETT, *Rev. Sol.*, who served as Capt. under Gen. Francis Marion, "The Swamp Fox" of S. C. Came to Wilkes Co., Ga. Mar. Dortha Lane, of Wilkes Co., Ga. Only child: Devereaux, was reared and resided in Oconee Co., S. C. Removed to Ga., 1810. Mar. Sarah Patton, of Buncombe Co., N. C. They had 4 children.

LEWIS JENKINS, b. 1760; d. Meriwether Co., Ga.; received pension for service as private 5th N. C. Regiment under Capt. Tidd and Major Tiller. Mar. MARY JONES.

WILLIAM JENKINS, b. Md., 1746; d. Morgan Co., Ga., 1806. Served as private Ga. Line. Mar. DEMARIUS ROBERTS.

NOTE: A meeting was held at the cantonment of the American Army on June 19, 1783 at the request of GENERAL GEORGE WASHINGTON to establish the *Society of the Cincinnati*. At the meeting attended by the General Officers of the Continental Army and the gentlemen designated by their respective Regiments, this society was established. (From Historical Sketch of the Society by Charles Lukens Davis).

ROBERT JENNINGS, b. Va.; d. Oglethorpe Co., Ga. Served as private Va. Line; received bounty land in Ga. for his service. Mar. (1) ELOISE BROWN; mar. (2) ELIZABETH ARNOLD.

JOHN JOHNSON drew land as a *Rev. Sol.* in Ga. Mar. ELIZABETH ASHFIELD; both d. in Ga. Their son, Silas Johnson, a *Sol. of the War of 1812*, b. 1795; d. 1864, mar. Mary B. Lankford.

JONATHAN JOHNSON, *Rev. Sol.*, d. Tattnall Co., Ga. His son, Benjamin Johnson, of Tattnall Co., Ga., mar. Patsey Lane.

THOMAS JOHNSON, b. Va.; d. Oglethorpe Co., Ga., 1805. Served as a private Ga. Line in Capt. James McNeil's Co.; received bounty land in Ga. for his service. Mar. 1765, PENELOPE SANDERS, d. 1839.

THOMAS JOHNSON, with wife, Agnes, sold to Thomas Standley 287½ acres of land, Greene Co. granted to him for his service as a *Rev. Sol.*

WILLIAM JOHNSON, b. Charlotte Co., Va., 1758; d. Hancock Co., Ga., 1802. Served as private Va. Militia. Mar. Rebecca Moseley (1762-1843), moved to Ga. 1788. Son: Malcom, mar. Catherine Smith Davenport. Their son was Richard Malcom Johnston.

WILLIAM JOHNSON, b. Amelia Co., Va., 1753; d. Bibb Co., Ga., 1839; placed on Pension Roll, 1835 for service, 1777, in Capt. Wm. Lewis' Co., Col. Richard Parker's Va. Regiment; also served 1781 under Captains Payne and Archer. Mar. —. Their dau., Martha Johnson (1818-1894), mar. 1834, John Holliman, d. 1849.

PHILIP JONES, b. N. C., 1759; d. Burke Co., Ga., 1789. Served as private N. C. Line; received bounty grant of land for his service in Ga. Mar. ELIZABETH JONES.

THOMAS JONES, b. England, 1755; d. Richmond Co., Ga., 1809. Mar. (2) Elizabeth Boyd (1769-1831). Served as private Ga. Line.

WILLIAM JONES, b. Va.; d. Ga. Served in the first Co. (Volunteers) of Va.; was in the Southern campaign. His commission signed by Benjamin Harrison. Mar. SUSAN WILSON.

WILLIAM JORDAN, b. Va., Mar. 31, 1744; d. Ga., Sept. 23, 1826. Served as Lieut., Continental Army; received land grant for his service, Warren Co., Ga. Mar. 1786, ANNE MEDLOCK (1756-1817).

DEMPSEY JUSTICE (1766-1827), *Rev. Sol.*, buried in family cemetery near Salem Church, Baldwin Co., Ga.

JACOB KELLY, b. Robinson Co., N. C., 1755; d. Jasper Co., Ga., 1835. Served as private, 1779 in Col. Elijah Clarke's Ga. Troops. Mar. SUSANNA —.

JOHN KIMBROUGH, b. Anson Co., N. C., 1745; d. Wilkes Co., Ga., 1799. Served as Lieut. under Gen. Elijah Clarke. Mar. ANNE LE GRANDE. Children: Elizabeth, mar. WILLIAM BALDWIN, *Rev. Sol.*; Thomas (1788-1847), mar. Sarah Garrett (1790-1864). Perhaps other children.

PETER KITTLES, b. S. C.; d. Ga. Served as private under Gen. Francis Marion. Mar. SARAH WILLIAMSON. One of their sons, John R. Kittles, of Screven Co., Ga., mar. Clarky Lovett (dau. of Fens Lovett, and grand-dau. of THOMAS LOVETT, *Rev. Sol.* of S. C. and Ga.)

JOHN KING, b. Va., 1754; d. Jackson Co., Ga., 1840; received pension for his service as a private Va. Troops. Mar. 1792, ELEONE KARR (1770-1860).

NOTE: Three brothers, all *Rev. Sols.* are buried in Upson Co., Ga., viz: HENRY KENDALL; MAJOR JOHN KENDALL; and DR. JAMES KENDALL.

WILLIAM KIMBROUGH, b. 1735; d. Greene Co., Ga., 1803. Served as private Ga. Line under Gen. Clarke. Mar. Gracey —. Children (known): John; Elizabeth; Hannah; Thomas; Nancy; William.

JOHN LAMAR, b. S. C., 1763; d. Jones Co., Ga., 1842. Served as private S. C. Troops under Gen. Marion and Gen. Pickett; twice wounded. Mar. FRANCES BREEDLOVE (1766-1841).

RICHARD LAKE, b. N. J.; d. Ga., 1800. Served as private in Capt. Longstreet's Co.; 3rd. Regiment Middlesex Co., N. J. Mar. SARAH LANDON.

RICHARD LEDBETTER, *Rev. Sol.* Lived to be 100 years of age; buried Lumpkin Co., Ga.

ANDREW LEBEY was one of six brothers who came with Count d'Estang's fleet from France to assist the Continental Army in its efforts to take Savannah, Ga., from the British in 1779. He was wounded in the assault on the British at Springfield Redoubt near Savannah and his five brothers, JEROME; LOUIS; PHILIP; AUGUSTINE, and JOHN LEBEY were all killed. After the war he settled at Ebenezer, Ga. Mar. MARY (HINES) ANDERSON. Had issue; d. Savannah, Ga.

JAMES LESTER, d. 1820; buried Smith — Lester Cemetery, Baldwin Co., Ga. Name found on record book, Baldwin Co. Court House, labelled "Watson's Battalion Dist." He was a *Rev. Sol.* and a *Sol. of War of 1812.* Also a J. P., Burke Co., Ga.

JAMES LASSITER, b. Halifax Co., N. C., 1759; d. Ga. Enlisted N. C. 1776; served later as private in Lieut. John Pope's Co., Col. Marbury's Ga. Regiment of Light Dragoons. Mar. 1782, ELIZABETH BUTT, b. 1760, Halifax Co., N. C.

THOMAS LEVERETT, b. 1755; d. Troup Co., Ga., 1834. Served as private Ga. Line, under Capt. John Clarke, Col. Alexanders' Regiment. Mar. 1789, MARY GRIFFIN.

WILLIAM LEVERETT, b. 1760; d. Putnam Co., Ga., 1812. Served as private, received bounty land in Cherokee Co., Ga. Mar. CELIA ANN MOSELEY.

JOHN LEWIS, b. Va., 1753; d. Ga., 1817. Served as a private in Va. and Ga. Line. Mar. 1776, ELIZABETH KENNORE (1754-1826). Dau., Elizabeth (1801-1858), mar. Wm. Desarix Stone; son, Ulysses (1799-1856), mar. Sarah Abercrombie.

RICHARD LEWIS, b. Va., 1747; d. Greene Co., Ga., 1809. Served as Sergt. 10th Regiment N. C. under Capt. Lytles. Mar. Caroline Booker.

REV. ELIJAH LINCH, b. S. C.; d. Ga. He and four bros. were *Rev. Sols.* He mar. MISS CHAPMAN.

MATTHEW LIVELY (son of Abraham Lively, who came from Scotland), b. Ga., 1750; d. Burke Co., Ga., 1834. Served in Ga. Line, received bounty land in Ga. for his service. Mar. ELIZABETH ODOM.

ADAM LIVINGSTON, b. Ireland. Served as a *Rev. Sol.* in Penn.; removed to Va., then to Greene Co., Ga., where he was killed by the Indians. He had 13 children, living in Greene Co., Ga.

DAVID LOWRY, b. 1764; d. Jackson Co., Ga., 1848. Served as a *Rev. Sol.*; received bounty land in Ga. for his service. Mar. 1806, MARTHA McLEULLER.

ISAAC LOW, SR., b. —; d. Richmond Co., Ga., May 17, 1790. Was a J. P. in Richmond Co., 1782; received a bounty grant of land in Ga., upon certificate of COL. JAMES McNEIL. Mar. —. Mentions children (in will): ESTHER, mar. Samuel Hart; William; Ann; Burrey; Hickenbotham; Grace; Isaac, Jr.; and George.

ELIJAH MARTIN, b. Penn., 1751; d. Jones Co., Ga., 1819. Served as private, S. C. Militia. Mar. 1774, MARY VAN DER BERG (1753-1833).

JOHN MARTIN, d. Augusta, Ga., Feb. 14, 1843, aged 105 years. On monument in St. Paul's Churchyard, Augusta, Ga.: "He served in the Cherokee War, 1735. Was wounded in the head by a tomahawk. He served throughout the whole of the Revolution with honor. Erected as a tribute of respect by the Ladies of Augusta, Ga."

MARSHALL MARTIN (son of Abram Martin and his wife, Elizabeth Marshall), b. —; d. Augusta, Ga., 1819; was wounded at the Siege of Augusta. His mother, ELIZABETH (MARSHALL) MARTIN, was a *Heroine* of the Rev., and lived to be 96 years of age.) He had six bros. who were *Rev. Sols.*. One bro., WILLIAM, was b. S. C., and killed at the Siege of Augusta, Ga. Mar. GRACE WARING, of Dorchester, S. C., one of the *heroines* of the Rev.

JOHN MASON, b. Ga., 1755; d. Ga., 1795. Served as Sergt.-Maj., Ga. Line. Mar. Elizabeth Hix, b. 1765.

TURNER MASON, b. Va. In 1793 he moved to Jefferson Co., Ga., where he d. Served as Lieut. in Continental Army of Va. Mar. (1) in Va., ELIZABETH BURNS, d. 1783; 3 children; mar. (2) in Halifax Co., N. C., 1785, MARY LOWE; 14 children.

JEREMIAH MATTHEWS, b. Halifax Co., N. C.; d. Ga. Served as private, N. C. Troops. Mar. SARAH BRINKLEY.

WILLIAM MATTHEWS, b. England; d. Baldwin Co., Ga. Served as private *Rev. Sol.* Mar. DORCAS WRIGHT.

SILAS MERCER, b. Currituck Co., N. C., 1745; d. Wilkes Co., Ga., 1793. Served as Chaplain, N. C. Troops. Mar. DORCAS —, d. 1791. Son, MOUNT MORIAH MERCER (1784-1822), mar. 1816, Nancy (Ann) Edge; son, Herman, mar. Elizabeth Andrews, of Greene Co.; son, Jesse, mar. (1) —; mar. (2) Nancy (Mills) Simons, widow of Abram Simons.

WILLIAM MEAD, b. Va., 1727; d. Augusta, Ga., 1805. Gave active service, Bedford Co., Va. Troops. Col. in Va. Mar. (2) MARTHA ANN HAILE, d. 1769. Their son, JOHN HAILE. b. 1755, Bedford Co., Va., d. Augusta, Ga., 1798; *Rev. Sol.* Served as Ensign, 14th Va. Regiment, Mar. ELIZABETH CRUMP, d. 1813. Dau., Elizabeth, mar. Col. Ambrose Gordon.

DAVID WOOD MERIWETHER, b. Louisa Co., Va., 1754; d. Clarke Co., Ga., 1797. Served as private and Lieut., Va. Line. Mar. 1782, MARY LEWIS, d. 1801.

CHARLES MIDDLETON, b. Westmoreland Co., Va., 1750; d. Dooly Co., Ga. Served as 2nd Lieut., Ga. Troops. Mar. 1773, MARGARET —.

DAVID MELSON, b. Md.; d. Hancock Co., Ga. Served as private, Md. Line. Mar. Mary Grace.

JOHN MOFFETT, b. Va., 1742; d. De Kalb Co., Ga., 1829. Early settled Chester Co., S. C. Served as Capt. in Snow Campaign against the Cherokee Indians, 1776; *Rev. Sol.* under Sumpter, in S. C., 1780.

NATHANIEL MILLER, b. Ireland, 1738; d. Laurens Co., Ga., 1834. Served as private in Col. James McCay's Troops. Mar. 1756, Mary Neile, d. 1770.

JAMES MONTGOMERY, b. Scotland, 1736; d. Franklin Co., Ga., 1808. Served as 2nd Lieut., Ga. Troops; received bounty land grant in Ga. for his service. Mar. (1) 1756, ELIZABETH McCONNELL.

FRANCES MORELAND and ROBERT MORELAND, buried in Jasper Co., Ga., near Shady Dale; both *Rev. Sols.*

WILLIAM MORAN, b. Ireland, came to N. C.; removed to Ga. Buried in family cemetery, Hancock Co., Ga.

JOHN MURPHREE, b. Dublin, Ireland, 1735; d. Burke Co., Ga., 1798. Served as private in Capt. John Johnson's Co., Col. John Collins' N. C. Regiment. Mar. Martha —. (Grave marked by D. A. R.)

ABEDNEGO MOORE, *Rev. Sol.* from Effingham Co., Ga., mar. Letty Strong (dau. of Josiah Strong, nephew of JOSIAH TATNALL, who was at Siege of Augusta). They settled in Jackson, Ga.

WILLIAM MURDOCK, b. Ireland, 1759; d. Franklin Co., Ga., 1840. On Pension Roll Elbert Co. for service as private. Mar. Mary Mills.

JAMES McCORMICK, d. Baldwin Co., Ga., 1813. Served in S. C. Militia. Received land in Wilkes Co., Ga., for his service. Mar. (1) MARY ANN FLETCHER, b. Santee S. C., 1759. (Their dau., Patsey, mar. Samuel Neal.) Mar. (2) Katherine Oliver.

DAVID McCULLOUGH, b. Ireland, 1738; d. Savannah, Ga., 1795. Served as Capt. on the Cruiser "Rattle-Snake" and captured many prizes from the British. Mar. 1765, PHOEBE BOYD.

JOHN McCULLOUGH, *Rev. Sol.*, was an early school teacher in Savannah, Ga. Mar. NANCY BUTT and settled in Hancock Co., Ga.

JAMES McFAIL, d. Lowndes Co., Ga. Mar. Judith —. She received land, 1838 Lottery as widow of *Rev. Sol.* Children (known): Nancy (1786-1840), mar. 1807, William Hendry (1783-1840), son of ROBERT HENDRY (1752-1830), *Rev. Sol.*, and his wife, Ann Lee (1752-1834).

WILLIAM McCUTCHEON, b. Augusta Co., Va., 1760; d. Spalding Co., Ga., 1827. Served as private Va. Militia. Mar. (2) ANN SHAW (1772-1832).

JAMES McAFEE, b. N. C., 1762; d. Habersham Co., Ga., 1844. Enlisted 1776 N. C. Troops. Served until close of War. Mar. MARGARET COLE.

DANIEL McGEHEE, b. Amelia Co., Va., 1747; d. Augusta, Ga., 1801. Served as *Rev. Sol.* Mar. 1778, JANE BROOKE HODNETT (1749-1801).

JOHN NEELY, b. Ireland, 1744; d. Coweta Co., Ga., 1837. at the age of 93. Enlisted as a *Rev. Sol.* while a resident of Waxhaw Settlement, S. C., 1776. Private under Capt. Eli Kershaw 3rd S. C. Regiment; was in Georgia 10 months under Capt. Pettigrew, Col. Jack's Regiment; with State Troops in S. C.; wounded in an engagement with the Tories at Camden, S. C.; received pension in 1832 while a resident of Coweta Co., Ga.

JAMES NEAL, d. Warren Co., Ga. A *Rev. Sol.* Mar. MARY RUCKER.

DAVID NEAL, of Warren Co., Ga., served as Capt. 1st Ga. Battalion under MAJ. JOHN LAWSON, Commander Ga. Troops.

JEREMIAH NELSON, *Rev. Sol.*; received bounty grant of 490 acres of land for Rev. service in Irwin Co., Ga., Mar. 28, 1820; signed George M. Troup, Governor. He was living in Lucas District, Hancock Co., Ga., 1820.

WILLIAM NIBLACK, b. N. C., 1761; d. Camden Co., Ga., 1828. Served as private N. C. LINE. Mar. DIANA TISON.

JESSE NORMAN, b. N. C.; d. Wilkes Co., Ga.; served as *Rev. Sol.* under Count Pulaski at Siege of Savannah, Ga. Mar. Elizabeth Southward. Their dau., Sophia Morman, b. 1783-1841.

WILLIAM NORMAN, b. Fauquier Co., Va.; d. Lincoln Co., Ga. Enlisted as a private 1776 in Capt. George Stubblefield's Co., 5th Va. Regiment, under Lieut. Col. Josiah Parks; wounded at the Battle of Brandywine. Mar. MISS SHEPHERD.

GEORGE W. NORWOOD, b. N. C., 1760; d. Ga., 1840. Drew a pension 1833, living in Campbell (now Fulton) Co., Ga. Served as Orderly-Sergt. in Capt. James Richard's Co., Col. Benj. Seawell's N. C. Regiment. Mar. MARISH WALL.

WILLIAM OSBORNE, b. Ga., 1749; d. Ga., 1796. Mar. MARY —. Served as private, 3rd Battalion Ga. Regiment.

EPHRIAM OWENS, a *Rev. Sol.*, received bounty land April 26, 1784, Washington Co. Certificate of Col. G. Lee.

GEORGE PALMER, b. N. C., 1750; d. Burke Co., Ga., 1826. Served as private in 4th Ga. Battalion. Mar. MARY CURETON.

RICHARD PARHAM, *Rev. Sol.* of Ga., buried in family cemetery, 13 miles east of Milledgeville, Baldwin Co., Ga.

JOHN PATTERSON, b. Ireland, 1736; d. Burke Co., Ga., 1822. Served as private in Capt. Abner Beckham's Co., Col. John Twiggs Ga. Regiment. Mar. CATHERINE MOSSMAN. Their son, William (1776-1862), mar. 1803, Eleanor Little.

WILLIAM PATTERSON, b. Ga., 1743; d. Jefferson Co., Ga., 1801. Enlisted from St. George's Parish, Ga., at the beginning of War. Mar. 1759, NANCY MOSSMAN.

RICHARD PAULETT, b. Va., 1753; d. Campbell Co., Ga., 1835. Ensign 1778; Lieut. under Col. Francis Taylor, Va. Continental Line. Mar. CATHERINE SMITH.

JOHN PECK, b. Va., 1743; d. Ga., 1800. Mar. Tabitha —; was in Ga. Troops under Col. Elijah Clarke, at the Siege of Augusta, Ga.

WILLIAM PENN, b. Charles City, Md., 1760; d. Ga., 1836. Served in Ga. Line. Buried Baptist Cemetery, Monticello, Ga., and engraved on his tombstone is an account of his service as a *Rev. Sol.* He mar. MARTHA A. SLADE.

JAMES PERRY, b. N. C., 1759; d. Jasper Co., Ga., 1843. Served as private N. C. Line; received bounty grant for his service in Jasper (formerly Baldwin) Co., Ga. Mar. ELIZABETH VALENTINE (1768-1853). Two children (known): Penny, mar. John Hand; Kesiah, mar. Joseph J. Henderson.

WILLIAM PENTECOST, b. Dinwiddie Co., Va., 1763; d. Jackson Co., Ga., 1839; received a pension for service as *Rev. Sol.*; as private, Va. Troops. Mar. Delilah Wood.

ARCHIBALD PERKINS, b. N. C., 1746; d. Greene Co., Ga. Served as private, N. C. Troops. Mar. ELIZABETH GIBBS. Their dau., Elizabeth, b. 1766, mar. 1780, ISAAC MIDDLEBROOKS (b. Va., 1755; d. Morgan Co., Ga., a *Rev. Sol.*).

JESSE POPE, b. Chowan Co., N. C.; d. Hancock Co., Ga., 1820; received bounty grant of land in Ga. for his service in N. C. Troops. Mar. MARY FORT.

MARK PHILLIPS, b. Ireland, 1755; d. Ga., 1839. Applied for pension, 1819, which was granted; served as private N. C. Militia under Capt. Samuel Jones. Mar. Raney Moore, b. 1753.

GEORGE PHILLIPS, b. Va., 1758; d. Ga., 1849. Served as private Va. Line. Mar. 1790, SARAH LAVELL.

ISAAC PHILLIPS, b. Savannah, Ga., 1741; d. Henry Co., Ga., 1837. Served as private, Ga. Troops. Mar. MARY DAWSON.

JOSEPH PHILLIPS, b. 1734; d. Morgan Co., Ga., 1800. Served as Minute Man under Col. Elijah Clarke in Ga.; received bounty land of 550 acres for service in Washington Co. Mar. Sarah Lindes (Lyndes).

WILLIAM PILCHER, b. N. C., came to Wilkes Co., Ga. Killed by the Tories. Buried in (now Glascock Co.), Ga.

WILLIAM PINDAR, b. Wales; d. Savannah, Ga., 1793. Was a *Patriot*; supplied the Continental Troops with provisions during the Siege of Savannah. When the British captured Savannah, they burned his home and made him prisoner; he was sent to Nassau Island, where he remained until the end of the War. Mar. REBECCA HUCHINS; she d. 1799.

WILLIAM POLLARD, b. Culpeper Co., Va., 1737; d. Greene Co., Ga., 1802; a *Rev. Sol.* Served as private, Va. Militia under Capt. Berry and Col. Bowman. Mar. (2) TABITHA COLLINS, Children: Frances, b. 1784, mar. John Spencer Shropshire; Joseph; Sallie, mar. John Jeffries.

DUDLEY POOL, b. Va., 1753; d. Wilkes Co., Ga., 1826; received bounty land grant in Wilkes Co., Ga. for his service. Mar. Elizabeth Hyde.

HENRY AUGUSTINE POPE, b. Aug. 6, 1760; d. Oglethorpe Co., Ga., 1801. Served as *Rev. Sol.* Mar. (1) Clara Hill (1763-1798); mar. (2) 1799, MARY DAVIS, d. 1843; received bounty land in Ga.

WYLIE POPE (bro. of Henry Augustine Pope), b. 1758; d. Ga., 1808. Served as private under Gen. Elijah Clarke at Kettle Creek.

JOHN HENRY POPE, b. 1756; d. Wilkes Co., Ga., 1821; received bounty land in Ga. for his service with N. C. Troops. Mar. MARY BURWELL.

JAMES POWERS, b. N. C., 1747; d. Ga., 1818. Served in Col. Hogan's 7th N. C. Regiment, as Lieut. Mar. PENELOPE HARDY.

ROBERT PULLEN, b. July 6, 1756; d. Jan. 12, 1851. Buried Covington, Ga., *Rev. Sol.* Grave marked by D. A. R.

NOTE: PULASKI COUNTY, GA. was created from Laurens Co., 1808. Named in honor of Count Pulaski, a Polish nobleman who lost his life in Ga. fighting in behalf of the Americans. Was wounded at the Siege of Savannah, Ga., Oct. 9, 1779.

JOHN RAIFORD, b. New Bern, N. C., 1750; d. Jefferson Co., Ga., 1812. Served as Lieut. 2nd N. C. Troops 1780-1; received bounty grant of land for his service in Ga. Mar. 1769, Lucy Spell (1753-1823). Had issue.

ROBERT RAINES, b. 1766; d. Twiggs Co., Ga., 1816. Served as Capt. Co. 4, 1st Regiment of Ga. Troops, Ga. Line. Mar. SARAH T. HAMILTON b. Amelia Co., Va., Nov. 28, 1775; d. Thomas Co., Ga., July 13, 1850. (dau. of JOHN HAMILTON, b. Amelia Co., Va., 1747; d. Hancock Co., Ga., 1805; served as private Ga. Line, and his wife, Tabitha Thweatt, b. Va., 1747). Children (in will): John W.; Lucien H.; Robert H.; Martha, mar. — Terrell; Henrietta, mar. — Murphy; Angelina, mar. — Chaires; Emily, mar. — Blackshear.

SAMUEL REID, had pension granted him as a *Rev. Sol.* Enlisted Abbeville, S. C. (District); b. Lancaster, Penn., Jan. 26, 1749; d. Gwinnett Co., Ga., Feb. 5, 1843; received pension 1832 while living with his children in St. Clair, Ala.

ROBERT ROZAR, b. Halifax Co., N. C., 1756; d. Wilkinson Co., Ga., 1840. Enlisted Bladen Co., N. C. in Col. Brown's N. C. Regiment, 1775. Moved 1781, to Georgetown Parish, S. C. and enlisted in Col. Horry's S. C. Regiment; moved to Wilkinson Co., Ga; received pension. Mar. Mary —. Two children (known): Robert, Jr., mar. Nancy; Alexander.

JOHN RICHARDSON, b. Va., 1760; d. Oglethorpe Co., Ga. Served in the Va. Line; received bounty land in Oglethorpe Co. for his service. Mar. 1790, ELIZABETH TATE.

WALKER RICHARDSON, b. Va.; d. Elbert Co., Ga. (Will made Mar. 13, 1819, pro. 1822.) Served as Lieut. in 1st Va. Regiment. commanded by Col. Charles Harrison. Came to Ga., 1792. Mar. PRUDENCE —.

CATO RIDDLE, b. Chatham Co., N. C., 1755.; d. Washington Co., Ga., 1823. Served as Capt. N. C. Troops; was at Cowpens and Guilford C. H. Mar. MARTHA TOMLINSON (1770-1840).

JAMES ROBERTS, b. Ga., 1744; d. Screven Co., Ga., 1814. Served as Lieut., Ga. troops; received bounty grant of land for his service. Mar. 1785, EMILY WILLIAMSON (dau. of ROBERT WILLIAMSON, *Rev. Sol.* of Ga., and his wife, Lucy Conyers).

FREDERICK ROBINSON, b. N. C.; d. Wayne Co., Ga. Served in N. C. Line. Mar. JANE THOMAS in N. C. and moved to Ga.

JAMES ROQUEMORE, b. France; d. Warren Co., Ga. Served as private Ga. Line. Mar. ELIZABETH —.

BRITTAIN ROGERS, b. N. C., Oct. 11, 1761; d. Monroe Co., Ga., April 22, 1835. Mar. 1782, Elizabeth Lockett (1767-1845). *Rev. Sol.* and *Sol. of War of 1812.* His son, OSBORNE (1783-1857), mar. 1813, Mary Thorn.

JAMES ROWAN, b. Ireland, 1752; d. Warren Co., Ga., 1795. Served as private S. C. Troops; received bounty land in Ga. for his service. Mar. ANN —, b. 1758.

WILLIAM RYALS, b. N. C., 1748; d. Montgomery Co., Ga., Feb. 1, 1828; buried 3 miles from Uvalda, Ga. at old Dead River Cemetery. Served as private 2nd N. C. Regiment under Capt. Hall and Col. John Patten. Mar. EDITH CHILDS (1765-1835). (Grave marked by D. A. R, 1921).

WILLIAM A. RYALS, *Rev. Sol.*, d. Ga. Mar. Miss McDonald. Children: Joe, mar. Miss. Conner; John, mar. Maria Conner; Thomas, mar. — Burch; David, James, mar. Becky Yarbrough; and other children.

PHILIP RYAN, b. Henry Co., Va., about 1755; d. Jackson Co., Ga., 1822. Served as private Ga. Troops. Buried in the old Ryan Cemetery, 4 miles from Athens, Ga. Mar. OBEDIENCE

WOODLIEF (1760–1838).   Children: Christiana, mar. John Nance; Angelica, b. 1782, mar. Lewis Lampkin; Whitehead; Philip, mar. Rachel Pinkard; Elizabeth, mar. — Hall.

MOSES SANDERS, b. England, 1742; d. Banks Co., Ga., 1817. Served as Rev. Sol. Mar. ELIZABETH —. Son, Moses, Jr. Found on tombstone, Banks (formerly Franklin) Co., Ga.: "A Baptist preacher and Rev. Sol."

JESSE SANDERS, b. Lancaster Co., Va., 1743; d. Ga. Capt. 6th Regiment, N. C. Troops. Mar. 1765, Ann Yancey.

DILL SAPP (and wife, Lydia), of Burke Co., drew 287½ acres of land on Rocky Creek, Washington Co., for his service as a Rev. Sol.

THOMAS SCOTT, WOODLIEF SCOTT, and FREDERICK SCOTT, bros., b. Va.; were Rev. Sols., Va. Line; came to Ga. and settled in Hancock Co.

WILLIAM SCURLOCK, b. Va., 1763; d. Ga., 1840. Placed on Pension Roll, 1833. Served under Col. Benjamin Cleveland, N. C. Regiment. Mar. 1796, RHODA SIMMONS (1771–1831).

JOHN SEAY, b. 1758; d. Ga. Served in Ga. under Gen. Micajah Williamson. Mar. (1) MISS WEST; mar. (2) SARAH McALPIN.

JOHN SESSIONS, b. N. C., 1758; d. near Griffin, Ga., 1836. Served in the N. C. Troops, under Capts. Bright and Heritage. Mar. MARY —.

JOHN SHARPE (SHARP), b. Halifax Co., Va., 1762. Served as private, Ga. Troops, under Capts. Lewis and Grant; Col. Emanuel and Col. Jackson. Mar. BETSEY WYNN, d. 1835. He died Tattnall Co., Ga., 1835. Their son, John Thomas (1795–1846), mar. Rebecca Lasseter (1795–1878). Other children.

LEVI SHEFTALL, b. Ga., Jan. 11, 1739; d. Savannah, Ga. Enlisted and served in Ga. Troops. Mar. in the West Indies, SARAH De LEMOTTA. Had 7 sons; three of them were: Benjamin; Mordecia; and Solomon.

SHEFTALL SHEFTALL (son of Mordecia Sheftall, who came to Savannah, Ga., with the first Jewish settlers), was a Rev. Sol.; was at the Siege of Savannah, and taken prisoner by the British. He was b. Savannah, 1762; d. there Aug. 17, 1847.

JOHN SHELLMAN, b. Md., 1756; d. Savannah, Ga., 1838. Granted a pension, 1836, for his service in the Md. Line. Mar. CLARISSA MONTFORT, d. 1845.

ARCHIBALD SIMPSON, b. Md., 1750; d. Wilkes Co., Ga., 1828. Served in Md., and under Col. Elijah Clarke's Ga. Troops at Kettle Creek. Mar. CATHERINE (Kitty) NELSON (sister of JOHN NELSON, Rev. Sol., of Wilkes Co., Ga.).

WILLIAM SIMMONS, b. Va., 1745; d. Jasper Co., Ga., 1828; received bounty land in Ga. for service in Va. Line. Mar. 1793, ANN KING (1759–1810). Children: William, Jr.; Allen G., mar. 1820, Mary Cleveland.

ROBERT SIMMS, b. N. C., 1757; d. Hancock Co., Ga., 1815. Served as private in Capt. John Dickinson's Co., N. C. Troops. Mar. (1) 1774, SARAH DICKINSON (dau. of CAPT. JOHN DICKINSON, Rev. Sol. of N. C., and his wife, Mary Barnes).

JAMES SPANN, b. Red Banks, S. C., 1754; d. Savannah, Ga., 1796. Served as Lieut. in Col. Samuel Hammond's S. C. Regiment. Mar. ELIZABETH FOX (1758–1827).

ALEXANDER SMITH granted a pension as Rev. Sol., 1840, while a resident of Meriwether Co., Ga.

ABNER SMITH, b. Ireland, settled in S. C.; wounded in Battle at Sullivan's Island; received pension as a Rev. Sol., while a resident of Coweta Co., Ga., where he d.

CHARLES SMITH, b. Md., 1760; d. Morgan Co., Ga., 1822. Served as 2nd. Lieut., Md. Line; received bounty land in Ga. Mar. JANE PINCKARD.

COLESBY SMITH, b. Va., 1765; d. Washington Co., Ga., 1840. Served as private, Va. Militia; granted bounty land in Ga. for his service. (Grave marked by Ga. D. A. R.) Mar. 1792, ANNA HENRY.

ISAAC SMITH, b. New Kent Co., Va., 1758; d. Monroe Co., Ga., 1834. Enlisted as Sergt., 1st Va. Regiment; in 1831 he was placed on the Pension Roll of Ga. Mar. REBECCA GILMORE.

NATHAN SMITH, b. 1751; d. Wilkes Co., Ga., 1816. Mar. Sarah Foster. Served as private, Ga. Troops.

DANIEL SMITH, b. Conn.; d. Savannah, Ga., 1814. A *Rev. Sol.* A Custom Officer of Savannah. Left wife and children.

JAMES SMITH, b. N. C.; d. Greene Co., Ga.; served with N. C. Troops. Mar. ELIZABETH COWAN, b. Scotland; d. Cobb Co., Ga., age over 100 years.

THOMAS SMITH, b. Va.; d. Warren Co., Ga., 1785; a *Rev. Sol.*; received bounty land in Ga. for his service. Mar. PHOEBY —.

LARKIN SMITH, b. Va., 1760; d. Oglethorpe Co., Ga., Oct. 20, 1834.; received pension for his service as private in Capt. James Baytop's Co., Col. Heth's Va. Regiment. Mar. AVEY BRADLEY (1767-1807).

GEORGE SLAUGHTER, b. Va., 1764; d. Greene Co., Ga., 1840. Served as private, Va. Line; placed on Pension Roll. Mar. 1788, MARTHA SMITH, d. 1813.

JOHN SPARKS, b. N. C., 1755; d. Washington Co., Ga., 1834. Enlisted in Wilkes Co., N. C.; received pension for his service. Buried near Sandersville, Ga. Mar. 1779, MARGARET HAMPTON.

STEPHEN STAPLES, b. Hanover Co., Va., about 1749; d. Wilkes Co., Ga., 1805. Served as private, Ga. Line, under Gen. Elijah Clarke and Col. Stephen Heard. Mar. 1778, MARY STARKE (dau. of JOHN STARKE, COL. of Hanover Co., Va., Militia, 1775; member of Va. Assembly, and his wife, Ann Wyatt), b. 1762. They had 14 daus. and two sons.

JOHN STEPHENS, b. S. C., 1737; d. Liberty Co., Ga., 1777. He was *Delegate* to the *Provincial Congress* which met at Savannah, Ga., 1775. Mar. Margaret McCarty. Their son, John, Jr. (1777-1832), mar. Amarinthia Monroe.

JOHN STEPHENS, b. N. C.; d. Ga. Served in N. C. Militia; came to Wilkinson Co., Ga., 1822. Buried two miles south of Toomsboro, Ga. Grave marked by D. A. R. Mar. in N. C., ELIZABETH MATTHEWS. Their son, James, b. N. C., 1817, mar. Jerusha Barnes; other children.

LEWIS STOWERS, b. Orange Co., Va., 1764; d. De Kalb Co., Ga., 1844. Served as private in Capt. Richard White's Co, Col. Taylor's Va. Regiment. Mar. 1786, JOYCE SHEFLETT (1765-1842).

JOHN STANTON, b. Prince George Co., Va., 1756; d. Ga., 1832. Buried near Sandersville, Ga. Served as private in Capt. Howell Tatum's Co. N. C. Line; Sergt,. 1780. Mar. 1778, ELIZABETH SHORT.

GRAVERNER STEWART, received bounty grant of 287½ acres of land in Washington (now Greene) Co., Ga., for his services as a *Rev. Sol.* He mar. JANE —.

Heirs of JOHN STEWART, dec., *Rev. Sol.*, Nov. 2, 1786, sold to Joseph Philips, 287½ acres of land in Greene Co. granted him for his service, 1785. Heirs were his children: James, Robert, Charles and Lydia Stewart.

SAMUEL STILES, b. in the Bermudas; settled in Bryan Co., Ga., 1769. Was a *Rev. Sol.* and was at the Siege of Savannah, Ga. Mar. CATHERINE CLAY (dau. of JOSEPH CLAY, *Rev. Sol.* Savannah, Ga.)

JAMES STOVALL, b. Va.; d. Elbert Co., Ga., of wounds received during *Rev. War*; served with Va. Troops; received land grant in Elbert Co., Ga. for his service. Mar. MISS BRADLEY and moved to Ga., 1787.

JOSIAH STOVALL and BENJAMIN STOVALL, both *Rev. Sol.* from Granville Co., N. C. (sons of JOHN STOVALL, *Rev. Sol.* of N. C.); received land in Wilkes Co., Ga., for their services. JOSIAH STOVALL, d. Lincoln Co., Ga., 1798; BENJAMIN STOVALL d. Oglethorpe Co., Ga., 1828.

PETER STROZIER, b. Germany, 1748; d. Wilkes Co., Ga., 1823. Served as private Ga. Militia under Col. John Dooly at Kettle Creek. Mar. MARGARET DOZIER.

FRANCIS STROTHER, b. Culpeper Co., Va.; d. Lincoln Co., Ga. *Rev. Sol.* Mar. SARAH HOLLIDAY, Wilkes Co., Ga.

JAMES STUBBS, b. Va., 1746; d. Putnam Co., Ga., 1822. Served as private Ga. Line. Mar. 1770, MARY ELIZA SCOTT (1750-1820).

WILLIAM SUTTLES, b. Va., 1731; d. Ga., 1839; received bounty land in Ga. for his service as a private in Va. Troops. Mar. MARGARETTE HARLEY.

JOSEPH SUMNER, SR., was a *Rev. Sol.* of Emanuel Co., Ga.; drew land for his service, and also in Lottery of 1827.

JOHN TATE, b. Ireland, 1758; d. Ga., 1838; received a pension for service as private Penn. Troops under Col. Dunlap. Mar. 1790, Anne Olipharit (1768-1841).

CLARK TAYLOR, b. Mecklenburg Co., Va., 1759; d. Oglethorpe Co., Ga., 1846. Served as a *Rev. Sol.*; received a bounty grant of land in Ga. for his service. Mar. 4 times. Name of one wife: Elizabeth Whitehead (1766-1819).

WILLIAM TAYLOR, b. N. C., 1760; d. Ga., 1812. Served as private 1777, N. C. Troops, 10th Regiment under Col. Abraham Shepard. Mar. 1780, MARY BILLINGSLEY, d. 1804. Had issue. One dau., Nancy, mar. 1821, David Blackshear (1793-1868).

RICHMOND TERRELL, b. Charlottesville, Va., 1760; d. Newton Co., Ga., 1856. Served at the Battle of King's Mt. Mar. 1782, CECILIA DARRACOTT.

JAMES THOMAS, b. Va.; settled at Augusta, Ga. Was presented a sword "for his gallant service" under Gen. Nathaniel Greene. D. 1844 and is buried in Baldwin Co., Ga., 8 miles from Milledgeville.

WILLIAM THOMAS, b. Culpeper Co., Va., 1763; d. Franklin Co., Ga., 1835. Served as private Capts. Leah's, Chapman, and Varnum under Col. Paisley.

ISHAM THOMPSON, b. Chesterfield Co., Va.; d. Elbert Co., Ga., 1795. Served as private in Gen. Elijah Clarke's Regiment; received bounty land in Ga. for his service. Mar. 1760, MARY ANN OLIVER, b. 1742.

WILLIAM THOMPSON (Buried in St. Paul's Church Yard, Augusta, Ga.) From tombstone: "Member Order of the Cincinnati. Here lies the body of William Thompson, Esq. Who was an Officer in the 9th Pennsylvania Regiment of the late American Army. From its formation in 1776 to its dissolution and amongst his American Bretheren made an offering of his blood on the Altar of Liberty. He departed this life on the 19th of March, 1794. Aged 45 years. And as a Testimony of regret, and in remembrance of him, his disconsolate widow hath caused this stone be placed as a covering to his Bed of Rest." Granted bounty land Mar. 9, 1785.

THOMAS TRAMMELL, b. S. C., 1747; d. Upson Co., Ga., 1823. Served as private in Capt. Hughes Co., Col. Brandon's S. C. Regiment. Mar. 1775, MARY TURNER (1759-1859).

ABSOLOM TARVER, b. N. C., 1757; d. Hancock Co., Ga., 1831. Served as private, N. C. Continental Line; received grant of land in Ga. for his service. Mar. 1776, URSULA SMITH.

WILLIAM TURK, b. Ireland 1744; came with his parents, James and Mary Turk, to America and settled, 1757, in S. C. Served as Express Courier under Gen. Pickens, of S. C. Mar. Margaret Archibald (dau. of John Archibald, of Rowan Co., N. C.; moved to Elbert Co., Ga. D. Franklin Co., Ga., 1795.

FRANCIS TRIPLETT, b. Va., 1756; d. Richmond Co., Ga., 1806. Served under Col. E. Clarke in Ga. Mar. 1783, Rachel Brock. Buried "Twigg's Cemetery," near Augusta, Ga.

WILLIAM TWITTY, b. S. C., 1761; d. Broad river settlement, 1816. Aided in the defense of Graham's Fort when it was attacked by the Tories; served with the Lincoln Co. Boys at King's Mt. Mar. 1784, FRANCES RHODES LEWIS (1768-1838).

JOSEPH TURNER, b. Dinwiddie Co., Va., July 27, 1764; moved to Hancock Co., Ga.; d. Putnam Co., after 1807. Served as Maj. in Va. Line. Mar. RHODA HINES.

ISAAC WALKER, SR., b. 1707; d. Jefferson Co., Ga., 1781. Served with Ga. Troops, and was a *Patriot*. Mar. MARY MORGAN. Their son, ISAAC, JR., b. 1730; d. Sumter Co., Ga., 1810. Served as private, Ga. Troops. Mar. IDA WOLF. Their son, Henry I. (1789-1862), mar. Winifred Jackson.

JOEL WALKER, b. Franklin Co., N. C., 1758; d. Ga., 1800. Served in Ga. Militia. Was at the Battle of Guilford C. H.; received bounty land in Warren Co., Ga., for his service. Mar. HOLLY BERRY PERSONS (1765-1846) (dau. of JOSIAH PERSONS, *Rev. Sol.* of N. C., and his wife, Rachel —).

JOHN H. WALKER, b. Prince Edward Co., Va., 1763; d. Ga., 1836. Buried in family cemetery, Monroe, Ga. Enlisted in Loudon Co., Va.; served as private, Va. Regiment, under Capt. John Henry, Col. Alexander's Va. Regiment, then transferred to Capt. Call's Light Infantry. Mar. (1) —; mar. (2) 1797, ELIZABETH JOHNS; mar. (3) 1814, MARIA LEVERETT.

MOSES WATKINS, b. Va., Mar. 1745; d. Oglethorpe Co., Ga., 1814. Served in Va. Continental Line; received bounty land in Ga., Feb. 12, 1784. Mar. Margaret —.

ROBERT WATSON, of Habersham Co., Ga., *Rev. Sol.*, Rev. service certified to Jan. 9, 1837. Witt: by Absolem Holcombe, J. I. C., and John H. Sterrett, J. P. Enlisted Jan. 1781 in Co. A., S. C., under Capt. William Alexander and Col. Wade Hampton, Continental Line. Discharged from service, Orangeburg, S. C. A resident of Ga., Mar. 8, 1818.

WILLIAM WARD, b. Va., 1757; d. Ga., 1850. Served as *Rev. Sol.* Mar. SARAH VERNON. Children (known): Sarah; Vernon; Nancy.

WILLIAM WARTHERN, b. Va., 1761; d. Washington Co., Ga., 1823. Served as private, Va. Line; received bounty land for his service. Mar. (1) Mary Mott, d. 1808; mar. (2) 1810, Rebecca Beckham.

JOHN WATSON, buried in old Family Cemetery, West Baldwin Co., Ga. (Name found in old Land Lottery Book, 1819, Baldwin Co., Ga.) He was a *Rev. Sol.*

JAMES WEST, b. England, 1735; d. Ga., 1800. Served in Va. and Ga. Took Oath of Allegiance in Md. Settled in Nacoochee Valley, Habersham Co., Ga. Mar. ELIZABETH CHADWICK.

WILLIS WALL, b. Va.; d. Wilkes (now Elbert) Co., Ga. A *Rev. Sol.* Mar. MARTHA PAGE.

JOHN WANSLEY, b. Louisa Co., Va., 1738; d. Elbert Co., Ga., 1833; allowed pension as a private, Albemarle Co., Va. Line. Enlisted 1776. Mar. 1761, AMELIA BARBER, b. 1744. They had children (known): Sarah (1766-1800), mar. John Beck; Martha (1781-1868), mar. Benjamin Davis, Jr.

DANIEL WHATLEY, b. Dec. 25, 1744; d. Taylor Co., Ga., Sept. 28, 1857; resided in Orange Co., N. C., 1779. Served as a *Rev. Sol.*, private, Capt. Trousdale's, Col. O'Neal's Regiment. He also served as a *Sol. of 1812.* Moved to Ga. in 1785; to Houston Co. in 1834; to Macon Co. in 1839; applied for pension, 1847, while a resident of Talbot Co., Ga. (Grave marked).

THOMAS WILBURN, b. N. C.; d. Greene Co., Ga.; received bounty land in Ga. for service as private Ga. Troops. Mar. MARTHA —.

EDWARD WHITE, b. Brookline, Mass., 1758; d. Savannah, Ga., 1812. Served as Ensign, Mass. Line 1777; transferred as Lieut. Light Infantry, Yorktown, Va. Mar. (1) 1792, MILDRED SCOTT STUBBS.

RICHARD WHITE, b. Va., 1758; d. Columbia Co., Ga., 1814. Served as Lieut. Convention Guards, Va. Continental Line; then as Capt. Mar. 1782, MARY MERIWETHER (1763-1840).

THOMAS WHITE, b. Dublin, Ireland, April, 1753; d. Wrightsboro, Ga., April, 1844. Served in the Ga. Line as Capt.; commanded a Fort on Upton Creek, Ga.; received bounty grant of land in Ga. for his service. Mar. MARY ANNIE HUNT, b. Dublin, Ireland, Nov. 4, 1758; d. Ga., Sept. 7, 1835. Children (known): Susan, mar. Daniel Massengale, Jr.; Thomas, Jr.; Lucy, mar. Mark A. Candler.

FREDERICK WILLIAMS, b. N. C., 1751; d. Bulloch Co., Ga., 1821. Served as private Ga. Militia under Col. Elijah Clarke. Mar. MISS GOFF.

JOHN WILLIAMSON, b. Ireland; d. Butts Co., Ga., 1831. Served as private Va. Troops. Mar. Margaret (Leslie) Mitchell. Their son, Adam Williamson, mar. 1810, ELIZABETH HORTON, d. 1868 (dau. of PROSSER HORTON, b. 1756; d. Jackson Co., Ga., 1823, and his wife, Sarah —. He served as a private Ga. Line).

EDWARD WILLS, b. England, 1758; d. Clarke Co., Ga., 1820. Enlisted 1777 as private in Capt. Thomas Thweatts Co. 10th Va. Regiment. Mar. SARAH VAUGHN.

JESSE WINFREY, b. Prince Edward Co., Va., 1764; d. Columbia Co., Ga., 1808. Served as private Ga. Line. Mar. 1788, FRANCES SPENCER. One of the daus.: Martha Hughes Winfrey, mar. 1826, William Drane, Jr. (son of WILLIAM DRANE, SR., a *Rev. Sol.*, and his wife, Cassandra Magruder).

JOHN WINN, b. S. C., 1720; d. Liberty Co., Ga., 1781. Member of the *First Provincial Congress* of Ga. His name appears on the famous "Blacklist" sent by the Royal Governor of Ga. to England.

PETER WINN, b. S. C., 1750; d. Liberty Co., Ga. Private Ga. Militia. Mar. (1) 1777, MARY FARLEY.

JAMES WILLIAMS, b. England, 1750; d. Wilkes Co., Ga., 1824; mar. 1788, Elizabeth Blackburn (1752-1812). He was Capt. of 6th Va. Regiment; received bounty land in Ga. Children (known): Thomas Blackburn; James T.; Sarah; Elizabeth.

JAMES WILLIAMS, b. N. C., 1757; d. Bulloch Co., Ga., 1817. Served as private under Gen. Elijah Clarke at Battle of Kettle Creek. Mar. 1777, ELIZABETH CALLAWAY (1759-1815, Bulloch Co.). Their son: Rev. Ezekiel James Williams (1803-1888), mar. Flora McDermid.

JAMES WILLIAMS (1740-1780), *Rev. Sol.* Mar. Mary Wallace. Children: Daniel, Joseph; James; Washington; Sarah; Elizabeth; Mary.

JOSHUA WILLIAMS, *Rev. Sol.* Drew land for his service in Franklin Co., Ga.; on list certified troops. D. Jones Co., Ga.

JOHN WYATT, b. Va., a *Rev. Sol.*; moved to Clarke Co., Ga., 1802, then Butts (formerly Henry) Co., where he d., age 99 years.

JAMES WRIGHT, of 7th Va. Regiment under Col. Dangierfield, granted land in Ga. as a *Rev. Sol.*, Dec. 26, 1793.

MAJOR SAMUEL WRIGHT came from England to Frederica when that town was the military capital of Ga. He was a *Rev. Sol.* of Ga., and his grave has been marked by the D. A. R. in the Colonial Cemetery at Frederica Church, St. Simons Island, Ga.

WILLIAM WRIGHT, b. Va., 1736; d. Wilkes Co., Ga., 1795. Enlisted as private Va. Militia and served until 1781. Mar. Mary Philpot.

JAMES YOUNG, b. S. C.; d. Walker Co., Ga., 1857. Served as private 1776, 6th S. C. Regiment. Mar. ANNA FOSTER.

PETER ZACHARY, b. Va.; d. Columbia Co., Ga., 1791. Served as private Va. Troops. Mar. Mary —. Their dau., Mary, b. 1770, mar. 1790, THOMAS WARD, who served as private in Capt. Dean's Co., 7th Md. Regiment. He was b. Md.; d. Jefferson Co., Ga., 1800.

REVOLUTIONARY SOLDIERS

PART III

Copy of letter written by EDWARD BUTLER, *Rev. Sol.*, to his brother-in-law, JOHN SHACK-ELFORD, *Rev. Sol.*, of Halifax Co., Va.:

(Edward Butler and John Shackelford d. in Ga.)

Hanover, 12th of June, 1783.

DEAR SIR:

This leaves us in tolerable good health at present. Thanks be to God. How long we may continue so, I can not tell, as we have a strange disorder raging in these parts at present. Some say it is not fatal, but only the effects of frenzy and imagination. (But this I know, it is very catching.) The effects of it are as follows (not only men, but women feel the effect of this disorder). They are at first somewhat thoughtful and melancholy, and after some time, appear pretty cheerful. Then appear to be in a frenzy, and after turning around a few times, they stand still with their faces somewhat towards the South, and then you will hear them utter with a loud voice: "GEORGIA." Was this word repeated only for a day or so, and then something else, I would not think much of it, but this is the last you hear at night, and the first in the morning. It is called here the GEORGIA FEVER. Not all the sleep nor dreaming will make them repeat any other word. At our last Court, there appeared to be half the people there with the symptoms on them, but I expect if we have a good crop of corn, etc., this fall, which is promising at present, it will cure some of us. I, myself though laughing at the rest, still find others (I mean the home party) laughing at me. But—enough of this—

Let us turn now to serious matters. MR. WINGFIELD, his son, GARLAND; WILLIAM TERRELL and PETER, have been to GEORGIA this Spring, and have purchased land at 10 and 12 Sterling per acre, in the NEW purchase in the neighborhood of WASHINGTON TOWN, and also for several others of their acquaintance. I would not consent to go with them expecting great bargains would be sold in lands here. To which end I have ever since last winter offered my lands very cheap in comparison to what others ask that intend to move, but it seems now as if I should be caught at it, as I have an offer for my land, and if I sell, I suppose I must go to GEORGIA, too. If I sell my land, I shall go off this fall, pack and package. If I do not, I shall go myself. As Mr. Falkner once said of Caroline and Halifax, we will have HANOVER in GEORGIA. Should be glad to have a line from you by the first opportunity, as I want to know respecting the treaty with the Indians at Georgia, as I expect much depends on that.

If Col. Lewis, of your County, has not made up his complement of families to fill up his grant, and you think it worth-while, get me down on his list. I want a thousand acres of land, if to be had. Let me know by the first opportunity. Also when you intend setting off. I have advertised your land here agreeable to your ticket by Mr. Pate.

I have no more to add, but our love to Sister and children and remain

Your friend, etc.,

EDWARD BUTLER.

"At a Court held at Hanover Co., Va., Nov. 6, 1783, the court being informed of a law passed by the State of Ga., requiring any persons emigrating from other States in the Union to the said State of Ga., before they become citizens of the same to bring with them a certificate from the court of the County where they reside, of their being good citizens and, a friend to the rights and liberties of America.

"EDWARD BUTLER, who informs the said court of his intention of moving himself to the State of Georgia have desired a certificate of the same.

"Therefore, this court do certify that the said EDWARD BUTLER hath been long an inhabitant of the said County of Hanover, Va., and hath conducted himself in every instance as a good and worthy citizen, and uniformly given, undeniable of his attachment to the cause of America, and the Independence thereof."

RICHARD CHAPMAN (*Lt. H. Co.*)
THOMAS TRAVILIAN
WILLIAM JOHNSON

PARK GOODALL,
GEORGE CLOUGH

EDWARD BUTLER, b. Va., Feb. 18, 1748; d. Ga., Dec. 15, 1809. Mar. 1770, Elizabeth Wingfield. A *Rev. Sol.* of Va. Will in Wilkes Co., Ga.

Children:

1. John W., b. Va., Dec. 4, 1775; d. Columbia Co., Ga., Jan. 1867.
2. Nancy Wingfield, b. June 9, 1784.
3. David, b. Nov. 19, 1788; d. Aug. 11, 1822; mar. Jan 18, 1816, Frances W. Shackelford (1791–1827).
4. Kitty G., mar. — Terrell.
5. Frances, mar. — Terrell.
6. Zacariah.
7. Lucy.

JOHN SHACKELFORD, b. Parish Stratton Major, King and Queen Co., Va., 1750; d. Hancock Co., Ga., April 3, 1800. Mar. in Hanover Co., Va., 1775, FRANCES WADE BUTLER, b. Hanover Co., Va., 1755; d. Hancock Co., Ga., Sept. 23, 1811. He served with the Va. Troops as a *Rev. Sol.*; received bounty land in Ga. for his service. (See page 151).

JESSE WOMACK (son of Richard Womack), b. Va., 1739; came to Ga. in 1760, settling in what was afterwards Burke County. He d. Ga., 1815. Mar. (1) Dorothy Prior, b. about 1740; d. Ga., 1777; mar. (2) Phoebe —. He was a *Rev. Sol.* in the Continental Army under Gen. John Twiggs; served as Lieut. in 10th Co. under Capt. Blasingame Harvey, Col. John Thomas; received bounty grant of 287½ acres of land in Washington Co. for his service, Mar. 21, 1787.

Children by (1) wife:

1. Elizabeth.
2. John, b. Dec. 25, 1776; mar. Frances Coleman.

Child by (2) wife:

William, b. May 25, 1779.
(Perhaps other children).

FRANCIS COLEMAN, b. Va., Aug. 16, 1744; d. Washington Co., Ala., Aug. 13, 1825. Mar. about 1767, Margaret —, b. Dec. 29, 1750; d. April 19, 1804. He moved to Ga. about 1760. Served as a *Rev. Sol.* under Col. Elijah Clarke; given 250 acres of land as a bounty for his service, as per certificate of Elijah Clarke, Col.

Children:

1. Isaac, b. Sept. 25, 1768.
2. William, b. May 13, 1770, mar. Nancy (Dean) Lawrence, widow. Lived in Perry Co., Ala. 10 children.
3. Francis, b. June 8, 1772.
4. Margaret, mar. Robert Tillman. Lived in Ala.
5. John, b. Jan. 3, 1776.
6. Frances, b. Feb. 14, 1781, mar. John Womack, b. Dec. 25, 1776 (son of JESSE WOMACK, a *Rev. Sol.* of Ga., and his wife, Dorothy Prior).
7. Benjamin, b. April 29, 1778; d. Dec. 24, 1816.
8. Abner, b. 1783; d. 1789.
9. Elius, b. 1784; d. 1786.
10. Vashti, b. Dec. 19, 1786, mar. (1) John Williamson; mar. (2) Matthew Shaw.
11. Robert, b. 1789; d. 1789.
12. Daniel, b. Sept. 5, 1792, mar. Sarah H. —.

NOTE: The compiler wishes to acknowledge her indebtedness in this public way, to Dr. Jean Stephenson, National Chairman of Genealogical Research, N. S. D. A. R., and Mrs. Lue Reynolds Spencer, Genealogical Editor, N. S. D. A. R.

WILLIAMSON BIRD, b. Va., 1728; d. Wilkes Co., Ga., 1802. Mar. 1750, Phoebe Price. Served as Capt. of Militia of Prince Edward Co., Va. Moved to Wilkes Co., Ga.; received bounty land for his service.

Children (not in order of birth):

1. Price.
2. Dyce.
3. Williamson.

4. John.

5. Philemon, mar. Mary —.

6. Fanny, mar. Daniel Price.

7. Elizabeth (Betsey), mar. —Woodall.

8. Caty, mar. — Switcher.

9. Tabitha.

WILLIAM BLAIR, *Rev. Sol.* (son of James Blair, the immigrant, who came to Ga. about 1770 from Northern Ireland, and settled at Queensborough—now the site of Louisville, Ga., known as "Irish Town"; d. prior to end of Rev. War, for his grant of land for Rev. service went to "heirs of WILLIAM BLAYER Feb. 10, 1784" (Blair). He was mar. Oct. 26, 1771 at Jerusalem Church, Ebenezer, Effingham Co., Ga. to SIBBIAH EARL (dau. of John Earl, who came to Ga. from N. C. in 1760). They lived in Screven Co., Ga.

Children:

1. Jane, d. after 1838; mar. ROBERT STAFFORD, *Rev. Sol.*, d. 1829.

2. William, d. 1840, Brooks Co., Ga.; mar. Mary Joyce. (His record in House of Representatives, Senate from Lowndes Co., Ga. and J. I. C. for Society of the *War of 1812*.)

3. Henry, Clerk of Court, etc. Lowndes Co.

4. Mary.

5. Martha.

NOTE: Names of some of the "LIBERTY BOYS" of St. George's Parish, Ga., viz: William Blair; Thomas Burton; Thomas Chaser; John Conyers; John Green; John Gasper Greiner; James Herbert; Thomas Howell; Joseph Humphreys; Thomas Lewis; Abraham Lundy; Thomas Owens; Thomas Simmons; John Williams.

BENJAMIN BUCHANAN, b. Newberry District, S. C., 1754; d. Jasper Co., Ga., 1821. Served as private and Corporal S. C. Troops, Continental Line. Mar. Mary Wood.

JOHN BUCHANAN, b. Va., 1736; d. Greene Co., Ga., 1801. Served as private Ga. Troops. Mar. 1760, Ann —; had issue.

Child:

JOSEPH BUCHANAN, b. 1761; d. Ga., 1811; served as private Ga. Troops. Mar. 1784, Mary —.

CHARLES BRAWNER applied for bounty land, certificate of Lieut. Col. James Jackson, July 30, 1784 that he served in the Ga. State Legion Infantry, from the reduction of Augusta to the evacuation of the State by the British forces. Prays for 287½ acres of land in Washington Co., which was granted.

WILLIAM CHEEK, b. Randolph Co., N. C., 1752; d. Franklin Co., Ga., 1845; received pension 1832 in Ga. for service as private S. C. Regiment under Col. JOHN HUNTER. Mar. (2) Cinthia Coker (1755-1860).

JOHN CLEMENTS, b. Mecklenburg Co., N. C., 1763; d. Houston Co., Ga., 1807. Served as *Rev. Sol.* Mar. Mary Erwin.

JAMES CODY, b. Ireland, prior to 1750; came to Va. Mar. Sarah Womack. Lived in Halifax Co., Va. Served as *Rev. Sol.* of Va.; came to Ga. 1792. He and his wife d. Warren Co., Ga., 1795.

Children:

1. Mary, mar. George Lumpkin, and had issue: John, b. 1763, mar. Lucy Hopson; (they came to Ga. 1784;) George; Robert; Mary.

2. Aisle.

3. Jacob.

4. Edmund, b. Halifax Co., N. C., 1754; d. Warren Co., Ga., 1832. Mar. Catherine Donelson (1758-1814).

5. John.

6. Jesse.

7. Richard.

8. Michael, b. Halifax Co., N. C., 1768; d. Warren Co., Ga., 1832. Mar. (1) Mary Hodo (dau. of Peter and Susanna Hodo); Mar. (2) Rebecca Rogers (dau. of REUBEN ROGERS, *Rev. Sol.* of Ga.)

9. David.

GEORGE CLIFTON, b. 1761; d. Clarke Co., Ga., 1840. Applied for pension as a *Rev. Sol.*, which was allowed. Enlisted, 1777, with Del. Troops, under Capt. Daggett, Col. Vaughn's Regiment. Mar. (1) ELIZABETH DICKERSON; mar. (2) Milly —. Will signed Jan. 7, 1831, Pro. 1847.

Children by (1) wife:
1. Elizabeth.
2. Isaiah.
3. Elijah.
4. Mary.
5. Thomas.
6. Coke.
7. Nancy.
8. Caroline.

Child by (2) wife:
Hiram. (Perhaps other children).

From *GA. GAZETTE*, June 15, 1786: *Rev. Sols.:* A. D. CUTHBERT, JOHN BRADDOCK, J. O. DAY, J. HARDY, ARTHUR HAYES, GEORGE MELVIN, JOHN MYERS, SR., JOHN MYERS, JR., THOMAS MYERS, WILLIAM MYERS.

NOTE: LUKE MANN—Certificate of Col. John Baker, Col., Mar. 18, 1784—Files power of attorney to draw bounties for ABRAHAM LAND, ANDREW WALTHOUR, LABAN THOMPSON, JOSEPH PLUMER, JOSIAH NAYLOR, WILLIAM SAPP, JOHN SAPP, ELIGER SAPP, EMANUEL SAPP; ANDREW DICK, all *Rev. Sols.*

PETER COFFEE, *Rev. Sol.* of Ga., mar. Sarah Smith. Had issue.

One son, John, b. 1782; d. 1836, mar. 1809, Penelope Bryan (1784–1865) (dau. of John Hill Bryan (1761–1826, Thomas Co., Ga., and his wife, Elizabeth Harrison; g.-dau. of JOHN BRYAN, *Rev. Sol.* of N. C., and his wife, Rebecca Martin).

THOMAS COLE, b. R. I., 1758; d. Savannah, Ga. Served as private in Capt. Thomas Allen's R. I. Co. Mar. 1781, Anna Vose.

THOMAS CONNER, JR. (son of Thomas Conner, Sr., b. 1678; d. 1768), b. Md., 1726; d. Ga., Sept. 12, 1802. Mar. about 1751, Margaret —. Served as private, Capt. Nathaniel Ewing's 1st Md. Regiment, 1776.

Children:
1. Elizabeth, mar. Ananias Lang, d. 1807.
2. James, b. 1755.
3. Lewis.
4. Ann.
5. William.
6. WILSON.
(Perhaps other children).

WILSON CONNER, b. Md., July 7, 1768; d. Montgomery Co., Ga. Buried in Dead river Cemetery (grave marked by D. A. R.). Served as a *Rev. Sol.*; in the *War of 1812*, and in the *Fla. Indian War*. Mar. in Tattnall Co., Ga., Oct. 8, 1789, Mary Cook, b. Aug. 1, 1774.

Children:
1. Martha, mar. Jesse Hall.
2. Louisa, mar. John Wilcox.
3. Wilson, Jr.
4. Eliza, mar. William Rials (or Ryals).
5. James G., b. 1790, mar. 1818, Penelope Rials.
6. Nancy, b. 1792, mar. 1810, George Cooper.
7. Harriet Elizabeth, b. 1793, mar. John Griffin.
8. Thomas Benton, mar. Sarah Wall.
9. Lucy Ann, mar. Joseph Ryals.
10. Mary Jane, mar. 1824, Thomas G. Sullivant.
11. Maria, mar. John Ryals.
12. Elizabeth.

JOHN COOPER, b. Frederick Co., Va., 1742; d. Wilkes Co., Ga., 1835. Served as private, Henry Co. Militia, 1777; received bounty land. Mar. 1778, Elizabeth Wilson.

JOHN DANIEL, b. 1757; d. Washington Co., Ga., 1788. Served as private, Ga. Troops; received bounty land for his service. Mar. 1787, Mary Mason.

CHRISTIAN DASHER, served as private, Ga. Troops, under Col. Jenkins Davis. D. in service. Mar. Anna Christiana Moyer.

JOSEPH DAVIDSON, b. Scotland, 1750; d. Wilkinson Co., Ga., 1846. Served as private, Ga. Troops, under Col. Elijah Clarke; received bounty land. Mar. Fanny Winifred May. Had issue.

One son, Joseph, Jr., b. 1777, buried Monroe Co., Ga., mar. April 6, 1818, Mary Ingram (dau. of John and Mary Ingram).

JEREMIAH DUCKWORTH, *Rev. Sol.* of Ga.; mar. Christian —. She drew land in 1827 Lottery as widow of a *Rev. Sol.*, while a resident of Jones Co., Ga.

JOHN BURKHALTER (son of Michael and Martha (Newsome) Burkhalter), joined the Rev. Army, when his father, a *Rev. Sol.*, was brought home wounded. He mar. May 29, 1792, Sarah (Hardin) Loyless (dau. of HENRY HARDIN, *Rev. Sol.*, and his wife, Judith Lynch). She was widow of James Loyless, b. 1763.

Children:
1. Harriet, b. 1793, mar. Moses McKinney.
2. Redan.
3. Samuel.
4. Martin H.
5. Averilla, mar. Kitchen McKinney.
6. David Newsome, b. 1803, mar. Ann Eliza Short.

JOHN BURNETT, b. N. C.; came to Bulloch Co., Ga.; d. Ga., 1827; *Rev. Sol.* of N. C.; received land in Ga. Mar. Molsey —. She drew land as widow of *Rev. Sol.*, 1838, while a resident of Lowndes Co., Ga., d. Clinch Co., Ga., 1860. They had issue.

One dau., Nancy Burnett, b. 1808, mar. David Johnson, b. 1802 (son of David and Martha Johnson, of Tattnall Co., Ga.).

JOHN BURNETT, of Glynn Co., was a *Rev. Sol.* of Ga., and served in the N. C. Troops. He came to Ga. and was in charge of troops against the Indians, the allies at that time of the British in this section of Ga. In 1788 the Creek Indians again became hostile. John Burnett, in charge of the troops, was wounded and his son, John, Jr., was placed in charge. The inhabitants of Glynn Co., on the then frontier, fled to Sea Island for protection as the Indians burned homes in this section. John Burnett was appointed Lieut.-Col. of the 25th Co., 7th Brigade, Nov. 1793.

WILLIAM CATO, b. Halifax Co., N. C., 1750; d. Greene Co., Ga., 1800. Served as private, *Rev. War.* Mar. 1775, Amanda —.

NATHANIEL DURKEE, b. New Milford, Conn., 1757; d. Franklin Co., Ga., 1823.; received a pension for service as quartermaster under Col. Herman Swift, Conn. and Continental Line. Mar. (2) 1791, Catherine McRea (1760-1820). (See page 193.)

JAMES GILMORE, b. Cumberland Co., N. C., 1755; d. Washington Co., Ga., Jan. 3, 1835; received a pension for his service as a private, corporal, and sergt., N. C. Troops, under Capts. Gilmore and Welch. Mar. 1779, Mary Hughes, of Wilkes Co., Ga. (1764-1850).

EDWARD HARDEN, b. S. C., Aug. 11, 1757; d. Savannah, Ga., 1802. Served as Major, S. C. Troops. Assisted his brother, WILLIAM HARDEN, in the capture of Fort Balfour, S. C. Settled in Savannah, Ga. Mar. Jane Reid.

Children:
1. Edward, mar. Mary Ann Randolph.
2. Robert Raymond, mar. Marie Antoinette Claudine Rosa Gouvaine (who came to Athens, Ga., from Paris, France).
3. Jane, d. y.

ABIMELECK HAWKINS, served as a *Rev. Sol.* and was granted 287½ acres of land in Franklin Co., Ga., on the Oconee river.

WILLIAM HAWTHORNE (son of JOHN HAWTHORNE, *Rev. Sol.* of Roberson Co., N. C., who came to Ga., 1820), b. N. C., 1762; d. Ga., May 15, 1846. He served in N. C. Troops; drew land as a *Rev. Sol.* in the 1827 Ga. Lottery. Lived in Pulaski and Decatur Cos., Ga. Mar. Meleachy Cliburn.

Children (known):
1. Jonathan, mar. Nancy Harrison.
2. Elias Owen, mar. Thelma Lee.
3. Timothy, mar. Martha Kelly.
4. William Bryant, mar. Elizabeth Jones.
5. Patsie, mar. Robert Jones.

JORDAN HOLCOMBE, b. Bute Co., N. C., Nov. 19, 1762. Moved, 1776, to Spartanburg, S. C. (His father was killed in an engagement with the Tories during the *Rev. War.*) He served as private in Capt. John Lawson's Co., Col. Thomas' S. C. Regiment; discharged 1781. Served also in Capt. Jeremiah Dixon's Co., Col. Roebuck's S. C. Regiment; allowed pension 1836. D. Hall Co., Ga. (One dau. and one son living with him, 1836, Hall Co., Ga.)

JOHN HUBBARD, b. Va., 1763; d. Ga., 1831; received bounty land for his service as private, Ga. Troops. Mar. Elizabeth Flint in 1785.

MATTHEW GALLAWAY (GALLOWAY), b. Dec. 15, 1759; d. Oglethorpe Co., Ga., Feb. 14, 1824.; drew bounty land as a *Rev. Sol.* in 1806 Lottery in Oglethorpe Co., Ga. Mar. (1) — Beaver; mar. (2) Mary (called Polly) East.

Children by (1) wife:
1. William, b. 1782, mar. 1805, Polly Ragan.
2. Levi.

Children by (2) wife:
1. Wiley, b. Sept. 9, 1791.
2. Anderson, b. 1793.
3. Brittain, b. Dec. 12, 1795.
4. James, b. 1797.
5. Thomas, b. 1801.
6. Sarah, b. 1805.
7. Nathan Johnson, b. Oct. 26, 1807.

(His widow moved to Ala. with her children. Returned to Ga., 1847. At the age of 81 years, she mar. Elder Hutchinson, a Baptist minister. She was buried in the Lester burying ground, Walton Co., Ga.)

ABSOLEM JACKSON (son of Walter Jackson), b. Va.; lived in Wilkes Co., Ga.; d. Miller's Bluff, St. Mary's, Ga. Served as *Rev. Sol.*, private in Ga. Troops; received bounty grant of land for his service. Mar. 1782, Phereba Webster, b. Nov. 6, 1763; d. Miller's Bluff, Point Peter, Ga., Feb. 12, 1839. She mar. (2) Peter Bryson.

Children:
1. William, b. 1786, mar. Ann Eliza Fox.
2. Mary Scott, b. 1783; d. 1855; mar. Thomas Harvey Miller.
3. Harriet Ann (1788–1865), mar. Lieut. Samuel Elbert, U. S. N. (son of Samuel Elbert, *Rev. Sol.* of Ga.).
4. Francis W.

WALTER JACKSON, b. Va.; came to Wrightsboro, Ga., 1768; d. Wilkes Co., Ga., 1816. Mar. Mary Chauncey Clark. She d. Antauga Co., Ala., 1832, age 93. He was a *Rev. Sol.*, private in Ga. Troops; received bounty land for his service.

Children:
1. ABSOLEM, a *Rev. Sol.*
2. Sarah.
3. Robert.

4. James, mar. Temperance Motley.

5. William.

6. Jeremiah.

NOTE: WILLIAM WEBSTER was a *Rev. Sol.* of Ga.; killed by the Tories in Wilkes Co., Ga.; mar. Elizabeth Bostic. BENJAMIN WEBSTER, *Rev. Sol.* of Ga., was killed at the Siege of Augusta, Ga. Both were sons of Jonathan Webster and his wife, Caledonia Johnson, of Wilkes Co., Ga.

ROBERT MORROW, b. Va.; came to Ga., 1785; *Rev. Sol.* of Va.; received bounty land for his service. Mar. in Va., Nancy Herley. Had issue.

One son, William H., b. Morgan Co., Ga., 1788; mar. in Jasper Co., Ga., Nancy Elliott (dau. of George and Mary (Cloud) Elliott), b. 1790.

NOTE: DAVID MURRAY, b. Prince Edward Co., Va., 1760; d. Ala., Nov. 8, 1840. Served as *Rev. Sol.* of Va. Moved to Ga., and Murray Co., Ga., is named for him.

JAMES McCORMICK, b. N. J., 1740; d. Baldwin Co., Ga., 1814. Served as a *Rev. Sol.* of N. J. Mar. Mary Ann Fletcher, b. S. C., 1759.

Their dau., Patty, mar. Samuel Neal.

WILLIAM McINTOSH, b. 1726; d. Ga., 1796; Lieut. in 1st Batt. of Troops raised in Ga., later Col. in Continental Army. Mar. Janie Mackey.

Children:

1. John.

2. William.

3. Lachlan, mar. his cousin, Anne Baillie.

4. Marjorie, mar. James Spalding.

5. Barbara, mar. her cousin, William McIntosh.

6. Helen, mar. Alexander Baillie.

LACHLAN McINTOSH, Col., 1st Reg., Ga. Batt., 1775; later Major-Gen., Continental Army. After his duel with Button Gwinnett, he was transferred from Ga. and put in command, as Major-Gen., Continental Troops, by Gen. George Washington. He d. 1806, at 79 years of age.

JOHN McINTOSH (son of William), b. (now McIntosh Co., Ga.), 1755; d. there, 1826. Served as Capt. and Lieut.-Col., Ga. Troops. Taken prisoner at Briar Creek, Ga.; was Brig.-Gen. in the *War of 1812.*

NOTE: LIBERTY POLE—The first "Liberty Pole" in Ga., was erected on June 4, 1775, the anniversary of the birth of King George, III, of England, who was b. June 4, 1738. It stood in front of Tondee's Tavern in Savannah, Ga., and became a rallying point for friends of Independence. After it was raised, two toasts were given—one to the King and one to "American Liberty." On June 22, 1775, upon the occasion of the appointment of the Council of Safety, the Union flag was hoisted upon the Pole and 13 patriotic toasts were drunk, one to each of the 13 Colonies, and each was followed by a salute from two pieces of artillery and martial music.

WILLIAM OAKMAN, of Savannah, Ga., served in the 2nd Ga. Regiment under Lieut. Francis Tennille, in 1775. Mar. Mary Lilybridge. They had twin sons, b. Savannah, Ga., Oct. 12, 1792.

Children:

1. William Henry, d. 1860, mar. 1820, Eliza Ann Hagood, b. near Barnwell, S. C., 1800. They had 15 children.

2. Henry William, mar. Frances Jennings. They had 2 children.

THOMAS NEWELL, b. Va., June 8, 1746; d. Ga., Oct. 15, 1792. Served as a *Rev. Sol.* under Col. Elijah Clarke, in Ga. Mar. Catherine Swann.

Children (known):

1. William.

2. Mary Virginia, mar. James McConnell.

3. Lucinda, mar. — Sharpe.

CADER POWELL, b. 1752; d. Ga., 1835. Served as a *Rev. Sol.* in Ga. Campaign under Gen. Nathaniel Greene; received bounty land. Mar. Frances Foote (1750-1846).

Children:

1. Jacob, b. 1773.

    2. Frances, b. 1774, mar. Edward Knight.
    3. Henry, b. 1778.
    4. Isaac, b. 1780.
    5. Allen (1783–1835), mar. Mary Johnson (1786–1831).
    6. Theophilus.
    7. Annie.
    8. George.
    9. Mary.

NOTE: From 1830 Census, LIBERTY CO., Ga.: *Rev. Sols.*, viz: ROBERT HENDRY; LEVY MORGAN; JAMES SCOTT; DAVID DELK; WILLIAM H. PARKER; JOHN BENTON; ABRAHAM DANIEL.

JOHN PITTS, b. N. C.; d. Effingham Co., Ga. Commanded a Co. of N. C. Inf., 1780. Mar. Frances Griffin.

HENRY RAWLINGS, b. Va.; d. Hancock Co., Ga., 1807. Served as Capt. in Va. Militia, under Col. Bowman. Mar. 1769, Sarah Allen.

RICHARDSON ROUNTREE, b. 1751; d. Ga., 1819. Served as a *Rev. Sol.* Mar. 1777, Mildred Hart.

Children:
    1. Maria.
    2. James.
    3. Martha, mar. Cary Cox, Jr.
    4. Isabella, mar. William Stephens, Jr.
    5. Mildred, mar. — Goldsmith.
    6. William.
    7. Daniel, mar. Fannie Nelson.
    8. Thomas, mar. — Nesbit.

SHADRACK ROWE, b. 1762; d. Harris Co., Ga., Sept. 1853. Served as private in *Rev. War.* Mar. Mary Bynum.

JAMES SMITH was a *Sol.* in the Continental Line of N. C. Was at the Battle of Cowpens and other engagements. Removed to Lincoln Co., Ga., where he d. Mar. Elizabeth Cowan, who d. in Cobb Co., Ga., at more than 100 years of age.

Children (known):
    1. Ebenezer, mar. Cynthia Lewis.
    2. Dau., mar. Jesse Oslin.
    3. Dau., mar. Rev. William Collins.

JOHN SMITH, b. England; d. Washington Co., Ga. Served as Lieut., Va. Militia, under Col. Thomas Walker. Mar. Elizabeth Taylor.

LAZARUS SOLOMON, b. Washington Co., N. C., 1765; d. Jeffersonville, Ga., 1837. Enlisted, 1781, in 9th N. C. Regiment. Mar. Elizabeth Bedgood.

Children:
    1. Delilah (1789–1815).
    2. Henry, b. 1791, mar. Lucinda Griffin.
    3. William, b. 1792.
    4. Mary, b. 1795.
    5. John, b. 1797.
    6. Dicey, b. 1799.
    7. James, b. 1800.
    8. Sarah, b. 1802.
    9. Fannie, b. 1804.
    10. Peter, b. 1806.
    11. Hardy, b. 1808.
    12. Carol, b. 1810.
    13. Lewis, b. 1812.
    14. Elizabeth, b. 1814.

JOHN SPARKS, b. N. C., Feb. 27, 1755; d. Ga., 1834. *Rev. Sol.* Mar. Jan. 13, 1779, Margaret Hampton, b. S. C., Oct. 14, 1757.
Children:
1. Sarah Ann, b. Dec. 5, 1779.
2. Mary.
3. Rachel, b. 1784, mar. Enoch Gray.
4. Benjamin, b. 1786, mar. Sarah May.
5. Isabel.
6. Stephen.
7. Margaret.
8. George H.
9. John.
10. Thomas, b. 1799, mar. Ann McNeal Collins.
11. Elizabeth, mar. David Curry.

JOHN SPEARMAN, b. Caroline Co., Va., 1764; d. Jasper Co., Ga., 1827. Served as private, Ga. Troops; received bounty land. Mar. 1787, Mary Witherspoon.

JOHN THOMAS, b. Va., 1746; d. Hancock Co., Ga., 1807. Served as a *Rev. Sol.* in Burke Co., Ga., Militia. Mar. (1) 1770, Martha Grigsley, b. 1751.

CHARNEL HIGHTOWER THORN, b. Buncombe Co., N. C.; d. Gwinnett Co., Ga. Buried near Lawrenceville, Ga. Served as a *Rev. Sol.* in the Brig. of Light Horse Harry Lee. Mar. —.
Their dau, Ann, b. Edgefield Co., S. C., Jan. 1804; d. April 20, 1858; mar. William Sanders Howard (1793–1885) (son of John Howard, *Rev. Sol.* of S. C., b. Granville Co., N. C., Aug. 23, 1756; d. 1832, and his wife, Margaret Fudge, d. 1834). A *Sol. of the War of 1812.*

PURNAL TRUITT, b. Feb. 26, 1757; d. Wilkes Co., Ga., 1841. He served as private in Del. Regiment. In 1827 drew land in Lottery, as a *Rev. Sol.* Mar. (1) Polly Godfrey, b. N. J., 1758; d. 1810; mar. (2) Nancy Render (dau. of Joshua Render, Sr., and wife, Susanna, of Wilkes Co., Ga.).
Children:
1. Sarah, b. 1784.
2. Nancy, b. 1786.
3. Riley, b. Wilkes Co., Ga., 1788; d. Jasper Co., Ga.; mar. 1813, Bonetta Smith (1793–1844).
4. Nathan, b. 1792.
5. Purnal, Jr., b. 1795.
6. John, b. 1798.

JAMES TURNER, b. Orange Co., Va., 1752; d. Franklin Co., Ga., 1804. Served as private, Ga. Troops, under Capts. Davis and Burroughs. Mar. 1772, Martha Seals (1754–1812).

MATTHEW VARNER, b. Md., 1765; d. Oglethorpe Co., Ga. Served as private in Col. Wade's N. C. Regiment. Mar. 1787, Susanna Henley.

THOMAS WAGNON, b. Va., 1727; d. Ga., 1810. Served as private, Ga. Line. Mar. 1748, Frances Vaughn (1730–1805).

DANIEL WALKER, b. Augusta, Ga., 1764; d. Ga., Mar. 13, 1839. Mar. in Newberry Dist., S. C., Hannah Richardson, b. July 1791; d. at the home of her son, Daniel, Jr., in Richmond Co., Ga., Aug. 11, 1854. He served as private in Capt. James Cartledge's Co., and Col. Few, Ga. Troops; later he was promoted to Col.; moved to S. C., then returned to Richmond Co., Ga., where he drew a pension Nov. 13, 1833. His wife drew a pension for his service, Feb. 22, 1845.

JOHN WALKER (son of George Walker and his wife, Mary Duchart, mar. 1756 and settled on Briar Creek, now Burke Co., Ga.), b. Sept. 5, 1760(in now Burke Co.); d. Morgan Co., Ga., Dec. 7, 1836. Served as *Rev. Sol.* in Ga. Troops. Mar. 1810, Frances Byne (1767–1831).
Children:
1. Isaac.
2. Edmund, mar. (1) Susan Smith; mar. (2) Mary Gautier Corley.
3. John.
4. Eliza, mar. — Dawson.

JOHN WATSON, b. S. C., 1753; d. Franklin Co., Ga., 1848. Served as private in Capt. William Butler's S. C. Regiment. Mar. Charity Hillen (1752–1850).

SAMUEL WHATLEY, b. N. C., 1755; d. Wilkes Co., Ga., 1820. Served as private, Ga. Troops, under Col. Elijah Clarke; widow received pension for his service. Mar. Catherine Anglin (1762–1857).

JOHN WILLIAMS, b. Va. —; d. Ga. Served as a Rev. Sol. Mar. 1767, Frances (Bustin) Slatter.

Their dau., Sallie, b. Halifax Co., Va., 1774; d. Russel Co., Ala., 1861; mar. 1796, Thomas Turner Persons, d. Warren Co., Ga., Oct. 11, 1827. They had 15 children.

JOHN WISE, b. Accomac Co., Va., 1733; d. Oglethorpe Co., Ga., 1800. Served as Corp., 9th Va. Regiment of Inf. Mar. 1755, Anne Smith (1735–1799). Had issue.

One son, Patton (1765–1828), mar. 1787, Sarah Johnson.

JOHN SEAY, b. 1758; d. Ga. Served as a Rev. Sol. in the Ga. Troops, under Gen. Micajah Williamson. Mar. Miss West.

Their son, John Seay, Jr., b. Aug. 26, 1790; d. Gordon Co., Ga., Aug. 6, 1862; mar. Jan. 11, 1816, Sarah Wilson (1791–1863) (dau. of JAMES WILSON; a Rev. Sol. of Greene Co., Ga., and his wife, Phoebe White).

JAMES BLAIR, b. Va., 1761; d. Habersham Co., Ga., 1839. Served as a Rev. Sol., private under Col. McDowell, N. C., and was at King's Mt. Mar. Elizabeth Powell.

Their dau., Annie (1792–1834), mar. Joseph Terrell.

THOMAS CHISHOLM, Rev. Sol., Capt. and Lieut.-Col. Member of the Supreme Executive Council of Ga.

JOSEPH CLAY, Rev. Sol. Member Provincial Congress, Ga.; Quartermaster General and Paymaster General; Delegate to Continental Congress.

SETH JOHN CUTHBERT, Rev. Sol., Capt. and Major. Member of the Council of Safety of Ga.; also member of Provincial Congress.

MAJOR BERNARD ROMAN (DeLISLE), commanded a Regiment of Penn. Artillery from Feb. 8, 1776 to Nov. 28, 1779. Afterwards served in the Ga. Continental Line.

GRAY ELLIOT, a Son of Liberty, elected by the Ga. Assembly as an assistant to Dr. Franklin to plead the cause of the Colonies in England.

BENJAMIN FISHBOURNE, Rev. Sol., Capt. and Major. Commanded, in 1779, the Fourth Regiment, Penn. Continental Line. Removed to Savannah, Ga., 1780. Was a member of the Ga. Society of the Cincinnati.

JOHN BOHUN GIRADEAU, Rev. Sol. Member of the Provincial Congress of Ga., and Commissary General of Issues.

ANDREW BURNS, b. Scotland, 1718; came with parents to Ga., 1735; d. Ga., 1793. Mar. 1740, Mary Johnson, d. 1793. Member Richmond Co., Ga., Militia. Member First Provincial Congress of Ga.

JACOB COLSON of the Province of Ga., 1773, was a Rev. Sol., Capt. of Ga. Batt. April 28, 1776. Made will, Wilkes Co., Ga., Nov. 5, 1777, probated Feb. 5, 1778. (From will): "I leave all estate 'rale' and personal to be divided between my son Abraham and my daughter Nancy, lawful heirs by my beloved wives SARAH and MILBY COLSON, except $500.00 to Milby the day of her marriage, she to be provided for during her widowhood. Two children to be thoroughly educated in the English tongue." Trusty friends, GEORGE TURENAN, a Rev. Sol., EVAN RAGLAND, a Rev. Sol., and JOHN COLEMAN, a Rev. Sol., all of Wilkes Co., Ga., Excrs. MILLY COLSON, widow, mar. as (2) wife, JEREMIAH WALKER, d. Elbert Co., Oct. 1792. He was a J. P., Wilkes Co., 1788. (War of 1812 record).

In his will (made Sept. 14, 1792), JEREMIAH WALKER mentions wife, Milly; dau., Polly, mar. — Coleman; sons, Henry Graves, Memorable; Jeremiah; James Sanders; John Williams; dau., Elizabeth, mar. — Marshall; and brother, Sanders Walker.

JOHN COMBS, SR., d. Wilkes Co., Ga.; received bounty land, 1784, for his service as a *Rev. Sol.*, on certificate of Col. Elijah Clarke. Drew land also in 1819 Land Lottery. Sold land in 1791 on Rocky Creek, Wilkes Co., adjoining lands of JOHN CARTER, *Rev. Sol.*, GABRIEL JONES, *Rev. Sol.*, who mar. Elizabeth Russell (dau. of John Russell), and DANIEL TERONDET, a *Rev. Sol.*, who drew 575 acres bounty land, 1785, in Franklin Co., Ga. Mar. Milly Russell (dau. of John Russell). They had issue.

One son, John, Jr., was a *Sol. of the War of 1812.*

PHILIP COMBS, SR. Estate administered Mar. 24, 1838, Wilkes Co., Ga. He was a *Rev. Sol.*; received bounty grant of land 1784, and drew in the Land Lottery of 1819. The legatees of his estate were his sons.

Children:

    1. Philip, Jr.

    2. James, d. before 1838; mar. Mildred.

    3. Nancy, mar. William Hammack (or Hammock). They had children: William, Nancy, and Jane.

    4. Dau., mar. James Woodroofs.

    5. Pamelia.

    6. Jane.

    7. Mary Ann.

    8. Martha, mar. Daniel C. Jackson.

    (Perhaps other children.)

    NOTE: DANIEL TERONDET, a *Rev. Sol.*, received 575 acres of bounty land for his service, 1785. D. June 1795. Mar. (1) Nancy —; mar. (2) Sarah —. One son, James Carter Terondet. (From will "that my son be given instruction in English, French, Latin, and mathematics.")

JOHN CLEVELAND (son of Col. Benjamin Cleveland, *Rev. Sol.* of N. C. and S. C., and his wife, Mary Graves), b. N. C.; d. Tugalo District, Franklin Co., 1803. A *Rev. Sol.*; drew land of Capt. Walter's Dist., Franklin Co., Ga., in the 1825 Lottery. Mar. in N. C., Catherine Montgomery Sloan. Moved to Ga.

Children:

    1. Benjamin, mar. Arglin Jones.

    2. Nancy, mar. Chapley Ross Welborn of Wilkinson Co. (son of William and Mary Welborn). (Perhaps other children).

LITTLETON JOHNSTON (son of Larkin and Mary (Rogers) Johnston of Va.), b. Va., Feb. 18, 1761; d. Jasper Co., Ga., July 7, 1842. Buried at (Cross Roads) graveyard, Jasper Co. He served in the Va. army, and drew land in 1827 Lottery of Ga., in Jasper Co., as a *Rev. Sol.* Mar. (1) Jan. 4, 1781, LUCY CHILDS, b. Jan. 30, 1756; d. Jasper Co., Ga., June 9, 1826. Mar. (2) Sarah Dirbin, widow, Feb. 12, 1828.

Children by (1) wife:

    1. John Chew, b. N. C., Mar. 17, 1782; d. 1792.

    2. Larkin, b. N. C., Sept. 13, 1783; d. Monroe Co., Ga., May 12, 1834; mar. Sally Underwood.

    3. Elizabeth, b. N. C., April 26, 1785, mar. Wiley Thornton.

    4. William, b. Mar. 19, 1787, mar. Nov. 17, 1805, Sarah Grizel.

    5. Thomas, b. Feb. 5, 1789; d. Jasper Co., Ga., Sept. 17, 1848; mar. 1816, Margaret (Peggy) Gaines.

    6. Nathan, b. June 27, 1790; d. Jasper Co., Ga., Aug. 10, 1843; mar. 1812, Biddy Thornton.

    7. Franky, b. N. C., Mar. 18, 1792; d. Jasper Co., Ga., 1871; mar. June 2, 1808, Joseph Henderson.

    8. John, b. N. C., Oct. 14, 1793; d. Jasper Co., Ga., July 1844.

    9. James, b. N. C., Dec. 13, 1795; d. Dec. 1, 1863; mar. 1816, Jane Gaines.

    10. Lucy, b. Elbert Co., Ga., 1800; d. 1801.

    11. Richard, b. Elbert Co., Ga., Dec. 16, 1802; d. Jasper Co., Ga., Feb. 1859.

    (Mary Rogers, wife of Larkin Johnston, had brother, Henry Rogers, of Granville Co., N. C.)

JOHN MAXWELL (son of Thomas Maxwell and his wife, Mary Pemberton), b. Va., May 9, 1763; lived in Elbert Co., Ga.; d. Milton Co., Ga., Oct. 5, 1840. Mar. Feb. 6, 1792, AGATHA HENRY, d. Ala. Was a *Rev. Sol.*, and drew land in 1827 Lottery in Ga.; a member of Major Dobbs'

Batt., Capt. Horton's Dist., Elbert Co. Buried in Maxwell's Cemetery, S. W. of Alpharetta, Milton (now Fulton) Co., Ga. Grave marked by the Ga. D. A. R.

Children:

1. Simeon, b. June 24, 1793; d. Ala.; mar. Dec. 9, 1819, Elizabeth Fortson.
2. Reuben, b. Nov. 4, 1795; d. Ala.; mar. Dec. 13, 1821, Elizabeth Thornton.
3. Nancy, b. Nov. 9, 1797; d. 1880; mar. Arthur T. Camp.
4. Benson, b. Dec. 11, 1799; d. Talbot Co., Ga.; mar. July 25, 1826, Eliz. B. Johnston.
5. Clara, b. Oct. 18, 1801.
6. Mary, b. Dec. 31, 1803; d. July 22, 1851; mar. Dec. 6, 1833, Isham Teasley.
7. Elizabeth, b. Sept. 12, 1807; d. near Griffin, Ga.; mar. Oct. 4, 1830, Allen Shackleford.
8. William, b. Dec. 28, 1810; d. Jan. 31, 1885; mar. June 26, 1837, Serepta Rucker.
9. Ann, b. Nov. 12, 1813; mar. John Upshaw.

THOMAS MAXWELL (son of Thomas Maxwell, Sr., and his wife, Keziah Blake of Va.), b. Middlesex Co., Va., Sept. 7, 1742; d. Elbert Co., Ga., Dec. 12, 1837. Mar. 1761, Mary Pemberton, b. 1740; d. Dec. 18, 1827. He was a *Rev. Sol.* of Va., and was a prisoner during the Rev. Drew land in 1825 Lottery as a *Rev. Sol.*; a member of Major Dobbs' Batt. of Elbert Co., Ga. Thomas Maxwell and his wife are buried at Old Maxwell Cemetery, in Centerville District, Elbert Co., Ga. A minister of the Baptist Church.

Children:

1. John, b. May 9, 1763; d. Oct. 5, 1840; mar. Feb. 6, 1792, Agatha Henry.
2. Keziah, b. Jan 11, 1766, mar. Benson Henry.
3. Thomas J., b. Jan. 1, 1768; d. Dec. 12, 1825.
4. James, b. Sept. 12, 1770.
5. Elijah, b. May 1, 1773; d. Jan. 22, 1842; mar. Elizabeth Jordan.
6. William, b. Dec. 22, 1775, mar. Jane Higgenbotham.
7. Jesse, b. Dec. 11, 1780.
8. Joel, b. Sept. 30, 1783; d. Aug. 23, 1863; mar. Mary (Polly) Brown.
9. Sara, b. Jan. 4, 1786; d. 1850; mar. 1807, W. Payne Christian.
10. Jeremiah, b. July 14, 1789.
11. Elizabeth, b. Sept. 25, 1791, mar. Sept. 3, 1812, W. McMullan.

THOMAS MIDDLEBROOKS (son of JOHN MIDDLEBROOKS (1726–1817), a *Rev. Sol.* of Caswell Co., N. C., and his wife, Miss Sims). b. Caswell Co., N. C., 1763; d. Jones Co., Ga., May 13, 1825. He served as a *Rev. Sol.* of N. C. Came to Ga. Mar. 1790, Ann Selman (or Selmon), b. Mar. 20, 1778; d. Jones Co., Ga., 1859.

Children (from will in Jones Co., Ga.):

1. William Sims, b. Nov. 18, 1793; d. 1836.
2. Elizabeth, b. Apr. 26, 1795, mar. — Willis.
3. Nancy, b. Hancock Co., Ga., June 2, 1797; d. Upson Co., Ga., Aug. 8, 1866; mar. Mar. 16, 1812, William Willis, b. Nov. 5, 1784; d. Upson Co., Ga., Aug. 11, 1851.
4. Mary, b. June 1, 1799.
5. Frances, b. Oct. 25, 1800; mar. (1) — Johnson; mar. (2) 1825, Benjamin Haygood (1799–1887).
6. Alley, b. Sept. 26, 1803.
7. Biernetta, b. Aug. 25, 1805; d. 1865; mar. John Knight.
8. James Madison, b. Mar. 13, 1809; d. Dec. 16, 1885.
9. Sarah, b. Mar. 12, 1811; d. 1834.
10. Thomas J., b. Feb. 1, 1814; d. 1866.
11. Micha, b. July 12, 1816; d. 1885.

PHILIP MINIS, b. Savannah, Ga., July 11, 1734, the year following the founding of the Ga. Colony by Oglethorpe, said to be the first male white child b. in Ga.; d. Savannah, Ga., Mar. 6, 1789. Mar. Judith Pollock, a member of one of the first families that settled Newport, R. I., just as Philip Minis belonged to a family numbered among the first settlers of the Colony of Ga. It is an interesting fact that R. I. and Ga. were the only two Colonies where Jews were not prohibited from settling. He gave active aid and support to the Colonists, and on this account he was named in the Royal Disqualifying Act of 1780. In 1779 he was a *Rev. Sol.*, serving as guide when the French auxiliaries arrived in Savannah, and afterwards continued as a soldier. During the darkest hours of the Rev., PHILIP MINIS, b. of Hebrew parents, contributed $7,000.00 towards paying the Troops of Va. and N. C.

Children (known):

1. Isaac, a *Sol. of 1812*, mar. Dinah Cohen.

2. Philip, Jr., mar. Sarah A. Livingston, of N. Y.

3. Sarah Ann, mar. Dr. Isaac Hays, of Philadelphia.

4. Phillippa, mar. Edward Johnson Etting, of Philadelphia.

NOTE: It is interesting to note that connected with the WESTMORELAND, TIDWELL, and SIMMONS families of Va. and Ga. are the following *Rev. Sols.*: WILLIAM STUART of S. C.; TSCHARNER DE GRAFFENREID of Va.; OLIVER HALE and MOSES EMERY of Mass.; WILLIAM JONES of Va.; STILES CURTIS, DANIEL JUDSON; SILAS JUDSON, and SAMUEL WHITING of Conn.

WILLIAM PENTECOST, b. Dinwiddie Co., Va., 1763; d. Jackson Co., Ga., 1839. He was a *Rev. Sol.*; served in Buford's detachment, 14th Va. Regiment, 1780, at Battle of Waxhaw, S. C., where he lost an arm. Received pension. Mar. Delilah Wood. His widow received pension as widow of *Rev. Sol.*, 1848.

Their dau., Frances (1799-1852), mar. Jonathan Clark Coker.

(Perhaps other children).

NOTE: Rev. Daniel Marshall, b. Conn; was, in 1772 and throughout the Rev. War, the Pastor of the Kiokee Church, the first Baptist Church in Ga. After his death, his eldest son, Abraham, carried on his work as Pastor. Daniel Marshall had eight sons, all of whom where *Rev. Sols.* of Ga.

BENJAMIN POWELL (son of Moses Powell, Sr.), b. S. C., 1756; came to the Ceded Lands of Ga. (now Wilkes Co.) in 1773, with his parents; d. Wilkes Co., Ga., 1824. Mar. MARY LYBAS, formerly of Rockingham Co., N. C.; d. at the same place, 1825. A *Rev. Sol.*; received bounty land, 287½ acres, in Washington Co., Ga., for his service 1784.

BENJAMIN POWELL had three brothers and two sisters: LEWIS, CADER, and MOSES POWELL, JR., all *Rev. Sols.* of Ga.; Charity, mar. Harvy —; Henelephy, mar. — Lamar.

JOHN ROBINSON, SR., b. about 1753; d. Jasper Co., Ga., 1815; mar. in Chowan Co., N. C., Mar. 30, 1778, Lydia Brinn. Enlisted Chowan Co., N. C., 1782, 10th N. C. Regiment, Capt. Evan's Co., Col. Abraham Shepard; 18 months' service as private and musician. Moved to Jasper Co., Ga.

Children:

1. Christian, b. 1779; mar. Clinton Webb, d. 1872.

2. Luke J. (Baptist minister), b. June 22, 1781; mar. in Jasper Co., Ga., Jan. 23, 1823, Matilda Falkner; d. Newton Co., Ga.

3. Lucy, b. 1782; mar. in Oglethorpe Co., Ga., Oct. 17, 1806, Alexander Northcutt; d. Marietta, Ga., Oct. 2, 1866.

4. Lydia, mar. in Jasper Co., Ga., April 10, 1810, Chesley Burks.

5. William, mar. in Jasper Co., Ga., Sept. 3 1813, Polly Williams.

6. John, Jr., b. Apr. 10, 1786; mar. in Jasper Co., Ga., July 6, 1813, Mary Knox Croll, widow; d. Jasper Co., Ga., June 14, 1857.

7. Martha (Patsey), b. 1793; mar. in Jasper Co., Ga., Sept. 19, 1811, James Lyon Burks; d. Talbot Co., Ga., 1834.

8. Jesse Jones, d. unmar., Sabine Co., Texas, 1862.

9. Angelina, mar. (1) Warwick Smith; mar. (2) — Johnson.

NOTE: ELEMELECK SANDEFORD, b. Va., 1784; d. Wilkes Co., Ga. Applied for a pension Mar. 15, 1825. Stated he had enlisted for a term of 3 years Aug. 16, 1777, Brunswick Co., Va., Capt. Laurence House, Col. David Mason, State of Va. Continental Line. Lived in Northampton Co., N. C. Came to Washington, Ga., 1820. Wife living 1825. Children.

PHILIP TIGNER, b. Accomac Co., Va., Dec. 25, 1760; d. Ga., Jan. 6, 1819. A *Rev. Sol.* of Va., and Capt. of 5th Co., 2nd Batt., Ga. Troops, 1796. (*War of 1812 Sol.*) Mar. (1) May 7, 1780, Nancy Forbish; mar. (2) Nancy Hall, b. 1766.

Children by (1) wife:

1. Sarah, b. Jan. 22, 1781; mar. 1798, William Gremmett.

2. James, b. 1783.
3. William, b. Jan. 14, 1787; mar. 1808, —.
4. Elizabeth, b. Nov. 15, 1789; mar. 1809, John Hodnett.
5. Hope Hull, b. May 28, 1792; mar. 1819, Eliza Glenn.
Children by (2) wife:
1. Nancy F., b. Oct. 28, 1794; mar. 1810, Edward Elder.
2. Innocence, b. Apr. 30, 1796; mar. 1817, William L. Fambrough.
3. Pamela, b. June 24, 1798; mar. 1817, Hartwell Elder.
4. Freeborn G., b. Nov. 29, 1801.
5. John W., b. Jan. 18, 1803.
6. Young F., b. Aug. 22, 1805; mar. Sarah Frances Tinsley.
7. Urbane C., b. Oct. 16, 1808; mar. Susan Slaton.
8. Philip, Jr., b. Jan. 25, 1813; mar. Eliza Ann Stokes.

ROBERT WALTON (son of George Walton and Martha Hughes, of Va. and Ga.), b. Feb. 4 1754; was of "Frog Hill," Richmond Co., Ga. He was a *Rev. Sol.*, a Capt., and was among the list of 151 prescribed Patriots published by the British, 1780. He mar. 1775, Blanche Glasscock (dau. of WILLIAM GLASSCOCK, a *Rev. Sol.*, whose name appears among the prescribed Rebels in 1780. His son, THOMAS GLASSCOCK, was a *Rev. Sol.*, Capt., and afterwards, General).
Children:
1. Martha, mar. Col. Zachariah Williams of Columbia Co., Ga.
2. Elizabeth, mar. Col. James McClannahan of Va.
3. Mary, mar. — Scott of Va.
4. Augustus, mar. —. Moved to Miss.
5. William.
6. Thomas, d. unmar.
7. Robert (1791–1870), mar. Evelina Sarah Watkins. 10 children.

CALEB WELCH, b. —; d. Jefferson Co., Ga., Jan. 1830. Record of service as a *Rev. Sol.* found in the records at courthouse, Louisville, Ga. Children mentioned in will made Aug. 28, 1828, probated Louisville, Ga., Jan. 11, 1830. Marriages recorded same place. Name of wife unknown.
Children:
1. Asa, mar. 1815, Sallie Starling.
2. William, mar. 1811, Charlotte Brown.
3. James, mar. Jan. 11, 1810, Martha (called Patsey) Davis. He d. before 1828. 4 children.
4. Elizabeth, mar. 1815, Jacob Young.
5. Melinda, mar. 1830, Lorenzo Barrow.
6. Falby (dau.).
7. Jane.

PETER WILLIAMSON, b. —; d. Franklin Co., Ga., 1798. Served as private, Ga. Troops. *Rev. Sol.* Received bounty land for his service. Mar. Elizabeth —.
Children (mentioned in will, probated June 1798):
1. Elizabeth, mar. Richard Allen.
2. Patsey, mar. Josiah Pritchett.
3. Jennett, mar. — Hamby.
4. Mary, mar. William Henby.
5. Fanny.
6. Nancy.
7. Sally.
8. Robert.
9. Richard.
10. John.
11. Peter Griffin.

JOHN WILLIAMS, b. Powhatan Co., Va., 1757. From his statement, Mar. 15, 1825, when he applied for a pension in Wilkes Co., Ga., he enlisted as a Minute Man, Powhattan Co., Va., Capt. Carrington's Co.; later he served in the 1st Va. Regiment, commanded by Gen. Charles Scott. Discharged at Kemp's Landing in Va. Lived in N. C. after the War, and came to Wilkes Co., Ga., 1820.

WILLIAM STUART (sometimes spelled Stewart), b. S. C., 1764; lived in Augusta, Ga.; d. Beech Island, S. C. (formerly known as Fort Moore), across the Savannah river from Augusta, Ga., 1818. Served as private, Capt. Zachary Brooks', S. C. Regiment. Enlisted as a *Rev. Sol.* at 16 years of age, July 7, 1780. Mar. Dec. 24, 1787, Edgefield District, S. C., MARY PARKER (dau. of JOHN PARKER, *Rev. Sol.* of S. C., b. S. C.; d. 1784; mar. Susanna —, d. after 1790; had 6 children), b. S. C., 1768; d. Beech Island, S. C., Aug. 6, 1802.

WILLIAM STUART was for many years the "Head Master" of the Beech Island Academy.

Children (from records):

1. James, b. Mar. 13, 1789.
2. Jane, b. Mar. 2, 1791.
3. William, b. Sept. 9, 1793. Lived in Columbia Co., Ga., moved to Ala.
4. Elizabeth, b. July 14, 1799; d. Sept. 6, 1815.
5. Ann (called Nancy Stewart), b. Beech Island, S. C., April 8, 1796; d. Warrenton, Ga., April 28, 1851; mar. Augusta, Ga., Jan. 19, 1819, Eliphalet Hale, b. Newburyport, Mass., Mar. 17, 1793; d. Warrenton, Ga., Mar. 2, 1860 (son of OLIVER HALE, a *Rev. Sol.* of Mass. (1762–1837) and his (1) wife, Lydia Coffin (1764–1801), dau. of Eliphalet Coffin and his wife, Lydia Emery, of Newbury, Mass.

REVOLUTIONARY SOLDIERS

PART IV

Graves of Revolutionary Soldiers located but not listed in the Proceedings of the Ga. Society, D. A. R. Published in "Georgia's Roster of the Revolution," by Knight (pages 459–466).

Name	County	Name	County
Epps Brown	Hancock	John Macomsen	Fulton
Col. Joseph Clay	Savannah, Ga.	John Martin	Augusta, Ga.
James Comer, age 108	Jones	Col. John Milledge	Augusta, Ga.
Elijah Cornwall	Jasper	George Matthews	Augusta, Ga.
Daniel Cresswell	Wilkes	George Palmer	Burke
Rev. Francis Cummings	Greene	Daniel Phone	De Kalb
Seth John Cuthbert	Savannah, Ga.	Jeremiah Sanford	Greensboro, Ga.
David Emanuel	Burke	Sheftall Sheftall	Savannah, Ga.
Benjamin Few	McDuffie	Mordecai Sheftall	Savannah, Ga.
Ignatius Few	McDuffie	Daniel Skehee	Washington
Samuel Freeman	Cherokee	James Spalding	Savannah, Ga.
Thomas Glascock	Richmond	John Sparks	Washington
William Glascock	Augusta, Ga.	Edward Telfair	Savannah, Ga.
Ambrose Gordon	Augusta, Ga.	William Thomas	Augusta, Ga.
Thomas Grant	Jasper	William Thompson	Jackson
James Habersham, Jr.	Savannah, Ga.	Sherwood Thompson	Gwinnett
Hugh Hall	Hancock	C. H. Thorn	Oconee
John T. Hughes	Cherokee	Francis Triplett	Richmond
James Jackson	Washington, D. C.	John Twiggs	"Twigg's Cemetery"
Batte Jones	Burke	Thomas White	McDuffie
John Jones	Burke	Graner Whitley	DeKalb
Noble Wimberly Jones	Savannah, Ga.	John Williams	St. Mary's, Ga.
Seaborn Jones	Augusta, Ga.	(Now "Arlington Cemetery")	
Henry Kendall	Upson	Joseph Williams	Telfair
John Lamar	Jones	Richard Wylly	Savannah, Ga.
Lachlan McIntosh	Savannah, Ga.	Austin Dabney—negro	Pike
John McMullen	Hart		

REVOLUTIONARY SOLDIERS WHO DIED IN GEORGIA

MICHAEL BUFF, d. Oglethorpe Co., Ga., May 28, 1839, age 102 years. Was a Rev. Sol. in the Battles of Germantown and Brandywine.

MATTHEW COCHRAN, a Rev. Sol., d. Augusta, Ga., Nov. 1844, age 102 years.

JOHN FRANCIS WILLIAM COURVOISER, b. Vevey, Switzerland, 1750; d. Savannah, Ga., 1823. Was a Signer of the Resolution presented by the City of Savannah, in reference to the conditions of the Country in 1775. He mar. 1778, Mary Fox (1762–1816).

EMANUEL PETER DELEPLAIQUE, d. on his passage from Charleston, S. C., to Martinico, on July 17, 1778. He was a Rev. Sol.; "Captain in the late Continental Army, Batt. of Infantry raised in the State of Ga."

BARON DE KALB, a German officer, who fought with the American forces in the Rev., and was mortally wounded at the Battle of Cowpens, S. C. A Ga. Co. bears his name.

WILLIAM FLETCHER, b. Va.; d. Telfair Co., Ga., age 110 years. Buried at the Concord Church graveyard (near McRae, Ga.). "A Revolutionary S. C. Soldier," from the pension record of his son, JOHN FLETCHER, who served as a Rev. Sol. of S. C., and d. in Fla.

JOSEPH GOUGE, b. Va.; d. Gwinnett Co., Ga., Jan. 24, 1838, age 109 years. A Rev. Sol.

ANDRE JENVANCEALE, a Rev. Sol., b. Marseilles, France; d. Savannah, Ga., 1809, age 78 years. Left widow living in Savannah, Ga.

JOHN MARTIN, d. Augusta, Ga., Feb. 14, 1843, age 107 years. "A Revolutionary Soldier."

HENRY MITCHELL, b. Va., 1762; d. Hancock Co., Ga., May 7, 1837. Lived also in Warren Co., Ga. Served as Ensign, at 18 years of age, in Va. Army. Was wounded and captured at Hanging Rock. Served as *President of Ga. Senate*.

THOMAS NAPIER, *Rev. Sol.*, b. Va., 1758; d. Ga., Sept. 3, 1838. Buried in the old "Cherry St. Cemetery," Macon, Ga., age 80 years.

COL. JAMES M. C. MONTGOMERY, b. Lancaster Dist., S. C.; d. "Standing Peachtree," De Kalb Co., Ga., Oct. 6, 1842, age 73 years.

ISHAM McDANIEL, d. at the home of his son, William, in Lowndes Co., Ga., April 1845, age nearly 100 years.

JAMES WALDROUP, d. Fayette Co., Ga., Dec. 3, 1846, age 104 years. A *Rev. Sol.*, who was at the Battle of Yorktown.

FADDY WHITTINGTON, b. Johnson Co., N. C.; d. Pike Co., Ga., age 105 years. A *Rev. Sol.* of N. C. Buried at the Seagraves graveyard on the old Macon Road, near Griffin, Ga.

From notices in Ga. newspapers:

Capt. James Alford, d. Hancock Co., Nov. 6, 1812, age 72 years.
James Allen, d. Burke Co., Mar. 2, 1841, age 85 years.
Capt. Jeffrey Barksdale, d. Hancock Co., Nov. 1832.
Sion Barnett, b. Warren Co., N. C.; d. Jasper Co., Mar. 25, 1843.
Gen. David Blackshear, b. N. C.; d. "Springfield," Laurens Co., July 4, 1837, age 74 years.
Prescott Bush, d. Stewart Co., June 23, 1846, age 90 years.
Rev. Edmund Byne, d. Burke Co., Feb. 1814.
Sampson Chance, d. Houston Co., Dec. 22, 1837, age 90 years.
Hugh M. Comer, b. Va.; d. Jones Co., May 13, 1836, age 70 years.
Major Nicholas Conry, d. Washington Co., Feb. 23, 1827, age 67 years.
Robert Cresswell, b. Md.; d. Augusta, May 1814, age 61 years.
Richard Curd, b. Va.; d. Henry Co., May 16, 1827, age 65 years.
James Darsey, b. N. C.; d. Laurens Co., Feb. 1832, age 90 years.
John Dismukes, d. Milledgeville, April 1, 1818, age 93 years.
Jesse Doles, Sr., d. Baldwin Co., July 26, 1831, age 80 years.
Isaac Du Bose, d. Columbia Co., June 14, 1816, age 75 years.
Capt. Robert Flournoy, b. Va.; d. Chatham Co., July 6, 1825.
Peter Fair, b. France; d. Ga., Aug. 21, 1826, age 68 years.
James Glenn, b. Hanover Co., Va.; d. Jackson Co., Oct. 11, 1837, age 74 years.
Major Davis Gresham, b. Orange Co., N. C.; d. Ga., April 11, 1819, age 64 years.
Littleberry Gresham, d. West Point, Feb. 20, 1834, age 72 years.
Henry Graybill, b. Lancaster Co., Penn.; d. Hancock Co., Oct. 29, 1822, age 67 years.
Thomas P. Hamilton, b. Va.; d. Randolph Co., Aug. 12, 1833.
Arthur Harrup, d. Jones Co., Sept. 3, 1836, age 85 years.
Thomas Hill, d. on Little Spirit Creek, Mar. 5, 1814.
David Hudson, d. Heard Co., Jan. 9, 1839, age 77 years.
Capt. Henry Hughes, d. Burke Co., April 27, 1814, age 58 years.
Capt. David Jameson, d. Twiggs Co., Aug. 30, 1825, age 72 years.
Sergeant Jonathan Jones, d. Laurens Co., Mar. 31, 1836, age 80 years.
William Jones, b. Va.; d. Columbia Co., Dec. 27, 1833, age 73 years.
Conrad Keller, b. S. C.; d. Washington Co., April 1839, age 84 years.
John Lamar, b. S. C.; d. Jones Co., Oct. 18, 1842, age 81 years.
Simeon Lowery, b. Sept. 12, 1762; d. Burke Co., Sept. 7, 1838, age 79 years.
James Malcom, b. Va.; d. Morgan Co., Feb. 23, 1829, age 77 years.
John Miles, d. Baldwin Co., Sept. 22, 1825, age 67 years.
William McGehee, Sr., b. Va.; d. Baldwin Co., Feb. 1829, age 80 years.
Charles McCall, b. Penn., near Va. Line; d. Bulloch Co., 1816, age 84 years.
William McCall, b. on Lynch's Creek, Peedee river, near Society Hill, S. C.; d. Screven Co., Jan. 12, 1830, age 64 years.

Thomas McCall, b. N. C., Mar. 19, 1764; d. Laurens Co., 1839, age 75 years.
Jesse Sanford, d. Baldwin Co., Feb. 18, 1827, age 64 years.
Major Benjamin Samuels, d. Lincoln Co., May 24, 1834, age 71 years.
Gilbert Shaw, d. Jasper Co., Feb. 3, 1842, age 85 years.
George Slaughter, b. Cumberland Co., Va.; d. Greene Co., Feb. 25, 1845, age 81 years.
Robert Smith, b. Cumberland Co., Va.; d. Oglethorpe Co., Oct. 9, 1834, age 85 years.
Capt. John Staunton, b. Hampton Co., N. C.; d. Washington Co., June 16, 1833, age 94 years.
John Torrance, d. Warren Co., July 4, 1827, age 78 years.
Samuel Turner, b. Md.; d. Hancock Co., Jan. 15, 1834, age 74 years.
John Turner, b. Worcester Co., Md.; d. Putnam Co., Jan. 25, 1848, age 87 years.
Nathaniel Ward, d. Irwinton, Ga., Jan. 20, 1840, age 98 years.
Francis Ward, b. Isle of Wight Co., Va.; d. Putnam Co., Feb. 8, 1830, age 65 years.
Gen. John McIntosh, b. Ga.; d. McIntosh Co., Nov. 12, 1826, age 70 years.
John Oslin, b. Va.; d. Henry Co., Nov. 9, 1843, age 80 years.
George Paschal, b. N. C.; d. Oglethorpe Co., Sept. 14, 1832, age 73 years.
William Patrick, d. Clarke Co., June 18, 1833, age 77 years. Lived in Newton Co.
William Patman, d. Oglethorpe Co., July 2, 1821.
Ezekiel H. Park, d. Greene Co., Dec. 30, 1826.
James Park, b. Prince Edward Co., Va.; d. Ga., 1823.
Archibald Perkins, b. Goochland Co., Va.; d. Baldwin Co., Oct. 15, 1830, age 94 years.
Major Oliver Porter, b. Prince Edward Co., Va.; d. Greene Co., Ga., Aug. 29, 1838, age 74 years.
Otey Prosser, d. Baldwin Co., July 3, 1839, age 80 years.
Reuben Ransome, Sr., d. Clarke Co., Feb. 18, 1833, age 79 years.
James G. Russell, d. Baldwin Co., May 4, 1873, age 81 years.
Col. Benjamin Whittaker, d. Jefferson Co., Aug. 29, 1821, age 56 years.
Capt. James Wilson, d. Monticello, Ga., Feb. 1824, age 79 years.

FROM *Ga. Gazette:*

"Died on Sunday, last, Dec. 1, 1799, at St. Simon's Island, MAJOR WILLIAM McINTOSH, Rev. Soldier of Ga. Born in Ga., 1759. He obtained his rank and was a distinguished officer in the late Continental Revolution Army of America, from the beginning of that war to the end of it. Alas! our firm disinterested patriots of 1776 are daily decreasing."

NAMES AND AGES OF PENSIONERS FROM GEORGIA FOR REVOLUTIONARY SERVICE FOUND IN THE CENSUS OF PENSIONERS FOR REVOLUTIONARY MILITARY SERVICE, UNDER THE ACT FOR TAKING THE 6TH CENSUS IN 1840

(From Book of Pensioners Published in Washington, D. C., by Authority of the Secretary of State)

CAMPBELL COUNTY					
Name	Age	Name	Age	Name	Age
Gunnell, William R.	88	Brewster, Hugh	80	McDowell, Robert	86
Clinton, William	80	Harris, Benjamin	81	Barnwell, John	88
Norwood, George	77	Baker, Chas.	79	Collins, John	80
Bledsoe, Benjamin	77			Eastwood, Israel	82
Akins, James	90	CLARK COUNTY		Edwards, Adonijah	73
		Farrar, Francis	76		
CHATTOOGA COUNTY		Oliver, John	78	CRAWFORD COUNTY	
O'Rear, Daniel	83	Espy, John	84	Mathews, Philip	88
		Parr, Benjamin	83	Meador, Jason	81
CHEROKEE COUNTY		Wilson, George	88	Bailey, James	80
Smith, Charles	75			Ethridge, Joel	77
Willaford, Nathan	82	CAMDEN COUNTY		Turner, Thomas	89
Martin, Ephriam	80	Wilford, Lewis	95 to 100	Hartley, Daniel	97
				Goodwin, Lewis	74
CASS COUNTY		COBB COUNTY		Fudge, Jacob	82
Lewis, John	83	Nesbit, Jeremiah	105		
Edwards, Reuben	82	Grover, Peter	79	CARROLL COUNTY	
		Sumner, John	77	Stedman, Zacheriah	89

Name	Age	Name	Age	Name	Age
Rowell, Jesse	87	Edenfield, David	79	Dobs, Nathan	85
Robinson, John, Sr.	88	Curl, Matthew	78	Harris, Stephen	86
		Drew, William	75	McDade, John	93
Coweta County		Brown, Henry	70	Andes, Owen	87
Gay, Allen	75	Sutton, A	82	Lawrence, John	80
Smith, William	91	Durden, Jacob	85	Iseley, Philip	91
Neely, John	83			Jackson, Edward	86
Akens, James	74	**Effingham County**		Pateson, Robert	78
Brewster, William	83	Rahn, Jonathan	78	Bramblett, Reuben	75
				Hunt, Littleton	97
Burke County		**Early County**		Gowers, Abel	86
Thomas, Abraham	86	Wells, Redman		Benson, Enoch	84
Allen, James	84	Baggett, Josiah	78	Thrasher, George	85
		Jordan, Elizabeth	57	Herrington, Joseph	77
Baldwin County		(Living with Charles B.			
Anderson, William	78	Jordan)		**Gilmer County**	
Talbot, Benjamin	76			Cox, Richard, Sr.	79
Robinson, Joseph	70	**Franklin County**		Smith, Enoch	81
Russell, James G., Sr.	78	Cash, Ann	75	Kell, James	81
		(Living with Howard Cash)		Fain, Hezekiah	78
Bulloch County		Dyer, Elisha	77	Ellis, Mary	84
Banks, John	84	Mendock, William	81	(Living with Elijah Ellis)	
		Stonecypher, John	84		
Butts County		Fuller, Stephen	88	**Greene County**	
Price, E.	79	Clarke, Thomas	79	Slaughter, George	77
		Aaron, William	93	Pullin, Robert	85
Dade County		Holbrook, Jesse	76	Gaiter, Stephen	
Perkins, Moses	87	Spears, William	95	Harris, Matthew	88
		McCoy, Samuel	79	Shurr, John	77
De Kalb County		Fleming, Robert	70		
Stowers, Lewis, Sr.	76	Sheridan, Abner	80	**Heard County**	
Terrell, William	84	Mitchell, William	81	Stewart, James	75
Copeland, William	75			(Living with John Stewart)	
Brooks, George	79	**Fayette County**			
Roberts, Thomas	95	Mills, Karew-Harpuck	79	**Hall County**	
Maconeson, John	84	Waldrup, James	85	Bonds, Joseph	84
Reeve, William	84	Suddeth, Jared	76	Anderson, James	72
		Black, William	76		
Elbert County		Gilleland, Susan	80	**Hall County**	
Cook, John	79			Reed, Isaac	87
Kelly, William	82	**Forsyth County**		Moore, John	83
Carter, David	82	Wells, Leonard	84	McClesky, James	86
Riley, James	82	Browne, Ambrose	83	Flanigan, William	91
Gulley, Richard	85	Nolen, James	90	Kell, Robert	89
Davis, John	87	Lagraw, John M.	87	Gilmor, James, Sr.	80
Brown, Benjamin	77	Whiten, Philip	95	Albread, Elias	82
Ward, William	82	Carroll, James	75	Childers, Milliner	77
Daniel, John	80			Hulsey, Jesse	81
Gaines, William	83	**Gwinnett County**		Pitts, James	71
Richardson, Amos	76	Davis, John	109	Nicholson, John	77
Trammell, William	83	Conger, Benjamin	84	Gunter, Charles	78
Rice, Leonard	81	Clower, Daniel	79	Baker, Beal	84
Glasgow, William	78	Horton, Isaac	81	Robertson, Robert	83
		Curbo, Joseph	86	Clark, William	9–
Emanuel County		McRight, William	91	Shaw, Basil	92
Terulauth, Benjamin	83	Williams, Nathan	89	West, Benjamin	81

HENRY COUNTY

Name	Age
Cloud, Ezekiel	78
Adams, Francis	77
Gilbert, James	87
Cook, Thomas	88
Upchurch, Charles	85
Chandler, Sheildcake	88

HARRIS COUNTY

Norris, William	84
Swan, William B	82

HABERSHAM COUNTY

McColloms, Daniel	86
Pilgrim, Thomas	74
Vandergriff, Garret	89
Turner, Robert	80

HANCOCK COUNTY

Mullins, Malone	80
Sheffield, William	70
Rossiter, Timothy	80
Hill, John	80
Dennis, John	70

HANCOCK COUNTY

Brasel, Bird	70
Blount, Isaac	80
Grant, Joseph	80
Howel, Mills	70
Faison, William	70

JONES COUNTY

Morton, Oliver, Sr	75
Roberts, Reuben	85
Slocumb, John C	80

JASPER COUNTY

Barnett, Sion	79
Waters, David	105
Davidson, John	79
Jones, William, Sr	82
Spears, John	89
Yancey, Lewis D	78

JEFFERSON COUNTY

Sodown, Jacob	80

JACKSON COUNTY

Mathews, Isaac	79
Mathews, William	77
Saxon, Solomon	73
Cunningham, Ansell	77
Lowrey, Levi	76
White, Jesse	79
King, John	85

Name	Age
Levay, George	85
Anglin, Henry	81
Thompson, Sherrod	83
Wheeler, James	85

LIBERTY COUNTY

Hart, Mary	
(Living with Joseph Jones)	

LUMPKIN COUNTY

Allen, William	101
Fleming, William	79
Hames, John	94
Hill, Reuben	69
Ledbetter, Richard	101
Singleton, Edmund	85
(Living with Overstreet Singleton)	
Nix, John	75
Pilgrim, Michael	86

LINCOLN COUNTY

Linville, William	85
Guise, John	79

MACON COUNTY

Whatley, Daniel	87
Passimore, Joseph	79
Baker, Dempsey	77

MORGAN COUNTY

Barkly, William	80
Cochran, M.	83
Campbell, George	86

MADISON COUNTY

Tate, Robert L	76
Tugle, Charles	87
Thompson, James	77
Hanan, Alexander	80
Cheek, William	89

MURRAY COUNTY

Stone, William	

MARION COUNTY

Buchanan, George	81
Mayo, John	81

McINTOSH COUNTY

White, George	81
Calder, John	77

MONROE COUNTY

Davis, Toliver	84

Name	Age
Stewart, William	87
Jones, William	..
(Living with David Woolsey)	

MERIWETHER COUNTY

Smith, Alexander	81
Bowen, Samuel	83
Jenkins, Lewis	87
Black, John	77
Keily, Giles	78
Earnest, George	80

MUSCOGEE COUNTY

Hodge, Philemon	83
Christmas, Richard	77

NEWTON COUNTY

Webb, John	85
Terrell, Richmond	80
Fretwell, Richard	87
Weathers, Valentine	76
Hewell, Wyatt	84
Carter, Robert	84
McLane, Thomas	80

OGLETHORPE COUNTY

Finch, William	76
Dunn, Thomas Sr	76
Woodall, Joseph	76
Bledsoe, Miller	78
(Living with Whitfield Landrum)	
Ward, Samuel	85
Eberhart, Jacob	83
Carter, Charles	88
Kidd, William, Sr	77
Strong, Charles	77

UNION COUNTY

Tanney, Michael	81

UPSON COUNTY

Chellfinch, Hiram	85

PIKE COUNTY

Jenkins, John, Sr	85
Wise, John	84
Harper, William	88
Gresham, David	83
Whittington, Faddy	87

WILKINSON COUNTY

Rosier, Robert, Sr	84
Meadows, John	78
Jenkins, William	83

WILKES COUNTY

Name	Age
Combs, John	75
Williams, William	78
Woolf, Andrew	88

WASHINGTON COUNTY

Name	Age
Williams, William	86
Thompson, Lustatia	74
(Living with Greene H. Warthen)	
Howard, George F.	97
Peacock, Uriah	88
Love, Thomas	90
Cox, Moses	86
Jones, Isaac	79

WALTON COUNTY

Name	Age
Hardin, Henry	89
Harris, Benjamin	87
Swords, James	92

WALKER COUNTY

Name	Age
Newnan, Daniel	..
Story, Robert	..

WARREN COUNTY

Name	Age
Cason, William	93
Doud, John	85
Draper, James	89
Wilson, John	85
Rickerson, Benjamin	80

Name	Age
Jackson, John	85
Studivent, Charles	80

RABUN COUNTY

Name	Age
Williams, Edward	102
McLain, John	81
Dillard, John	81
Callahan, Josias	81
Dunlap, Jonathan	81

RICHMOND COUNTY

Name	Age
Martin, John	103

RANDOLPH COUNTY

Name	Age
Bucholler, Peter	77
Brown, Ezekiel	75
Brown, John	77
Davis, Thomas	85
Darby, Richard	102

TALIAFERRO COUNTY

Name	Age
McCormack, Thomas	90
King, Richard	88
Evans, William	98
Stewart, Henry	81

TELFAIR COUNTY

Name	Age
Williams, Joseph	80

TALBOT COUNTY

Name	Age
Ellis, Shadrack	80

TWIGGS COUNTY

Name	Age
Keith, John	90
Lile, Ephriam	77
Taylor, Thomas, Sr.	77

TROUP COUNTY

Name	Age
Thomason, William	92
Jourdan, Fountain	77
Johnson, Joseph	86

PULASKI COUNTY

Name	Age
Parkerson, Jacob	79

SUMTER COUNTY

Name	Age
Flanigan, Daniel	83

CITY OF SAVANNAH

Name	Age
Sheftall, Sheftall	78
Bullough, Elias	77
Cabos, John	94

SCREVEN COUNTY

Name	Age
Arnett, John	80

STEWART COUNTY

Name	Age
Elliott, Zacheriah	84
Smith, Benjamin	88
Melton, Robert	82
Bush, Prescot	81
Glenn, Thomas	81
Statham, Nathaniel	76

NAMES OF REVOLUTIONARY SOLDIERS WHO DREW LAND IN CHEROKEE LAND LOTTERY IN 1838 AND THE COUNTIES IN WHICH THEY LIVED

(Compiled from "*The Cherokee Land Lottery*," by James F. Smith of Milledgeville, Georgia; published, 1838.)

A

Name	County
Adams, Benjamin	Warren
Adams, James	Elbert
Affut, Nathaniel	Washington
Alexander, Matthew	Habersham
Allen, John	Franklin
Allen, William	Franklin
Alsabrook, J., Sr	Jones
Anthony, David	Franklin
Aikens, James	Fayette
Arnaud, John Peter	Chatham
Arnett, John	Thomas
Arnold, Charles	Tattnall
Arnold, William	Oglethorpe
Atkins, Ici	Talbot
Atkinson, Robert	DeKalb
Angley, Conrad	Decatur
Auldridge, Absolem	Houston

Name	County
Auldridge, William	Wilkes
Austin, John	Walton
Ayers, Baker	Habersham

B

Name	County
Bailey, Stephen	Monroe
Baker, Charles	Habersham
Baldassee, Isaac	Tattnall
Barnett, Joel	Oglethorpe
Barnwell, John	Henry
Barnwell, Michael	Houston
Barnwell, Robert	Hall
Barton, John	Hall
Bassett, Richard	Harris
Beall, Nathaniel	Richmond
Beasley, Thomas Sr	Henry
Beard, Moses	Clark
Bearden, Humphrey	Clark

Name	County	Name	County
Blair, James	Habersham	Comer, James, Sr	Jones
Boring, Isaac	Jackson	Conden, John	Oglethorpe
Bowden, James	Monroe	Connor, William	Putnam
Bowen, Elijah	Tattnall	Connell, John	Montgomery
Bowen, John	Gwinnett	Conyers, John	Screven
Bowles, Nathan	Jackson	Cook, James W	Jackson
Bozeman, Ralph	Thomas	Cooksey, John	Newton
Brady, Samuel	Marion	Copeland, Benjamin	Greene
Bradley, John	Jackson	Cotten, George, Sr	Warren
Branch, James	Laurens	Cowart, Zachariah	Early
Branch, William S	Greene	Crabbe, Asa	Putnam
Brannon, Michael	Gwinnett	Crawford, Jay	Chatham
Brooks, John	Columbia	Crawford, Philip	Newton
Brooks, Robert	Houston	Christopher, William	Oglethorpe
Brown, James	Clark	Crosby, Urill	Wilkes
Brown, Jesse	Early	Cross, John	Muscogee
Brown, Joseph	Rabun	Crumbley, Anthony	Henry
Brown, Lewis	Monroe		
Brown, Mordeaci (orphans of)	Henry	**D**	
Brown, Wallis	Pike	Daniel, Frederick	Pike
Bryan, Thomas, Sr	Franklin	Daniel, Littleberry	Heard
Burch, Edward	Pulaski	David, Isham	Madison
Burford, Wm	Butts	Davidson, Joseph	Pike
Burgess, Josiah	Jasper	Davies, Daniel	Montgomery
Burkett, Uriah	Dooly	Davis, John, Sr	Habersham
Butler, Patrick	Elbert	Davis, John	Lowndes
Bynant, Sugars	Houston	Davis, William	Fayette
		Dawson, Brittain	Burke
C		Dawson, Joseph	Butts
Cabaniss, Henry	Elbert	Dean, Richard	Houston
Caison, Willoughby	Ware	Dennis, Josiah	Morgan
Callahan, John	Oglethorpe	Denson, Joseph, Sr	Putnam
Campbell, William, Sr	Oglethorpe	Dickerson, Harry	Washington
Cannup, Thomas	Habersham	Dickey, Patrick	Putnam
Cantrell, Charles	Rabun	Dillard, James	Elbert
Carithers, Robert	Madison	Dobbs, Nathan	Gwinnett
Carlisle, Benjamin	Columbia	Dobson, Henry	Hall
Carithers, Samuel	Gwinnett	Doby, John	Jasper
Carroll, John	Jasper	Dorton, Benjamin	Pike
Carson, Adam	Jones	Dowd, John	Warren
Carter, Charles, Sr	Oglethorpe	Downs, Wm	Effingham
Carter, James	Elbert	Drake, James	Telfair
Carter, Robert	Newton	Durham, Isaac	DeKalb
Cartledge, J., Sr	Columbia	Dunn, John	Fayette
Cash, Dorson	Columbia	Dyer, Jacob C	Putnam
Cason, Willis	Henry	Durvuzieaux, Stephen	Jefferson
Chestnut, Needham	Houston		
Choice, Tully	Hancock	**E**	
Clayton, Stephen, Sr	Carroll	Eagin, John	Richmond
Clark, George	Jackson	Elder, Joshua	Fayette
Coker, Isaac	Henry	Elrod, Samuel	Habersham
Cobbett, Thomas	Elbert	Ellis, Shadrack	Talbot
Coleman, Jesse	Burke	Elton, Anthony W	Jackson
Collins, Joseph	Twiggs	Elvington, Gideon	Lowndes
Colquitt, Robert	Oglethorpe	Epperson, Thompson	Franklin
Comer, Hugh M	Jones	Espy, James	Clark

Name	County
Eubanks, George	Butts
Evans, John	

F

Name	County
Fain, Ebenezer, Sr.	Habersham
Fairish, William	Rabun
Faison, William	Hancock
Finch, William	Oglethorpe
Fitzpatrick, Rene	Heard
Flanningan, Wm	Hall
Fould, James	Wilkinson
Franklin, Zepheniah	Warren
Funderburg, John	Monroe

G

Name	County
Gainey, Reedy	Tattnall
Garner, Thomas	Hall
Gates, Charles, Sr.	Gwinnett
Gibbs, Cornelius	Rabun
Gilbert, John	Jackson
Gilleland, Wm., Sr.	Fayette
Gilmer, James, Sr.	Hall
Glasgow, Wm	Madison
Glenn, Thomas	Jones
Glaze, Reuben	Oglethorpe
Goodwin, Lewis	Twiggs
Gower, Abel	Gwinnett
Grace, John	Tattnall
Gray, James	Pike
Greene, Daniel	Ware
Gregory, Richard	Oglethorpe
Griffin, Joseph	Troup
Grumbles, George	Burke
Guise, John	Lincoln
Guise, Peter	Lincoln
Gurnill, Wm	DeKalb

H

Name	County
Habersham, George	Crawford
Hall, Isaac	Meriwether
Hall, Wm. G.	Putnam
Ham, William	Crawford
Hames, John	Hall
Hammett, John	Warren
Hancock, Isaac	Habersham
Handy, Nathaniel	Habersham
Harmon, John, Sr.	Elbert
Harper, George	Jones
Harper, John	Habersham
Harper, William	Habersham
Harrell, Ethelred, Sr.	Pulaski
Harris, John	Newton
Harrup, Arthur	Jones
Hatcher, Henry	Pike
Hatcher, Josiah	Richmond
Hayman, Henry	Lowndes

Name	County
Hayman, Stephen	Burke
Hays, John	DeKalb
Heggie, Thomas	
Henderson, Robert	Hall
Henderson, Robert	Jackson
Hendrick, John	Pike
Hendricks, Elias	Madison
Hendricks, Samuel	Muscogee
Henry, Robert, Sr.	Walton
Harriden, Joseph	Newton
Harrington, Ephriam	Emanuel
Hewell, Wyatt	Newton
Hickman, John	Monroe
Higgs, John	Montgomery
Higgs, Thomas	Hall
Hines, John	Burke
Hinton, Pester (Peter)	Elbert
Hodges, Philemon	Muscogee
Holbrooks, Edy	Franklin
Holcombe, Moses	Cherokee
Holliman, Samuel	Columbia
Holliday, William	Twiggs
Holmes, Thomas	Franklin
Hooper, Richard	Franklin
Hopkins, Isaac	Wilkes
Horsley, Valentine	Monroe
Horton, Isaac	Gwinnett
Hudson, John	Henry
Huey, Henry	DeKalb
Hunter, Moses	Habersham

J

Name	County
Jackson, Ebenezer	Chatham
Jenkins, Lewis	Washington
Jennings, Robert	Oglethorpe
Jett, Daniel	Greene
Jester, Levi	Butts
Johnson, Angus	Putnam
Johnson, Hardy	Emanuel
Johnson, Jesse	Jackson
Joiner, Abraham	Bibb
Joiner, Benjamin	Pike
Jones, Gabriel	
Jones, William	Bibb
Jones, William	Jasper
Jordan, Benjamin	Meriwether
Jordan, Charles, Sr.	Meriwether
Jordan, Job	Marion
Jordan, William	Newton
Jordan, Edmund	Oglethorpe

K

Name	County
Kelly, Edward	Pulaski
O Kelly, Francis	Oglethorpe
Kellmer, George	Talbot
Kendall, James Key	Habersham

Name	County
Kent, John	Twiggs
King, John	Jackson
King, William	Ware

L

Name	County
Lambert, James, Sr	Burke
Landrum, John	Wilkes
Lanier, Lewis	Screven
Lard, William	Jackson
Lawrence, John	Putnam
Leach, Burdette	Franklin
Leak, James	Jasper
Leansley, Thomas	Coweta
Lee, John	Washington
LeGrand, John	Elbert
Lesley, Wm	Oglethorpe
Lewis, Nathaniel	Chatham
Liles, Ephriam	Twiggs
Lindsey, Isaac, Sr	Hall
Little, William, Sr	Putnam
Litton, John	Habersham
Lockhart, James	Elbert
Loyd, Thomas	Jasper

Mc

Name	County
McCall, Thomas	Laurens
McClain, John	Ware
McDade, John	Gwinnett
McDonald, John	Jackson
McGinty, John	Pike
McGruber, W. R.	Richmond
McKenzie, Wm	Monroe
McMullen, John R	Franklin
McMurrah, David	Newton
McNeil, Jesse	Bibb
McVicker, John	Henry

M

Name	County
Maddox, John	Gwinnett
Maginty, John	Pike
Mangham, Howell	Franklin
Mason, Gideon	Jones
Massey, Allston S	Harris
Martin, Alexander	Oglethorpe
Matthews, Isaac	Clark
Matthews, Wm	Jackson
Mayes, Thomas	Franklin
Mead, Minor	Carroll
Meriwether, Thomas	Jasper
Middlebrook, John	Newton
Mikell, James	Bulloch
Miller, Jesse	Harris
Miller, Wm	Habersham
Millican, Thomas	DeKalb
Mitchell, Robert	Bibb
Mitchell, Wm., Sr	Franklin

Name	County
Meitzger, David	Effingham
Monk, John	Monroe
Moore, Isaac	Henry
Moore, John	Hall
Moore, John	Hancock
Morgan, John, Sr	Morgan
Morris, John	Pulaski
Moseley, Samuel	Franklin
Mott, Nathan	Washington
Murray, Thomas	Columbia

N

Name	County
Nall, Reuben	Tattnall
Nead, George	Effingham
Newnan, Thomas	Richmond
Nix, John	Hall
Nobles, Lewis S	Montgomery
Norman, John	Wilkes
Nunnellee, James F	Elbert

O

Name	County
Oates, Richard W	Harris

P

Name	County
Paine, John	Greene
Palmer, William	DeKalb
Parker, Daniel, Sr	Upson
Patrick, David	Oglethorpe
Patrick, Wm	Emanuel
Peacock, Archibald	Washington
Peavy, Dial	Fayette
Pennington, Neddy	Jones
Pentecost, William	Jackson
Perkins, Archibald	Greene
Phillips, Benjamin	Camden
Phillips, Levi	Carroll
Pinson, Moses	Hall
Pledge, Thomas	Elbert
Pollock, Jesse	Houston
Potts, John	Habersham
Price, Ephriam	Greene
Prince, John	Habersham

R

Name	County
Raines, Edmund	Morgan
Ratchford, Joseph	Jackson
Ray, John, Sr	Harris
Reddick, Abram	Jasper
Redwine, Jacob	Elbert
Renfroe, Stephen H	Jones
Rahn, Jonathan	Effingham
Rice, Leonard	Elbert
Richardson, Amos	Elbert
Richardson, Jesse	Habersham
Roach, Samuel	Early
Roberts, John	Gwinnett

Name	County
Rutherford, John	Baldwin
Ryles, James, Sr	Hall
Ryall, Wright	Telfair

S

Name	County
Sanders, James	Madison
Sanders, John	DeKalb
Sandridge, Clayborn	Elbert
Sappington, John	Henry
Savage, Thomas, Sr	Hall
Scott, James	Liberty
Scott, William	Coweta
Shockley, Jonathan	Monroe
Seal, Anthony	Harris
Seale, William	Hancock
Sellers, Solomon	Appling
Selman, William	Upson
Setzger, Jacob	Franklin
Shackleford, Edmund	Elbert
Simmons, Richard	Gwinnett
Simmons, Thomas	Ware
Sisson, John	Jackson
Slaton, George	Jackson
Stacy, Thomas	DeKalb
Smith, Benjamin	Coweta
Smith, Colesby	Washington
Smith, Ivy	Appling
Smith, James	Oglethorpe
Smith, Jesse	Franklin
Smith, Joshua	Hall
Smith, Larkin	Oglethorpe
Smith, Robert	Butts
Smith, Samuel	Chatham
Snyder, Godlip	Effingham
Speak, Richard	Butts
Spears, John	Newton
Spears, William	Franklin
St. John, James	Newton
Starrell, James	Habersham
Stewart, Hardy	Wilkinson
Stewart, Henry	Jasper
Stewart, John	Monroe
Stillwell, Jacob	Troup
Stone, Henry	Ware
Stone, William	Jasper
Strauther, James	Rabun
Stroud, Sherwood	Walton
Stuart, John	Jasper
Sword, James	Walton
Suttles, William	DeKalb

T

Name	County
Tanner, Thomas	DeKalb
Taylor, Richard C	Morgan
Tedder, William	Montgomery
Telly, Lazarus	Rabun

Name	County
Terrell, William	DeKalb
Terrell, James	Franklin
Thaxton, James	Greene
Thomas, John	Troup
Thomas, Massa	Putnam
Thompson, Frederick	Walton
Thompson, Seth	Meriwether
Thompson, William	Habersham
Thompson, William	Ware
Tillary, John	Butts
Tilley, William	Monroe
Tomalson, William	Washington
Treadwell, Stephen	Heard
Tucker, Allen	Greene
Tucker, Robert	Elbert
Tuhett, John	Pike
Tully, Henry, Sr	Newton
Turner, John	Oglethorpe
Turner, John	Putnam

U

Name	County
Usury, Thomas	Crawford

V

Name	County
Vaughan, Felix	Franklin
Varner, George	Franklin
Varner, Matthew, Sr	Oglethorpe
Vickers, William	Meriwether

W

Name	County
Waites, George	DeKalb
Waites, Samuel	Troup
Walker, James	Upson
Wallace, William	Greene
Walton, Josiah	Wilkes
Warden, Samuel	Madison
Warthern, William	Washington
Waters, Clement	Habersham
Watkins, W., Sr	Washington
Watson, Isham	Lowndes
Watson, Samuel	Troup
Weatherton, Thomas	Walton
Weeks, Theophilus	Camden
West, John	Talbot
Wcotbrook, John	Franklin
Wetter, William	Clark
Whitaker, Joshua	Richmond
White, Zeceriah	Effingham
Whitfield, Lewis	Burke
Wight, John	Butts
Wilhite, Lewis	Elbert
Williams, Anderson	Effingham
Williams, John	Habersham
Williams, Solomon	Laurens
Wills, Leonard	Gwinnett
Wilson, George	Walton

Name	County
Wilson, James, Sr.	Jackson
Wilson, John, Sr.	Greene
Wilson, John	Columbia
Wilson, Samuel	Screven
Wilson, Williams	Jackson
Wood, James	Monroe
Woodall, Joseph	Oglethorpe
Woodruff, Richard	Wilkes

Name	County
Wright, John	Butts
Wright, William	Clark
Y	
Young, George	Oglethorpe
Z	
Zinn, Henry	Richmond

NAMES OF WIDOWS OF REVOLUTIONARY SOLDIERS WHO DREW LAND IN THE CHEROKEE LAND LOTTERY OF 1838, AND THE COUNTIES IN WHICH THEY LIVED

A

Name	County
Alexander, Sarah	Gwinnett
Alexander, Susanna	Talbot
Allison, Martha	Greene
Arrant, Elizabeth	Upson

B

Name	County
Bacheler, Nancy	Wilkinson
Bailey, Keziah	Washington
Baker, Jane	Chatham
Baker, Sarah	Gwinnett
Barnett, Caroline	Clark
Barnett, Margaret	Jackson
Barron, Frances	Upson
Barr, Elizabeth	Houston
Bateman, Tabitha	Houston
Battle, Sarah	Taliaferro
Bayless, Sarah	Warren
Blalock, Eleanor	Upson
Boggs, Eve	Jackson
Bohanan, Lydia	Appling
Bolton, Mary	Warren
Bostwick, Mary	Morgan
Brach, Sarah	Wilkinson
Bradford, Ann	Putnam
Branch, Hester	Tattnall
Brantley, Mary	Putnam
Brewer, Elizabeth	Elbert
Broadwell, Christian	Jackson
Brookins, Nancy	Washington
Brooks, Rachel	DeKalb
Brown, Elizabeth	Burke
Brown, Frances	
Brown, Laonie	Dooly
Brown, Mary	DeKalb
Brown, Mary	Campbell
Brown, Rebecca	Henry
Browning, Margaret	Clark
Bruson, Frances	Houston
Bruce, Elizabeth	Wilkes
Bryan, Ann	Burke
Buchanan, Mary	Jasper
Buise, Margaret	Newton
Burnett, Molsey	Lowndes
Butler, Hannah	Lee
Butler, Marcy C.	Gwinnett

C

Name	County
Cannon, Ann	Walton
Cannon, Elizabeth	Jasper
Cannon, Mary	Bulloch
Carnes, Rosanna	Rabun
Carroll, Mary	Wilkes
Cash, Sarah	Jackson
Chambers, Martha	Fayette

Name	County
Cheshire, Sarah	Monroe
Chesser, Easter	Clark
Chickonimy, Mary	Monroe
Childs, Elizabeth	Jones
Clark, Mary	Jefferson
Cohom, Elizabeth	Taliaferro
Coleman, Elizabeth	Bibb
Coleman, Nancy	Appling
Connaway, Elizabeth	Hall
Cook, Deborah	Washington
Cook, Elizabeth	Jackson
Cook, Lydia	Effingham
Copeland, Martha	Bibb
Crawford, Mary	Carroll
Crawford, Mary Ann	Columbia
Creeny, Rebecca	Appling
Cronich, Rachel	Walton
Culbertson, Celia	Troup
Culver, Nancy	Hancock
Cummings, J.	Washington
Cumming, Sarah	Greene
Cunningham, Nancy	Elbert

D

Name	County
Daniel, Mary	Washington
Daniel, Sarah	Richmond
Darris, Elizabeth	Jackson
Davis, Mary	Montgomery
Davis, Mary Ann	DeKalb
Deadwyler, Alice	Elbert
Deason, Hannah	Campbell
Denton, Emily	Jones
Dickson, Mary	Screven
Dobbs, Sarah	Hall
Doles, Elizabeth	Baldwin
Doherty, Elizabeth	DeKalb
Douglass, M. A.	Meriwether
DuBose, Sarah	Burke
Duffel, Lucy	Oglethorpe
Duke, Nancy	Morgan
Dunnaway, Mary	Warren
Durracott, Rebecca	Elbert
Dyson, Esther	Lee

E

Name	County
Edmunds, W.	Wilkes
England, Margaret	Habersham
English, Sarah	Franklin
Estes, Isabella	Putnam
Eubanks, Susanna	Hall
Evans, Jane	Fayette

F

Name	County
Fairchild, Elizabeth	Wilkinson
Faris, Rebecca	Gwinnett

Name	County	Name	County
Fincher, Jemina	Henry	Jenkins, Rosanna	Oglethorpe
Fitzpatrick, Elizabeth	Twiggs	Johnson, Martha W	Fayette
Fitts, Mary	Elbert	Johnson, Rosannah	DeKalb
Flood, Jane	Henry	Johnson, Sarah	Heard
Floyd, Sarah	Madison	Johnson, Sivel	Warren
Fowler, Martha	Morgan	Jones, Mary	Hall
Fogil, Mary	Morgan		
Fox, Wilmouth	Jasper	**J**	
Freeman, Elizabeth	Jasper	Jones, Margaret	Jefferson
Fuller, Elizabeth	Greene	Jones, Nancy	Fayettc
Fuller, Keziah	Columbia	Jordan, Winnefred	Washington
		Jourdan, Elizabeth	Warren
G			
Gaines, Ann	Thomas	**K**	
Gamage, Charity	Houston	Kellebrew, Elizabeth	Warren
Gammill, Jane	Harris	Kendall, Elizabeth P	Muscogee
Garr, Catherine	Morgan	Kesterson, Nancy	Bibb
Gideons, Elizabeth	Talbot	King, Elizabeth	Warren
Giles, Celia	Washington	King, Mary	Talbot
Ginn, Sarah	Elbert	Kirklin, Mary	Troup
Glazier, Sarah	Newton	Knight, Bethany	Emanuel
Glenn, Ann	Jasper		
Glenn, Elizabeth	Jackson	**L**	
Glenn, Elizabeth	Troup	Lacy, Sarah	Newton
Glynn, Lucy	Greene	Lambert, Sarah	Jackson
Golden, Elender	Walton	Lansford, Elizabeth	Jasper
Golden, Frances	Wilkes	Lawless, Agnes	Madison
Golightly, S	Washington	Lawson, Martha	Wilkinson
Goodwin, Nancy	Franklin	Lewis, Catherine	Henry
Goolsby, Mary	Oglethorpe	Lewis, Nancy	Coweta
Grady, Mary	Franklin	Lewis, Selia	Gwinnett
Gray, Diana	Franklin	Lindsey, Mary	Wilkes
Gray, Susanna	Elbert	Lockland, Charlotte	Monroe
Gressam, Sally	Hall	Long, Louisa	Bibb
Grizzard, Susanna	Warren	Long, Martha	Hancock
		Lovejoy, Jemina	Pike
H		Loyd, Mary	Gwinnett
Hamilton, C	Montgomery	Lucas, Mary	Hancock
Haney, Elizabeth	Gwinnett	Lynn, Sally	Jasper
Haney, Ursula	Putnam		
Hanson, Peggy	Morgan	**Mc**	
Harper, Mary	Hancock	McCibben, Margaret	Henry
Harris, Clara	Troup	McClain, Mary	Gwinnett
Harris, Lavania	Oglethorpe	McCollum, Margaret	Franklin
Harris, Mary	Rabun	McCoy, Ann	Taliaferro
Harvey, Sarah	Twiggs	McCutcheon, Jane	Hall
Hartley, Ferebe	Washington	McDaniel, Elizabeth	Jones
Head, Sarah	Elbert	McDaniel, Mildred	Hancock
Hendrix, Mary	Screven	McFail, Judith	Lowndes
Hendry, Ann	Liberty	McMinn, Jane	Habersham
Herndon, Frances	Heard	McRee, Mary	Clarke
Hester, Diana	Jones	McWhorter, Margaret	Oglethorpe
Hewell, Susanna	Clarke		
Hicks, Susanna	Upson	**M**	
Higgenbotham, Jean	Elbert	Magbee, Rachel	Butts
Highsmith, Sarah	Wayne	Magee, Elizabeth	Putnam
Hinds, Martha	Chatham	Manley, Temperance	Franklin
Hines, Nancy	Jackson	Mappin, Mary	Columbia
Hobbs, Margery	Habersham	Matthews, Elizabeth	Jefferson
Holbrook, Hannah	Gwinnett	Matthews, Elizabeth	Pike
Holbrooke, Prisillon	Gwinnett	Mattox, Amelia C	Wilkes
Holcombe, Frances	Chatham	Merritt, Barbara	Jasper
Holloman, Levicy	Pulaski	Middlebrooks, Milly	Newton
Horn, Dorcas	Pike	Miller, Lucretia	Early
Hubbard, Elizabeth	Oglethorpe	Moffett, Mary	Meriwether
Hubbard, Susanna	Oglethorpe	Monk, Susanna	Putnam
Hunter, Elizabeth	Gwinnett	Moody, Anna	Oglethorpe
		Moreland, Frances	Putnam
J		Morrow, Ann	Newton
Jackson, Mary	Washington	Morrow, Elizabeth	Franklin

Name	County	Name	County
Murphy, Martha	Wilkes	Starr, Mary	Morgan
Myers, Mary	McIntosh	Strad, Priscilla	Monroe
		Stewart, Tabitha	Screven
N		Stringer, Celia	Burke
Napp, Mary	Greene	Sutton, Sarah	Putnam
Nash, Mary	Jones		
Newsome, Lucy	Wilkinson	**T**	
Newsome, Nancy	Morgan	Tabor, Elizabeth	Franklin
Nichols, Mary	Twiggs	Talbot, Elizabeth	Clarke
Nix, Rebecca	Talbot	Tammons, Zipporah	Cherokee
		Tatum, Molly	Monroe
O		Terry, Hannah	Warren
Oliver, Jane	Elbert	Thomas, Mary	Washington
		Thomas, Sarah	Newton
P		Thrower, Sarah	Newton
Paine, Winefred	Crawford	Tomlinson, M. W.	Jefferson
Paris, Jane	Habersham	Tool, Jane	Jones
Park, Phebe	Greene	Trainum, Elizabeth	Morgan
Parrish, Elizabeth	Warren	Twitty, Sally	Fayette
Patterson, Jane	Monroe	Turke, Margaret	Franklin
Peacock, Amy	Walton	Tyler, Elizabeth	Newton
Phillips, Mary	Twiggs		
Pool, Dicey	Pike	**V**	
Porter, Elizabeth	Columbia	Verdin, Winnie	Oglethorpe
Proctor, Biddy	Gwinnett	Vernon, Patsey	Houston
Pruitt, Peniny	Newton	Vickers, Sarah	Hancock
		Visage, Elizabeth	Rabun
R		**W**	
Randolph, Dorothy	Wilkes	Walker, Elizabeth	Washington
Ray, Jane	Talbot	Walker, Luraney	Meriwether
Reese, Silva	Hall	Ward, Elizabeth	Pike
Richardson, Clara	Monroe	Ward, Jane	Elbert
Rivers, Mary Ann	Warren	Warren, Mary	Hall
Roberts, Elizabeth	Walton	Waters, Judith	Franklin
Robinson, Polly	Carroll	Weaver, Mary	Randolph
Rooke, Mary	Wayne	Wense, Mary	Chatham
Ross, Mary	Harris	Wesson, Sarah	Washington
Ruddell, Lee Ann	Wilkes	Wheeler, Mary	Franklin
Rudolph, Elizabeth	Camden	Wheeler, Susanna	Walton
Rushing, Sarah	Washington	*(See Gordon Co. History.)	
Rutherford, Mary	Gwinnett	Wilcher, Elizabeth	Newton
Rye, Elizabeth	Harris	Willis, Susanna	Wilkes
		Williams, Diana	Twiggs
S		Williams, Mary	Bulloch
Sager, Ann	Greene	Williams, Rebecca	Hall
Scott, Frances	Greene	Williamson, Nancy	Thomas
Sett, Susanna	DeKalb	Willingham, Jane	Oglethorpe
Shell, Elizabeth	DeKalb	Wilkes, Nancy	Elbert
Sims, Caty	Jasper	Willoughby, Unity	Bibb
Simmons, Sarah	Upson	Willson, Ann	Effingham
Singletary, Martha	Decatur	Willson, Rebecca	Greene
Slatter, Elvira	Twiggs	Windham, Lucy	Butts
Smith, Elizabeth	Greene	Wingate, Mary	Richmond
Smith, Mary	Warren	Worsham, Mary	Walton
Smith, Mary	Meriwether	Wright, Amis	Butts
Smith, Sarah	Morgan	Wright, Susan	Hancock
Smith, Susan	Montgomery	Wylie, Jane	Pike
Sparks, Jane	Troup		
Spence, Mary	Burke	**Y**	
Springer, Ann	Wilkes	Yates, Susanna	Fayette
Stamps, Mary	Warren	Yarbrough, Rachel	Muscogee

ROLL OF OFFICERS AND PRIVATES IN CAPT. PATRICK CARR'S CO. OF RANGERS, COL. JAMES MACKAY'S REGIMENT, BURKE CO., GA., 1781–1782

Patrick Carr, Capt.	William Patterson	John Murray
Mich'l Jones, 1st Lt.	William Moore	Tim Rickerson
Josiah Hatcher, 2nd Lt.	Anderson Berryhill	Tephan Bell

Daniel Evans
John Hatcher
John Leith
Theodk Goodwyn
Urek Hatcher
John Mammin
Hillery Phillips
Nath'l Bell
Charles Burch
Edward Burch
Edward Bugg
John Doris
John Hix
William Jones
Peter Brown (Besoon)

...... Epperson
William Caletrop
Henry Doolin
Patrick Maloga
Isaac Ardis
Ezekiel Oxford
Jefse Oxford
Ezekiel Harris
Thomas Galphin
William Holmes
George Galphin
John Milledge
John McElhoney
William Collins

William Hatcher
William Stewart
John Kitts
Sud Outlaw
Edward Outlaw
...... Ballard
John Jolly
Jake Durban
...... Hill
Martin Shirley
Samuel Griffin
James Harvin
William Hunt
Peter Connalley

Note: (Original record at State Dept. of Archives, Atlanta, Ga.)

Revolutionary Soldiers of Ga.

Name	Lived in Co.	Drew land in year
Baker, Dempsey	Hancock	1842
Barber, Charles	Glynn	1827
Barson, David	Pulaski	1829
Boyd, John	Warren	1830
Brown, John, Sr.	Franklin	1828
Brown, Starke	Walton	1831
Brunfield, John	Elbert	1825
Bullock, Daniel	Twiggs	1836
Buchanan, James P., Sr.	Jasper	1822
Christian, Turner	Elbert	1831
Crawford, John	Twiggs	1822
Curry, Cary	Baldwin	1823
Dantigal, John	Richmond	1832
Doles, Jesse	Baldwin	1834
Duck, John	Morgan	1837
Felts, James	Jones	1823
Geddins Thomas	Pulaski	1842
Gilbert, Thomas	Franklin	1838
Harbin, William Sr	Elbert	1831
Heidt, Christian J.	Effingham	1821
Hinsley, Thomas	Jasper	1826
Hodges, Joseph	Bulloch	1826
Horn, Richard	McIntosh	1837
Hubbard, Manvah	Baldwin	1839
Jameson, David	Twiggs	......
Joyce John	Tattnall	1823
Knight, John	Wayne	1821
McCall, John	Effingham	1820

Name	Lived in	Drew land in year
McClendon, Thomas, Sr	Walton	1822
McCullers, William Sr	Morgan	1827
McCullough, Jacob	Richmond	1836
Moore Joseph	Jasper	1833
Morris, John	Clarke	1822
Morris, William, Sr	Jackson	1821
Mullen, Malone	Hancock	1842
Perkerson, Joel	Jackson	1825
Pilgrim, Michael	Franklin	1831
Pollett, Richard	Clarke	1824
Ramey, John, Sr	Clarke	1839
Ridge, James	Gwinnett	1842
Shavely, Edward	Jones	1832
Shay, David	Clarke	1823
Thornby, Thomas	Pulaski	1829
Trammell, William	Elbert	1821
Usher, Daniel	Richmond	1821
Williams, Thomas, Sr	Jackson	1836
Williby John	Twiggs	1822
Willis, Joseph, Sr	Effingham	1822
Whelons, Lewis, Sr	Morgan	1827
Yates, Peter	Clarke	1842

Names copied from a copy of *"The Original List"* of the drawing of "Old Irwin" Co., Ga., together with a list of the "reverted lots" giving the names, dates of the Grant, and the names of the Counties in which the grantees lived at the time of the issuing of the grants. "Old Irwin" comprised the counties of Irwin, Berrien, Lowndes, and Colquitt, together with portions of Clinch, Worth, Coffee, and Thomas Counties.

Certified to by E. R. De Graffenreid and printed at Milledgeville, Baldwin Co., Ga., 1857.

Name	County	Date
Allgood, John	Elbert	Feb. 24, 1831
Bellinger, John	Elbert	Mar. 19, 1825
Binum, Drury	Warren	Oct. 13, 1834
Brantley, Amos	Hancock	Dec. 26, 1828
Brooks, Samuel, Sr	Wilkes	Nov. 3, 1830
Brumfield, John	Elbert	Dec. 13 1830
Bryant, Isaac	Putnam	Sept. 21, 1836
Buford, John, Sr	Screven	Dec. 19, 1823
Capeheart, John	Jefferson	1824
Casey, Daniel	Elbert	Nov. 11, 1821
Collins, James	Richmond	Dec. 22, 1821
Collins, Joseph	Morgan	Sept. 4, 1837
Conner, Daniel	Clarke	Mar. 1, 1830
Cook, Elisha	Hanock	Nov. 13, 1832
Easterling, James	Twiggs	Dec. 24, 1839

Name	County	Date
Gi bert, Thomas	Franklin	1824
Gilbert, William	Morgan	Dec. 17, 1829
Goore, Thomas, Sr.	Hancock	Dec. 23, 1828
Grant, Joseph	Hancock	Nov. 3, 1828
Greene, Forrest	Jackson	Nov. 26, 1821
Greer, Robert	Morgan	Nov. 4, 1829
Gully, Richard	Elbert	1828
Harvey, John	Clarke	July 31, 1821
Herndon, John, Sr.	Jackson	Dec. 18, 1837
Hendley, John	Morgan	Feb. 2, 1835
Hill, John	Hancock	Sept. 17, 1840
Hollinsworth, Isaac	Twiggs	Oct. 30, 1827
Inger John	Jackson	Dec. 17, 1823
Jarrell, Richard	Baldwin	July 20, 1824
Johnson Jacob	Twiggs	Oct. 5, 1837
Johnston, John B	Clarke	Aug. 27, 1841
Judkins, Zachariah	Hancock	Jan. 27, 1840
Kent, John	Warren	Dec. 6, 1820
McCleland, Mack	Screven	Dec. 19, 1825
McGamary, John	Warren	Sept. 30, 1824
Mercer, Jacob	Jasper	Jan. 31, 1828
Moreland, Robert, Sr.	Wilkes	May 19, 1826
Morris, W. M., Sr.	Jackson	Mar. 31, 1824
Myhand, James	Morgan	Nov. 3, 1822
Nelson, Jeremiah	Hancock	Jan. 12, 1826
Pressnell, W.lliam	Jackson	Dec. 21, 1839
Rives, Joel	Hancock	Nov. 23, 1825
Rooks, Hardeman	Jackson	Nov. 5, 1827
Sanders, David	Putnam	Dec. 14, 1836
Smith John, Sr.	Morgan	Aug. 29, 1841
Smith William	Walton	Jan. 29, 1821
Snow, Mark	Gwinnett	Nov. 1, 1830
Thompson, W lliam	Jackson	Dec. 29, 1825
Tinney, Ed R.	Chatham	Dec. 9, 1825
T:son, James	Effingham	Feb. 14, 1833
Webb, Clarence	Jackson	Dec. 19, 1826
Willeby, John	Twiggs	Dec. 19, 1829
Wright, John	Walton	Nov. 4, 1829

LA FAYETTE'S VISIT

The much heralded coming of La Fayette to Milledgeville, Ga., in 1825 was a red letter day for the citizens of Wilkinson Co., Ga. Within her borders still lived at that time about 30 of the veterans of the *Rev. War*, among whom were:

Major John Hatcher, John Ussery, Jesse Vaughn, Solomon Wright, William Statham, Hardy Stewart, Brice Ragan, John Nunn, William Lindsey, William Lord, Hansell Lasseter, William Kemp,

Spencer Douglass, Nathaniel Cannon, Peter Buckles, Lemuel Burkett, Ezekiel Boggs, John Bowen, William Bivins, Cornelius Bachelor, Robert Barnett, Henry Adkerson, Robert Rozar, John Tomberlin and others.

These grizzled veterans had fought in the Battles of the Revolution, some of whom had perhaps fought under the command of the great Frenchman, and hearing of his coming doubtless would have been willing to sacrifice the remainder of their days for one last opportunity to grasp his hand.

In his book, "*Bench and Bar of Ga.,*" Stephen F. Miller tells us of how the great La Fayette embraced in Milledgeville, Ga. one after another, the Veterans of the Revolution, how down the line of Sols. he walked, shaking hands with each man, and complimenting the splendid appearance of the Military companies. (From *Wilkinson Co. History*.)

REVOLUTIONARY SOLDIERS

TERRELL Co. (DRAWERS OF LAND IN DISTRICTS OF OLD LEE Co., WHICH BECAME TERRELL Co.) (FROM TERRELL Co. HISTORY (NOT PUBLISHED), MRS. IVY MELTON, Co. HISTORIAN)

Name	County	Date
Akridge, Ezekiel	Newton	1830
Anderson, William, Sr	Wilkes	1836
Armstorph, George, Sr	Effingham	1836
Beasley, Henry	Walton	1836
Beasley, William	DeKalb	1844
Bohan, Joseph	Putnam	1827
Booker, John	Wilkes	1839
Brazil, Bird W	Hancock	1842
Brinkley, Eli	Washington	1845
Brown, John R	Washington	1837
Burton, John	Franklin	1841
Burkhalter, Jacob	Warren	1837
Cash, John	Jackson	1830
Clower, Daniel	Gwinnett	1838
Clare, George	Madison	1835
Connell, Daniel	Jefferson	1835
Cooper, Henry	Putnam	1838
Cox, Moses	Washington	1836
Crawford, Lemuel	Clark	1839
Culver, Nathan	Hancock	1837
Daugherty, Joseph	Screven	1831
Denton, John	Hancock	1836
Dillard, John	Rabun	1844
Donaldson, William	DeKalb	1831
Duncan, Pearson	Elbert	1836
Eastward, John, Sr	Washington	1836
Freeman, Daniel	Jasper	1831
Futch, Onesimur	Bryan	1830
Gailer, James	Gwinnett	1827
Gay, William	Irwin	1828
Glenn, James	Jackson	1835
George, Jesse	Gwinnett	1836
Gressup, James	Elbert	1829
Grant, Joseph	Hancock	1828

Name	County	Date
Harmon, Henry	Warren	1843
Heath, Jordan	Burke	1834
Herring, George	Bibb	1829
Houston, Samuel	Henry	1828
Inlow, Thomas, Sr	Walton	1831
Jackson, Moses	Greene	1836
Jones, David	Monroe	1833
Jones, Reuben	Jasper	1834
Jones, Moses	Lincoln	1836
Johnson, Emanuel	Richmond	1831
Johnson, William	Bibb	1832
Jordan, Aven	Laurens	1837
Knight, Thomas	Walton	1828
Leathers, Samuel	Hall	1837
Lee, Samson	Washington	1845
Lewis, Peter	Henry	1836
Miles, Thomas	Baldwin	1839
Morris, Thomas	Jasper	1840
McCutcheon, Joseph	Hall	1843
McNeese, James	Jackson	1836
Newsom, John	Warren	1835
Parker, Daniel	Morgan	1837
Pichard, John H	Monroe	1846
Poss, Henry, Sr	Walton	1832
Posey, Bennett	Jasper	1845
Ray, Benjamin	Twiggs	1836
Raley, Henry	Warren	1845
Rhyme, Willis	Warren	1836
Roddenberry, George	Bulloch	1833
Sandiford, Elmerick	Wilkes	1832
Salmon, Ezekiel	Richmond	1835
Sparks, Jeremiah	Morgan	1838
Smith, William	Gwinnett	1831
Smith, John	Wilkes	1832
Shuffield, William	Putnam	1845
Triplet, William	Wilkes	1834
Triplett, William	Tatnall	1834
Tindall, James, Sr	Burke	1843
Vincent, Isaac	Clarke	1833
Wayne, George	Jasper	1830
Welch, Nicholas	Newton	1831
Williamson, John	Henry	1831
Wilson, James	Franklin	1828
Womack, William	Effingham	1830

The Following Names of Revolutionary Soldiers Are Not in Knight's "Roster of the Revolution of Ga." (Found in Lottery Lists in Milledgeville, Ga.)

Isaac Ardis
Nathaniel Bell
Tephan Bell
Anderson Berryhill
William Caletrop
Peter Connally
Henry Doolin (Dulin)
Drury Harris
Urek Hatcher
William Holmes
Peter Du Bose
John Jolley

Doster Jordan
Overoff Jordan
John Leith
Jeremiah Loftus
Patrick Maloga
John Murray
Sud Outlaw
Ezekiel Oxford
Jesse Oxford
Lovick Pierce
Martin Shirley
Isaac Stocks

Revolutionary Soldiers Found in Records, Department of Archives (Not Published)

Isaac Ardis
John Bechner
Nathaniel Bell
Andrew Berryhill
Jacob Bousman
Daniel Brunson
Nicholas H. Bugg (Camden Co.)
Edward Bugg
Elizabeth Bush (Widow *Rev. Sol.*)
Joseph Carson
David Caudell
Wiatt Cleveland
William Coletrap
Charles Dameron
Henry Doolin (Dulin)
John Duncan, Sr.
Lewis Flemister
Sherrard de Langig, Jr.
Samuel French
Christopher Gardner
John Gaster
John Germany, Jr.
Charles Guffis
Archible Griggsberry
William Hannett
Arthur Hayer
Edmund Henry

William Holmes
James Jackson (1825 Lottery)
Stephen Kitchens
John Leith
Patrick McCullough
John McElheny
Thomas Macher
James Martin
James Miller, Sr.
Samuel Morgan
Edmund Murphy
John Murray
(2) John Nelson's
Daniel Newman
Jacob Oates
Sud Outlaw
Ezekiel Oxford
Isaac Patterson
John Payne
Hillery Phillips
Stephen Powell
Major Romand
Moses Sanders
Martin Shirley
Lt. Francis Tennill
Matthew Zettler

Laurens County Revolutionay Soldiers (From Original Records)

Jonathan Bacon
Simon Beck
John Bennett
James Branch
William Bush
Samuel Cason
John Coats
Jonathan Coleman

Theophilus Coleman
Sampson Culpepper
Benjamin Darsey
John Dean
William Dean
Thomas Duncan
Thomas Farmer
John Fullwood

James Glass
Henry Goodman
Edward Hagan
Benjamin Hampton
Jonathan Holly
John Hudson
Jonathan Jones
William Livingston
Amos Love
Benjamin Manning
Drury Manning
John Manning
Dennis McLendon
Dr. Thomas Moore
William O'Neal
Burrell Phillips
Mark Phillips

Wylie Pope
Thomas Pullen
John Rowland
Wright Ryals
John Shine
Hardy Smith
David Spear
George Tarvin
John Thomas
Peter Thomas
Thomas Vickers
Josiah Warren
William Whitehead
Solomon Williams
William Yarbrough
Oren (Wren) Young

Revolutionary Soldiers Who Applied for Pensions in Georgia
(Under Act of 1832)

Name	County	Name	County
David Andrew	Fayette	Christopher Gardner, Private	
Absolem Awtry		John M. Griner	Bulloch
Thomas Beatty		Thomas Guthrie, Private	
William Bobbitt, Private		John Hammond	Hall
Peter Cash	Henry	Arch Henderson, Private	
Ephriam Cassell	Campbell	James Hughes	De Kalb
Silas Caster	Washington	William Merry	Carroll
David Comer, Lieut.		William Nevis	Early
John Conway, Private		William Pentecost, Lieut.	
James Dawson	Rabun	Henry Pool, Sr.	Baldwin
Joseph Davie	Muscogee	James Quillen	Habersham
Jeremiah Drew, Private		James Sleigh	Camden
Alexander Dunn	Monroe	Henry Spalding	Columbia
John Halcondale Edge	Bulloch	Elisha Talley	Heard
Arthur Elliott, Private		James Town	Madison
Liddall Ester	Troup	James Vassels, Private	
James Findall	Burke	Alexander Walden	Coweta
James Flournoy	Talbot	Thomas Wilson	Gwinnett

Widows of Revolutionary Soldiers Who Applied for Pension

Name	County	Name	County
Susan M. Evans, W. *Rev. Sol.*		Drusilla Holbrook, W. *Rev. Sol.*	
George Evans	Clarke	Caleb Holbrook	Gwinnett
Harriet Ann Elbert, W. *Rev. Sol.*		Elizabeth Kiker, W. *Rev. Sol.*	
Lieut. Elbert		George Kiker	Cass
Bethany, Fuller W. *Rev. Sol.*	Warren	Mary G. Levert, W. *Rev. Sol.*	
		Thomas Levert	Walton

Revolutionary Soldiers, Pensioners of 1835, Henry County

Francis Adams
Robert Beard
John Barnhill
Ezekiel Cloud

John Cook
Thomas Cook
Reuben Edwards
James Hannegan

Joseph Hand
David McCance
Isaac Moore, Sr.
Charles Upchurch

REVOLUTIONARY SOLDIERS, PENSIONERS OF 1832, UPSON COUNTY

Charles Adkins
William Black
Thomas Cannon
William Carraway
William Duke
Henry Garland

Christopher Flannigan
William Hudgins
Benjamin Hamrick
Michael Kelly
Peter McKenzie
Daniel Parker

Samuel Pool
Henry Peeples
Patrick Roach
William Stephens, Sr.
William Shepherd
Thomas E. Sullivan

NAMES OF REVOLUTIONARY SOLDIERS MENTIONED IN THE ORIGINAL RECORDS OF JACKSON COUNTY
(FROM DEEDS, WILLS, ESTATES, AND LOTTERIES)

Miles Angley
James Barr, Sr.
Thomas Barrow
Robert Beavers
Francis Bell
William Bennett
Josiah Bondurant
Nathan Bowly
Peter Boyle
Jacob Brazelton, Sr.
Bond Veal Brown
William Burns, Sr.
Isaac Burson
Middleton Brooks
Thomas Carter (Franklin)
Thomas A. Carter (Elbert)
John Carter
John Cash
Patrick Cash
James Cochran
James W. Cook
Joseph Cowan
Ansel (Ancil) Cunningham
Charles Damron
William Dial
John Duncan
Thomas Eaves
Anthony W. Elton
Sharod Gean
James Glenn
William Gober
Charles Gunter

John Hampton, Sr.
Joseph Harper, Sr.
Joseph Harris
John G. Henderson
Robert Henderson
Lewis Hines
John Justice
Samuel Knox
John King
Levi Lowry
Jesse Johnson
William Lord
Isaac Lynch
Isaac Matthews
William Matthews, Sr.
William Moore
Robert Morgan
Alexander Morrison
John Mickelhannon
Daniel McDaniel
John McDonald
John McCarty
James McKilgore
Charles McKinney
John Nix
John Orr, Sr.
William Pentecost
William Potts
Edward Pharr
William Patton
Samuel Pool
Alexander Reid

John Robinson
Philip Ryan
John Sesson
Solomon Saxon
George Slaton
Christopher Sailors
John Nix
John Orr, Sr.
William Patton
William Pentecost
Edward Pharr
Samuel Pool
William Potts
Alexander Reid
John Robinson
Philip Ryan
Solomon Saxon
Christopher Sailors
John Sesson
George Slaton
William Smith
Thomas Staples
Henry Stoneman
Robert Taylor
Sherrod Thompson
Levi Wallace
Claiborne Webb
James Wilson, Sr.
William Wilson
John Winters
John Wright

REVOLUTIONARY SOLDIERS IN BALDWIN COUNTY
(NAMES REGISTERED IN 1819)

John Asbell
William Asbell
Hugh Davice
Charles Francis

John Griggs
Monsah Hubbard
Thomas Humphries, Jr.
James Lester, Sr.

William Jones
Luke Moore
John Sims, Sr.
Samuel Tinsley

REVOLUTIONARY SOLDIERS IN BURKE COUNTY (FROM RECORDS)

Benjamin Brack
Alexander Carswell
John Carswell
Daniel Inman

Joshua Inman
Gov. Jared Irwin
Abraham Jones
Col. John Jones

Seaborn Jones
John Lawson
Abraham Lively
Matthew Lively

John Murphree
Miles Murphree
Joseph A. Roe

Revolutionary Soldiers in Butts County (from Records)

Joseph Benton (Pension)
William Buford
Joseph Dawson
George Eubanks
Alexander Harbin
Levi Jester

William Jester
Henry Lee
William McCoy
Abner Piggott
E. Price (Pension)
David Ramsdill

Richard Speake (Pension)
Robert Smith, Sr.
John Tillery, Sr.
John Wright

Revolutionary Soldiers in Effingham County (from Land and Rev. Records)

(This is not a complete list. The records of these Soldiers are found also in Screven and Bulloch Counties, Ga. Many went "West" to Miss. and La.)

Paul Beville
Robert Beville
William Cone
Benjamin D'Oiley (Aley)
Philip Dell
William Fletcher and his 4 sons:
  Henry Fletcher
  George Fletcher
  John Fletcher
  Joseph Fletcher
McKeen Green, Sr.
McKeen Green, Jr.
John Groover
Samuel Hearn
William Hearn
Joshua Hodges
David Harris
Caleb Howell

Daniel Howell
Robert Hudson, Sr.
Robert Hudson, Jr.
Joseph Hodges
Joseph Humphries
Clement Lanier
Lewis Lanier
Theophilus Lundy
Nathaniel Lundy
John McCall
Charles McCall and his 3 sons:
  David McCall
  George McCall
  William McCall
Thomas McCall and his 2 sons:
  Sherrod McCall
  Thomas McCall, Jr.
Nathaniel Miller

James Moore
John Moore
George Palmer
Joshua Pearce, Sr. and his 3
  sons:
  Joshua Pearce, Jr.
  Stephen Pearce
  William Pearce
William Porter
Abraham Ravot
John Rupert
Solomon Thornton
David Thorn
Jeremiah Warren
James Willson
William Willson

Revolutionary Soldiers in Jasper County (1825) Lottery

Sion Bennett
Freeman Blunt
James Brooks
Josiah Burgess

John Seal Cardin
John Carrell
John Chatfield
William Germany

Robert Hester
Mordecai Hill
Thomas Morris

Revolutionary Soldiers in Jefferson County (from Records)

Hugh Alexander
John Arrington (d. 1827)
John Boutin
Ezekiel Causey
William Clements, Sr. (d. 1828)
James Cotter
Michael Cowart
James Cook
John Darby, Sr.
Stephen Durougeaux (d. 1833)

George Fowler, Sr.
Dempsey Hall, Sr.
Hudson Hall, Sr.
Benjamin Green
John S. Holder
James Johnson
William Lions
Norman McCloud
John Patterson
William Patterson

Morris Murphy
Moses Newton
Seth Pierce
John Thompson
William Thompson
Joshua Watson
Caleb Welch
Jerry Wilsher

Revolutionary Soldiers in Coweta County (from Records)

James Aikens
John Benton
John Dickson (d. 1835)
John Endsley
John Faver
Allen Gay

O. M. Houston
Isham Huckaby
Zedic Hudson
Benjamin Hughes
Abner Johnson
Joseph McClendon

John Neely
Randal Robinson
William B. Smith, Sr.
John Thurmond (Thurman)
Major James Wood
William Wood

Revolutionary Soldiers in Ware County (from Records)

William Cason	Levi Lee	Thomas Simmons
Willeford Cason	John McClain	Ivey Smith
Willis Cason	William Miller	Henry Stone
Charles Griffis	Specey Rushin	David Sutton
William King	Solomon Sellers	William Thompson
John Lee	Joshua Sharp	

Revolutionary Soldiers in Thomas County (from Records)

Joseph Anderson	Simon Hadley	Shadrack Pugh
Ralph Bozeman	Ignatius Hall	

Revolutionary Soldiers of South Carolina

(Descendants came to Georgia)

Found in "*Old Records Division,*" Washington, D. C. Adj. General's Office. No. 30189. (Never published)

"We whose names are hereunder written, being deeply impressed with the Calamitous Circumstances of the Inhabitants of America from the Opressive Acts of the British Parliament Tending to Enslave this Continent—Do find it necessary for the Security of our Lives and Fortunes and above all our Liberty and Freedom, to associate ourselves into a volunteer Company under the command of JAMES JONES.

And that we will hold ourselves in Readiness for our Mutual Security and Defense to obey all such Orders as shall be Directed by our Provincial Congress.

Henry Jourdan, Sr.	Martin Loadholt	Daniel Reaves
Henry Jourdan, Jr.	Jacob Haders	John Morris
Wm. Stanley	Jacob Heir (Hiers)	Wm. Wood
Moses Bennett	Edmund Jones	Mark Tapley
Samuel Pickings	Wm. Wournell	Michael Odom
Josiah Brunston	George Kierse	Joshua Elkins
Gustavus Gulfies	James Morris	Thomas Reavs, Sr.
Thomas Jovas, Sr.	Henry Peoples	Thomas Reavs, Jr.
Jacob Colson	Timothy Caffle	Thomas Lennox, Sr.
Wm. Kierse	John Maders	Thomas Lennox, Jr.
Wm. Brunston	George Brunston	Amox Lennox
John Taylor	William Jones	Jacob Besinger
Joseph Sykes	Henry Taylor	Ephriam Jones
Wm. Lunnix	Jeremiah Brown	Joseph Doelittle
Alexander Brunston	Benjamin Byrd	Daniel Buddest
John Ayers	Lewis Lee	Charles Morris
Wm. Ayers	Solomon Peters	Benjamin Odom
Stephen Frank	John Tedden	William Jones"

Original paper in possession of A. S. Salley, State Historian of S. C. No. 503202. Certified to by Mr. Wintermeyer of the Old Records Division Office Washington, D. C. Many descendants of these men came to Ga.

Revolutionary Soldiers from Georgia

The following applied for PENSIONS under Act of Congress, June 7, 1832. From Minutes of Franklin Co., Ga., Court of Ordinary, commencing May 4, 1829 and ending Nov. 4, 1844. (Applications Abstracts) can be found in Georgia D. A. R. Historical Collections, Vol. I—Pages 137 to 182.

Albritton, John—b. Hanover Co., Va., 1747.

Bond, Richard—b. Amherst Co., Va., 1763; d. Ga., 1837.

Cash, James—b. Fairfax Co., Va., 1764.

Cheek, William—b. N. C., 1752.

Clark, Thomas—b. Granville Co., N. C., 1761.

Dyer, Elisha—b. Potomac river, Va., 1763; d. Ga., Sept. 4, 1839.
Downs, Ambrose—b. Richmond Co., Ga., 1761.
Edwards, Joseph—b. Md., 1756.
Epperson, Thompson—b. Albemarle Co., Va., 1757.
Farrar, John—b. N. C., 1760.
Guest, Moses (Capt.)—b. Fauquier Co., Va., 1750.
Glover, William—b. Prince George Co., Md., 1760.
Lee, Andrew—b. Augusta, Ga., 1761.
Leach, Burdette—b. Virginia, 1760.
Murdock, William—b. Ireland, 1759.
Mitchell, William—b. Va., 1761.
Moseley, Samuel—b. Bute Co., N. C., 1759.
Nichols, Julius—b. Granville Co., N. C., 1759.
Parks, Henry—b. Albemarle Co., Va., 1758; d., 1840.
Stoneycipher, John—b. Culpepper Co., Va., 1756.
Smith, Jesse—b. Montgomery Co., N. C., 1765.
Stow, Warren—b. Sheffield, Conn.
Smith, Gabriel—b. Montgomery Co., N. C., 1764.
Smith, William—b. Moore Co., N. C., 1763.
Tate, John—b. Ireland, 1758.
Thomas, William—b. Culpepper Co., Va., 1763.
Wilson, James—b. Pa., 1758.
Wilkerson, Elisha—b. Sussex Co., Va., 1763.
Ray, William—Pension No. 19360.
York, William—Pension No. 19185.

Wilkes County Revolutionary Soldiers

WILKES COUNTY was named for John Wilkes, a *member of Parliament,* who opposed the policy of Great Britain toward the American Colonies which brought about the *Rev. War.* It was created 1777 from the northern part of St. Paul's Parish and land acquired from the Creek and Cherokee Indians in payment of their debts to the Indian traders, and called the "Ceded Lands." It was called "The Hornet's Nest" by the Tories.

Many of the Counties of Ga. were named for English friends of the Colonists, Champions of American Liberty in England, viz: Edmund Burke, the Earl of Camden, William Pitt, the Earl of Chatham, the Earl of Effingham, John Glynn, the Duke of Richmond, John Wilkes.

Then Washington County was created in 1784 and named in honor of GEORGE WASHINGTON. At the time of the organization, it included all the land "from the Cherokee corner north, extending from the Ogeechee river to the Oconee river, south to Liberty Co." It was settled by many refugee Soldiers who were given bounty lands, 287½ acres for their services in the *Revolutionary Army.*

"War Woman's Creek" in Wilkes (now Elbert) Co., Ga. This is a small tributary of Broad river, and which acquired the name of "War Woman's Creek" during the Revolution. It was near this stream that Benjamin Hart and his wife, Nancy Hart, Georgia's Revolutionary heroine, lived. The name was conferred on the Creek because of the heroic deeds of Nancy Hart, who was known among the Indians of that section, as the War Woman.

Note: PETITION—"Petition of practitioners of Law in the Western District to Superior Court of Wilkes Co., Ga.," that no person be admitted to the Bar without three years' study with an Attorney or Judge of the Superior Court, and of good moral character, except those who have competent knowledge of Latin and Geeek or Latin and French, who shall be admitted after two years' study, for which a certificate must be furnished. Lawyers from other States not to be allowed to practice till after one year's residence in Georgia."

"Recommendation of members of the Bar to enforce the law requiring practitioners of law to appear at the Bar in black silk surplice or gown." (From Records.)

THEY FOUGHT AT THE BATTLE OF KETTLE CREEK, THROUGH WHICH GEORGIA WAS
FREED OF THE TORY DOMINATION, AND A MONUMENT HAS BEEN
ERECTED TO THEIR MEMORY ON THIS BATTLE GROUND
IN WILKES CO., GA.

A

Anderson, Alexander
Anderson, Henry
Anglin, William
Alexander, Asa
Alexander, James
Aycock, Richard
Atkins, John
Austin, Richard
Aldridge, James
Anthony, John
Anthony, Alexander

B

Bird, John
Barnes, Richard
Barnes, William
Brown, James
Bird, Benjamin
Bazelwood, Richard
Brannon, Moses
Barnett, Nathan
Butts, Solomon
Butler, William
Butler, Edmund
Branham, Samuel
Beasley, Richard
Beasley, Ambrose
Beasley, William
Beasley, James
Bedell, Absolem
Bedingfield, Charles

C

Catchings, Benjamin
Catchings, Seymour
Catchings, Joseph
Clark, John
Coleman, Daniel
Coleman, Thomas
Coleman, Benjamin
Coleman, John
Coleman, James
Crosby, William
Crutchfield, John
Cheshire, John
Compton, William
Clower, Peter
Carter, James
Chandler, John
Cade, Drury
Carr, Henry
Cantey, Jeceriah

Cohron, Cornelius
Clarke, Gibson
Cloud, Ezekiel
Cloud, Nehemiah
Cloud, Jeremiah
Cain, John
Combs, John
Crain, Spencer
Cook, George
Catchings, Merideth
Catchings, Philip

D

Davis, Samuel
Davis, Absolem
Davis, Joel
Davis, Hardy
Dautham, Elijah
Dullins, Henry
Downs, William
Downs, Jonathan
Dooly, George
Dooly, John
Darden, George
Day, Robert
Day, Joseph
Durkee, Nathaniel

E

Edison, Shelton
Evans, Daniel
Evans, Benjamin
Ellis, Jerry

F

Favour, John
Ferrington, Jacob
Freeman, Daniel
Freeman, John
Freeman, George
Freeman, James
Freeman, Holman Jr.
Freeman, William
Flynn, John
Franklin, David
Franklin, David, Jr.
Farr, John
Farr, Benjamin
Fowler, Peter
Fowler, Henry
Foster, Francis
Foster, William
Fluker, John

Fluker, Owen

G

Gillons, James
Gouze, Henry
Glass, John
Glass, Joseph
Glass, Joel
Grant, Thomas
Graves, James
Graves, William
Graves, Thomas
Griffin, Randolph

H

Howard, William
Howard, John
Huggins, Robert
Hamilton, William
Hawkins, Stephen
Holliday, William, Sr.
Hubbard, John
Harvie, James
Harvie, Joel
Hill, James
Heard, Richard
Heard, Barnard
Heard, George
Heard, Joseph
Hart, John
Harris, John
Harris, David
Harris, Buckner
Harper, Samuel
Harper, Robert
Heard, Jesse

J

Jordan, Dempsey
Jordan, Samuel
Jiles, Thomas
Jiles, Samuel
Johns, Thomas
Johnson, John
Jones, Jesse
Joiner, Benjamin
Joiner, Thomas

K

Kilby, Daniel

L

Lowe, Jesse
Lowe, William

Lamar, James
Lamar, Zecheria
Lamar, Samuel
Lamar, Basil
Loyd, James
Little, Archibald
Little, James
Little, David
Lindsey, Dennis
Lindsey, John

Mc

McLendon, Jacob, Sr.
McLendon, Jacob, Jr.
McLendon, Isaac
McLean, James
McCall, Hugh (uncle of State Historian)
McCall, Thomas
McBurnett, Daniel
McMurray, Frederick

M

Marney, Thomas
Manaduc, Henry
Meriwether, Daniel
Mathews, Isham
Mercer, Jacob
Mercer, James
Mercer, Joshua
Mercer, William
Morgan, Asa
Morgan, William
Morgan, Luke
Moseley, William

N

Nelson, John

O

Ollens, Daniel
Oliver, Dionysius
Oliver, Peter
Oliver, John

P

Powell, Joshua
Prickett, William
Prickett, John
Persons, Samuel
Persons, Henry
Pratt, Edward

Pickins, Joseph
Poullain, Anthony
Poullain, William
Philips, Joseph
Philips, Zachariah

R

Roberson, Hugh
Roberson, David
Rogers, Reuben
Reddens, Scott
Rice, John
Rice, Nathan
Rice, David

S

Smith, Peyton
Smith, Nathan
Smith, James
Summerlin, Samuel
Summerlin, John
Summerlin, Dempsey
Summerlin, Richard
Summerlin, James
Stots, John
Stots, Peter
Smith, Thomas
Sinquefield, William
Sinquefield, Samuel
Spikes, Nathan
Simmons, William
Spurlock, George
Steward, William
Swan, John
Stephens, John
Stubblefield, Jeter
Sutton, William
Stroud, Thomas
Sampson, Archibald
Sampson, William
Simmons, James
Simpson, James
Strozier, Peter
Snead, Dudley
Stone, Charles
Stone, Joshua
Stephens, Benjamin
Stripling, Francis
Shannon, Thomas, Sr.
Shannon, Thomas, Jr.
Simby, William
Simby, James

Simby, Thomas
Shepard, Benjamin

T

Thompson, Reuben
Thompson, Peter
Terrell, David
Triplett, Francis
Tyner, Richard
Tyner, Benjamin
Tunis, Nicholas
Tate, Richard

V

Veazey, James
Vance, Patrick

W

Weller, Jacob
Wood, James
Worth, Thomas
Williams, James
Williams, John
Whatley, Samuel
Whatley, Walton W.
Wilkinson, Benjamin
Wilkinson, Elisha
Walton, George
Walton, Jesse
Walton, John
Walton, Nathan
Walton, Robert
Wellbourne, Daniel
Walker, John
Walker, Thomas
Wallace, John
Williamson, Micajah, Sr.
Williamson, Micajah, Jr.
Wellbourne, David
Waller, Benjamin
Winn, Benjamin
Watson, Zacheriah
Watson, George
Wooten, Thomas
Willis, Robert
Willis, Brittain
Willis, Josiah
Watson, Benjamin
Watson, Jacob
Watson, John

*Dabney, Austin (Mulatto)

Ga. Land Lottery, 1819

The land given in this Lottery, 1819, was obtained from the Creek and Cherokee Indians by the United States in several treaties, one at Fort Jackson, Aug. 9, 1814; one at the Chreokee Agency, July 8, 1817; one at the Creek Agency on the Flint River, Jan. 22, 1818; and included the original boundaries of Early, Irwin, Appling, Walton, Hall, Gwinnett, and Habersham Counties of Ga. Act was passed ...., 1818, and was amended Dec. 21, 1819, to include territory acquired from the Cherokee Indians by a Treaty held by John C. Calhoun at the City of Washington, Feb. 27, 1819, which was the original Rabun Co. Many *Rev. Sols.* drew land in this Lottery.

The land given out in the Lottery of 1803 was obtained from the Creek Indians in a Treaty at Fort Wilkinson, June 16, 1802, and included "the Territory south of the Oconee and Altamaha rivers." This land was divided into three counties, Wayne, Wilkinson, and Baldwin. No mention is made of military service in this Act.

The following names are found in 1819 Land Lottery as *Rev. Sols.* of Wilkes Co., Ga., viz: NATHAN BLACKBURN; JOHN COMBS, SR. (wife Milly Russell); PHILIP COMBS, SR.; EZEKIEL HARRIS; WILLIAM HUDGENS; JOHN KELLY (wife Elizabeth); ANDREW MELOY; GANNAWAY MARTIN; JOHN MURPHY (wife Martha); CHRISTOPHER POSS; JOHN RIDLEY, SR. (dec. 1824, wife Jane); MATHEW TALBOT; WILLIAM TRIPLETT, SR. (wife Sarah); MOSES WADE; JOHN WILLIAMS; ANDREW WOLFE, SR.

Revolutionary Soldiers
Franklin Co., Ga., Records

(These names are not found in Knight's "Roster of Ga., *Rev. Soldiers.*") Certificate of Service signed by Lieut.-Col. Leonard Marbury for Continental Bounties for *Rev. Sols.*

John Adamson	Robert Harrod
Arthur Allen	James Henson
Edmund Anderson	Thomas James
Henry Barclay	Simon Jackson
Thomas Bolling	William Jeans
William Booth	Robert Jenkinson
Reuben Bryan	Henry Johns
John Bullman	William Johns
Henry Daniel	Russel Jones
Thomas Davison	Henry Kass
William Davison	John Keble
Peter Downey	Joseph McLain
Robert Dennis	John McRae
Peter Eaton	Frederick Michael
James Edwards	William Owens
Robert Farling	Peter Turley
James Fenton	Jonathan Turner
William Finley	Robert Watson
Ephriam Hardy	Eli Williams
Robert Hardy	Thomas Williams
James Harley	

Names of *Rev. Sols.* found in the records of Franklin Co., Ga. (State Dept. of Archives); names not in Knight's "Roster of *Rev. Soldiers.*" They received certificates for bounty lands for their service, signed by COL. ELIJAH CLARKE, COL. SAMUEL JACK, and COL. GREENBERRY LEE.

Hugh Anderson	Robert Carey
Peter Anderson	David Cooper
George Beall	John Cooper
John Beall	Richard Cowsley
John Bratcher	William Cucksey
Moses Bruer	Alexander Davis
Elisha Burrus	John Dennison
Catlatt Cawley	Sabry Dinkins
John Cawley	James Dunman
Richard Cawley	Joshua Edwards

Conrod Ellrod
John Ferguson
Ambrose Gaines
Dennis Gay
Joshua Gillison
Peter Gillison
Augustus Harris
John Hartford
Cezer Hawkins
John Hawkins
Walter Harrison
James Hays
Robert Higgins
Peter Holland
Peter Hill
John Horner
Henry Howard
Isaac Johnston
Levy Johnston
Noel Jones
Benjamin Kemble
William Kemble
David Langston
Richard Leavens
James Lloyd
Peter Lucas
Archibald Mickson
John Milder
Brantley Moseley
Andrew McGruen
Robert Owsley

Hugh Paskins
Stephen Pennington
Elisha Peters
Benjamin Pinkins
Jeremiah Polhill
Demcy Pollard
Peter Price
Amos Razor
Jonathan Reese
Harris Roberts
David Rowling
John Rowling
Darby Rozar
Richard Runnals
Thomas Runnals
John Ryley
Edward Simol
Philip Sommerhill
John Soulter
John Stedorne
Peter Stockwell
John Taylor
Abraham Turner
Ralph Vann
Edward Wardman
Hugh Wardman
Isaac Wardman
Peter P. Ward
Cooper Welborn
John Woods

Jefferson Co., Ga., Revolutionary Soldiers
(1821 Lottery in Ga.)

Hugh Alexander
John Arrington (d. 1827)
John Boutin
Ezekiel Causey
William Clements, Sr. (d. 1828)
James Cotter
Michael Cowart
James Cooke
John Darby, Sr.
Stephen Durougeaux (d. 1833)
George Fowler, Sr.
Dempsey Hall, Sr.
Hudson Hall, Sr.

Benjamin Green
John S. Holder
James Johnson
William Lions
Norman McCloud
Morris Murphy
Moses Newton
Seth Pierce
John Thompson
William Thompson
Joshua Watson
Caleb Welch
Jerry Wilsher

NOTE: The names of WILLIAM, OWEN, and EPHRIAM BALDWIN (sons of DAVID BALDWIN, SR., Rev. Sol. of Richmond Co.), all Rev. Sols., appear on the land records of Greene Co., Ga., 1790. DAVID BALDWIN, SR., Capt. Certificate of Col. John Stewart, May 15, 1784, "Capt. of a Co. of Minute Men, on the Florida Expedition, and is entitled to a bounty of land." On May 25, 1784, the heirs of Capt. David Baldwin, Sr., were awarded 575 acres of land in Washington Co.

Ga. Sons of Liberty
(From "Harvey List")

Philip Allman
Benjamin Andrew, Sr.

William Bacon, Jr.
John Baker, Sr.

William Baker, Sr.
William Baker, Jr.
Abraham Baldwin
Sutton Banks
Peter Bard
John Benefield
T. Bierry
Henry D. Bourquin
Oliver Bowen
Adam Fowler Brisbane
Hugh Bryan
Jonathan Bryan
William Bryan
Edmund Bugg
Archibald Bulloch
Andrew Burney
Thomas Burton
Joseph Butler
Shem Butler
Jonathan Cochran
John Coleman
Thomas Corbett
Christopher Cramer
Daniel A. Cuthbert
Isaac Cuthbert
Stephen Drayton
Gray Elliott
William Ewen
Samuel Farley
John Flerl
John Fulton
Samuel Fulton
John Germany
Samuel Germany
Joseph Gibbons
William Gibbons
Robert Gibson
William Glasscock
John Glen
James Habersham
Joseph Habersham
Lyman Hall
Robert Hamilton
William Holzendorf
George Houston
John Houston
Richard Howley
James Jones
Noble Wimberly Jones
Paul Judton
Charles Kent
Thomas King
Edward Langworthy
John Eaton Le Conte
Joseph Le Conte
William Le Conte
Thomas Lee

Benjamin Lewis
David Lewis
William Lord
Charles McCay
John McClelland
Samuel McClelland
John McCullough, Sr.
Seth McCullough
Charles McDonald
George McIntosh
Roderick McIntosh
Joseph Maddock
John Mann
Luke Mann
James Maxwell
John Milledge
Samuel Miller
Andrew Moore
Jiles Moore
John Morel
John Neufville
Jones Newson
William O'Bryan
William Peacock
William Pierce
James Pugh
Joseph Reynolds
James Robertson
Matthew Roche, Jr.
John Roland
Daniel Ryan
Peter Sallens, Jr.
James Screven
Peter Shuttleworth
Reuben Shuttleworth
John Smith
John Stacy
John Stephens
Samuel Stephens
John Stirk
Joseph Stobe
Thomas Stone
William Stone
Allen Stuart
Edward Telfair
George Threadcraft
Peter Tondee
John Adam Treutlen
Jacob Walthour
George Walton (Gov.)
John Walton
Parmenas Way, Sr.
Andrew Elton Wells
Humphrey Wells
John Wereat
William Williams, Sr.
John Winn, Sr.

John Witherspoon, Sr.
John Witherspoon, Jr.
Ambrose Wright

George Wyche
Isaac Young
William Young

Names of Revolutionary Soldiers from Original Documents on File in State Department of Archives and in Secretary of State's Office, State Capitol, Atlanta, Ga.
(Not published in Knight's "Roster of the Revolution")

Archibald Adams
Matthias Adams
Laban Beckham
Lewis Bentley
Absolem Biddle
Samuel Bishop
George Bledsoe
Bedford Brown
Herbert Brown
John Bruce
Morris Brunner
Joseph Buchanan
William Buchanan
David Burney
Joseph Carter
Henry Chandler
Robert Christmas
Archibald Christy
Lewis Cook
William Cook
Caleb Cowley
Richard Cowley
Peter Crawford
Charles Daniel
Jacob Darden
Amory Day
Thomas Deal
Ralph Edwards
John Ellis
Charles Finley
Daniel Fraser
Henry George
Edwards Gilmore
James Graham
William Gray

Benjamin Griffin
James Grymes
Benjamin Hall
George Harris
Lard Harris
Samuel Hearn
Thomas Hearn
William Hearn
Joseph Henderson
Thomas Hensley, Jr.
James Henry, Jr.
Nicholas Higgins
David Howard
Joshua Houghton
William Irons
Nathaniel Jackson
Elijah James
Job Johnson
Nathaniel Lindsay
Gabriel Long
William Lockhart
Jesse Love
George Mills
Burgess Moore
Benjamin Nixon
William O'Neil
Joseph Oswald
Thomas Oswald
Darby Rozar
John Sebert
Edward Simmons
Robert Simmons
James Starritt
Edward Swinner
Solomon Turner

Revolutionary Soldiers

REV. SILAS MERCER: "This is to certify that the REV. SILAS MERCER, in the beginning of these times, was very active and useful in convincing the people of the justice of the cause of America, and after the British took possession of Savannah, Ga., he spent much of his time in preaching to the armies, and obtained an excellent recommendation from Col. Hammond to Gen. Lincoln in order that he might preach to his army. As he was on his way to Purysburg he came to Burke Jail to preach to my Regiment and was there at a time of a very warm engagement, and behaved himself exceedingly well at the time of the action, and soon after he left the State at the expense of the chief of his property, rather than surrender to the British Government. I have been creditably informed that he hath behaved himself honorably during his absence, and has spent much of his time in preaching to armies and has at all times supported the character of a good Whigg. Therefore, I believe he is entitled to as much land as any gentleman of his rank. Benjamin Few, Colonel, Richmond Co., Ga., Daniel Coleman, Zacheus Fenn. Granted 650 acres as a refugee *Chaplain*, with the rank of Major, Feb. 24, 1784. (Wife Dorcas —.)" (Record at State Department of Archives.)

WILLIAM READ: "This is to certify that WILLIAM READ was appointed second Surgeon of the General Hospital in the Middle District, July 9, 1778. He was promoted to Hospital Physician, May 15, 1781, and continued to serve in that capacity to the end of the War. Petitioner prays for bounty land in the forks of the Oconee River, Ga." Signed by Lachlan McIntosh, Major-General, Feb. 26, 1784.

JOHN FARRELL, THOMAS TURNER, SR., THOMAS TURNER, JR., DENNIS TURNER: "This is to certify that JOHN FARRELL, THOMAS TURNER, SR., THOMAS TURNER, JR., and DENNIS TURNER were *Rev. Sols.* under me in Continental Regiment, Light Horse." Signed by Leonard Marbury, Lieut.-Col., Jan. 24, 1785.

GEORGE FREEMAN (son of HOLMAN FREEMAN, SR., and brother of HOLMAN, JR., JOHN, JAMES and WILLIAM FREEMAN, all *Rev. Sols.* of Ga., who lived in the "Ceded Lands," now Wilkes Co., Ga.); *Rev. Sol.* of Wilkes Co., Ga. Certificate of Col. Elijah Clarke. Warrant dated Dec. 4, 1783. Received 250 acres of bounty land for *Rev.* service, on the Waters of Clark's Fork, Long Creek, Wilkes Co., Ga., adjoining the lands of Anderson Brown, John Cloud, and Col. Elijah Clarke. Mar. Frances Taylor.

JOHN SIMMONS, b. 1793; d. Hancock Co., Ga. *Rev. Sol.* Certificate of Col. Elijah Clarke, warrant dated June 8, 1784; received 287½ acres of bounty land in Washington Co., Ga., bounded North by Col. William Candler, East by Shoulderbone Creek, South by Thornton, West vacant. Survey 578. Grave marked by D. A. R.

McKEEN GREEN, SR., *Rev. Sol.* Certificate of Col. James McKay, Jan 29, 1784, received 287½ acres of land in Washington Co., Ga., on the Altamaha river. His son, McKEEN GREEN, JR., *Rev. Sol.*, upon certificate of Col. Caleb Howell, received 287½ acres of bounty land on the Altamaha river, Washington Co.

JOSEPH PHILLIPS, *Rev. Sol.* of Ga. Certificate of Col. Elijah Clarke, warrant signed Feb. 2, 1784, for bounty land for his service. After his death CASANDER PHILLIPS, widow, prays for a warrant issue to her son, ISHAM PHILLIPS, of the 575 acres of land granted to her late husband for his service as a *Rev. Sol.* Warrant granted. ISHAM PHILLIPS received also 287½ acres of bounty land in Washington Co., Jan. 25, 1785, for his service as a *Rev. Sol.*

JOHN RAMSEY, JR. Certificate of James Jackson, Col. Ga. State Legion, Mar. 24, 1784. Your petitioner is heir and surviving brother to SAMUEL RAMSEY, who fell fighting for the Independence of the country. Prays two bounties of 287½ acres each in Franklin Co., Ga. James Jackson certifies that "SAMUEL RAMSEY, JR., served under me as a good and faithful soldier and citizen, and was killed in the service of this State, under my command, doing his duty."

THOMAS PACE. Certificate of James McNeil, Col., Feb. 21, 1784. He was taken prisoner by the British but finally escaped and renewed service as a *Rev. Sol.* under Col. James Martin, July 26, 1784. Prays for two bounties of 287½ acres each in Washington Co.

JOHN MATTHEWS, upon certificate, received bounty land of 287½ acres in Franklin Co., bounded North and East vacant; South by Fred Winters; West by John Allen. Crossed by Indian Trading Path. Cut by Eastanaula Creek. Dec. 16, 1784.

WILLIAM JONES, *Rev. Sol.*, and his wife, Abigail, sold, on Oct. 10, 1785, to Robert Flournoy, a *Rev. Sol.* of Augusta, Ga., 287½ acres of bounty land in Washington Co., on Shoulderbone Creek, granted to the said William Jones by his Honor the Governor of Ga., Samuel Elbert, on Oct. 15, 1784 for his service as a *Rev. Sol.* (Greene Co., Ga., Records.)
Names found in List of *Rev. Sols.* of Ga.:

PETER ZAVADOOSKI, invalid Pensioner, Chatham Co.; ERNEST ZITTRAUER; BARTHOLOMEW ZACHARY; JAMES ZACHARY; NATHANIEL ZETTLER; JACOB ZINN; HENRY ZINN, of Richmond Co.

Note: SAMUEL ELBERT, Brig.-Gen., Continental Army, July 15, 1784 certified that ROWLING LANCASTER, ISAAC REYFIELD, DAVID CRAWFORD, and BASIL MAXWELL were *Rev. Sols.* of 2nd Batt., Ga. Troops; that all four d. in service, and the heirs of said sols. are entitled to Ga. State bounty grants for their service.

Note: The bounties of the *Rev. Sols.* were paid for their service in the Head-Right Territory, most of them in the Cos. of Washington and Franklin. (By Act passed Aug. 20, 1781, and also Act passed Feb. 17, 1783.) This Head-Right Territory of the State consists now of thirty-five (35) Cos. (See pages 193–197, for Explanation of Head-Rights and Lottery Land Grants of Ga., in Knight's "Roster of the Revolution," copied from "Historical Collections of the Joseph Habersham Chapter, D. A. R. of Ga.," Vol. I, pages 303–309.)

Note: REAL DAUGHTERS (of the National Society of the American Revolution), 757 daus. of *Rev. Sols.* have become members of this Society. Two are now (1941) living, one in N. H., and one in Pa.

BENJAMIN BLEDSOE, of Warren Co., GEORGE BLEDSOE, of Wilkes Co., MILLER BLEDSOE, of Oglethorpe Co., PEACHY BLEDSOE, JOHN BLEDSOE and WILLIAM BLEDSOE, of Wilkes Co., were all *Rev. Sols.* and received bounty grants of land in Ga. for their service.

Note: Richmond Academy, Augusta, Ga., is Georgia's oldest educational institution; chartered in 1783 by the State Legislature. The original building was also used as the State House and for Federal and State courts. GEORGE WASHINGTON, *President of the United States*, was entertained there on his memorable visit to Georgia in 1791. (Marker placed by the D. A. R.)

JOHN CARTER, b. Mecklenburg Co., Va.; d. 1838. Will made Mar. 20, 1838, recorded in Oglethorpe Co., Ga., Sept. 4, 1838. He was a *Rev. Sol.* and served in the N. C. Line. Mar. (1) Dec. 12, 1788 in Va., Polly Stevens, d. 1826; mar. (2) Dec. 23, 1829 in Oglethorpe Co., Ga., Amelia Elkins, widow. He moved from Va. to Granville Co., N. C., then to Oglethorpe Co., Ga., and settled on Beaver Dam Creek, where they died and were buried.
Children:
1. Wiley, mar. — Pinson.
2. Paul, mar. Winny Bridges.
3. Magnus (1800–1886), mar. Theodocia Farmer.
4. Edna (1803–1887), mar. James Pinson.
5. Hixey, mar. Thomas Carter.
6. Holly, mar. William Carter.

Note: THOMAS and NANCY CARTER, of Mecklenburg Co., Va., had children:
1. John.
2. Charles.
3. Thomas.
4. Elizabeth.
5. Judith.
6. Sallie.
7. Robert.
8. Mary.
Will of THOMAS CARTER dated Aug. 8, 1796.

JOSEPH HENDERSON, b. Va., 1737; d. Wilkes Co., Ga., 1810. Mar. 1758 in N. C., ISABELLA DELPHIA LEA, b. N. C.; d. Wilkes Co., Ga., Jan. 13, 1813 (dau. of WILLIAM LEA, a *Rev. Sol.*, d. Wilkes Co., Ga., April 1794, and wife, Nancy —). He was a *Rev. Sol.* of S. C. and received bounty grant of land in Ga. for his service.
Children:
1. Nancy (1758–1849), mar. 1777, Lawrence Bankston.

2. Sarah, mar. John Petit (or Peteet).
3. Isabella, mar. Joshua Callaway.
4. Adelphia, mar. Richard Petit.
5. Mary (1768–1861), mar. Israel Miller (1764–1833).
6. John, mar. Hannah Shaw.
7. Joseph, Jr., mar. (1) Margaret Reynolds; mar. (2) Helen B. Dearing.
8. Major (*Sol. of the War of 1812*), mar. Mary Strozier.

JOHN HOOD, b. Amelia Co., Va., 1759; d. Wilkes Co., Ga., 1827. Was a *Rev. Sol.* Served 1778 as a private in Capt. Charles Pelham's Co., 1st Va. Regiment. Mar. 1785, REBECCA REEVES. She drew land in the 1827 Lottery as the widow of a *Rev. Sol.*
Children (not in order of birth; see Page 92):
    1. William.
    2. Joel.
    3. Ichabod.
    4. Stephen W.
    5. Avery B.
    6. Nancy, mar. — Crain.
    7. Patsey, mar. — Crain.
    8. Lucy.
    9. Polly.

WILLIAM KIDD, b. Mecklenburg Co., Va., Dec. 16, 1763. Will made 1843, probated Jan. 27, 1845. Moved to Oglethorpe Co., Ga., 1799, where he d. Was a *Rev. Sol.* Served in Va. Army in Capt. Anderson's Co. Wounded 1780. Enlisted again 1781 in Capt. Swepton's Co., Col. Munford's Va. Regiment. Allowed pension in Oglethorpe Co., Ga., 1832. Mar. Oct. 8, 1781, JUDITH (called Judy) CARTER; she d. before 1843. (His brother, JAMES KIDD, was also a *Rev. Sol.* of Va.)
Children (mentioned in will):
    1. William, mar. Dec. 20, 1813, Nancy Carter.
    2. Mary, mar. Edward Carter.
    3. Lucy, mar. Johnson Wright.
    4. Elizabeth, mar. Dean Tucker.
    5. Webb, mar. Malinda Kidd.

(See page 105.)

REV. JOSIAH LEWIS, Chaplain, deceased, is entitled to a bounty of 750 acres of land in Ga. as a refugee from N. C., and 250 acres as a citizen after his return to this State. Certificate of John Twiggs, Brig.-Gen., April 10, 1784. Petition of SUSANNA LEWIS, widow of JOSIAH LEWIS—for self; for Jonathan Rees Lewis, 10 years old; for Benjamin Thomas Lewis, 8 years old; for Susanna Lewis, Jr., 3 years old; and for Josiah Lewis, 1 year old—praying that four separate bounties in Washington Co. be granted BENJAMIN LEWIS, brother of JOSIAH LEWIS, deceased, in trust for the four minors.

BENJAMIN LEWIS was given a bounty grant of 575 acres of land in Washington Co., as a refugee *Rev. Sol.*, upon certificate of Maj.-Gen. John Twiggs, 1784.

DR. EVAN LEWIS. Certificate that he was regularly appointed Surgeon Mate in Southern Hospital of Continental Army and served until time of his death. Brothers and lawful heirs were THOMAS LEWIS and JACOB LEWIS (both *Rev. Sols.*).

    NOTE: Other *Rev. Sols.* of this name in Ga. included DAVID LEWIS, SR. (wife Keziah); DAVID LEWIS, JR.; BENJAMIN LEWIS (Son of Liberty); ELEZIUR LEWIS; JACOB LEWIS; JAMES LEWIS; JOEL LEWIS; and THOMAS LEWIS. All had certificates for bounty land for their service.

JOHN HAILE MEADE, b. Bedford Co., Va., 1755; d. Augusta, Ga., 1798. Served as a *Rev. Sol.* Ensign in 14th Va. Regiment. Mar. Elizabeth Crump.

WILLIAM SHEFFIELD (sometimes spelled SHUFFLE), b. N. C.; d. Ga. Served as *Rev. Sol.* in the Ga. State Troops, 1st Regiment, 4th Co., under Capt. Robert Raines. Received certificate for bounty land as a *Rev. Sol.*, Jan. 19, 1799.

JAMES STARRITT (son of Benjamin Starritt, of Md. and Guilford Co., N. C.), b. Cecil Co., Md., 1751; d. Habersham Co., Ga., 1849, age 98 years. He enlisted as a *Rev. Sol.* from Guilford Co., N. C.; served as second Lieut. in Capt. Wilson's Co., Col. Saxon's Regiment of N. C. Line. Mar. NANCY —, b. 1759; d. 1850, age 91 years. They moved to Habersham Co., Ga. (about four miles from Clarkesville, Ga.). Both are buried in the Bethlehem Church cemetery, near the Burton Road highway, Habersham Co., Ga. (Grave marked 1940 by the TOMOCHICHI Chapter, D. A. R., Clarkesville, Ga.)

GEORGIA COUNTIES

COUNTIES in GEORGIA (Named for *Rev. Sols.* and English friends of the Colonists.)

BAKER CO., created from early 1825, named for COL. JOHN BAKER, *Rev. Sol.*, of Liberty Co.

BALDWIN CO., laid off in the lottery Act of 1803, organized 1805, named in honor of ABRAHAM BALDWIN, b. Guilford, Conn., Nov. 6, 1754.

BRYAN CO., organized 1793; named for JONATHAN BRYAN, *Rev. Sol.* of Ga. On Sept. 16, 1769, he presided over a meeting of merchants and traders in Ga., and was by order of the King, dismissed from the Governor's Council, of which for some time he had been a member. Thus he was the first object of the Royal vengeance in Ga. When the British captured Savannah, Dec. 29, 1778, he was made a prisoner, because of his deep loyalty to the cause and notwithstanding his age of nearly four-score years, he was confined on one of the British ships. He was very prominent in the affairs of the Colony and took an active part in the stirring events just preceding and during the Revolution.

BULLOCH CO., which was a part of Screven, was created in 1796 and was named for ARCHIBALD BULLOCH, member of the *Provincial Congress*, and *Governor of Ga.*, Jan. 1776 to Feb. 1777. (called President and also served as Commander-in-chief of the Army.)

BURKE CO., was laid out in 1758 as St. George's Parish. It received its present name Burke in honor of Edmund Burke, the great champion of American Liberty in England.

CARROLL CO., laid out after Campbell 1828, named for CHARLES CARROLL, of Md., signer of the Declaration of Independence.

CAMDEN CO., which was once included in the parishes of St. Thomas' and St. Mary's, was formed 1777, and named in honor of the Earl of Camden, a champion of Colonial rights in the English Parliament.

CHATHAM CO., is the nucleus around which the present State of Georgia has developed. The Colonists first landed at Yamacraw Bluff, the site of the present city of Savannah, Feb. 12, 1773. In 1758 this part of Ga. was laid out into St. Philips and Christ Church parishes. In 1777 the parishes were changed to counties. Christ Church Parish, with part of St. Philip's, was erected into a county which was named Chatham, in honor of William Pitt, Earl of Chatham, who in the British Parliament ably defended the rights of the Colonists. During the *Rev. War*, Chatham Co. was the scene of a number of engagements between the Americans and the British and their Indian and Tory allies. The first Legislative body ever convened in Ga. assembled at Savannah, Jan. 7, 1755.

CLARKE CO., created from Jackson Co. in 1801, named in honor of the rugged *Rev. Hero* of Ga., GENERAL ELIJAH CLARKE.

DeKALB CO., laid out by Act of Legislature on Dec. 9, 1822, organized on Dec. 22, 1822, and named for BARON de KALB, the German officer who fought with the American forces in the *Rev.* and was mortally wounded at the Battle of Camden, S. C.

DOOLY CO., laid off under lottery act of 1821, and named for COL. JOHN DOOLY, one of Georgia's *Rev. Sols.* b. of Irish parents in Wilkes Co., Ga.

EFFINGHAM CO., once a part of the parishes of St. Matthew and St. Philip, which were formed in 1758. It was changed to a county 1777, and named for the Earl of Effingham, who in Parliament so gallantly defended the interests of the American Colonists, and who resigned his commission in the British Army when his regiment was ordered to America. In 1793, a part of this Co. was given to Screven, and in 1794, a part was given to Screven, and in 1794 a part was given to

Bryan Co. (EBENEZER was one of the first places outside of Savannah to be founded. Here is found one of the most historic landmarks in Ga., the old "Jerusalem Church of this Salzburgers.")

EMANUEL CO., laid off from Bulloch and Montgomery 1812, and named for DAVID EMANUEL, *Rev. Sol.* of Ga., and *Governor of the State,* 1801.

GLYNN CO., formed into a county 1777, and named in honor of JOHN GLYNN, an English nobleman who was an ardent supporter of the Colonists in their demands.

GREENE CO., surveyed 1784, laid out from Washington Co. 1786. Named in honor of GEN. NATHANIEL GREENE. He was Commander of the South during the *Rev. War.*

GWINNETT CO., laid out by the lottery Act of 1818, and named in honor of BUTTON GWINNETT, one of Georgia's Signers of the Declaration of Independence.

HABERSHAM CO., laid out by the Lottery Act of 1818, and named for JOSEPH HABERSHAM, of Savannah, b. 1751, who as a Major of the Ga. troops captured Governor Wright. He was one of the most active and resourceful advocates of Liberty.

HALL CO., was created by Lottery Act of 1819 and named for DR. LYMAN HALL, one of Georgia's Signers of the Declaration of Independence. Also *Governor of the State* 1783-84.

HANCOCK CO., laid out in 1793, and named in honor of JOHN HANCOCK, of Mass., *President of the Continental Congress.*

HENRY CO., created in 1821 from lands acquired by treaty with the Indians, and was named for PATRICK HENRY, the renouned Patriot and orator of Va.

IRWIN CO., laid out by the Lottery Act of 1818, named for JARED IRWIN, who distinguished himself as a *Rev. Sol.* and served two terms as Governor.

JACKSON CO., formed in 1796 and named for JAMES JACKSON, of Savannah, Brig.-Gen. in the Rev. army and *Governor of Ga.* 1798-1801.

JASPER CO., formed Randolph Co. 1807 name changed to Jasper Co. 1812, in honor of SERGEANT JASPER who, when the flag at Fort Moultrie was shot from the staff, recovered it at the risk of his life and held it aloft until a new staff could be procured.

JEFFERSON CO., laid out from Burke and Warren Cos. in 1796, and named for THOMAS JEFFERSON, author of the Declaration of Independence, *President of the United States* 1801-1809. Louisville, the county seat, was the first official capital of the State of Ga.

LAURENS CO., laid out in 1807 and named in honor of LIEUT-COL. JOHN LAURENS of S. C., who was killed near Combahee, S. C. during the *Rev. War.*

LIBERTY CO., was formed from the parishes of St. John, St. Andrew, and St. James in 1777. Its name is derived from the eagerness of its inhabitants to send a delegate to the Continental Congress before the rest of the Province had decided to join the other Colonies in a fight for Independence. Dr. Lyman Hall was sent as delegate. Liberty Co. is rich in history, Medway Church is in this Co.

LINCOLN CO., was formed from part of Wilkes in 1796 and named for GEN. BENJAMIN LINCOLN, of Mass., who for a time commanded the American forces in the South during the *Rev. War*

MACON CO., created 1837, and named for NATHANIEL MACON, of N. C. who served throughout the Rev. War as a private, declining promotion.

MERIWETHER CO. created Dec. 1827 from Troup, and named for DAVID MERIWETHER, of Va. and Ga. Served and Brig.-Gen. at the Siege of Savannah, captured by the British and held prisoner.

MONTGOMERY CO., laid out from Washington Co. 1793 and named in honor of Gen. Richard Montgomery, who was killed in an attack upon the fortifications at Quebec in 1775.

MORGAN CO., laid out from Baldwin in 1807 and named for Gen. Daniel Morgan, the hero of Cowpens.

MURRAY CO., named for DAVID MURRAY, b. Prince Edward Co., Va., 1760. Came to Wilkes Co., Ga.; d. Ala., Nov. 8, 1840. A *Rev. Sol.*

PICKENS CO., created 1853 and named in honor of Gen. Andrew Pickens, of S. C.

PULASKI CO., laid out from Laurens in 1808, and named for the Polish nobleman Count Pulaski, who fell in defense of American Liberty at Savannah Oct. 9, 1779.

PUTNAM CO., laid out in 1807 and named in honor of GEN. ISRAEL PUTNAM, of Mass., the *Rev. Hero.*

RICHMOND CO., laid out as St. Paul's Parish; in 1777 when the parishes were changed to counties, the name of Richmond was conferred on this section of the Province, in honor of the Duke of Richmond, who as a member of the British Parliament, stood as the stanch friend of the American Colonists. Augusta is the county seat.

(COLUMBIA CO., laid out from Richmond Co. 1790, was named for Christopher Columbus, the discoverer of America.)

SCREVEN CO., formed from the counties of Burke and Effingham 1793, was named for GEN. JAMES SCREVEN, who was killed at the battle of Medway Church. The Battle of Brier Creek was fought in this county.

STEWART CO., formed from Randolph 1830, named for GEN. DANIEL STEWART, of Liberty Co., who achieved fame as a *Sol.* of the *Rev.* and in subsequent Indian wars. (Ancestor of Mrs. Franklin D. Roosevelt, wife of the President of the United States, 1938.)

SUMPTER CO., laid out from Lee 1831, and named for GEN. THOMAS SUMPTER, of Va. who commanded the S. C. troops during the War of the Rev.

TALIAFERRO CO., formed in 1825 and named for COL. BENJAMIN TALIAFERRO, of Va. who d. Wilkes Co., Ga., 1821. Served under Morgan during the Rev. and was captured by the British at Charleston.

TATTNALL CO., formed from Montgomery 1801, and named in honor of JOSIAH TATTNALL *Rev. Sol.* and *Governor of Ga.* 1802.

TELFAIR CO., laid out in 1807, and named in honor of Edward Telfair, a Son of Liberty, member Council of Safety, and twice *Governor of Ga.*

TREUTLEN CO., named for JOHN ADAM TREUTLEN, member *Provincial Congress, Rev. Sol.* and *Governor of Ga.*, 1777.

TWIGGS CO., laid out from Wilkinson 1809, and named for COL. JOHN TWIGGS, who during the *Rev. War* won distinction in many battles with the British and their Indian allies.

WALTON CO., laid out by the Lottery Act of 1818 and named for GEORGE WALTON, one of Georgia's Signers of the Declaration of Independence and *Governor of Ga.*

WASHINGTON CO., created in 1784 and named in honor of GEORGE WASHINGTON. At the time of the organization, it included all the land "from the Cherokee corner north, extending from the Ogeechee to the Oconee, south to Liberty County." It was settled by many refugee Sols. who were given bounty lands, 287½ acres for their service in the Rev. Army.

WARREN CO., laid out in 1793, and named for GEN. JOSEPH WARREN, *Rev. Sol.* of Mass. who fell at the Battle of Bunker Hill.

WILKINSON CO., laid out by the Lottery Act of 1803, organized 1805. Named for GEN. JAMES WILKINSON, a *Sol.* of the *Rev.* and a *Sol. of the War of 1812.*

WILKES CO., was created in 1777 from land acquired from the Indians in 1773. It was first called the "Ceded Lands of Ga." Named for JOHN WILKES, a great champion of American Liberty. WASHINGTON, the county seat of Wilkes Co., claims the honor of being the first place in the United States to bear the name of GEORGE WASHINGTON, the first President of the United States.

WAYNE CO., laid out under the Lottery Act of 1803 and named for ANTHONY WAYNE, b. Penn., Jan. 1, 1745; d. Penn., Dec. 15, 1796. A *Rev. Sol.*, who settled in Ga., and was a delegate to the Convention that framed the First State Constitution after independence was established.

Battles of the Revolutionary War in Georgia
April 1775 to December 1783

Battles. In the War of the Revolution many battles and skirmishes were fought on Georgia soil.

Following is a list of these engagements: Fights occurred at Augusta; Beards' Bluff; Baillon's Causeway; Beard's Creek; Belfast; Brewton's Hill; Brier Creek; Broad river; Brownsborough; Buckhead Creek; Bull Town Swamp; Burke Co. Jail; Carr's Fort; Cherokee Ford; Cockspur Island; Ebenezer; Etowah river; Fishing Creek; Forts Charlotte, Cornwallis, Heard, McIntosh, Morris and Tybee; Fulsum's Fort; Galphin's; Gibbons' Plantation; Hawk's Creek; Herbert's Place; Hickory Hill; Kettle Creek; Lockhart's; Matthews' Bluff; Medway Church; Ogeechee Ferry; Paris' Mill; Riceboro; Savannah; Sharon; Sunbury; Tybee Island; White House; Wiggin's Hill; Wright's Fort; Yamacraw Bluff, Mar. 4, 1776; and Yamassee Bluff.

The capture of Savannah, Ga., by the British, Dec. 29, 1778.

Capture of Augusta, Ga., by the British, Jan. 1779.

Battle of Kettle Creek, Feb. 14, 1779.

Capture of Charleston, S. C., by the British, May 12, 1780. (Many Georgians fled to S. C. after the capture of Savannah, when Ga. was overrun by the British and the Tories.)

Surrender of the British at Yorktown, Oct. 19, 1781.

Savannah, Ga., evacuated by the British, Nov. 3, 1781.

Treaty of Peace, July 2, 1782, and formally ratified at Versailles, Sept. 3, 1783.

The withdrawal of British forces from Savannah, Ga., began on July 11, 1783. On that day Col. James Jackson, at the head of the Colonial forces, marched in and took possession of Savannah. This place had been in the hands of the enemy for three years, six months, and thirteen days.

It was not until Sept. 3, 1783, that definitive treaties between England, France, and America were finally ratified. Thus success crowned the American Revolution and the terrible War for Independence was ended. In the eyes of all Europe the thirteen Colonies were free and Independent States.

GEORGIA LAND

(Tune, "Maryland, My Maryland")
"Love, light, and joy forever more,
    Georgia Land, dear Georgia Land,
The world finds welcome at thy door,
    Georgia Land, dear Georgia Land.
The Star-crowned hills and valleys sweet
    Their litanies of love repeat
At night and morning, singing sweet,
    Georgia Land, dear Georgia Land.

"Where'er thy loving children roam,
    Georgia Land, dear Georgia Land,
With thee their hearts are still at home,
    Georgia Land, dear Georgia Land.
Where'er the wanderer's pathway lies,
    In dreams he sees thy blessed skies,
And hope doth like a star arise,
    Georgia Land, dear Georgia Land.

"Blest be thy holy hills and plains,
    Georgia Land, dear Georgia Land,
The sunlight twinkling through thy rains,
    Georgia Land, dear Georgia Land.
God have thee ever in His keep,
    From mountain wall to stormy deep,
Until upon thy breast we sleep,
    Georgia Land, dear Georgia Land."

FRANK L. STANTON,
Poet-Laureate of Ga.

INFORMATION

GEORGIA SOCIETY, Daughters of the American Revolution was organized 1891 by Mrs. Augustus Ramon Salas, Waynesboro, Ga. First State Regent, 1891.

ATLANTA CHAPTER, Atlanta, Ga. organized April 15, 1891 (the second Chapter organized in the National Society Daughters of the American Revolution).

XAVIER CHAPTER, Rome, Ga. organized July 15, 1891.

See "Georgia's Roster of the Revolution," by Lucien Lamar Knight.

Pages 315-316. List of *Rev. Sols.* who drew in 1825 Lottery, and who resided in Major Dobb's and Major Allen's District, Elbert Co., Ga.

Pages 313-314. The Original Lists of the Irwin Co. Land Lottery. Both lists compiled by Miss Helen M. Prescott, of Atlanta, Ga.

Pages 374-401. Certified Lists of Ga. Troops — Sols. of the Line, Rev. War; copied under the direction of Mrs. William Lawson Peel, of Atlanta, Ga., from the original papers in the office of the Secretary of State.

See "Reprint of Official Register of Land Lottery of Georgia, 1827," compiled and published by Miss Martha Lou Houston, Columbus, Ga.

REFERENCES

The list of *Rev. Sols.* in this book is not complete. It includes the names of many *Rev. Sols.* who enlisted from Ga. or settled in Ga. after the close of hostilities, and are buried in Ga. Many graves have been marked, and many graves have been located. The list of the children of these sols. is not complete, as it has not been possible to obtain the names of all children. It is confidently believed that the list, as given, is correct, and will help to obtain other names not known to the compiler.

At the close of the Rev. War, Ga. gave grants of land, called bounties, not only to the *Rev. Sols.* of Ga., but to all *Rev. Sols.* from other States who settled in Ga. These grants are officially recorded in the Secretary of State's office, State Capitol, Atlanta, Ga.

From "Unpublished Genealogical Records," placed in the McCall Genealogical Library, of the Ga. Society, D. A. R., at Rhodes Memorial Hall, State Department of Archives, Atlanta, Ga.

(This Library was a GOLDEN JUBILEE PROJECT of Ga. D. A. R., 1940, MRS. WILLIAM HARRISON HIGHTOWER, State Regent, 1938–1940.)

LOTTERY LISTS, compiled by Miss Helen Prescott, Atlanta, Ga., and CERTIFIED LISTS OF GA. TROOPS, prepared under direction of Mrs. William Lawson Peel, of Atlanta, Ga. Both published in ROSTER OF REV. SOLS. OF GA., compiled by Lucien Lamar Knight.

"Cherokee Lottery of 1838," by James F. Smith.

"Reprint of 1827 Lottery," by Miss Martha Lou Houston, Washington, D. C. and Columbus, Ga.

"Smith's History of Ga."

"McCall's History of Ga."

"Indents of Rev. Soldiers of S. C.," by A. S. Salley.

"Roster of North Carolina Soldiers," by N. C. Daughters of the American Revolution.

Vols.: I, II, III of the Joseph Habersham Chapter, D. A. R., Historical Collections.

"Historical Collections," published by the Ga. Society, D. A. R., Vol. I, Franklin Co., Ga., and (other records); Vol. II, Richmond Co., Ga.; Vol. III, Elbert Co., Ga.; Vol. IV, Family Bible Records.

County Histories of Ga.

Vols. I and II, "Wilkes Co. Records," by Grace G. Davidson.

Bureau of Pensions and War Department, Washington, D. C.

White's Historical Collections of Ga.

Genealogical Reference Department, Carnegie Library, Atlanta, Ga.

Military service records, lottery lists, and land grants; official records on file in Secretary of State's Office, State Capitol, Atlanta, Ga., and in State Departments of Archives, Atlanta, Ga.; Columbia, S. C.; Richmond, Va.; and Raleigh, N. C.

"Southern Lineages," by Adelaide Evans Wynn of Ga.

"History of Medway Church," by Stacey.

"History of the Cheraws," by Gregg of S. C.

"McCall, Tidwell, and Allied Families," by Ettie Tidwell McCall of Ga.

Lineage Books of National Society, D. A. R.

Official Records from various courthouses in Va., N. C., S. C., and Ga., collected by the compiler.

INDEX

Key to Abbreviations

Rev. Sol.....................Revolutionary Soldier.
W. R. S.....................Widow of Revolutionary Soldier.
Rev.......................Revolution.
Wid........................Widow.
W.........................Wife.
Dau.......................Daughter.
Co..........................County.
Rank of Soldier:
    Gen..................General.
    Col....................Colonel.
    Maj...................Major.
Names of States abbreviated—as Ga. for Georgia; N. C. for North Carolina, etc.
Reg.......................Regiment.

Part I—Part II—Part III

Name A	*Page*	*Name*	*Page*
		Allen, Robert	22
Abercrombie, Charles	19	Allison, Benjamin	22
Abercrombie, Robert	19	Allison, Henry	22
Adair, James, Sr.	20	Anciaux, Nicholas	187
Adair, John	19	Alston, James	22-129
Adair, Joseph, Sr.	19	Alston, Philip	129
Adair, Joseph, Jr.	19	Alston, Solomon	77
Adams, David	187	Alston, William	22-51
Adams, James	20-165	Anderson, George	187
Adams, Nathaniel	187	Anderson, William	23-188
Adams, Thomas	187	Andrew, Benjamin	89
Addington, William	187	Andrew, John	24
Adkins, Charles	187	Andrews, Garnett	24
Adkins, William	187	Andrews, John	24
Aikens, James	187	Andrews, Mark	25
Albritton, John	187	Andrews, William	25
Alderman, Daniel	21	Anglin, James	187
Alderman, David	20	Ansley, Thomas	25
Alderman, John	21	Anthony, Christopher	23
Alexander, Adam	21	Anthony, James	24
Alexander, Hugh	187	Anthony, Joseph	23-51-55
Alexander, John	187	Appling, John, Sr.	25
Alexander, Samuel	21	Appling, John, Jr.	25
Alexander, William	21	Arnaud, Jean Pierre	25
Alford, James	225	Arnold, James	25-188
Alford, Lodowick	187	Arnold, James	26
Allen, David	87	Arrington, Hannah	14
Allen, Drury (Drewry)	21	Asbury, Henry	188
Allen, James	21-187-225	Asbury, Richard	188
Allen, John	187	Ashe, William	26
Allen, Philip	187	Atkins, Ici	26

Name	Page
Hawthorne, John	195
Hawthorne, Joshua	196
Hawthorne, Stephen	195
Hawthorne, William	195
Hayes, Arthur	212
Hays, John	196
Haygood, Benjamin	196
Haynes, Moses	86
Haynes, Parmenas	86
Haynes, Thomas	196
Hazzard, William	151
Head, James	87
Heard, Bernard	87
Heard, Jesse	87
Heard, John	88
Heard, Stephen	17–88
Heard, Thomas	87
Heard, William	116
Hearn, Elisha	88
Hearn, Jonathan	88
Heath, Jurdan	44
Henderson, Joseph	30–255
Henderson, Michael	76
Henderson, Robert	196
Hendley, William	89
Hendrick, John	196
Hendry, Robert	196–201–216
Herbert, James	211
Heuston (Huston), James	89
Heuston, John	89
Hewell, Wyatt	196
Hicks, David	196
Hicks, Nathaniel	196
Highsmith, James	91
Hightower, James	196
Hightower, Mrs. Wm. Harrison	256
Hill, Abraham	89–164
Hill, Abraham, Jr	99
Hill, Henry	90
Hill, Isaac	90–196
Hill, Thomas	225
Hill, William	90
Hillary, Christopher	90–118
Hillhouse, David	91
Hillyer, Asa	70
Hines, James	196
Hobby, Wm., Jr	14
Hobson, Matthew	196
Hodges, Joshua	91
Hodnett, Benjamin	197
Hogg, Lewis	197
Holbrook, Jesse	197
Holbrook, Nathan	197
Holcomb, Henry	91
Holcombe, Jordan	214
Holland, Thomas	20
Holliday, Thomas	49–197
Holliday, William, Sr	91
Holliday, William, Jr	91
Holliman, David	92
Holloway, William, Sr	92
Hood, John	92–256
Hopson, Elizabeth	42–81
Horseley, Valentine	107
Horton, Prosser	208
Howard, John	93–181–217
Howard, Mary Ann	93
Howard, Nehemiah	93
Howard, Rhesa	67
Howard, Solomon	197
Howe, Robert	58

Name	Page
Howell, Daniel	72
Howell, Joseph	93
Howell, Thomas	211
Houston, John	15–18–42–197
Houston, Martha Lou	255
Hubert, Matthew	94
Hubbard, John	94–214
Hubbard, Joseph	93
Hudgins, William	250
Hudson, Cuthbert	94
Hudson, David	32–94–225
Hudson, Irby	20–94
Hughes, Henry	197–225
Huling, James	169
Hull, Hope	197
Hull, John	197
Hull, Thomas	197
Hulsey, Jennens	197
Humphries, Joseph	211
Humphries, Thomas	197
Hunt, James	95
Hunt, Moses	95
Hunt, Turner	197
Hunter, Jesse	77
Hunter, John	211
Hurt, William	197
Hyde. James	141

I

Name	Page
Inlow, Lewellyn	21
Inman, Daniel	95
Inman, Shadrack	95
Irwin, Alexander	15–197
Irwin, Hugh	96–197
Irwin, Jared	15–18–96–178–197
Irwin, John Lawson	15–96–197
Irwin, William	15–197
Irvine, Christopher	30–96
Irvine, William	30

J

Name	Page
Jack, James	96
Jack, John	34–96
Jack, Patrick	31–96
Jack, Samuel	250
Jackson, Absolem	214
Jackson, Andrew	181
Jackson, Charles	77
Jackson, Edward	198
Jackson, Daniel	97
Jackson, Drury	97
Jackson, Ebenezer	140
Jackson, Edward	96
Jackson, James	15–18–211
Jackson, Michael	140
Jackson, Walter	214
Jameson, David	225
Jarrett, Robert	198
Jasper, Sergeant	195
Jenkins, Lewis	198
Jenkins, Charles F.	14
Jenkins, William	198
Jennings, Robert	198
Jennings, William	97
Jenvaceale, Andre	224
Jeter, Oliver	97
Johnson, Angus	97
Johnson, Archibald	97
Johnson, John	97–98–198

Part IV

Contents

The names of all *Rev. Sols.* in Part IV (with the exception of the 1840 Pension List) are in alphabetical order and are not listed by page number.

Part IV contains names of *Rev. Sols.* living in Ga., found in lists of Pensioners; Lottery Lists; in original records of different counties and have been listed as follows:

NAMES NOT INCLUDED IN INDEX

*NOTE: Supplement contains names of *Rev. Sols.* and widows of *Rev. Sols.* who drew land in the 1827 Lottery.

APPENDIX

LOTTERY LIST OF 1827—REVOLUTIONARY SOLDIERS

Compiled from the official Register of the Land Lottery of 1827, printed by Grantland and Orme in 1827, and from the reprint published in 1928 by Martha Lou Houston, of Columbus, Ga. and Washington, D. C. Also from land grants found in the Secretary of State's office, State Capitol, Atlanta, Ga.

NAMES OF REVOLUTIONARY SOLDIERS WHO DREW LAND IN GEORGIA IN THE "LOTTERY OF 1827" AND THE COUNTIES OF GEORGIA IN WHICH THEY LIVED

Name	County
A	
Adams, Aaron	Hall
Adams, Dancy	Columbia
Adams, David	Jasper
Adams, Thomas, Sr.	Elbert
Adkins, William	Monroe
Ajohns, Eli	Chatham
Aiken, John	Morgan
Aikins, James	Greene
Akridge, Ezekiel	Clark
Akridge, William	Baldwin
Alberson, William	Newton
Albritton, John	Franklin
Alexander, Isaac	Elbert
Allen, David	Morgan
Allen, John	Franklin
Allen, Joseph	Elbert
Allen, Philip	Clark
Allen, Robert	Burke
Allen, William	Elbert
Allen, Woodson	Walton
Allison, Benjamin	Habersham
Amison, Jesse	Washington
Anderson, Henry	Wilkinson
Anderson, William	Wilkes
Andrew, John	Clark
Andrews, Owen	Gwinnett
Angelly, Alexander	Twiggs
Anglin, John	Madison
Armistorph, George, Sr.	Effingham
Armor, John	Greene
Arthur, Matthew	Habersham
Astin, Robert	Greene
Atkinson, Robert	DeKalb
Austin, Harris D.	Jefferson
Austin, Michael	Fayette
Ayers, Frances	Jackson
B	
Bachlott, John	Camden
Bagby, John	Gwinnett
Bagley, Herman	Gwinnett
Bailey, Christopher	Effingham
Bailey, Stephen	Monroe
Baker, Charles	Habersham
Baker, Christopher, Sr.	Gwinnett
Baker, Joshua	Franklin
Baker, Real	Hall
Ballard, Frederick	Effingham
Ballard, James	Greene
Bandy, Lewis	Morgan
Banks, Drury	Warren

Name	County
Banks, William	Wilkes
Bankston, Abner	Monroe
Barker, John	Twiggs
Barker, Joseph	Crawford
Barkley, William	Morgan
Barnett, Robert	Wilkinson
Barnett, William	Greene
Barnes, William	Jones
Barron, Joseph	Houston
Bates, John	Burke
Bay, Moses	Henry
Bazemore, Thomas	Jones
Beard, Robert	Henry
Beazley, Henry	Walton
Beasley, William	DeKalb
Beckham, Samuel	Baldwin
Beckham, Sol	Monroe
Bedgood, John	Washington
Bellah, Samuel	Morgan
Bennett, Daniel	Habersham
Benson, Enoch	Gwinnett
Benson, Isaac	Jackson
Bentley, Jesse	Walton
Benton, John	Liberty
Benton, Joseph	Henry
Berry, Isham	Newton
Bethune, Peters	Richmond
Bevins, William	Wilkinson
Biffle, John	DeKalb
Bird, Thomas	Habersham
Birdsong, John	Oglethorpe
Black, Lemuel	Oglethorpe
Black, Thomas	Habersham
Black, William	Effingham
Blackburn, Nathan	Wilkes
Blakely, William	Jones
Blanford, Cark	Washington
Blanks, James, Sr.	Jackson
Bledsoe, Benjamin	Warren
Bledsoe, Miller, Sr.	Oglethorpe
Blount, William	Jones
Blythe, Rogers	Habersham
Boen, Stephen	Telfair
Boggs, Ezekiel	Wilkes
Boham, Joseph	Putnam
Boile, Charles	Montgomery
Bolles, John	Hall
Bond, Richard C.	Franklin
Bone, Archibald	Washington
Booker, John	Wilkes
Booker, William	Wilkes

Name	County	Name	County
Boon, Jess	Greene	Burkhalter, Jacob	Warren
Boring, Isaac	Jackson	Burkhalter, Michael	Warren
Bowen, John	Wilkinson	Burnley, Henry	Columbia
Bowen, S., Sr.	Wilkes	Burton, John	Franklin
Bowling, Edward	Clark	Burton, Thomas	Elbert
Boyd, Thomas	Burke	Bush, Levi	Pulaski
Brack, Elezur, Sr.	Wilkinson	Bush, Samuel	Burke
Bradberry, Lewis	Clark	Butler, John	Gwinnett
Braddy, Lewis	Warren	Butril, William, Sr	Henry
Bradley, John	Jackson	Butt, James	Hancock
Bragg, William	Madison	Burwell, William, Sr.	Jackson
Bramblett, Henry	Elbert	Bynum, Drewry	Warren
Brand, William	Walton	Byrd, John	Hall
Branch, William S.	Greene		
Braswell, Britton	Jones	**C**	
Braswell, Samuel	Newton	Cabos, John	Chatham
Braziel, Britton	Jackson	Camp, Edward	Franklin
Brewster, Hugh	DeKalb	Campbell, William, Sr.	Oglethorpe
Bridges, Wiseman	Jasper	Cameron, James	Jasper
Brinkley, Ely	Washington	Cameron, William, Sr	Oglethorpe
Britt, Edward	Henry	Candell, Benjamin	Habersham
Brockman, Lewis	Oglethorpe	Cannon, Allen	DeKalb
Brooks, James	Jasper	Cannon, Nathaniel	Wilkinson
Brooks, Micajah	Henry	Carlisle, Benjamin	Columbia
Brooks, Robert	Crawford	Carlisle, Edmund	Morgan
Brooks, William, Sr.	Greene	Carson, Ephriam	DeKalb
Brown, Ambrose	Newton	Carr, William	DeKalb
Brown, Benjamin	Elbert	Carrell, John	Jasper
Brown, Dempsey	Twiggs	Carroll, Brittain	Columbia
Brown, Edward	Elbert	Carroll, Douglas	Greene
Brown, Edward	Baldwin	Carroll, Owen	Laurens
Brown, Elisha	Jones	Carter, Charles	Oglethorpe
Brown, Frederick	Columbia	Casey, William	Henry
Brown, James	Clark	Cash, Dorson	Columbia
Brown, John P.	Baldwin	Cash, Howard	Habersham
Brown, Larkin	Richmond	Cash, James	Franklin
Brown, Meridith	DeKalb	Cash, John	Jackson
Brown, Moses	Newton	Causey, Ezekiel	Jefferson
Brown, Samuel	Chatham	Chambless, Chris	Bibb
Brown, William P	Baldwin	Champion, John	Warren
Brown, Uriah	Badwin	Chance, Simpson	Jefferson
Bryan, David	Monroe	Chandler, John, Sr	Gwinnett
Bryan, James	Effingham	Chapman, Abner	Jasper
Bryan, John	Franklin	Chapman, John	Warren
Bruce, William	DeKalb	Chapman, Nathan	Newton
Buchanan, George H	Jasper	Chappell, John	Monroe
Buchanan, James	Jasper	Childress, Thomas	Walton
Buckles, Peter	Wilkinson	Clanton, Holt	Columbia
Buckner, Benjamin	Putnam	Clark, David	Elbert
Bullock, Hawkins	Madison	Clark, George	Jasper
Bullock, Richard	Bibb	Clements, Clement	Bibb
Burch, Edward	Houston	Cleveland, Absolem	Franklin
Burgamy, William	Washington	Cleveland, Jeremiah	Habersham
Burke, Joseph	Wilkes	Cliatt, Isaac	Richmond
Burke, William	Walton	Clore, George	Madison
Burket, Lemuel	Wilkinson	Cloud, Ezekiel	Henry
		Clower, Daniel	Gwinnett

Name	County
Cobb, Thomas	Columbia
Cockburn, George	Franklin
Cockrell, Thomas, Sr	Newton
Cockrum, Matthew	Morgan
Coil, James	Madison
Colby, Samuel	DeKalb
Coleman, Abner	Gwinnett
Coleman, John	Jefferson
Coleman, Samuel	Walton
Colley, James, Sr	Oglethorpe
Collins, John	Hall
Collins, Joseph	Twiggs
Collins, Matthew, Sr	Lincoln
Colquitt, James	Oglethorpe
Cone, John	Bibb
Congo, Benjamin	Gwinnett
Connell, Daniel	Jefferson
Connell, Elisha, Sr	Jasper
Connors, William	Putnam
Cook, Archibald	Franklin
Cook, Henry	Putnam
Cook, George	Elbert
Cook, James	Jefferson
Cook, John	DeKalb
Cook, Theodosie	Elbert
Cook, Thomas	Elbert
Cooper, Henry	Putnam
Cooper, James	Madison
Cooper, John	Wilkes
Cooper, Richard	Tattnall
Cooper, Samuel	Putnam
Copeland, Benjamin	Greene
Corhon, Cornelius	Monroe
Cotten, James	Jefferson
Couch, Shadrach	Putnam
Cowan, George	Jackson
Cowan, James	Jackson
Cowle, Samuel	Monroe
Cox, John	Hall
Cox, Moses	Washington
Cox, Richard	Habersham
Cox, Thomas	Gwinnett
Crabb, Asa	Putnam
Crabtree, William	Houston
Crawford, Gay	Camden
Crawford, Lemuel	Clark
Credilla, William, Sr	Greene
Crelington, Jonathan	Rabun
Crittenden, J	Twiggs
Crockett, David	Bibb
Croison, John	Lincoln
Cronan, James	Morgan
Cross, Stephen	Bibb
Crow, Stephen	Clark
Crumbley, Anthony	Henry
Crumbley, Thomas	Habersham

Name	County
Culpepper, Malakiah	Morgan
Culver, Nathan	Hancock
Cummings, F	Greene
Cunningham, Andrew	Twiggs
Curry, Peter	Wilkes
Cutliff, Abraham	Putnam
Cutts, Joseph	Houston

D

Name	County
Dabbs, John	DeKalb
Dalton, Randolf	Gwinnett
Damron, Charles	Jackson
Daniel, John	Liberty
Daniel, Jeptha	Oglethorpe
David, Isaac	Madison
Davidson, John	Jasper
Davidson, Joseph	Pike
Davis, Clement	Morgan
Davis, Henry	Gwinnett
Davis, Samuel	Bulloch
Davis, Surry	Habersham
Davis, Thomas	Oglethorpe
Davis, Toliver	Baldwin
Davis, William	Warren
Davis, William	Wilkes
Davis, Zion	Ware
Davies, Daniel	Montgomery
Daughtry, Jacob	Emanuel
Daughtry, Joseph	Screven
Dawson, Brittain	Burke
Dean, Charles	Clark
Deason, Zacheriah	Henry
Delk, David	Liberty
DeLaunay, James	Jones
DeLoach, Hardy	Liberty
Denham, Arthur	Fayette
Dennis, Matthias	Hancock
Denton, John	Hancock
DeVeaux, Peter (Major)	Chatham
Dias, John	Tattnall
Dickerson, Zechariah	Elbert
Dickinson, Winborn	Hancock
Dickson, David	Fayette
Dickson, John	Jones
Dicky, Patrick	Putnam
Dillard, James	Elbert
Dillard, John	Rabun
Dillon, Thomas	DeKalb
Dodd, James, Sr	Oglethorpe
Dolton, John	Bibb
Dooly, Thomas	Habersham
Dossett, Philip	Richmond
Doster, Jonathan	Wilkes
Douglass, Stephen	Wilkinson
Dover, Francis J	Habersham
Dowdy, Richard	Chatham
Downey, Joseph	Gwinnett

Name	County
Downs, Ambrose	Wilkes
Downs, John	Henry
Drake, Epaphroditus	Hancock
Drake, James	Telfair
Dubberly, John	Tattnall
Dudley, James	Elbert
Duke, Thomas	Morgan
Duncan, Edmund	Jones
Duncan, John, Sr	Elbert
Dunham, William	Richmond
Dunn, Gatewood	Oglethorpe
Durozeaux, Stephen	Jefferson
Duty, Thomas	DeKalb
Dye, Avery	Burke
Dykes, John	Effingham
Dyson, John	Wilkes

E

Name	County
Eady, John	Wilkinson
Eagan, John	Richmond
Earnest, George	Clark
Eastwood, John	Newton
Eavinson, Edi	Elbert
Edwards, John	Franklin
Edwards, John	Henry
Edwards, Joseph	Columbia
Edwards, Reuben	Henry
Edwards, William	Madison
Eidson, Shelton	Oglethorpe
Eidson, Thomas	Wilkes
Ellis, Hicks	Putnam
Elliott, James	Warren
Elsberry, Benjamin	Clark
Etton, Abram	Washington
Embry, Joseph	Oglethorpe
Embry, William	
England, Charles	Habersham
English, Parmenius	Oglethorpe
Espy, John	Clark
Evans, Burwell	Early
Evans, James	Hancock
Evans, John	Jackson
Evans, Thomas	Habersham
Evans, William	Morgan
Evans, William	Habersham
Evans, William D	Baldwin
Everett, Abraham	Hancock
Evers, John	Effingham
Ezell, Hartwell	Jasper

F

Name	County
Faircloth, John	Screven
Fane, Thomas	Decatur
Faris, William	Rabun
Farmer, James	Henry
Farrar, Francis	Clark
Feagan, William	Morgan

Name	County
Fears, William	Jasper
Fiveash, Elias	Tattnall
Finch, William	Oglethorpe
Findley, John	Fayette
Flanigan, Wm	Franklin
Fleming, Robert	Jefferson
Fletcher, William, Sr	Telfair
Florence, Thomas, Sr	Lincoln
Fluker, John	Jasper
Foster, Arthur	Liberty
Foster, John	Putnam
Foster, William	Monroe
Fownley, Nathan, Sr	Morgan
Franklin, David	DeKalb
Fraser, Simeon	Liberty
Freeman, Daniel	Jasper
Friday, Joseph	Montgomery
Fulcher, James	Richmond
Fuller, James	Baldwin
Fuller, William, Sr	Jackson
Fulton, Thomas	Twiggs
Fulwood, John	Laurens
Funderburk, John	Monroe

G

Name	County
Gaiter, James	Gwinnett
Gaines, William	Elbert
Gainer, William	Elbert
Gainey, Reddick	Tattnall
Gancy, Bartholomew	Laurens
Garland, John	Jones
Garner, Charles	Clark
Garrotte, Samuel	Washington
Gates, Hezekiah	Walton
Gay, Joshua	Emanuel
Gay, William	Irwin
Gibson, Henry B	Wilkes
Gibson, John	Warren
Gibson, John	Wilkes
Gibson, John S	Butts
Gideon, Benjamin	Bulloch
Gilbert, William	DeKalb
Giles, John M	Morgan
Gilleland, William	Fayette
Gillis, James	Henry
Glass, Levi	Laurens
Glaze, Reuben	Oglethorpe
Glenn, James	Jackson
Glover, William	Franklin
Golden, Andrew	Bulloch
Goodwin, Jacob	Jefferson
Goodwin, James	Wilkes
Goodwin, Shadrack	Jones
Goolsby, Richard	Jones
Gordon, Thomas	Gwinnett
Goulding, Palmer	Liberty

Name	County	Name	County
Grady, Arthur	Houston	Harrison, Benjamin	Franklin
Grantham, Nathan	Telfair	Harrison, Edward	Hall
Grantham, William, Sr	Early	Harrison, Elijah W	Jones
Grant, Jesse	Burke	Harrison, Joseph	Wilkes
Gray, Allen	Henry	Harrison, Reuben	Putnam
Greaves, William	Burke	Hartsfield, Richard	Oglethorpe
Greassup, James	Elbert	Haslett, Wm	Oglethorpe
Green, Burwell	Jasper	Hatcher, Henry	Richmond
Green, Richard	McIntosh	Hatcher, Thomas	Twiggs
Greer, James	Clark	Hatcher, William	Washington
Greethouse, John, Sr	Oglethorpe	Ha(w)thorn, Thomas	Monroe
Gresham, John	DeKalb	Hawthorn, William	Putnam
Griffin, James	Irwin	Haynes, Moses	Elbert
Griffin, John, Sr	Hancock	Hays, Edward	Gwinnett
Griffin, Joseph	Monroe	Hays, Jonathan J	Franklin
Grimmer, Wm	Jasper	Haval, Hardy	Jefferson
Guice, Nicholas	Lincoln	Head, John S	Gwinnett
Gunn, Richard, Sr	Warren	Heard, John G	Morgan
Gunter, James	Walton	Heard, William	DeKalb
Guthrie, John	Gwinnett	Heath, Jordan	Burke
Guthrie, William	Gwinnett	Heaton, James	Gwinnett
Guttery, Francis	Morgan	Heeth, Roiston	Warren
		Hemphill, Jonathan	Jackson
H		Hendon, Robert	Oglethorpe
Hackney, Robert	Greene	Hendrick, Jesse	Bulloch
Hadaway, David	Jackson	Hendrick, Hezekiah	Monroe
Hale, James, Sr	Clark	Hendrick, Siah	Walton
Hall, Benjamin	Jasper	Hendrix, John	Screven
Hall, Dempsey	Jefferson	Herndon, Joseph	Walton
Hall, John	Gwinnett	Hester, David	Burke
Hall, Ignatius	Montgomery	Hester, Zecheriah	Jones
Hall, Instant	Laurens	Heyman, Stanton	Bryan
Ham, John	Monroe	Hicks, David	Pike
Hamilton, Bartow	Greene	Higden, Daniel	Hancock
Hamilton, John	Hall	Higgins, Reuben	Gwinnett
Hammond, Abner	Baldwin	Hill, Isaac	Clark
Hamron, Henry	Warren	Hill, Mordeaci	Jasper
Hamrick, Benjamin	Jasper	Hill, William	Warren
Hampton, John	Jackson	Hine, Nathaniel	Greene
Hand, Joseph	Henry	Hines, Lewis	Jackson
Hand, William	Baldwin	Holbrook, Jesse	Franklin
Harrington, James	Henry	Holcombe, James	Richmond
Haralson, J	Greene	Holcombe, Sherwood	Habersham
Harbuck, Nicholas	Warren	Hodges, Sherwood	Clark
Harden, Henry	Walton	Holder, John S	Jefferson
Harkness, Robert	Gwinnett	Holland, Thomas	Greene
Harley, Joseph	Columbia	Holley, William	Washington
Harley, Joseph	Wilkes	Holman, George	Twiggs
Harley, William	Elbert	Holman, Jacob	Richmond
Harper, Samuel, Sr	Crawford	Holmes, Jonathan	Morgan
Harrell, Simon	Warren	Holt, James	Houston
Harrin, Alexander	Butts	Holt, Thomas	Washington
Harrington, Elijah	Emanuel	Holtzclaw, John G	Oglethorpe
Harris, Benjamin	DeKalb	Hood, John	Wilkes
Harris, Graves	Morgan	Hook, Thomas	Putnam
Harris, John, Sr	Elbert	Hooper, James	DeKalb
Harris, Mathew	Greene		

Name	County
Hooten, Henry	Upson
Horn, Sherwood	Bibb
Hoskins, John, Sr	Jones
Howard, Abraham	Hall
Howard, Solomon	Washington
Howe, Elisha	Burke
Howell, John	Houston
Hornsley, Val	Monroe
Houston, Samuel	Henry
Hubbard, Burwell	Oglethorpe
Hubbard, John	Oglethorpe
Hubbard, Winaford	Camden
Huckaby, William	Oglethorpe
Hudgins, Ansel	Newton
Hudler, John	Bulloch
Hudson, Daniel	Elbert
Huie, James	Jackson
Hulsey, James	Hall
Human, Alex	Madison
Hunt, Daniel	Jones
Hunt, George	Greene
Hunt, Turman	Jasper
Huston, John, Sr	Jasper
Hutchinson, James	Franklin
Hutton, John	Laurens

I

Name	County
Ingram, John	Hall
Inman, Daniel	Burke
Ivey, Ephriam, Sr	Warren
Izely, Philip	Gwinnett
Ivey, Henry, Sr	Jasper

J

Name	County
Jackson, Ebenezer	Chatham
Jackson, Edward	Gwinnett
Jackson, Jeremiah	Greene
Jackson, Moses	Greene
James, Eliasha	Putnam
James, George	Gwinnett
Jarvis, Elisha, Sr	Morgan
Jenkins, Francis	Burke
Jenkins, James	Greene
Jester, Barnet	Elbert
Jeter, Andrew	Bibb
Johns, Eli	Burke
Johns, Robert	Columbia
Johnson, Bar	Wilkes
Johnson, Emanuel	Richmond
Johnson, Jacob	Burke
Johnson, John	Oglethorpe
Johnson, Joseph B	Wilkes
Johnson, Martin	Houston
Johnson, William	Warren
Johnson, William	Columbia
Johnson, William	Liberty
Johnson, William	Morgan

Name	County
Johnston, William	Bibb
*Johnston, Willis	Columbia
(This name is spelled Johnson or Johnston.)	
Jones, David	Monroe
Jones, Harrison	Newton
Jones, Isaac	Telfair
Jones, John	Jones
Jones, Josiah	Dooly
Jones, Matthew	Liberty
Jones, Moses	Lincoln
Jones, Nimrod	Columbia
Jones, Stephen	Putnam
Jones, Thomas	Twiggs
Jones, Thomas B	Crawford
Jones, Wm. Jones	Columbia
Jordan, Aven	Jefferson
Jordan, Dempsey	Greene
Jordan, John	Warren
Jordan, William	Washington
Jott, Daniel	Greene
Jourdain, Edmund	Oglethorpe
Jourdain, Fountain	Elbert
Joyner, Benjamin	Putnam
Justice, Aaron	Houston
Justice, Isaac	Richmond

K

Name	County
Kelly, Lloyd	Hancock
Kelly, William	Hall
Kendrick, Hezekiah	Monroe
Kennedy, Seth	Hancock
Kendal, William	Jasper
Kent, Daniel	Oglethorpe
Kent, Sampson	Oglethorpe
Kercy, Alcy	Burke
Key, William Bibb	Elbert
Key, John Waller	Franklin
Killard, James	Jones
Kimball, David	Clark
King, John	Franklin
King, John	Putnam
King, Thomas, Sr	Putnam
King, William	Elbert
Kitchens, Zacheriah	Jasper
Kits, Henry	Gwinnett
Knight, Aaron	DeKalb
Knight, Thomas	Walton
Knowlton, A	Oglethorpe
Kolb, Peter	Jones

L

Name	County
Lacy, Noah	Oglethorpe
Ladd, Amos	Habersham
Latta, David, Sr	Hall
Lamar, John	Jones
Lamb, Isaac	Jefferson
Lambert, Elisha	Fayette

Name	County	Name	County
Lambert, George	Putnam	McDuff, William	Henry
Lambert, Thomas	Clark	McFarland, Robert	Franklin
Landers, Tarpell	Gwinnett	McGee, Reuben	Warren
Landrum, Timothy	Jasper	McGlancy, John	Warren
Lane, Wm., Sr	Morgan	McIntyre, John	Habersham
Langham, James	Upson	McKee, John	Oglethorpe
Larissey, William	Screven	McKie, Samuel	Franklin
Lassiter, Hansell	Wilkinson	McKenzie, Samuel	Monroe
Lawless, John	Washington	McKinney, Charles	Jackson
Lawrence, John	Oglethorpe	McLain, Thomas	Oglethorpe
Leathers, Samuel	Hall	McLendon, Samuel	Henry
Lee, Andrew, Sr	Lincoln	McMichael, John, Sr	Jasper
Lee, James	Morgan	McMillion, Alexander	Franklin
Lee, Jesse	Morgan	McNeese, James	Jackson
Lee, John	Ware	McRae, Alexander	Clark
Lee, Sampson	Washington	McRee, William	Clark
Lee, Timothy	Newton	McWhorter, John	Hancock
Leigh, Benjamin	Columbia		
Leshley, Edmund	Columbia	**M**	
Lewis, Elizur	Burke		
Lewis, George	Tattnall	Mabry, George	Morgan
Lewis, Joseph	Hancock	Mackie, Thomas	Franklin
Lewis, Peter	Henry	Maddox, Charles	Wilkes
Leverett, Richard, Sr	Wayne	Maddox, John	Fayette
Lindsey, Dennis	Warren	Maddox, Walter	Wilkes
Lindsey, James	Hall	Mainer, Samuel	Walton
Lindsey, William	Wilkinson	Male, John	Warren
Linton, John	Twiggs	Male, Levi	Habersham
Liverman, Con	Richmond	Malone, William	Clark
Lloyd, James	Fayette	Mallory, Stephen	Wilkes
Lockett, Solomon	Warren	Manning, Benjamin	
Loggus, James, Sr	Hall	Martin, David	Warren
Lokey, William	Madison	Martin, Jesse	Oglethorpe
Lord, William	Wilkinson	Martin, James	Laurens
Love, James	Walton	Martin, James	Irwin
Lowrey, Levi	Jackson	Martin, James	DeKalb
Lowrey, Simeon	Bulloch	Martin, John	Richmond
Lumpkin, Dickson	Jackson	Mash, Nathan	Warren
Lumpkin, John	Oglethorpe	Massey, Seaborn	Lincoln
Lumsden, Jeremiah	Jasper	Mathis, John	Washington
		Matthews, Joel	Warren
Mc		Matthews, John	Twiggs
McClane, Ephriam		Maulden, Amos	Jones
McClain, John	Rabun	Maxwell, John	Elbert
McClelland, McClain	Screven	May, Elias	Columbia
McCorkle, Archibald	Lincoln	Mayberry, Stephen	Wilkes
McCormick, John	Warren	Meacham, Jason	Jones
McCuller, Thomas	Wilkinson	Meador, Jason	Jones
McCutcheon, Joseph	Hall	Meadows, Jacob	Oglethorpe
McDerman, Joseph	Madison	Meeks, Britton	Gwinnett
McDaniel, Jacob	Jones	Menefee, George, Sr	Jackson
McDaniel, Jeremiah	Habersham	Meriwether, David	Clark
McDonald, Isom	Pulaski	Meroney, Nathan	Madison
McDonald, J	Franklin	Merritt, Torem	Elbert
McDonald, James	Bibb	Middlebrook, John	Newton
McDowell, Robert	Jackson	Middleton, John	Washington
		Middleton, Hugh	Houston

Name	County
Miles, John, Sr.	Greene
Miles, Thomas	Baldwin
Miller, George	Jones
Miller, Richard	Hall
Miller, William	Jackson
Miller, William	Bulloch
Miller, William, Sr.	Jasper
Mitchell, Henry	Jones
Moreland, Robert	Jasper
Monk, John	Monroe
Monk, Silas	Putnam
Moore, Francis	Clark
Moore, John	Upson
Moore, Joseph	Jasper
Moore, William	Jackson
Moore, William	Clark
Morgan, James	Richmond
Morgan, John	Morgan
Morgan, William	Fayette
Morris, Burrel	Monroe
Morris, Jesse, Sr.	Columbia
Morris, John	Baldwin
Morris, Osten	Gwinnett
Morris, Nathaniel	Jones
Morrow, Ewing	Morgan
Moseley, James	Bibb
Moseley, Joseph	Bibb
Moseley, Lewis	Greene
Mote, William	Warren
Mott, Nathan	Washington
Murphy, Edmund	Richmond
Mushborn, John	Gwinnett
Myrick, John	Baldwin

N

Name	County
Nash, John	Columbia
New, Jacob	DeKalb
Newsome, John	Warren
Niblack, William	Camden
Niblet, Tillman	Monroe
Nichols, James	Franklin
Norris, Alexander	Wilkes
Norris, James	Warren
Norris, William	Monroe
Norris, William	Gwinnett
Nunnellee, James F.	Elbert
Nunnally, Israel	Greene

O

Name	County
Odum, Archibald	Pulaski
Oglesby, Thomas	Elbert
Oglitree, William	Monroe
O'Kelly, Francis	Oglethorpe
Oliver, James	Pulaski
Oliver, Peter	Elbert
Oman, John	Butts
O'Neal, Ross	Warren

Name	County
Osborne, Reps	Henry
Owens, John	Camden

P

Name	County
Pace, Barnabas	Elbert
Pace, Thomas, Sr.	Oglethorpe
Paine, John	Greene
Palmore, Elijah, Sr.	Greene
Parker, Aaron	Henry
Parker, Daniel	Morgan
Parker, Richard	Hancock
Parker, Samuel	Morgan
Parkerson, Levi	Wilkes
Parr, Benjamin	Clark
Parris, William	Rabun
Paschall, George	Oglethorpe
Paul, Robert, Sr.	Jones
Paulett, Richard	Clarke
Paulos, Robert	Greene
Peace, John	Monroe
Peacock, Archibald	Washington
Peacock, Isham	Tattnall
Peacock, Uriah	Washington
Pearce, John	Camden
Peavy, John	Gwinnett
Peddy, Jeremiah	Monroe
Penn, William	Jasper
Penny, Ed	Twiggs
Perkins, John	Bibb
Perryman, Herman	Twiggs
Persons, Jones	Upson
Peters, Edmund	Walton
Peters, Moses	Bibb
Peters, William	Twiggs
Pettis, Moses	Bibb
Pharoah, Joseph	Richmond
Phelps, Thomas	Jasper
Philips, Daniel	Early
Philips, Isham	Jones
Philips, Thomas	Jackson
Phinazee, John	Monroe
Pinckard, J. H.	Monroe
Pierce, Hugh	Habersham
Pierce, Seth	Jefferson
Pinson, Joseph	Rabun
Pittman, John	Gwinnett
Pitts, John	Telfair
Pledger, Thomas	Elbert
Poe, Stephen	Habersham
Polk, John	Wilkinson
Pollard, John	Jones
Pool, Henry	Warren
Pool, Samuel	Monroe
Pool, Walter	Newton
Porter, John	Jasper
Porter, William, Sr.	Jasper
Porter, William G.	Effingham

Name	County
Portwood, B., Sr	Jasper
Posey, Bennett	Jasper
Pose, Henry, Sr	Walton
Potter, Augustin L	Jasper
Potts, James	Jasper
Powell, Benjamin	Bulloch
Powell, Francis	Wilkes
Powell, Lewis	Columbia
Powell, Seymour	Newton
Powledge, George	Effingham
Presslay, Peter, Sr	Hall
Pressley, Moses	Henry
Pressley, John	Henry
Price, Lucius	Crawford
Prigden, David	Bulloch
Prince, Noah	Clark
Proctor, Stephen	Monroe
Prosser, Otey	Washington
Pryor, John	Jasper
Pugh, Shadrack	Upson
Pullen, John	Hancock
Pulliam, William	Franklin
Pullin, Thomas, Sr	Laurens
Purvis, Needham	Jefferson
Pye, James	Oglethorpe

R

Name	County
Ragan, Bruce, Sr	Wilkinson
Ragan, Buckner	Hall
Bailey, Charles	Twiggs
Bailey, Henry	Warren
Rainey, Isham, Sr	Oglethorpe
Ramsdell, David	Burke
Randolph, Robert	Columbia
Ransome, Reuben	Clark
Rawls, Isaac	Jackson
Rawls, William	Wayne
Ray, Andrew	Oglethorpe
Ray, Benjamin	Twiggs
Ray, John	Wilkes
Ray, Mark	Monroe
Ray, Philip	Oglethorpe
Red, Job	Gwinnett
Rees, Hugh	Columbia
Respess, Richard	Upson
Reeves, John	Columbia
Reynolds, Benjamin	Jones
Reynolds, Daniel	Jones
Reynolds, Thomas	Monroe
Rhodes, Richard	Oglethorpe
Rice, Leonard	Elbert
Rich, John	Hall
Richardson, John	Oglethorpe
Rickerson, Benjamin	Warren
Riley, James	Greene
Roberson, James	Newton

Name	County
Robert, Astin	Greene
Roberts, Aaron	Franklin
Roberts, Reuben	Jones
Roberts, Rollin	Screven
Robinson, Freyer	Clark
Robinson, James	Newton
Robinson, John	Irwin
Roe, John	Hancock
Rogers, Brittain	Monroe
Rogers, John	Gwinnett
Rogers, Robert	Rabun
Rogers, William, Sr	Tattnall
Rooks, John	Wayne
Ross, George	Jones
Ross, Jesse	Jones
Rowe, Joshua	Newton
Rowe, Shadrack	Putnam
Royalston, John	Bulloch
Rucker, William	Elbert
Rutherford, Claiborn	Newton
Rutherford, James	Irwin
Russell, George	Madison
Rutledge, John	Gwinnett

S

Name	County
Sailors, Christopher	Jackson
Sandiford, Elim	Wilkes
Samples, Nathaniel	Jefferson
Sanford, Jeremiah	Greene
Sanders, James	Madison
Sanders, John	Franklin
Sanders, Thomas	Upson
Sapp, Shadrack	Tattnall
Savage, Thomas	Hall
Sawyer, John Jones	Hancock
Scott, John	Bibb
Scott, William	Putnam
Scroggins, George	Jones
Scroggins, Thomas	Pike
Selman, John	Franklin
Seals, Wm	Hancock
Searcy, George	Baldwin
Sewell, Chris	Franklin
Sewell, Wm	Franklin
Sharp, John	Tattnall
Sharp, Joshua	Ware
Shaw, John	Hall
Sheffield, West	Pulaski
Sheffield, West	Wayne
Sheftall, Sheftall	Chatham
Shelman, John (Col.)	Chatham
Sherley, Edward	Crawford
Shurling, Ison	Putnam
Sims, Jeminy	
Sims, Robert	Clark
Simmons, John, Sr	Pike

Name	County	Name	County
Simmons, William	Jones	Strange, John	Franklin
Slack, John, Sr	Wilkes	Strickland, John	Richmond
Slocumb, John C	Jones	Strickland, Joseph	DeKalb
Smalley, Michael	Columbia	Strong, Charles, Sr	Oglethorpe
Smether, Gabriel	Elbert	Strong, William	Jones
Smith, Abner	Jasper	Stroud, Philip	Jasper
Smith, Ezekiel	Laurens	Sturdivant, Abner	Warren
Smith, Ezekiel	Richmond	Sturdivant, John	Hancock
Smith, Hardy	Laurens	Sumner, Joseph, Sr	Emanuel
Smith, Henry	Franklin	Sutley, James	Franklin
Smith, Henry	Monroe	Sutton, David	Ware
Smith, George	Richmond	Sweatman, John J., Sr	Monroe
Smith, Job	Washington	Swan, William	Newton
Smith, John	Pulaski		
Smith, John	Clark	**T**	
Smith, John	Wilkes	Tabor, Zekekiah	Oglethorpe
Smith, John	Jones	Tallant, John	Hall
Smith, John	Wilkes	Tapley, Adam	Baldwin
Smith, Lawrence	Morgan	Tarbutton, Joseph	Hall
Smith, Leonard	Columbia	Tarver, Absolem	Hancock
Smith, Mathew	Columbia	Tate, John, Jr	Franklin
Smith, Nathan	Emanuel	Taylor, Clark	Oglethorpe
Smith, Reuben	Greene	Taylor, Dempsey	Irwin
Smith, Robert	Oglethorpe	Taylor, Edward	Monroe
Smith, William	Newton	Taylor, James	Jones
Smith, William	Jackson	Taylor, John	Tattnall
Smith, William	Gwinnett	Taylor, Richard	Morgan
Smith, William	Twiggs	Taylor, Theophilus	Habersham
Smokes, William C	Jefferson	Taylor, William	Henry
Snead, Philip	Jones	Teal, Emanuel	Jasper
Solomon, Lazarus	Twiggs	Teal, Ludowick	Jasper
Sowell, Zadoc	Wilkes	Teasley, Silas	Elbert
Sparks, Jeremiah	Morgan	Terrill, Micajah	Henry
Spearman, John, Sr	Jasper	Tellers, James	Oglethorpe
Spinks, Pressly	Warren	Terrell, James	Franklin
Spurlock, Wm	Baldwin	Tidd, David	Jones
Stanford, Joshua, Sr	Warren	Tilley, William	Monroe
Stanton, John	Newton	Tindall, James, Sr	Burke
Staples, Thomas	Jackson	Themby, Thomas	Houston
Sterling, John	Tattnall	Thigpen, Nathan	Warren
Statham, Wm	Wilkinson	Thomas, Benjamin	Washington
Steel, Henry	Jasper	Thomas, Carl	Tattnall
Stephens, Barnett	Madison	Thomas, Ethelred	Laurens
Stephens, Burrell	Jefferson	Thomas, James	Oglethorpe
Stephens, James	Burke	Thomas, James	Baldwin
Stephens, John W	Burke	Thomas, Massa	Putnam
Stephens, Joseph	Monroe	Thomas, Richard	Monroe
Stephens, Reuben	DeKalb	Thomas, William	Franklin
Stephens, Richard	Twiggs	Thompson, Andrew	Oglethorpe
Stewart, Charles	Monroe	Thompson, James, Sr	Madison
Stewart, James	Forsyth	Thompson, Moses	Warren
Stewart, William	Jones	Thompson, Samuel	Newton
Stoneycipher, John	Franklin	Thompson, William	Jackson
Stovall, George	Franklin	Thrasher, George	Habersham
Stovall, William	Monroe	Tomlinson, Aaron	Washington
Stowers, Lewis	Elbert	Tomlinson, Nathaniel	Putnam

Name	Couny	Name	Count
Toller, Lewis	Henry	Ward, Nathaniel	Warren
Toole, James	Richmond	Ward, Samuel	Oglethorpe
Towns, John	Monroe	Watkins, Benjamin	DeKalb
Townsend, Thomas	Habersham	Watkins, James C	Hall
Trimble, John	DeKalb	Watkins, William	Washington
Trimble, Moses	Newton	Watson, Ezekiel	Washington
Triplett, William	Wilkes	Watson, John, Sr	Monroe
Tripler, William	Tattnall	Watson, Joshua	Jefferson
Trout, George	Hall	Webb, John	Jasper
Truitt, Purual		Weeks, Theophilus	Camden
Tucker, Henry C. (Henry)	Montgomery	Welborn(Wilborn), Elias	Columbia
Tucker, Robert	Columbia	Welch, Nicholas	Habersham
Turner, Abrahal	Bulloch	Welsher, Jeremiah	Jefferson
Turner, Henry	Burke	West, Benjamin	Hall
Turner, John	Madison	West, Willis	Fayette
Turner, Reuben	Wayne	Wetherton, Thomas	Walton
Turner, Robert	Habersham	Whateley, Michael, Jr	Bibb
		Wharton, Benjamin	Hall
U		Wheeler, Amos	Pulaski
Umphlet, Asa	Warren	Wheeler, Thomas, Sr	Elbert
Usurey, John	Wilkinson	White, John M	Fayette
		White, Vincent	Hall
V		Whitfield, Lewis	Burke
Vanbrackel, John	Bryan	Whitington, B. G	Liberty
Varner, George	Oglethorpe	Whitten, Philip	Habersham
Vassar, Micajah	Laurens	Wiggins, Richard	Warren
Vaughan, Jesse	Wilkinson	Wilbanks, Gillam	Franklin
Veal, William	Putnam	Wilder, Willis	Jones
Veasey, Zebulon	Hancock	Wilder, William	Jones
Vickery, Hezekiah	Screven	Wiley, John	Washington
Vickery, Joseph	Elbert	Wilhight, Lewis	Elbert
Vincent, Isaac	Clark	Williby, William	Clark
Vinson, Elijah	Henry	Williams, Abraham	Jackson
Voicle, Lewis	Hancock	Williams, Benjamin Z	Gwinnett
		Williams, Joseph	Warren
		Williams, Lewis	Franklin
W		Williamson, John	Henry
Wade, John W	Hall	Williamson, Zach, Sr	Bibb
Wade, John W	Columbia	Willingham, Jesse	Madison
Waggoner, William	Wilkes	Willis, George	Wilkes
Wagnon, Daniel	Greene	Willis, John	Walker
Wainslow, John	Elbert	Wilson, James	Franklin
Waldrop, James	Fayette	Wilson, John	Columbia
Walker, Elijah	Warren	Wilson, John	Warren
Walker, James	Irwin	Wimberly, John	Jones
Walker, Samuel	Jackson	Wilmoth, William	Franklin
Walker, Samuel	Jasper	Winburn, Josiah	Pulaski
Walker, Thomas	Gwinnett	Winslett, Samuel	Greene
Wall, Henry	Twiggs	Woodall, John, Sr	DeKalb
Wall, John, Sr	Jackson	Woodall, Joseph	Oglethorpe
Wall, Myall	Greene	Woodcock, William	Bulloch
Wallace, John	Putnam	Wofford, Absolem	Jackson
Wallace, William	Newton	Wolf, Andrew	Wilkes
Waller, Elijah	Warren	Womack, A	Monroe
Walls, Charles	Gwinnett	Womack, William	Effingham
Walls, Samuel	Franklin	Wood, Abraham	Pulaski
Walters, Peter	Franklin		

Name	County	Name	County
Wood, Ellet	Newton	Wylie, William	Hancock
Wood, James	Columbia		
Wood, John	Wilkes	**Y**	
Wood, Thomas	Clark	Yancey, Lewis D	Jasper
Wooten, Thomas	DeKalb	Yarborough, Benjamin	Laurens
Wright, Elisha	Jones	Yarborough, L	Morgan
Wright, Reuben	Early	York, John	Lincoln
Wright, William	Clark	Young, James	Clark
Wright, William	Crawford	Young, James	Oglethorpe
Wyatt, John	Henry	Young, John	Tattnall
		Yates, William	Montgomery

NOTE: See "Certified List of 1827 Lottery," compiled by Capt. B. F. Johnson, Chief Clerk in office of Secretary of State, Ga., and "The Reprint of Land Lottery of 1827" (printed by Grantland and Orme, 1827), by Martha Lou Houston, of Columbus, Ga., in 1928.

NAMES OF THE WIDOWS OF REVOLUTIONARY SOLDIERS WHO DREW LAND IN GEORGIA IN THE "LOTTERY OF 1827," AND THE COUNTIES OF GEORGIA IN WHICH THEY LIVED

Name	County	Name	County
A		Baxter, Elizabeth	Madison
Achison, Winnefred	Warren	Beall, Rutha	Pulaski
Adams, Abigail	Putnam	Beard, Eve	Oglethorpe
Adams, Mary	Jasper	Beavers, Elizabeth	Morgan
Adams, Nancy	Jasper	Beck, Sarah	Elbert
Akins, Jane	DeKalb	Bell, P. (widow of T. Bell)	Burke
Aldredge, Elizabeth	Appling	Bell, Sarah	Jackson
Alexander, Mary	Elbert	Bellamy, Mary	Franklin
Alford, Rebecca	Greene	Bellinger, Mary	Chatham
Allen, Catherine	Jefferson	Benson, Elizabeth	Wilkinson
Allen, Chloe	Putnam	Bentley, Abi	Wilkes
Allen, Elizabeth C	Columbia	Benton, Mary	Jones
Allison, Chris	Oglethorpe	Bevers, Jane	Jackson
Alred, Margaret	Clark	Blackwood, Jane	Jasper
Also, Elizabeth	Houston	Blair, Nancy	Washington
Amos, Learry	Hancock	Blanchard, Sarah	Columbia
Anders, Mary	Wilkes	Blanks, Nancy	Greene
Anderson, Ann	Greene	Bledsoe, Margaret	Morgan
Anderson, Mary	Wilkes	Blitch, Ann	Effingham
Arendell, Susanna	Franklin	Blount, Lucy	Jones
Armstrong, Mary	Warren	Boatright, Margaret	Emanuel
Armstrong, Sarah	Pulaski	Bogan, Elizabeth	Richmond
Arnold, Bethany	Walton	Bolton, Chris W	Wilkes
Atkinson, Martha	Greene	Boswell, Sarah	Franklin
		Bradford, Mary	Jackson
B		Bragg, Mary	Oglethorpe
Babb, Elizabeth	Baldwin	Branham, Elizabeth C	Putnam
Baker, Ann	Walton	Brewer, Mary	Pike
Baker, Sarah	Gwinnett	Bridges, Rebecca	Washington
Barker, Mary	Wilkinson	Bridges, Susanna	Morgan
Barfield, Winny	Morgan	Bridges, Susanna	Greene
Bargeson, Elizabeth	Burke	Brinson, Mary	Burke
Barksdale, F	Lincoln	Brinson, Unity	Pulaski
Barnes, Mae	Monroe	Brooks, Mary	Warren
Barrett, Sarah	Fayette	Brooks, Sarah	Madison

Name	County
Brown, Ann	Wilkinson
Brown, Sarah	Monroe
Browning, Margaret	Clark
Brownson, Elizabeth	Screven
Bryan, Dorcas	Monroe
Bryan, Mary	Pulaski
Bryan, Nancy	Gwinnett
Bryan, Sue	Twiggs
Bruce, Elizabeth	Wilkes
Bull, Elizabeth	Pike
Burden, Hannah	Elbert
Burney, Elizabeth	Washington
Burnside, Ann	Columbia
Burson, Nancy	Warren
Burton, Rachel	Hall
Burton, Rhoda	Twiggs
Busbin, Sarah	Oglethorpe
Bynum, Silvey	Pulaski

C

Name	County
Calef, Letisha	Jones
Carden, Milly	Pulaski
Cargyle, Jane	Columbia
Carrington, W	Madison
Cary, Elizabeth	Warren
Carter, Elizabeth	Wilkes
Cates, Hannah	Newton
Chambless, S	Jones
Chance, Mary	Burke
Chapman, Lydia	Monroe
Cheatham, Sarah	Franklin
Christian, Sally	Pulaski
Christopher, Elizabeth	Greene
Clark, Lucy	Morgan
Clark, Rebecca	Elbert
Clark, Sarah	Elbert
Clark, S. B	Baldwin
Clements, Anna	Putnam
Clements, Frances	Hall
Clemmons, Jeninay	Jones
Cobb, Catherine	Hancock
Coffee, Nancy	Rabun
Cofield, S	Twiggs
Collins, Bridget	DeKalb
Collins, Diana	Burke
Collins, Sarah	Burke
Comer, Ann	Jones
Connor, Sarah	Tattnall
Cook, Elizabeth	Jackson
Cook, Susannah	Appling
Cooper, Hollandberry	Oglethorpe
Cowan, M	Jefferson
Cowles, Judith	Monroe
Crain, Juda	Rabun
Crawford, Vic	Franklin
Crosby, Elizabeth	Columbia

Name	County
Cruse, Sarah Ann	Chatham
Culbreath, Jane	Jones
Cureton, Martha	Hancock

D

Name	County
Dabney, Hannah	Jasper
Dannielly, Elizabeth	Jasper
Davenport, Dicy	Clark
Davis, Elizabeth	Walton
Davis, Fanny	Oglethorpe
Davis, Jane	Greene
Davis, Mary	DeKalb
Davis, Sarah	Greene
Dawson, Mary	Twiggs
Dean, Mourning	Gwinnett
Defual, Mary	Pulaski
DeLoach, Elizabeth	Tattnall
Dennis, Cath	Warren
Dickey, Sarah	Putnam
Dingler, Nancy	Jasper
Dismukes, Elizabeth	Richmond
Dixon, Martha	Putnam
Dodd, Catherine	Franklin
Dooly, Elizabeth	Habersham
Douglass, M. A	Jones
Duckworth, Christian	Jones
Duke, Ann	Jones
Dukes, Sarah	Henry
Dunn, Winnefred	Columbia
Dupree, Martha	Twiggs
Durham, Isabel	Clark

E

Name	County
Eccola, Zippy	Washington
Ector, Elinor	Monroe
Eldridge, Jane	Twiggs
Ellis, Percilla	Crawford
Evans, Elizabeth	Morgan
Evans, Elizabeth	Wilkes
Evans, Lucy	Hancock

F

Name	County
Farley, Delina	Jones
Featherstone, Jane	Jasper
Fitzpatrick, Elizabeth	Twiggs
Fitzpatrick, S	Morgan
Fleming, Sarah	Jefferson
Flemister, E. G	Jasper
Flowers, F. Elizabeth	Warren
Floyd, Sarah	Madison
Flud, Jane	Greene
Flynn, Elizabeth	Columbia
Fogel, Mary	Morgan
Fountain, L	Jefferson
Fountain, Sarah	Jefferson
Freeman, Mildred	Jasper

Name	County
G	
Gadden, Mary	Franklin
Gailey, Mary	Madison
Gainer, Elizabeth	Morgan
Gainer, Phebe	Wilkinson
Gant, Mary	Bulloch
Garnett, Elizabeth	Columbia
Garrard, Elizabeth	Wilkinson
Garvin, Rebecca	Jefferson
Giles, Elizabeth	Walton
Gilmore, Elizabeth	Tattnall
Girtman, Catherine	Jefferson
Glover, Drucilla	Jefferson
Godbee, Mary	Burke
Goolsby, Caty	Jasper
Gordon, Mary	Gwinnett
Goodwin, Elizabeth	Henry
Grace, Hez	Tattnall
Gray, Rebecca	Jasper
Green, Charity	Warren
Green, Mary	Henry
Green, Mary	Jackson
Griffin, Comfort	Richmond
H	
Hagan, Frances	Appling
Hale, Drucilla	Burke
Hall, Ann	Jefferson
Hall, L. M.	Washington
Hall, Nancy	Tattnall
Ham, Betsey	Elbert
Hambleton, Mary	Monroe
Hamesburger, Mary	Liberty
Hamilton, Abigail	Gwinnett
Hammond, Susanna	Greene
Hand, Rachel	Henry
Hand, Sarah	Baldwin
Haney, Jemina	Oglethorpe
Hanson, Peggy	Morgan
Harbuck, Mary	Warren
Hardagree, Eleanor	Clark
Hardeman, Zilla	Oglethorpe
Hardwick, Judith	Jasper
Hardy, Winnie	Putnam
Harper, Ann	Morgan
Harris, Charity	DeKalb
Harrington, Cath	DeKalb
Harris, Catherine	Washington
Harris, Mary	Rabun
Harris, Rebecca	Elbert
Harrison, Charity	Laurens
Harrison, Elizabeth	Columbia
Harrison, Mary	Oglethorpe
Hartley, Fere	Washington
Harvey, Betsey J	Burke
Hasty, Jemina	Jones
Hatcher, Sarah	Burke

Name	County
Haynes, Martha	Monroe
Haynes, Sarah	Oglethorpe
Haynie, Elizabeth	Richmond
Hays, Jane	Greene
Hays, Nancy	Jasper
Hughes, Jane	Burke
Hughes, Sarah	Newton
Huling, Elizabeth	Wilkes
Hunter, Elizabeth	Crawford
Hunter, Martha	Jackson
Head, Margaret	Morgan
Heath, Louisa	Burke
Heeth, Winnefred	Warren
Heflin, Sarah	Warren
Hemphill, Elizabeth	Morgan
Henderson, Mary	Jasper
Henderson, Mary	Jones
Henderson, Sally	Hancock
Hendrick, Mary	Jones
Henley, Sarah	Gwinnett
Herren, Dulcy	Appling
Herrin, Mary Ann	Habersham
Herring, Hollin	Morgan
Hicks, Susanna	Clark
Hill, Catherine	Jasper
Hill, Frances	Warren
Hill, Percilla	Habersham
Hill, Sarah	Jasper
Hines, Elizabeth	Laurens
Hines, Martha	Chatham
Hinson, Sarah	Jackson
Hirresly, Elizabeth	Jones
Hogans, Nancy	Baldwin
Holbrook, Priscilla	Gwinnett
Holland, Elizabeth	Jasper
Hollis, Elizabeth	Jasper
Holsey, Susanna	Hancock
Hood, Rebecca	Wilkes
Horn, Sarah	Greene
Hoskins, Maryan	Crawford
Howard, Edith	Baldwin
Howard, Elizabeth	Baldwin
Howard, Jane	Columbia
Howard, Lucretia	Clark
Howard, Sarah	Jackson
Howard, Sarah	Wilkinson
Howell, Franky	Fayette
Howell, Mary	Houston
I	
Irving, Mary	Greene
Irwin, Nancy	Bibb
Irwin, Nancy	DeKalb
J	
Jackson, Mary	Monroe
James, Elizabeth	Pike

Name	County
Jameson, Mary	Twiggs
Jarman, Ruth	Greene
Johnson, Dorcas	Morgan
Johnson, Elizabeth	Hancock
Johnson, Mary	Elbert
Johnson, Molly O	Jasper
Johnson, Patty	Pulaski
Johnson, Rebecca	Morgan
Johnson, Sivel	Warren
Jones, Elizabeth	Jones
Jones, Elizabeth	Rabun
Jones, Elizabeth H	Oglethorpe
Jones, Fanny	Elbert
Jones, Jane	Gwinnett
Jones, Jemina	Burke
Jones, Margaret	Jefferson
Jones, Nancy	Houston
Jordan, Milly	Oglethorpe
Joy, Elizabeth	Jackson

K

Name	County
Kelly, Elizabeth	DeKalb
Killabrew, Elizabeth	Washington
King, Elizabeth	Warren
King, Mary	Jasper
King, Mary	Monroe
Kitchens, Sarah	Monroe

L

Name	County
Lantern, Elizabeth	Columbia
Lawrence, Let	Oglethorpe
Lawson, Jane	Wilkinson
Lavare, Mary	Monroe
Ligon, Tabitha	Morgan
Liles, Bathesba	Columbia
Lindsey, Mary	Wilkes
Lipham, Elizabeth	Monroe
Lipham, Nancy	Henry
Little, Fanny	Screven
Lockhart, Polly	Wilkes
Lord, Martha	Tattnall
Lord, Milly	Wilkinson
Lurisford, Elizabeth	Putnam
Lyle, Elizabeth	Jackson
Lyon, Jemina	Oglethorpe

Mc

Name	County
McAhaney, Ann	Jasper
McCants, Sarah	Crawford
McCarty, Mary	Warren
McCommon, Sue	Clark
McConnell, Agnes	Gwinnett
McDonald, Esther	Pike
McFarling, C. M	Jones
McKenzie, N	Twiggs
McLelland, Elizabeth	Gwinnett

Name	County
McLeod, Muriel	Pulaski
McLeroy, Christiana	Jones
McLeroy, Sarah	Oglethorpe
McNeely, Elinor	Jefferson
McRae, Cath	Telfair
McWalters, Margaret	Henry

M

Name	County
Maclin, Jane	Wilkes
Malone, Nancy	Clark
Martin, Edy	Washington
Massa, Nancy	Walton
Mathews, Dicey	Wilkinson
Mathews, Elizabeth	Jefferson
Mathews, Nancy	Walton
Mathews, Sarah	Washington
Mathis, Jane	Jasper
Maxwell, Hanney	Washington
Mayo, Susan	Pulaski
Mayo, Temper	Washington
Megahee, Susan	Columbia
Metcalf, Martha	Burke
Miller, Martha	Warren
Miller, Sally	Newton
Mills, Elizabeth	Burke
Mills, Sarah	Jones
Mims, Elizabeth	Upson
Minchen, Martha	DeKalb
Modiset, Isobel	Monroe
Montgomery, Mae	Wilkinson
Montfort, Elizabeth	Laurens
Moore, Lucy	Walker
Moore, Nancy	Greene
Moore, Synthia	Laurens
Mophit, Mary Ann	Lincoln
Morgan, Charlotte	Hancock
Morgan, Elizabeth	Jasper
Morgan, Mary	Jackson
Morris, Elizabeth	Gwinnett
Morris, Hannah	Clark
Morris, Lucy	Warren
Morrow, Elizabeth	Franklin
Moseley, Sarah	Walton
Munden, Levina	Hancock
Murphy, Cherry	Jones
Murray, Elizabeth	Warren
Murray, Nancy	Elbert

N

Name	County
Nalah, Frances	Elbert
Nation, Catherine	Gwinnett
Nelson, Ann	Morgan
Newsom, Elizabeth	Warren
Newsom, Lucy	Wilkinson
Newton, Ann	Screven
Newton, Catherine	Clark
Nicholson, Elizabeth	Screven

Name	County
Norris, Jemina	Hall
Nunnelee, Elizabeth	Habersham
Nunnally, Mary	Wilkes

O

Name	County
O'Kelly, Elizabeth	Habersham
O'Kelly, Elizabeth	Oglethorpe
Orrick, Celia	Putnam
Owens, Barsheba	Wilkes
Owens, Nancy	Burke
Oxford, Susanna	Jones

P

Name	County
Pace, Meldridge	Wilkinson
Page, Mary	Warren
Palmer, Elizabeth	Jackson
Parham, Asa	Monroe
Parris, Elizabeth	Warren
Parrish, Rhoda	Greene
Payne, Mary	Henry
Pearce, Lucy	Franklin
Pearson, Winnefred	Pike
Penn, Frances	Oglethorpe
Penn, Martha	Elbert
Petit, Betsey	Columbia
Philips, Ruth	Warren
Philips, Sarah	Pike
Philips, Sarah	Putnam
Powell, Ann	Liberty
Powell, Rachel	Columbia
Prescott, Fanny	Newton
Priddy, Judith	Newton
Pryor, Mary	Jefferson
Psalmonde, S.	Wilkes
Purdue, Sarah	Putnam

R

Name	County
Radford, Elizabeth	Walton
Radford, Patsey	Richmond
Rahn, Hannah Elizabeth	Effingham
Raiford, Patience	Baldwin
Railey, Ruth	Warren
Rainer, Sarah	Jones
Ramsey, Rachel	Franklin
Reaves, Sarah	Jasper
Reeves, Hanney	Wilkes
Reese, Elizabeth	Columbia
Reynolds, Sarah	Warren
Reynolds, Susanna	Hancock
Richards, Lyddy	Greene
Rickerson, Prucy	Henry
Right, Alsy	Jackson
Rivers, Mary Ann	Warren
Roberts, Tabitha	Camden
Robertson, Silva	Newton
Robinson, Jane	Newton

Name	County
Rogers, Luraney	Bulloch
Ross, Sarah	Columbia
Rowland, Elizabeth	Oglethorpe
Rouse, Mary	Twiggs
Royal, Sarah	Burke
Rundle, Susanna	Hancock
Russell, Elizabeth	Monroe
Rye, Mary	Wilkinson

S

Name	County
Saffold, Sarah	Wilkes
Sanders, Mary	Rabun
Sapp, Zilpha	Burke
Saxon, Elizabeth M	Elbert
Scarborough, Sarah	Burke
Seals, Elizabeth	Elbert
Sharp, Patty	Lincoln
Shaw, Margaret	Morgan
Sheerer, Ann	Wilkes
Shofner, Elizabeth	Wilkinson
Shell, Elizabeth	Newton
Simmons, Nancy	Burke
Simpson, Euphamy	Houston
Sims, Amis	Franklin
Sinclair, Mary	Upson
Sisson, Hannah	Greene
Skinner, Sarah	Burke
Smith, Afamy	Liberty
Smith, Ann	Jackson
Smith, Elizabeth	Jones
Smith, Elizabeth	Greene
Smith, Margaret	Gwinnett
Smith, Mary	Columbia
Smith, Mary P	Clark
Smith, Sarah	Habersham
Smith, Sarah	Baldwin
Smith, Sarah	Jasper
Smith, Rebecca	Walton
Smithwick, Elizabeth	Walton
Sorrels, Mildred	Madison
Sorrow, Mary	Morgan
Sosebee, Elizabeth	Franklin
Spann, Lamey	Jefferson
Spell, Mary	Laurens
Spratlin, Winnefred	Monroe
Stanford, Elizabeth	Washington
Starr, Mary	Morgan
Stephens, Caley	Twiggs
Stephens, Desire	Bulloch
Stephens, Mary	Bibb
Stephens, Sarah	Habersham
Steward, Judith	Jasper
Stewart, Elizabeth	Greene
Stinson, Phebe	Wilkes
Stokes, Sarah	Wilkinson
Street, Mary	Jackson

Name	County
Stringfellow, Amy	Greene
Summerell, Sarah	Bibb
Sutton, Sarah	Putnam
Swan, Nelly	Screven
Switley, Sarah	Liberty

T

Name	County
Teaver, Rebecca	Madison
Terry, Priscilla	Morgan
Tharp, Ruth	Twiggs
Thomas, E. C.	Clark
Thomas, Hannah	Gwinnett
Thomas, Nancy	Twiggs
Thomas, Polly	Clark
Thompson, Sarah	Clark
Thompson, Sarah	Jefferson
Timmons, Elizabeth	Appling
Tomlinson, Joanna	Hancock
Tredeway, Mary	Monroe
Tumlin, Mary	Gwinnett
Twiggs, Ruth	Richmond

V

Name	County
Veal, Elizabeth	Putnam
Veasy, Martha	Greene
Volloton, Rachel	Burke

W

Name	County
Waldraven, Elizabeth	Gwinnett
Walker, Rebecca	Jones
Wall, Ann	Twiggs
Ward, Charity	Madison

Name	County
Ware, Jane	Jackson
Warren, Unity	Morgan
Watson, Mae	Richmond
Webb, Margaret	Elbert
Whatley, Elizabeth	Newton
Whatley, Fannie	Jones
Wheeler, Mourning	Jackson
White, Barsheba	Jasper
Whitlock, Elizabeth	Hall
Wiggins, Almey	Ware
Wilkerson, Ester	Wilkerson
Willeford, Lucy	Oglethorpe
Williams, Dilly	Bulloch
Williams, Martha	Chatham
Williams, R.	Fayette
Williamson, Letysha	Gwinnett
Williamson, Margaret	Laurens
Williamson, Sarah	Jasper
Willis, Sarah	Jones
Wilson, Ann	Pulaski
Wilson, Margaret	Hall
Winburn, Sarah Ann	Gwinnett
Winn, Ann	Liberty
Wood, Nancy	Greene
Woodly, Milly	Hall
Wooten, H.	Elbert
Worsham, Nancy C.	Baldwin
Wyhand, Rosanna	Morgan
Wyndham (Windham) Permely	Laurens

Y

Name	County
Yarborough, Margaret	Laurens
Young, Susan	Laurens

CPSIA information can be obtained
at www.ICGtesting.com
Printed in the USA
FFOW03n1947281117
43695933-42561FF